Transistor physics
and circuits

PRENTICE-HALL INTERNATIONAL, INC., *London*
PRENTICE-HALL OF AUSTRALIA, PTY., LTD., *Sydney*
PRENTICE-HALL OF CANADA, LTD., *Toronto*
PRENTICE-HALL OF INDIA (PRIVATE) LTD., *New Delhi*
PRENTICE-HALL OF JAPAN, INC., *Tokyo*

Transistor physics and circuits

SECOND EDITION

MARLIN P. RISTENBATT
Research Engineer
University of Michigan

ROBERT L. RIDDLE
Technical Vice President
HRB Singer, Inc.

Prentice-Hall, Inc.   Englewood Cliffs, N. J.

© 1958, 1966 by Prentice-Hall, Inc., Englewood Cliffs, N. J.

All rights reserved. No part of this book may be reproduced in any form, by mimeograph or any other means, without permission in writing from the publisher.

Current Printing (last digit):

10 9 8 7 6 5 4

Library of Congress Catalog Card Number 65-27830

Printed in the United States of America
C-93013

Preface

Transistor technology has developed rapidly during recent years. The transistor can now be produced in large quantities at a fairly low cost, and the characteristics can be held within useable limits. Practically every electronic consumer product is now available in solid state form.

The advantages of using transistors are well known and need only cursory mention. Chief among the advantages are the small physical size and the extreme ruggedness of the transistor. Although designed to perform many of the functions of the vacuum tube, this device requires no filament power and operates with very low bias voltages. One of the greatest boons to the ready acceptance of the transistor has been the fact that it has a life expectancy measured in years rather than hours.

Although the disadvantages of the transistor are steadily being diminished, present limitations to its use exist. There is still a basic limitation on the power handling ability, and the temperature dependence of its characteristics are often a challenge. In the past noise was a troublesome factor, but transistors are now equal to or better than vacuum tubes in this respect. The low resistance of transistors to radiation fields from nuclear reactors is another disadvantage.

With the increased utilization of transistors it has become essential that all electrical engineers, electronic designers, and technicians acquire an understanding of transistors. The main purpose of this book is to treat those fundamental aspects which underlie all serious transistor circuit work. Thus this book serves directly as a source of transistor circuit theory for circuit designers and technicians. The material here is a necessary prerequisite for the electrical engineering student who wishes to continue into more specialized transistor circuit work. Also, we hope this book will be a direct aid to any person wishing to obtain an understanding of transistors, such as the radio amateur.

In choosing the material for this book, the objective has always been to elicit those fundamental principles and techniques which underlie the varied design techniques and practices. These principles remain valid and valuable even as the transistor itself is changed and improved, so that the material here should be valuable to the reader for many years. Also with this treatment, the electronic designer comes to understand the reason for the particular analysis method in the given area, and lays the groundwork for further specialized knowledge. Treatment of this basic material is most sensible, it is felt, for the classroom or self-study situation.

We present this material on transistors from the vantage point of a person having a basic high school knowledge of physics and algebra and either classroom or practical experience with electronic circuits. Emphasis is placed on illustrating the practical results of any theory. The use of mathematics for calculating the performance of transistors is limited to algebra; knowledge of the basic theory of electronic circuits will be of help but is not necessary. The equivalent circuits which depict the operation of the transistor are expressed in terms of the h parameters. These are the parameters that are being supplied by all transistor manufacturing companies, and most parameter measuring equipment on the market measures the h parameters.

Problems are included at the end of each chapter, where applicable. These problems are used to help explain important points throughout the book.

The bulk of the material in Chapters 2 and 6 is included for those who wish to review the basic physics and electrical circuitry applicable to an understanding of the rest of the book. This material may easily be omitted without destroying the continuity of the remainder of the book.

The material is divided into two parts, covering the physics of transistors and the circuit aspects of transistors. The section on physics includes the first five chapters. A practical approach is taken to the fundamental principles of physics in Chapter 2. Using these principles the physical action of transistors is then developed in a logical fashion. Semiconductors are first studied, and then applied to the transistor. The section culminates with a chapter describing the various types of transistors. With this second edition we have updated the entire section. Chapter 5, the summary of various types of transistors, has been entirely rewritten because the transistor manufacturing art has changed greatly since the first edition.

The section on the circuit aspects includes Chapters 6 through 17. In these chapters the performance calculations and some design procedures are

Preface

studied. Following an electrical circuit review transistor circuits are first considered in terms of small signal and large signal circuits. The basic mathematical and graphical methods are introduced here. Bias circuits and frequency response are studied next, followed by bias stability. A study of feedback and noise completes the coverage of those items pertinent to all transistor amplification and circuit design.

In the chapter on transistor oscillators, heavily revised with this edition, we then consider the analytic techniques for this important area. The subject of the following chapter, new with this edition, is digital switching circuits. This chapter first considers the basic transistor *switch*, and then the various digital circuits built with switches.

This circuit section concludes with a brief chapter on high frequency description of transistors, and circuit aspects of field effect transistors.

Although the physics of semiconductors is essential to understanding the physical action of transistors, the two parts are written in such a manner that the reader may begin with the section on circuit aspects. In addition, each chapter has been made as self-explanatory as possible in order that the book may serve usefully as a reference. Even though this requires a certain amount of repetition, it is felt that the goals of the book are best served by this technique.

A set of selected transistor characteristics is given in the Appendix, as an illustration of transistor properties and to aid in solving the problems. The Appendix also includes a short treatment of determinants and the necessary relations between the various matrices used with transistors.

With this treatment it is believed that a clear, practical approach to the subject of transistors has been achieved.

In addition to many people to whom we are indebted for discussion and comments, we would like to acknowledge the following people: Eric M. Aupperle for his help in preparing the new Chapter 15 on digital circuits, and for reviewing Chapter 14; B. G. Finch for his critical help in preparing the material on field effect transistors in both Chapter 5 and Chapter 17; finally, sincere appreciation is expressed to Mr. Joseph Gershon for his technical review of the entire revision.

M. P. R.
R. L. R.

Contents

PART ONE: PHYSICS

1 INTRODUCTION   3

    Development of the Transistor and Its Early Applications, 5
    Applications, 7
    Present State, 8
    Stargazing, 8

2 PHYSICS REVIEW   10

    Newtonian Physics, 11
    Application of Newton's Laws to the Solar System, 16
    Energy, 17
    The Isolated Atom, 20
    Atoms in Association to Form Crystals, 28
    Summary, 32

3 SEMICONDUCTORS   35

    Crystal Structure and Properties, 35
    Crystals with Impurities, 43
        N-type crystal, 44
        P-type crystal, 46
    Effect of Heat and Light on Semiconductors, 49

4 THE PHYSICAL ACTION OF TRANSISTORS 55

P-N Junctions, 55
N-P-N Junction Transistor, 60
P-N-P Junction Transistor, 69
Summary, 71

5 SUMMARY OF VARIOUS TRANSISTORS AND DIODES 72

Junction-Type Transistors, 73
    Grown Junction Transistors, 73
    Alloy Junction Transistors, 75
    Electrochemical Etched and Plated Transistors, 77
    Diffusion Techniques, 78
    Epitaxial Transistors, 78
    Physical Construction, 79
Field Effect Transistors, 80
    Junction Field Effect Transistor, 81
    Insulated Gate Field Effect Transistor, 83
    Physical Construction of FET, 85
Other Semiconductor Devices, 86

PART TWO: CIRCUITS

6 ELECTRICAL REVIEW 93

Basic Circuit Quantities, 93
    Current, 93
    Voltage, 95
    Power, 96
Passive Circuit Elements, 97
    Resistance, 97
    Capacitance, 97
    Inductance, 99
Basic Circuits, 100
    Series circuits, 100
    Parallel circuits, 104
    Resonance, 108
Voltage and Current Sources, 111
Methods of Circuit Analysis, 113
Circuit Theorems, 117
Black-Box Concept, 120
Maximum Power Transfer, 125
Frequency Response, 128
Transient Response, 134
Transformers, 136

Contents   xi

7   THE TRANSISTOR AS A CIRCUIT ELEMENT   142

    Method of Graphical Analysis, 143
        Junction transistor characteristics, 144
        Amplifier illustration, 149
    Method of Small Signal Equivalent Circuits, 155
        The equivalent circuit, 155
        Common-emitter amplifier illustration, 161
    Comparison of Methods, 164

8   SMALL SIGNAL AMPLIFIERS   168

    The Important Quantities, 169
        Power Gain, 170
        Current and voltage gain, 171
        Input and output resistances, 172
    Single Stage h-Parameter Analysis, 173
    Common-Emitter Amplifier, 179
    Common-Base Amplifier, 184
    Common-Collector Amplifier, 191
    Comparison of Three Connections, 194
    Transducer and Available Power Gain, 199
    Example of Small Signal Analysis, 203

9   POWER AMPLIFIERS   214

    Performance Quantities, 215
        Physical limitations, 216
        Power output, 219
        Distortion, 221
    Class A Power Amplifiers, 222
        Operating point, 226
        Load, 226
        Performance equations, 227
        Distortion, 231
        Common-base class A amplifier, 234
        Design example, 235
    Class B Power Amplifiers, 239
        Performance calculations, 242
        Load line, 247
        Distortion, 247
        Common-base class B amplifier, 248
        Design example, 249
    Other Power Circuits, 253
        Class A push-pull, 254
        Complementary symmetry, 255
        Single-ended class B circuits, 258

10 CASCADE AMPLIFIERS 265

    Biasing Circuits, 267
    Frequency Response, 276
        Mid-frequency gain calculations, 278
        Low-frequency gain calculations, 284
        High-frequency gain calculations, 290
    Design Considerations, 297
        Design example, 298
        RC-coupled amplifier, 305
    Comparison of the Two Designs, 317

11 BIAS EQUATIONS AND BIAS STABILITY 324

    Important Factors, 325
        Temperature variation, 325
        Unit-to-unit variation, 330
    D-C Equivalent Circuit, 330
    Stability Factor, 333
    Stabilized Bias Circuits and Equations, 335
        D-c current feedback, 335
        D-c voltage feedback, 341
    Additional Stabilizing Techniques, 346
        Temperature-sensitive elements, 346
        Tandem operation, 348
        Comment on common-base stabilized circuits, 349
    D-C Amplifier, 349

12 FEEDBACK 359

    Effects of Using Feedback, 360
        Gain, 363
        Gain stability, 363
        Frequency response, 364
        Input and output impedances, 365
        Nonlinear distortion, 365
    Methods of Treating Feedback in Transistors, 365
    A Transistor Connection Using Current Feedback, 366
    A Transistor Connection Using Voltage Feedback, 370
    Multistage Feedback, 373

13 NOISE 380

    General Noise Considerations, 381
        Description of noise, 382
        Thermal noise, 383
        Other thermal-type noises, 385
        Equivalent circuit of a noise source, 386

Contents

Transistor Noise Sources, 387
Noise Figure, 389
Methods of Measuring Noise Figure, 392
    Two-generator method, 392
    Direct noise figure measurement, 394
Use of Manufacturer's Stated Noise Figure, 395
Use of the Noise Figure, 398

14 TRANSISTOR OSCILLATORS AND NEGATIVE IMPEDANCE DEVICES   401

General Description of Oscillators, 402
Feedback Oscillators, 404
    Mathematical analysis of oscillators, 406
Negative Impedance Considerations, 411
    Use of the input characteristic, 413
    Negative resistance input characteristics, 415
Tunnel Diode as an Example of a Negative Impedance Device, 422

15 DIGITAL SWITCHING CIRCUITS   428

Basic Transistor Switch, 429
    OFF condition, 431
    ON condition, 432
    Transient conditions, 433
Triggered Digital Circuits, 438
    Flip-flops, 438
    Astable multivibrators, 444
    Monostable multivibrators, 449
    Schmitt trigger, 452
Logical Gating Circuits, 454
    Resistor-transistor logic, 455
    Direct-coupled transistor logic, 457
Analytical Expressions for the Transistor, 460

16 HIGH FREQUENCY DESCRIPTION OF TRANSISTORS   467

h parameter description, 470
y parameter description, 472
The hybrid-π equivalent circuit, 475

17 CIRCUIT ASPECTS OF FIELD EFFECT TRANSISTORS   480

Small signal performance quantities, 483
Common source connection, 485
Common drain condition, 486

APPENDICES

    I. Determinants, 487
   II. Parameter Conversions, 492
  III. Transistor Parameters, 497

INDEX   539

List of symbols

A_i	amplifier current gain
α	short circuit, common-base current gain; refers to either d-c or a-c value
A_p	power gain
A_v	voltage gain
β	short circuit, common-emitter current gain; refers to either d-c or a-c value
B	bandwidth
B_C	capacitive susceptance
B_L	inductive susceptance
BV_{CBO}	breakdown voltage, collector to base, emitter open
BV_{CEO}	breakdown voltage, collector to emitter, base open
BV_{EBO}	breakdown voltage, emitter to base, collector open
BW	bandwidth in cycles per second
C	capacitance
C_{ob}	common-base collector capacitance
C_{oe}	common-emitter collector capacitance
C_W	wiring capacitance
db	loss of interstage in decibels
Db	gain of transistor stages in decibels
Δ	small change in
Δ^h	determinant value of h parameters

List of symbols

E	electric field in volts per centimeter; also, sometimes source voltage
E_n	rms value of transistor noise voltage squared
E_2	voltage (effective value of sine wave)
e_N	rms noise voltage, short circuit test
F	noise factor
$f_{hfb} = f_{\alpha b}$	common base, small signal short circuit forward current gain cutoff frequency
$f_{hfe} = f_{\alpha e}$	common emitter, small signal short circuit forward current gain cutoff frequency
f_H	upper 3-db frequency point
f_{Hf}	upper 3 db frequency with feedback
f_L	lower 3-db frequency point
f_{Lf}	lower 3 db frequency with feedback
F_0	noise factor at 1000 c for a 1-c bandwidth
G	conductance
γ	conductivity in mhos per centimeter
h	refers to hybrid parameters in general
h_{11}	general input resistance
h_{12}	general voltage feedback ratio
h_{21}	general forward current ratio
h_{22}	general output admittance
h_{fb}	common base, small signal short-circuit forward current transfer ratio
h_{fe}	common emitter, small signal short-circuit forward current transfer ratio
h_{fc}	common collector, small signal short-circuit forward current transfer ratio
h_{FE}	common emitter, static or d-c value of forward current transfer ratio
h_{ib}, h_{ie}, h_{ic}	(common base, common emitter, common collector) small signal input impedance, output a-c short circuited
h_{IE}	common emitter static or d-c value of the input resistance
h_{ob}, h_{oe}, h_{oc}	(common base, common emitter, common collector) small signal output admittance, input a-c open circuited
h_{OE}	common emitter static or d-c value of output admittance
h_{rb}, h_{rc}, h_{re}	(common base, common emitter, common collector) small signal, reverse voltage transfer ratio, input a-c open circuited
h_{RE}	common emitter static or d-c value of reverse voltage ratio
$h*$	parameters for series feedback
h'	parameters for shunt feedback
I	current (effective value of sine wave)
i_e, i_b, i_c	instantaneous incremental current for emitter, base, and collector
i_E, i_B, i_C	instantaneous total current for emitter, base, and collector
I_e, I_b, I_c	rms or effective value of a-c incremental currents for emitter, base, and collector
I_E, I_B, I_C	d-c or operating point currents for emitter, base and collector

List of symbols

$I_{CBO}(I_{CO})$	d-c collector current when collector junction is reverse biased and emitter is open-circuited
I_{CEO}	d-c collector current with collector junction reverse biased and base open-circuited
I_{CES}	d-c reverse collector current with base shorted to emitter
J	current density in amperes per square centimeter
L	inductance
M.A.G.	maximum available gain
NF	noise figure in decibels
pf	pico-farads, equal 1×10^{-12} farads
P	power
P_{RN}	thermal noise power of R_g
P_{TN}	transistor input noise power
$P_C(T)$	maximum permissible collector dissipation as a function of temperature T
P_C	maximum permissible dissipation at reference temperature (usually 25°C)
Q	d-c operating point
R	resistance
R_F	feedback resistance
R_g	parallel combination of R_o and R_L
$R_s(R_g)$	source resistance
R_i	input resistance
R_L	load resistance
R_o	output resistance
R_p	parallel combination of R_B and R_i
R'_T	parallel combination of R_L, R_B and R_i
R_T	parallel combination of R_o, R_L, R_B and R_i
S	stability factor for changes in I_{CBO}
T	temperature in degrees centigrade
T_r	reference temperature (usually 25°C)
T_1	cycle time in triggered switching circuits
v_e, v_b, v_c	instantaneous incremental voltages of emitter, base, and collector
v_E, v_E, v_C	instantaneous total voltages of emitter, base, and collector
V_e, V_b, V_c	effective or rms value of a-c incremental voltages of emitter, base, and collector

V_{CB}	d-c collector to base voltage
V_{CE}	d-c collector to emitter voltage
V_{BE}	(for N-P-N) base to emitter voltage (positive in active region)
V_{EB}	(for P-N-P) emitter to base voltage (positive in active region)
V_{BB}, V_{EE}, V_{CC}	d-c supply voltages for base, emitter and collector
X_L	inductive reactance
X_C	capacitive reactance
Y	admittance
Z	impedance
$|Z|$	magnitude of impedance

Actual current direction.

PART ONE

PHYSICS

1
Introduction

Before delving into the physical and circuitry aspects of transistors it is useful to deal first with the question, "What is a transistor and what does it do?" A typical first answer is, "The transistor is an electronic device that performs the same functions as the vacuum tube." Taking into consideration the wide publicity afforded the vacuum tube by radio and television, this definition seems sufficient. However, it is useful to consider for a moment the basic function of both the vacuum tube and the transistor.

In a very basic sense, either of these two devices serves mainly to *amplify* electronic communication signals. Note that this definition does not restrict the devices to amplifiers as such; amplification is intrinsic to oscillators, electronic switches, function generators, and some mixers and detectors. In other words, the property of amplification is essential to each of the applications to which either transistors or vacuum tubes, excluding diodes, may be put. In this sense then, either of the two devices produces at its output, when an electric signal appears at its input, some sort of amplified signal. The output signal is usually uniquely related to the input, but this does not mean that the output is necessarily a replica of the input.

Another concept that is useful for electronic devices is that they function as continuous controls. The implication here is that an input signal causes the device to *control* a larger output signal. As in any control circuit, the fact that the output signal is larger stems from the fact that there is a source of power in the output circuit. Thus in both vacuum tubes and transistors the object that allows the "enlargement" is the battery (or power supply) in the output side. The device itself acts as a converter in the sense that it converts such battery power to power that is in the form of the input signal.

In any of its many applications, then, the vacuum tube and the transistor can be thought of as acting primarily as amplifiers or as continuous controls.

Whereas the basic vacuum tube requires a plate, cathode, grid, and heater (to cause the cathode to emit electrons), the transistor appears, on the surface, to be far simpler. It consists essentially of a piece of prepared semiconductor to which three leads are attached. The fact that it appears thus so simple does not mean that it is a simple device to manufacture or apply. The preparation of the semiconductor is indeed a very difficult process, and many phenomena have to be taken into account when applying the transistor in a circuit.

Since the transistor consists essentially of a solid piece of material, it is seen that physically the transistor differs in conception from the vacuum tube. Whereas the vacuum tube requires the passage of electrons from the cathode to the plate within an evacuated bulb, all the electronic action in a transistor occurs within a solid piece of material. Although there are many differences between the two devices, as we shall see in the following chapters, the above is certainly the difference which strikes one at the beginning.

Considering this physical difference, it is clear that the transistor requires no such element as a heater. The saving in power requirements as a result of this is probably the greatest boon resulting from the use of transistors. Also, as a result of the physical construction described, the transistor is very small and extremely rugged. Another asset, not evident from the construction, is the long life expectancy of transistors.

In developing the transistor, various difficulties had to be overcome. Two of the major problems associated with transistors have been the difficulty of producing units with uniform characteristics, and the temperature dependence of the characteristics. Improved fabrication and circuit design techniques have permitted satisfactory solutions to these issues. Formerly noise and low power-handling

Introduction

ability were also disadvantages, but these considerations have been successfully solved early in the transistor history. For some applications, the low impedances of the transistor are undesirable. The newer field-effect transistor is now available for such cases.

With this brief over-all look at the transistor, we will scan the history and development of this device.

**DEVELOPMENT OF THE
TRANSISTOR AND ITS
EARLY APPLICATIONS**

In 1948 Brattain and Bardeen of the Bell Telephone Laboratories were studying the surface properties of germanium semiconductor rectifiers. During these studies they noted that the conduction properties of a semiconductor diode could be controlled by an additional electrode attached to the semiconductor. This simple phenomenon resulted in what we now know as the *point contact transistor*. It consists essentially of a small slab of germanium (semiconductor) upon which two metal contacts are placed. In terms of the original experiment, the semiconductor and the one contact (called the collector) make up the rectifier and the additional control contact is called the *emitter*.

It was found that when an input current was inserted in the emitter contact a larger current resulted in the collector contact. This, coupled with the fact that the input impedance was much smaller than the output impedance, resulted in a revolutionary amplifying device.

Although the principle involved held great potential, this basic point contact unit had several drawbacks. Its internally generated noise was much higher than that for the vacuum tube; it reacted adversely to high humidity and temperature; and its structure was rather fragile.

The next major step in the transistor history occurred in July 1949. W. Shockley, also of the Bell Telephone Laboratories, published an analysis that predicted the possibility of a *junction transistor*. Soon thereafter experimental evidence that corroborated the theory was published and the junction transistor was brought into being. The basic difference from the previous device is that here the important action occurs wholly *within* the semiconductor instead of at the metal contacts. The emitter-collector action is achieved by providing three regions within the semiconductor; one region acts as the emitter and another as the collector. This is often described as utilizing an *area* contact instead of a point contact.

A basic operational difference between the two types is that the junction type has an emitter-to-collector current gain slightly less than unity, while the point contact type a current gain greater than unity. It still has emitter-to-collector voltage and power gain, however, because of the ratio of input to output impedance.

This junction transistor showed greater promise than its predecessor because it had better noise properties and was immediately more rugged. Also, it was deemed that the characteristics of the three-region semiconductors were more amenable to improvement than the characteristics of the point contact type. The progress that followed was devoted mostly to the junction type and consisted of attempts to improve the techniques of producing the semiconductor junctions, and also different schemes to acquire the junction action. Point contact transistors were abandoned entirely fairly early in the history of transistors.

The first junction transistors were prepared by a process called the *grown-junction* technique, and this process resulted mainly in N-P-N junction devices. A significant development occurred in 1951 when the alloy method of producing junctions was perfected. The semiconductors resulting from this process are largely of the P-N-P type. Present-day commercial transistors are usually made with this process.

During attempts to raise the upper frequency limit of transistors, electrochemical etching and plating was applied to transistor fabrication. This led to the development of the surface-barrier transistor. Many new types of junction transistors have been developed since these early types. These are discussed in Chapter 5.

Throughout the entire period of these changes in junction transistors, efforts were constantly directed toward improving the basic properties of the semiconductors themselves. A most significant development occurred when the techniques of handling silicon were perfected, permitting the fabrication of silicon junction transistors. Silicon devices will operate at higher temperatures than those made from germanium.

More recently, new fabrication techniques have made the field-effect transistor more important. In addition an array of integrated circuit techniques has been evolved.

Introduction

The great interest in nuclear energy has created the need for electron devices that will work in high-density neutron and gamma fields. Transistors have been investigated with this in mind and it has been discovered that semiconductors are very sensitive to gamma and neutron bombardment. Efforts throughout the industry continue on the problem of producing transistors which are insensitive to the radiation from nuclear reactors.

APPLICATIONS

From the very beginning the electronics industry was keenly interested in the transistor. The possibility of light weight, small size, and low power consumption devices was very intriguing. The first application of any commercial importance was in hearing aids where the size and operating expense of these devices were drastically reduced.

Other early applications were in the telephone switching circuits and portable radios. The applications at present are as numerous as there are applications for amplifiers, multivibrators, oscillators, etc. In other words, transistors are being used in all electronic applications except special cases where vacuum devices may be necessary. The military and space electronics industry were the first to effect a complete switch over from vacuum tubes. The entire commercial industry soon followed, and now practically all electronic equipments are available in transistor form. The change over has depended, of course, on economic factors as well as technical factors.

The small size, reliability, and low power consumption of the transistor have permitted space missions and experiments not otherwise possible. In addition, many military equipments were made feasible by the transistor. In the domestic and industrial sphere the most important development has been the phenomenal growth of the computer and data processing area. In addition, the transistor has resulted in exploiting the general advantages of extreme portability. This is particularly true for communications. The portable radio and television is being used in the domestic and industrial spheres.

More or less as a by-product of the interest stimulated by transistors, a whole family of semiconductor devices has come into being.

These include the photodiode, phototransistor, Zener diode for voltage regulation, double-base diode, tunnel diode, and the solar and atomic batteries.

PRESENT STATE

It is useful to summarize the state of the art in transistor performance and applications. Because of the greater emphasis, in the past twenty years, on research in the technical fields, it may safely be said that the transistor has advanced farther in fifteen years than the technology of vacuum tubes advanced in fifty.

At the present time experimental transistors are being built which have a frequency response up to thousands of megacycles. Other transistors are available having a power dissipation of up to hundreds of watts. At present commercial transistors exist that have noise figures below 4 db and a life expectancy measured in years rather than in hours—a life expectancy of forty years is estimated by some authorities. Transistors have been produced that will operate at temperatures of 375°C (centigrade) and may be stored at temperatures up to 500°C. Also, as would be expected with a solid device, the transistor is free from shock and vibration effects to a great extent.

STARGAZING

In the future, transistors will continue to influence all aspects of electronics. The application of computers and data processing to all spheres of life has been taken for granted in recent years. The general trend toward evermore complex equipment in increasingly smaller space will continue.

In the future the trend toward microelectronic or integrated circuit packaging, yielding complete functional units with multiple transistors, will accelerate. This will permit another generation of size reduction.

Many concepts, still seeming far-fetched, are made more feasible by these developments. For example, automatic highways upon which the driver may relax after dialing the location to which he wants to travel are feasible. The nation-wide telephone dialing system, which is partially completed already, is being made possible in part by the transistor. Communication satellites, which will permit easy communication with any part of the world are already being developed. In addition, long distance space missions will require use of these transistor developments. In addition, the long predicted wrist watch radio is now nearly a reality.

In totality, it is expected that the transistor will make possible many new devices that will make everyday living easier and more enjoyable.

2
Physics review

In this chapter the salient points of basic physics are reviewed. Since the transistor is a semiconductor device, and since these devices are still generally unfamiliar, their operation is explained by utilizing the fundamental laws of physics.[1]

The basic building block of all matter is the atom; therefore this physics review is directed toward providing an understanding of the structure of the atom. In order to accomplish this understanding, Newtonian physics and the concepts of energy are considered. Following consideration of the atom, the action of combined atoms in a solid is studied. This leads to considering three types of solids: conductors, semiconductors, and insulators. Of these, the semiconductor is of interest here, but comparison to the other two is useful.

[1] The initial material in this review may be unnecessary for those readers having adequate background in elementary physics. The purpose of this material is to act as a refresher for those whose physics training is far in the past and to establish a consistent, continuous development of the physical action of semiconductors. For the readers of adequate background the authors suggest merely scanning the initial material and beginning with the section on "The Isolated Atom."

NEWTONIAN PHYSICS

A basic picture of a simple isolated atom can be obtained by applying the classical laws of mechanics to the two charged particles that form the atom. Therefore we will quickly review the classic Newtonian laws.

It is maintained by many authorities that Newton's formulation of the fundamental physical laws was the beginning of modern science. Newton's studies, although originally directed toward the movement of the planets in the universe, led to the development of the fundamental laws of all motion. These laws have remained unchanged since Newton's time in spite of the fact that refinements are necessary when dealing with extremely small quantities at high velocity, such as the quantitative behavior of individual atoms. Since we are interested here in acquiring a fundamental concept of the atom, we shall rely on Newton's basic laws without delving into quantitative calculations requiring the refinements mentioned.

Newton's four laws consist of three laws of motion plus one law concerning gravitation.

Newton's first law of motion:

A body at rest will remain at rest, and a body in motion will remain in motion with constant velocity as long as no unbalanced external forces act on it.

Newton's second law of motion:

If an unbalanced force acts upon a body, the body will be accelerated; the magnitude of the acceleration will be proportional to the magnitude of the unbalanced force and the direction of the acceleration will be in the direction of the unbalanced force.

Newton's third law of motion:

If one body exerts a force on a second body, the second body exerts a force of equal magnitude but in the opposite direction on the first body.

Newton's law of universal gravitation:

Every body in the universe attracts every other body with a force which is directly proportional to the product of their masses and inversely proportional to the square of the distance between them.

It is worthwhile to utilize common experience in obtaining an understanding of these four laws. Newton's first law specifies that every body possesses a resistance to a change of motion. Inertia is the measure of this tendency of a body to remain in its present state of motion. This occurs when the body is at rest as well as when it is moving. The property of inertia can be demonstrated by placing a coin on a slip of paper and then pulling the paper out from under the coin with a quick jerk. Although the paper has moved, the position of the coin remains unchanged. It is the inertia of the coin that keeps it from moving when it is initially at rest.

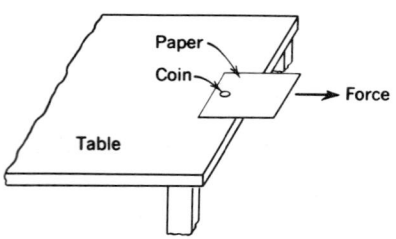

Fig. 2-1. Demonstration of the property of inertia for a body at rest. Pull the paper rapidly and the coin remains on the table top.

Another common experience exhibits the property of inertia in a moving body. When riding in a car in which the brakes are suddenly applied, the car will stop quickly. The rider will continue forward however, unless he is braced. This forward movement continues until he places his hand against the dashboard or some other object to check his motion.

To restate Newton's first law, we can say that a body tends to remain in its present state of motion unless acted upon by an unbalanced external force.

Newton's second law specifies the magnitude and direction of the change in motion when an unbalanced external force is applied to a body. This change in motion is measured by the acceleration of the body. When a force is applied, the acceleration will be proportional to the force, and inversely proportional to the mass of the body. Before proceeding further it is useful to consider the property of mass.

The mass of an object is a measure of the amount of material it contains as indicated by its inertia. Since weight is often confused with mass, it is necessary to note the distinction. Mass is an intrinsic property of a body, whereas weight is the property that specifies the effect of the earth's gravitation on the mass. If the weights of a number of bodies are measured at sea level, the weight and mass of each body will be related by a single constant. Now, if measurements are made at Pike's Peak on the same bodies, the weight and mass will again be related by a constant; but this constant is different from the former constant. The masses of the bodies remain the same but the measured weights change. This is shown in Figure 2-2 and results

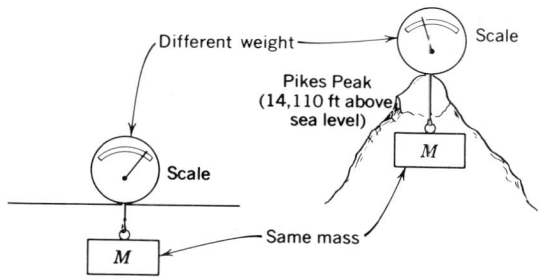

Fig. 2-2. Difference between weight and mass. Weight depends on position; mass is independent of position.

from the fact that the effect of the earth's gravity varies with different altitudes. This difference, however, is so small as to be negligible in practically all cases where the body is relatively close to the earth's surface.

Returning to Newton's second law then, the acceleration experienced by a body is proportional to the force applied and inversely proportional to its mass. In the usual set of units the proportionality factor is unity so that acceleration equals the force divided by the mass. The acceleration of a body is expressed as the rate of change of velocity. Thus the force on a body can be determined by noting its mass and the rate of change of its velocity. An easily demonstrated example of this consists of rolling a ball bearing across a table top and causing it to strike a block of wood. It is the motion of the wood that will be studied. As shown in Figure 2-3, the ball bearing will apply a force to the block of wood upon striking it. Depending upon the mass of the wood, the block will be accelerated from a velocity of zero to some finite velocity. In this example the ball bearing acts as the source of external force that causes the block to experience an acceleration. This same experiment can be done with two coins on a smooth surface.

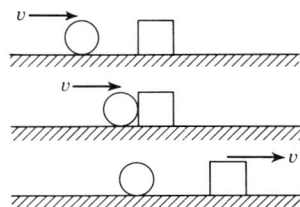

Fig. 2-3. Example of acceleration resulting from an external unbalanced force.

Whereas the first two laws consider the properties of a single body, Newton's third law of motion deals with the forces associated between two bodies. This law may be restated thus: For every action there is an equal and opposite reaction. Although the forces on the two bodies are equal and opposite, they do not cancel each other since they act on different bodies. Thus when one steps from a boat the person is moved toward the shore while the boat is propelled backward. In order to move forward one exerts a force on the boat; the boat exerts an equal and opposite force on the person. In spite of the equality of forces, the boat will move a smaller distance than the person if the boat's effective mass is greater.

Another example of action and reaction is experienced when walking across a smooth floor upon which a rug is placed. The rug tends to move backward when one tries to push forward on it. The reason for the rug movement lies in the fact that since there is little friction between the rug and the floor, there is no sufficient force available to push back on the person. Therefore, the rug moves according to its mass and the force applied. Figure 2-4 depicts two familiar situa-

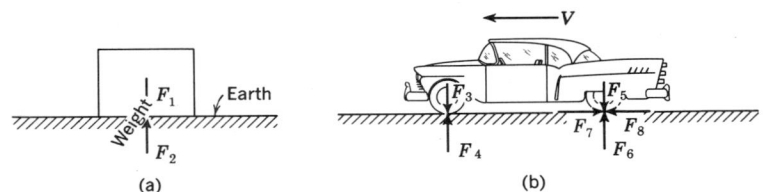

Fig. 2-4. Diagrams showing the forces associated with a weight at rest upon the earth and the forces between a moving car and the earth: in (a) $F_1 = F_2$; in (b) $F_3 = F_4$, $F_5 = F_6$, and $F_7 = F_8$.

tions that illustrate this third law of motion. Part (a) shows a weight lying on the earth; the force exerted on the earth by the body's weight is equaled by the force that the earth exerts on the body. In (b) the same condition applies to the vertical forces of the automobile tires. In the horizontal direction, the tire exerts a force (F_7) on the road. The road in turn exerts a force (F_8) on the tire so that $F_7 = F_8$. If F_7 were greater than F_8 the tire would be spinning on the road; if F_8 were greater than F_7 the tire would be skidding.

It has been noted that the first three laws deal with motion; the fourth law concerns the attraction between any two bodies of the universe. This law states that all bodies of the universe experience an attraction toward each other. When one of the bodies concerned is the earth, this attraction is simply gravity. It was stated earlier that the weight which a body possesses is the effect of the earth upon the

Physics review

mass of the body. This effect is caused by the attraction between the earth and the body (gravity). Newton's law states that the magnitude of the weight determined by gravity is equal to the product of the mass of the earth and the mass of the body divided by the square of the distance between the body and the center of the earth. Although gravity is the clearest example of this universal attraction between bodies, it must be remembered that all bodies attract each other. Thus two books lying on a table attract each other; however, because the attraction between the earth and each of the books (their weight) causes a much greater frictional force on the table, the force between the books is hardly measurable.

An example of the application of this universal law of gravitation is shown in Figure 2-5. Two situations are depicted: a certain mass

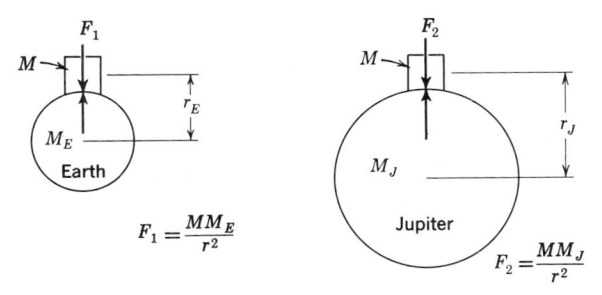

$$F_1 = \frac{MM_E}{r^2} \qquad F_2 = \frac{MM_J}{r^2}$$

Fig. 2-5. Universal gravitation. F_2 is $2\frac{1}{2}$ times F_1 due to the larger mass of Jupiter.

is shown lying on the surface of the earth, and the same mass is considered on the surface of the planet Jupiter. The product of the mass of the earth and the mass of the body divided by the square of the distance between the body and the center of the earth determines the force (weight) that the body experiences on the surface of the earth. If this same quantity is calculated, using the mass of Jupiter and the distance to its center, the weight experienced on the surface of Jupiter would be $2\frac{1}{2}$ times as much as in the case of Earth. This is caused by the fact that the mass of Jupiter is much larger than the mass of Earth. Thus if one weighs 200 pounds on Earth, one would experience a weight of 500 pounds on Jupiter. It should be noted that one's own mass remains unchanged but the force experienced would increase.

This concludes the review of Newtonian physics. Since the goal of this physics review is to obtain an understanding of the atom, Newtonian laws will be applied to the solar system. When attempting to picture an atom, it is useful to begin by considering an analogy between certain aspects of the solar system and a simple atom. This affords us an elementary picture of the atom that will then be modified to form a more accurate picture.

APPLICATION OF NEWTON'S LAWS TO THE SOLAR SYSTEM

Before considering Newton's explanation of the solar system, it is interesting to trace the various concepts that preceded Newton's discovery. Ptolemy explained the action of the planets and the sun from the standpoint that the earth was the center of the solar system and the other planets and sun revolved about the earth in circular paths This appeared correct until refined measurements proved that the orbits of the planets are not circular. Copernicus expounded the theory that the sun is the center, and the planets, including the earth, revolve around the sun. Kepler proved that this was true and postulated laws which, he contended, govern the motion of the planets. These laws, which will not be stated here, led Newton to discover his law of universal gravitation and his three laws of motion.

The current concept of the solar system is as follows. The sun is the center of our solar system and the planets revolve about the sun in elliptical orbits. The forces which hold the planets in their relative positions can now be developed from Newton's three laws of motion and his law of universal gravitation.

Without reflecting upon the philosophical question of how the universe began, we shall assume that the planets are located in their orbits and possess their respective velocities. Thus we are dealing with the question of how the planets maintain this original movement. In accordance with Newton's universal law of gravitation each planet exerts an attractive force on all the other planets. The forces between the planets, however, are small in comparison with the forces between the planets and the sun; therefore we may neglect all forces except those between any planet and the sun. The forces between planets do affect the respective orbits, but this is a minor consideration.

We shall consider the application of Newton's three laws of motion to the solar system by considering the earth. Newton's first law, specifying that a body maintains its present motion unless acted upon by a force, predicts that the earth will tend to continue in a straight path with its present velocity. The attraction between the sun and the earth, however, provides the force that causes the earth to follow a curved orbit about the sun. This is somewhat analogous to the action that takes place when a weight is whirled around on the end of a string. Here the tension force provided by the string keeps the weight in a curved path. Newton's second law, which specifies that the result of any unbalanced force is an acceleration, is fulfilled when it is realized that the continuously changing direction of the earth's velocity represents an acceleration (of the earth) toward the sun. Figure 2-6 illustrates the force that acts upon the earth and the continuously changing direction of its velocity. The velocity is always tangent to the orbit at any position on the path. The third law of motion dealing with action and reaction is already illustrated. The force exerted by the sun on the earth is exactly equal and opposite to the force required by the earth to keep it in the curved orbit. If these forces were not equal, the earth would move closer to or farther from the sun until the forces became equalized.

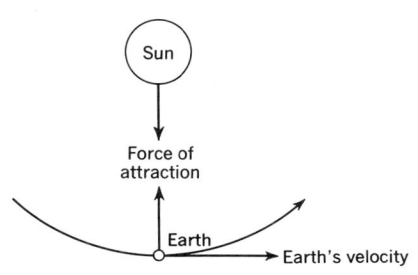

Fig. 2-6. Earth's orbit and gravitational force. Force of attraction pulls earth into a curved orbit around the sun.

The same conditions described for the earth also apply to the other planets. Their initial velocities, their distances from the sun, the sun's mass, and their masses determine their orbits as required by Newton's laws of motion. As stated before, this role of the planets and sun will later be used to suggest an elementary picture of an isolated atom, where we deal with electrons instead of planets, and a nucleus instead of the sun. Also, the force of attraction will be electrostatic instead of gravitational.

ENERGY

The concepts of energy are a necessary consideration in any physical problem and they are especially vital in understanding the action in atoms. The properties of semiconductors will later be illustrated by considering the energies of electrons. For these reasons the basic concepts of energy will now be reviewed.

Having discussed forces from the standpoint of Newtonian physics, we may now consider what happens when a force acts over a given distance. If we push a block of wood across a table top we are doing work. Work is defined as the product of a force and the distance over which it operates. It should be noted that distance is an important concept in work; if we hold a weight stationary, no work is being done on the block even though our muscles will tire. Energy is closely related to work, for energy is a measure of the ability to do work. Energy is generally considered in terms of three basic types: potential energy, kinetic energy, and heat energy.

Kinetic energy is the measure of the ability of an object in motion to do work. A simple illustration of how a moving object can perform work by exerting a force over a distance is afforded by considering the action when the moving body strikes another stationary body. Upon impact, the second body will experience a force and will move accordingly. Thus the first body has exerted work on the second body. The amount of work that a moving body can perform is proportional to the product of the square of its velocity and its mass:

$$\text{kinetic energy} = \text{K.E.} = \tfrac{1}{2}mv^2$$

Figure 2-7 shows two bodies of equal mass but with different velocities. The second object can perform more work than the first since its kinetic energy is higher.

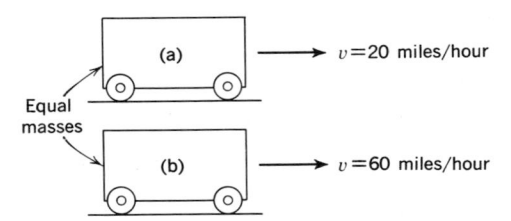

Fig. 2-7. Kinetic energy. Object (b) has the larger kinetic energy as its velocity is higher than that of object (a).

Potential energy is an energy of position. Position here refers to distance from an ever-present force. The most familiar force in this respect is the gravitational force. This force is ever present in the

Physics review

sense that it is a permanent force which acts everywhere in the vicinity of the earth. If the surface of the earth is considered the reference point or datum plane, we can see how any body positioned above the surface is capable of doing work. If a book is resting on a table of one foot height, work can be done by allowing the book to drop to the floor. If the book is tied to a heavy object on the table, the falling of the book will exert a force over a distance on the heavy object. If the table is now made three feet in height, more work can be done by the book. In this manner, position above the earth determines the potential energy of a body in the gravitational field. Figure 2-8 is an illustration of the potential energy of two objects.

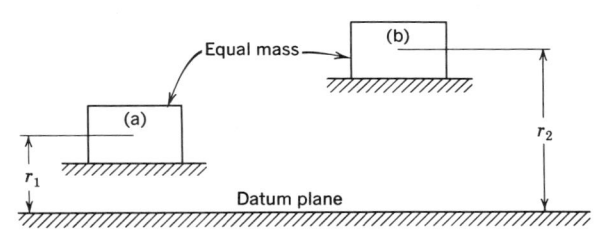

Fig. 2-8. Potential energy. In this diagram, object (b) has the larger potential energy because it is located higher above the datum plane than object (a).

Although heat energy is one of the basic forms of energy, heat energy is not usually considered in terms of its ability to do work by exerting a force over a distance. Usually heat energy is considered in terms of its equivalent mechanical ability for exerting such a force. A familiar example will illustrate, however, the manner in which heat can do work directly. If heat is applied to an air-filled balloon, the air will expand and increase the volume of the balloon. The force exerted in expanding times the distance expanded is the measure of the work performed by the heat. A frequent source of heat energy in physical motion problems is friction. Whenever two objects are caused to slide on each other, the friction, which produces a force that opposes the sliding, causes the sliding objects to receive heat energy.

Having discussed three of the basic types of energy, we may now consider a very important relationship between the three forms. The first law of thermodynamics specifies that energy cannot be destroyed but only converted from one form to another. This is also called the *law of conservation of energy.*

The changing of energy from one form to another can be illustrated by the following simple experiment. Place a piece of paper as a bridge between two books that are separated about two inches. Place a pencil on each end of the paper where it lies on the book. If another pencil is now held about two inches above the paper, the pencil possesses a certain amount of potential energy. If the pencil is released, it immediately gains kinetic energy by virtue of its motion; meanwhile its potential energy is decreasing since the pencil is losing height. In this manner potential energy is converted into kinetic energy. When the pencil has struck the paper and stopped, the kinetic energy has decreased to zero. A measure of the kinetic energy possessed by the pencil is the amount by which the paper is deflected. When the kinetic energy is reduced to zero, that energy is converted to heat energy (frictional) at the points of support on the book and the heat energy of impact of the falling pencil onto the paper.

Another example of the energy conversions is exhibited by tossing a box onto a shelf. The stored energy in the body is converted into kinetic energy of the box as it leaves the hand. As the box goes higher into the air some of the kinetic energy is converted to potential energy due to the continually increasing height. When the box reaches its maximum height it has zero kinetic energy and maximum potential energy. As it descends toward the shelf potential energy is changed to kinetic energy due to the downward motion. Upon striking the shelf, the accrued kinetic energy is changed to heat energy of impact.

THE ISOLATED ATOM

Since the most fundamental unit of all matter is the atom, we shall now consider materials eventually leading to semiconductors by studying the properties of single atoms as they would appear if they were isolated. We shall then proceed to investigate the action when many atoms are combined to form a crystal of a solid material.

The arrangement and action of the separate components of an isolated atom can be crudely visualized as similar to a minute solar system. In analogy to the sun of the solar system, which is the center of attraction, each atom possesses a nucleus which is the center of attraction forces. Corresponding to the planets of the universe the electrons of an atom rotate in orbits about the nucleus. The forces and relationships between the nucleus and electrons of an atom are similar to those existing between the sun and its planets.

In spite of a basic analogy between the solar system and atoms, three major differences should be noted. The most obvious is the extreme difference in size; whereas the solar system is several billion miles in diameter, the diameter of the atomic solar system is so small that 1×10^{23} (1 with 23 zeros following) such systems can be placed in a cubic centimeter. The second way in which they differ is the nature of the attraction forces. The action of our solar system is determined by gravitational forces. The forces existing in the atomic system are electrostatic forces; electrostatic forces are the attractional force that always exist between two electric charges. The attractional forces referred to here pertain to Coulomb's familiar law, which specifies that like charges repel and unlike charges attract each other. The charges may be either single charges such as electrons, or may be solid objects that possess an excess or deficiency of electrons. If a body is uncharged it is said to be electrically neutral. The electrostatic forces act much like the gravitational forces; a charged object creates a field that affects any other charges in the field much like gravity affects any bodies with mass. One difference lies in the fact that an electric field may repel another charge, whereas the gravitational field always attracts objects. A third difference distinguishing the solar system and the atom is a matter of orderliness. The electrons corresponding to the planets all possess the same mass; the planets of the solar system do not have equal masses. Furthermore, we will see later that this basic model constructed from classical mechanics and electrostatics will have to be altered in certain ways. For example, it will be found that only certain discrete orbits can exist out of the many possible. Nevertheless is it worthwhile, for visualization, to draw the basic analogy between the solar system and a simple isolated atom.

As a first approximation, the electron may be pictured as an extremely small particle with a known mass and possessing one unit of negative electronic charge. It is important to note that every electron has exactly the same mass and charge. The nucleus, the center of the atom, is made up of protons and neutrons. The proton has a mass 1800 times that of the electron and has one unit of positive charge. Thus electrically the proton is equivalent to the electron except for the difference in mass and the opposite sign for the charge. The neutron has a mass approximately equal to the proton but has no electric charge. These two quantities, the proton and the neutron, combine to form the nucleus.

In accordance with the analogy to the solar system, the atom is made up of a nucleus around which one or more electrons are spinning in orbits. For all atoms there are a certain number of orbits available. These orbits also represent energy levels for the electrons; each orbit corresponds to a certain energy, and no more than two electrons may exist in one level or orbit. It is very important to note that these energy levels, or orbits, exist in discrete levels for the atom. No electron may exist at any level (or orbit) other than one of the permissible levels. Thus the electrons are restricted in the sense that their energies must occur in one of the permissible levels for the atom. For purposes of considering the chemical properties of the atoms a group of permissible orbits are combined into electron "shells." The amplitude difference in energy between shells is much greater than the difference between energy levels within a shell. Thus the shells can be regarded as appropriate groupings of the possible orbits. The number of electrons that appear in the various shells determine the chemical properties of the atom, and the state of the energies or orbits within the shells determine the electrical properties of the atom.

There is a definite maximum to the number of electrons that may appear in each of the shells. A smaller number than this may appear but not a larger number. The first shell, or inner shell, may possess two electrons. The second may have up to eight electrons, and the third, eighteen. The fourth shell may have as many as 32 electrons. The atoms or elements that we shall be concerned with do not have more than four shells. A law that holds for the first three shells is that whenever one of these shells has any electrons it is certain that the lower shells are filled. The fourth shell may have electrons after the third one has at least eighteen. Each of the existing atoms or elements differs in the total number of electrons which occur in the various shells; there are 98 different elements and each one differs in this manner. For example, hydrogen has one electron in the first shell; helium contains two electrons in the first shell (this is the maximum for the first shell); lithium has two electrons in the first shell and one in the second shell; neon contains two in the first shell, and eight in the second shell.

A very important property of all atoms is that the electric charge on the nucleus is always equal to the negative charge as determined

Physics review

by the number of electrons. Thus for hydrogen the nucleus has a positive charge of one unit, helium has a positive charge of two units, and lithium has a charge of three units. This means that the atom by itself is always electrically neutral; however, if an atom gains or loses some electrons it will be in a charged condition. If an atom is in the charged state it is said to be an *ionized atom* and it is called an *ion*. Figure 2-9 represents the electron shells and nuclei of the hydrogen

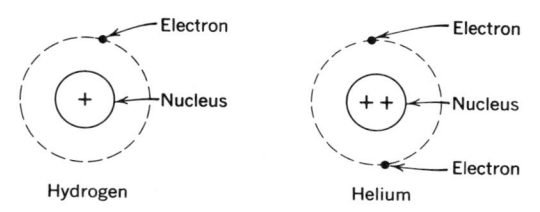

Fig. 2-9. Hydrogen and helium atoms.

and the helium atoms. It is seen that the charge on the nucleus equals the number of electrons in the atom. The *atomic number* refers to the number of positive charges on the nucleus. Thus, the atomic number also equals the total number of electrons in the atom.

The electrons in the outermost shells (the higher order shells) are called *valence electrons*, because it is these electrons that determine the action of the atom when it combines with atoms of another element to form compounds. When the outermost shell of an atom is completely filled, that element is stable and not capable of combining with the atoms of another element to form a compound. If this outer shell is not completely filled, however, the atom is susceptible to forming a compound. The general nature of these formations is that an atom will accept valence electrons from another atom so that the combined electrons will fill the outer shell. In turn an atom may contribute its valence electrons to those of another atom to form a compound. A general rule is that if the atom contains more than four valence electrons it will usually receive valence electrons from another atom. If the atom contains fewer than four valence electrons it will usually contribute its electrons to those of the other atom.

Having considered the construction of the various elements in terms of the electrons and nucleus, we can now consider those forces and actions which bind the atom together. As mentioned earlier, the forces acting within the atom are similar to the forces acting in the solar system. The nucleus contains an electric charge which is greater than the charge of any one electron (except for the case of hydrogen); it will be remembered that the total charge of the nucleus is equal to the total charge of all the electrons of the atom. The electric attraction between the nucleus and any one of the electrons exerts a force on the electron that is very similar to the gravitational force exerted by the sun on the planets. Therefore the electrons can be thought of as following curved orbits, much as the planets. In this way the basic classical laws of mechanics can be used to picture certain aspects of the motion of electrons. The inward force needed to constantly change the direction of motion of the electron is supplied by the force of attraction between the electron and the nucleus. As in the case of the solar system, the law of action and reaction must hold; the orbit is determined by the energy that the electron possesses. In other words, the force needed to change the direction of the electron (to keep it moving in a curved orbit) must be exactly equal to the force of attraction provided by the electrostatic force of attraction. If by some means the electron is provided with more energy, the orbit, and hence the energy level, of that electron must change. Since it is very easy to give additional energy to an atom, it should be clear that any one electron has the ability to have its orbit or energy level changed. When it is thus changed, however, the energy supplied must be of such a value that the electron energy can jump from one permissible level to another.

The energy that an electron possesses in any orbit consists of two parts. The electron has kinetic energy due to its motion, and potential energy due to its position with respect to the nucleus. When energy is added to an electron, both the kinetic component and the potential component are increased. It can easily be seen that, since any electron must jump from one discrete level to another, the amount of energy which it is capable of receiving is discrete in value. This reaffirms the fact that electrons cannot exist between permissible orbits.

To reiterate the essential facts concerning the orbits or energy levels of the electrons in an isolated atom: the atom possesses many levels corresponding to orbits in which it is permissible for an electron to be and there are many more possible orbits than electrons. All the electrons of the atom must exist in one of the permissible energy levels. For purposes of defining chemical composition these many orbits are grouped into collections of orbits called electron shells. Those electrons in the orbits of the outermost shell are called valence electrons, and these are active in forming compounds. Since there are many more orbits then electrons, the implied fact is that electrons may move from orbit to orbit if proper energy is provided.

Although it is useful to envisage the atom in terms of the analogy to the basic mechanics situation, this classical model does not yield accurate results for cases other than a single electron atom. In general, the electron must be considered as having both the properties of a *particle* (as we have implied heretofore) and properties of a *wave*. Consideration of the wave properties of the atom resulted in the mathematical theory called *quantum mechanics* or *wave mechanics*. The most famous tool in this theory is Schrödinger's wave equation. As a result of this theory, four quantum numbers are defined that correspond to a solution of this basic wave equation. Each of these four quantum numbers must be given to completely specify the energy (or state) of an electron.

It is necessary to consider how the wave mechanical theory alters our picture of the atom. Dealing with the wave equation, it is found that the electron is more precisely a *wave packet* rather than a single particle. An interpretation of this is that one cannot specify the exact position of the electron particle; the effect of the electron is spread over a region rather than being concentrated at a definite point. Thus one is confined to talking about the probability of finding the electron at a given point at a particular time. When many electrons are involved, the wave treatment in effect treats the individual electron as a statistical quantity. Accurate statements can be made only on a statistical basis.

In spite of the complications introduced by the dual (wave and particle) nature of the electron, it is still useful for many purposes to visualize the basic model in terms of a particle.

We will now consider ways in which the energy of electrons within an atom can be increased. The application of heat is one of the most convenient ways to apply energy to an atom. If we can envisage having a single atom isolated in space, the application of heat would act to raise the energy level, and thus change the orbit, of some electrons in the atom. The determination of which electrons will receive an increase in energy is decided by the ease with which they can receive the energy; those electrons that previously had the highest energy will be the first to have their orbits changed. It is these electrons that exist in the outermost orbits of the atom. If the proper reference is taken it can be shown that those electrons in orbits closest to the nucleus have less energy than the electrons in the farther orbits. Thus it is the electrons that are in the outermost orbits that will have their orbits changed first by the application of external additional energy such as heat.

Since the electrons must exist in certain discrete levels, it is seen that when the energy is applied to an atom the amount of heat absorbed will be in discrete quantities. These discrete quantities, called *quantums of energy*, correspond to the difference in energy between the permissible levels for the electrons. If a sufficient amount of heat energy is absorbed by any one electron, that electron can be completely removed from the influence of the atom. This process is called ionization and is discussed in the next chapter.

When an atom absorbs heat energy then, the energy levels of some of the electrons are raised and the atom is said to be *excited*. The energy level that an electron possesses should not be confused with the permissible energy levels of the atom; the permissible levels for the atom do not change with heat. The electron moves from one permissible level to another when heat energy is applied.

Another way to increase the electron energy of the atom is to direct light onto the atom. Light represents the visible portion of the entire electromagnetic spectrum. Thus light consists of the same radiation as radio waves but the frequency (of vibration of the electric and the magnetic fields) is higher for the visible portion. Whenever a body absorbs electromagnetic radiation, the radiation absorbed will be converted into energy. Thus electromagnetic radiation represents a source of energy for raising the electron levels of an atom.

Because the electrons have discrete energy levels at which they may exist, the energy (as for the case of heat) must be absorbed in *quanta*. The electromagnetic field may be considered as possessing little bundles or *quanta* of energy. The amount of energy in a quantum depends upon the frequency of the radiation; the higher the frequency, the higher the energy. In order for the radiation to excite an electron of an atom, the quantum of energy of that radiation must be equal to or greater than the energy needed to raise the electron to the next permissible level. It is for this reason that only a portion of the entire electromagnetic spectrum is capable of giving energy to the electrons of solids. Thus the application of light is a suitable method of applying energy to the electrons of an atom. In the energy sense, the effect of light on an atom is similar to the effect of heat.

Physics review

The two elements that we are interested in to the greatest extent in this text are silicon and germanium. Silicon is number 14 of the elements. This means that an atom of silicon contains fourteen electrons and thus the nucleus contains a positive charge of fourteen. The two inner shells of electrons are filled and the third shell contains four electrons. Thus silicon has a valence of 4 since it has four electrons that may be used in combining with another element to form a compound. Germanium is element number 32 and also has four electrons in its outer orbit. In this case the outer orbit is the fourth shell; the first three shells are filled with the first having two, the second eight, and the third eighteen electrons. It can be seen that electrically the atoms of silicon and germanium are similar since they each have a valence of 4. Figure 2-10 represents the electron shells

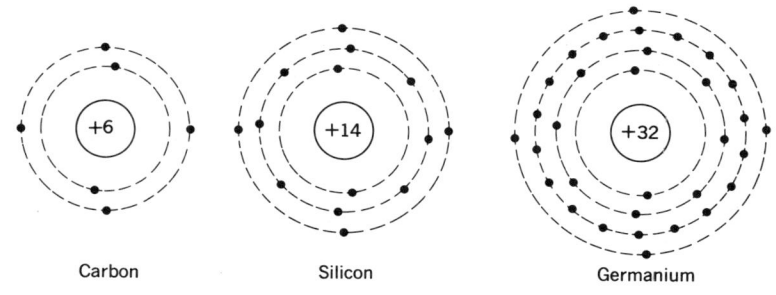

Fig. 2-10. Carbon, silicon, and germanium atoms.

and nuclei of the three atoms silicon, germanium, and carbon. Carbon is included in this group because it too has four valence electrons. The three atoms have an additional property in common; they all assume the shape of the diamond crystal when more than one atom (of the same element) are combined. This, of course, applies to material in the solid state. The chapter on semiconductors discusses silicon and germanium at greater length.

Although the models above picture the electrons as particles, it must always be remembered that this is symbolic only. In actuality, the dualism of matter requires that we think of both the wave and particle nature of the electrons. As stated, a major result of this is that one cannot determine exactly the position of an electron at a given time. Instead one must talk about the probability of finding the electron at a given point within an energy range.

ATOMS IN ASSOCIATION TO FORM CRYSTALS

Having discussed the properties of single isolated atoms, we are now in a position to consider combinations of atoms as they occur in nature. We refer here to combinations of atoms of the same material and the combination of atoms of different materials to form compounds. Also, we shall here be interested only in the solid state of any material without considering the properties of gases or liquids.

The first fact to be noted about atoms in combination is that the solid state of any inorganic material possesses a *crystal* state; this means that in the solid state the atoms of the material are oriented with respect to each other in a definite orderly manner. Thus, if one views a single crystal of a solid material, one sees a definite arrangement of all the atoms within that crystal; if one views another crystal of the same material, the identical arrangement of the atoms will be noted as formerly. Although the structure within the crystal is always defined, it should be noted that crystals may be oriented with respect to each other in various ways. The area where one crystal is joined to another crystal is called a grain boundary. Another way to define a single crystal is to state that it is the smallest repetitive structure of atoms found in any solid material.

The combination of atoms to form a crystal in a solid material should not be confused with another combination of atoms, the molecule. A molecule is a unit that specifies the number of single atoms required to form a basic unit of chemical composition. Thus the common gas, oxygen, contains two atoms per molecule and is written O_2. Carbon dioxide, CO_2, requires one atom of carbon and two atoms of oxygen to form one molecule of carbon dioxide.

When discussing a single atom we considered the forces that bind the components of the atom together. It is now pertinent to discuss those forces binding the atoms within a crystal together and also those binding the crystals themselves together. The forces that bind atoms together are electrostatic in nature, and therefore are similar to the forces operating within the atom. These electrostatic forces can be divided into three categories: (1) ionic binding forces, (2) covalent binding forces, and (3) metallic binding forces. Although our interest shall be chiefly in the covalent type, all three will be discussed briefly.

The ionic binding forces occur when the valence electrons from one atom are joined to those of another atom to fill the outer shell of the latter atom. If an atom has four or more valence electrons (in a shell where the normal number is eight) it has a tendency to gain additional electrons when joining with other atoms. When this happens the outer shell contains the filled amount of eight, and the binding forces are considered ionic. It is these binding forces that usually occur when compounds are formed. The term "ionic" is derived from the fact that ions are always formed when this interaction of valence electrons takes place. An ion is defined simply as an electrically charged atom. If an atom, which is always intrinsically electrically neutral, acquires any additional electrons (or loses some) its resultant charged state is called an ion. If an atom has four valence electrons and receives four more to fill its shell, it becomes an ion of four negative charges, and the atom contributing four electrons becomes an ion of four positive charges. An example of an ionic bound molecule is salt, or sodium chloride. Sodium, having one valence electron, gives the valence electron to the chlorine atom with seven valence electrons. Thus the chlorine atom acquires a filled shell of eight electrons. Meanwhile, the sodium, in losing one electron, has become positively charged and the chlorine atom has become negatively charged due to the additional electron. Thus each atom has become an ion and the forces that bind them together are regarded as ionic forces.

Covalent forces occur when the valence electrons of neighboring atoms share their electrons with each other. If an atom of a material contains four valence electrons, it may share one electron from each of four neighboring atoms. The concept of sharing valence electrons should be distinguished from the previous situation of gaining (or losing) valence electrons. One important difference is that no ions are formed when the binding forces are covalent. The covalent forces are set up when two electrons coordinate their motions in a manner so as to produce an electrostatic force between the electrons. More will be said about covalent binding forces in the chapter on semiconductors.

The concepts dealing with the atomic binding forces in metals include metallic binding forces. Here neither ion forces nor covalent forces are the major consideration. Metallic forces are construed as occurring when positive ions float in a cloud of electrons. There is a constant electrostatic force present between the positive ions and the negative electrons. The important feature here is the great mobility of electrons of a metal. Since they move about relatively freely, the electrons cannot be associated with particular atoms. Thus a more or less stable state occurs where ions are continuously being formed by electrons leaving any particular atom, but the atoms are held in place by the attraction between the resulting ions and the electron cloud.

In the previous section, it was pointed out that any single atom possesses many permissible energy levels in which electrons can exist and that no electron can exist at an energy level other than one of these permissible levels. This situation remains the same for atoms in combination if the spaces between the atoms are large enough. For example, the atoms of a gas fulfill this condition. In any solid, however, the atoms of the material are very close to each other and important changes occur in the state of the energy levels.

When atoms are brought into close proximity as in a solid, the energy levels that existed for single isolated atoms break up to form *bands* of energy levels. Within each band there are still discrete permissible levels rather than a continuous band. The important fact is that many more energy levels are now permissible, and these levels are grouped into separate bands. For a comparison of the energy levels in a relatively isolated atom and in a solid, Figure 2-11 and Figure 2-12 show the levels for an isolated hydrogen atom and for an atom in a germanium crystal, respectively.

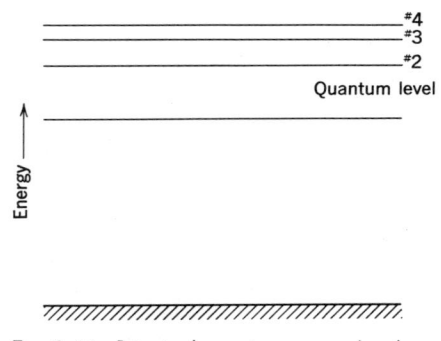

Fig. 2-11. Principal quantum energy levels of a hydrogen atom.

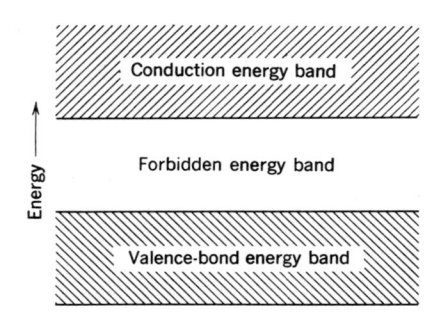

Fig. 2-12. Energy levels of germanium in a crystal structure.

Figure 2-12 shows only the two upper bands of energy levels. There are numerous bands below the level of the *valence-bond* band shown in this figure. In considering electrical properties, however, only the two upper bands are of interest. The two upper bands are called the *conduction band* and the *valence-bond band*.

The conduction band is a band of energies in which the level of energy (of the electrons) is high enough so that electrons in these levels will move readily under the influence of an external field. If the electrons are thus mobile, they are capable of sustaining a current if an external field in the form of a voltage is applied. For our purposes here, an electric current is defined as the familiar concept of moving electrons. The more general concept is that any moving charge constitutes an electric current; this will be dealt with later. Therefore solids which have many electrons in the conduction levels are known as conductors.

The valence band is a band of energies in which the energy is of the same level as the energy of valence electrons. The electrons in these levels are more or less attached to individual atoms and are not free to move about as were the former conduction electrons. This valence band would be of little interest if it were not for the fact that, with proper addition of energy, electrons in the valence band may be caused to be elevated to the conduction band. In order to do this, they have to bridge the gap between the valence band and the conduction band. This gap is known as the *forbidden energy band*. It is the energy difference across this forbidden region that determines whether a solid acts as a conductor, a semiconductor, or an insulator.

A conductor is a solid which contains many electrons in the conduction band at room temperature. In fact, there is no forbidden region between the valence band and the conduction band of a conductor; the two bands may be considered to be joined. A semiconductor is a solid that contains a forbidden gap as shown in Figure 2-12. Normally, it would be considered that a semiconductor has no electrons in the conduction band; however, by virtue of the energy provided by the heat of room temperature, there is sufficient energy available to overcome the atomic force on a few valence electrons so that some appear in the conduction band. Therefore at room temperatures semiconductors are capable of sustaining some electric current. It is the semiconductors in which we shall be interested, but not the pure material; we shall be concerned with semiconductors in which certain impurities are placed.

To complete the picture of energy bands, insulators are those materials in which the forbidden gap is so large that practically no electrons can be given sufficient energy to bridge this gap. Therefore, unless extremely high temperatures are available, these materials will not conduct electricity.

SUMMARY

The part of the physics review just completed has been directed toward acquiring a simple concept of the nature of atomic action. Our explanation has started with classical mechanics, as defined by Newton, and then was modified accordingly to describe the more accurate situation, including the wave nature of electrons. Here we will briefly retrace the steps from the classical to the wave mechanical model.

The fact that only discrete energy levels are available in an atomic structure is described by a basic formulation of quantum mechanics. Newton's concepts considered alone would imply that any of a continuum of energy levels would be permissible. However, problems such as those posed by the photoelectric effect and black-body radiation led to Planck's discovery of the discrete energy levels in atomic structure. The basic unit in this theory is the *quantum of energy*, which is the energy difference between adjacent levels.

Although, for purposes of visualization it is often satisfactory to consider the electron as a particle; any serious attention will invoke its wave nature. One of the results of this wave nature of the electron is that one cannot specify the exact position of the electron at a given time, but must speak of the probability of finding it in an energy region. Further, this wave mechanical treatment calls for specifying four quantum numbers to describe the electron energy states. The first quantum number is the principal one and is related to the probability of finding the electron in a region around the nucleus. This wave treatment considers the individual electron as one part of a large statistical group of electrons.

When atoms are brought into close proximity it was noted that the discrete energy levels of the isolated atom break up to form bands of energy levels. Materials can then be classified as conductors, insulators, or semiconductors, depending on the arrangement of these bands of energy levels. The semiconductor has a forbidden gap between the valence band of energies and the conduction band.

REFERENCES

1. *Proceedings of I.R.E.*, December, 1955, p. 1787.
2. Coblenz, A. and H. Owens, *Transistors—Theory and Application* (New York: McGraw-Hill Book Company, 1955).
3. Currier, A. and A. Rose, *General and Applied Chemistry* (New York: McGraw-Hill Book Company, 1948).
4. Ryder, J. D., *Electronic Engineering Principles* (Englewood Cliffs, N. J.: Prentice-Hall, Inc., 1961).
5. Slater, J. and N. Frank, *Mechanics* (New York: McGraw-Hill Book Company, 1947).
6. White, M., et al., *Practical Physics* (New York: McGraw-Hill Book Company, 1953).

PROBLEMS

1. Explain Newton's laws of physics and give an example of these laws in operation that you have experienced.
2. Explain Newton's law of universal gravitation.
3. What is the difference between weight and mass?
4. What is acceleration and when does it occur? (Explain this with respect to the forces acting upon a body.)
5. How do Newton's laws apply to the solar system?
6. What is energy? Describe its two most common forms (potential and kinetic).
7. Compare the isolated atom to the solar system (point out their differences).
8. What is the total electric charge of an atom? What is the electric charge of an ion?
9. What are electron shells?
10. Sketch the energy diagrams of isolated hydrogen and helium atoms.
11. Name the three types of binding forces for atoms within a crystal. Describe each.

12. What is the main change in the energy diagrams of the electrons from an isolated atom to atoms associated in a crystal structure?
13. Explain what insulators, conductors, and semiconductors are.
14. What are valence and conduction electrons?
15. What is the forbidden region of a semiconductor?

3
Semiconductors

The transistor is a device that utilizes the semiconducting properties of such elements as germanium or silicon. Although transistors are a relatively recent development, semiconductors have been used for decades in such devices as dry rectifiers of the selenium and copper oxide type. In spite of the frequent use of such semiconductors, understanding the theory of operation had to await the development of the transistor.

This chapter aims to clarify the physical principles of semiconductors and prepare for studying their application in transistors. The structure and properties of intrinsic semiconductor crystals will be considered first. Since certain impurities are essential to the transistor semiconductors, the study will proceed to crystals containing impurities and consideration of single crystals possessing two types of impurities in two distinct regions. At this point we will be ready to study the physical action of a junction transistor.

**CRYSTAL STRUCTURE
AND PROPERTIES**

The heart of a transistor is a piece of single crystal germanium or silicon. It is very important that the piece of semiconductor be part of a single crystal. The concepts of a crystal in a solid state material were mentioned in the previous chapter on physics review but are repeated here for the specific case of germanium and silicon.

A single crystal of any material specifies that all the atoms are oriented with respect to each other in a definite orderly manner. Every atom in the crystal is related to its neighbors in exactly the same way. The *lattice* of a crystal refers to the geometrical arrangement that the atoms assume in the crystal. Germanium and silicon have a lattice structure of the crystals that is called the *face-centered cubic lattice*. This type of cubic lattice occurs when each atom has four neighbors that are all at an equal distance from it, and the neighbors are all at an equal distance from each other. Figure 3-1 shows a three-dimensional representation of the atoms of the cubic lattice. It is interesting to note that the diamond also has the face-centered cubic lattice for its crystal structure.

In the natural state, any piece of a solid material would contain many crystals. Thus the material would be made up of many units as shown in Figure 3-1, and these units would be oriented with respect to each other in various ways. The boundary between such crystal units is called a *grain boundary*. Therefore if a material contains any grain boundaries it is necessarily polycrystalline; that is, it contains more than one crystal. All the crystals will be identical in structure (except size), but they will have various orientations with respect to each other. As stated then, a solid material usually is polycrystalline. Only by careful processing can a large piece of single crystal material be formed. Producing large single crystal specimens was one of the early difficulties in manufacturing transistors.

The crystal structure in Figure 3-1 is held in place by forces between the atoms. As is the case for most semiconductors, germanium and silicon crystals are bound by the forces resulting from *electron-pair bonds*. Forces resulting from such bonds are called *co-valent forces*. An electron-pair bond or covalent bond is formed when a valence electron of one atom coordinates its motion with a valence electron of another atom in a manner so as to produce an electrostatic force between the electrons. This bond is often described as a sharing process. Thus an atom shares one of its valence electrons with a valence electron of another atom.

Germanium and silicon are both from the fourth column of the periodic table; this means that their atoms possess four valence electrons. In a crystal of pure germanium or silicon, each atom shares

Semiconductors

one of these valence electrons with each of its four neighbors. Instead of depicting this electron sharing on a three-dimensional diagram such as Figure 3-1, we can consider a representation of that figure.

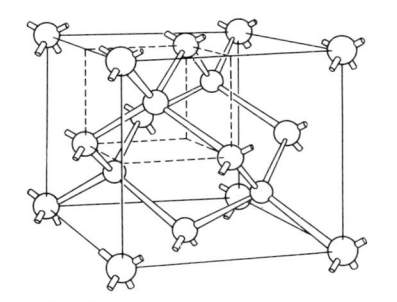

Fig. 3-1. Structure of atoms in face-centered cubic lattice.

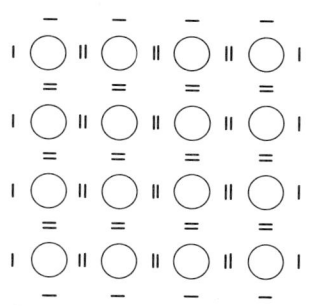

Fig. 3-2. Germanium and silicon crystal structure.

Figure 3-2 shows the resultant two-dimensional representation of the cubic lattice. The status of each atom having four equally spaced neighbors remains true for this representation also, so that this simplified view is quite valid. The circles in Figure 3-2 denote the nucleus of the atoms, and the short lines the valence electrons. The valence electrons that appear adjacent to each other are involved in covalent bonds. Electrons other than the valence electrons are not shown. In this figure it is seen that each atom shares one of its valence electrons with each of four neighboring atoms.

In order to understand the physical action in semiconductors it is necessary to investigate the energies of electrons in the crystal. In Chapter 2 the permissible energy bands of both isolated and crystalline atoms were discussed. It was noted that when atoms are in extremely close proximity as in a solid material, the discrete energy levels of the isolated atom are converted into bands of energy levels with finite gaps between the bands. Although there are a great number of energy bands available, only the valence and the conduction bands enter into the consideration of electrical properties. Both of these bands in turn contain many discrete levels, but for most purposes they can be considered as continuous bands. Figure 3-3 shows the same diagram as Figure 2-12 of Chapter 2 and depicts the conduction band and the valence-bond band for a crystal of germanium or silicon. It is noted that the gap between the valence and the conduction bands, called the forbidden energy band, is a region in which no electrons can exist.

Thus far we have described those energy bands in which electrons can exist in semiconductors, but have not specified under what conditions they do exist in any of these bands. Let us begin by saying that if the atomic structure of the crystal is exactly as shown in Figure 3-1, then all the electrons of the crystal are involved in covalent bonds. This situation also specifies that each electron is associated with its parent atom. The two foregoing facts clearly indicate that each electron has an energy equivalent to the energy of valence electrons. Therefore, referring to Figure 3-3, the valence band of energy levels

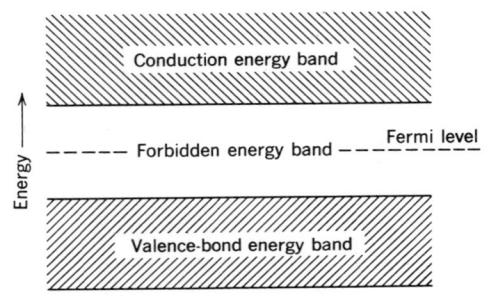

Fig. 3-3. Energy diagram of a silicon or germanium crystal.

will be filled, and no electrons will appear in the conduction band. The situation just described occurs if a crystal is at a temperature of 0° Kelvin (273° centigrade below 0°).

It was stated earlier that the application of heat is an effective method of adding energy to the electrons of any material. If a crystal is at room temperature (25°C) some electrons will have energies above those of a temperature of 0°K due to the effect of the added heat. This room temperature heat is sufficient, in a semiconductor, to break some of the covalent electron bonds. The electrons freed in this process are now capable of moving about in the crystal. The energy added accomplished two things: it broke the bond between two electrons, and also freed the concerned electrons from the electrostatic attraction of the parent atomic nucleus. Since energy had to be added to accomplish this, the affected electrons necessarily have a higher energy than in the bonded state. It is these electrons then which will appear in the conduction band of Figure 3-3, and it is seen why the conduction band is at a higher level than the valence band. The number of electrons which are thus moved from the valence band to the conduction band is determined both by the

Semiconductors

width of the forbidden region and the energy given the electron as evidenced by its temperature (assuming heat is the only source of energy).

When any electrons go from the valence band into the conduction band the crystal is said to be in an ionized state. This is based on the fact that when the conversion is made, the electron in effect leaves the parent atom. Therefore that atom is missing one unit negative charge and hence is ionized. Although we have here considered heat as the source of external energy, an electric field or incident light can also provide this ionizing energy. It should also be noted that when an electron leaves the valence band for the conduction band an empty energy level occurs in the valence band.

A semiconductor, by definition, is a material whose forbidden gap is such that at room temperature only a small current is conducted. Since electrons are one of the current carriers, this specifies that only a small number of electrons appear in the conduction band of a pure semiconductor at room temperature. A conductor, on the other hand, possesses a forbidden energy gap whose width is zero; therefore many electrons are available for current conduction at room temperature.

It is useful to introduce here a very important concept concerning energy levels. This concept is the *Fermi level* of a material, and is a property of every solid material; we shall here be interested in semiconductors only. This property is especially important whenever two different materials are joined, or when a single material has two types of impurities (as we shall encounter later). The Fermi level is a reference energy level from which all other energies may be conveniently measured. The Fermi level can be defined as that energy level at which the probability of finding an electron n energy units above the level is equal to the probability of finding an "absence" of an electron n energy units below the level.

This level, for a crystal of a pure semiconductor, falls midway in the forbidden region between the valence and the conduction bands. This seems reasonable when it is considered that for every electron in the conduction band there is an empty level in the valence band. It is not likely that an electron from a lower band will enter the valence band. Therefore the state of having an electron in the conduction band correspond to an empty level in the valence band fulfills the above definition of the Fermi level. This reference level of energies is shown for the pure crystal in Figure 3-3.

Having considered the structure and the energy levels of a pure semiconductor, we now wish to study the methods of current conduction. However, before entering the topic of current conduction in a semiconductor crystal it is helpful to clarify the concepts of current conduction in any solid. We are all familiar with the use of Ohm's law[1] to calculate the current in a circuit where $I = V/R$. We are usually not so familiar with considering current in solid materials where the dimensions of the conducting element become important. For the case of a circuit resistance we consider the voltage as being the force which, when applied to the resistance, causes a movement of conduction electrons. The current specifies the amount of electrons moved and could be measured, at a certain point on the wire, by counting the number of electrons which passed per unit time. The resistance of the material determines the difficulty with which the electrons are moved, and thus

$$I = \frac{V}{R} \tag{1}$$

In the case of solid materials the current is again expressed by Ohm's law, but slightly different quantities are used.

When discussing the current in a solid where the dimensions of the conductor are important, current density is the parameter used. The current density is the current per unit cross-sectional area of the conductor. Instead of speaking of voltage, the electric field is used as the force quantity. Conductivity, instead of resistance, is used as the measure of the difficulty with which the current carriers are moved. Figure 3-4 shows a portion of a solid conductor in which we wish to study the current. Ohm's law for the current expressed in terms of the above quantities is

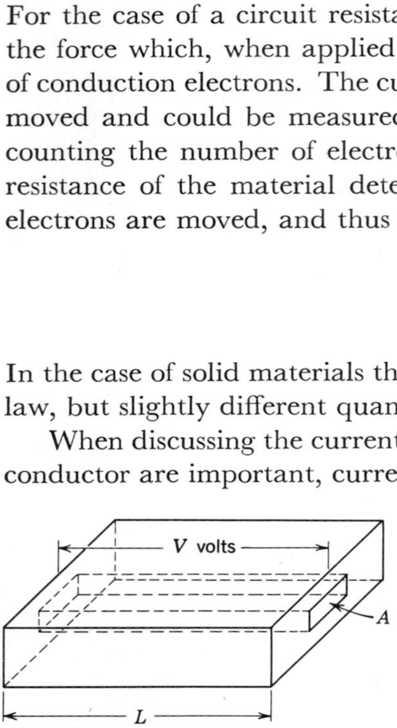

Fig. 3-4. Current-carrying element of a solid.

$$J = \gamma \mathcal{E} \tag{2}$$

where J = current density in amperes per square centimeter,
γ = conductivity of the solid in mhos per centimeter,
$\mathcal{E}$ = electric field in volts per centimeter.

[1] The basic circuit laws are briefly reviewed in Chapter 6, "Electrical Review."

Semiconductors

The electric field (for a homogeneous medium) is defined as the voltage per unit length. Conductivity is equal to the reciprocal of resistivity and, therefore, is proportional to the inverse of the resistance. In order to convert current density J to total current I we have to multiply J by the cross-sectional area

$$JA = I$$

and
$$I = \gamma A \varepsilon = \frac{V}{R} \qquad (3)$$

Equation (3) shows the analogy between the two forms of Ohm's law.

In conclusion then, we shall be speaking of the conductivity and the electric field when discussing the current in a crystal of a semiconductor. It is to be remembered that the electric field varies as the voltage, but the conductivity varies as the inverse of the resistance. Also, the electric field ε is regarded as the force that causes movement of the charge carriers in a solid material.

We now return to the current conduction which occurs in a crystal of a pure semiconductor. It was stated earlier that when some covalent bonds are broken and the affected electrons are raised to the conduction band, these electrons are capable of supporting a current. If an electric field is applied to the crystal these conduction band electrons are capable of moving, and this movement constitutes a current. The movement of these conduction electrons, under the influence of the electric field, is identical to the movement of the electrons in a metallic conductor. There is still another method of supporting a current in a pure semiconductor, however. When a covalent bond is broken, the removal of the electron leaves a vacancy in the parent atom since that atom has now only three valence electrons. It has been found to be the case that an electron from a nearby covalent bond may break its own bond and move to fill the previous vacancy. When the electron arrives at the vacancy, it enters into a covalent bond. The electron, to make this jump, does not have a conduction band energy; rather its energy has remained in the valence band. When the electron moves from the nearby bond to the original vacancy, a new vacancy is created at the bond which the electron left. Another electron, in turn, may leave its bond and move into this new vacancy. In this manner current is supported by electrons which are not in the conduction band; rather their energies lie in the valence band. Even though the movement has been that of an electron moving from one bond to another bond, the more important effect is that the vacancy has moved. Thus this manner of conduction resembles more the movement of the vacancies than the movements of the electrons themselves. This type of conduction is called *conduction by holes*.

It has been noted that this conduction by holes occurs in the valence energy band; the electrons concerned with the movement of the holes do not have conduction band energies. Since the absence of an electron from a normal covalent bond represents a localized positive charge (the atoms are electrically neutral only when all valence electrons are present), the hole may be thought of as a particle similar to the electron but having a positive charge. On this basis, the hole is considered a particle that moves much like the electron under the influence of an electric field, but in an opposite direction to that of the electrons. For this conception the hole is regarded as possessing a definite mass, like the electron. It should always be remembered, however, that the concept of a hole is simply a convenient device for describing the "jumping" movement of the electrons. The concepts of conduction by holes will again be considered when discussing current conduction in semiconductors in which certain impurities have been added.

We have just seen that, for a crystal of a pure semiconductor, current may be conducted by two processes. One process is the normal one in which electrons are allowed to move (more or less) throughout the crystal. The other process is one in which the movement of the electrons is relatively restricted—they move from one atom to another—and therefore resembles the movement of the holes, which may be depicted as positive charges with properties similar to the negative electron.

We have already stated that when a covalent bond is broken, both an electron and a hole are made available for carrying current. The process of elevating the electron to the conduction band creates a hole at the region where the electron was freed. These charge carriers, when created by the breaking of covalent bonds, are called electron-hole pairs. Since, in a semiconductor containing no impurities, the only charge carriers are such electron-hole pairs, the number of holes is always equal to the number of conduction electrons. This condition is expressed by saying that the semiconductor is *intrinsic*. The term "intrinsic" is used to distinguish a pure crystal from one containing impurities.

Since, in the intrinsic crystal, the number of holes is equal to the number of conduction electrons, the Fermi level can be defined in terms of the two charge carriers thus: the Fermi level is the average energy of the charge carriers. Comparison will show that this definition is equivalent to the one stated earlier.

The current conduction in an intrinsic semiconductor is dependent on both temperature and the electric field applied. At absolute zero temperature there is no conduction by either method since no covalent bonds are broken. At a higher temperature small currents will flow, by both electron and hole movement, depending on the applied electric field. At excessively high temperatures a pure semiconductor can be made to act like a conductor since more and more covalent bonds are broken to furnish the current carriers.

It should be noted that, under equilibrium conditions, the thermal generation of electron-hole pairs must be accompanied by the reverse process since the total number remains constant. This reverse process, called *recombination*, occurs whenever an electron enters a hole to eliminate an electron-hole pair. It appears that the recombination process involves an intermediate step, wherein electrons are temporarily held in *traps* or *deathnium centers*. These traps appear at crystal impurities and defects.

Whenever electrons and holes are available as current carriers, a net movement (or current) can occur either by *diffusion* or by *drift*. Diffusion implies that there is temporarily an unequal distribution of charges; diffusion current is always in a direction then to equalize the distribution. Drift occurs when an electric field is applied to the semiconductor; the available charges will drift in the direction of the field. As in a conductor, the movement of the individual charges themselves is not smooth, because of collisions between the electrons and the atoms of the solid. However, the total effect of the many electrons in a current appears to be a smooth movement in the direction of the current.

CRYSTALS WITH IMPURITIES

Thus far we have been concerned with the crystal structure and the properties of an intrinsic semiconductor; that is, no impurities were considered to be present. For transistors, however, a semiconductor in this pure state is of little value. To be used in a transistor the semiconductor has to possess a small, but nevertheless important, quantity of impurities. The amount and type of such impurities have to be closely controlled during the preparation of the single crystal. We shall now consider crystals which contain impurities. As was done for the pure crystal, the concepts of energy and the conduction properties will be considered.

There are two types of impurities which, when added to a crystal of germanium or silicon, produce either N-type material or P-type material. A transistor is made of a crystal that contains regions of both impurities, and these impurities are very important to the operation of the device. We shall consider the alteration of the energy states and the conduction properties of both of these impure crystals.

N-TYPE CRYSTAL. Both germanium and silicon are in the fourth column of the periodic table; this specifies that each of their atoms has four valence electrons. If, during the preparation of a single crystal of material, some atoms from the fifth column of the periodic table (5 valence electrons) are inserted, these atoms will take various positions throughout the crystal. They will supplant some atoms of the pure germanium. The two-dimensional representation of a crystal containing such impurities is shown in Figure 3-5. Because any one atom has only four immediate neighbors, there are four valence electrons from these neighboring atoms available for forming covalent bonds. This means that one of the electrons from the impurity atom is not utilized in a covalent bond. This electron represents a surplus particle in the regular structure of the crystal. For this reason, an impurity of this type is called a *donor* impurity since it donates an extra electron. Also, the crystal resulting from the addition of this donor impurity is called *N-type*, where N is derived from the negative charge of the surplus particle. This unbound electron is not immediately free to move about, however. Since the foreign atom has a nucleus containing a positive charge of 5, an electrostatic force is exerted on the unbound electron to keep it in the immediate vicinity of the foreign atom. This force, however, is reduced from what would normally be expected by the dielectric effect of the

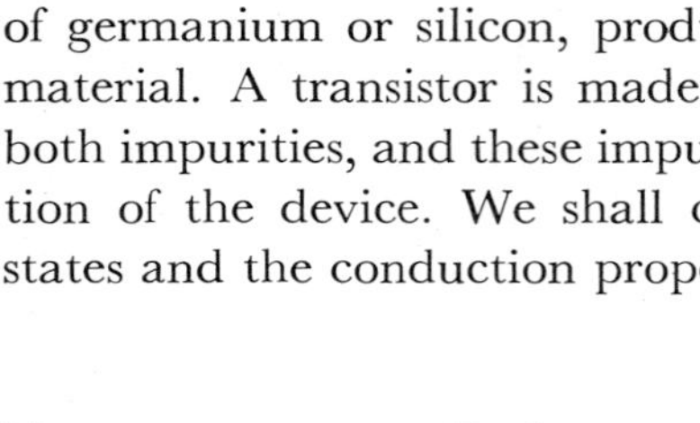

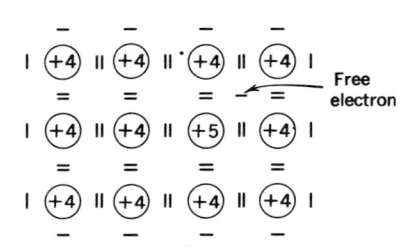

Fig. 3-5. N-type semiconductor.

Semiconductors

crystal; i.e., the surplus electron is partially shielded from the attraction to the parent atom. The result is that this electron is only loosely bound to the parent atom. Therefore we would expect that, although the energy of the donor electron (in the un-ionized state) is not in the conduction band, it is not far below this band. This has been found to be the case and Figure 3-6 shows the position of the

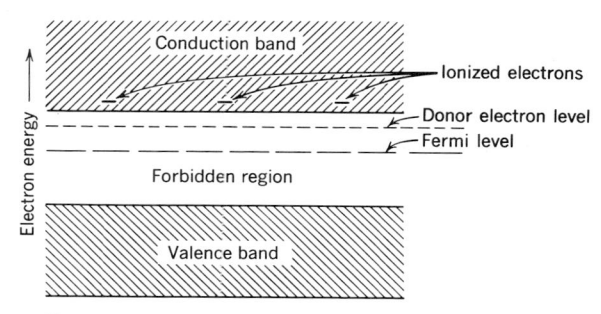

Fig. 3-6. Energy diagram for an N-type semiconductor.

energy of the donor electron. Its energy is 0.05 electron volt below the conduction band of energies, in the forbidden region. (The term "forbidden" applies only to the energies of a pure crystal.) Thus it is seen that, in terms of energy, the donor impurity has added an energy level to the levels of the pure crystal. In addition, this added level appears in a region which was excluded to the pure crystal.

These donor electrons require 0.05 electron volt (of energy) to raise them to the conduction band; for germanium, 0.7 electron volt is required to elevate an electron from the valence band to the conduction band, and silicon requires 1.1 electron volts. Thus it is seen that the energy required to ionize a donor atom is much less than that required to break a covalent bond.

With the addition of impurities to form N-type material, it would be expected that the Fermi level will change. It moves, from midway in the forbidden region for the pure crystal, to a place between this position and the conduction band. This is shown in Figure 3-6. For a crystal with impurities, the Fermi level will vary both with the amount of impurities and with the temperature of the crystal. More will be said of this when studying the effects of temperature on a semiconductor.

For this N-type semiconductor, current will again be conducted by the electrons and holes as for the pure crystal, where the electron-hole pairs are derived from broken covalent bonds. However, in this case there are many electrons available which require only a small energy to elevate them to the conduction band. Therefore when an electric field is applied to a crystal of N-type material, the effect of the donor electrons will greatly overshadow the effect of the electron-hole pairs achieved by the breaking of covalent bonds. For most purposes, then, the current in N-type material may be considered to be completely carried by the donor electrons. With the exception of the small energy needed to raise these electrons to the conduction band, this current resembles that of an ordinary conductor.

Since there are now more electrons than holes, the electrons in an N-type material are called the *majority* carrier. The hole, of course, is the *minority* carrier. Although both carriers play a role in the conduction, the status of majority and minority depicts the predominance of the one over the other.

The amount of impurity necessary for proper operation of an N-type semiconductor varies, but the order of magnitude is 10^{15} atoms per cubic centimeter. This means that for every impurity atom there are about 10^7 atoms of germanium or silicon. Thus it can be readily seen that extreme care must be taken in the manufacture of semiconductor devices in order to hold the impurity concentration to the desired values. Any impurity from the fifth column of the periodic table will theoretically result in an N-type semiconductor. However, the larger heavy atoms are not generally used. The most common types of N-type impurities are arsenic and antimony.

P-TYPE CRYSTAL. The other type of impurity crystal is called a *P-type* material. P-type material is formed by adding an impurity from the third column of the periodic table to the crystal of the semiconductor. An element from the third column has three valence electrons in the outer orbits of its atoms. When such atoms are added to a pure crystal the foreign atoms will replace some of the germanium or silicon atoms. Since the foreign atom has only three electrons to share with the four neighboring semiconductor atoms, one electron will be missing from a potential covalent bond of the impurity atom. This situation is shown in the two-dimensional representation of Figure 3-7. The impurity atom has a nucleus containing a positive charge of three; for the intrinsic atoms, the charge is four. This means that one hole (one electron short of forming a complete co-

Semiconductors

valent bond structure) exists for each impurity atom. The concept of holes was first encountered when discussing the current conduction methods of the pure crystal. As in the intrinsic crystal, the presence of this hole, in turn, creates the possibility for an electron to jump into this region and form the covalent bond. It is remembered that

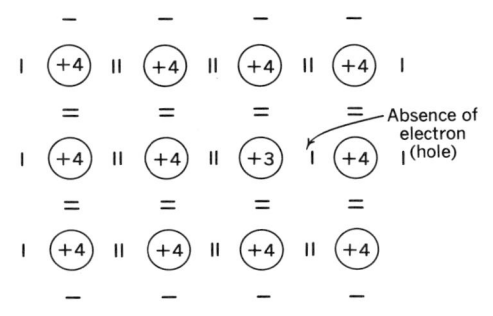

Fig. 3-7. P-type semiconductor.

electrons may leave an existing bond to fill the vacant bond without possessing a conduction band energy. If an electron leaves a covalent bond to fill the bond of the foreign atom, it leaves a hole at the region which it left. This hole may in turn be filled by another electron, and so forth. Figure 3-8 depicts this method of hole movement. The

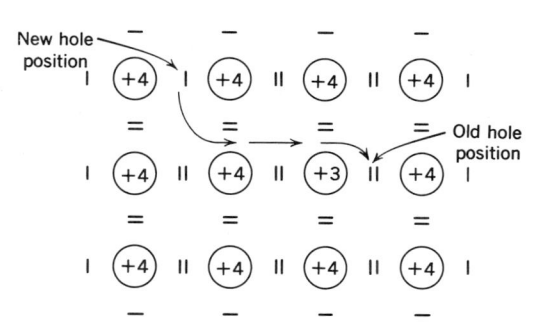

Fig. 3-8. Conduction process in a P-type semiconductor.

course of the arrows represents the motion of the electrons. This motion shows that the hole may be considered as moving in the opposite direction of the electrons.

We are now in a position to understand more clearly the concept of current conduction by holes. Usually current is taken to be the movement of electrons through a solid or a wire, and the electrons must be free to move. In this situation, however, the electrons are continuously going from a bound state in one covalent bond to a bound state in another covalent bond. Thus in this case it is not profitable to consider the action of the electrons in causing the current. Rather it is more useful to consider the hole—the absence of the electron—as being the charged particle carrying the current. Although in a P-type material there are always some electrons available for movement, due to the constant breaking up of covalent bonds from the heat energy, by far the greater part of the current is conducted by the manner just described.

In the P-type material, the number of holes present due to the impurity greatly overshadows the number of electron-hole pairs created by the breaking of covalent bonds. Thus when an electric field is applied to a crystal of such material, the current can be considered to be carried completely by the positive impurity particles, the holes. This condition is usually expressed by calling the hole the majority carrier in a P-type material. The electron, of course, would be the minority carrier. The properties of the majority and the minority carriers are discussed later in connection with the complete crystal of a transistor. The name P-type is derived from the positive charge of the majority carrier of this material. An impurity that results in P-type material is called an *acceptor* impurity since it accepts one electron to complete its covalent bonds.

Figure 3-9 shows how the presence of the P-type impurity atoms affects the energy levels of the semiconductor. It is seen that the presence of this impurity can be represented as holes having energies slightly above the upper edge of the valence band. As in the case of the donor impurity and its surplus electron, the hole of the acceptor atom is loosely bound to the parent atom. If 0.08 electron volt is applied to this hole, the hole will be freed from its parent atom and will be able to support current. Since a hole is a positive particle, as compared to the negative electron, application of energy to a hole will result in the hole moving downward in the diagram of Figure 3-9. This reaffirms that conduction by holes occurs in the valence band.

The effect of the acceptor impurity, then, is to provide an energy level in addition to those of the pure crystal. Since the only other possible means of achieving a hole is to raise an electron from the valence band to the conduction band, leaving a hole in the valence band, it is seen that the acceptor impurity provides a current carrier. Only 0.08 electron volt is required to ionize the acceptor impurity,

Semiconductors

whereas 0.7 electron volt is required to generate a hole by the breaking of a covalent bond in germanium.

As for the case of the N-type material, the Fermi level shifts when P-type impurities are added to a pure crystal, and the level is moved from the middle position to a position nearer the valence band.

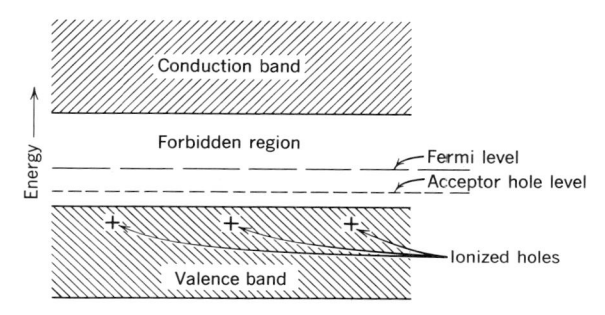

Fig. 3-9. Energy diagram of P-type semiconductor.

The Fermi level for a P-type material is shown in Figure 3-9. Again this level varies with the amount of impurities and the temperature of the crystal.

The impurities used in P-type semiconductors include indium, gallium, and aluminum. The heavier atoms are not used because of their physical size.

EFFECT OF HEAT AND LIGHT ON SEMICONDUCTORS

In Chapter 2, when discussing the isolated atom, it was mentioned that the application of heat and light are two methods by which energy can be supplied to an atom so as to raise the energy levels of its electrons. Again, when considering current conduction in intrinsic and impurity type crystals in this chapter, it was pointed out that the heat of room temperature provides sufficient energy to break some covalent bonds of the crystal structure. It is this property of having a few current carriers available, at room temperature, that specifies that germanium and silicon are semiconductors. In this section we are interested in studying more explicitly the effects of heat and light upon semiconductors. As before, we shall investigate the properties of the energy levels and the current conduction. It is felt that the method of energy diagrams provides a convenient way to study the current conduction.

The temperature of absolute zero, or 0°K, is defined as that temperature at which the electrons of any atom are in the lowest possible energy states. It is to be noted that absolute zero is not the absence of all energy, but only the condition of lowest energy. For a semiconductor such as germanium or silicon this means that all the electrons, whether valence electrons or impurity electrons, are bound by electric forces. At this temperature the valence electrons are all associated in covalent bonds. The surplus electrons of N-type impurities are bound to their parent (or donor) atoms, and the holes of P-type impurities are attached to their parent (or acceptor) atoms. Thus no current can flow at this temperature. As the crystal rises to a higher temperature the forces holding the impurity holes and electrons are overcome, so that these carriers are released first. The carriers are released by virtue of the heat energy gained from the rising temperature. At some higher temperature the heat energy gained will be sufficient to cause the generation of electron-hole pairs by the breaking of covalent bonds. At room temperature all the impurity atoms are usually ionized and some covalent bonds have been broken. Thus at room temperature the current is conducted in the manner described in the previous sections for the intrinsic, the N-type, and the P-type crystal.

As temperatures above that of room temperature are reached, the effect produced is that covalent bonds continue to be broken but no additional impurity carriers are released, since they were all ionized previously. This is a very important effect since this condition changes the properties of an impurity type crystal. The consequence of this change is that the impurity crystal begins to become more and more like an intrinsic crystal. As more and more covalent bonds are broken the ratio of electron-hole pairs thus created begins to overshadow the impurity electrons (or holes). Thus the crystal begins to take on the properties of the intrinsic crystal and the effect of the impurities is overcome. This is a completely undesirable effect since the specified amount of impurities is important to the operation of the transistor, as is seen in the next chapter.

The effects of temperature on a crystal of germanium or silicon are shown in Figure 3-10. The representation here shows both N- and P-type impurities in the crystal. Since the temperature determines the amount of current carriers available, it is seen that the conduc-

Semiconductors

tivity varies with temperature. It is remembered that conductivity varies inversely with resistance; a high conductivity means a low resistance. At 0°K the conductivity is zero since there are no free holes or electrons. At the normal operating temperature (room temperature, 25°C) the conductivity is determined mainly by impurity carriers—holes for P-type and electrons for N-type material—as discussed earlier. When the temperature increases to the high range (100°C to 500°C), the conductivity increases greatly due to the generation of electron-hole pairs from the breaking of covalent bonds. At these high temperatures, then, the current appears the same as for a pure crystal but its value is larger than previously.

Another important effect of high temperatures in an impurity

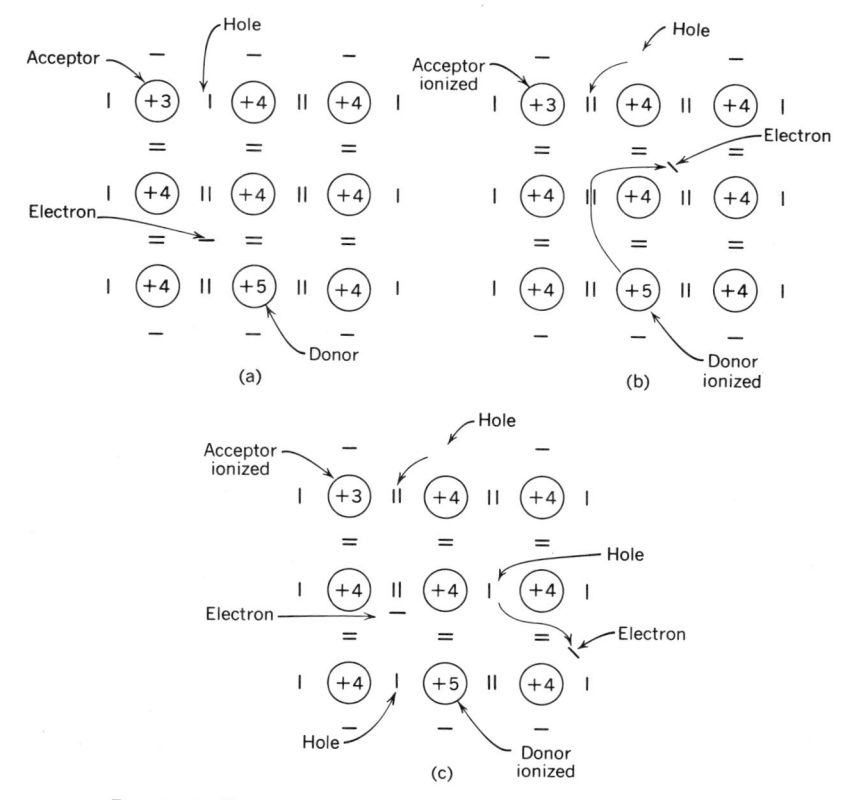

Fig. 3-10. Temperature effects in germanium and silicon. (a) 0° Kelvin. All of the electrons and holes are in their lowest energy state. (b) Middle range of temperature. The acceptors and donors are ionized. (c) High temperature. The donors and acceptors are ionized and also there are electron-hole pairs generated.

type crystal is that the Fermi level shifts toward the center of the forbidden energy gap. This again results because the electron-hole pairs from broken covalent bonds overshadow the effect of the impurities. Therefore the Fermi level returns toward the Fermi position of an intrinsic crystal. This effect, it will be seen, changes the properties of a crystal containing both N- and P-type regions.

The application of light is another means available for applying energy to a solid material. When light of the correct wavelength or frequency shines upon a germanium or silicon crystal, electron-hole pairs are created. This increase in the number of current carriers will act again to increase the conductivity of the crystal. As mentioned before, light can be considered to contain small bundles of electromagnetic energy, and the amount of energy in a bundle depends upon the frequency of the light. For a quantum of light to be able to create an electron-hole pair, the quantum must possess an energy equal to or greater than the energy of the forbidden gap between the valence and the conduction band of the crystal. If the light is of such a frequency that the energy is less than this amount, it will pass right on through the crystal. The crystal is then said to be transparent to this frequency of light. When the light frequency is above this value, the light energy will be absorbed by the process of creating an electron-hole pair and the crystal is said to be opaque to this light frequency.

Since the generation of electron-hole pairs will result in an increased conductivity, we may consider the conductivity in studying the effect of the band of light frequencies. Figure 3-11 shows how the

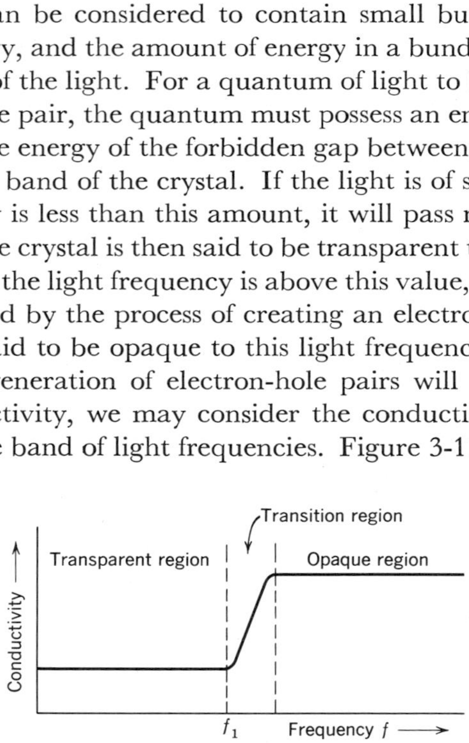

Fig. 3-11. Effects of light of varying frequency upon conductivity.

conductivity of a semiconductor crystal varies with different frequencies of light. When the energy contained in a quantum of light is below the energy gap of the semiconductor, the material is transparent. When the energy is above this value, the semiconductor is

Semiconductors

opaque. There is a region of transition between these two conditions as shown in Figure 3-11.

If the frequency of light is above the value of f_1, the amount of light falling on the crystal will affect the conductivity in the manner

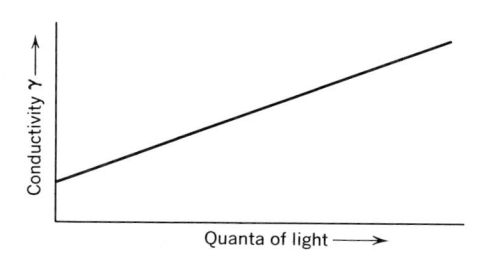

Fig. 3-12. Effects of light strength upon conductivity.

shown in Figure 3-12. The stronger the light the greater the effect upon the conductivity since more electron-hole pairs are created.

REFERENCES

1. *Proceedings of I.R.E.*, November 1952, pp. 1289–1313.
2. *Proceeding of Transistor Short Course.* University Park, Pa.: The Pennsylvania State University, 1954, pp. IV-1–VII-7.
3. *Electrons and Holes in Semiconductors*, Shockley. Princeton, N. J.: D. Van Nostrand Co., Inc., 1955.
4. *Transistors*, Dennis LeCroissette. Englewood Cliffs, N. J.: Prentice-Hall, Inc., 1963.

PROBLEMS

1. What is a single crystal?
2. How do silicon and germanium form single crystals and what is their crystal structure called?
3. Sketch a two-dimensional diagram depicting the crystal structure of germanium and silicon.
4. Sketch the energy band diagram for a typical semiconductor.
5. What is the Fermi level?

54 Semiconductors

6. What is an electron-hole pair, and what is its importance?
7. Assuming that temperature rises, what happens to the electron-hole pairs in a semiconductor?
8. What is an intrinsic semiconductor?
9. Describe an N-type crystal and sketch its two-dimensional crystal diagram.
10. What is the net electrical charge of an N-type crystal?
11. What is a donor?
12. Sketch the energy diagram for an N-type crystal.
13. Describe a P-type crystal and sketch its two-dimensional crystal diagram.
14. What is an acceptor?
15. Sketch the energy diagram for a P-type crystal.
16. Explain how a hole carries current.
17. What is the effect of heat and light upon a semiconductor, especially with respect to the Fermi level?
18. What is the energy difference between the Fermi level and the valence band in a P-type crystal, and between the Fermi level and the conduction band in an N-type crystal? *Note:* Use room temperature conditions.
19. Assume that an intrinsic semiconductor has a constant voltage applied to it. Sketch the behavior of the current as temperature increases, and explain reasons.
20. Do problem 19 for an N-type semiconductor. Sketch the current on the same graph for comparison, and explain.

4

The physical action of transistors

Having explored the principles of semiconductors, we can now study the physical operation of transistors. Although there are various types of transistors, as discussed in the next chapter, we will here concentrate on the junction transistor, by far the most prominent. In addition, the important physical action in this type of transistor is often found in the other types as well. To distinguish them from the unipolar field effect transistors, these transistors are also called *bipolar*.

The study begins with consideration of P-N junctions, which are the critical areas of a transistor. Following this, the N-P-N junction transistor is analyzed in some detail; since the P-N-P type is directly similar to the N-P-N only a brief comment on it is given.

P-N JUNCTIONS

A transistor utilizes a single crystal of semiconductor that contains regions of both N-type and P-type material. Having discussed both types of impurity materials, and the method of conducting current, we are now prepared to consider the interaction when both N-type and P-type materials occur in a single crystal.

When discussing the properties of the pure semiconductor and the semiconductor with impurities, the concept of the Fermi level was used to describe the energy states. The importance of the Fermi level will now become evident. Whenever two materials are joined together in equilibrium conditions *their Fermi levels will always be the same.* Although N-type and P-type materials represent the same basic semiconductor containing different impurities, we have noted that the Fermi level is different for the two materials. The law just stated then demands that their Fermi levels "line-up" when both materials occur in the same crystal. This aligning of the Fermi energy level is somewhat analogous to the situation depicted in Figure 4-1. When

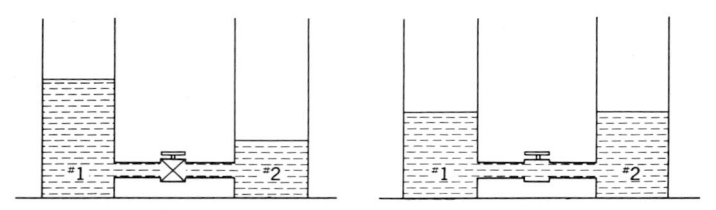

Fig. 4-1. Water levels before and after valve in pipe is opened.

the columns of water are considered separately each may have its own water level; when the two levels are joined, so to speak, the levels of the two columns are no longer independent and they reach a common level. Water flows from the first container into the second container until the water levels in both are equal. The original level of both columns determines the resultant level when the two are joined.

The similar process occurs when an N-type and a P-type material are joined. Figure 4-2(a) shows the energy levels of both the N-type and the P-type material when they are separate. This portion of the figure is a combination of the levels shown previously in Figures 3-6 and 3-9. Figure 4-2(b) shows the resultant energy relations when the two materials are joined. The two situations shown in Figure 4-2 should not lead us to believe that the N- and P-type materials, after existing separately, may be mechanically joined. A P-N junction can be formed only by a chemical process in which the P- and the N-type material are made to form a single crystal. A process for making P-N junctions will be discussed later.

If separate crystals of N-type and P-type materials were mechan-

The physical action of transistors

ically joined, a polycrystalline semiconductor would result and this would not produce transistor action. To understand transistor action in the simplest terms possible, however, it is useful to consider the change from the separate state to the joined state.

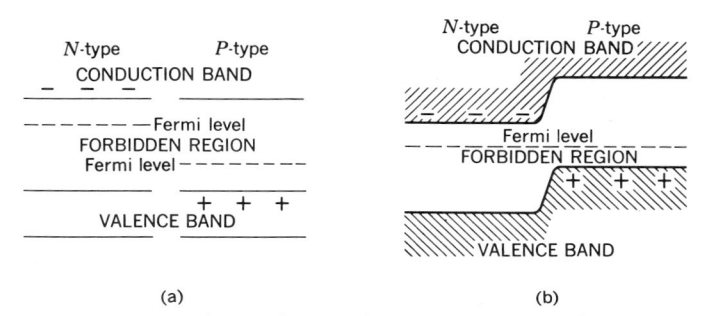

Fig. 4-2. Energy diagram for an N-P junction: (a) energy diagram for N- and P-type semiconductors; (b) equilibrium energy diagram for an N-P junction.

In Figure 4-2(b) the region of transition from the N-type to the P-type is the critical region in terms of producing correct transistor action. It is this specific region that is referred to when the term "P-N junction" is used. We shall now explain what takes place in the conversion from (a) to (b) in Figure 4-2. First, however, it may be best to repeat the salient facts about the impurity materials in the separate condition as shown in (a). In the N-material the electrons are the majority carriers and therefore the mobile particles; for the P-material, holes are the free particles and therefore the majority carriers. Each material, when considered as a unit, is electrically neutral. This means that in the N-material the negative charge from the free electrons is exactly balanced by the surplus positive charge from each of the impurity atom nuclei; and likewise for the P-material the total positive charge of the free holes is balanced by the total negative charge contributed from each of the impurity nuclei. As a last point, the energy diagrams we have been investigating refer to energies of *electrons*, and energy bands shown depict the permissible energy levels; the *permissible* levels are not necessarily filled with electrons at any one time.

We proceed then to discuss the transition from (a) to (b) of Figure 4-2. The over-all consequence of the transition is that the permissible energy levels of both N- and P-regions have been altered. To wit, the P-region now has higher levels permissible in the conduction band, but some of the levels at the bottom of this band have been removed. The same thing has happened for the valence band. For the N-region, the exact reverse has occurred; this region has lost some of the high conduction levels and gained some levels at the low end. The two actions, the change in the N-levels and the change in the P-levels, occur simultaneously (when the materials have been hypothetically joined) until an equilibrium is reached; that is, until the Fermi levels are aligned. During this period, a very important change in the electrical properties of the junction region has occurred. In order for the P-region to change its permissible energy levels, holes had to leave the P-region and move to the N-region. Likewise for the N-region to change its permissible energy levels, electrons had to leave the N-region and shift to the P-region. In view of the actual status of holes, both actions mean that electrons shifted from the N-region to the P-region. This movement of electrons means that current flowed momentarily when the materials were joined. The current ceases when equilibrium conditions (alignment of Fermi levels) are achieved.

This being the case, it is no longer true that each material is electrically neutral. In the region of the junction, the P-region has more electrons than before, and necessarily the N-region has fewer electrons. This specifies that the P-region has achieved a net negative charge and the N-region a net positive charge. Thinking of the junction momentarily as being two charges of opposite sign, we readily see that an electric field (and hence a voltage) exists at the junction. The voltage caused by this electric field is a permanent feature of the P-N junction and its magnitude depends upon the amount of impurities in both regions. This voltage is often called the *potential barrier* of a P-N junction. The current which flowed upon the joining of the two materials was stopped when the potential barrier was high enough to prevent further flow. This is simply another way to view equilibrium conditions. We can alter the magnitude of this junction voltage by applying external bias, and this will be considered next. It should be noted, however, that the intrinsic voltage of a P-N junction is the critical feature in determining transistor action. In fact, this voltage difference at the junction of two dissimilar materials has long been exploited. It is this property that is used to produce the ordinary wet cell battery of your automobile or the dry cell batteries used in flashlights.

We shall now consider the influence of applying an external bias

The physical action of transistors   59

to a P-N junction. Since, in any semiconductor, the direction of any applied voltage is significant we shall investigate both forward and reverse bias. It is clear that any external bias will destroy the equilibrium conditions of the P-N junction as depicted in Figure 4-2(b). This being the case, we should expect that current will flow due to the loss of equilibrium.

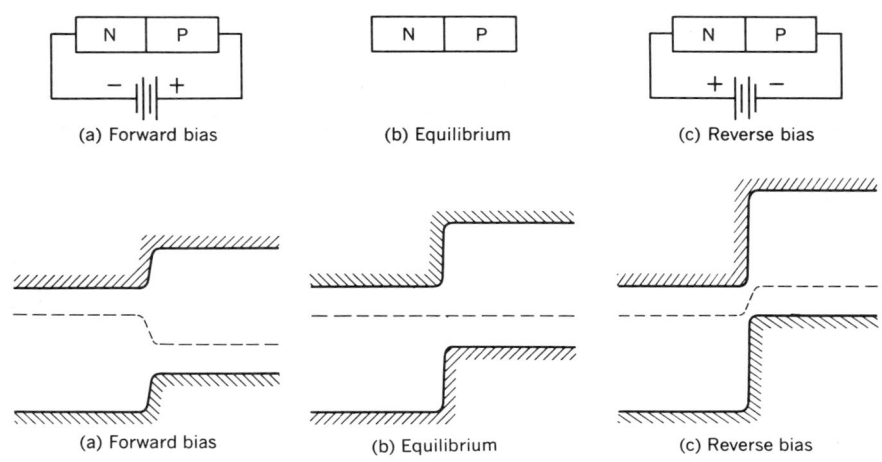

(a) Forward bias   (b) Equilibrium   (c) Reverse bias

(a) Forward bias   (b) Equilibrium   (c) Reverse bias

Fig. 4-3. Energy diagrams for N-P junction under forward bias, equilibrium, and reverse bias. Note: In (a), (b), and (c) the upper band is the conduction band, the lower band is the valence band; the region between these two bands is the forbidden region, and the broken line is the Fermi level.

Figure 4-3 shows the bias direction for both forward and backward bias and the unbiased equilibrium state with the associated energy levels. Figure 4-3(b) shows the unbiased junction and hence is a repetition of Figure 4-2(b). In (a) of Figure 4-3 the forward bias shows that a positive voltage is applied to the P-region. The effect of this, in the energy structure, is to lower the Fermi level, and hence both the conduction and the valence band of the P-region with respect to the N-region. This result is justified when it is remembered that for an unbiased P-N junction, the P-region has a net negative charge. With the external positive voltage applied, the negative charge of the P-region is reduced. With external bias of this polarity, the energy bands of the two regions *tend* to become aligned. In effect this reduces the voltage barrier between the N- and the P-region at the junction. With the voltage barrier of the junction thus reduced, additional electrons from the N-region move into the P-region, and holes from the P-region move to the N-region. Again both of these movements constitute a flow of electrons from the N- to the P-region. A continuing supply of electrons from the battery assures that this process continues. Thus the application of forward bias to a P-N junction provides the facility for easy current flow.

Reverse bias, as the name implies, provides also for the flow of current, but in this case the polarities are such that the current cannot easily flow. The effect on the energy structure is such as to increase the difference between the energy bands of the two regions. Thus the potential barrier is increased, and it is now more difficult for electrons to move from N to P or for holes to move from P to N. The direction of the external bias is such as to move electrons to the left in the material and move holes to the right. Thus the majority current carriers in both regions move away from the junction producing a *depletion region*. Depletion refers to the reduced number of majority carriers in the region on both sides of the reversed biased junction. At first thought, this would lead one to believe that no current can be carried under these conditions. However, the P-region does contain some electrons (the minority carrier for this region) and the N-region some holes. It is these minority carriers that conduct the current for reverse bias, for these carriers allow movement of electrons from the P- to the N-region and holes from the N- to the P-region. The current which occurs when reverse bias is applied is generally referred to as *back current*; it is also called I_{co} or *cutoff current* for the transistor.

The P-N junction just discussed is a *diode* of the junction type. To obtain a useful diode (one with extremely small back current) the impurities in the N- and P-regions must be controlled rigorously.

N-P-N JUNCTION TRANSISTOR

In essence a junction transistor may be thought of as a single crystal semiconductor containing two P-N junctions. For proper operation these two junctions must be formed back-to-back. Having considered the energy relations and current conduction of P-N junctions, we now investigate these properties when two junctions occur in the same crystal. This is merely an extension of the material just discussed and so we proceed directly to the biased N-P-N junction, which fully illustrates the action of a transistor.

Figure 4-4(a) shows the position of the energy levels for the

The physical action of transistors

unbiased N-P-N junction transistor. This diagram can be quickly verified by referring to Figure 4-3(b), which shows the diagram for a single junction. As noted before, the Fermi level is aligned throughout the crystal under the equilibrium conditions. The valence and the conduction bands are warped by the amount necessary to assure the constant Fermi level.

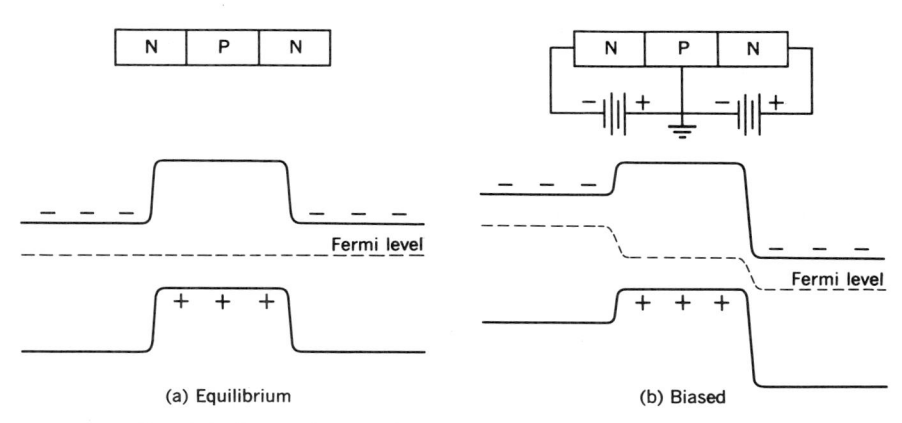

Fig. 4-4. Energy diagrams for an N-P-N junction transistor in equilibrium and when biased.

Although the transistor can be biased to various regions, we will here concentrate on that region where the transistor *amplifies*. This region is called the *active* region; two others are the *saturation* and the *cutoff* regions.

By far the most important region is the amplifying active region. The d-c bias conditions necessary to provide transistor (amplifying) action are that one junction be biased in the forward direction (the direction of easy current flow) and the other junction be biased in the reverse direction. Whenever the junctions are biased thusly, we will say that the transistor is in the *active* region. The bias of either of the two junctions is stated with respect to the center region, and this center region is called the *base*. The portion of the transistor that is biased in the forward direction (with respect to the base) is called the *emitter* and the portion biased in the reverse direction is called the *collector*. Figure 4-4(b) shows the bias connection necessary to bias the emitter junction in the forward direction and the collector junction in the reverse direction. The positions of the energy levels for the biased transistor are also shown in this figure. Again the positions of these energy levels may be verified by referring to Figure 4-3 (a) and (c).

Figure 4-4(b), then, shows the biases which must be applied to a junction transistor in order to be used in any electronic application. We shall use this figure to study the fundamental action of the charge carriers in the transistor. Although a few separate currents exist, we shall consider first the most important one: the current of the base region minority carrier.

Based upon the discussion in the previous section about the currents across biased P-N junctions, it will be seen that the emitter can very easily emit electrons from the N-type emitter into the P-type base region since the emitter junction is biased in the forward direction. These electrons, upon reaching the base region are minority carriers in the base region since the majority carrier of a P-region is the hole. In the base region, since there is no electric field, these minority carriers move by a process of diffusion. This diffusion process, depicted in Figure 4-5, results from the fact that any bunched

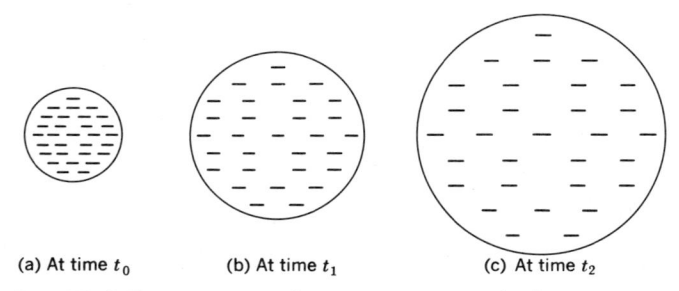

(a) At time t_0 (b) At time t_1 (c) At time t_2

Fig. 4-5. Diffusion process of minority carriers in the base region.

group of electrons will diffuse by the same laws as those that govern a group of gas molecules. At time t_0 the electrons are rather compactly spaced after being emitted into the base region. At a later time t_1 the same electrons cover a larger area, and at t_2 they have spread out still farther from each other. If the individual path of an electron could be observed during this diffusion process it might look like that represented in Figure 4-6. The electron will start off in one direction and retain it until it collides with a crystal lattice or another electron; it will then rebound in another direction until another collision. An erratic motion of this sort is typical of the paths of electrons in any sort of conduction medium. It may seem that this diffusion process is a flimsy sort of basis for transistor action, but

The physical action of transistors

remember there are always more electrons entering at the emitter junction, with the result that the minority carriers (electrons) in the base region are crowded toward the collector junction.

In the above manner, then, the injected electrons tend to distribute themselves uniformly throughout the base. Most of the electron carriers reach the collector by this means; some, however, recombine with holes in the base region.

When the electrons reach the collector junction they experience a force due to the reverse bias which pulls them into the N-type collector region. It will be remembered that for the reverse bias, the current is carried by minority carriers. If a single N-P junction is being used, there is a very small number of minority carriers available to conduct current with the reverse bias so that only the back (cutoff) current flows—a very small current. In the case here, however, the presence of the emitter junction acts as a continuous *source* of minority carriers for the collector junction. With this supply of minority carriers available the reverse-bias collector junction experiences a relatively large current. In fact, in the manufacture of transistors, an attempt is made to form the width of the base region narrow enough so that practically all the electrons emitted by the emitter junction arrive at the collector junction and pass into the collector region.

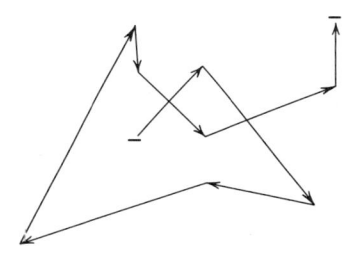

Fig. 4-6. Path of an electron during diffusion process.

We have now seen that the essential physical action of a junction transistor consists of the emitter injecting current carriers into the base region. For the N-P-N transistor these carriers are electrons. In the P-type base region the electrons are minority carriers and move by diffusion to the collector junction. Due to the reverse bias of the collector junction the minority carriers of the base region are attracted into the collector region. From this over-all view of the operation we have gained a very important fact: the basic action in a junction transistor is controlled by current carriers; therefore the transistor is a current-operated device. This is in contrast to the vacuum tube, for example, which is basically a voltage-operated device. For the vacuum tube the basic action is controlled by applying *voltages* to the control grid. The next chapter shows that the newer field effect transistor is also basically a voltage-operated device.

We can now consider the action of the transistor in a simple common-base amplifying circuit shown in Figure 4-7 and discuss all the current carriers that enter into the transistor action. This action can be interpreted by first noting the bias currents[1] and then noting the change when a small signal is applied to the emitter circuit. Figure 4-7 shows the base grounded, the signal applied to the emitter,

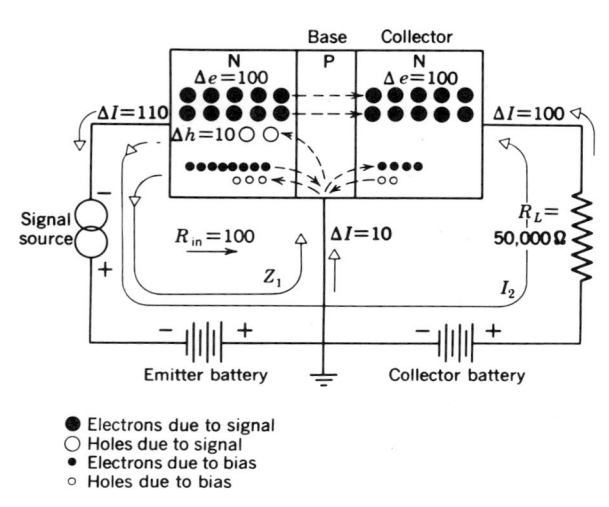

[Figure 4-7 diagram showing N-P-N transistor circuit with Signal source, $R_{in} = 100$, Z_1, Emitter battery, Collector battery, $R_L = 50{,}000\,\Omega$, I_2, $\Delta I = 110$, $\Delta e = 100$, $\Delta h = 100$, $\Delta I = 10$, $\Delta e = 100$, $\Delta I = 100$]

- ● Electrons due to signal
- ○ Holes due to signal
- • Electrons due to bias
- ○ Holes due to bias

Fig. 4-7. Physical action in an N-P-N transistor in the common-base connection.

and the load resistor connected to the collector. This method of connection is known as the *common-base* connection. The small solid circles in the diagram represent the electrons that take part in the bias current, and the small unfilled circles represent the bias holes. Since the bias current flows continuously after the batteries are connected, these holes and electrons can be considered to be in continuous movement. The large circles represent those holes and electrons that are made to move due to the small signal applied.

Considering the bias currents, it is seen that electrons flow from the N-emitter to the P-base region. This flow of carriers is justified when it is noted that the emitter junction is biased in the forward direction. The section on P-N junctions explained that the current across a junction biased in the forward direction is carried by the

---

[1] The bias concepts for transistors are similar to those for vacuum tubes. The need for bias currents in transistors is first treated on page 143 and is dealt with throughout Chapter 7.

The physical action of transistors

majority carriers. Likewise, this accounts for the flow of holes from the P-base to the N-emitter region. The emitter battery has a voltage of the order of 0.1 volt and this causes a current, due to the combined action of the electrons and holes, of about 1.0 milliampere.

For the bias currents across the collector junction, it is seen that electrons flow from the P-base to the N-collector region, and holes flow from the N-collector to the P-base region. Again this can be accounted for in terms of the backward bias applied to the collector junction. For backward bias it is the minority carriers that support the current. It was pointed out earlier that the source of these minority carriers are the relatively few holes and electrons generated from the breaking of covalent bonds. A normal collector voltage is about 6.0 volts (from the collector to the base) and this results in a current of the order of 0.010 milliampere. As mentioned before, these currents flow continuously when the batteries are applied to the circuit. For purposes of considering the amplification of the circuit we can disregard these bias currents and concentrate on the *change* in currents when a signal is applied to the emitter. We are interested in discovering what effect this signal has on the output side of the circuit—the load resistor.

Disregarding the bias currents then, we shall consider the action when a small negative voltage is applied to the emitter. This negative voltage will change the emitter-to-base voltage (from that of the bias) in the forward direction. Therefore electrons will move from the N-emitter to the P-base region. As an example, let us consider that 100 electrons per unit time are moved thus. From the same signal voltage, holes will move from the P-base to the N-emitter region. For reasons which will become evident later, it is necessary that this hole flow be less than the electron flow. Let us assume that only 10 holes flow due to the signal. This disparity in amount of electron and hole flow due to the same signal can be controlled mainly by adjusting the amount of impurities in the N- and the P-region. For the above example, the N-emitter region would have approximately 10 times as many impurities as the P-base region.

For good transistor action the P-base region is constructed narrow enough so that practically all the electrons move by diffusion to the collector junction. Since the electrons are minority carriers in such a P-region, there is a tendency for the electrons to combine with the holes of the P-region through recombination. However, for our example, we shall consider that all the electrons arrive at the collector junction. When they arrive at this junction they are attracted into the collector region because of the reverse bias of this junction.

In order to clarify the input and output currents of this simple amplifier, let us consider the current in the wires connected to each of the three transistor regions. Since both holes and electrons contribute to the current, the emitter wire is conducting a current of 110 units. The wire connected to the base has a current of 10 units; this current is due only to the hole flow from the base region to the emitter region. It was noted that the electron flow across the emitter junction does not contribute to this base wire current since all the electrons were assumed to move to the collector region. (In practice a few per cent of the electrons will combine with holes in the base region, and these holes will be replaced from the base lead and contribute a small amount to the base current.) Since the signal then did not change the collector junction current in any manner other than the electron current noted above, the collector wire current has increased by 100 current units. For our example, then, we are applying 110 units to the input and achieving 100 units at the output. The current amplification for this case is 100/110 and this figure would be the α for this transistor.[2] The current amplification α is a very important parameter of the transistor. We have found that the current amplification is less than one, and it is always true that, for a junction transistor operating in the common-base connection, the current gain is slightly less than one.

We have considered current flow through the transistor regions without mentioning ohmic voltage drop; a comment on this is warranted at this point. The ohmic voltage drop in the emitter and collector region can be ignored because their conductivity is very high from heavy impurity doping. In the base region the minority carrier (electron) movement is by diffusion, and hence no ohmic drop appears with this current. The majority carrier (hole) current in the base region, however, is a normal current caused by an electric field; therefore an ohmic drop appears in the base region. Later the equivalent circuit of the transistor will include a base resistor to account for this ohmic drop.

One might readily wonder how this transistor circuit is capable of exhibiting power gain since we have found above that the current

---

[2] The measurement of α requires a constant collector voltage which is ignored in this simple example; see Chap. 7.

The physical action of transistors

gain is less than one. The answer lies in the impedance levels at the input and output.[3] Because of the forward bias of the emitter, the input impedance is fairly low, let us say about 100 ohms. The output impedance, determined by the collector junction, is very high due to the reverse bias of this junction. For a good junction transistor the collector impedance is in the order of one megohm. Having such a high output impedance for the transistor, we can easily make the load resistor of the same order—for our example we shall make $R_L = 50{,}000$ ohms. Assuming that each of the current units we considered corresponds to one microampere, we find, using $P = I^2 R$ that the power input to the circuit is 0.0012 milliwatt. Calculating the power in the load resistor we find that 0.5 milliwatt is available. Thus this transistor circuit, for the assumed values, exhibits a power gain of 417.

We have now seen in some detail how the basic transistor circuit provides power gain. Along with this power gain, of course, voltage gain is provided. In the example given, the input signal voltage ($V = IR$) is 0.011 volt and the voltage across the load resistor is 5 volts. Thus a voltage gain of 455 is available. It is essential to note that the important feature of a transistor is that it utilizes a current carrier, and that the important carrier in a junction transistor is the minority carrier of the base region.

For many purposes it is convenient to consider an amplifying circuit in terms of its control properties rather than in the detailed terms just considered. Any amplifying circuit can be considered to be a control circuit in the sense that, by inserting a small signal at the input, a larger reproduction of the signal is attained at the output. For the transistor circuit shown in Figure 4-7, this concept can be exhibited by considering the current I_1 and I_2 as shown. I_2 flows in the load resistor, I_1 flows in the base lead, and $I_1 + I_2$ flows through the source. We can simplify the concept of the action of this circuit by saying that I_2 is the major current of this circuit and that I_1 controls this current. In this sense the action of the transistor is made analogous to the vacuum tube, where the grid voltage controls the current between the cathode and plate. It is very important to note that, for the transistor, a current controls another current. It may be considered that I_1 effects its control over I_2 by varying the conductivity

---

[3] These impedance levels stem largely from active diode impedance, and not ohmic drop. This is discussed in Chapter 7.

of the material through which I_2 passes. This effect of varying the conductivity is brought about by the way in which the emitter junction responds to a signal, as was described earlier.

Although the common-base circuit is the most basic in terms of physics and for describing all the junction currents, it is the *common-emitter* connection which is the most important in applications. This is simply a circuit rearrangement of the same transistor regions, and is shown in Figure 4-8. For this example we shall assume that the

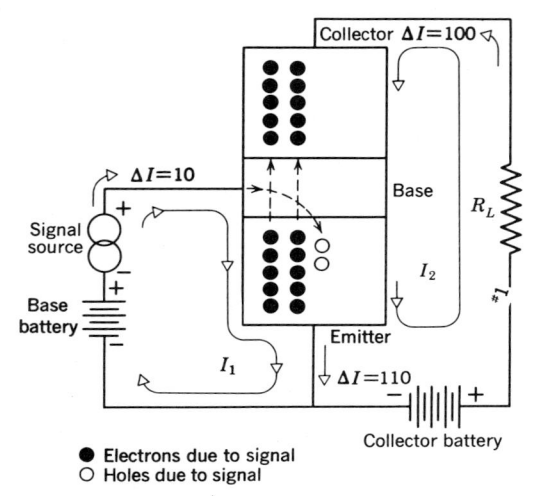

Fig. 4-8. Physical action of N-P-N transistor in the common-emitter connection.

same transistor is used and the same biases are applied as for the previous case of the common-base circuit. Also, the magnitude of the applied signal voltage will be the same. It can be seen then that Figure 4-8 is identical to Figure 4-7 except that the signal is applied to the base instead of the emitter. We shall see, however, that this change in insertion of signal greatly changes the current gain of the circuit. Since the same value of signal voltage is applied as in the previous case, the emitter junction will experience the same change in forward bias. Therefore the amount of electrons and holes moving across the emitter junction will be the same. (The bias holes and electrons are not shown in Figure 4-8.) The result is that the currents in the transistor leads due to the signal are the same for both cases.

For this case the input current is 10 current units and the output

The physical action of transistors

is 100 units. The current gain, therefore, is 100/10 = 10. We now see that the common-emitter connection has a current gain greater than 1. If α is the current gain of the common-base circuit, it is always true that the current gain (β) for the common-emitter circuit is related to α by the equation

$$\beta = \frac{\alpha}{1-\alpha} = \frac{100/110}{1-100/110} = 10 \tag{1}$$

The power gain of this connection will also be greater than that for the common base. The input resistance is increased over that for the common base, and the output resistance is decreased. These changes are discussed in detail when studying the parameters of the transistor. It is sufficient for the purposes here to consider the physical action of electrons and holes in the two basic connections of the transistor.

Viewing Figure 4-8 in terms of control, it may be considered that I_2 is the main current of the circuit and I_1 is the control current. If we visualize transistor action in this respect, the operation of the transistor in the grounded-emitter connection is analogous to the physical action of a vacuum tube. The current I_2 may be considered analogous to the current flowing from cathode to plate in a vacuum tube, and the current I_1 can be considered to be the control quantity analogous to the control voltage on a grid. To exert this control, the current I_1 in effect varies the conductivity of the semiconductor path between the collector and the emitter. This is a completely different control concept from the vacuum tube where the voltage on the grid controls the current through the load.

P-N-P JUNCTION TRANSISTOR

Since the critical feature of a transistor is the action at the junctions, a P-N-P transistor will operate just as satisfactorily as the N-P-N just discussed. The action in the P-N-P junction transistor is directly similar to the N-P-N if the roles of the N- and P-type semiconductors are reversed. This entails two major differences in the electrical operation: (1) the biasing polarities are reversed (the emitter is biased positive with respect to the base and the collector is biased negative with respect to the base) and (2) the minority carriers in the base region are holes rather than electrons. It is noted that with the biases as stated, the emitter junction is again biased in the forward direction and the collector junction in the reverse direction. In the base region the holes are now the minority carriers since the base consists of N-type material.

Since the holes are the important current carriers involved for the P-N-P transistor, the energy diagram of Figure 4-9 illustrates the

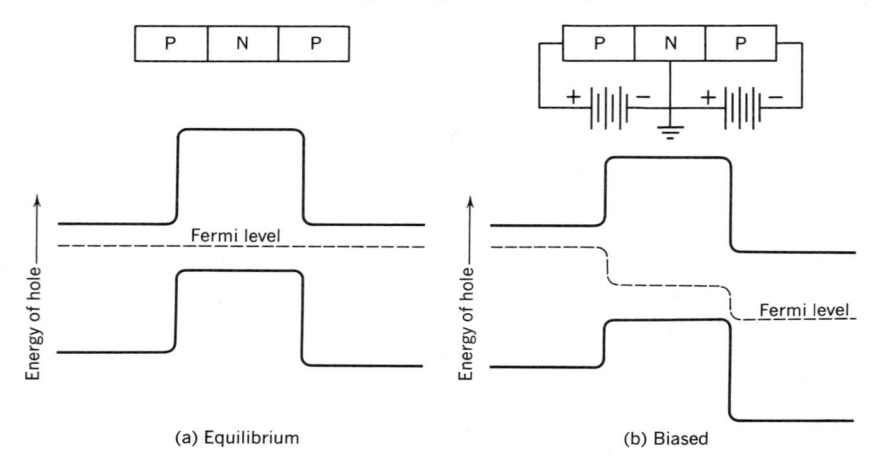

Fig. 4-9. Energy diagrams for P-N-P junction transistor.

energy levels for the holes at the three regions of the semiconductor. Note that all the previous energy diagrams depicted the energy levels of electrons. Since we have thus changed the ordinate from electron energy to hole energy, the diagram remains the same as for the N-P-N transistor of Figure 4-4. Thus the emitter injects holes into the base region and these holes diffuse to the collector junction where they are collected. The examples of two amplifiers discussed for the N-P-N transistor can be applied here if the roles of the electrons and holes are reversed. There is no difference in physical operation of the two types of junction transistors except for this current carrier reversal.

SUMMARY

We have seen that the junction transistor is formed from a combination of two P-N junctions. For transistor action the emitter junction is forward biased and the collector junction is reverse-

The physical action of transistors

biased. The important current carrier in a junction transistor is the minority carrier of the base region. In effect, the emitter junction supplies base-minority carriers that are then collected at the collector junction.

The junction transistor is by far the most prevalent transistor in current use. However, more recently use of the field effect transistor has increased. The physical action of this field effect type is described in the next chapter as well as the various junction type transistors.

PROBLEMS

1. Sketch the energy diagram for a P-N junction in a semiconductor.
2. What part does the Fermi level play in a P-N junction?
3. What is the potential barrier in a P-N junction?
4. What are the required polarities for forward and reverse bias on a P-N junction?
5. If the impurity content of either or both the P- and the N-region is increased, what happens to the potential barrier, and why? Does temperature affect the potential barrier?
6. Sketch the biased and unbiased energy diagrams for an N-P N junction transistor.
7. What are the required biasing conditions for an N-P-N junction transistor in the active region? For a P-N-P?
8. Explain diffusion in the base region of a transistor.
9. What is the essential action permitting amplification in a transistor?
10. Explain the reason for a current gain less than one for the grounded-base configuration.
11. Explain the reason for a current gain greater than one for the grounded-emitter configuration.
12. Sketch the energy diagrams for a P-N-P junction transistor.
13. State the bias conditions for a P-N-P transistor to be saturated. To be cut-off.
14. In the amplifier illustrations, assume that temperature increases. What changes will occur?

5

Summary of various transistors and diodes

In the preceding chapters we have considered the fundamental physical action of the junction transistor. This action was built upon a somewhat detailed analysis of the action in semiconductors. It was noted that the transistor depends critically upon the action in a semiconductor at a *junction* between two impurity materials. The junction transistor is by far the most prevalent transistor in use today. Different methods of manufacture for junction transistors have been evolved as a result of the constant attempt to improve the desired transistor properties. This chapter briefly introduces the various basic methods of fabricating the basic junction transistor and summarizes the various types of transistors. We will not enter into a detailed discussion but will simply indicate the various types of transistors that are available.

Because of the increasingly important role of the field effect transistor, this chapter also describes the basic physical action of the field effect type. The circuit aspects of the field effect are treated in the last chapter of this book.

In addition to the junction and the field effect transistor, the Zener diode and the tunnel diode are introduced in this chapter. Each of these are important semiconductor devices deserving discussion. We begin then by considering the various junction-type transistors.

JUNCTION-TYPE TRANSISTORS

For purposes of clarification, the term *junction-type transistors* refers to all types that utilize a junction. Thus this category includes the basic type described in the previous chapter as well as any allied types. We begin by describing the manufacturing methods for the basic N-P-N or P-N-P junction transistor. It will be remembered that the basic junction transistor consists of two P-N junctions with the impurity material arranged in a N-P-N or P-N-P fashion. Often times the junction transistor is categorized by its manufacturing method. Although there are a variety of methods for producing junction transistors we will basically discuss five different techniques.[1] They are: (1) grown junction, (2) alloy junction, (3) electrochemical etching and plating, (4) diffusion, and (5) epitaxial. The ordering of these is somewhat aligned with their historical order of development. The grown junction was the first method used; the diffusion and epitaxial methods have been developed more recently.

GROWN JUNCTION TRANSISTORS. The first and most direct method employed in achieving an N-P-N (or P-N-P) semiconductor is by a method of growing the crystal, and is called the *grown junction* method. This process begins by placing high purity germanium along with granules of N-type impurity into a small graphite crucible which is capable of being heated to very high temperatures. This furnace-like device is equipped with a vertical rod capable of being drawn upward at a very slow rate while turning. In its crudest form, the vertical-pulling furnace resembles a slow-operating drill press with an attached heating unit. After the N-type germanium is heated sufficiently to achieve the molten state, a small seed crystal is lowered into the melt until it just comes in contact with the surface. This seed is a single crystal of germanium in which precaution is taken to cut the crystal perfectly along the face of the cubic lattice. Because of surface tension between atoms of the seed and atoms of the melt,

---

[1] The grouping used here has been suggested in "A Guide to Modern Junction Transistor Types," R. L. Pritchard, *Electronics*, August 17, 1962.

the melt will cling to the seed after contact. The seed is then pulled slowly away from the melt while being rotated. That portion of the melt which is in contact with the seed begins to solidify because of the cooling provided by heat conduction through the seed. Thus, as the seed is withdrawn, a solid piece of germanium is continuously accumulated. The germanium changes from the molten state to the solid state as it rises slightly above the surface of the melt, the cooling always being provided by the solid material preceding it. The material that freezes out of the melt takes on the same crystal orientation as that of the seed. If the process continues smoothly the resultant grown material will be a single-crystal specimen.

It is noted that the original material in the crucible was N-type. If now, during the pulling process, some pellets of P-type impurity are dropped into the melt they will counteract the N-type impurity and change the material to P-type. The rotating of the material as it is withdrawn insures that any such additions are properly mixed throughout the melt. In this manner a P-region is formed adjacent to the N-region. After a short length of P-type is grown, N-impurities are again added to form N-material. In this manner a single-crystal N-P-N semiconductor is formed. This method has often been referred to as "double doped" method. This refers to the fact that one first starts with an N-type doping or impurity, changes to P, and then returns to N.

This relatively large crystal is then sliced into small pieces, each of which contains the P-layer sandwiched between two N-layers. Metal contacts are then placed on all three regions with the middle P-layer acting as the base. Although the result here is an N-P-N transistor, a P-N-P can be made in exactly the same manner. All that remains to be done is to enclose the semiconductor in a solid plastic material to seal it from the contaminating effects of humidity.

Another form of the grown junction method of fabricating a transistor consists of using the *rate-grown* method. This method is similar to the double doped method described above except that several N-P-N (or P-N-P) sandwiches may be obtained from a single growing process. Instead of explicitly changing the material by addition of impurities, the melt always contains both N- and P-impurities. In this case the type of material grown is determined by the rate at which the pulling occurs. When the crystal is being grown, a slow rate of pulling produces N-type material because the P-impurities tend to stay in the molten state. If the rate is increased suffi-

Summary of various transistors and diodes

ciently the P-impurities which are being constantly rejected from the growing crystal form a concentration directly under the crystal. The increased supply of P-impurities from this concentration will produce a P-layer. Let us say that the growing rate is adjusted so that an N-type region is being grown. When the rate is changed properly a P-region is grown and a P-N junction is formed. The rate is then returned to that suitable for an N-region. This process may be repeated several times during the growing of a single crystal, which results in a more economical use of materials than for the former method.

ALLOY JUNCTION TRANSISTORS. As mentioned the first junction transistors were manufactured by the grown junction technique. The second method of achieving junction transistors consists of an alloy process. Instead of the process of growing a crystal from the molten state, this process depends on an operation similar to soldering.

The essential treatment is to begin with an N-type crystal and "fuse" or "alloy" a P-producing material into the N-region. It was noted in Chapter 3 that indium acts as an impurity to produce P-type material when it is combined with germanium. Therefore indium is used to combine with the N-type germanium so as to produce a P-N-P junction transistor. The operation is begun by taking an N-type crystal and slicing it into small wafers about one-quarter inch long by one-eighth inch wide. These slices are then placed in a graphite jig with a "dot" of prepared indium on either side, as shown in Figure 5-1 (showing five such units). The use of a

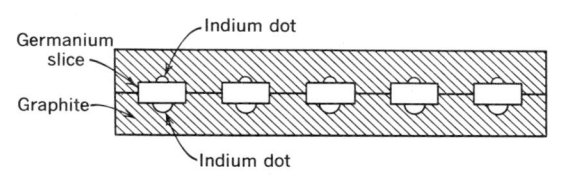

Fig. 5-1. Jig arrangement for alloy transistor.

jig is necessary because the indium dots must be perfectly aligned on opposite sides of the slice, and its graphite construction is necessary to withstand the heat.

The jig is placed in a furnace and the temperature is raised to about 500°C for a short period of time. During this heating the jig is surrounded with hydrogen gas in order to prevent contamination. As a result of the extreme heat, the indium melts and starts combining with the germanium. The combining action is similar to that of soldering, in that a mechanical bond is created by the heat; however, in this case a much more important effect is the *chemical* bonding that takes place. This chemical bonding results in two abrupt P-type regions being formed from the indium-germanium alloy, which then forms the emitter and collector regions. This action can be considered as a "recrystallizing" of the melted area during cooling.

After the jig is removed from the furnace and has cooled, metal leads are attached to the three areas. The amount of indium placed on one side of the slice was larger than on the other side. A collector lead is attached to the larger indium dot and an emitter lead to the smaller dot. The N-type slice becomes the base. The result is a P-N-P junction transistor and is shown in Figure 5-2. It is important to note that, after the alloying process, the indium enters into the crystal structure of the germanium so that the resultant P-N-P junctions form a *single* crystal.

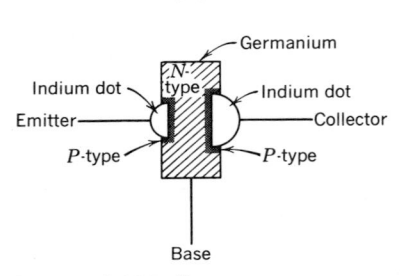

Fig. 5-2. P-N-P alloy junction transistor.

N-P-N transistors may also be constructed by this alloying process if a P-type slice is used and antimony or arsenic is substituted for indium. Originally the usual practice was to construct P-N-P transistors by the alloying method, and N-P-N transistors by the grown or rate-grown method. For the grown junction method it was found that the impurities can be controlled better if the operation is started with N-type material; thus an N-P-N junction results. For the alloying process, germanium heavily dosed with indium provides a convenient material to alloy to a central N-layer, thus providing a P-N-P junction. It is possible, however, to obtain P-N-P from the grown method, and N-P-N from the alloy method.

In the past, most commercial transistors were made by the alloy method. Although this method is somewhat less controllable than the grown junction method, it does lend itself to mass production more readily. Thus, unless a high degree of accuracy is needed— accuracy in amount of impurities and width of the center region—

Summary of various transistors and diodes

the alloy method is used. If the accuracy is necessary, the grown junction method is used.

ELECTROCHEMICAL ETCHED AND PLATED TRANSISTORS. Electrochemical etching is a technique in which one can very precisely control the physical dimensions of a process (i.e., width of base region). Electroplating allows one to precisely control the amount of material deposited (or plated) onto a surface. Electrochemical etching and plating resulted from attempts to increase the high-frequency response of the alloy transistors. A direct result of this was the *surface-barrier* transistor. This transistor is somewhat unique in that the junctions are formed from a metal-to-semiconductor alloy rather than the conventional semiconductor-to-semiconductor alloy.

To achieve such junctions, two jets of an electrolyte are squirted against a small slice of N-type germanium. From basic chemistry it will be remembered that an electrolyte is any solution capable of conducting electricity. With current of the right polarity through the electrolyte, the jet acts as an abrasive and etches the surface of the germanium. This process is continued until the germanium thickness is reduced to a desired value, and then the polarity of the current through the electrolyte is reversed. This stops the etching action and the jet begins plating the germanium with a metal electrode. The use of this electrolyte method permits a great degree of accuracy in controlling the thickness of the germanium slice. It is for this reason that the surface-barrier transistor can be operated at very high frequencies.

In the manner described then, a thin slice of N-type germanium is obtained between two metal electrodes. Figure 5-3 shows a cross section of the surface-barrier transistor. The proper "junction action" from these metal-to-semiconductor junctions depends upon the surface states of the germanium. At the surface of a piece of pure germanium an electric field exists such as to exclude both holes and electrons from a thin region near the surface. For N-type germanium, the

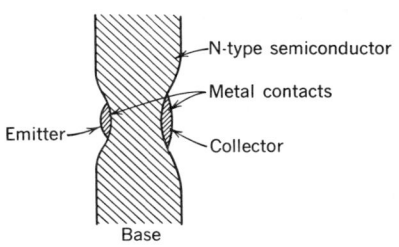

Fig. 5-3. Cross section of surface-barrier transistor.

field is such as to repel the free electrons (majority carrier) away from this surface region. If a metal is joined to the germanium, the free electrons are still repelled, but a concentration of holes (minority carrier) is produced directly under the surface.

When the emitter contact is biased positive with respect to the base, some of these holes will move into the region between the emitter and the collector. These holes then diffuse across the base region, as in the P-N-P transistor. If the collector contact has a reverse bias the holes will be collected. In this way the metal-to-semiconductor junctions perform similar to the semiconductor-to-semiconductor ones.

Another transistor which utilizes etching and plating methods is the *micro-alloy* transistor. In this case the original slice (or wafer) is etched as above. Then either N- or P-type impurities are plated onto the etched parts. This plated surface is then alloyed into the original slice of semiconductor to produce semiconductor-to-semiconductor junctions.

DIFFUSION TECHNIQUES. Diffusion techniques here refer to exposing a semiconductor wafer, at a high temperature, to impurities in the gaseous (or vapor) state. Under these conditions the impurity atoms will diffuse through the surface and into the semiconductor material at a predictable rate. This permits accurate control of penetration depth, and hence close control of the dimension of the region.

The diffusion technique can be used in a variety of ways. It can be used simply to produce a nonuniform base region (drift transistor), or it can be used to form either a single or both P-N junctions of the transistor. The junctions (or regions) produced with diffusion are never abrupt, but are graded in some desired way. This generally reduces junction capacitances and permits higher operating voltages. Also, many desirable transistor characteristics are possible if the regions are nonuniform.

Diffusion is often combined with other techniques in forming a transistor. For example, one junction may be formed by a diffusion process, whereas the other may result from an alloy process. If both junctions are formed with diffusion, one may still need etching to shape the desired regions.

EPITAXIAL TRANSISTORS. The epitaxial technique refers to a more recently developed technique for depositing a thin film of semicon-

Summary of various transistors and diodes

ductor material onto another semiconductor wafer. The outstanding characteristic of this deposited film is that its single-crystal structure is a true continuation of the single crystal of the previous piece. Thus an entire single-crystal transistor could be formed by continuing successively the process of epitaxial deposition on the preceding layer.

One begins construction with a single-crystal wafer (called a *substrate*) of low resistivity. This substrate physically supports the ensuing layers but plays no role in the electrical performance. Following this, one can epitaxially deposit a thin film of like material, but of high resistivity, which will serve as the collector. One could continue this process for the other regions, or use other techniques for the remaining regions.

PHYSICAL CONSTRUCTION. In addition to the techniques outlined here, diverse physical arrangements for the regions have been evolved for use with these various techniques.

One basic physical arrangement is that for the alloy-type transistor, shown in Figures 5-2 and 5-3. Note that the junctions there are formed from opposite sides of the original semiconductor, and this bulk semiconductor is the base region.

More power capability and ruggedness are obtained by going to the *mesa* construction, which is shown in Figure 5-4. Here one begins

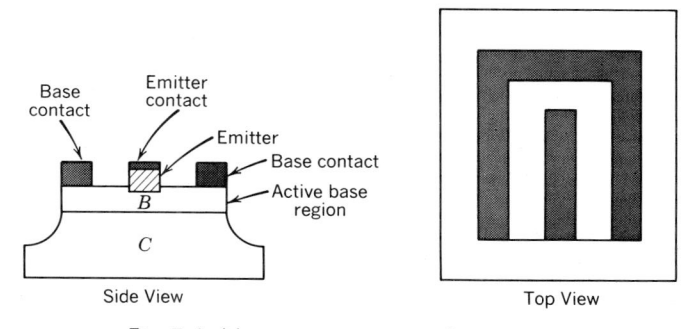

Fig. 5-4. Mesa-type construction for transistor.

with the semiconductor slice that will serve as the collector, and both junctions are formed on the same side of the original slice. The junctions can be formed with either alloy, diffusion, or epitaxial techniques. Note that now the bulk semiconductor serves as the collector. If the epitaxial method is used, one first starts with heavily doped (low resistivity) substrate, and then grows a high resistivity layer on top of this, to form the effective collector region.

The *planar* transistor construction is similar to the mesa, but here each of the junctions appear at a common surface. This results from the methods of forming the additional regions. When forming the base and emitter regions by diffusion, an oxide mask is used to accurately control the area to which the diffusant is exposed. The important characteristics of the planar type are similar to those in the mesa type.

Figure 5-5 shows the basic planar construction in which an epitaxial collector is depicted. Note that both junctions appear at the top surface.

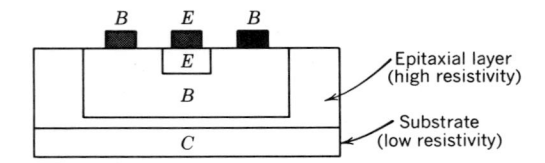

Fig. 5-5. Planar-type construction with epitaxial collector.

This concludes the summary of different methods of fabricating junction transistors. Usually a given transistor is the result of a combination of the techniques.

FIELD EFFECT TRANSISTORS

The operation of the field effect transistor (FET) differs radically from that of the junction type. Its chief advantage is a very high input impedance; in addition to this, it has a low noise figure. Although a relatively old device, this transistor has more recently received wide acceptance because of improvements in fabrication techniques. For this reason the physical action of this transistor is described in this section.

The essential idea in the field effect transistor is to use a semiconductor wafer as a conducting channel, and then vary the conductivity of this channel by means of an externally applied voltage. Two types of FET's have been constructed thus far: (1) a *junction FET* in which the channel conductivity is controlled by varying the

Summary of various transistors and diodes

voltage on reversed biased P-N junctions, and (2) an *insulated gate FET* in which an insulated metal electrode furnishes an electric field to alter the conductivity of the channel.

The field effect transistor differs from the junction type in two important ways. First, the FET is *unipolar* whereas the junction type is bipolar. Thus, while the conventional injection type is relatively symmetrical, so that the collector and emitter can sometimes be interchanged, the FET can only be operated in the forward direction. The renewed interest in FET's has led to calling the more conventional junction type the bipolar transistor. A second major difference involves the current carrier; the conventional junction transistor uses the minority carrier of the base region as its chief carrier, while the field effect transistor uses the majority carrier of the conductivity channel. Therefore the field effect transistor is a majority carrier device, whereas the junction type is a minority carrier device. Because of the above differences, the component parts of the FET have been given different names. Thus, instead of speaking of emitter, collector, and base, one speaks of the *source*, *drain*, and *gate*. This terminology applies to all types of FET's and will be defined shortly.

The first field effect transistor ever attempted was of the insulated gate type. However, in the early years fabrication techniques were not available to permit successful exploitation of the insulated gate idea. Therefore the first commercially practicable FET was the junction FET. This FET's fabrication technology was similar to that of the conventional junction transistors; this accounts for its earlier success.

Later fabrication techniques, however, have permitted return to the original insulated gate idea and it now appears that these insulated gate FET's will become the more important. This type is capable of a much larger frequency bandwidth than the junction FET. It is this frequency limitation that appears to be the chief limitation of the junction FET.

We will now summarize the basic physical operation of the junction FET, followed by the insulated gate FET.

JUNCTION FIELD EFFECT TRANSISTOR. The essential structure of the junction FET is that of a single-impurity semiconductor, to which impurity material of the opposite type is formed on both sides. This entire material again must be single-crystal material in order to obtain P-N junctions at the innerface. This basic construction is shown in Figure 5-6. The basic material is N-type, to which heavily doped P-material (denoted P+) is added. The major N-type semiconductor area forms the channel. Each end of this semiconductor has a heavily doped area (N+) which serves as contacts to the intervening material. The current input side to this semiconductor is known as the *source* (comparable to a vacuum tube cathode), and the opposite end of the main channel is called the *drain* (comparable to a vacuum tube plate). The opposite impurity control regions are called the *gate* (comparable to a vacuum tube grid). This source, drain, gate terminology applies to all types of FET's.

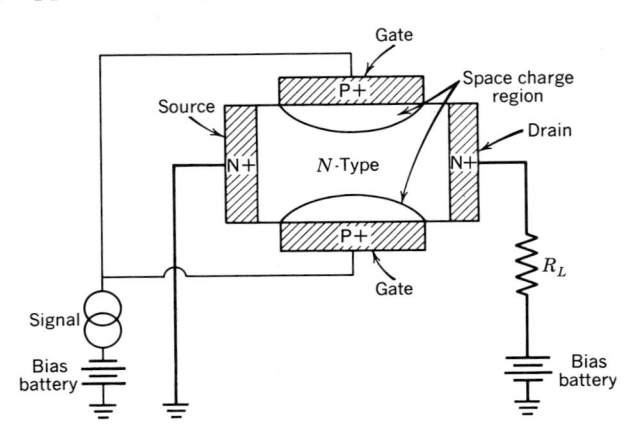

Fig. 5-6. Operation of junction FET in a simple amplifier circuit.

    The essential operation of this transistor can be explained by considering a main current and a controlled voltage. In Figure 5-6 the path of the main current, which contains the load resistor, is exhibited by a heavy line. The connections that provide the control voltage are shown in light lines.

    The N-type layer provides the path of main current through the transistor. Since electrons are the majority carrier in N-type, the main current is composed mostly of electrons. It is the function of the signal voltage to *control* the amount of electrons that flow through the N-layer, and thus control the main current. The signal voltage exerts this control by applying reverse bias to both the P-N junctions. (Due to the symmetry of the circuit any action on one junction also occurs on the other; consequently it suffices to discuss only one junction.)

Summary of various transistors and diodes

Let us now see why the application of reverse bias affects the control, and how amplification is provided in that the *controlled* signal is greater than the control signal. Reference to Chapter 4 [Figure 4-3(c)] shows that the bias battery of Figure 5-6 does provide reverse bias to the P-N junctions. It will also be remembered that the reverse bias causes the majority carriers, of both the P- and the N-regions, to be drawn away from the junction, and that this results in a depletion region. It is this depletion region that provides the increase in voltage barrier when reverse bias is applied. It is exactly this depletion effect that provides the control in the field effect transistor. As the reverse bias is increased, electrons in the N-layer are drawn away from the junction. Not only are they physically moved, they are also rendered incapable of conducting current. The depletion region acts much like a capacitor: the charges are moved and effectively stored in the battery. For example, a capacitor plate which has a positive charge has been robbed of some of its normal electrons.

The effect, then, is that the reverse bias causes the electrons normally near the junction to be withdrawn as available current carriers. When the reverse bias is varied, the volume of the depletion region is varied, so that the number of electrons affected varies with the bias. The total effect is that the area of the N-type material which provides current carriers is varied by the signal. Therefore the main current varies according to the number of carriers available.

Having established the manner of control, it is now easy to see why amplification results. Since the signal is providing reverse bias, only a very small current flows in the input. The output current, on the other hand, is not even passing through a junction. It is passing straight through an N-type material. Its magnitude is limited only by the size of the main battery and the impurity density of the N-material. Thus a small signal controls a much larger output signal. As mentioned, the junction type FET was the first FET to be commercially successful. The insulated gate type, to be described now, was developed later.

INSULATED GATE FIELD EFFECT TRANSISTOR. In its simplest form the insulated gate FET is a single-crystal slice of semiconductor, which is brought within the proximity of a metal electrode. The voltage on the metal electrode can be used to alter the conductivity properties of the main path semiconductor. This is indicated in Figure 5-7.

Typically the controlling electrode is called the gate, and the main semiconductor, on which the source and drain appear, is called a substrate. An insulator or dielectric appears between the gate and the substrate.

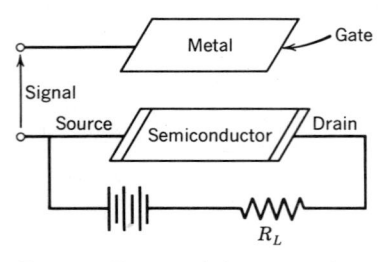

Fig. 5-7. Functional depiction of insulated gate FET.

The construction for an actual insulated gate transistor is shown in Figure 5-8. It is seen that a feature of the insulated gate transistor is that both the source and the drain are heavily doped regions within a larger substrate. The effective channel action occurs within the substrate, between the source and drain.

Using the basic structure shown in Figure 5-8, there are two possible types of insulated gate transistors; the depletion-type tran-

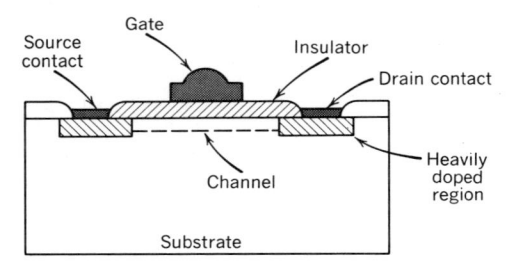

Fig. 5-8. End view of a planar insulated gate FET.

sistor, and the induced channel transistor. The two types depend on whether or not the source and drain are of the same impurity type as the channel.

Depletion Type. In the depletion-type insulated gate FET the source and drain contacts are of the same conductivity type as the channel. This depletion-type FET can be operated either in the depletion mode or the enhancement mode. In the depletion mode the gate is reversed biased so that carriers depart from the channel. This is based simply on like charges repelling and unlike charges attracting. In the enhancement mode the gate is forward biased so that the carriers are drawn into the channel region. Therefore one can use both positive and negative gate voltages with this depletion-type insulated gate FET.

Summary of various transistors and diodes

Induced Channel-Type Insulated Gate FET. The induced channel-type FET is fabricated by making the channel of the opposite conductivity-type from the source and drain contacts. Back-to-back diodes are then effectively formed between the source and drain contacts. Essentially no channel current flows with zero bias voltage on the gate. Assume that we are dealing with a P-type channel and N-type source and drain contacts. If the gate voltage is positive, holes will be depleted from the surface and an accumulation of electrons will result at the surface. Thus the surface channel goes from P-type, through intrinsic, to an inverted N-type layer. At this point conduction from source to drain commences. It is in this way that the induced channel is effected. For further increases in positive gate voltage the enhancement mode of operation is obtained. It is seen, then, that in the induced channel FET the gate voltage is effective in only one direction. Positive gate voltages are used with N-type sources and drains, and negative gate voltages with P-type.

PHYSICAL CONSTRUCTION OF FET. In general the planar type FET's can be constructed by using techniques similar to those described for the junction transistor. Typically the different areas are imposed by diffusion. In more recent techniques insulated gate FET's have been constructed by the use of thin film techniques, hence they are often called TFT's, thin film transistors. The basic construction of the TFT is indicated in Figure 5-9. The TFT is deposited upon an

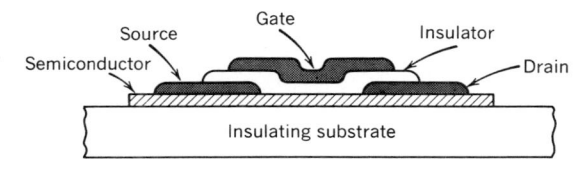

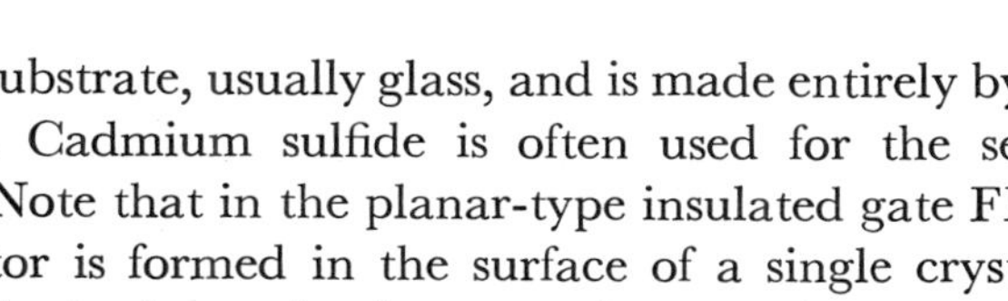

Fig. 5-9. Construction of thin film insulated gate FET.

insulating substrate, usually glass, and is made entirely by evaporation techniques. Cadmium sulfide is often used for the semiconductor substrate. Note that in the planar-type insulated gate FET (Fig. 5-8) the transistor is formed in the surface of a single crystal of silicon. Although the basic mechanisms are the same between the TFT and that planar form, there are differences in their characteristics and in their utilization.

Finally, it should be noted that the TFT insulated gate FET seems suitable for integrated circuit technology. It will be remembered that the main applications attraction for the FET's in general is their high input impedance. Also, they are generally much less susceptible to radiation than the other types and have a lower noise figure as well.

It is expected that the FET's will play an increasingly important role in transistor circuits. We consider the special circuit aspects of the FET's in the last chapter of this book.

OTHER SEMICONDUCTOR DEVICES

There are a number of semiconductor devices that can be considered as accessories to transistors. Those that are of interest here and which we shall summarize are: diodes or varistors, Zener diodes, thermistors, photodiodes, and tunnel diodes.

One of the earliest forms of a semiconductor diode was the *crystal detector*. The chief characteristic of any diode is that it readily conducts current in one direction, but offers a very high resistance to current of the opposite direction. If a diode and resistor are connected to an alternating voltage source, only that half of the alternating voltage of the correct polarity will appear across the load resistor; if a capacitor is added in parallel to the load resistor, a basic power supply is formed. In terms of a transistor, a junction diode consists of one-half of a transistor; that is, only one junction is used instead of two. From our previous study of P-N junctions, it is easily seen that a single junction acts as a diode. When the junction is biased in the reverse direction, the junction offers a high impedance, and little current flows. If forward bias is applied, the junction will permit a relatively large current to flow. In this way a semiconductor junction acts as a diode, and can be used as a circuit device.

A semiconductor diode may also be of the point contact variety. In a "point contact" a metal-to-semiconductor contact is concentrated at a point. A potential barrier similar to that appearing across a junction is produced. The early transistors were made with such contacts and were called point contact transistors. Although the basic action is the same, the point contact diode does not offer as

Summary of various transistors and diodes

high a "reverse impedance" as does the junction type. For this reason the junction type is the more efficient of the two.

The *Zener diode* is another useful circuit device. This type of diode makes use of the breakdown properties of a P-N junction. If the reverse voltage applied to a P-N junction is progressively increased, a value will be reached at which the current will increase greatly from its normal cutoff value. The voltage at which this occurs is called the *breakdown* voltage or the *Zener* voltage and occurs at 250,000 volts per centimeter for germanium. If, in biasing a transistor, the reverse bias is high enough to induce the Zener effect, the transistor may be ruined. In a Zener diode, however, the construction of the junction is such that the Zener effect may be used repeatedly in a circuit application. A graph showing the current characteristic of a Zener diode is given in Figure 5-10. These diodes are also called *voltage reference* diodes, since this is the chief circuit application.

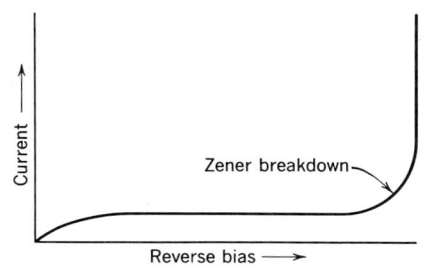

Fig. 5-10. Zener effect in a P-N junction diode.

A *thermistor* is any electronic device in which the proper operation is dependent upon temperature. If a particular electronic circuit has to operate over a temperature range that causes the circuit to show undesirable effects of temperature, a thermistor may be used in such a manner that it compensates, by its own temperature dependence, the undesirable properties of the rest of the circuit. A P-N junction, biased in the reverse direction, is intrinsically temperature sensitive. It was noted earlier that temperature affects the amount of minority carriers within an impurity semiconductor because of the generation of electron-hole pairs. It is also remembered that, when reverse bias is applied, the minority carriers are the current bearers. A thermistor, then, is a semiconductor diode in which special attention has been given to emphasize the temperature dependence of the current for any particular voltage. The thermistor will be mentioned again in connection with the bias stabilization of transistor circuits.

Still another useful circuit device is a semiconductor junction which makes use of the effects of light upon the junction. Such a device is called a *photodiode* and is simply another application of a

P-N junction in which special care has been taken to emphasize the light effects upon the junction. It is remembered that light, like temperature, is effective in generating electron-hole pairs in a semiconductor. Therefore if a diode is biased in the reverse direction, any incidence of light will modify the conductivity of the junction and thus provide a device that enables the incidence of light to control some desired function.

A more recent semiconductor diode is the *tunnel diode*. The reason for the interest in this device is that it exhibits negative resistance over part of its region of operation. The circuit aspects and values of negative resistance are treated in Chapter 14. The tunnel diode can be used to speed up transistor switching circuits, or as an amplifier or oscillator. The basic physical action of this diode is noted here because it is sufficiently unique and the tunnel diode's potential application in transistor circuits is sufficiently great to warrant inclusion.

It was learned in Chapter 4 that there is a potential barrier at any P-N junction. Intuitively one would expect that electrons could not cross from one region to the other unless their energy exceeded this potential barrier. Using the theory of quantum mechanics, however, one can show that there exists a small probability of an electron crossing the potential barrier even though its energy is less than the barrier height. This can take place only when electrons on both sides of the barrier have the same energy.

Electrons having the same energy on both sides of the barrier can be effected by forming a highly doped P-N junction. When the junction is highly doped, the Fermi level alignment causes a different situation from that of a normally doped junction. For a highly doped junction the Fermi level is now in the conduction band of the N-region, and extends across the valence band into the P-region, as shown in Figure 5-11. Here some of the electrons in the N-region conduction band can have the same energy level as some of the electrons in the P-region valence band. If there are vacant energy levels in the upper valence band of the P-material and electrons at the same level in the conduction band of the N-material, then electrons can "tunnel" through the barrier from the N-material to the P-material to fill the vacant energy levels.

With no applied voltage there will be an equal tunneling current of valence electrons from the P-type material to the empty levels in the N-material conduction band.

Summary of various transistors and diodes

If a small positive voltage is applied to the diodes the current increases because the tunneling of electrons from the N- to the P-type increases. This is because many of the filled energy states at the bottom of the N-conduction band are aligned with unfilled states in the P-valence band.

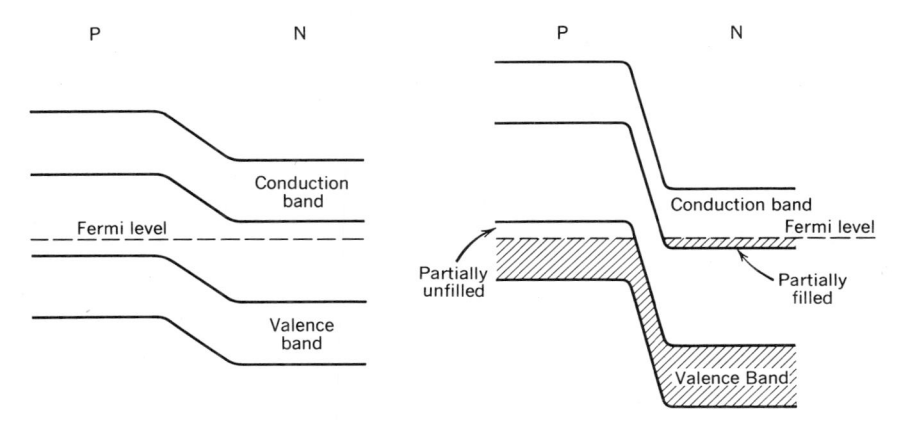

Fig. 5-11. Energy bands for conventional and for tunnel diode.

If the voltage is further increased, the current now begins to decrease, and this is the negative resistance region. This decrease is caused by the fact that the bottom of the N-conduction band moves up toward the forbidden region, so that the overlap of energy band decreases. Thus this decrease in tunneling produces the negative resistance region.

After the overlap ceases, the diode eventually begins to appear as a normal P-N junction diode and the current will again rise with voltage increase due to the usual junction behavior.

This concludes the summary of semiconductor devices which are allied to transistors.

REFERENCES

1. "A Guide to Modern Junction Transistors Types," R. L. Pritchard, *Electronics*, August 17, 1962.
2. "The Field Effect Transistor," J. T. Wallmark, *I.E.E.E. Spectrum*, March 1964.

3. *Transistors*, Dennis LeCroissette. Englewood Cliffs, N. J.: Prentice-Hall, Inc., 1963.
4. "The Silicon Insulated Gate Field Effect Transistor," Hofstein, Heiman, *Proc. I.E.E.E.*, September 1963, p. 1190.

PROBLEMS

1. What are the two major types of transistors?
2. What are the essential steps in producing the grown-junction transistor?
3. What are the essential steps in the alloy process of manufacturing transistors?
4. Name two attractive features of the field effect transistor.
5. Name two types of field effect transistors, and describe them.
6. What is the important application property of a Zener diode?
7. What is the important application property of the tunnel diode?

PART TWO

CIRCUITS

6
Electrical review

In order to provide a consistent approach to the circuit aspects of transistors, it is necessary to rely on the basic electric circuit theory. For this reason it is desirable to review, as briefly as possible, this basic circuit theory in the light of the material to follow. It is intended that this material act as a refresher and give the reader a frame of reference upon which the remaining chapters of this text are based. This chapter begins with the fundamental quantities of electricity and electric circuits. While the basic material is included only for easy reference, the more advanced material on frequency response, equivalent circuits, and impedance matching will be covered more completely.[1]

BASIC CIRCUIT QUANTITIES

CURRENT. Current is the measure of *flow* of electric charge in any conductor and is measured in amperes. The amount of current flow-

[1] The reader should note that, like the Physics Review, this chapter begins with a brief restatement of the most basic electric theory. For the reader who is quite familiar with these basic concepts the initial material will be unnecessary. For such readers the authors suggest skipping the first sections and beginning with the section on "Methods of Circuit Analysis."

ing corresponds to the number of coulombs of electric charge which pass a given cross section of conductor per unit time. In an ordinary conductor the current is carried by electrons so that the current flowing is directly related to the number of electrons flowing. Two major types of current are direct current and alternating current.

A *direct current* is a current in which the *direction* of flow of the electric charges is always the same. Although the direct current may vary in magnitude, it usually is constant. Therefore the equation for a direct current may be written

$$I = k \tag{1}$$

Alternating current is a current in which the direction of flow of the electric charges changes periodically. Thus in a circuit the electrons flow to the right for one-half cycle and to the left for the other half cycle. The most common alternating current is a sine wave current, and its equation is written

$$i = I_m \sin \omega t \tag{2}$$

where i = instantaneous value of current,
 I_m = maximum current value,
 $\omega = 2\pi f$ = electrical angular frequency in radians per second,
 t = time elapsed from some starting time.

This equation states that, in a circuit containing a sine-wave current, the current at any instant of time will be given by the product of the maximum value of the wave and the sine of an angle. It is noted that the product ωt indicates an angle measured in radians.

Figure 6-1 shows a graph of the instantaneous value of a sine-wave current. The *frequency* (f) of a sine wave is determined by the number of complete cycles which occur in one second. The *period* of a sine wave (T) is defined as the time required to complete one cycle. Thus the period is equal to the reciprocal of the frequency

$$T = \frac{1}{f} \tag{3}$$

Although it is sometimes necessary to know the equation of the current in a circuit, it is usually sufficient to consider only the effective value of a sine-wave current. The *effective value* is defined as that value of alternating current which produces the same amount of work (or

Electrical review

heat) in a circuit as does a direct current. Thus one ampere of effective alternating current does the same amount of work as one ampere of direct current. The effective value of a sine-wave current is equal to

$$I_{\text{eff}} = \frac{I_m}{\sqrt{2}} = 0.707 I_m \tag{4}$$

When dealing with any alternating currents for the rest of this text, the effective value will always be used unless noted otherwise. Because of the manner of deriving the effective value, it is also called the *root mean square* or *rms* value.

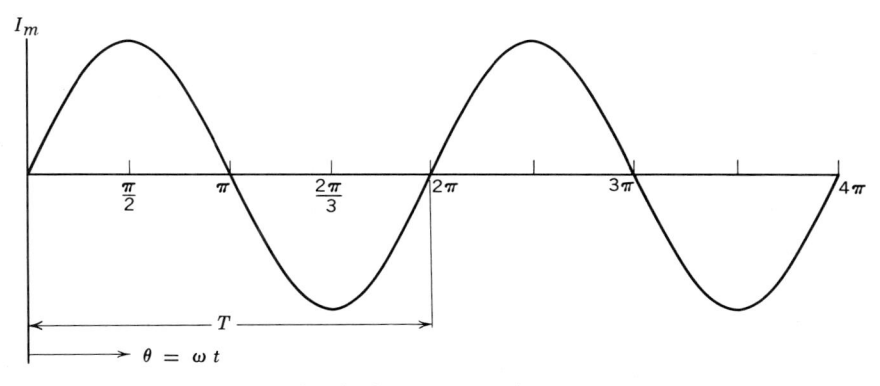

Fig. 6-1. Graph of a sine-wave alternating current.

It is important here to consider combinations of alternating and direct current. A unidirectional current that varies in magnitude is composed of both a-c and d-c components. In this case the d-c component is larger than the peak value of the a-c component. If the a-c component is larger, we no longer have unidirectional current flow, but alternating current with unequal periods. There may also be alternating currents composed of more than one sine wave.

VOLTAGE. Voltage plays two roles in electric circuit theory. In the one sense, voltage is the electromotive force (emf) that produces current in a circuit. In this sense the voltage of a battery, for example, is the force which produces a flow of current; the letter E will be used to designate a voltage source. Voltage is also used in the sense of describing the *effect* of a current passing through any passive circuit element. It is in this sense that we speak of the voltage across a resistor, a capacitor, or an inductor. This is also called *voltage drop* and will be designated by V.

Since voltages are directly related to currents, there are direct and alternating voltages. The equation for a direct voltage will be

$$E = k \qquad (5)$$

Corresponding to the current case, the equation for an alternating voltage is

$$e = E_m \sin \omega t \qquad (6)$$

where e = instantaneous value of voltage,
E_m = maximum voltage value,
$\omega = 2\pi f$ = electrical angular frequency in radians per second,
f = frequency or number of alternations per second,
t = time in seconds.

The effective or rms value of a sine-wave voltage is again calculated by the equation

$$E_{\text{eff}} = \frac{E_m}{\sqrt{2}} = 0.707 E_m \qquad (7)$$

Power. The remaining basic electrical quantity is power. There are two aspects of power in electric circuit theory. The first aspect concerns the rate of work done when electric power is converted to some form of mechanical power. Thus, in a motor, electric power is converted to mechanical rotation; in a radio speaker, electric energy is converted to acoustical energy. In both cases the electric energy consumed is the measure of the work done by the converting device.

The second aspect of power concerns the time rate of loss of energy in the form of heat. Whenever current flows through a resistance such as that of a transmission line, electric energy is changed to heat energy and is dissipated into the surroundings. This consumption of energy represents a loss of energy to the electric circuit, and is comparable to friction in mechanical systems.

In both of the above cases the *consumption* of energy implies that electric energy is changed to some other form of energy and is lost to the electric system. In the case of the motor the consumption can be regarded as intentional and useful, whereas in the second case it is

Electrical review

unintentional and represents a loss of efficiency for the electric circuit.

Having considered the basic electrical quantities—current, voltage, and power—the review continues to the circuit relations for the three passive circuit elements.

PASSIVE CIRCUIT ELEMENTS

In considering the basic circuit elements, we are interested in the relation between the applied voltage and the resulting current for resistance, inductance, and capacitance.

RESISTANCE. A resistance is an element that offers opposition to the flow of current and consumes power. Resistance is measured in ohms, and if a voltage is applied, current will flow according to the relation

$$I = \frac{E}{R} \qquad (8)$$

where I = current in amperes,
E = voltage in volts,
R = resistance in ohms.

Equation (8) is the statement of Ohm's law, and is one of the fundamental equations of electric circuitry. Ohm's law states that one volt impressed across one ohm of resistance results in one ampere of current flow. The power consumed by a resistance when a current flows through it is given by

$$P = I^2 R \qquad (9)$$

where P = power in watts.

Equations (8) and (9) apply for either direct or alternating currents. It must be remembered, however, that for the a-c case the effective or rms values must always be used.

CAPACITANCE. A *capacitor* is an element that offers opposition to the flow of current but in which no power is consumed. A capacitor, in its simplest form, consists of two conducting plates separated by a dielectric. At any instant of time the voltage across a capacitor is related to the electric charge on the plates by the equation

$$E = \frac{Q}{C} \tag{10}$$

where E = voltage across capacitor in volts,
Q = charge on capacitor in coulombs,
C = amount of capacitance in farads.

One of the important properties of a capacitor is that it is capable of *storing* an electric charge. Thus if a direct voltage source is applied to a capacitor, a charge will be stored whose amount is determined by Equation (10). If now the source is removed, the capacitor will retain the charge and a voltage will remain across the capacitor equal to the applied voltage. For this reason the capacitor has two applications in a circuit: (1) as an element capable of storing charge; and (2) as an element offering opposition to the flow of current in the same sense as a resistor.

If we are interested in the first application, we must consider the "transient" situation. That is, we want to know how long it takes to charge the capacitor and how long to discharge it after another element is applied. We note that, in the storage application, current flows as long as the capacitor is either charging or discharging. Current continues to flow until the conditions of Equation (10) are met.

If we are interested in the capacitor as a circuit element offering opposition to the flow of current, we deal with it in terms of a steady direct or alternating current. From the previous paragraph it is noted that, if a steady direct voltage is applied to a capacitor, no current will flow after the initial transient charging current. *Thus a capacitor blocks the flow of steady direct current.* If an alternating voltage is applied to a capacitor, the continuously changing value of voltage specifies that a continuous current flows. The fact that a capacitor blocks a steady direct current but allows an alternating current to flow makes it a very useful element for separating direct and alternating currents. This function represents its most important use in electronics.

If an alternating voltage is applied to a capacitor, a current will flow of value

$$I = \frac{V}{X_C} \tag{11}$$

where X_C = capacitive reactance in ohms.

Electrical review

Equation (11) states that X_C is the opposition which the capacitor offers to the flow of alternating current. X_C in turn, is defined by

$$X_C = \frac{1}{2\pi f C} \qquad (12)$$

where f = frequency of the alternating current,
C = capacitance in farads.

Note that Equations (11) and (12) may be used for direct currents also if a direct current is regarded as an alternating current of zero frequency. Then $X_C = \infty$ and no current flows (in the steady state).

X_C is measured in ohms and is called capacitive *reactance*. A reactance differs from a resistance in that a phase angle is associated with reactance; the phase angle refers to the angle between the voltage and the current. For a pure capacitance, the current leads the voltage by 90°. Thus if an alternating voltage is applied to a capacitor, the resulting current, at any time, will lead the voltage by one-quarter of a cycle. Another difference between a reactance and a resistance is that a pure reactance consumes no power.

A capacitor, then, does not consume power. When an a-c source is applied, the capacitor will store energy during one-half of the cycle and return the energy to the source during the other half cycle.

INDUCTANCE. Inductance is another passive element that offers opposition to the flow of current but in which no power is consumed. If an alternating voltage is applied to an inductor, a current will flow, given by

$$I = \frac{V}{X_L} \qquad (13)$$

X_L, in turn, is given by

$$X_L = 2\pi f L \qquad (14)$$

where X_L = inductive reactance in ohms,
L = inductance in henries.

From Equations (13) and (14) it is noted that, for a direct current ($f = 0$), the inductor offers no opposition. For direct current, then, a pure inductor is a short circuit (in the steady state).

X_L is called *inductive reactance* and is measured in ohms. The phase angle associated with inductive reactance is 90°, and the current lags the voltage. It is noted that this angle is opposite to that for the capacitor, where the current leads the voltage.

BASIC CIRCUITS

SERIES CIRCUITS. Whenever resistances are connected in series, the total resistance is simply the sum of all the resistances. If a resistance is in series with a reactance, either capacitive or inductive, the resistance and reactance must be added *vectorially*. The combination of resistance and reactance is called *impedance*. Since impedance generally has reactance present, a phase angle will be associated with it. Therefore, when specifying the impedance we must give the magnitude and the phase angle.

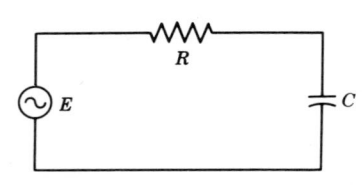

Fig. 6-2. Series RC circuit.

Figure 6-2 shows a series *RC* circuit. For an applied voltage, *E*, the magnitude of the current will be given by the impedance form of Ohm's law

$$I = \frac{E}{|Z|} \tag{15}$$

where $|Z|$ = the magnitude of the impedance in ohms.

The magnitude of the impedance is found by the relation

$$|Z| = \sqrt{R^2 + (-X_c)^2} \tag{16}$$

The minus sign preceding X_C is necessary to distinguish the *lead* phase angle of the capacitor from the *lag* angle of the inductor.

Note that a resistance and a reactance can never be added directly, but must be combined in the manner shown in Equation (16).

If we wish to know the phase angle between the current and the voltage of the circuit, we have to find the phase angle of *Z*. This is given by

$$\theta = \tan^{-1}\left(-\frac{X_C}{R}\right) \tag{17}$$

Electrical review

To write the complete expression for the impedance, then,

$$Z = \sqrt{R^2 + (-X_C)^2} \Big/ \tan^{-1}\left(-\frac{X_C}{R}\right) \qquad (18)$$

This equation gives the magnitude and the angle of the impedance phasor.

The phase relationship between the current and voltage is shown in Figure 6-3(a). It is seen that the current leads the voltage by an

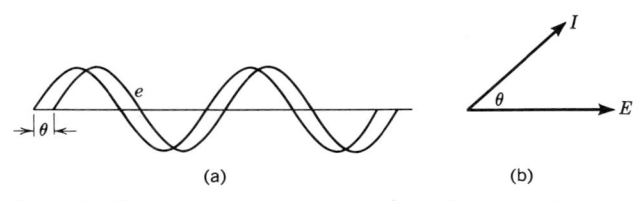

Fig. 6-3. Phase angle between current and voltage in an *RC* series circuit. (a) Actual waveform of current and voltage. (b) Phasor diagram representation.

angle θ, and this is the impedance angle as defined by Equation (17). Figure 6-3(b) shows a phasor representation of the current and voltage. A phasor diagram of this sort is very useful, in a-c circuitry, for providing a visual picture of the current-voltage relations. Such diagrams are usually used as an aid for the calculations.

The impedance itself may be represented by a phasor diagram. This is shown in Figure 6-4. From such a diagram Equations (16) and (17) can be verified by using simple trigonometry. The magnitude of the impedance is given by the hypotenuse of a right triangle, and the phase angle is determined by the angle whose tangent is $-X_C/R$.

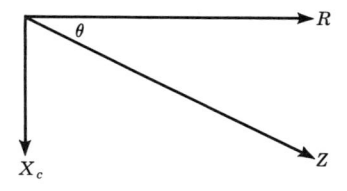

Fig. 6-4. Impedance phasor diagram of an *RC* series circuit.

A useful notation that fits the phasor representation of Figure 6-4 is the following:

$$Z = R - jX_C \qquad (19)$$

The j will always precede a reactive term when this notation is used and indicates that the reactance is to be plotted at right angles to the resistance component. The negative sign appears because the current leads the voltage in a capacitive reactance, and on the phasor diagram indicates that the Z phasor lies below the horizontal axis.

A circuit consisting of a resistor and an inductance in series is shown in Figure 6-5. Again the current is given by Equation (15) and the magnitude of the impedance is given by

$$|Z| = \sqrt{R^2 + X_L^2} \qquad (20)$$

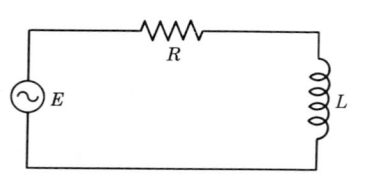

Fig. 6-5. Series RL circuit.

Since reactance is present, a phase angle will be associated with this circuit. This phase angle, which specifies the phase between the current and the voltage, is given by

$$\theta = \tan^{-1}\left(\frac{X_L}{R}\right) \qquad (21)$$

The complete expression for the impedance, then, is

$$Z = \sqrt{R^2 + X_L^2} \bigg/ \tan^{-1}\left(\frac{X_L}{R}\right) \qquad (22)$$

This equation gives the magnitude and the angle of the impedance phasor.

For the RL circuit, the current *lags* the voltage; it is remembered that current leads the voltage in the RC circuit. Figure 6-6(a) shows

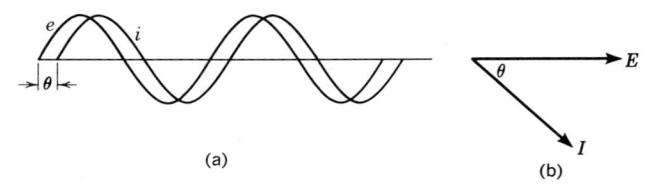

Fig. 6-6. Phase angle between current and voltage of an RL series circuit. (a) Actual waveform of current and voltage. (b) Phasor representation.

the actual waveforms of the current and voltage, and it is seen that the current lags the voltage by the impedance angle θ. The phasor representation of the current and voltage is shown in Figure 6-6(b).

The impedance phasor, for the series RL case, is shown in Figure 6-7. It is noted that in this case the X_L is plotted upward, and that the resultant Z lies above the horizontal axis.

Electrical review

Again the impedance can be written in the form

$$Z = R + jX_L \qquad (23)$$

We can now state a general rule concerning elements in series. When reactances and resistances are connected in series, *add the resistances separately, and then add the reactances by using a positive sign for inductive reactance and a negative sign for capacitive reactance.* The total impedance is found by the relation

$$Z = \sqrt{(R_1 + R_2 + R_3 + \ldots)^2 + (X_{L_1} + X_{L_2} - X_{C_1} - X_{C_2} - \ldots)^2} \bigg/ \tan^{-1} \frac{X_{L_1} + X_{L_2} - X_{C_1} - X_{C_2} - \ldots}{R_1 + R_2 + R_3 + \ldots} \qquad (24)$$

If all the circuit elements are in series, the current flowing through each element is the same. The voltage across each element, of course, depends upon the impedance of the element. The total voltage across the series circuit is equal to the phasor sum of the element voltages. It is important to remember that, for elements containing reactance, the voltages cannot be added directly but must be added vectorially.

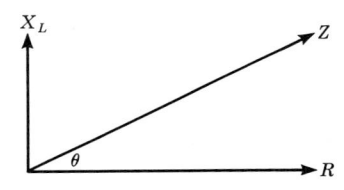

Fig. 6-7. Impedance phasor diagram of an *RL* series circuit.

Figure 6-8 shows a series circuit consisting of three series impedances. The phasor sketch shows how the three voltages add to

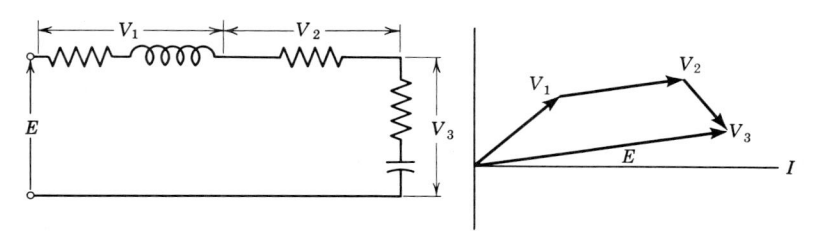

Fig. 6-8. Phasor diagram showing the voltage addition in a series circuit.

form the total applied voltage. Since the same current is common to all elements in a series circuit, the current is used as the reference for the phasor diagram.

Whenever a circuit contains reactance, the power consumed can be calculated by the relation

$$P = VI \cos \theta \tag{25}$$

The angle θ here is again the impedance angle. This equation can be applied to either a single impedance or a total circuit. Since any power is consumed only in resistance, the following relation must be true:

$$P = I^2 R = VI \cos \theta \tag{26}$$

Thus the power can be calculated by either of the two methods.

PARALLEL CIRCUITS. When resistances are connected in parallel, the total resistance can be found by first adding the reciprocals of all the resistances, and then inverting the result. Likewise, if reactances are connected in parallel, the total reactance is found by adding the reciprocals of all the reactances, and then inverting the result. For reactance, it is necessary to note the sign: a positive sign for inductive reactance and a negative sign for capacitive reactance.

When both resistance and reactance appear in a parallel circuit, the total resistance and total reactance must be found separately and then these totals must be combined according to the laws of a resistance and a reactance in parallel. Since this is relatively complicated, it is easier to deal with the *admittance* of a parallel circuit than with the impedance. The admittance is defined as the reciprocal of the impedance

$$Y = \frac{1}{Z} \tag{27}$$

where Y = admittance in mhos,
Z = impedance in ohms.

Since the admittance Y is the reciprocal of a phasor quantity, it will itself be a phasor and it is measured in mhos.

By substitution we find that Ohm's law can be written in terms of admittance thus

$$I = EY \tag{28}$$

where I = total current from source,
E = applied voltage.

Electrical review

We shall use a parallel RC circuit, shown in Figure 6-9, to illustrate the use of admittance. The essential step in using admittance is to take the reciprocal of the resistances and the reactances. The reciprocal of a resistance (G) is called a *conductance* and is found by

$$G = \frac{1}{R} \qquad (29)$$

where G = conductance in mhos,
R = resistance in ohms.

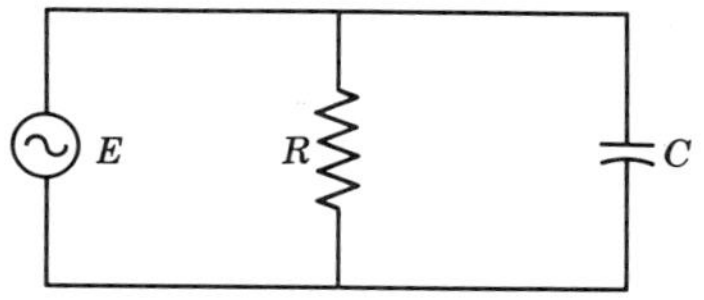

Fig. 6-9. Parallel RC circuit.

The reciprocal of a reactance is called a *susceptance* and is found by

$$B_C = \frac{1}{X_C} \qquad (30)$$

where B_C = capacitive susceptance in mhos,
X_C = capacitive reactance in ohms.

The conductance is analogous to the resistance of an impedance, and the susceptance is analogous to the reactance of an impedance. The magnitude of the admittance, then, is found by combining the conductance and the susceptance in the following manner:

$$|Y| = \sqrt{G^2 + B_C^2} \qquad (31)$$

where Y = admittance in mhos,
$G = 1/R$ = conductance in mhos,
$B_C = 1/X_C$ = capacitive susceptance in mhos.

Similar to the case for impedance, the phase angle between the voltage and the current is found by

$$\theta = \tan^{-1} \frac{B_C}{G} \qquad (32)$$

The complete expression for the admittance, which contains the magnitude and the phase angle, is then given by

$$Y = \sqrt{G^2 + B_C^2} \; \underline{/\tan^{-1} \frac{B_C}{G}} \qquad (33)$$

As for the impedance, the admittance can also be written in the form

$$Y = G + jB_C \qquad (34)$$

A phasor diagram showing the current and voltage of the parallel RC circuit is shown in Figure 6-10(a). Figure 6-10(b) shows the

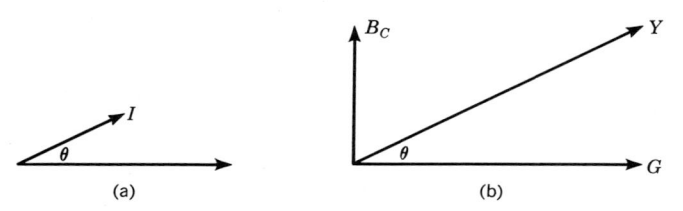

Fig. 6-10. Diagrams for a parallel RC circuit: (a) phasor diagram of current and voltage; (b) phasor diagram of admittance.

phasor representation of the admittance. Although this diagram is similar to that of Figure 6-4 for impedance, it should be noted that capacitive susceptance (B_C) is plotted upward, whereas capacitive reactance (X_C) is plotted downward. It is this difference which accounts for the use of the positive sign in Equation (34).

We have just seen that the use of admittance, for parallel circuits, is essentially a laborsaving device. The method consists of using the reciprocal quantities directly in Ohm's law rather than converting the reciprocal quantities to impedance and then using the impedance form of Ohm's law. It is important to note that, when an impedance is stated, the elements are effectively in series. When an admittance is stated, the elements are in parallel. In fact, if the impedance of a parallel circuit is found, this can be regarded as a series equivalent of the parallel circuit.

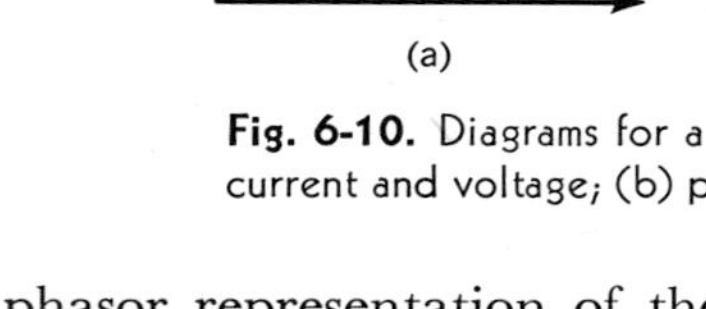

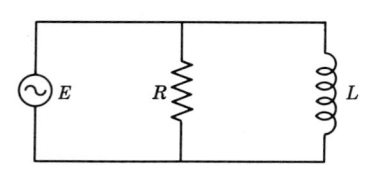

Fig. 6-11. Parallel RL circuit.

A parallel RL circuit is shown in Figure 6-11. If the voltage E is applied, the current flowing will be

$$I = EY \tag{35}$$

For the case of a resistance in parallel with an inductance, the magnitude of Y is given by

$$|Y| = \sqrt{G^2 + (-B_L)^2} \tag{36}$$

where Y = admittance of the circuit in mhos,
  $G = 1/R$ = conductance in mhos,
  $B_L = 1/X_L$ = inductive susceptance in mhos.

Electrical review

The phase angle between the voltage and current is given by

$$\theta = \tan^{-1} \frac{B_L}{G} \qquad (37)$$

As a result of Equations (36) and (37), the complete expression for Y is

$$Y = \sqrt{G^2 + (-B_L)^2} \bigg/ \tan^{-1} \frac{B_L}{G} \qquad (38)$$

As before, the admittance Y may be written in the form

$$Y = G - jB_L \qquad (39)$$

Figure 6-12(a) shows the phasor diagram of the current and voltage in the parallel RL circuit. Figure 6-12(b) depicts the phasor dia-

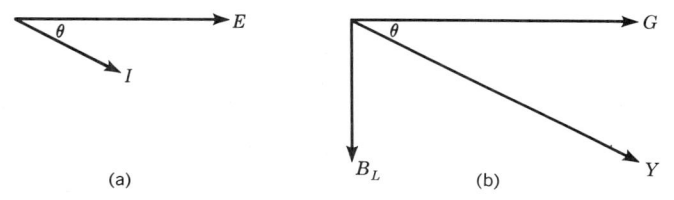

Fig. 6-12. Diagrams for a parallel RL circuit: (a) phasor diagram of current and voltage; (b) phasor diagram of admittance.

gram of the admittance. It is noted that B_L is plotted downward, whereas X_L (in impedance) is plotted upward. This agrees with the negative sign preceding the j term in Equation (39).

In circuits that contain many elements in parallel the general procedure is to add all the conductances, add all the susceptances (paying attention to sign) and then find the admittance by using the equation:

$$Y = \sqrt{(G_1 + G_2 + G_3 \ldots)^2 + (B_{C_1} + B_{C_2} - B_{L_1} - B_{L_2} \ldots)^2} \bigg/ \tan^{-1} \frac{B_{C_1} + B_{C_2} - B_{L_1} - B_{L_2} \ldots}{G_1 + G_2 + G_3 \ldots} \qquad (40)$$

If all the circuit elements are in parallel, the voltage across all the elements is the same. The total current flowing into the circuit consists of the *phasor* sum of the element currents. Again it is necessary to stress the fact that the currents must be added vectorially whenever susceptance appears in the circuit.

As in the series circuit, the power is all consumed in resistances and can be found by

$$P = I^2R = VI \cos \theta \qquad (41)$$

where θ = the admittance angle.

RESONANCE. In a circuit that contains both inductance and capacitance, the inductive reactance may cancel the capacitive reactance. When this occurs, the circuit is in *resonance*. Resonance may occur in series circuits or in parallel circuits.

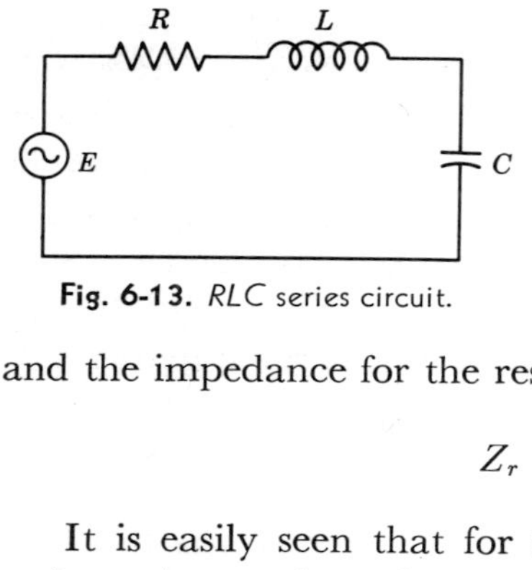

If a series circuit contains R, L, and C, as shown in Figure 6-13, the impedance is given by

$$|Z| = \sqrt{R^2 + (X_L - X_C)^2} \qquad (42)$$

Fig. 6-13. RLC series circuit.

If X_L is equal to X_C, then the reactive term in Equation (42) goes to zero, and the impedance for the resulting series resonance is

$$Z_r = \sqrt{R^2} = R \qquad (43)$$

It is easily seen that for such a circuit the lowest value of impedance is experienced at resonance. If a circuit contains inductance and capacitance, resonance can be achieved by: (1) varying the inductance, (2) varying the capacitance, or (3) varying the frequency. In any case, the basic condition that must be met is that

$$X_L = X_C \qquad (44)$$

If the inductance and capacitance are held constant, and the frequency is varied, the frequency at which resonance occurs is found by setting $X_L = X_C$ and solving for f:

$$X_L = X_C, \quad 2\pi f_r L = \frac{1}{2\pi f_r C}, \quad f_r = \frac{1}{2\pi \sqrt{LC}} \qquad (45)$$

At a frequency slightly higher than f_r, X_L will be greater than X_C, and the circuit appears inductive. At a frequency lower than f_r, the X_C predominates and the circuit appears as a capacitive circuit. The variation of impedance, as f is varied, is shown in Figure 6-14. The

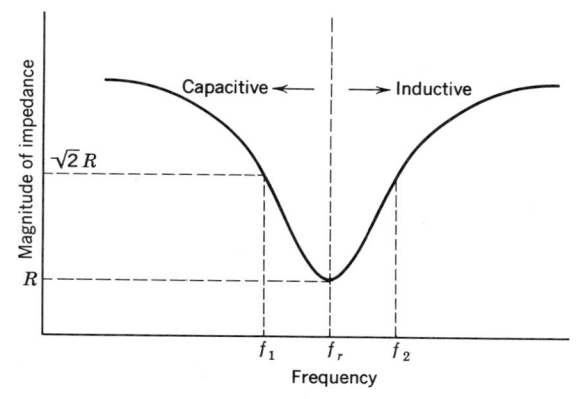

Fig. 6-14. Impedance versus frequency for an RLC series circuit.

capacitive and inductive regions are shown there, and it is seen that the lowest possible impedance is encountered at resonance.

The frequency-selective properties of a series resonant circuit are also shown by this figure. At the resonant frequency, and in its neighborhood, the circuit offers a low impedance. At any other frequencies the circuit offers a much higher impedance.

The selectiveness of a resonant circuit depends upon the sharpness of the peak or dip. If the dip, such as in Figure 6-14, is very narrow, the circuit will select only a narrow range of frequencies and reject the others. The parameter that measures the sharpness of the peak is the Q, and is defined by

$$Q = \frac{\text{resonant frequency}}{\text{frequency bandpass}} = \frac{f_r}{f_2 - f_1} \qquad (46)$$

The f_2 and f_1 of Equation (46), which specify the frequency bandpass, are those frequencies where the impedance curve is $\sqrt{2}$ times the minimum value of the curve. Here f_2 is the higher frequency and f_1 is the lower frequency; the bandpass is shown in Figure 6-14.

For the series resonant circuit, Q is also equal to

$$Q = \frac{X_{L_r}}{R} = \frac{X_{C_r}}{R} \qquad (47)$$

Although the parameter Q applies basically to the entire resonant circuit, many times the Q of an inductance alone is specified. In this case the Q is

$$Q = \frac{X_{L_{inductor}}}{R_L} \qquad (48)$$

where R_L = resistance of the inductor.

If an inductor whose Q is given is used in a resonant circuit with no additional resistance inserted, the Q of the coil closely approximates the Q of the circuit no matter what resonant frequency is used.

If an inductance and a capacitance are connected in parallel, as in Figure 6-15, the phenomenon of *parallel* resonance may be experi-

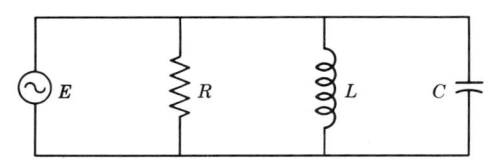

Fig. 6-15. Parallel *RLC* circuit.

enced. Since it is a parallel circuit, we shall deal with admittance. The admittance is found by

$$|Y| = \sqrt{G^2 + (B_C - B_L)^2} \qquad (49)$$

When the capacitive susceptance B_C is equal to the inductive susceptance B_L, parallel resonance will occur and the admittance will be a minimum, equal to

$$Y_r = \sqrt{G^2} = G \qquad (50)$$

Since admittance is the reciprocal of impedance, we see that parallel resonance exhibits *maximum* impedance. This is opposite to the case of series resonance, where minimum impedance occurs. Resonance may be achieved by the three means stated for the series case. If frequency is varied and the inductance and capacitance contain no series resistance, then the resonant frequency will be given by Equation (45), which was stated for the series case.

Figure 6-16 shows the curve of impedance versus frequency for a parallel resonant circuit. As noted, the impedance is maximum at resonance. Note also that the circuit is inductive below resonance and capacitive above. This is reversed from the case of series resonance.

Also shown in Figure 6-16 are the frequency-rejection properties

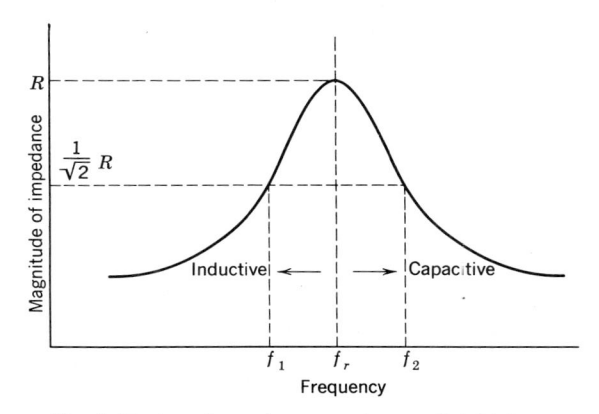

Fig. 6-16. Impedance function of a parallel *RLC* circuit.

of a parallel resonant circuit. At resonance the circuit offers a high impedance, but offers a lower impedance to the frequency bands on either side. As in the series resonance, the measure of the rejection property is the Q. The Q is defined in Equation (46). For the parallel resonant circuit, the Q may also be found by the equation

$$Q = \frac{R}{X_{L_r}} = \frac{R}{X_{C_r}} \tag{51}$$

It should be noted that Equation (51) differs from Equation (47).

VOLTAGE AND CURRENT SOURCES

Although all sources in an electric circuit are essentially power sources, they are called *voltage sources* or *current sources* depending upon whether they resemble an ideal voltage source or an ideal current source.

An ideal voltage generator is a power source that contains no internal series impedance. The concept of ideal stems from the fact that, no matter how much current is drawn, the voltage always remains the same. Figure 6-17(a) shows an ideal voltage source connected to a load; the voltage across the load will remain constant for any value of load impedance.

Any physical source of power necessarily has an internal impedance, so that a practical voltage generator appears as in Figure 6-17(b). The internal impedance is in series with the ideal generator.

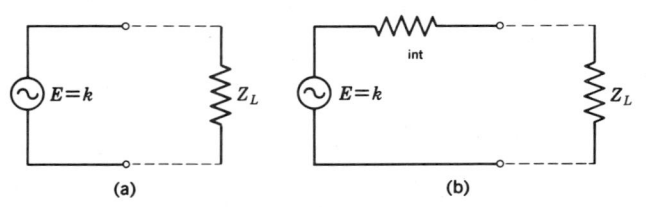

Fig. 6-17. Voltage sources: (a) ideal voltage source; (b) practical voltage source.

The voltage across the load now depends on the value of Z_L and is equal to

$$E_L = \frac{Z_L}{Z_{\text{int}} + Z_L} E_g \qquad (52)$$

As long as the internal impedance (Z_{int}) is small with respect to any load impedance (Z_L), the output voltage remains essentially constant with changing load. However, when Z_L is of the same order of magnitude as Z_{int}, the output voltage will change when the load impedance changes.

An ideal current generator is a power source that contains an infinite internal parallel impedance. It is ideal in the sense that it will force a constant current through a circuit no matter what the load impedance. An ideal current generator is shown in Figure 6-18(a),

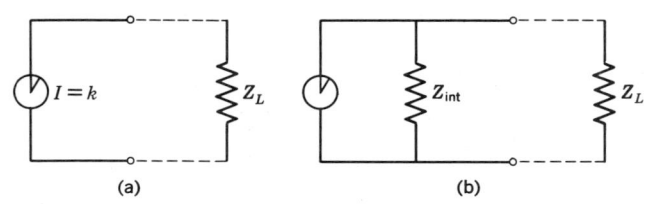

Fig. 6-18. Current sources: (a) ideal current source; (b) practical current source.

and the current through the load will remain constant for any load. A practical current generator will have a finite impedance in

Electrical review

parallel with the ideal current generator and is shown in Figure 6-18(b). The current through the load will now depend on the value of the load, and is given by

$$I_L = \frac{Z_{\text{int}}}{Z_{\text{int}} + Z_L} I \qquad (53)$$

As long as the load impedance (Z_L) is small compared with (Z_{int}), the load current will be essentially independent of the value of the load. If the value of Z_L is of the same order of magnitude as Z_{int}, however, the current will vary as the load impedance is changed.

Although the series representation is usually used for the voltage source, and the parallel representation for the current source, each can be converted from one form to the other. In conclusion, then, a voltage source is a power source that possesses a relatively low internal impedance, and a current source is a power source that has a relatively high internal impedance.

Before leaving the topic of "sources," it is useful to define *active* and *passive* circuits. An active circuit is one that contains an internal source. "Internal" here refers to being internal with respect to the input and output terminals defined for the circuit. Usually an active circuit implies that the internal source voltage (or current) is dependent upon other circuit quantities, and is not fixed. A passive circuit, of course, is one that does not contain such internal sources.

METHODS OF CIRCUIT ANALYSIS

In general, electric circuits are not of the simple series or parallel type. For these more complicated circuits general methods of analysis are required. There are two general methods of analyzing circuits; the *mesh* method and the *nodal* method; both are based on Kirchhoff's circuit laws. The mesh method is based on Kirchhoff's first law, which states that "the sum of all the voltage drops around a loop is equal to zero." The nodal method is based upon Kirchhoff's second law, which states that "the sum of all the currents into a node is equal to zero." We shall treat the mesh method first.

Figure 6-19 shows a series-parallel circuit which we shall use to illustrate the mesh method. The first step is to assume a separate positive direction of current for each mesh (or loop) of the circuit.

The curved lines of Figure 6-19 show the assumed positive directions. It should be noted here that no attention need be paid to the direction of any current; the direction may be chosen in any manner. The

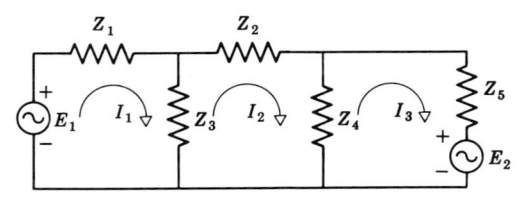

Fig. 6-19. Series-parallel circuit.

second step consists of writing an equation for each of the meshes; this equation consists of setting the sum of the voltage drops in each mesh equal to zero. We write the equation by starting at one point in the mesh and summing the voltage drops until the starting point is reached. If any voltage rises (batteries, etc.) are encountered, they may be written as negative voltage drops, and transferred to the other side of the equation. The three mesh equations which result from the circuit of Figure 6-19 are

First loop: $\quad E_1 = I_1(Z_1 + Z_3) - I_2 Z_3 + I_3 0 \quad$ (54)

Second loop: $\quad 0 = -I_1 Z_3 + I_2(Z_3 + Z_2 + Z_4) - I_3 Z_4 \quad$ (55)

Third loop: $\quad -E_2 = I_1 0 - I_2 Z_4 + I_3(Z_4 + Z_5) \quad$ (56)

These three equations, taken together, represent the equations necessary to analyze the circuit. They are three simultaneous equations, and hence must be solved by either the method of elimination or the method of determinants.[1] We note that, from the mathematics viewpoint, the voltage sources on the left side of the equations are the constants, and the three currents I_1, I_2, and I_3 are the three unknowns. It is remembered that as many equations are required as there are unknowns. In the three equations we may say that the voltages are written in terms of the currents.

We may solve, then, for each of the three currents by the use of the method of determinants. The current I_1 is found to be

[1] The solution of simultaneous algebraic equations is treated in Appendix 1.

Electrical review

$$I_1 = \frac{\begin{vmatrix} E_1 & -Z_3 & 0 \\ 0 & Z_2 + Z_3 + Z_4 & -Z_4 \\ -E_2 & -Z_4 & Z_4 + Z_5 \end{vmatrix}}{\begin{vmatrix} Z_1 + Z_3 & -Z_3 & 0 \\ -Z_3 & Z_2 + Z_3 + Z_4 & -Z_4 \\ 0 & -Z_4 & Z_4 + Z_5 \end{vmatrix}} \qquad (57)$$

In this manner the currents I_2 and I_3 can be determined. After the three currents have been evaluated, the current flowing in any element of the circuit can be found by noting the assumed currents on the diagram. For example, the current flowing through Z_3 is $I_2 - I_1$. The voltage across any element is found by multiplying the element current by the impedance.

We can now see why any positive direction may be chosen for the mesh currents; the currents will appear with a phase angle with respect to the assumed positive direction when evaluated.

We shall now discuss the second general method of solving electric networks, the nodal method. The object here is to write the currents of the circuit in terms of the voltages; thus the voltages are the unknowns in this case. To illustrate the nodal method the same circuit as was used for the mesh method in Figure 6-19 is shown in Figure 6-20. Since we are here dealing with nodes it is necessary to define

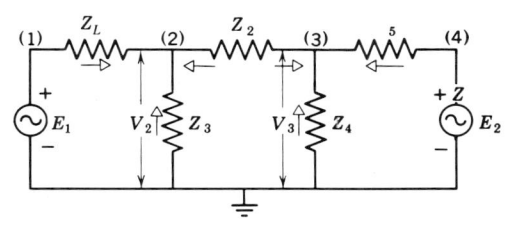

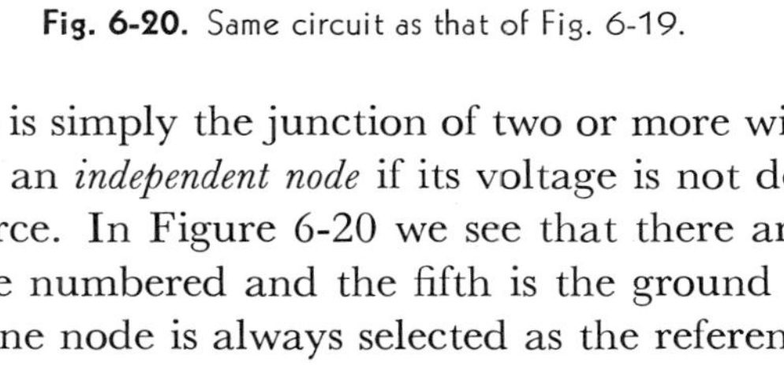

Fig. 6-20. Same circuit as that of Fig. 6-19.

a node. A node is simply the junction of two or more wires. Further, a node is called an *independent node* if its voltage is not determined by an external source. In Figure 6-20 we see that there are five nodes: four of them are numbered and the fifth is the ground node. In the nodal method one node is always selected as the reference node, and we have chosen the grounded node of Figure 6-20.

In using the nodal method, as many nodal equations must be written as there are independent nodes. Consequently, after the reference node has been selected, it is necessary to determine which of the remaining nodes are independent. Referring to Figure 6-20 we note that nodes 1 and 4 are not independent since both are already determined by the voltage sources E_1 and E_2, respectively. Thus the two nodes which must be considered are nodes 2 and 3. Writing the equation for node 2, we set the sum of the currents into the node equal to zero (see arrows).

$$\frac{E_1 - V_2}{Z_1} - \frac{V_2}{Z_3} + \frac{V_3 - V_2}{Z_2} = 0$$

rearranging, we have

$$V_2\left(-\frac{1}{Z_3} - \frac{1}{Z_1} - \frac{1}{Z_2}\right) + V_3\left(\frac{1}{Z_2}\right) = \frac{-E_1}{Z_1} \qquad (58)$$

Using the same process for node 3, the original and rearranged equations are

$$\frac{V_2 - V_3}{Z_2} - \frac{V_3}{Z_4} + \frac{E_2 - V_3}{Z_5} = 0$$

$$V_2\left(\frac{1}{Z_2}\right) + V_3\left(-\frac{1}{Z_4} - \frac{1}{Z_2} - \frac{1}{Z_5}\right) = -\frac{E_2}{Z_5} \qquad (59)$$

Combining the equations for the two nodes, the two resulting simultaneous equations are

Node 2: $\quad -\dfrac{E_1}{Z_1} = V_2\left(-\dfrac{1}{Z_3} - \dfrac{1}{Z_1} - \dfrac{1}{Z_2}\right) + V_3\left(\dfrac{1}{Z_3}\right)$

Node 3: $\quad -\dfrac{E_2}{Z_5} = V_2\left(\dfrac{1}{Z_2}\right) + V_3\left(-\dfrac{1}{Z_4} - \dfrac{1}{Z_2} - \dfrac{1}{Z_5}\right)$

(60)

It is seen that Equations (60) are two simultaneous equations in which the currents are written in terms of the voltages. Thus the voltages are the unknowns and the currents are essentially the constants. We can solve for both V_2 and V_3 by the use of determinants.

$$V_2 = \frac{\begin{vmatrix} -\dfrac{E_1}{Z_1} & \dfrac{1}{Z_3} \\ -\dfrac{E_2}{Z_5} & \left(-\dfrac{1}{Z_4} - \dfrac{1}{Z_2} - \dfrac{1}{Z_5}\right) \end{vmatrix}}{\begin{vmatrix} \left(-\dfrac{1}{Z_3} - \dfrac{1}{Z_1} - \dfrac{1}{Z_2}\right) & \dfrac{1}{Z_3} \\ \dfrac{1}{Z_2} & \left(-\dfrac{1}{Z_4} - \dfrac{1}{Z_2} - \dfrac{1}{Z_5}\right) \end{vmatrix}} \qquad (61)$$

Electrical review

The value of V_3 can be found in an identical manner. After the node voltages are thus found the current in any element of the circuit can be evaluated by taking the difference in voltage across the element and dividing by the impedance.

It is important to recognize that the mesh method and the nodal method are different ways of performing the same task: analyzing a given electric network. We also note that, in the example used, three mesh equations were required whereas only two nodal equations were needed. This is often the case, and then much labor can be saved by using the nodal method even though it may be less familiar, at first, than the method of meshes. The best method to use in any situation is determined by comparing the number of meshes to the number of independent nodes.

In conclusion let us stress the fact that the mesh and the nodal methods are the basic tools for solving any electric network.

CIRCUIT THEOREMS

Many times in dealing with an electric network, we are interested, not in the entire network, but in some single part of it. Often we are interested mainly in what takes place at the load impedance or what may be called the *output* of a network. When this is the case, two circuit theorems, Thevenin's and Norton's, are valuable tools. The essence of both of these theorems is that they greatly simplify that portion of the circuit which is of lesser interest, and enable us to view the action on the output part directly.

Figure 6-21 illustrates the application of Thevenin's theorem. Let us assume that, in the circuit of Figure 6-21(a), we are interested only in the current flowing through the load resistance. As shown in Figure 6-21(b), all the circuitry except the load resistance has been

(a) Network   (b) Thevenin's equivalent

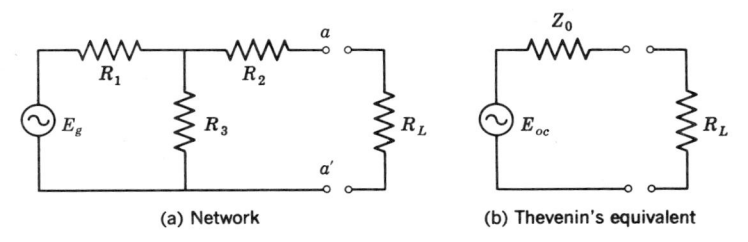

Fig. 6-21. An electrical network and its Thevenin equivalent.

simplified to a single generator and series impedance. No matter how complicated the original circuit, it can be simplified in this manner so that a single generator and series impedance form the equivalent of that part of the circuit connected to the output. Stated formally, Thevenin's theorem specifies that "any linear circuit may be replaced by an equivalent circuit consisting of a voltage generator in series with an impedance."

The open-circuit voltage (E_{oc}) is found by determining the voltage across points a-a' when R_L is disconnected. Since, with R_L disconnected, there is no drop across R_2, the voltage will be

$$E_{oc} = \frac{R_3 E_g}{R_1 + R_3} \qquad (62)$$

where E_{oc} = the open-circuit voltage of the Thevenin's equivalent.

The equivalent impedance is found by looking back from the points a-a'. In this process all sources are assumed to be zero and are replaced by their internal impedance: the Z_0 for Figure 6-21 with the ideal voltage generator shorted, is thus

$$Z_0 = R_2 + \frac{R_1 R_3}{R_1 + R_3} \qquad (63)$$

where Z_0 = the series impedance of the Thevenin's equivalent.

In a like manner the Thevenin's equivalent circuit can be found for any network as seen through two terminals. The procedure is to: (1) find the open-circuit voltage (i.e., the voltage with the output disconnected), and (2) determine the impedance looking back from the output terminals, with all sources replaced by their internal impedance—an ideal voltage source is short-circuited and an ideal current source is open-circuited. If the concerned network has no source in it, then the Thevenin's equivalent reduces to merely finding the equivalent impedance.

Norton's theorem deals with a similar situation. In this case, however, the resultant equivalent circuit contains a current generator instead of a voltage generator. Figure 6-22 shows the same circuit as that of Figure 6-21, but this time Norton's theorem is applied to form the equivalent circuit. Again the effect has been achieved that all the circuitry except the output has been simplified to a single current generator and a parallel impedance. The magnitude of the

Electrical review

current generator in the equivalent circuit (I_{sc}) is found by short-circuiting the output terminals. The current generator is made equal

(a) Network

(b) Norton's equivalent

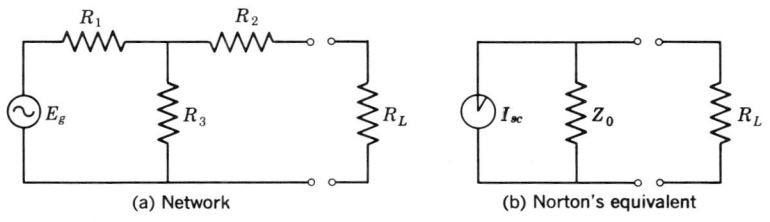

Fig. 6-22. An electrical network and its Norton equivalent.

to the current flowing through the short-circuited terminals. In Figure 6-22 this can be shown to be

$$I_{sc} = \frac{E_g R_3}{R_1 R_2 + R_1 R_3 + R_2 R_3} \tag{64}$$

The parallel impedance is found by exactly the same manner as for the Thevenin's case: the equivalent impedance is found by looking back from the output terminals. For doing this, all sources are short-circuited and replaced by their internal impedances. For Figure 6-22, the parallel impedance is, as before,

$$Z_0 = R_2 + \frac{R_1 R_3}{R_1 + R_3} \tag{65}$$

It seems clear that, since Thevenin's and Norton's equivalent circuits perform essentially the same function, we should be able to convert from one type of equivalent circuit to the other. This is the case, and Figure 6-23 shows the two types of circuit with the quantities to convert from one to the other.

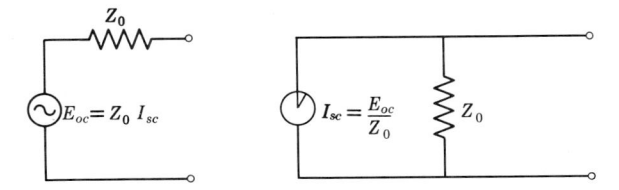

Fig. 6-23. Equivalence of Thevenin's and Norton's circuits.

It is interesting to relate the use of the theorems just described to that of the basic mesh and nodal methods. The mesh and nodal methods are used to analyze a circuit completely in the sense that every current and every voltage of the circuit is found. The circuit theorems, on the other hand, find their greatest use in the special case where only the current and voltage at an output are sought.

Thus far we have considered the two theorems in the application where a *known* electric network is simplified in order to be able to attack the output part of the circuit directly. There is still another aspect of the two theorems. This aspect concerns the taking of measurements to determine the electrical operation of an *unknown* network or electric device. Thevenin's theorem tells us that, for any two-terminal circuit or device, we can ascertain the electrical operation by making two measurements: (1) the open-circuit voltage, and (2) the input impedance with all sources replaced by their internal impedance. It is necessary, of course, that we be able to short-circuit (or open) any sources in the circuit or device.

In conclusion then, Thevenin's and Norton's theorems enable us to reduce any two-terminal network to a single generator and impedance. This can be done by manipulation of a known network or by taking measurements on an unknown network or device.

BLACK-BOX CONCEPT

Another situation that frequently occurs in electronics is that we are interested in both the input side and the output side. That is, we have a known generator on the input side and a known load on the output side, and we want to ascertain what output is produced by the generator. For this situation we wish to simplify the intervening network as much as possible in order to be able to view the generator and the load directly. We can regard the intervening network as a circuit having two input terminals and two output terminals. Thus this intervening circuit is called a *four-terminal* or a *two-terminal pair* *circuit*.

We have just seen, in the preceding section, that the circuit connected to a terminal pair can always be replaced by a single voltage generator and series impedance. It follows, then, that for the intervening circuit between a known source and a load, the circuit can be replaced by one Thevenin equivalent on the input side and another equivalent on the output side. Therefore, no matter how complex the intervening circuit, the resultant equivalent can consist of no more

Electrical review

than two generators and two impedances. Figure 6-24 shows an example of the application of this concept. (Note that, since Thevenin's and Norton's theorems are defined only for linear circuits, all the material in this section also implies *linear* circuits.)

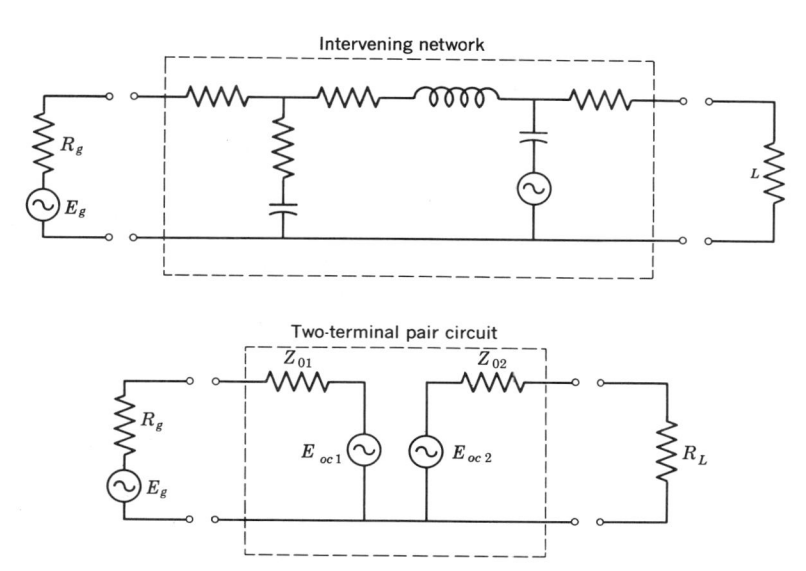

Fig. 6-24. Circuit showing use of two-terminal pair concept.

The concept of treating an intervening circuit in this manner is called the *black-box* concept because we need not know the actual circuit. We need only take two measurements on the input side and two on the output side to determine the action of the circuit. These measurements, as stated previously, are the open-circuit voltage and the impedance looking back into the circuit. For this reason, then, we can think of the intervening circuit as being in a black box whose contents we cannot examine directly.

This concept is most essential when dealing with electric devices. Any physical device most certainly has both input and output terminals. We can find the electrical operation of any device, then, by taking the measurements stated above and inserting the resulting equivalent circuit between the input source and the output load. This process can be regarded as a *method* for determining the electric equivalent circuit of a physical device such as a vacuum tube or a transistor, for example.

We can now apply this method to the derivation of an equivalent circuit for the transistor. By taking measurements on the input side—the open circuit voltage with a known voltage applied to the output, and the impedance looking into the transistor with the output short-circuited—we find the values for the Thevenin's equivalent of the input side, as shown in Figure 6-25. We do the same thing for the

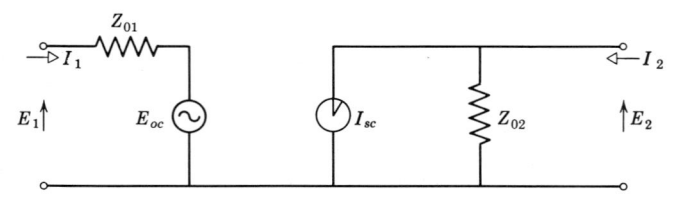

Fig. 6-25. General equivalent of a two-terminal circuit.

output side, except that this time we shall use a Norton's equivalent instead of Thevenin's. It was found earlier that a Thevenin's circuit can always be replaced by a Norton's. The reason for doing this is that, for a transistor, the measurements are much more appropriate to determining the Norton's values on the output side.

Since we have a series circuit and a voltage generator on the left-hand side of Figure 6-25, it is logical to write a mesh equation for this side. The equation will be

$$E_1 = Z_{01}I_1 + E_{oc} \tag{66}$$

For the output side, the presence of the current generator and the fact that it is a parallel circuit suggests the use of a nodal equation. The equation for the output side is

$$I_2 = I_{sc} + \frac{E_2}{Z_{02}} \tag{67}$$

The two equations that describe the electrical operation of the circuit of Figure 6-25, then, are

$$E_1 = Z_{01}I_1 + E_{oc}, \quad I_2 = I_{sc} + \frac{E_2}{Z_{02}} \tag{68}$$

It was mentioned earlier that the circuit of Figure 6-25 can be used to represent *any* electric circuit or device that has two input terminals and two output terminals. Therefore, the two Equations (68) are valid for *any* two-terminal pair circuit or device, provided that the proper values for the generators and resistances are found.

Electrical review

Equations (68) are of little use yet because there are more unknowns than equations. From Equation (62) it will be remembered that the open-circuit voltage is always related to the driving voltage; in Equations (68) the driving voltage, for the input side E_{oc}, is equal to a constant times E_2. Similarly, the current generator on the output side is related to the driving current; therefore I_{sc} is equal to a constant times I_1, because I_1 is the driving current for the output side measurement. With these substitutions, Equations (68) can be written

$$E_1 = h_{11}I_1 + h_{12}E_2, \quad I_2 = h_{21}I_1 + h_{22}E_2 \qquad (69)$$

It is seen that $h_{12}E_2$ has replaced E_{oc} and $h_{21}I_1$ has replaced I_{sc}. It is also seen that we have simply relabeled Z_{01} and called it h_{11}; also, $1/Z_{02}$ has been called h_{22}. Equations (69), then, are exactly the same as Equations (68) with the above substitutions.

It is interesting to note why the symbol h was selected to represent the values of the circuit constants. It is remembered that one of the two equations is a mesh equation and the other is a nodal equation. Thus these two equations make use of both the mesh method and the nodal method. For this reason they can be thought of as *hybrid* equations. The symbol h then is simply the abbreviation for the word hybrid.

Referring to Equations (69), we note that we now have two simultaneous equations. The unknowns are I_1 and E_2, and the constants for the equations are E_1 and I_2. It is remembered that these equations were written for the equivalent circuit of Figure 6-25. We can now change the labels of that circuit to suit the symbols that appear in the equations. The equivalent circuit appears as shown in Figure 6-26. It is necessary to repeat that this equivalent circuit can be used

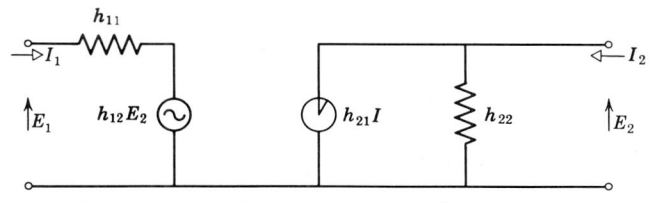

Fig. 6-26. Equivalent circuit in terms of h parameters.

to represent *any* electric circuit or device that has two input and two output terminals. However, for our purposes, we are interested in this circuit as the equivalent circuit of a transistor. This circuit is used throughout this book to represent the electrical operation of the transistor. Thus the h parameters are employed to describe the transistor operation.

Referring to Figure 6-26 it is seen that h_{11} is the input resistance seen when the output side is short-circuited, and h_{22} is the output conductance (reciprocal of resistance) when the input side is open-circuited. The factor h_{12} is a dimensionless constant and relates the open-circuit voltage of the input to the voltage appearing across the output; h_{21} is the constant factor that shows the current which appears in the output side when a current exists in the input side.

If we have a two-terminal pair circuit or device, such as a transistor, we can find the h parameters by taking the proper measurements. Looking at Equations (69), h_{11} may be measured by short-circuiting the output terminals (making $E_2 = 0$), applying a voltage E_1 to the input, and then measuring the resulting input current. Then h_{11} will be given by the ratio of the input voltage to the input current

$$h_{11} = \left.\frac{E_1}{I_1}\right|_{E_2=0} \tag{70}$$

In a similar manner, h_{21} is measured when $E_2 = 0$ by taking the ratio of the output current I_2 to the input current I_1.

$$h_{21} = \left.\frac{I_2}{I_1}\right|_{E_2=0} \tag{71}$$

Values of h_{12} and h_{22} are measured when the input side is open-circuited ($I_1 = 0$) and a voltage is applied to the output. The equations for h_{12} and h_{22} are

$$h_{12} = \left.\frac{E_1}{E_2}\right|_{I_1=0} \qquad h_{22} = \left.\frac{I_2}{E_2}\right|_{I_1=0} \tag{72}$$

In conclusion, then, the black-box or two-terminal pair concept is essentially the concept of simplifying the intervening network between a source and a load. Additionally, from the standpoint of measurements, this concept is useful in finding the electric equivalent circuit of a physical device. We have here treated the equivalent circuit in terms of h parameters, but it should be noted that other parameters can be used. The h parameters were chosen because they are most appropriate for transistors.

Electrical review

The two-terminal pair concept is also the basis of the matrix treatment of electric networks. This treatment is beyond the scope of this book and will not be considered.

MAXIMUM POWER TRANSFER

Whenever two circuits are connected together, or a device is connected in an electric network, the concept of *maximum power transfer* becomes important. This concept has to do with matching the impedances of both circuits so that the maximum possible power is transferred from one circuit to the other.

When dealing with connected circuits we can think of the one circuit as being a source and the other circuit as being the load on that source. The source part of the circuit may be either an actual voltage or current source, discussed previously, or it may be the output terminals of any electric network. From Thevenin's and Norton's theorems we remember that the output terminals of any network can be represented by a single generator and impedance. Therefore, whether the source part is an actual generator or the output of a network, it can always be written as an ideal current generator in parallel with an internal impedance.[2] For the load part of the circuit, we may have a single load impedance or a complex network. In the case of the latter, we can always find the equivalent impedance which the network presents at the input terminals.

Figure 6-27 shows a diagram that depicts two connected circuits in terms of a source and a load where both the internal impedance and the load are resistive. As noted before, this diagram can be applied to any two connected circuits, as well as to a generator connected to a single load.

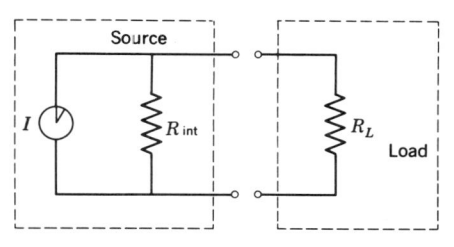

Fig. 6-27. Diagram showing two connected circuits in terms of a source and a load.

In order to achieve the maximum amount of power in the load of Figure 6-27, *the load resistance must be equal to the internal resistance of the source.*

---

[2] The use of Norton's theorem is selected instead of Thevenin's because the output of a transistor is essentially a current source.

$$R_{\text{int}} = R_L \qquad (73)$$

If the load resistance is either higher or lower than the internal resistance of the source, the power achieved in the load resistor will be less than for the case where Equation (73) is fulfilled. This is shown in the graph of Figure 6-28, where the load power is plotted

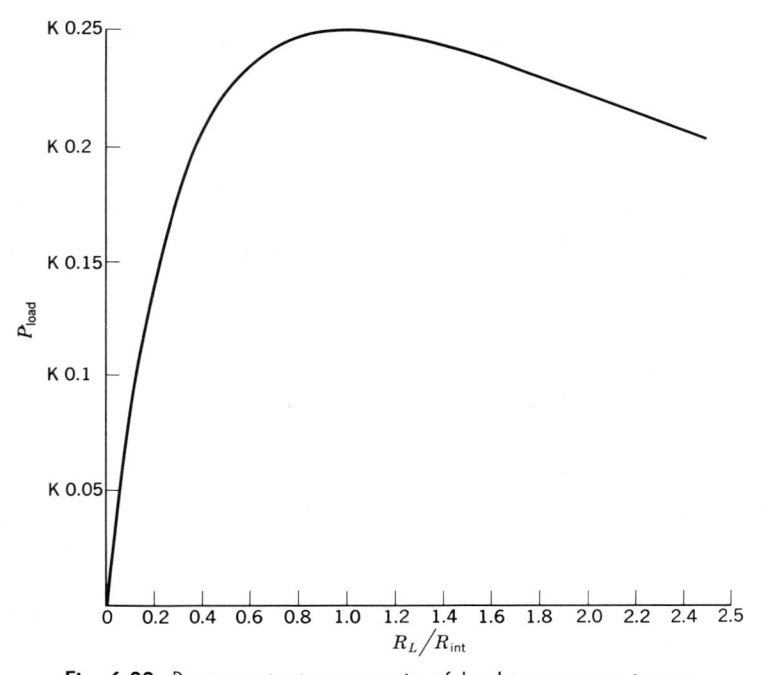

Fig. 6-28. Power output versus ratio of load-to-source resistance.

versus the ratio of R_L to R_{int}. It is seen that maximum power occurs when the ratio is equal to one.

If the resistances are matched according to Equation (73), the power achieved in the load resistance is

$$P_L = \frac{I^2 R_L}{4} \qquad (74)$$

where P_L = power consumed in R_L,
I = current from the current generator.

This is the maximum power available from any source, whether it be an actual generator or the output of a network.

Electrical review

If the internal impedance of a source *is not a pure resistance*, then slightly different matching conditions are needed. For a source impedance containing a reactive element, the load impedance should be

$$Z_L = R - jX \quad \text{if} \quad Z_{\text{int}} = R + jX \qquad (75)$$

We note that the resistance of the load is equal to the resistance of the source, and that, additionally, the reactance of the load is equal to the reactance of the source. However, the reactance of the load is of *opposite* sign from that of the source. Hence, if source impedance is inductive, the load impedance should contain a capacitance whose reactance is equal to that of the source inductive reactance. A source with an inductive reactance and consequent capacitive load is shown in Figure 6-29. If the source impedance were capacitive, then the

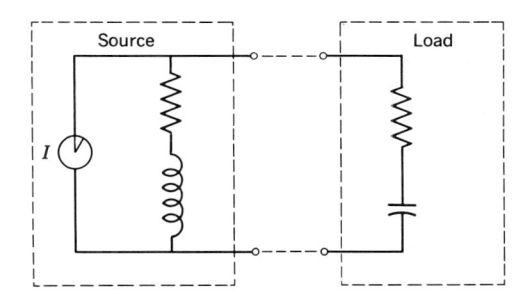

Fig. 6-29. Impedance matching if source is reactive.

load impedance would have to be inductive. The maximum power is transferred to the load, then, when Equation (75) is fulfilled.

Many times the source impedance is reactive, but it is not possible to make the load impedance matched by the use of Equation (75) because the load is restricted to a resistance. In this case the best solution is to make the *value* of the load resistance equal to the *magnitude* of the source impedance. This may be written

$$\sqrt{R_{\text{int}}^2 + X_{L_{\text{int}}}^2} = \sqrt{R_L^2} = R_L \qquad (76)$$

The conditions described above must be fulfilled if maximum power transfer is to be accomplished. In those cases, however, when it is impractical or too costly to match the source to the load, the closest match will have to suffice. We shall find that stage-to-stage matching is a prominent problem in the use of transistors.

FREQUENCY RESPONSE

In dealing with electronic circuits, one of the most important problems arising is the response of the circuits to signals of varying frequencies. If an amplifying electronic circuit, for example, is to reproduce faithfully a complex input signal, the circuit must amplify equally a variety of frequencies with sufficient accuracy to avoid distortion.

In general, any given electrical waveform (as a function of time) can be depicted in terms of its frequency content. Thus a waveform can be depicted either in the time domain or in the frequency domain. If one is given the time domain description, one must use a Fourier analysis to find the frequency description.

If an electronic circuit is to reproduce faithfully any given waveform, its frequency response must be sufficiently broad and regular so that it amplifies equally all important frequency components of the given waveform. Electronic circuits generally consist of devices, such as vacuum tubes and transistors, and interstage networks. The interstage networks are necessary to provide the proper biases to the devices and to enable connection of one stage to another. The problem of frequency response exists in both the electronic devices and the interstage networks. The frequency response of the transistor will be taken up later; we will here consider the frequency response of circuits that are typically used as interstage networks.

Whenever a circuit contains a reactance, the action of that circuit will vary with frequency since the reactance itself is dependent upon frequency. Before going into a mathematical analysis, let us investigate the general effect of capacitors and inductors. Capacitive reactance, it is remembered, is inversely proportional to frequency. Therefore, as the frequency goes up, the X_C approaches zero. Figure 6-30(a) shows a series capacitor connected between the input and

(a) Series capacitor   (b) Parallel capacitor

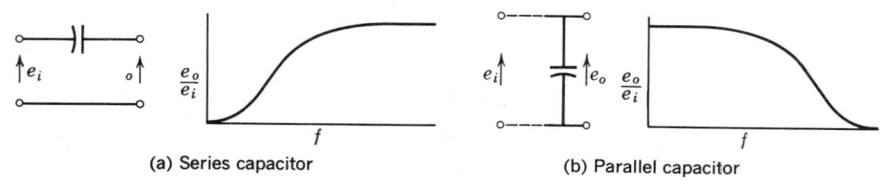

Fig. 6-30. Capacitor circuits and sketch showing frequency response.

output terminals of a simple circuit. Let us assume that a voltage (e_i) of constant magnitude but of varying frequency is applied to the input. We wish to know how the output voltage varies with frequency. Figure 6-30(a) shows a sketch of the variation in output voltage (e_o) with frequency. It is seen that, at zero frequency (direct current), all the voltage appears *across* X_C and hence e_o equals zero. As the frequency goes up, X_C decreases and less voltage drop appears across it. Finally, at a high enough frequency, X_C becomes effectively zero and all the input voltage appears at the output. Thus *a series capacitor tends to block the low frequencies* because of the high impedance it offers.

A parallel capacitor is shown in Figure 6-30(b). From this sketch it is seen that, *at high frequencies, the capacitor tends to short out the input signal*. At low frequencies, the X_C is high enough to exert no load on the signal.

Considering an inductance, it is remembered that X_L is proportional to frequency. Therefore, as shown in Figure 6-31(a), *a series inductance blocks the signal at high frequencies*. At low frequencies the inductive reactance causes little voltage drop and the entire input signal appears at the output.

(a) Series inductor

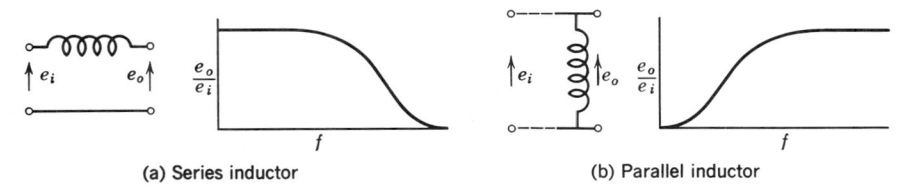

(b) Parallel inductor

Fig. 6-31. Inductor circuits and sketch showing frequency response.

Figure 6-31(b) depicts a parallel inductor. It is seen that a *parallel inductor tends to short out the input signal at the low frequencies*. For the high frequencies, the X_L is sufficiently large to cause no appreciable load on the signal.

These, then, are the general frequency relations for series and parallel reactances. We now proceed to show the analysis method used for interstage networks containing series and parallel reactances. The first circuit to be considered is shown in Figure 6-32(a). It is noted that both a series and a parallel capacitor are included. From our previous survey, we know that the frequency response will drop off at the low end because of C_1 and at the high end because of C_2. Thus we expect to find the frequency response as sketched in Figure 6-32(b).

The established procedure for solving the frequency response problems of circuits, in general, is to break the problem up into the three frequency areas; low-frequency, mid-frequency, and high-frequency. Thus in Figure 6-32(a), we do not solve the circuit as is, but

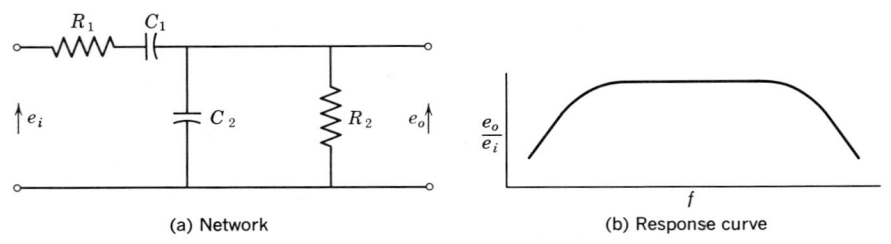

Fig. 6-32. An interstage network having a series and parallel capacitance: (a) network; (b) response curve.

first alter the circuit appropriately for each of the three frequency areas. Figure 6-33 shows the resulting three circuits, derived from

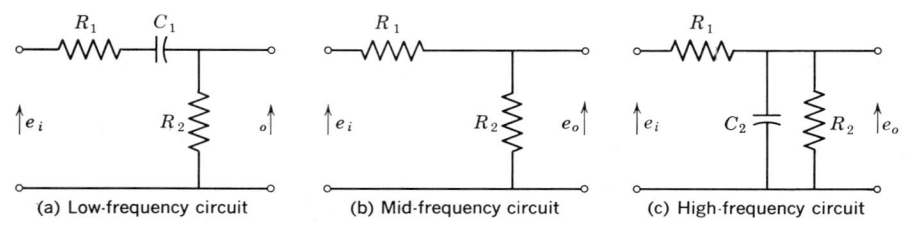

Fig. 6-33. Equivalent circuits for the network of Fig. 6-32(a).

Figure 6-32. It is seen that, for low frequencies, the parallel capacitor is removed; for high frequencies the series capacitor is removed; and for the frequencies between these ranges both reactive elements are dropped.[1]

We will begin the calculation of the frequency response by considering the mid-frequency circuit. For an input voltage (e_i), the output voltage (e_o) of Figure 6-33(b) will be given by

$$e_o = iR_2 = \frac{e_i}{R_1 + R_2} R_2 \tag{77}$$

The ratio of e_o to e_i will then be

$$\frac{e_o}{e_i} = \frac{R_2}{R_1 + R_2} \tag{78}$$

[1] Note that this procedure could not be used if there were no flat intermediate region. In such a case both reactances would have to be considered simultaneously.

Electrical review

This is the maximum response available from the circuit of Figure 6-32.

For the low-frequency circuit of Figure 6-33(a), the e_o will be given by

$$e_o = iR_2 = \frac{e_i R_2}{\sqrt{(R_1 + R_2)^2 + \left(\frac{1}{\omega C_1}\right)^2}} \quad (79)$$

The ratio of e_o to e_i is then

$$\frac{e_o}{e_i} = \frac{R_2}{\sqrt{(R_1 + R_2)^2 + (1/\omega C_1)^2}} \quad (80)$$

It is seen that, as the frequency decreases ($\omega \to 0$), the response of Equation (80) drops because the denominator is getting larger. Thus the low-frequency portion of the sketch in Figure 6-32(b) is verified.

Considering the high-frequency circuit of Figure 6-33(c), the output voltage will be

$$e_o = i\left|\frac{-jR_2/\omega C_2}{R_2 - j/\omega C_2}\right| = \frac{e_i R_2}{\sqrt{(R_1 R_2 \omega C_2)^2 + (R_1 + R_2)^2}} \quad (81)$$

Then the ratio e_o of e_i will be

$$\frac{e_o}{e_i} = \frac{R_2}{\sqrt{(R_1 R_2 \omega C_2)^2 + (R_1 + R_2)^2}} \quad (82)$$

From Equation (82) it is seen that as the frequency increases ($\omega \to \infty$), the response drops because of the growing denominator. Thus the high-frequency sketch of Figure 6-32(b) is verified.

Figure 6-34 shows the entire frequency response curve with the proper equations for each area.

When dealing with circuits in which the response drops at either the low frequencies or the high frequencies, or both, it is necessary to specify over what range the circuit is usable. The *half-power points* of the circuit are used to define that frequency range over which the response is acceptable. The half-power point is defined as "that point at which the power delivered to the load drops to one-half the maximum value." Since power is proportional to the square of voltage, the half-power point corresponds to that point where the voltage has dropped to $1/\sqrt{2}$ of the maximum value.

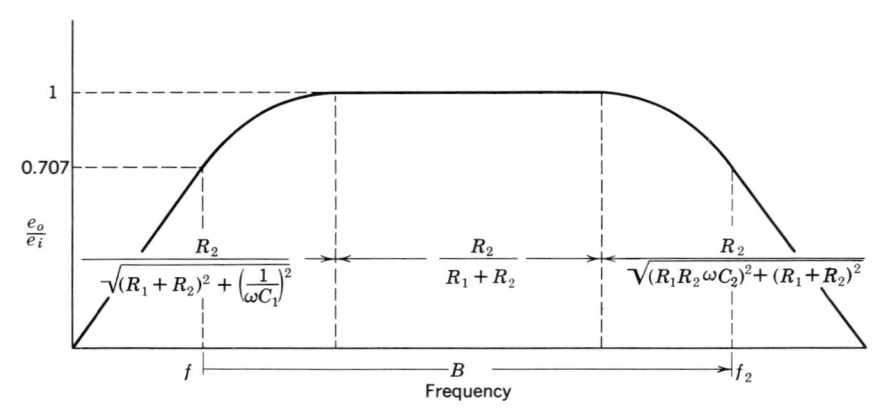

Fig. 6-34. Frequency response curve showing division into three areas.

From Figure 6-34 it is seen that the maximum voltage (hence maximum power) occurs in the mid-frequency range. Therefore we can find the half-power points by proceeding along the curve, on both sides of the maximum, until the e_o/e_i ratio has dropped to $1/\sqrt{2}$ of its mid-frequency value. The low and the high half-power points are shown in Figure 6-34 as f_1 and f_2, respectively. The frequency range between f_1 and f_2, for any frequency-dependent circuit, is defined as the *bandwidth*.

$$\text{BW} = f_2 - f_1 \qquad (83)$$

where BW = bandwidth in cycles per second.

The frequency response of the series-parallel inductance circuit of Figure 6-35(a) will be considered next. The reduced circuits that apply to each frequency range are shown in part (b), (c), and (d) of this figure. Note that here it is the parallel inductance that causes the low-frequency drop-off, and the series inductance decreases the high-frequency response.

Without doing the intermediate steps, the response curve and the equations that apply to each region are shown in Figure 6-36. The equations specify the ratio of e_o/e_i for the concerned region. The half-power points may again be found by determining where the response

Electrical review

curve has dropped to $1/\sqrt{2}$ of the maximum value. The consequent bandwidth is shown on the figure.

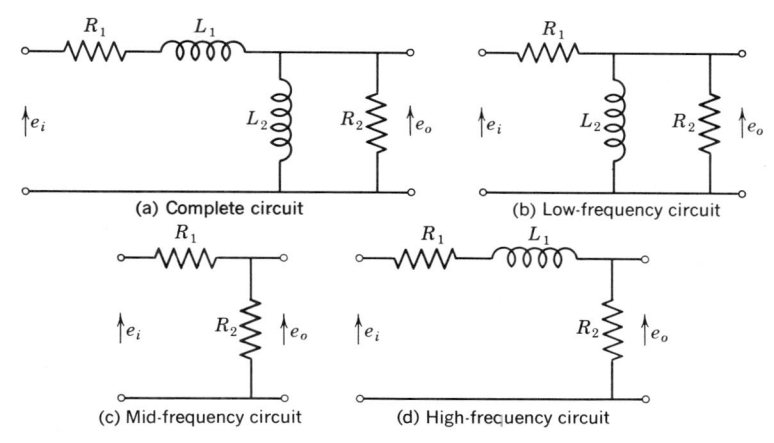

Fig. 6-35. An interstage network having series and parallel inductances.

Although the response curves of Figures 6-34 and 6-36 are typical of the ones encountered, the presence of both capacitors and inductors may cause resonance to occur at some frequency. This will result in

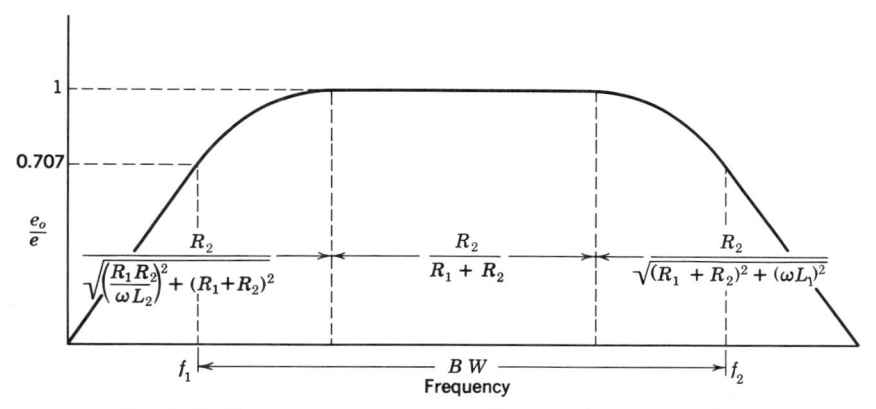

Fig. 6-36. Frequency response curve showing division into three areas.

the response curve having a peak at the resonant frequency. If such circuits are encountered, the basic ideas used in the foregoing paragraphs will serve to find the response curve. Again the solution is found by dividing the problem into the three frequency areas. The difference is, that in the area containing the resonance peak, the equation will be a corresponding resonance equation rather than the more simple equations given above.

TRANSIENT RESPONSE

The transient response of an electronic circuit refers to the speed with which the circuit is able to follow the input signal; it is an especially important issue in switching circuits. Here the signals involved are usually sudden "stepped" voltages or sharp pulses. Since an electronic circuit can seldom follow such signals instantaneously, the finite time required to follow is of interest.

The transient response of the transistor itself is considered in Chapter 15. Here we will discuss the basic transient conditions for simple (and frequently encountered) RC and RL circuits and will note the response of these circuits to a *voltage step*.

The transient response of a circuit is directly related to its frequency response. In general, if a circuit has a high-frequency response, its transient response will be short. Thus it will follow fast inputs rapidly. A circuit with a low cutoff frequency response will have a long transient response.

Figure 6-37 shows the transient response of a step voltage for a

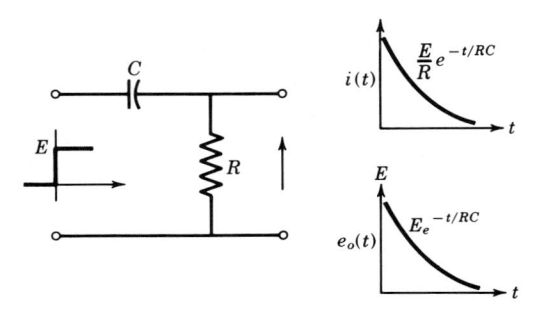

Fig. 6-37. Response of a series capacitance RC circuit to a voltage step.

series capacitance RC circuit. It is remembered that this circuit passes high frequencies, but attenuates at the low end. Thus one would expect a very rapid response. It is seen that the output voltage follows the input rise immediately, and then decays toward zero as the charge builds up on the capacitor. This simple circuit is often

Electrical review

used as a *differentiator*, since the output pulse is similar to the differential of the input step. If one differentiates a waveform, one gets a waveform which is the "rate of change" of the original waveform.

A basic rule for capacitor transients is that the *voltage across a capacitor can never change instantaneously*, but the current can do so. This can be seen to hold in Figure 6-37.

The other RC circuit of interest involves parallel capacitance. As noted before, this circuit attenuates high frequencies, so that we expect a long transient in this case. This is indicated in Figure 6-38. It is seen that the output voltage is quite slow in following the input *step*. The current here if the same as before since the elements are simply exchanged. Again it is seen that the voltage across the capacitor cannot change instantaneously. This circuit is often used as an integrator; its output initially resembles the integral of the input step. If one integrates a waveform, one gets a waveform whose value at any time t equals the area under the original waveform at that time t.

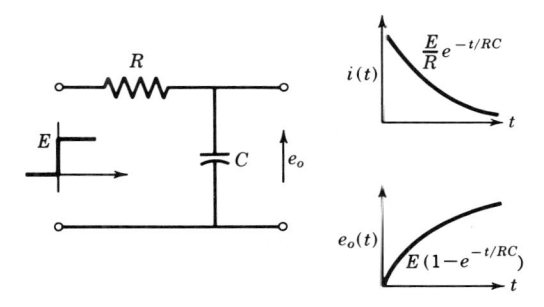

Fig. 6-38. Step response of parallel capacitance RC circuit.

If the series RC circuits of Figures 6-37 and 6-38 had an initial voltage stored on the capacitor, of voltage E_o, the $i(t)$ would be given by

$$i(t) = \frac{E - E_o}{R} e^{-t/RC} \qquad (84)$$

where E = step voltage
  E_o = initial voltage on capacitor

In this case the voltage across the capacitor would be given by

$$e_c(t) = E - (E_o - E)e^{-t/RC} \qquad (85)$$

where $e_c(t)$ = voltage across capacitor

Although inductors are seldom used in transistor circuits, Figure 6-39 shows the transient responses of the two *RL* arrangements. In

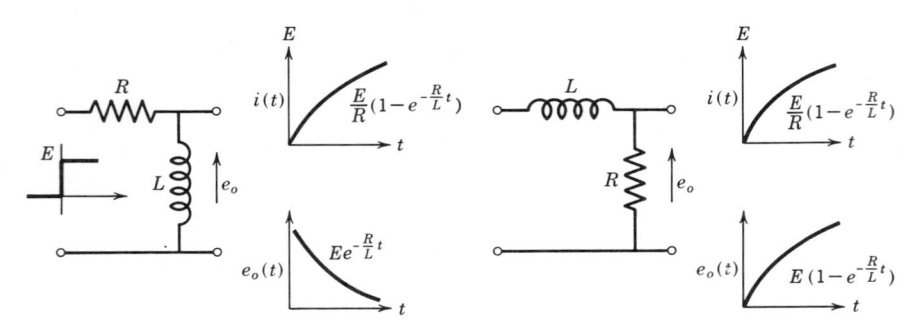

Fig. 6-39. Transient response of *RL* circuits.

inductors the basic rule is that the current cannot change instantaneously, but the voltage can change immediately. Again one can note the relation between the frequency and the transient response.

Since capacitance is such a universal element in all electronic circuits, it is especially useful to remember the basic action in the above *RC* circuits.

TRANSFORMERS

The last topic to be considered in this electrical review is the transformer. This device, very important to electronic circuits, consists of two inductances (coils of wire) which are physically adjacent to each other. When an alternating voltage is applied to the one coil, the resulting current induces a voltage in the other coil. The amount of voltage thus induced depends upon the physical construction and the number of wire turns on each coil.

The transformer is used to transform voltages, currents, or impedances to a higher or lower level, and to isolate direct and alternating currents. It should be noted that no voltage is induced if a direct voltage is applied to a coil.

We will consider here only the *ideal* transformer; that is, a transformer in which there are no resistances. As a result, this transformer has no losses, and the power in is equal to the power out. The symbol for an ideal transformer is shown in Figure 6-40(a). If an alternating voltage E_1 is applied to the primary side, the voltage on the output side will be

$$E_2 = \frac{N_2}{N_1} E_1 \tag{86}$$

where E_2 = voltage on secondary side,
N_2 = number of turns on secondary,
N_1 = number of turns on primary.

If a load is attached to the secondary side, the primary current (I_1) will cause a secondary current equal to

$$I_2 = \frac{N_1}{N_2} I_1 \tag{87}$$

where I_2 = current in secondary and through the load.

One of the most important uses of the transformer in electronic circuits lies in impedance matching. If a resistance R_2 is connected to the secondary, the load *appearing on the primary side* will be

$$R_1 = \left(\frac{N_1}{N_2}\right)^2 R_2 \tag{88}$$

Therefore, if the actual resistance load of a circuit is of an undesirable value, a transformer may be used, as shown in Figure 6-40(b), to

(a) Voltage transformation   (b) Resistance transformation

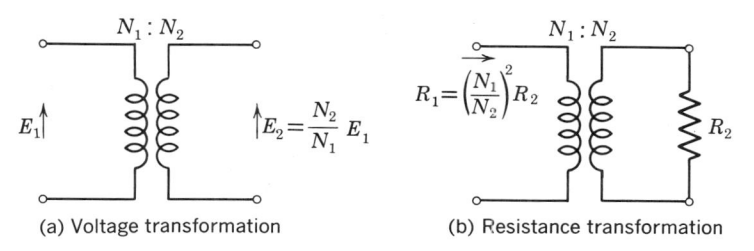

Fig. 6-40. Action of an ideal transformer: (a) voltage transformation; (b) resistance transformation.

transform the resistance to a suitable value. When meeting this situation in a circuit, the analysis procedure is to find the transformed resistance and use this as the load on the circuit.

PROBLEMS

1. Define the ampere and explain which particle or particles carry current.
2. What is voltage and how does it produce current flow?
3. What is power? (Explain in terms of current and voltage.)
4. What are resistance, capacitance, and inductance, and explain how they perform differently in a-c and d-c circuits?
5. Explain Ohm's law and how it functions with respect to a-c and d-c circuits.
6. How does inductive and capacitive reactance differ from resistance?
7. What is the definition of a series circuit?
8. What is the definition of a parallel circuit?
9. What is impedance? (Explain with respect to resistance and reactance.)
10. What does a phasor diagram of current and voltage show about an electric circuit?
11. How is admittance related to impedance?
12. How are conductance and susceptance related to resistance and reactance?
13. Define resonance of an electric circuit.
14. What is meant by the Q of a circuit?
15. Describe an ideal voltage source. How does a practical voltage source differ?
16. Describe an ideal current source. How does a practical current source differ?
17. What is the voltage drop across each resistor of the circuit of Figure 6-41 and what is the power consumed by each resistor?

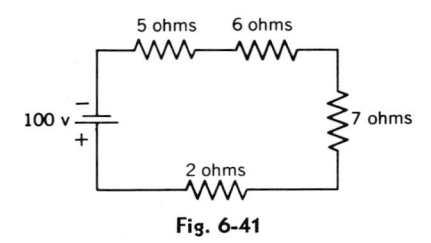

Fig. 6-41

Electrical review

18. What is the current through each branch of the circuit of Figure 6-42 and what power is consumed by each branch?

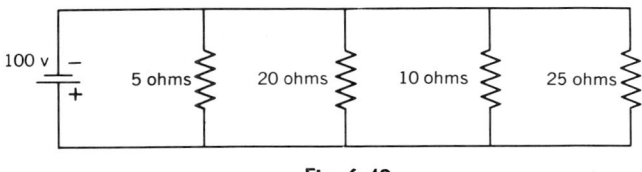

Fig. 6-42

19. What is the total resistance to the flow of current in circuits of Figures 6-41 and 6-42?

20. What are the current, voltage, and power for each resistor of the circuit of Figure 6-43? What is the total current drawn from the 100 v battery?

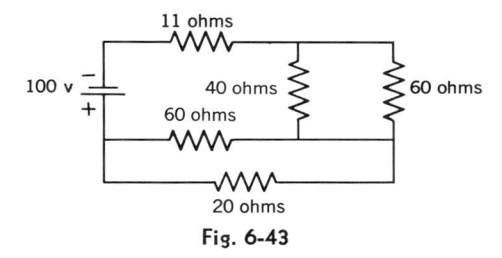

Fig. 6-43

21. There is a set of resistors connected as shown in Figure 6-44. It is desired to know what proportion of the input voltage appears across the 3 K resistor. This is a simulated d-c biasing circuit used in transistor circuits. (*Hint:* Use nodal method.)

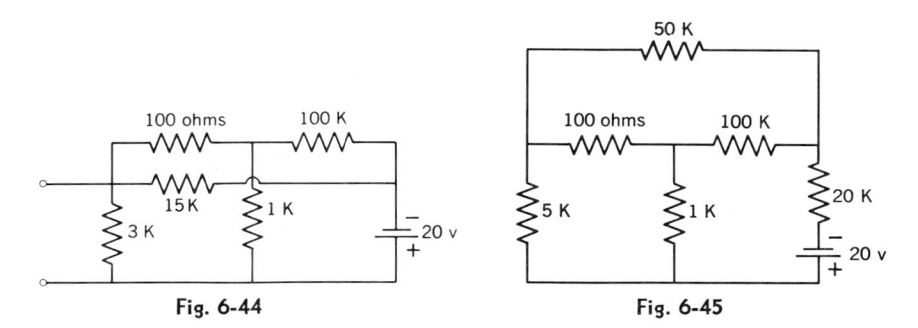

Fig. 6-44

Fig. 6-45

22. In Figure 6-45 is shown another transistor biasing circuit. What is the current flowing through the 100 ohm resistor? (*Hint:* Use mesh method.)

23. What is the Thevenin equivalent of the circuits shown in Figure 6-46?

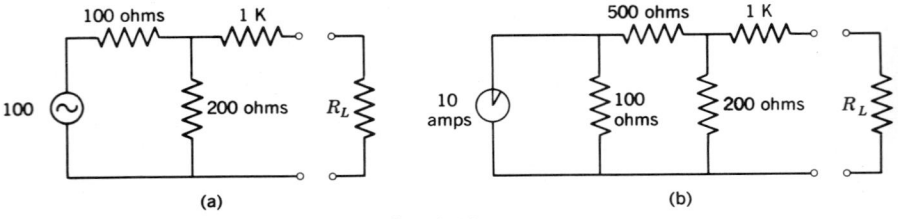

Fig. 6-46

24. What is the Norton equivalent of the circuit shown in Figure 6-46?
25. Find the hybrid equivalent circuit of the four-terminal devices shown in Figure 6-47.

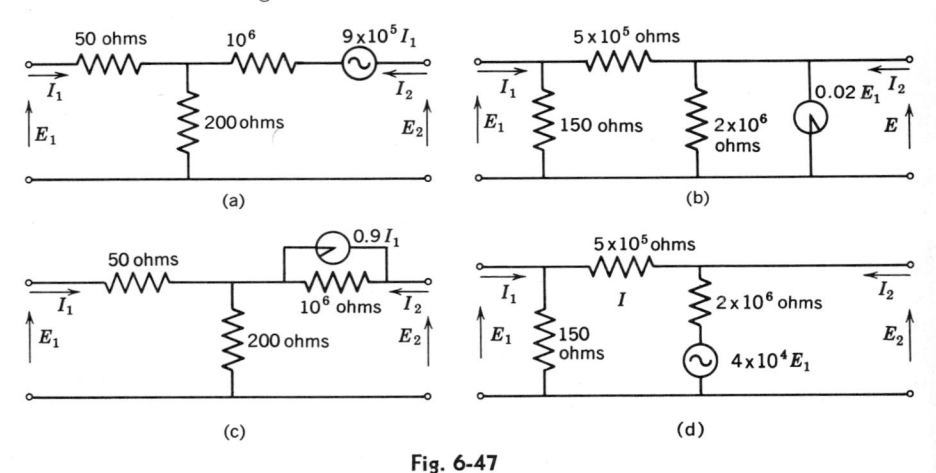

Fig. 6-47

26. What load resistance R_L should be used in the circuits of Figure 6-46 to obtain maximum power transfer to the load?
27. Determine the upper and lower half-power frequencies for the circuit shown in Figure 6-48.

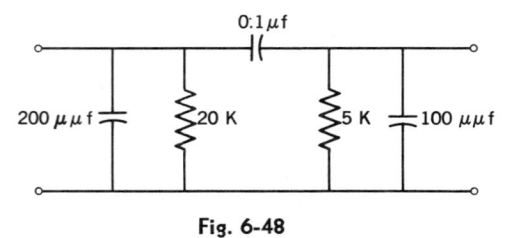

Fig. 6-48

Electrical review

28. Assume that an "impulse" (the rate of change of the step) is applied to the currents of Figures 6-37 and 6-38. Sketch the responses to this impulse. This response will be the rate of change of the responses to the square wave.

29. Assume that a capacitor in a series RC circuit has an initial stored charge, with voltage E_o. Assume that this capacitor is suddenly discharged through a resistance R. What is the equation and sketch of the discharge current? The capacitor voltage during discharge?

30. The time constant of a simple RC circuit is $T = RC$. What percentage "change" has taken place (between initial and final value) if a step voltage is applied to a series RC circuit?

7

The transistor as a circuit element

Thus far, in dealing with transistors, we have concentrated on their physical operation. In Chapter 4 the basic operation of the P-N junction was described. We shall now study the circuit aspects of the transistor; that is, the transistor as an electric device.

In this chapter emphasis is placed on the *methods* by which the transistor is analyzed as a circuit element. Because some circuitry methods for the transistor are similar to those for vacuum tubes, some of this material will seem familiar to those readers proficient in vacuum tube theory. Nevertheless, it is helpful to reinvestigate the fundamental methods as they apply to transistors.

In usual applications transistors are used to form either an amplifier, an oscillator, or a switching device. Of these three the most basic is the amplifier, operating in the "active" region of transistor operation. The circuit methods described here are concerned with transistor operation in this active region. Later, when discussing switching circuits, we will also have to consider the operation in the *cutoff* and the *saturation* regions.

The first circuitry method considered is the *method of graphical analysis*. After the philosophy and basis of this method is explained, the simple amplifier of Chapter 4 will be analyzed as a circuit element. Following this, the *method of small signal equivalent circuits* is treated, and again the simple amplifier is used to illustrate the use of the method.

METHOD OF GRAPHICAL ANALYSIS

When dealing with its circuit aspects, the first fact to be noted about a transistor is that it is an *active* device. In the preceding chapter, an active electric circuit was defined as a circuit that has an electrically internal power source. The output of this source is not fixed, but is dependent upon other circuit quantities. The transistor behaves as an active circuit element in the following way: when a signal is applied to the input, an internal (and amplified) signal causes an enlarged signal in the output which is controlled by the applied input signal. To realize this active action, the transistor must be connected to a d-c power source which is of course external to the transistor. In effect, then, the transistor causes d-c power from the d-c sources to be converted to desired signal power. Thus it is seen that the active property of the transistor is the source of amplification in a transistor circuit.

The second fact to be noted about a transistor is that it is a *biased* active device. The basic idea here is that the desired action may take place about any one of a large number of possible *operating* or *bias* points. It is usually the case that bias batteries (or bias circuitry) are applied to both the input and the output sides of the transistor circuit; however, in some cases the input side has no overt bias circuitry.

In order to consider all possible action of a transistor in a circuit, then, we must know its action about any and every possible bias point. The most convenient way of specifying the transistor action in the entire active region is to find the graphical characteristics of the transistor. If we have ascertained the characteristics of both the input and the output side, we then know the circuit action of the transistor at any and all bias points. It can be concluded that the only way to specify the complete electric (static) action of a biased active device is to specify the input and output characteristics.[1]

[1] For completeness, these characteristics would have to be given for a range of temperatures. Also, note that the characteristics do not indicate the frequency or the noise behavior of the device.

JUNCTION TRANSISTOR CHARACTERISTICS. We will deal with both output and input characteristics. For reasons to be seen later the output characteristics are used much more frequently than the input ones, and we shall concentrate on them here.

Consider first the common base connection. The output characteristics will consist of collector current (I_C) plotted versus collector voltage (V_{CB}). Since the emitter is the input for the common base connection, the collector characteristics will be plotted with emitter current (I_E) as the parameter. The collector curves for a junction transistor along with the symbolic circuit diagram are shown in Figure 7-1. Along any one curve on this graph the input (emitter)

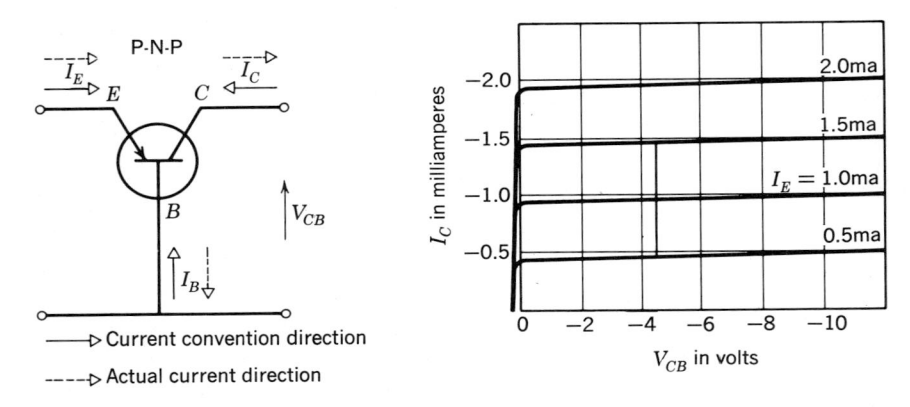

Fig. 7-1. Collector curves for common-base junction transistor.

current is constant. This series of curves tells us what emitter current must exist to achieve any combination of V_{CB} and I_C. It is noted that these curves are very linear, and practically parallel to the V_{CB} axis. This leads to a very important observation: the collector current, for constant emitter current, does not change appreciably with large changes in collector voltage.

A comment on the convention regarding current direction is required here. When specifying transistor characteristics it is useful to agree on a fixed convention for current direction. The accepted convention is that the *positive* current direction is *into* the terminals, as shown by the solid arrows in Figure 7-1. This convention is applied to both P-N-P and N-P-N transistors.

The *actual* current direction for the P-N-P transistor is shown by the dashed arrows in Figure 7-1 (each current would be reversed for

The transistor as a circuit element

the N-P-N transistor). It is seen that both I_C and I_B are negative, in terms of the stated convention, for the P-N-P. (I_E is negative for the N-P-N). This convention is the reason for showing a negative I_C on any P-N-P characteristics (as in Figure 7-1).

The reader is warned that we will abandon this convention in later chapters, when writing the d-c equations. There it will be considerably more convenient to adopt the actual current directions as the definition for positive currents. (Hence, the positive directions for N-P-N will be opposite those of P-N-P). The reader should be constantly prepared to switch from one convention to the other, since adopting one convention for all purposes would be unwieldy.

It is interesting to note that one could have selected emitter voltage (V_{EB}) as the parameter for the collector characteristics instead of I_E. If the V_C-I_C characteristics were plotted versus V_{BE}, the curves would not be uniformly spaced. The reason for this is that the input resistance is not linear; i.e., its value changes as the input current increases or decreases. For this reason transistors are usually driven with approximate *current sources;* consequently the output characteristics usually use input constant current as the parameter. As the curves suggest, the characteristics of Figure 7-1 are measured by varying the collector voltage and then adjusting the emitter current so as to keep it constant for any particular curve. Such characteristics give us information only about the transistor; there is no circuitry added thus far.

It is useful to point out the basic current gain stressed in Chapter 4. For example, the common-base current gain (α) of a transistor is determined by the straight line shown in Figure 7-1. As defined in Chapter 4, the current gain is

$$\alpha = -\frac{\Delta I_C}{\Delta I_E} \quad \text{for } V_{CB} \text{ constant} \tag{1}$$

The negative sign simply accounts for the fact that, by our convention, the I_C is negative for the P-N-P (while the I_E is negative for the N-P-N). The α is always positive.

If, in Figure 7-1, we read the change in I_C and in I_E across the short vertical line, then the α is determined by Equation (1), and it is seen to be about 0.980/1.00. A word of caution is necessary here; the current gain (α) is: (1) a parameter of only the transistor, independent of circuitry, and (2) is valid only for the common-base connection. Later we shall be dealing with the current gains of various circuits; those should not be confused with α.

The output characteristics of a common-emitter connection are shown in Figure 7-2. This connection is the one most used. Therefore, whenever characteristics are supplied by the manufacturer, it will usually be the common-emitter characteristics.

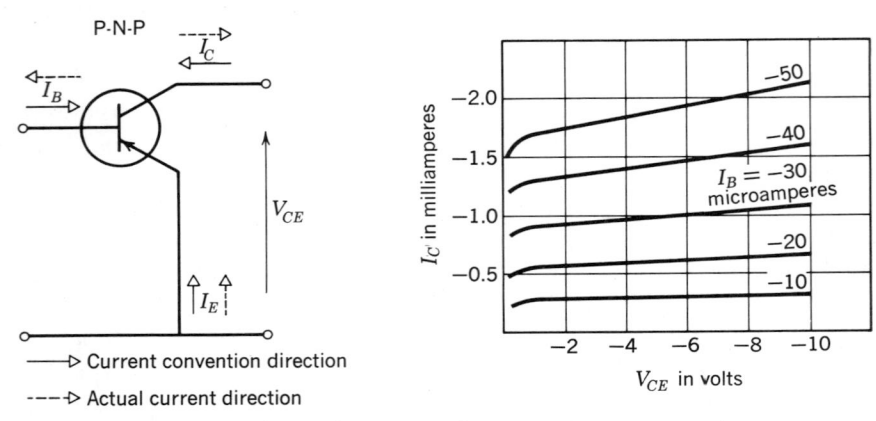

Fig. 7-2. Collector characteristics for common-emitter connection.

Although the curves of Figure 7-2 look similar to those of Figure 7-1 (common base), there are two important differences. First, the base current (I_B) is now the input variable instead of I_E. This results from the fact that the signal is now applied to the base. Second, the collector voltage is measured from collector to emitter (V_{CE}). The voltage V_{CE} differs only slightly in value from V_{CB}, so that for many purposes they can be regarded as identical.

In terms of the current convention (into the terminals) both I_C and I_B are negative, as depicted on the characteristics.

In Figure 7-2 it is seen that the curves are nearly linear and approximately uniformly spaced, although there are deviations from uniformity of spacing. The fact that these curves have more slope than those of Figure 7-1 means that the collector resistance is lower, and the variation in spacing means that the variation of current gain will be more than that for the common-base case.

As a result of I_B being the input current, the short-circuit current gain of the common-emitter transistor will be

$$\beta = \frac{\Delta I_C}{\Delta I_B} \quad \text{with } V_{CE} \text{ constant} \qquad (2)$$

As read from Figure 7-2, the current gain is $\beta = 40$. β is always

The transistor as a circuit element

positive and is related to α, the current gain of the common base, by the equation

$$\beta = \frac{\alpha}{1-\alpha} \qquad (3)$$

This relation was pointed out in Chapter 4, and we see that the current gain of the common-emitter junction transistor is always greater than that of the common base. Note that the current gain β is a parameter of only the transistor, independent of circuitry, and is valid only for the common-emitter connection.

It should be emphasized that the *actual* current directions shown in Figure 7-2 are for a P-N-P transistor. If an N-P-N is considered, the directions of all three currents would be reversed. This would also mean that each of the quantities on the collector characteristics would be positive, rather than negative.

The most common use of output characteristics is to help locate the bias point. In order to be accurate, one must measure the individual transistor curves with a characteristic plotter. Characteristics given by a manufacturer can only show typical values since there is substantial variation from unit to unit.

Note that the emitter characteristics are more important than the base ones since: (1) the common-emitter connection is most frequently used, and (2) the common-base curves are so *regular* that one can essentially draw the curves by knowing only a few parameters.

The other set of characteristics needed to specify the electrical action is the input set. For the common-base case this would be a plot of emitter current (I_E) versus emitter-to-base voltage (V_{EB}), with collector voltage (V_{CB}) as the parameter.

For the common-emitter case, the input characteristics appear as shown in Figure 7-3. Here the curves plot I_B versus V_{BE} with constant collector voltage as the parameter. When the collector voltage is equal to zero, the forward emitter current increases with V_{BE} similar to the forward characteristic of a diode. As the collector voltage is increased, a larger part of I_E flows to the collector and become I_C so that I_B is smaller for the same V_{BE}.

It is interesting to note why V_{CE} is chosen as the parameter rather than I_C. If I_C were the parameter then the characteristics would only be short segments. This is because, if collector current is kept constant, the V_{BE} can be varied over only a small range. Such characteristics would not be very useful in designing transistor circuits.

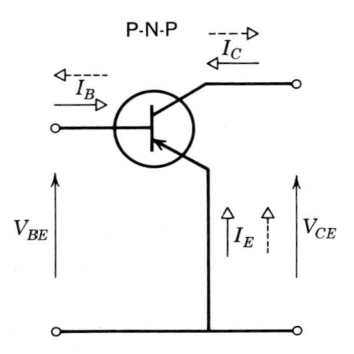

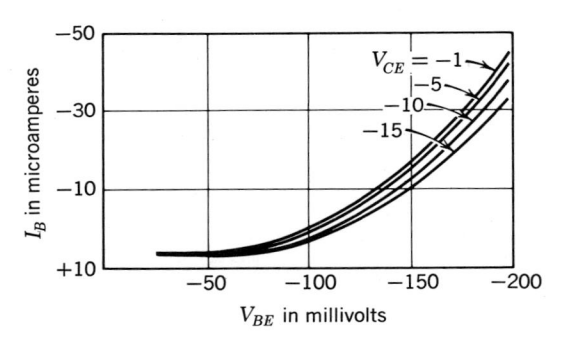

Fig. 7-3. Input (base) characteristics for common-emitter connection.

The transistor as a circuit element

The idea being stressed here is that the combined set of the input and the output characteristics serve to indicate the electrical operation of the transistor as a circuit element for all values of bias. With these characteristics, one can see the entire picture of the transistor operation. We shall see later that the equivalent circuit depicts the operation only about a particular bias point.

The above characteristics then are graphical ways of describing the electrical operation of the transistor. They are frequently used to help locate the bias point, and to picture the signal operation in large signal cases.

AMPLIFIER ILLUSTRATION. Having the characteristics which depict the transistor operation anywhere in the active region, we will now add the most elementary circuitry to the transistor to illustrate the basic action of the transistor in an amplifier circuit, which was used in Chapter 4 to explain the physical action. Figure 7-4 shows the basic common-emitter amplifier circuit and is the same amplifier as in Figure 4-7. The method of biasing shown in Figure 7-4, in which the bias battery is connected directly in series with the electrode, is the simplest and the most direct. Circuit methods for accomplishing the bias will be treated later. As in the circuit discussed in Chapter 4, the bias battery provides reverse bias for the collector junction.

Since, for both vacuum tubes and transistors, the output circuit is usually the more important, we shall consider the output side first. When using the characteristics to depict the operation of any biased active device, we must in effect also find the graph of the circuit to which the device is attached. Our object, then, is to find the graph of the output circuit to which the output side of the transistor is attached. Thus in Figure 7-4 we wish to find that I_C-V_C graph of the circuit to the right of points *e-f*. We get this by taking the limit points; when the circuit is short-circuited and when it is open-circuited. If *e* is short-circuited to *f*, the voltage across *e-f* is zero and the current flowing is (using the *actual* current direction)

$$I = \frac{V_{CC}}{R_L} = \frac{10}{5000} = 2 \text{ ma} \qquad (4)$$

This results in point 1 of Figure 7-4(b). When *e-f* is open-circuited the current is zero, and $V_{CE} = V_{CC}$, resulting in point 2. The graph of the *circuit*, then, is the straight line connected between the two

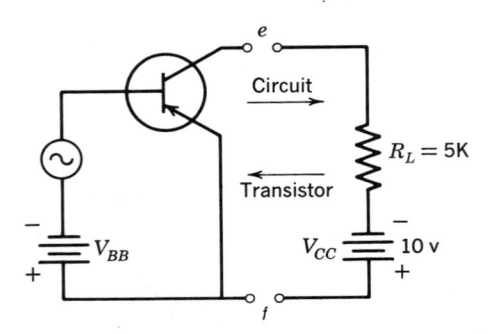

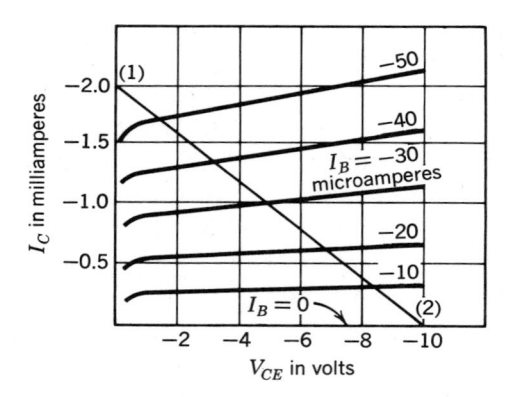

Fig. 7-4. Use of characteristics on output side of transistor.

The transistor as a circuit element 151

points. This is the "load line" for the circuit shown. Since the circuit to the right of *e-f* is connected to the transistor to the left, we, in effect, have to achieve a graphical solution of the two conditions. Thus we superimpose the load line on the characteristics, and have as a result a sort of simultaneous graphical solution.

It is advantageous, whenever using characteristics and load lines, to consider them in the terms just described. The following summarizes the method: (1) momentarily break the circuit so that the device with the characteristics appears on one side and the attached circuitry appears on the other side; (2) find the graph of the attached circuitry; (3) superimpose the circuitry graph on the characteristics.

We have yet to determine where the operating point is on the load line. This will be determined by the value of I_B, which is dependent on the emitter bias. Let us assume that the emitter battery causes an I_B of 30 μa. The operating point will then appear at the intersection of the $I_B = 30$ μa curve and the load line as shown in Figure 7-4.

Using the output characteristics of Figure 7-5, we can now view the circuit operation of the basic amplifier. In Chapter 4 an input signal was assumed to cause a signal current of 10 μa. Electrically this means that the signal has caused the transistor to follow the dotted path of the load line in Figure 7-5. It is seen that the dotted path

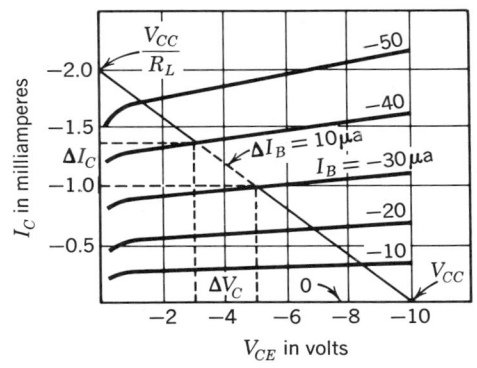

Fig. 7-5. Output characteristics showing basic amplifier action.

covers a length corresponding to $I_B = 10$ μa. Reading the change in collector current along the vertical axis, we see that the change is $\Delta I_C = 1.37 - 1.0 = 0.37$. Reading the change in collector voltage, we find it to be $5.2 - 3.2 = 2$ volts. Therefore, using $P = VI$, the power output is 0.74 milliwatts. This then is the electrical operation which was described physically in terms of electrons and holes in Chapter 4.

Since frequently the source impedance driving a transistor amplifier is much higher than the input impedance (hence acting as a current source), it is often sufficient to consider the output characteristics and load line as above. However, the input side may also be subjected to a load line analysis, if desired. Again the main idea is to find the graph of the circuitry attached to the input (base) side, and superimpose this graph on the base characteristics.

One cannot use the input characteristics of Figure 7-3 directly, however, unless the load is effectively zero (for constant V_C). Therefore one must first construct the *dynamic input transistor characteristic* for the particular load being used (shown in dashed line in Figure 7-3). This dynamic input curve can be obtained by combining the points from the input curves with those of the output curves-plus-load line. It is left to the student to derive this dynamic characteristic.

This dynamic curve can then be combined with an input load line. Since we may consider the signal source to be a pure voltage generator in series with an internal resistance, the input circuitry consists of a bias battery, a resistance, and a voltage source. The input load line, then, will be similar to that for the output side. The voltage generator of the signal source, however, will serve to *move the load line* along the V_B axis. This movement corresponds to the voltage applied by the voltage source.

The input graphical analysis, then, differs in two respects from the output analysis: (1) a dynamic input characteristic must first be derived, and (2) the load line itself moves back and forth as the signal voltage varies. Thus the input side can be graphically analyzed in a manner similar to the output analysis.

Before leaving the discussion of the basic amplifier, it is useful to describe the output characteristic analysis when an a-c sine-wave signal is applied. This is simply an extension of the principles just described and illustrated in Figure 7-6.

If a current source is supplying a sine-wave signal, the transistor will follow the dashed path on the load line of Figure 7-6. This operation results in a variation of collector current I_C shown to the right. With this collector alternating current flowing through the load resistor, an alternating voltage will be developed across the

The transistor as a circuit element 153

load resistor. This voltage V_{CE}, also shown, can be read directly from the characteristics.

When considering a-c amplifiers, we are mainly interested in the operation just described—that is, the operation *about* the bias point. Although the load resistor will have a direct voltage due to the bias current, we would be concerned primarily with the alternating voltage shown as V_{CE}. For the a-c amplifiers, then, after the bias point is established, we pay little attention to it, and concentrate on the operation *around* the bias point.

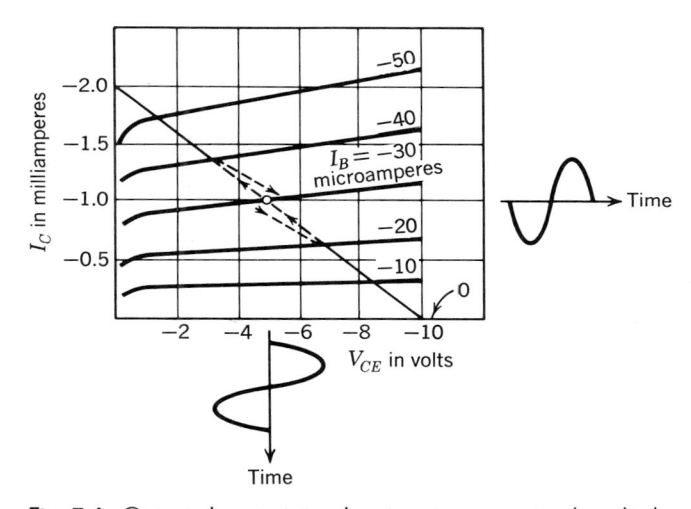

Fig. 7-6. Output characteristics showing sine-wave signal applied.

Often the a-c load of any electronic circuit differs in value from the d-c load. Therefore an actual amplifier unit will usually involve two distinct load lines: the d-c one treated here, and an a-c load line. The most frequent example of the d-c load differing from the a-c load is in *R-C* coupling between stages (to be discussed in Chapter 10). Figure 7-7 shows a single stage of such a "capacity-coupled" situation. The d-c load line is formed by R_L above, while the a-c one is formed by R_L in parallel with R_1. When the a-c and d-c load line differ, the d-c load line establishes the bias point, and the a-c load line determines the path on which the action takes place *around* the bias point. Thus, in Figure 7-7, the varying (I_B) waveform applied to this amplifier would travel along the (more vertical) a-c load line. This action is treated in more detail in Chapter 9, where transformer

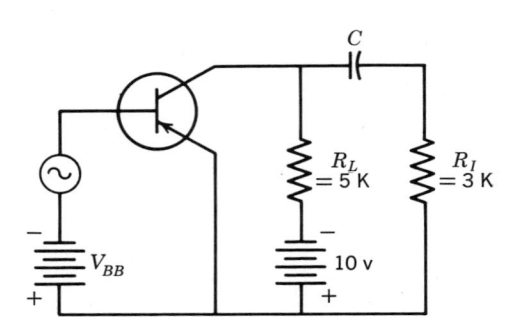

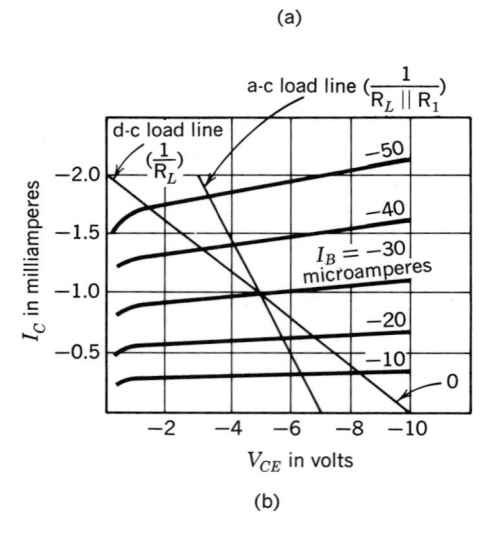

Fig. 7-7. (a) A basic amplifier (b) showing d-c and a-c load lines.

The transistor as a circuit element

coupling is considered. The object here is to deal with the basic aspects of transistor characteristics in conjunction with load lines.

In conclusion, it should be emphasized that the characteristic curves depict the operation of the transistor at any point in the active region.

METHOD OF SMALL SIGNAL EQUIVALENT CIRCUITS

When using the transistor as an amplifier, we are often interested in getting the maximum amplification under the prescribed conditions. In general, this demands that we analyze the transistor as an element in an electric network. It is for this purpose that small signal *equivalent circuits* of active devices are required.

In its simplest light, we may consider an equivalent circuit (of a physical device) as a combination of electric elements which, when given the proper values, produces the identical electrical operation in a circuit as does the physical element. The most general type of equivalent circuit would represent the transistor for all possible modes of operation. However, to be useful, an equivalent circuit must be relatively simple so that network laws can sensibly be applied to it. For this reason equivalent circuits are specialized and the three basic types are: (1) small-signal, low-frequency equivalent circuits, (2) small-signal, high-frequency equivalent circuits, and (3) large-signal equivalent circuits. The high-frequency equivalent circuit is treated in Chapter 16 and the large-signal equivalent circuit in Chapter 11. Here we are concerned with the small-signal, low-frequency equivalent circuits. Our object is to find that combination of electrical elements which simulates the transistor under conditions of small-signal input.

THE EQUIVALENT CIRCUIT. In a biased active device, such as the transistor, the small-signal equivalent circuit is always constructed without regard to the bias; i.e., the bias circuit and conditions are left out of the equivalent circuit. The reason for this is quite obvious. Within the operating limits of a given region in the transistor, the method of operation is always the same, regardless of bias. Although the operation is identical, the *values* of the equivalent circuit elements may change with bias (and temperature).

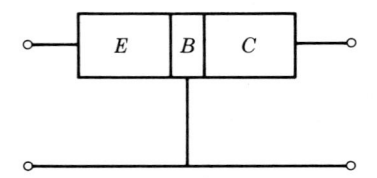

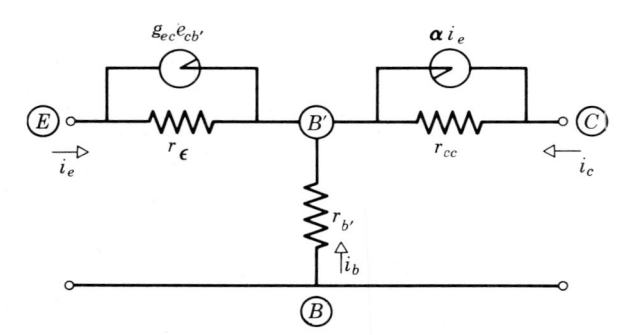

Fig. 7-8. An equivalent circuit that closely resembles the physical construction.

The transistor as a circuit element

Since the values of the small-signal equivalent circuit do change with bias, an equivalent circuit must necessarily represent the transistor only for a small variation *about* the operation point. In other words, only when *small* signals are applied does the equivalent circuit accurately represent the transistor. The change in circuit element value with bias is what specifies that the transistor, like a vacuum tube, is a nonlinear device.

When considering the relation of the equivalent circuit to the characteristics, we can regard the circuit as representing the operation *in a region of a particular operating point*. Now it is seen why the characteristics constitute the complete specifications of the electrical action; for by their use, the operation is depicted at *any* operating point and for any variation about that point. The small-signal equivalent circuit, on the other hand, depicts the operation only in the region of a specified bias point. These restrictions, however, do not make the equivalent circuit less useful than the characteristics. It is our purpose here merely to stress the relationship between the two methods; when and where these methods are used will be discussed later.

We return then to the problem of finding that combination of electric elements which, when connected in a circuit, acts exactly as does the transistor when connected in the same circuit. Since the transistor can be connected in any of three configurations, an equivalent circuit for each connection must be achieved. We will concentrate on the common-emitter connection because it is most frequently used. It is reasonable, however, to begin with the common-base connection, since this is the historical *reference* connection for the transistor. Also, physical considerations are easiest in this case. Consequently, we shall begin with the equivalent circuit of the common-base connection. The circuit for any other connection can be derived from the common-base connection.

In finding the equivalent circuit, we might logically start by considering the physics of the device. We know, for example, that the transistor consists of three areas of bulk material (the emitter, the base, and the collector) with the two junctions between these areas. Also, it is remembered that the emitter junction is forward biased and the collector junction is reverse biased in the active (amplifying) region. A small-signal equivalent circuit closely related to this physical description is shown in Figure 7-8. In this circuit the quantities can be identified as follows:

r_ϵ = resistance of the forward biased emitter *junction*
$g_{ec}e_{cb'}$ = feedback term giving effect of $e_{cb'}$ on i_e
$r_{b'}$ = base spreading resistance, due to ohmic resistance of base
r_{cc} = resistance of the reverse biased collector *junction*.

Although the circuit of Figure 7-8 is closely related to the physical operation, a simpler circuit (derived from that of Figure 7-8) is shown in Figure 7-9. The early transistor design work used this equivalent

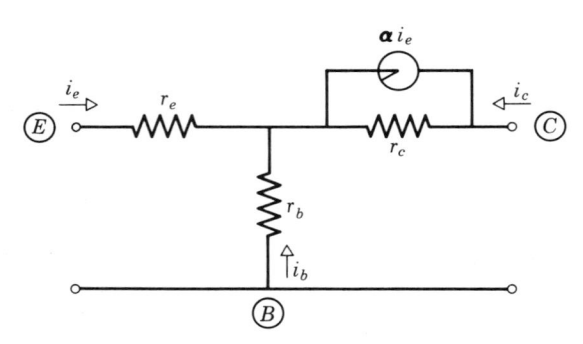

Fig. 7-9. Common-base T-equivalent circuit.

circuit almost exclusively; however, now it is used only infrequently. The relations between the parameters of this T-equivalent circuit and the one of Figure 7-8 are given in Appendix II. In this equivalent circuit the resistances are also related to the respective junctions of the transistor. When a voltage is applied to the input, a current i_e flows through r_e. Voltage and power amplification results since αi_e occurs at the output across a very high resistance (much higher than the input resistance). An internal feedback also occurs since r_b is common to input and output currents.

Since the common-emitter connection is the most prevalent case, the emitter equivalent circuit is of greatest importance. The circuit of Figure 7-9 can be rearranged to form the common-emitter version, shown in Figure 7-10. This circuit was widely used in past years.

The equivalent circuits of Figures 7-9 and 7-10 are a valid representation of the electric operation of the transistor for low frequencies. Furthermore, they grossly resemble certain aspects of the actual physical action. Also, this type of circuit, if modified to incorporate capacitances, is useful when high frequencies must be taken into ac-

The transistor as a circuit element 159

count. For low-frequency circuits, however, equivalent circuits that are based on matrix methods of analysis are most convenient. Such equivalent circuits are based on the *black-box* concept described in Chapter 6. Within this concept, there are a number of equivalent circuits. It is expedient to consider the various *types* in terms of the parameters by which the circuits are defined. The parameters, in turn, are determined by the basic circuit method used to analyze the circuit. For example, if mesh equations are used, the voltages are always written in terms of the current; the currents are the un-

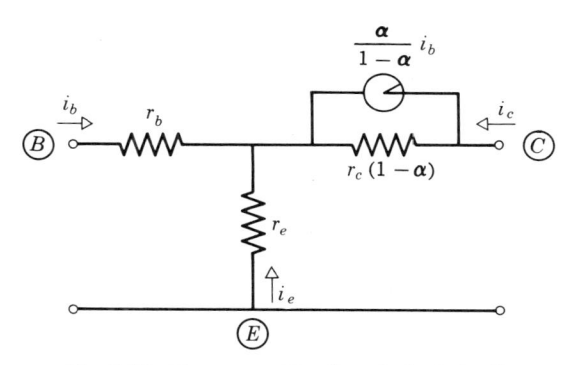

Fig. 7-10. Common-emitter T-equivalent circuit.

knowns. The parameters, in this case, are impedances (Z's) of which resistance is the real part. If nodal equations are used, the currents are written in terms of the voltages; the voltages are the unknowns. For this case the parameters are admittances (Y's), since an admittance multiplied by a voltage results in a current. In a particular situation we may combine the nodal and the mesh method. We may write a mesh equation for the input side of a circuit, and a nodal equation for the output side. In this case the parameters will consist of both impedances and admittances. Since impedances of both types are present, such parameters are called hybrid parameters, and it is these in which we shall be most interested. The reason for choosing the hybrid parameters is twofold: (1) the circuit analysis involves less complicated formulas, and (2) the parameters are much easier to measure on an actual transistor.

We shall not stop here to give a mathematical derivation of the conversion from the circuit of Figure 7-8 to an h-parameter circuit. We want to determine what information the equivalent circuit gives us and how it is used. The reader is referred to the equivalent circuit material in the electrical review in Chapter 6.

The equivalent circuit which makes use of the h parameters is shown in Figure 7-11. Although this circuit is perfectly general and

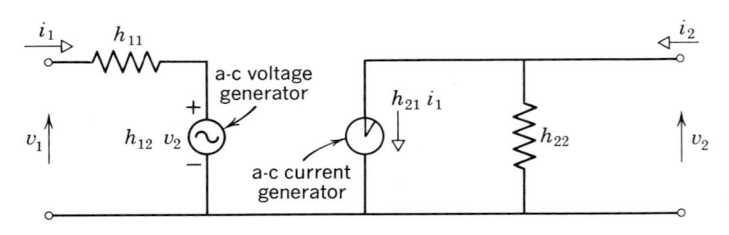

Fig. 7-11. h-parameter equivalent circuit of a transistor.

will depict any electric circuit, we can make it represent the transistor by simply substituting the right values for the four parameters h_{11}, h_{12}, h_{21}, and h_{22}. We note that this equivalent is made up by writing a mesh equation for the input side and a nodal equation for the output side. Therefore h_{11} is a resistance, and h_{22} is a conductance; i.e., the resistor labeled h_{22} is a resistance whose value is $1/h_{22}$. Both h_{12} and h_{21} are dimensionless ratios.

We can gain some intuitive notion of how this equivalent works by considering the following. Let us for the moment neglect the voltage source on the input side. Then, when a voltage (v_1) is applied to the input, a current i_1 flows through the resistor h_{11}. This current causes a current, $h_{21}i_1$ to flow in the output current source. Thus h_{21} is the current gain of this equivalent circuit and is equal to $(-\alpha)$. Placed across the output is a resistor of value $1/h_{22}$. Therefore the current divides between this resistor and that circuitry which is connected to the transistor. A voltage v_2 will be developed across the output as a result of this current and this is the output voltage. We can now look at the voltage generator, $h_{12}v_2$. When any voltage v_2 appears on the output side, a portion of this voltage, $h_{12}v_2$ will be fed back to the input side. Thus the initially applied voltage meets this feedback voltage in addition to the input resistor h_{11}. Thus the transistor may be regarded as having an internal feedback. We shall consider external feedback in a later chapter. It is especially important to remember, both here and for the rest of the book, that h_{11} is a resistance, h_{22} is a conductance, and both h_{12} and h_{21} are dimensionless ratios.

The transistor as a circuit element

Note that the circuit of Figure 7-11 will represent any of the three transistor connections, so long as the proper values are used for the h's. We shall now illustrate how the equivalent circuit is used for circuit analysis in the common-emitter case.

COMMON-EMITTER AMPLIFIER ILLUSTRATION. It will be our purpose now to treat the basic amplifier, which was considered in the physics section and in the previous section on the graphical analysis method, in the light of equivalent circuits. Figure 7-12 shows the basic common-emitter amplifier and its representation using the equivalent circuit. We note, first of all, that the bias batteries do not appear in the equivalent circuit diagram. This agrees with the condition mentioned previously—that the equivalent circuits do not contain the bias conditions. A general rule can be stated thus: when finding the equivalent circuit of an active network, first remove the circuitry (or batteries) that provides the bias.

The h subscripts shown in Figure 7-12, and as used in Chapter 6, are perfectly general and apply to any four-terminal network. These subscripts are useful when writing equations since they denote their correct position in the equation. To particularize these h parameters to a given physical situation, one need simply substitute correct values (as defined in Chapter 6). For the common-emitter transistor shown in Figure 7-12, the correct substitution is given by

$$h_{11} = h_{ie} = \text{input impedance parameter}$$
$$h_{12} = h_{re} = \text{reverse voltage gain parameter}$$
$$h_{21} = h_{fe} = \text{forward current gain parameter}$$
$$h_{22} = h_{oe} = \text{output admittance parameter.}$$

In these parameters the second subscript identifies the connection. The first subscript identifies the "function" as follows: i—input, r—reverse (feedback), f—forward (gain), and o—output.

It is these emitter parameters that are usually given by the manufacturer. Since any matrix-type parameters (such as the h parameters) apply to all three connections, it is often wise to do any circuit calculations in terms of the numerical subscripts. The parameters can then be particularized at the conclusion. This procedure is used in the following amplifier calculations, and we will note that, after the equivalent circuit is substituted in Figure 7-12, a general electric network results. The next step is to use the basic network

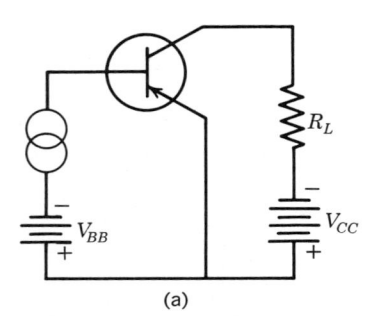

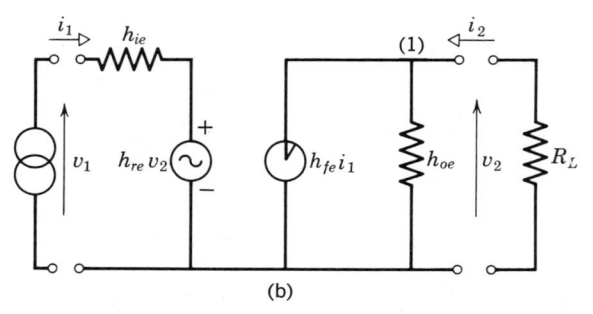

Fig. 7-12. Common-emitter transistor amplifier and its a-c equivalent circuit: (a) transistor amplifier; (b) equivalent circuit.

The transistor as a circuit element

tools to analyze this circuit. For this illustration, the voltage gain is found by use of mesh and nodal equations. Two simultaneous equations will suffice to analyze this circuit: one mesh equation on the input side and one nodal equation on the output side.

The input equation, since an internal voltage source is present, suggests the use of a mesh equation. Equating the source voltage, v_1, to the sum of the voltage drops, we have

$$v_1 = h_{11}i_1 + h_{12}v_2 \tag{5}$$

Here it is reaffirmed that $h_{12}v_2$ is a voltage; i.e., h_{12} must be dimensionless.

For the output side a current source is present; therefore a nodal equation is easiest. Using Kirchhoff's current law at the node 1 we can write

$$i_2 = h_{21}i_1 + i_3 = h_{21}i_1 + h_{22}v_2 \tag{6}$$

where $i_3 = \dfrac{v_2}{1/h_{22}} = h_{22}v_2$.

It is remembered that, in a current source, the current is always constant, regardless of voltage. Therefore the term $h_{21}i_1$ is always the current flowing to the left of the node. Also, the resistance across the output has a value $1/h_{22}$. Therefore the current flowing in this resistance is $h_{22}v_2$.

The equations are summarized thus

$$v_1 = h_{11}i_1 + h_{12}v_2, \quad i_2 = h_{21}i_1 + h_{22}v_2 \tag{7}$$

We see that these are two simultaneous equations, and i_1 and v_2 are the unknowns. These equations may be solved by any of the conventional methods for simultaneous equations.[2] The method of determinants is the most general way, and is recommended; however, elimination of one variable is sometimes simpler. For the illustration here we will use determinants.

The voltage gain is

$$A_v = \frac{v_2}{v_1} \tag{8}$$

We have then to use Equations (7) to find v_2 and v_1. Using the method of determinants we have

[2] The solution of simultaneous algebraic equations is treated in Appendix I.

$$v_2 = \frac{\begin{vmatrix} h_{11} & v_1 \\ h_{21} & i_2 \end{vmatrix}}{\Delta h} = \frac{h_{11}i_2 - h_{21}v_1}{\Delta h} \tag{9}$$

where $\Delta h = h_{11}h_{22} - h_{12}h_{21}$.

But
$$i_2 = -\frac{v_2}{R_L}; \quad \text{therefore } v_2 = -\frac{h_{21}v_1}{\Delta h + h_{11}/R_L} \tag{10}$$

Then
$$\frac{v_2}{v_1} = -\frac{h_{21}}{\Delta h + h_{11}/R_L} = -\frac{h_{fe}}{\Delta h + h_{ie}/R_L} \tag{11}$$

We have just seen that when an equivalent circuit is substituted for a transistor in a network, we return to the use of the basic network tools to analyze the network. We can now summarize the equivalent circuit method.

The equivalent circuit is an electric network which, at a particular bias point of the transistor, represents the electrical operation of the device. Thus, after the bias point has been determined, one has to determine the values of h_{11}, h_{12}, h_{21}, and h_{22} at that bias point. In practice, the manufacturer of the transistor will specify one or more recommended bias points and also the values of the h parameters at these points. If parameters other than the h ones are specified, they may be converted into h parameters by using the table in Appendix II. Because a particular set of h parameters is accurate only within a region of the bias point, it is to be kept in mind that the equivalent circuit method is only accurate for small applied signals.

In making use of the small signal equivalent circuit, the essential technique, whenever analyzing a transistor in a network, is to substitute the equivalent circuit at the same terminals. The result is a network that is made up of the familiar electric elements. The next step is to analyze the resulting network by the use of the ordinary network tools, consisting mainly of Kirchhoff's voltage and current laws. The former specifies the writing of mesh equations, and the latter the writing of nodal equations.

COMPARISON OF METHODS

The graphical analysis method consists of using the characteristics of the transistor in conjunction with a graph of the associated circuitry. The equivalent circuit method, on the other hand, consists of reducing the transistor to an electric network which, in conjunction with the associated circuitry, results in an analyzable network. As was mentioned, the characteristics of the transistor specify completely the electrical action of the transistor; that is, they are a graphical presentation of the operation of the transistor at any bias point. A particular equivalent circuit with its parameter values, in comparison, represents the transistor only within the region on the bias point where the parameter values hold. The equivalent circuit can depict different bias points by correcting the parameter values.

The characteristic method then is a *graphical* method whereas the equivalent circuit method is an *analytic* one. As with all graphical methods, there are many times when the only effective manner of getting certain information is by trial and error. The network analysis method makes use of the whole series of algebraic equations to enable one to find a direct solution to various circuit requirements.

Because the equivalent circuit is limited to small variations about the bias point, it is generally true that the equivalent circuit method is used for small-signal applications and the characteristics method is used for large-signal applications. There are many exceptions to this general rule, however.

For small-signal cases, the characteristics may be used to help find the bias point; the bias point may be determined by writing network equations, but a graphical picture would be helpful. Often, when treating a large-signal case, an equivalent circuit can be made to *approximate* the operation over a large swing. This facilitates the direct solution of many problems, which would be cumbersome graphically. This approximation is accomplished by using element values that represent the average of the values over the entire swing. In addition, an exact (but complicated) equivalent circuit for large signals can be found by implementing the Ebers-Moll equations (see Chapter 15).

Although the characteristics give the complete specification of the transistor, one limitation should be pointed out. A reactive load impedance, when analyzed at a single frequency, will appear as an ellipse when plotted on the characteristics. The elliptical load line may be plotted for a single frequency to obtain the operating conditions. This method gives a first-order approximation when nonlinear distortion is present and is usually sufficiently accurate for most applications.

166 The transistor as a circuit element

PROBLEMS

1. Using the curves of Figure 7-4, draw the load line for an R_L of 10,000 ohms and a V_{CC} of -10 volts. Assuming a quiescent I_B of $-20\mu a$, what is the V_{CE} and I_C?

2. Using the curves of Figure 7-4, draw the load line for an R_L of 2,500 ohms and a V_{CC} of -5 volts. Assuming a quiescent I_B of $-25\mu a$, what is the V_{CE} and I_C?

3. Estimate the I_B value at which the transistor of Figure 7-4 would go into saturation for: (a) $R_L = 5K$, $V_{CC} = -10$; (b) $R_L = 10K$, $V_{CC} = -10$; (c) $R_L = 2,500$ ohms, $V_{CC} = -5$.

4. Estimate the I_B value at which the transistor will cut off for the three cases in Problem 3.

5. Assume the curves of Figure 7-4, with an R_L of 2,500 ohms and a V_{CC} of -5 volts. Assume that an input signal current (sine wave) I_B has a peak-to-peak swing of $40\mu a$. Using a quiescent I_B of $-30\mu a$, draw to scale both the V_{CE} and the I_C as the I_B takes on its various values.

6. With everything else the same as in Problem 5, assume that the quiescent I_B is shifted to $I_B = -10\mu a$. Again draw the V_{CE} and the I_C to scale as I_B traverses its sine wave.

7. With everything else the same as in Problem 5, assume that the quiescent I_B is shifted to $I_B = -40\mu a$. Again draw the V_{CE} and the I_C to scale as I_B traverses its sine wave.

8. Give the three load line situations described in Problem 3. What is the quiescent I_B in each case which will permit maximum undistorted I_B "swing" in both directions?

9. Using the curves of Figure 7-3, and an R_L of 5K with a $V_{CC} = -10$, draw the dynamic characteristic on the I_B versus V_{BE} curves. The procedure is as follows: choose an I_B. Using the load line on the output characteristics, note the V_{CE} for that I_B. Return to the I_B versus V_{BE} set and plot a point at the I_B, V_{CE} intersection.

10. Starting with equivalent circuit shown in Figure 7-9, derive the one in Figure 7-10. Start by simply rearranging the circuit of Figure 7-9. Then write mesh equations for both cases and rearrange equations to derive Figure 7-10.

11. What are the units of h_{11}, h_{12}, h_{21}, h_{22}? Describe the electrical relation provided by each of these.

The transistor as a circuit element 167

12. Solve for the v_2 of Equation 9 by using the elimination method described in Appendix I, rather than the determinant method. Take the ratio of v_2 to v_1, and verify the voltage gain of Equation 11.

13. In Figure 7-4, write the linear equation which describes the load lines. Using the form $(y - y_0) = m(x - x_0)$, show that the slope of the load line is $-1/R_L$.

14. Assume now that an R_E is inserted in the emitter lead of Figure 7-4, with R_L still included in the collector lead. Now write the output d-c equation which describes the load line. Assume that I_C approximately equals I_E. Show that the slope of the load line is now $-1(R_L + R_E)$.

15. In Figure 7-7, verify that the a-c load line shown is the correct one for the parallel combination of 5K and 3K. For simplicity one assumes that the capacitor is a short-circuit at the frequency of interest.

16. Assume that the 2N1097 transistor (Appendix III) uses a d-c load line given by $V_{CC} = -15$, $R_L = 1.5K$. Assume also that an I_B of 0.15 ma is used. Assume that the effective a-c load resistance is 80 ohms. Find the operating point, and draw the a-c load line on the 2N1097 characteristics. At what a-c peak value of I_B will the transistor (a) cut off? (b) saturate?

17. For the conditions of Problem 16, what value of a-c resistance would give an approximately symmetrical distortion (between cut-off and saturation) in the output?

8
Small-signal amplifiers

It was stated in the preceding chapter that equivalent circuits are usually used when analyzing electronic circuits for small-signal applications, and a graphical analysis is used for large-signal applications. It will be our purpose here to consider the analysis procedures that are used for small-signal amplifiers; hence we are dealing with an electric network in which the active electronic device is replaced by its equivalent circuit.

Sometimes we encounter an electronic circuit that consists of a single stage; however, in most cases the circuit involves a number of connected stages. It will be remembered that the two general means for analyzing electric networks are the mesh and the nodal methods. Therefore the multistage electronic circuit can be analyzed in its entirety by the use of either of these methods. However, such an analysis quickly results in a large number of simultaneous equations and consequently the solution becomes fairly difficult. For this reason it is profitable to consider the multistage circuit not in terms of the entire circuit, but in terms of single stages that are connected together. This breaking up of a complex circuit into its separate stages represents a powerful and natural tool for the analysis of electronic circuits.

Small-signal amplifiers 169

When analyzing one stage of a multistage circuit by the use of this method, the previous stage will become the source and the following stage will become the load. Thus we can effectively analyze a cascaded complex electronic circuit by analyzing carefully only a single stage with its source and load and using this single-stage analysis repeatedly in the complex network.

It is for this reason that, in this chapter, we will consider carefully the analysis of single-stage transistor amplifiers. Since the transistor can be connected in three different ways in a circuit—common base, common emitter, and common collector—these three single-stage connections will be analyzed. It is important to stress that the concept of treating a complex circuit by means of the single-stage method is essentially a time- and worksaving device that avoids the large number of simultaneous equations that would result from considering the entire circuit as a whole.

The techniques treated in this chapter can be used for both low- and high-frequency amplifiers, so long as the proper parameters are used. However, these techniques are most appropriate for low-frequency cases. The high-frequency amplifiers are more conveniently treated by a different equivalent circuit, as is discussed in Chapter 16.

When considering the three types of single-stage circuits in this chapter, the first objective will be to obtain the basic formulas for each connection. The resulting formulas can be applied for any stage within a complex circuit if the proper source and load are determined. While deriving the formulas, an additional objective will be to illustrate the analysis method so that the principles may be extended to a multistage network considered in its entirety.

THE IMPORTANT QUANTITIES

The two issues of greatest concern when dealing with amplifying circuits are the *gain* or *amplification* and the power output. In this chapter we are concerned with small signal amplifiers and here it is implied that the amplification is the most important quantity. In the next chapter we discuss power amplifiers where the amount of obtainable output power is the important criterion.

When using the single-stage method of analysis, the important quantities that determine the amplifying capabilities of the stage are: (1) the power gain, (2) the current gain, (3) the voltage gain, (4) the input resistance, and (5) the output resistance.

POWER GAIN. Power gain is one of the most basic criteria for the performance of any device that both accepts input power and delivers output power. It is this quantity that determines how much power will be available for conversion into useful work in an output circuit. Thus if a circuit comprises a radio, the power gain, considered from the input to the output, specifies what power is available for conversion into acoustical energy for a certain input.

The power gain is defined simply as the ratio of the a-c power out to the a-c power in.

$$A_p = \frac{\text{a-c power output}}{\text{a-c power input}} \qquad (1)$$

Since conventional transistor circuits have moderate input and output impedances, they both accept and deliver power (as opposed to solely voltage or current). Hence, power gain is an important performance quantity for conventional transistor amplifiers.

The particular role for the power gain of single-stage electronic amplifiers depends somewhat on the terminations. For example, if input and output impedances are matched, the power gain is maximized (see Chapter 6) and is the basic quantity to consider. Consequently, power gain is the figure of merit for transformer-coupled amplifiers. On the other hand, the current gain is the figure of merit for *RC*-coupled stages since the stage coupling is greatly mismatched. Even for *RC*-coupled amplifiers, however, the power gain is still a quantity of interest since it tells how far one has moved from the optimum (in gain).

It is interesting to diverge here, for a moment, and compare the matter of power gain in the conventional transistor to that in the vacuum tube or in the field effect transistor. Typically a vacuum tube is basically controlled by a voltage and draws no current (in the Class A condition). Hence it is relatively meaningless to form a power gain ratio in such circumstances. This applies to the field effect transistor as well—it is also a voltage-controlled device and the input impedance is sufficiently high to make the concept of power gain less important.

The basic reason that the power gain is so important for the con-

Small-signal amplifiers

ventional transistor amplifier lies in the fact that the transistor is basically a current-operated device and hence has a relatively low input impedance. Consequently it draws current from any typical sources. Hence, if all other conditions were equal, it could be said that the optimum conditions are achieved only if one achieves maximum power gain.

The basic criterion of a vacuum tube and the field effect transistor, on the other hand, is the voltage gain. Many times, however, one does speak of a Class A vacuum tube power amplifier. This does not mean that the vacuum tube is other than a voltage amplifier; it means that the voltage amplification is used to convert power efficiently from the plate supply battery to a-c power in the load.

In conclusion, devices such as the conventional transistor, which have relatively low input impedances, perform optimally in the amplification sense only when maximum power gain is realized. If any mismatch occurs (due to other overriding reasons) some potential amplification is lost. The vacuum tube, on the other hand, requires a mismatch between stages so that the following stage does not load down the preceding stage. For the vacuum tube the maximum voltage is desired for the next stage, and not the maximum power.

The property of some devices to accept input power whereas others do not is a very important factor in electronics.

In addition to the straight forward power gain treated here [Equation (1)] there are *transducer* and *available* power gain concepts that are best treated after discussing amplifiers in more detail. These will be described after comparing the three transistor configurations.

CURRENT AND VOLTAGE GAIN. Sometimes the final output of an electronic circuit is not converted to some form of work, but is utilized directly. In these cases we may be interested in the current gain or the voltage gain. The current gain is defined as the ratio of the current through the load to the input current.

$$A_i = \frac{I_{\text{load}}}{I_{\text{input}}} \qquad (2)$$

This current gain should not be confused with the α (for the common base) or the β (for the common emitter). It is remembered that α

and β are parameters of the transistor alone and specify the current gain *if the a-c load is zero*. Their importance is in specifying a parameter of the transistor equivalent circuit. For many applications, however, the circuit current gain A_i will be approximately equal to the transistor current gain (α or β).

In transistor amplifiers with *RC* coupling the current gain is the basic figure of merit since the output impedance of a stage is much greater than the load impedance.

The voltage gain is defined by the ratio of the output voltage to the input voltage

$$A_v = \frac{V_{\text{load}}}{V_{\text{input}}} \tag{3}$$

The voltage gain is usually involved when an electronic circuit has a high input and load impedance.

INPUT AND OUTPUT RESISTANCES. Since reasonable resistance match is usually desired for the transistor amplifier, it becomes necessary to know the input and the output resistance of a transistor stage. As explained in the electrical review in Chapter 6, maximum power transfer from one stage to another depends upon the resistance match between the two stages. In general, the input and the output resistance greatly affect the power gain that a transistor stage will exhibit for a given generator and a given load.

The input resistance is defined as the resistance exhibited by the input terminals *when the load is connected*. As such, it is defined as the ratio of the input voltage to the input current with the load connected.

$$\text{input resistance} = R_i = \frac{V_i}{I_i} \tag{4}$$

The output resistance is defined as the resistance which appears looking back from the output terminals, with the source replaced by its internal impedance. The source may be an actual generator or a previous stage. Output resistance can be calculated by the relation

$$\text{output resistance} = R_o = \frac{V_o}{I_o} \tag{5}$$

Small-signal amplifiers

When considering the three single-stage amplifiers in this chapter we shall be interested in finding the equations for the quantities discussed above. Although frequency response is an important factor for amplifiers, we shall restrict the discussion to those frequencies where the transistor exhibits resistive parameters only. Frequency response is dealt with in Chapters 10 and 16.

SINGLE-STAGE h-PARAMETER ANALYSIS

The h-parameter equivalent circuit of the transistor was developed in the electrical review and treated again in Chapter 7. Here we will use this basic h-equivalent circuit to calculate the single-stage performance quantities described above.

We will first determine the performance quantities in terms of the general h parameters, which will include all three possible transistor connections. These results can then be particularized to each of the three connections by simply inserting the proper h parameters.

The general h parameters will use subscripts labeled in the ordinary matrix fashion, as depicted in the general equations[1]

$$V_1 = h_{11}I_1 + h_{12}V_2$$
$$I_2 = h_{21}I_1 + h_{22}V_2 \qquad (6)$$

In order to refer to a particular connection, such as common emitter, the *first* subscript is used to identify the matrix position of the element, and the *second* subscript identifies the circuit connection. The h-parameter substitution for the three connections is given below in Table 8-1.

Table 8-1. h-PARAMETER SUBSTITUTION

Description	General h parameter	Common-base parameter	Common-emitter parameter	Common-collector parameter
Input resistance	h_{11}	h_{ib}	h_{ie}	h_{ic}
Reverse voltage gain	h_{12}	h_{rb}	h_{re}	h_{rc}
Forward current gain	h_{21}	h_{fb}	h_{fe}	h_{fc}
Output admittance	h_{22}	h_{ob}	h_{oe}	h_{oc}

[1] We will use capital V's and I's, with subscripts, to depict either rms values of (incremental) sinewaves, or complex rms values at a given frequency.

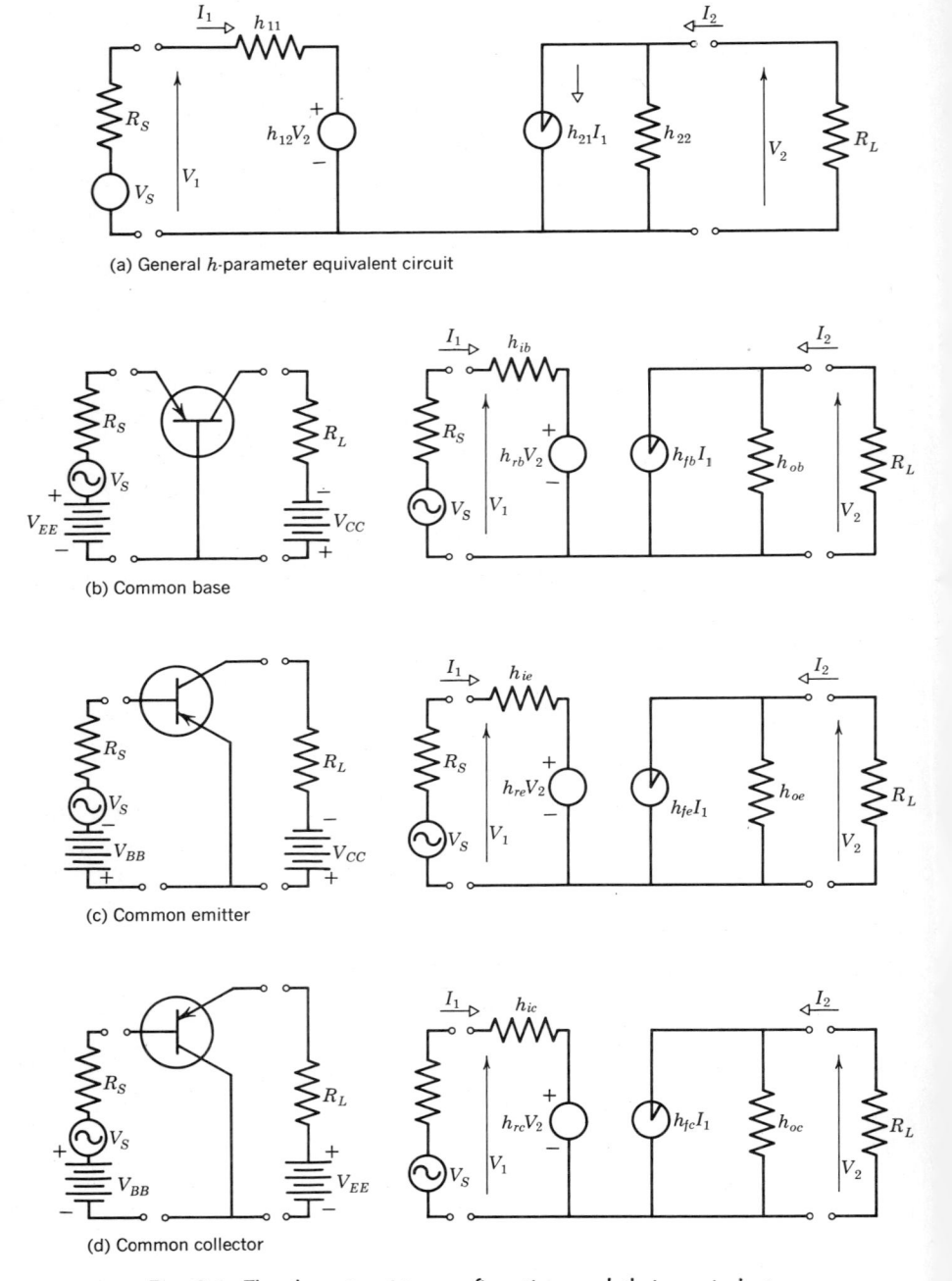

Fig. 8-1. The three transistor configurations and their equivalent circuits.

Small-signal amplifiers

Figure 8-1 shows the basic circuit and h-parameter equivalent circuit for each of the transistor connections. One of the advantages of using a matrix-type equivalent circuit is that one can derive general relationships with the general parameters, which can then be applied to a variety of situations by inserting the proper parameters. We will make use of this feature now by finding the performance quantities in terms of the general h parameters.

Let us begin by determining the input resistance at the source terminals. For this calculation the source is removed and the ratio of V_1 to I_1 at the source terminals, with the load attached, is found. Figure 8-2 shows the proper circuit.

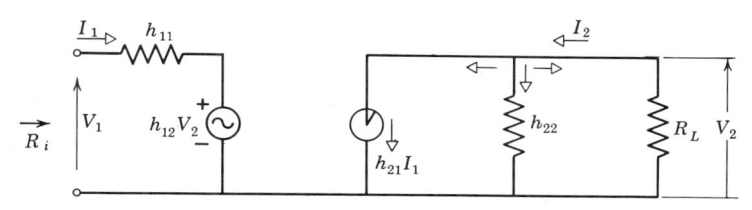

Fig. 8-2. General h-parameter equivalent circuit used for calculating R_i, A_i, A_v, and A_p.

Equating the sum of the voltage drops, in the input mesh, to the voltage rises, we have

$$V_1 = h_{11}I_1 + h_{12}V_2 \tag{7}$$

For the output side the sum of the currents (nodal equation) flowing out of node 1 are set equal to zero (see arrows).

$$0 = h_{21}I_1 + h_{22}V_2 + \frac{V_2}{R_L} \tag{8}$$

The two simultaneous equations for Figure 8-2 then, are

$$\begin{aligned}V_1 &= h_{11}I_1 + h_{12}V_2 \\ 0 &= h_{21}I_1 + (h_{22} + 1/R_L)V_2\end{aligned} \tag{9}$$

We note that I_1 and V_2 are unknowns and V_1 is the constant of these equations. Solving for I_1 by the use of determinants, we find

$$I_1 = \frac{\begin{vmatrix} V_1 & h_{12} \\ 0 & h_{22} + 1/R_L \end{vmatrix}}{\begin{vmatrix} h_{11} & h_{12} \\ h_{21} & h_{22} + 1/R_L \end{vmatrix}} = \frac{V_1(h_{22} + 1/R_L)}{h_{11}(h_{22} + 1/R_L) - h_{12}h_{21}} \tag{10}$$

To find R_i we divide V_1 by I_1 of Equation (10).

$$R_i = \frac{V_1}{I_1} = \frac{h_{11}(h_{22} + 1/R_L) - h_{12}h_{21}}{h_{22} + 1/R_L}$$

$$= \frac{h_{11}(h_{22}R_L + 1) - h_{12}h_{21}R_L}{h_{22}R_L + 1} \quad (11)$$

$$\text{input resistance} = \boxed{R_i = \frac{R_L \Delta^h + h_{11}}{h_{22}R_L + 1}}$$

where $\Delta^h = h_{11}h_{22} - h_{12}h_{21}$.

Given the h parameters of the particular transistor connection and the value of the load resistance, we find the input resistance by using Equation (11). For example, the common-emitter input resistance is given by:

$$R_i = \frac{R_L \Delta^{h^e} + h_{ie}}{h_{oe}R_L + 1} \quad (12)$$

It is necessary to emphasize that the input resistance depends somewhat upon the value of R_L. In the vacuum tube or field effect transistor (at low frequencies), for example, this is not the case. The R_L dependence means that the input and output side of a transistor are not isolated. That is, what is done to the output side directly affects the input side. This situation is basically different for the vacuum tube, where a change in load resistance does not change the grid-to-cathode resistance appreciably.

To find the voltage gain (A_v) we can use the same circuit (Figure 8-2), and hence the simultaneous Equations (9) apply. This time we shall solve for the other unknown, V_2.

$$V_2 = \frac{\begin{vmatrix} h_{11} & V_1 \\ h_{21} & 0 \\ h_{11} & h_{12} \\ h_{21} & h_{22} + 1/R_L \end{vmatrix}}{} = \frac{-h_{21}V_1}{h_{11}(h_{22} + 1/R_L) - h_{12}h_{21}}$$

$$= \frac{-h_{21}V_1 R_L}{h_{11}(h_{22}R_L + 1) - h_{12}h_{21}R_L} \quad (13)$$

Taking the ratio of V_2 to V_1, we find

Small-signal amplifiers

$$\text{voltage gain} = \frac{V_2}{V_1} = \boxed{A_v = \frac{-h_{21}R_L}{R_L\Delta^h + h_{11}}} \quad (14)$$

To find the current gain (A_i) we have merely to note that, from Figure 8-2,

$$V_2 = -I_2 R_L \quad (15)$$

If we substitute Equation (15) into Equation (8), we find

$$0 = h_{21}I_1 - h_{22}I_2 R_L - I_2 \quad (16)$$

The ratio of I_2/I_1 is then found to be

$$\text{current gain} = \frac{I_2}{I_1} = \boxed{A_i = \frac{h_{21}}{1 + h_{22}R_L}} \quad (17)$$

In previous chapters we used α for the common-base current gain, and β for the common-emitter current gain. In h-parameter terms we have

$$\begin{aligned} h_{fb} &= -\alpha \\ h_{fe} &= \beta \end{aligned} \quad (18)$$

Note that h_{fb} or h_{fe} apply only to the transistor.[1] Equation (17) now shows us the relation between the current gain of the transistor (h_{fb} or h_{fe}) and the circuit current gain when that transistor is used in an amplifier. For many cases of amplifier applications the load resistances are such that the current gain A_i approximately equals the transistor current gain (h_{fb} or h_{fe}).

To find the power gain (A_p) we have only to use the quantities already calculated. The power gain equals

$$A_p = \frac{I_2}{I_1} \times \frac{V_2}{V_1} = \frac{I_2^2}{I_1^2} \times \frac{R_L}{R_i} \quad (19)$$

[1] The sign of these matrix quantities is determined by the convention of current direction—*into* input and output terminals. Since α and β are positive, h_{fb} is a negative number, while h_{fe} is positive.

By using either of the two relations shown in Equation (19), the power gain is found to be

$$\text{power gain} = A_p = \frac{h_{21}^2 R_L}{(1 + h_{22}R_L)(h_{11} + \Delta^h R_L)} \qquad (20)$$

The remaining quantity to be calculated is the output resistance, R_o. To calculate this we need to find the resistance looking into the output terminals with the generator connected. For this calculation

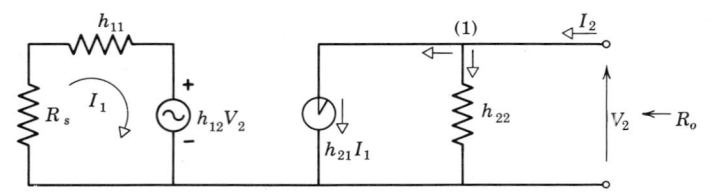

Fig. 8-3. General h-parameter equivalent circuit for calculating R_o.

the circuit of Figure 8-3 is used, and the two simultaneous equations are

$$0 = (R_s + h_{11})I_1 + h_{12}V_2$$
$$I_2 = h_{21}I_1 + h_{22}V_2 \qquad (21)$$

The unknowns are I_1 and V_2. Solving for V_2, we find

$$V_2 = \frac{\begin{vmatrix} R_s + h_{11} & 0 \\ h_{21} & I_2 \end{vmatrix}}{\begin{vmatrix} R_s + h_{11} & h_{12} \\ h_{21} & h_{22} \end{vmatrix}} = \frac{(R_s + h_{11})I_2}{(R_s + h_{11})(h_{22}) - h_{12}h_{21}} \qquad (22)$$

To find the output resistance we need to find the ratio of V_2 and I_2.

$$\text{output impedance} = \frac{V_2}{I_2} = R_o = \frac{R_s + h_{11}}{R_s h_{22} + \Delta^h} \qquad (23)$$

We note that the R_o is dependent upon R_s. This again tells us that the transistor output is not isolated from the input. This phenomenon was noted before for R_i. Any changes in the generator

Small-signal amplifiers

resistance affect the output resistance of the transistor. Again, this phenomenon does not occur for a vacuum tube.

The above performance quantities are collected below in Table 8-2.

Table 8-2. GENERAL PERFORMANCE QUANTITIES

Circuit quantity	Symbol	Equation
Input resistance	R_i	$\dfrac{R_L \Delta^h + h_{11}}{h_{22} R_L + 1}$
Current gain	A_i	$\dfrac{h_{21}}{h_{22} R_L + 1}$
Voltage gain	A_v	$\dfrac{-h_{21} R_L}{R_L \Delta^h + h_{11}}$
Output resistance	R_o	$\dfrac{R_s + h_{11}}{R_s h_{22} + \Delta^h}$
Power gain	A_p	$\dfrac{h_{21}^2 R_L}{(1 + h_{22} R_L)(h_{11} + \Delta^h R_L)}$

In the manner shown above, the performance quantities for a single stage amplifier are calculated. Our purpose here was twofold: (1) to provide the equations for the various quantities, and (2) to illustrate the method by which they are calculated.

It should be emphasized again that the above equations, stated in terms of the general h parameters, are to be used for any of the three transistor connections. In order to make the equations apply to any of the configurations, one simply substitutes the correct parameters as depicted in Table 8-1 and Figure 8-1.

We will now evaluate the general equations of Table 8-2 for each of the transistor configurations.

COMMON-EMITTER AMPLIFIER

As stated, the common-emitter connection is by far the most frequently used amplifier in transistor circuits. The reasons for this will become clear in this section.

A common-emitter amplifier and its equivalent circuit is shown in Figure 8-4. In order to evaluate the performance quantities for this amplifier we simply need to substitute the common-emitter h parameters into the general equations developed above. As an example of the application of these performance quantities, we shall use the same transistor as used before in the amplifier shown in Figure 8-4. Usually the common-emitter parameters are given by

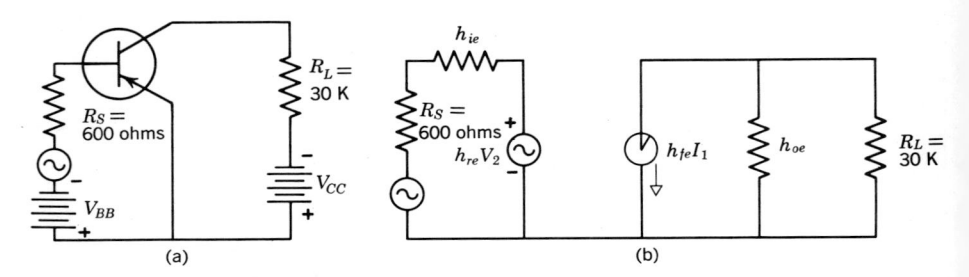

Fig. 8-4. (a) Common-emitter amplifier (b) and its equivalent circuit.

the manufacturer; we will see later in this section how the common-emitter parameters are related to the common-base ones. Some common-emitter parameters typical of a junction transistor are given as follows:

$$h_{ie} = 2000 \qquad h_{fe} = +49$$
$$h_{re} = 16 \times 10^{-4} \qquad h_{oe} = 5 \times 10^{-5}$$

Terminations that are somewhat typical for a common-emitter stage, if striving for high gain with a low to medium power output, are a load and source resistance of 30,000 and 600 ohms, respectively. The performance quantities then appear as:

$$\Delta^{h^e} = h_{ie}h_{oe} - h_{re}h_{fe}$$
$$= (2 \times 10^3)(5 \times 10^{-5}) - (16 \times 10^{-4})(49) = 0.0216$$

$$R_i = \frac{R_L \Delta^{h^e} + h_{ie}}{1 + h_{oe}R_L} = \frac{(3 \times 10^4)(2.16 \times 10^{-2}) + 2000}{1 + (5 \times 10^{-5})(3 \times 10^4)} = 1060$$

$$R_o = \frac{h_{ie} + R_s}{\Delta^{h^e} + h_{oe}R_s} = \frac{2000 + 600}{(2.16 \times 10^{-2}) + (5 \times 10^{-5})(6 \times 10^2)}$$
$$= 50{,}400 \tag{24}$$

$$A_i = \frac{h_{fe}}{1 + h_{oe}R_L} = \frac{49}{1 + (5 \times 10^{-5})(3 \times 10^4)} = 19.6$$

Small-signal amplifiers

$$A_v = \frac{-h_{fe}R_L}{\Delta^{h^e}R_L + h_{ie}} = \frac{-(49)(3 \times 10^4)}{(2.16 \times 10^{-2})(3 \times 10^4) + 2000}$$
$$= -554$$

$$A_p = A_i A_v = (19.6)(-554) = -10{,}850$$

Later it will be seen that the difference between the input and the output resistance is much less for the common-emitter case than for the common-base case. Thus the impedance match between cascaded similar stages is better for the common emitter than for the common base. For this reason, the common-emitter amplifier forms the backbone of the RC-coupled transistor amplifiers.

Since the common-emitter case is used so frequently we will examine it in more detail. First of all it is instructive to note how the A_i and the R_i vary with R_L for the emitter case. Figure 8-5 shows

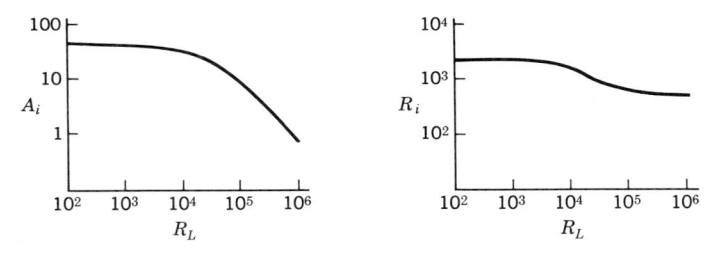

Fig. 8-5. Common emitter A_i and R_i versus R_L.

both A_i and R_i plotted versus R_L on log-log paper. (Note how the axes here differ from the normal linear axes.) It is seen that both A_i and R_i do not vary appreciably with R_L so long as R_L is below 10^4. ($R_L \ll 1/h_{oe}$.)

Since the R_L for many amplifier situations will be much less than $1/h_{oe}$, one can many times ignore the dependence of A_i and R_i on R_L. This is tantamount to having a negligible feedback term ($h_{re}V_2$) in the transistor equivalent circuit. Furthermore, consider the R_o given in Equation (25). If R_s is sufficiently high so that $R_s \gg h_{ie}$ and $h_{oe}R_s \gg \Delta^{h^e}$, the R_o is given by $1/h_{oe}$. This too, then, behaves as though $h_{re}V_2$ is negligible.

The above conditions on R_L and on R_s occur quite frequently for common-emitter stages. In particular, they occur for cascaded emitter stages, where the load impedance of a given stage is the input impedance of the next stage. For such cases, then, an equivalent circuit which deletes the $h_{re}V_2$ term is suitable. Since the R_L must be moderately low for this approximation, one can also delete the h_{oe} term from the equivalent circuit. The resulting simplified common-emitter equivalent circuit is shown in Figure 8-6. Note that now the tran-

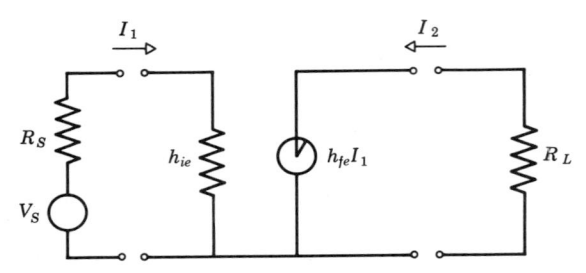

Fig. 8-6. Equivalent circuit for simplified analysis of common-emitter stages.

sistor appears as a unilateral device, and the output is *isolated* from the input. Using this equivalent circuit results in many simplifications of transistor circuit analysis. In particular, for any given stage, the performance quantities reduce to

$$R_i = h_{ie}$$
$$A_i = h_{fe}$$
$$A_v = -\frac{h_{fe}}{h_{ie}} R_L \tag{25}$$
$$R_o = \infty \; 1/h_{oe}.$$

Note that the output resistance R_o is infinite only with respect to the much lower R_L. Actually the R_o is given by $1/h_{oe}$.

The above performance simplifications should be used whenever the relative values of R_s and R_L warrant it. They are additionally attractive since one may not know the transistor parameters precisely (unless they are measured for each transistor). Also, the simplifications of Equation (25) are another advantage of using h parameters for transistor small-signal analysis.

Since the common-emitter configuration is the most important one for small-signal amplifiers, it is worthwhile noting the variation of the emitter h parameters with operating point by plotting the variation versus both I_E and V_{CE}.

Figure 8-7 shows the variation of the h^e and h^b parameters versus I_E for the typical alloy-junction transistor using 1 milliampere as a reference. This information is often supplied by the manufacturer's specifications. Figure 8-8 shows the parameter variation versus V_C, using 5 volts as the reference.

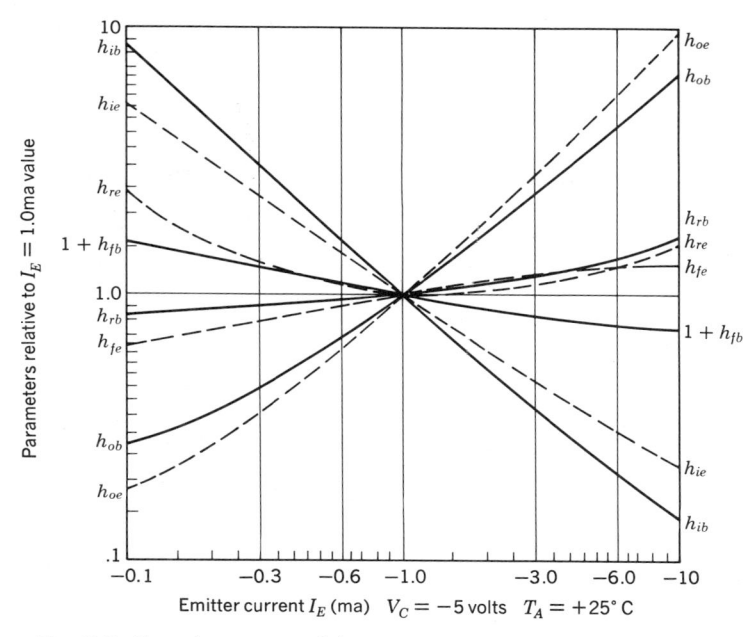

Fig. 8-7. Typical variation of h parameters with emitter current.

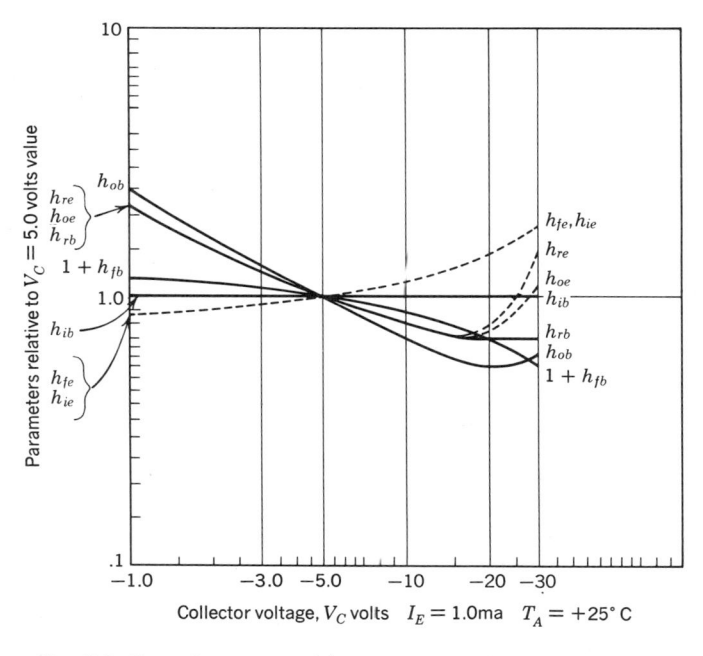

Fig. 8-8. Typical variation of h parameters with collector voltage.

183

184   Small-signal amplifiers

If only an approximate analysis is required, the manufacturer's typical values and correction curves such as the above are sufficient. If more accuracy is required, however, one should measure the particular transistor under the desired conditions.

COMMON-BASE AMPLIFIER

The common-base amplifier, shown in Figure 8-9, is the historical reference connection, but is used only infrequently in low-frequency

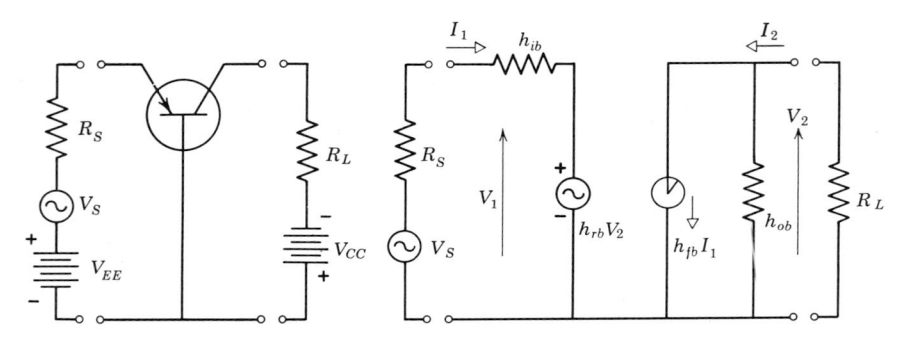

Fig. 8-9. Common-base transistor amplifier.

amplifiers. It will be useful, however, to note the typical parameters for the common-base case, and evaluate the performance quantities derived previously. We will need these to make a comparison of the various connections.

Since it is the h^e parameters that are usually given by the manufacturer, we will now derive the common base parameters in terms of the h^b parameters. In doing this we will gain some facility and understanding for manipulating matrix quantities in general, and h parameters in particular.

We will begin, then, with the common-emitter equivalent circuit and derive the common-base parameters. To do this, we rearrange the common-emitter equivalent circuit so as to form the common-base equivalent circuit. This is shown in Figure 8-9.

The objective now is to use the circuit of Figure 8-10(b) to find a circuit identical in form to that of (a). The resulting circuit will simply be the common-base h-parameter circuit.

We can accomplish this determination of the h^b parameters by using the basic defining equations, as stated before (Chapter 6):

Small-signal amplifiers 185

$$h_{ib} = \left.\frac{V_1}{I_1}\right|_{V_2=0} \qquad h_{rb} = \left.\frac{V_1}{V_2}\right|_{I_1=0}$$

$$h_{fb} = \left.\frac{I_2}{I_1}\right|_{V_2=0} \qquad h_{ob} = \left.\frac{I_2}{V_2}\right|_{I_1=0}$$

(26)

By applying these definitions to the circuit of Figure 8-10(b), we can evaluate the h^b parameters in terms of the h^e parameters.

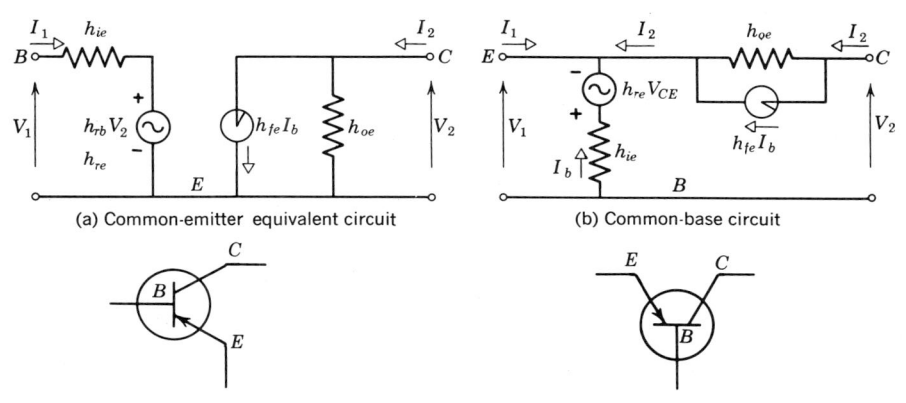

Fig. 8-10. Common-base equivalent circuit from rearranged common-emitter circuit.

The definitions of both h_{ib} and h_{fb} specify that $V_2 = 0$. Figure 8-11 shows the circuit of Figure 8-10(b) with the output (V_2) short-circuited. We need to solve this circuit for the ratios of V_1 to I_1 and I_2 to I_1.

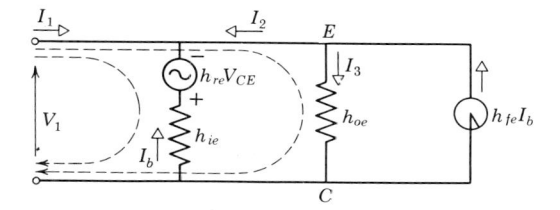

Fig. 8-11. Circuit of Fig. 8-10(b) when output is shorted.

This circuit consists essentially of two meshes, so we write two mesh equations. The two meshes selected are shown by dashed lines. The equation for the first mesh is

$$V_1 = -h_{re}V_{ce} - h_{ie}I_b \qquad (27)$$

For the second mesh, we first note that I_3, the current through the conductance h_{oe}, is

$$I_3 = h_{fe}I_b - I_2 \qquad (28)$$

The equation for the second mesh is then

$$V_1 = \frac{h_{fe}I_b - I_2}{h_{oe}} \qquad (29)$$

From Figure 8-11 we verify that $I_b = -(I_1 + I_2)$ and $V_1 = -V_{ce}$. Making these substitutions, the two simultaneous equations are

$$\begin{aligned} V_1 &= h_{re}V_1 + h_{ie}I_1 + h_{ie}I_2 \\ V_1 &= -\frac{h_{fe}}{h_{oe}}I_1 - \frac{h_{fe}}{h_{oe}}I_2 - \frac{I_2}{h_{oe}} \end{aligned} \qquad (30)$$

Written more conventionally, they appear

$$\begin{aligned} V_1 &= \frac{h_{ie}}{1 - h_{re}}I_1 + \frac{h_{ie}}{1 - h_{re}}I_2 \\ V_1 &= -\frac{h_{fe}}{h_{oe}}I_1 - \left(\frac{h_{fe}}{h_{oe}} + \frac{1}{h_{oe}}\right)I_2 \end{aligned} \qquad (31)$$

Solving these equations for the unknown I_1

$$I_1 = \frac{\begin{vmatrix} V_1 & \dfrac{h_{ie}}{1-h_{re}} \\ V_1 & -\left(\dfrac{h_{fe}}{h_{oe}} + \dfrac{1}{h_{oe}}\right) \end{vmatrix}}{\begin{vmatrix} \dfrac{h_{ie}}{1-h_{re}} & \dfrac{h_{ie}}{1-h_{re}} \\ -\dfrac{h_{fe}}{h_{oe}} & -\left(\dfrac{h_{fe}}{h_{oe}} + \dfrac{1}{h_{oe}}\right) \end{vmatrix}} = -\frac{V_1[(h_{fe}+1)(1-h_{re}) + h_{ie}h_{oe}]}{h_{ie}h_{fe} - h_{ie}(h_{fe}+1)} \qquad (32)$$

After further simplification, the ratio of V_1 to I_1 is

$$h_{ib} = \frac{V_1}{I_1}\bigg|_{V_2=0} = \frac{h_{ie}}{\Delta^{h^\bullet} + h_{fe} - h_{re} + 1} \qquad (33)$$

Small-signal amplifiers

Equation (33) can be accurately simplified by referring to the h parameters given previously for a typical junction transistor. It is always true that $\Delta^{h^e} - h_{re}$ is small with respect to $1 + h_{fe}$. Therefore Equation (33) becomes

$$h_{ib} \approx \frac{h_{ie}}{1 + h_{fe}} \qquad (34)$$

To find h_{fb} we need the ratio of I_2 to I_1. Using Equations (31), we solve for the unknown I_2.

$$I_2 = \frac{\begin{vmatrix} \dfrac{h_{ie}}{1 - h_{re}} V_1 \\ -\dfrac{h_{fe}}{h_{oe}} V_1 \end{vmatrix}}{\begin{vmatrix} \dfrac{h_{ie}}{1 - h_{re}} & \dfrac{h_{ie}}{1 - h_{re}} \\ -\dfrac{h_{fe}}{h_{oe}} & -\left(\dfrac{h_{fe}}{h_{oe}} + \dfrac{1}{h_{oe}}\right) \end{vmatrix}} = V_1 \frac{\left[\dfrac{h_{ie}h_{oe} + h_{fe}(1 - h_{re})}{(1 - h_{re})(h_{oe})}\right]}{\dfrac{h_{ie}h_{fe} - h_{ie}(h_{fe} + 1)}{(1 - h_{re})(h_{oe})}} \qquad (35)$$

Taking the ratio of I_2 to I_1 given by Equation (32), we have

$$h_{fb} = \left.\frac{I_2}{I_1}\right|_{V_2=0} = -\frac{\Delta^{h^e} + h_{fe}}{\Delta^{h^e} + 1 + h_{fe} - h_{re}} \qquad (36)$$

Using the same simplification as above, plus the fact that Δ^{h^e} is small with respect to h_{fe}, we have

$$h_{fb} \approx \frac{-h_{fe}}{1 + h_{fe}} \qquad (37)$$

Since h_{fe} is the transistor current gain for the common-emitter connection, h_{fe} equals β (defined previously):

$$h_{fe} = \beta \qquad (38)$$

Remembering that h_{fb} equals $-\alpha$, we see in Equation (38) the same relation between β and α as was stated in Equation (3) of Chapter 7.
From the defining Equations (26) we see that h_{rb} and h_{ob} are

calculated for $I_1 = 0$. Therefore we return to Figure 8-10(b) and obtain the equations for the circuit when the input is open-circuited. The circuit is shown in Figure 8-12.

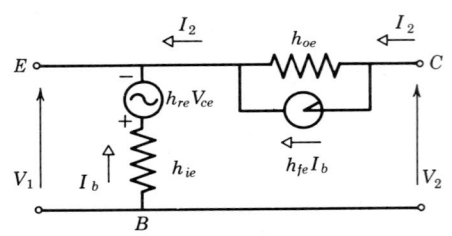

Fig. 8-12. Circuit of Fig. 8-10(b) when the input is open-circuited.

Since only one mesh exists for this circuit, we need write only one mesh equation.

$$V_2 = \frac{I_2 - h_{fe}I_b}{h_{oe}} - h_{re}V_{ce} - h_{ie}I_b \qquad (39)$$

From Figure 8-12 it can be seen that $I_e = -I_2$ and $V_{ce} = \frac{I_2 - h_{fe}I_b}{h_{oe}}$. Using these substitutions, the equation appears

$$V_2 = \frac{1 + h_{fe}}{h_{oe}} I_2 - h_{re}\left(\frac{1 + h_{fe}}{h_{oe}}\right) I_2 + h_{ie}I_2 \qquad (40)$$

Taking the ratio of I_2 to V_2, we find

$$h_{ob} = \left.\frac{I_2}{V_2}\right|_{I_1=0} = \frac{h_{oe}}{\Delta^{h^e} + h_{fe} - h_{re} + 1} \qquad (41)$$

Using the same simplifications as for Equations (37) and (34), this simplifies to

$$\boxed{h_{ob} \approx \frac{h_{oe}}{1 + h_{fe}}} \qquad (42)$$

To find the value of h_{rb} we need the ratio of V_1 to V_2. By referring to Figure 8-12, we see that V_1 is equal to

$$V_1 = -h_{re}\frac{(1 + h_{fe})I_2}{h_{oe}} + h_{ie}I_2 \qquad (43)$$

Small-signal amplifiers

Taking the ratio of this equation to that for V_2 given by Equation (41), it is found that

$$h_{rb} = \frac{V_1}{V_2} = \frac{\Delta^{h^e} - h_{re}}{1 + h_{fe} - h_{re} + \Delta^{h^e}} \qquad (44)$$

Using the simplifications as before,

$$\boxed{h_{rb} \approx \frac{\Delta^{h^e} - h_{re}}{1 + h_{fe}}} \qquad (45)$$

The equations we have just found give the common-base h^b parameters in terms of the common-emitter h parameters. They are listed here for easy reference.

$$h_{ib} \approx \frac{h_{ie}}{1 + h_{fe}} \qquad h_{fb} \approx -\frac{h_{fe}}{1 + h_{fe}}$$
$$h_{rb} \approx \frac{\Delta^{h^e} - h_{re}}{1 + h_{fe}} \qquad h_{ob} \approx \frac{h_{oe}}{1 + h_{fe}} \qquad (46)$$

Assuming the common-emitter parameters are given by the manufacturers, the above equations may be used to convert these to the common-base parameters.

We can now calculate the common-base parameters for the typical junction transistor used before. The given parameters are

$$h_{ie} = 2000 \qquad h_{fe} = +49$$
$$h_{re} = 16 \times 10^{-4} \qquad h_{oe} = 5 \times 10^{-5}$$
$$\Delta^{h^e} = 2.16 \times 10^{-2}$$

$$h_{ib} \approx \frac{h_{ie}}{1 + h_{fe}} = \frac{2000}{1 + 49} = 40$$

$$h_{rb} \approx \frac{\Delta^h - h_{re}}{1 + h_{fe}} = \frac{2.16 \times 10^{-2} - 16 \times 10^{-4}}{1 + 49} = 4 \times 10^{-4} \qquad (47)$$

$$h_{fb} \approx \frac{-h_{fe}}{1 + h_{fe}} = \frac{-49}{1 + 49} = -0.98$$

$$h_{ob} \approx \frac{h_{oe}}{1 + h_{fe}} = \frac{5 \times 10^{-5}}{50} = 1 \times 10^{-6}$$

Calculating Δ^{hb}:

$$\Delta^{hb} = h_{ib}h_{ob} - h_{fb}h_{rb}$$
$$= 40 \times 10^{-6} + (4 \times 10^{-4})(0.98) = 4.32 \times 10^{-4}$$

One important thing to note here is that h_{fe} is much larger than h_{fb}. Thus it is reaffirmed that the current gain of a junction transistor is less than 1 for the common-base connection, but is in the order of 50 for the common-emitter case. This will typically go as high as 150 in more recent transistors. Typical common-base terminations, if striving for high gain with low to medium power output, are a load resistance $R_L = 50,000$ and a source resistance $R_s = 100$ ohms.

The following performance quantities are then calculated:

$$R_i = \frac{\Delta^{hb}R_L + h_{ib}}{1 + h_{ob}R_L} = \frac{(4.32 \times 10^{-4})(5 \times 10^4) + 40}{1 + (1 \times 10^{-6})(5 \times 10^4)}$$
$$= 58.6$$

$$R_o = \frac{h_{ib} + R_s}{\Delta^{hb} + h_{ob}R_s} = \frac{40 + 100}{(4.32 \times 10^{-4}) + (1 \times 10^{-6})(1 \times 10^2)}$$
$$= 263,000$$

$$A_i = \frac{h_{fb}}{1 + h_{ob}R_L} = \frac{-0.98}{1 + (1 \times 10^{-6})(5 \times 10^4)} \tag{48}$$
$$= -0.933$$

$$A_v = \frac{-h_{fb}R_L}{h_{ib} + \Delta^{hb}R_L} = \frac{(+0.98)(5 \times 10^4)}{40 + (4.32 \times 10^{-4})(5 \times 10^4)}$$
$$= 795$$

$$A_p = A_iA_v = \frac{h_{fb}^2 R_L}{(1 + h_{ob}R_L)(h_{ib} + \Delta^{hb}R_L)}$$
$$= -742$$

The fact that A_i is preceded by a negative sign merely means that the actual output current I_2 is out of phase to the direction assumed as positive in Figure 8-8a. Thus the common-base connection has no phase shift since the output current flows in the same direction as the input current. The negative sign preceding the power gain is also a result of conventions; the power is actually consumed in the

Small-signal amplifiers   191

load, whereas a current and voltage as shown in Figure 8-8a would result in power being consumed by the transistor.

From the equations above is seen that the common-base amplifier has current gain less than 1, but does have substantial voltage gain. Also it is seen that the input resistance is quite low while the output resistance is relatively high. We will compare these results with those for the other connections in a later section. This concludes the single stage common base treatment.

COMMON COLLECTOR AMPLIFIER

The remaining connection to be examined is the common collector, shown with its equivalent circuit in Figure 8-13. The common-

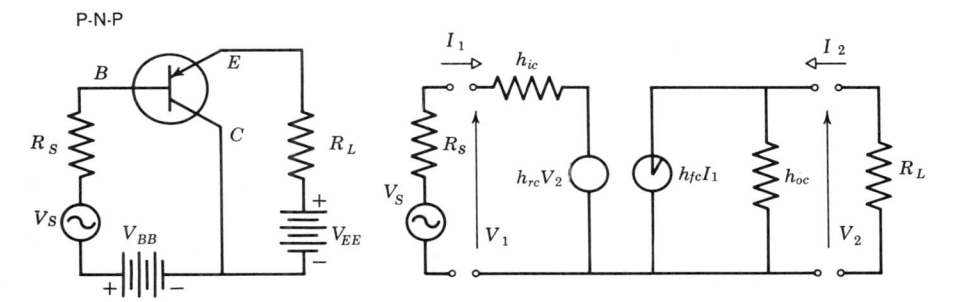

Fig. 8-13. Common-collector transistor amplifier.

collector circuit is also called the "emitter follower." We shall see that it performs in a manner similar to the vacuum tube cathode follower. We will quickly derive the common-collector h parameters in terms of the emitter parameters, and then we will evaluate the performance quantities. Since we are following rather closely the derivation for the common-emitter case, we shall here only sketch the derivation.

Figure 8-14(a) shows the common-emitter equivalent circuit rearranged to form the circuit for the common-collector connection. Figure 8-14(b) shows the base h-parameter circuit, and the parameters are suitably labeled h^c.

The h^c parameters are found by operating suitably upon the circuit of Figure 8-14(a). It is remembered from Equation (26) that, for h_{ic} and h_{fc}, the output is short-circuited to make $V_2 = 0$. For h_{rc} and h_{oc} the input is open-circuited to make $I_1 = 0$.

192   Small-signal amplifiers

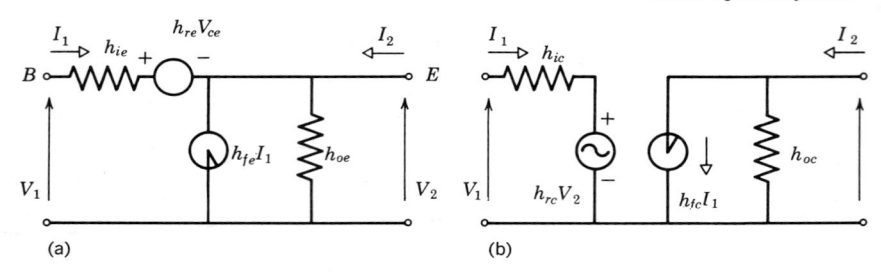

Fig. 8-14. Common-collector equivalent circuits: (a) circuit obtained from rearranging common-emitter circuit; (b) conventional circuit showing h^c parameters.

When the output of Figure 8-14(a) is short-circuited, the equation for the input is simply

$$V_1 = h_{ie}I_1 \tag{49}$$

Therefore, the h_{ic} is given by

$$h_{ic} = \left.\frac{V_1}{I_1}\right|_{V_2=0} = h_{ie} \tag{50}$$

$$\boxed{h_{ic} = h_{ie}}$$

For the h_{fc} calculation, summing the currents at the output node yields the equation

$$I_2 + I_1 + h_{fe}I_1 = 0 \tag{51}$$

Therefore, h_{fc} is given by

$$h_{fc} = \left.\frac{I_1}{I_2}\right|_{V_2=0} = -(1 + h_{fe}) \tag{52}$$

$$\boxed{h_{fc} = -(1 + h_{fe})}$$

If the input circuit of Figure 8-14(a) is left open-circuited, the output equation is simply

$$V_2 = I_2 \times \frac{1}{h_{oe}} \tag{53}$$

Then h_{oc} is

$$h_{oc} = \left.\frac{I_2}{V_2}\right|_{I_1=0} = h_{oe} \tag{54}$$

$$\boxed{h_{oc} = h_{oe}}$$

Small-signal amplifiers

The voltage equation, with $I_1 = 0$, is written

$$V_1 = h_{re}V_{CE} + V_2 \tag{55}$$

Noting that $V_2 = V_{EC} = -V_{CE}$, we have

$$h_{rc} = \left.\frac{V_1}{V_2}\right|_{I_1=0} = 1 - h_{re} \approx 1$$

$$\boxed{h_{rc} = 1 - h_{re} \approx 1} \tag{56}$$

Since h_{re} is considerably smaller than 1, h_{rc} is approximately 1.0.

Summarizing then, the common collector h^c parameters can be found in terms of the specified h^e parameters by the following:

$$\begin{aligned} h_{ic} &= h_{ie} & h_{rc} &= 1 - h_{re} \approx 1 \\ h_{fc} &= -(1 + h_{fe}) & h_{oc} &= h_{oe} \end{aligned} \tag{57}$$

Taking the same transistor as was used previously, the h^c parameters are

$$\begin{aligned} h_{ic} &= h_{ie} = 2000 \\ h_{fc} &= -(1 + h_{fe}) = -50 \\ h_{rc} &= 1 \\ h_{oc} &= h_{oe} = 5 \times 10^{-5} \end{aligned} \tag{58}$$

It is seen that these parameters are the same as for the common emitter, except for the value of h_{rc}. It will be found that this variation in h_{rc} causes a major difference between a common-emitter connection and a common-collector connection.

Using the above values, we can calculate the performance quantities for the common-collector amplifier. For purposes of a comparison with the other connections we will use a load resistance of 600 ohms and a source resistance of 30,000 ohms. Using these values in the basic circuit of Figure 8-13, the quantities are

$$\Delta^{hc} = h_{ic}h_{oc} - h_{rc}h_{fc} = (2000)(5 \times 10^{-5}) - (1)(-50) = 50.1$$

$$R_i = \frac{R_L\Delta^{hc} + h_{ic}}{1 + h_{oc}R_L} = \frac{(600)(50.1) + 2000}{1 + (5 \times 10^{-5})(600)} = 31{,}000$$

$$R_o = \frac{h_{ic} + R_s}{\Delta^{he} + h_{oc}R_s} = \frac{2000 + 30{,}000}{50.1 + (5 \times 10^{-5})(3 \times 10^4)} = 620$$

$$A_i = \frac{h_{fc}}{1 + h_{oc}R_L} = \frac{-50}{1 + (5 \times 10^{-5})(6 \times 10^2)} = -48.5$$

$$A_v = \frac{-h_{fc}R_L}{\Delta^{he}R_L + h_{ic}} = \frac{-(-50)(600)}{(50.1)(600) + 2000} = 0.938$$

$$A_p = A_i \times A_v = (-48.5)(0.938) = -45.5$$

(59)

With the sign of the current gain we see that the common collector, like the common base, has no phase shift. The negative power gain simply asserts that the power is consumed in the load.

COMPARISON OF THREE CONNECTIONS

Having considered the three types of single-stage connections, we can compare their properties as amplifiers. For this we will refer to Tables 8-3, 8-4, and 8-5. Table 8-3 summarizes the equations for expressing the base and collector parameters in terms of the common-emitter parameters. The quantities of Table 8-4 are the values of the h parameters for a typical junction transistor. Table 8-5 contains the performance values for a typical transistor calculated by using load and source impedances which are somewhat typical if one is striving for high gain and low to medium power output. (Note that

Table 8-3. THE BASE AND COLLECTOR h PARAMETERS IN TERMS OF EMITTER PARAMETERS

General	Common base	Common emitter	Common collector
h_{11}	$h_{ib} \approx \dfrac{h_{ie}}{1 + h_{fe}}$	h_{ie}	$h_{ic} = h_{ie}$
h_{12}	$h_{rb} \approx \dfrac{\Delta^{he} - h_{re}}{1 + h_{fe}}$	h_{re}	$h_{rc} = 1 - h_{re} \approx 1$
h_{21}	$h_{fb} \approx \dfrac{-h_{fe}}{1 + h_{fe}}$	h_{fe}	$h_{fc} = -(1 + h_{fe})$
h_{22}	$h_{ob} \approx \dfrac{h_{oe}}{1 + h_{fe}}$	h_{oe}	$h_{oc} = h_{oe}$

Small-signal amplifiers

Table 8-4. VALUES OF THE h-PARAMETERS FOR THE THREE CONFIGURATIONS, USING A TYPICAL JUNCTION TRANSISTOR

Parameters	Common base (h^b)	Common emitter (h^e)	Common collector (h^c)
h_{11}	$h_{ib} = 40$	$h_{ie} = 2000$	$h_{ic} = 2000$
h_{12}	$h_{rb} = 4 \times 10^{-4}$	$h_{re} = 16 \times 10^{-4}$	$h_{rc} = 1$
h_{21}	$h_{fb} = -0.98$	$h_{fe} = 49$	$h_{fc} = -50$
h_{22}	$h_{ob} = 10^{-6}$	$h_{oe} = 5 \times 10^{-5}$	$h_{oc} = 5 \times 10^{-5}$
Δ^h	$\Delta^{hb} = 4.32 \times 10^{-4}$	$\Delta^{he} = 0.0216$	$\Delta^{hc} = 50.1$

Table 8-5. VALUES OF PERFORMANCE QUANTITIES FOR THE THREE CONFIGURATIONS, USING A TYPICAL JUNCTION TRANSISTOR WITH HIGH GAIN LOADS AS USED IN EQUATIONS (20), (24), AND (59)

Quantity	Performance equation	Common base (use h^b parameter)	Common emitter (use h^e parameter)	Common collector (use h^c parameter)
$R_i =$	$\dfrac{\Delta^h R_L + h_{11}}{h_{22} R_L + 1}$	58.8	1,060	31,000
$R_o =$	$\dfrac{h_{11} + R_s}{\Delta^h + h_{22} R_s}$	261,000	50,400	620
$A_i =$	$\dfrac{h_{21}}{h_{22} R_L + 1}$	-0.933	19.6	-48.5
$A_v =$	$\dfrac{-h_{21} R_L}{h_{11} + \Delta^h R_L}$	793	-554	0.938
$A_p =$	$A_i A_v$	-740	$-10,850$	-45.5
M.A.G.*	$\dfrac{h_{21}^2}{[(\Delta^h)^{1/2} + (h_{11} h_{22})^{1/2}]^2}$	1,350	11,100	45.6

* The M.A.G. will be defined and discussed in the following section.

each configuration has a different source and load impedance.) The resultant performance quantities have no absolute significance, but only serve to demonstrate the trend between configurations.

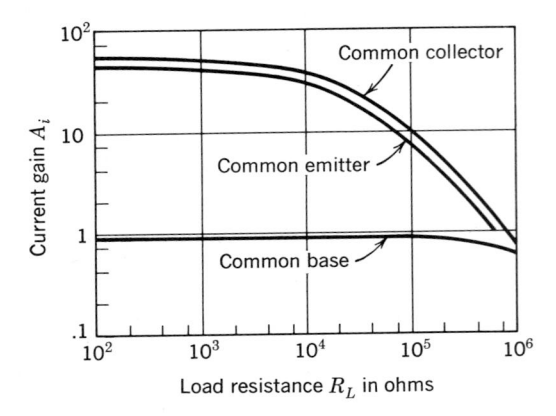

Fig. 8-15. Variation in current gain with load resistance for three connections.

In addition to Table 8-5, which represents a comparison under conditions where high gain with low to medium power is the criterion, we have plotted the variation of A_i, A_p, and R_i versus R_L for the three configurations. These curves facilitate a comparison at a particular R_L. These curves show not only the comparison of gains between the configuration, but also how they behave with respect to R_L.

Figure 8-15 shows A_i versus R_L for the three configurations. We shall see in Chapter 10 that the current gain is the primary figure of

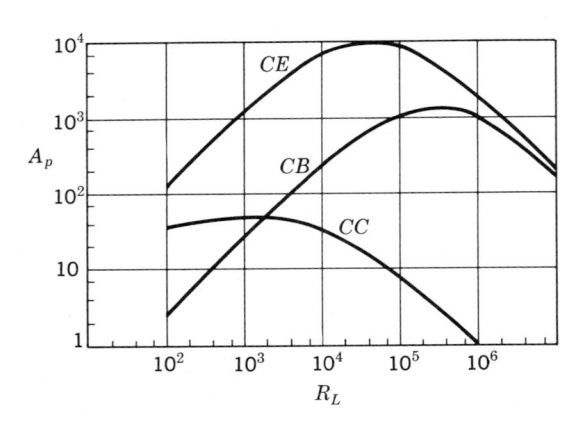

Fig. 8-16. Variation in power gain versus R_L for three connections.

Small-signal amplifiers

merit for *RC*-coupled stages. Figure 8-16 shows A_p versus R_L; this comparison is most useful for transformer-coupled stages.

Figure 8-17 shows R_i versus R_L for the three configurations. R_o versus R_s is plotted in Figure 8-18.

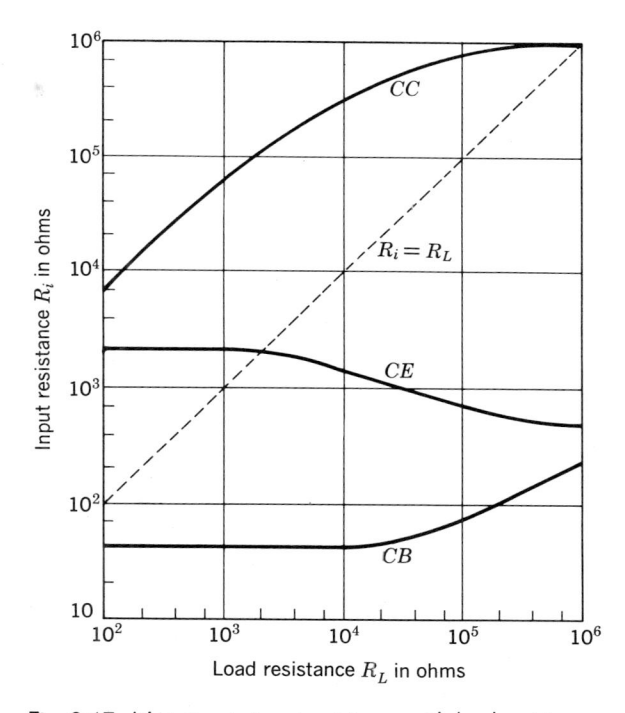

Fig. 8-17. Variation in input resistance with load resistance.

From Table 8-5 and Figure 8-16 we see that the common emitter has the largest power gain of the three connections. Since the output of most electronic circuits is converted to some form of work, the power gain is a basic criterion. This is a primary reason that the common-emitter connection is the most used connection for transistor amplifiers.

Table 8-5 and Figures 8-17 and 8-18 show that the emitter configuration has a better "impedance match" than the others—that is, the output impedance is closer to the input impedance. This factor is extremely important in cascaded stages if transformers are to be avoided.

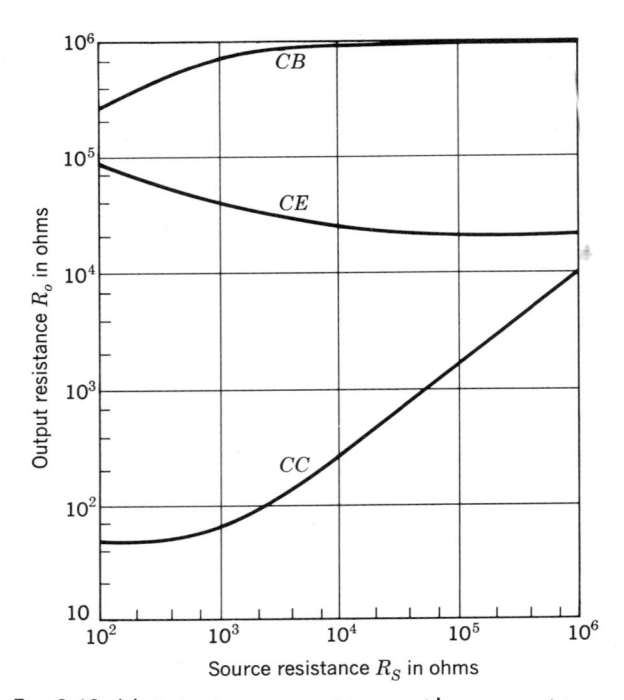

Fig. 8-18. Variation in output resistance with source resistance.

Nevertheless, it should be remembered that any impedance mismatch results in loss of potential power gain—this is the price paid to avoid the other undesirable effects of using transformers.

The common-base connection has a sizable power gain, but it is considerably smaller than that of the common emitter. It is seen that the voltage gain of the common base is the greatest of all the three connections. Thus if an application requires only a voltage output (such as to drive an oscilloscope trace where essentially no power is required), the common base is the best connection. It is also noted that the impedance mismatch for cascading stages is the poorest for the common-base connection. In fact, if two common-base stages are cascaded, transformers must be used for impedance matching, or the gain of two stages will be less than for a single stage. This is another reason for usually choosing the common-emitter connection for amplifiers.

Table 8-5 and Figure 8-15 show that, although the power gain

Small-signal amplifiers

of the common collector is small, the current gain is the highest. This, together with the fact that the input impedance is high and the output impedance is low, means that the common collector is most profitably used as an impedance-matching stage. This "emitter follower" is often used as a "driver" when a given transistor stage must drive a given low impedance. It is usually not used for impedance matching between amplifier stages since it is usually more profitable to use any transistor in an emitter configuration; the amplification overcomes the effect of the impedance mismatch.

To summarize: the common emitter is the best power amplifier, the common base is the best voltage amplifier, and the common collector is often useful as an impedance-matching connection. This simple comparison is somewhat altered, however, when bias stability and frequency response are considered. By bias stability we refer to the change in performance with a variation in bias voltages. Although these topics will be treated in detail later, it is useful to comment here on the major considerations in this connection. The common emitter has less stability and the frequency bandpass is smaller than for the common base. Therefore the higher power gain of the common emitter is acquired at the sacrifice of both the bias stability and the frequency response. Consequently measures must be taken to improve the bias stability and frequency response in many cases.

TRANSDUCER AND AVAILABLE POWER GAIN

Since the transistor amplifier is usually a low input impedance device, the power gain concepts are more important than for high impedance devices. The power gain, as treated thus far, was defined simply as the ratio of the power out to the power in:

$$A_p = \frac{P_{\text{out}}}{P_{\text{in}}} = \frac{I_2^2 R_L}{I_1^2 R_i} = A_i^2 \frac{R_L}{R_i} \qquad (60)$$

Using the value of power gain, we can find the power out if the input power is known.

Many times, when designing electronic circuits, we are given a certain source for the circuit and are not allowed to change its parameters. In other words, we are not allowed to change the internal impedance of the source so that it will match the electronic circuit input impedance; hence maximum power transfer cannot be effected. For this reason it is important to know how efficiently we are using the given source. Note that the power gain, given by Equation (60), gives no measure of how efficiently the source is used.

The transducer gain and the available gain have been defined in order to include the consideration of how efficiently the given source is utilized.

TRANSDUCER GAIN. The transducer gain is defined as the ratio of the actual output power in the load to the power available from the generator or source.

$$\text{transducer gain} = \frac{\text{power out}}{\text{power available from generator}} \quad (61)$$

By available power we mean the maximum power that can be drawn from the source. It is remembered from the electrical review in Chapter 6 that maximum power is achieved when the load impedance (for the source) is equal to the internal resistance of the source. The power achieved, under the matched conditions, for a source whose open-circuit voltage is V_s and whose internal resistance is R_s is

$$P_{\text{avail}} = \frac{V_s^2}{4R_s} \quad (62)$$

The transducer gain can then be written

$$\text{transducer gain} = \frac{P_0}{V_s^2/4R_s} = \frac{V_2^2/R_L}{V_s^2/4R_s}$$
$$= \frac{4I_2^2 R_L R_s}{V_s^2} = \frac{4I_2^2 R_L R_s}{I_1^2(R_s + R_i)^2} \quad (63)$$

If we now substitute the values for A_i and R_i as given by Table 8-5, the transducer gain is found to be

$$\text{transducer gain} = \frac{4R_L R_s h_{21}^2}{(R_s R_L h_{22} + R_s + \Delta^h R_L + h_{11})^2} \quad (64)$$

It is noted, of course, that the transducer gain is a function of source resistance R_s, as it must be since it takes into account the efficiency with which the source is utilized.

Small-signal amplifiers

Equation (64) can be used for either of the three connections if the appropriate h parameters (h^e for common emitter, etc.) are used.

For comparing two amplifiers with fixed loads that are to operate from the same source, the transducer gain will specify which circuit provides the higher output power. It is noted that the power gain, defined without respect to the source, would give no information for such a comparison.

AVAILABLE POWER GAIN. The available power gain is defined for a reason similar to that for the transducer gain. It includes the effect of the source, and in addition, concerns the power output if the load resistance were matched to the transistor output resistance. The available power gain is defined as the ratio of the power *available* from the transistor output to the power available from the source:

$$\text{available power gain} = \frac{\text{available power of transistor output}}{\text{available generator power}} \quad (65)$$

As mentioned, the available output power would be achieved if the load resistance were matched to the transistor output resistance. In terms of circuit quantities, then, the available power gain is

$$\text{available power gain} = \frac{V_{oc}^2/4R_o}{V_s^2/4R_s} = \frac{V_{oc}^2 R_s}{V_s^2 R_o} \quad (66)$$

where V_{oc} = output voltage when output is open-circuited.

To find V_{oc} the circuit Equations (9) indicate that, with $R_L = \infty$, the $V_{oc} = \dfrac{h_{21}}{\Delta^h} V_1$; R_i with $R_L = \infty$, is equal to Δ^h/h_{22}, and $V_s = I_1 R_s + \dfrac{h_{12}h_{21}}{h_{22}} I_1 + h_{11} I_1$. Making these substitutions in Equations (66), the available power gain is found to be

$$\text{available power gain} = \frac{h_{21}^2 R_s}{(\Delta^h + R_s h_{22})(R_s + h_{11})} \quad (67)$$

Note that the available gain is independent of R_L. For any particular transistor amplifier, the available gain is the same, regardless of the actual R_L. This gain figure has to do with what power is available; hence, what power could be realized *if* the R_L were equal to R_o.

The available gain is a function of R_s since the available output power depends upon how much of the generator power is inserted into the input. Again Equation (67) applies to all three connections providing the proper h parameters are used.

If we have two amplifiers that are to operate from the same source, and we can adjust the loads, then the available gain will specify which circuit would provide the higher output power. This is dependent upon being able to use the matched load resistance to *obtain* the available power. Even if the matched load is not used the available gain will remain the same; we simply do not achieve all the available power.

MAXIMUM AVAILABLE GAIN. The maximum available gain (M.A.G.) is the upper bound for the transducer gain, the available gain, and the power gain. If both the input side and the output side of the transistor are matched, maximum available gain will occur. This is, of course, the optimum condition. The value of the M.A.G. is determined solely by the parameters of the transistor. Therefore the M.A.G. can be regarded as a *figure of merit* for comparing various transistors or various connections of the transistors.

The transducer gain and the power gain are not so high as the M.A.G. is both the R_s and the R_L are not matched to the input and output, respectively. The available gain, since it is not dependent on R_L, is less than the M.A.G. if the R_s is not matched to the input. As mentioned, then, all three gains become equal when both input and output are matched, and the resulting gain is called M.A.G.

In order to find the correct value (for M.A.G.) of R_s and R_L for a certain transistor, we must write the following equations:

$$R_s = R_i, \qquad R_L = R_o \tag{68}$$

We remember that R_i is a function of R_L (Table 8-5) and R_o is a function of R_s. Therefore the two Equations (68) must be solved as simultaneous equations. Determinants can be used for this solution, and the results are

$$R_s = \sqrt{\frac{\Delta^h h_{11}}{h_{22}}}, \qquad R_L = \sqrt{\frac{h_{11}}{\Delta^h h_{22}}} \tag{69}$$

Knowing the h parameters of the transistor, we can find the matched values of R_L and R_s by using Equation (69). If these values

Small-signal amplifiers

are substituted in Equation (64) for transducer gain, or in Equation (67) for available gain, the M.A.G. is found to be

$$\text{M.A.G.} = \frac{h_{21}^2}{[(\Delta^h)^{1/2} + (h_{11}h_{22})^{1/2}]^2} \qquad (70)$$

It must be emphasized that the M.A.G. is a function of the transistor only and does not depend on R_L or R_s. Thus every transistor has its M.A.G.; whether that gain is achieved in an actual circuit is a question of whether the R_L and R_s fulfill Equation (69). If the matched conditions are used, then *the power gain, the transducer gain, and the available gain are all equal to the M.A.G.* The values of M.A.G. for a junction transistor in the three connections are shown in the bottom of Table 8-5. Again, all the above equations can be used for all three connections by using the proper h parameters.

In the design of transistor amplifiers M.A.G. can be achieved only by the use of impedance-matching transformers. The M.A.G. is therefore a figure of merit for transformed coupled cases. Since transformers are often undesirable, the M.A.G. remains as an optimum value of gain or as a figure of merit for comparison.

EXAMPLE OF SMALL SIGNAL ANALYSIS

It was noted in the beginning of this chapter that the single-stage analysis is useful, not only for single-stage amplifiers, but also for multistage circuits. Here we will illustrate the application of this single-stage method to a two-stage transistor amplifier.

The transistor amplifier is shown in Figure 8-19, and it is seen that two common-emitter amplifiers are connected in cascade. At this point we do not wish to discuss the function of the various elements of this circuit, or their values, as this will be considered later. We will regard this circuit as one whose various performance quantities can be found by the tools developed in this chapter. Note that both transistor stages are biased in the conventional manner: a battery for each lead. We will find later that a two-stage amplifier such as this can be entirely biased from a single battery.

When performing a small-signal analysis, the first step consists of reducing the circuit to its a-c equivalent. This means removing the bias batteries and replacing them by their internal impedance (if any) and removing those resistors that are by-passed by capacitors. Additionally, the coupling capacitors (in Figure 8-19) are removed if their reactance is sufficiently small. The a-c equivalent of Figure 8-19 then, is the circuit of Figure 8-20. Figure 8-20 also shows the

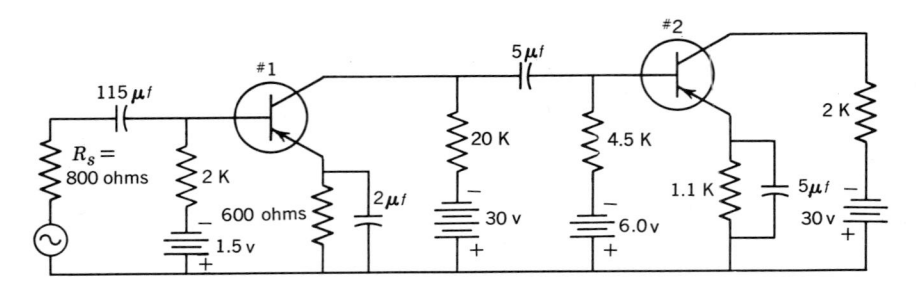

Fig. 8-19. A two-stage common-emitter amplifier.

values of the h^e parameters for both transistors. These values are typical for junction transistors.

Parameters of #1
$h_{ie} = 890$
$h_{re} = 5.89 \times 10^{-4}$
$h_{fe} = 21.2$
$h_{oe} = 2.22 \times 10^{-5}$
$\Delta^{h^e} = 7.25 \times 10^{-3}$

Parameters of #2
$h_{ie} = 2500$
$h_{re} = 2 \times 10^{-3}$
$h_{fe} = 49$
$h_{oe} = 5 \times 10^{-5}$
$\Delta^{h^e} = 2.7 \times 10^{-2}$

Here we do an analysis using the entire equivalent circuit. It is recommended that the reader do an independent analysis of this example using only h_{ie} and h_{fe}, as shown in Figure 8-6, as a comparison.

Since we are going to use the single-stage performance equations derived in this chapter, we need not analyze those parts of the circuit shown within the boxes; i.e., the transistor portion has already been analyzed.

Although we will use the single-stage method of analysis, it is necessary to emphasize its relation to that of the general mesh or nodal method. We could analyze the circuit of Figure 8-20 in its

Small-signal amplifiers

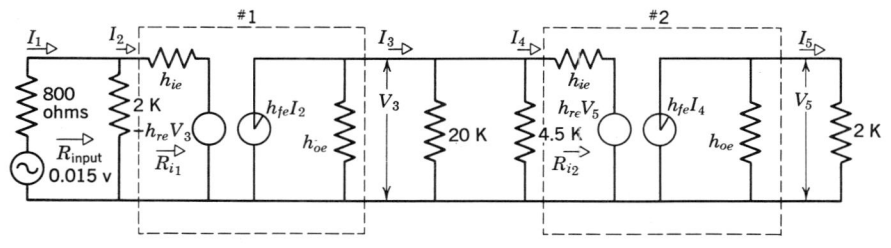

Fig. 8-20. The a-c equivalent of Fig. 8-19.

entirety by writing either mesh or nodal equations. If we did this, we would have to include the actual equivalent circuit of the transistor, as shown within the boxes. This would result in simultaneous equations, the number of equations being equal to the number of meshes (or nodes), and would be solved by determinants. Since even in the case of a two-stage amplifier the number of mesh equations is large, the solution of such simultaneous equations is difficult. This difficulty can be avoided by considering the circuit on a stage-by-stage basis, and using the results we have found in this chapter.

We will use the circuit of Figure 8-20, then, to illustrate the use of the single-stage method. We will find the power gain, the actual output power, and the transducer gain for this circuit.

To find the power gain, the relation equivalent to Equation (19) will be used:

$$A_p = \frac{I_5^2 R_L}{I_1^2 R_i} = A_i^2 \frac{R_L}{R_i} \tag{71}$$

The quantities we have to calculate are the A_i and the R_i. To do this we must begin with the last stage and work to the left.

SECOND STAGE. For the second stage the calculations are direct. Using the previously found equations,

$$A_{i_2} = \frac{I_5}{I_4} = \frac{h_{fe}}{h_{oe}R_L + 1} = \frac{49}{[(5 \times 10^{-5})(2 \times 10^3) + 1]} = 44.5 \tag{72}$$

$$R_{i_2} = \frac{\Delta^h R_L + h_{ie}}{h_{oe}R_L + 1} = \frac{(2.7 \times 10^{-2})(2 \times 10^3) + 2500}{(5 \times 10^{-5})(2 \times 10^3) + 1} = 2322 \tag{73}$$

206   **Small-signal amplifiers**

INTERSTAGE. We need to find the current gain of the interstage because not all of the first-stage output current (I_3) flows into the second-stage input (I_4). Therefore, we need to find the ratio of I_4 to I_3 by using basic circuitry methods. The interstage appears as in

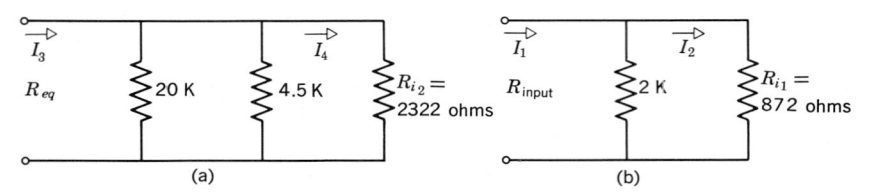

Fig. 8-21. The interstage networks of Fig. 8-20: (a) interstage between stages 1 and 2; (b) interstage between source and stage 1.

Figure 8-21(a). By use of the current division law, the value of I_4 is found to be

$$I_4 = \frac{(20K)(4.5K)/24.5K}{[(20K)(4.5K)/24.5K] + 2322} I_3 = 0.6215 I_3 \qquad (74)$$

The ratio, or current amplification is then

$$(A_i)_{\text{interstage}} = \frac{I_4}{I_3} = 0.6125 \qquad (75)$$

By combining the three parallel resistors of Figure 8-21, the equivalent resistance is found to be

$$\frac{1}{R_{\text{eq}}} = \frac{1}{2322} + \frac{1}{4500} + \frac{1}{20,000} \qquad (76)$$

$$R_{\text{eq}} = 1420$$

FIRST STAGE. It is necessary to know the R_{eq} above because *this forms the load resistance* (R_{L_1}) *of the first stage.* Calculating the current gain and input resistance with this value of R_{L_1},

$$A_{i_1} = \frac{I_3}{I_2} = \frac{h_{fe}}{h_{oe}R_{L_1} + 1} = \frac{21.2}{(2.22 \times 10^{-5})(1.42 \times 10^3) + 1} \qquad (77)$$

$$= 20.5$$

$$R_i = \frac{\Delta^h \cdot R_{L_1} + h_{ie}}{h_{oe}R_{L_1} + 1} = \frac{(7.25 \times 10^{-3})(1.4 \times 10^3) + 890}{(2.22 \times 10^{-5})(1.42 \times 10^3) + 1} \qquad (78)$$

$$= 872$$

Small-signal amplifiers

PRE-FIRST STAGE. We have yet to find the current gain and input resistance for the single resistor preceding the first stage. This must be charged to the amplifier since it is a bias resistor. The simple circuit for this appears in Figure 8-21(b).

$$(A_i)_{\text{pre}} = \frac{I_2}{I_1} = \frac{2000}{2000 + 872} = 0.697 \tag{79}$$

$$R_{\text{input}} = \frac{R_1 R_2}{R_1 + R_2} = \frac{(2 \times 10^3)(872)}{(2 \times 10^3) + 872} = 607 \tag{80}$$

TOTAL POWER GAIN. We can now find the total current gain by simply multiplying all the individual gains:

$$(A_i)_{\text{total}} = \frac{I_5}{I_1} = (0.697)(20.5)(0.6125)(44.5) = 390 \tag{81}$$

The R_i, of course, is equal to the R input found above:

$$R_{\text{input}} = 607 \tag{82}$$

Thus the total power gain is

$$A_p = A_i^2 \frac{R_L}{R_i} = (390)^2 \frac{2 \times 10^3}{607} = 501{,}000 = 57.1 \text{ db} \tag{83}$$

Now we see why it is necessary to begin with the last stage and work to the left. The last-stage input resistance depends upon its load resistance; the previous stage's load resistance depends upon the last-stage input, and so on.

Using this stage-by-stage method, any transistor circuit can be analyzed relatively quickly. Care is needed when finding the a-c equivalent circuit, since this is a critical step in the procedure. Unless great accuracy is required, the reactive elements may usually be eliminated (as was done here) at the frequencies of interest. Following the procedure illustrated above, then, the great number of simultaneous equations otherwise required is avoided.

OUTPUT POWER. Before leaving this example, it is interesting to find the transducer gain and the value of power output. Using the source values as shown in Figure 8-20, the input power supplied by the generator is

$$P_{in} = \frac{V_s^2 R_i}{(R_s - R_i)^2} = \frac{(1.5 \times 10^{-2})^2}{(800 - 607)^2} 607 = 6.9 \times 10^{-8} \text{ watts} \quad (84)$$

Multiplying this by the power gain found above, the power output is

$$P_{out} = P_{in} A_p = (6.9 \times 10^{-8})(5.01 \times 10^5) \\ = 34.6 \times 10^{-3} \text{ watts} = 34.6 \text{ milliwatts} \quad (85)$$

Thus if the load of the circuit consisted of a loudspeaker (with a transformer to transform resistance to 2000 ohms) there would be 34.6 milliwatts of power available for conversion into acoustical energy.

For calculating the transducer gain we need the available power from the generator. This is

$$P_{gen.\ avail.} = \frac{V_s^2}{4R_s} = \frac{(1.5 \times 10^{-2})^2}{4 \times 100} = 7.04 \times 10^{-8} \text{ watt} \quad (86)$$

The transducer gain is then

$$\text{transducer gain} = \frac{P_{out}}{P_{gen.\ avail.}} = \frac{34.6 \times 10^{-3}}{7.04 \times 10^{-8}} \quad (87) \\ = 4.92 \times 10^5 = 56.3 \text{ db}$$

It is noted that the transducer gain is nearly equal to the power gain. Therefore the generator is being utilized efficiently and this is verified by noting the near match between the generator 800 ohms and the input 607 ohms.

In conclusion, then, the single-stage method depicted in this example shows that a multistage network can be analyzed in a straightforward manner without incurring the set of simultaneous equations resulting from use of the general mesh or nodal method.

It is interesting to compare the situation encountered with vacuum tubes to the analysis method just described. For vacuum tubes, the single-stage method is natural because the input of a vacuum tube is isolated from the output. Thus if the equivalent circuit of a vacuum tube is inserted in a network, the resulting circuit is already broken

Small-signal amplifiers

up due to the isolation between grid and plate. Hence the stage-by-stage method is very appropriate. For the transistor, as we have seen, the output is not isolated from the input. This can be stated in this manner: the transistor has internal feedback. Consequently, any network containing a transistor equivalent circuit is a fully connected network and the general mesh or nodal equations seem applicable. However, a great amount of work is saved by using the stage-by-stage method and thus utilizing the performance equations derived in this chapter.

PROBLEMS

1. Assume that the 2N1097 transistor is used in a common emitter audio amplifier, with the h^e parameters (given in Appendix III) specified at $V_{CE} = -5$ v and $I_E = 1$ ma. What would the h parameters be at a V_{CE} of 2 v and an I_E of 10 ma? Use the h parameter curves shown for this transistor.

2. Assume that the 2N3392 transistor is used in a common emitter amplifier, with the h^e parameters being specified (Appendix III) at $V_{CE} = 10$ v, $I_C = 1$ ma. What would the h^e parameters be at a V_C of 2 v and an I_C of 10 ma? Use the correction curves given for this transistor.

3. Assume the 2N3638 transistor is to be used in a common emitter audio amplifier. Let the V_{CC} be -20 v, and an R_L of 2000 ohms. Assume the I_B is -0.10 ma. Use a d-c load line to find the operating point on the characteristics given in Appendix III. Find the new adjusted h^e parameters for this operating point, using the 2N3638 curves.

4. For the h parameters of the 2N1097 (at $V_{CE} = -5$, $I_E = 1$ ma), plot A_i versus R_L. Over what range of R_L is the A_i given approximately by h_{fe}? Plot R_i versus R_L, and find the range over which R_i is given approximately by h_{ie}.

5. Do Problem 3 for the 2N3392 transistor.

6. Using the h^e parameters of the 2N1097 (at $V_{CB} = -5$, $I_E = 1$ ma), plot the power gain A_p versus R_L using log-log paper. At what value of R_L is the power gain maximum?

7. Using the same matrix-equation methods as used in this chapter, derive the common-emitter h parameters in terms of the common-base ones. Start with the circuit arrangements analogous to those

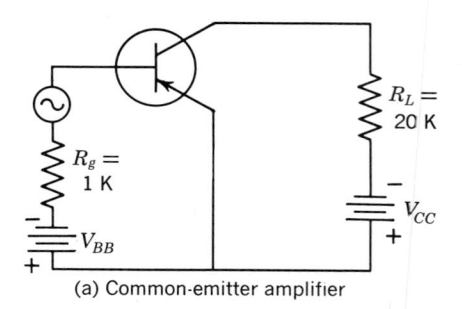

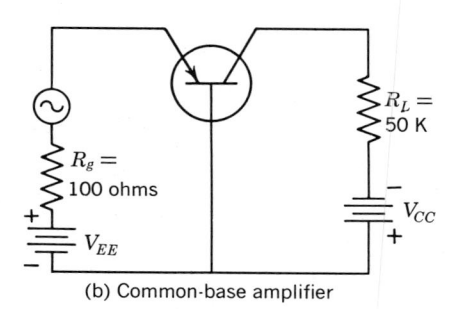

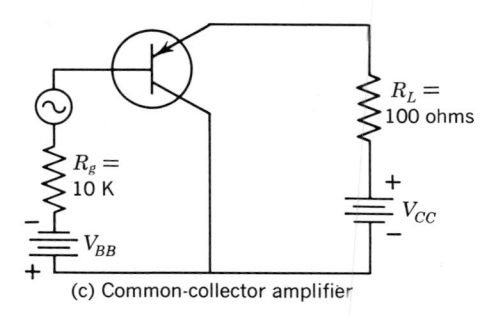

Fig. 8-22. Transistor amplifiers.

(a) Common-emitter amplifier

(b) Common-base amplifier

(c) Common-collector amplifier

Small-signal amplifiers

of Figure 8-10. Then, shorting the output, write two mesh equations for the resulting network. Proceed similarly leaving the input open-circuited. Check Appendix II for correct results.

8. In the same manner as described in Problem 7, derive the common-collector h parameters in terms of the common-base ones. Check Appendix II for correct results.

9. Using the 2N1097 parameters (at $V_{CE} = -5$, $I_E = 1$ ma), find the common-base parameters from the relations in Table 8-3. Plot the power gain A_p versus R_L for this transistor in the common-base connection. Plot on the same graph as the emitter-case (Problem 6) and compare to the emitter-case (use log-log paper).

10. Again using the 2N1097 parameters (at $V_{CE} = -5$, $I_E = 1$ ma) find the common collector parameters from the relations in Table 8-3. Plot the power gain A_p versus R_L for the transistor in the common-collector connection. Plot on the same graph as the A_p's of Problem 6 and 9, and compare them (use log-log paper).

11. Find and plot the current gain versus R_L for the 2N1097 (at $V_{CE} = -5$, $I_E = 1$ ma) for the common-emitter, the common-base, and the common-collector connection.

12. Assume that a given common-emitter stage, using the 2N1097 (at $V_{CE} = -5$, $I_E = 1$ ma) has an R_L of 5K ohms. Assume that a common-emitter stage precedes the given one (using same transistor). What is the current gain and power gain of the preceding stage (ignoring any bias circuitry)? Compare these values to those found if one used only the h_{ie} and h_{fe} equivalent circuit for both stages, as shown in Figure 8-6.

13. What is the power gain of each of the transistor amplifiers shown in Figure 8-22? The common-base h parameters for the transistor used in these circuits are $h_{ib} = 50$ ohms, $h_{rb} = 5 \times 10^{-4}$, $h_{fb} = -0.97$, and $h_{ob} = 10^{-6}$ mho. Find the emitter and collector parameters by using the relations of Problems 7 and 8, or Appendix II.

14. What are the transducer gains for the amplifiers of Figure 8-22?

15. Calculate the available gains for the circuits of Figure 8-22.

16. What are the maximum available gains for the circuits of Figure 8-22?

17. How do the stage gains compare with the transducer gains, available gains, and maximum available gains for the amplifiers of Figure 8-22?

212   Small-signal amplifiers

18. Analyze the total power gain of the circuit shown in Figure 8-19 by using only the simplified equivalent (transistor) circuit of Figure 8-6. Follow the same procedure as used in the "Example" section.

19. Calculate the gain of the two-stage amplifier shown in Figure 8-23. Show the gain of the two individual stages and the interstage losses. Use the same transistor parameters as in Problem 11. The internal resistance of the generator is 1000 ohms.

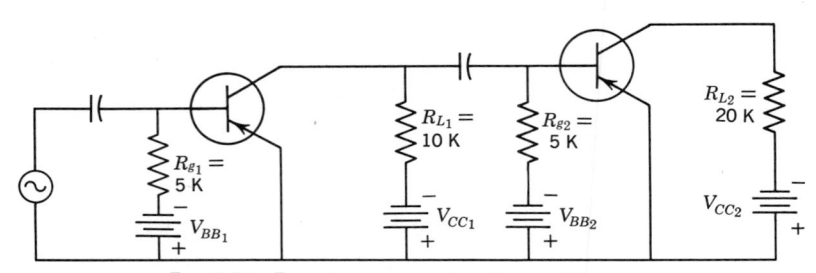

Fig. 8-23. Two-stage common-emitter amplifier.

20. Assume that the 2N3394 transistor is used in the circuit of Figure 8-24. Assume also that the typical h^e parameters given in the Appendix apply to the operating point for this transistor. Assume the capacitors are a short-circuit at the frequencies of interest. Find the power gain, current gain, voltage gain, and input resistance for this stage.

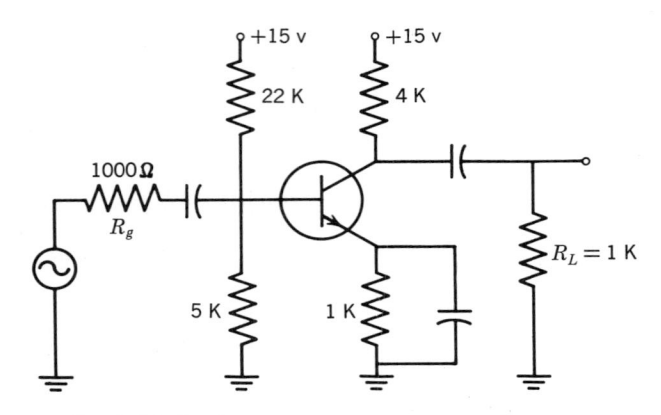

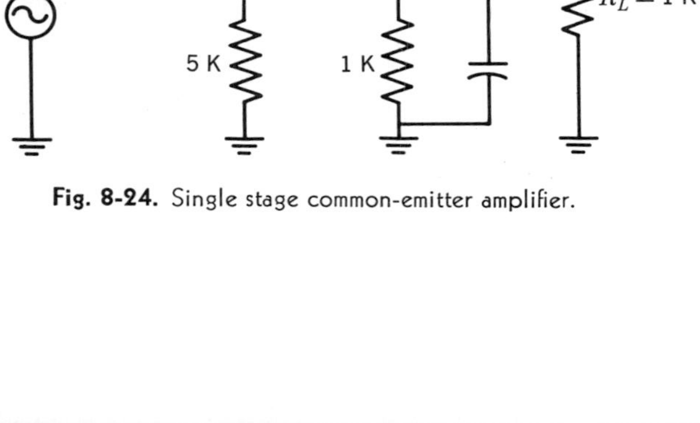

Fig. 8-24. Single stage common-emitter amplifier.

Small-signal amplifiers

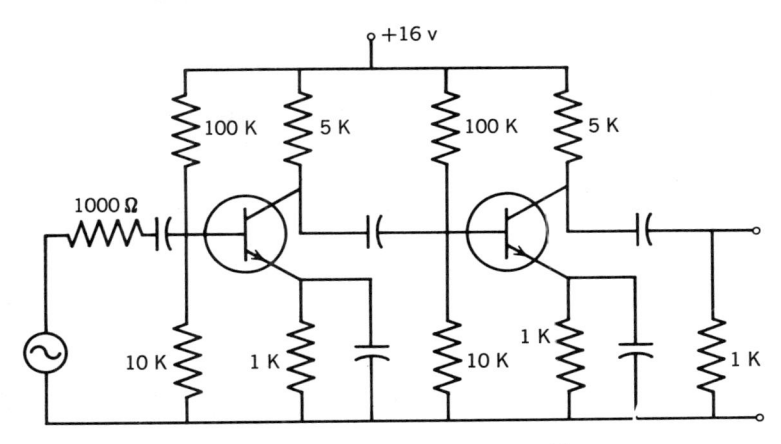

Fig. 8-25. Two-stage common-emitter amplifier.

21. Assume the 2N3394 transistor is used in the two-stage circuit of Figure 8-25. Use the typical h^e parameters and ignore any correction for operating point. What is the power gain, current gain, and input resistance for this circuit?

9

Power amplifiers

A general situation that occurs in electronic circuits consists of having a series of cascaded amplifiers that amplify a very small signal until sufficient power is available to perform some useful work (such as drive a radio speaker). In such a situation the signal level grows with each stage until the final stage is reached.

For analyzing such a series of cascaded amplifiers, the first few stages may usually be treated as small-signal amplifiers and the methods of the previous chapter are applicable. The stages following these small-signal amplifiers, however, will be operating at a higher signal level so that the equivalent circuit method is no longer accurate. It is remembered from Chapter 7 that the parameters of an equivalent circuit are applicable only within a small region of a specified operating point. If the transistor operation swings over a region greater than this, the equivalent circuit becomes inaccurate, and the graphical characteristics should be used to make design decisions. Many times, of course, a single large-signal amplifier will be encountered, and again the graphical characteristics should be consulted.

In general, the last stage of a series of cascaded stages is called the *power stage*. The power amplifier is distinguished from all the stages

Power amplifiers

that precede it in that here a concentrated effort is made *to obtain a maximum output power*. In this chapter it will be seen that, because of physical limitations, this criterion conflicts with the criterion of maximum power gain. Also the problem of distortion appears. A transistor that is suitable for a power amplifier is usually called a *power transistor*. Power transistors differ from other types in a number of ways. For one thing, they are always larger and contain means for conducting heat away from the collector junction.

Although specifically treating power amplifiers, *this chapter should also be construed as dealing with the methods of large-signal amplifiers in general*. In other words, this chapter will indicate a number of ways in which the graphical characteristics are useful in making design decisions. If the circuit of interest is not a power amplifier, the performance criterion will probably be the same as for the small-signal amplifiers—maximum *power gain*. For example, the stage (or stages) immediately preceding the power amplifier usually require a large-signal analysis, and are called *driver* stages. For these driver stages, *maximum* power gain is generally the basic criterion.

Power amplifiers are classified according to their mode of operation as Class A, Class B, or a combination of Class A and B referred to as Class A-B. For transistors, the important types are Class A and Class B. Class C, another type, is not discussed here since it is not useful at audio frequencies.

It is the object of this chapter to describe and analyze typical Class A and Class B power amplifiers. The transistor graphical characteristics will be used to portray the action and to help analyze the performance. Although the design of electronic circuits can never be reduced to a set procedure, a design example will be given for each type of power amplifier to illustrate the general approach.

PERFORMANCE QUANTITIES

As stated, the prime objective for a power amplifier is to obtain the maximum output power. Since the transistor, like every electronic device, has voltage, current, and power dissipation limits, the criteria for a power amplifier are: (1) power output; (2) distortion; and (3) power dissipation capability. An additional criterion is frequency response, but we shall here restrict the analysis to those frequencies where the characteristics are accurate.

PHYSICAL LIMITATIONS. Before considering the actual performance quantities it is necessary to consider the current, voltage, and power limitations of the transistor.

The voltage limitation applies mainly to the collector junction since this is the junction that experiences the high bias voltage in both the common-base and the common-emitter connections. At voltage breakdown the semiconductor crystal structure changes, and current rises rapidly. If the collector-to-emitter suffers such voltage breakdown it is due either to the collector-base junction breakdown or to a "reach through" or "punch through" from the collector to the emitter. The collector-base junction breakdown may be due either to the Zener effect or to the *avalanche* property; the effects of these two are similar. It was noted in Chapter 5 that the Zener effect or "tunneling" may be induced if an excessive voltage is applied to a semiconductor junction. For any of the above reasons, then, every transistor has a maximum allowable collector voltage that is specified by the manufacturer.

The manufacturer usually supplies a list of "maximum ratings" under which the breakdown voltages will be listed. This list usually includes the following:

BV_{CBO}, breakdown voltage, collector to base, emitter open
BV_{CEO}, breakdown voltage, collector to emitter, base open
BV_{EBO}, breakdown voltage, emitter to base, collector open.

The significance of these ratings is simply that the circuit designer must make sure that they are not exceeded under any conditions. All possible temperature variations and parameter changes between units must be considered.

The maximum limitation on collector current stems from one of two sources. Since the current gain falls at high currents, some manufacturers specify as the maximum that collector current at which the β has fallen by a certain percentage. The other current limitation occurs when the product of the maximum current and the accompanying voltage exceeds the allowed collector dissipation.

The allowable power dissipation of the transistor is a very important item for power transistors. Both of the transistor junctions have diode-type resistances which produce I^2R power losses. Since the reverse-biased collector junction has a much higher resistance than the emitter junction, the collector junction effectively produces all the heat. Since any temperature changes influence the semiconductor operation of the transistor (Chapter 4), the heat generated by these

Power amplifiers

power losses must be dissipated to the surroundings. The amount of heat that can be dissipated depends almost entirely upon the physical construction of the transistor and the temperature of the surroundings (ambient temperature). Sometimes provision is made to fasten the transistor on a heat-conducting body, such as a chassis, so that additional heat can be dissipated in this manner. Therefore every transistor will have a specified value of power which it can dissipate under specified conditions; this value is always stated by the manufacturer. If the design conditions specify a temperature higher than that quoted by the manufacturer, the given dissipation value must be derated accordingly (discussed below).

Manufacturers' methods of presenting dissipation data still vary considerably, and caution is essential. First of all, it is imperative to distinguish carefully between the dissipation data that are given for "free air ambient temperature" and the dissipation data that are given for "case temperature." If the data are stated for free air temperature, the dissipation data take account of the rate at which the transistor can be cooled in a given room or ambient temperature. If the data are indicated for the case temperature it is implied that there is an infinite heat sink available so that the case can be kept at the given temperature. It is clear that the dissipation data for the case temperatures will always be higher than for free air temperatures. With power transistors in which some overt heat sink capability is likely to be required, the manufacturer often quotes the dissipation both for a case and an ambient temperature. For low power transistors, it is more common to state the dissipation in terms of free air (ambient) temperature.

The allowable dissipation for a transistor, as a function of temperature, appears as shown in Figure 9-1. It is noted that a given

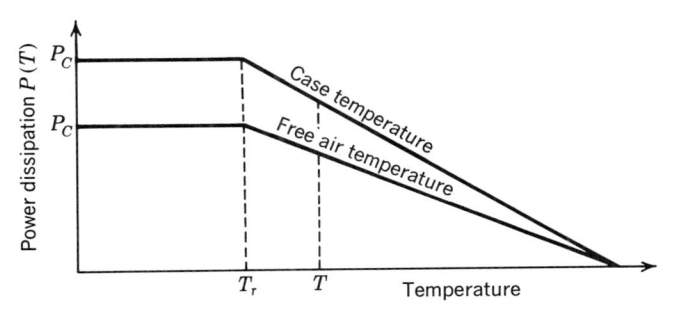

Fig. 9-1. Allowable transistor dissipation as a function of temperature.

power dissipation holds up to a certain temperature (this reference temperature is usually 25°C), and that above this temperature the stated dissipation figure must be derated according to some linear law. Note how the "case temperature" and the "free air temperature" curves differ. Either of these curves can be described by the mathematical equation

$$P_C(T) = P_C - \frac{(T - T_r)}{\Theta} \qquad (1)$$

where $P_C(T)$ = maximum permissible collector dissipation at a given case or a free air temperature,
P_C = maximum permissible collector dissipation at the reference temperature (usually 25°C),
T = the given case (or free air) temperature,
T_r = reference temperature (usually 25°C),
Θ = thermal resistance, junction to case (or junction to free air).

If the desired operating temperature is above the reference temperature, Equation (1) can be used to derate the stated (reference) power dissipation. The manufacturer always supplies the approximate derating factor (Θ). As noted, this standard derating equation may be applied to either the case temperature data or the free air room temperature data. To reiterate, in either case it is necessary to be cautious as to which one is stated in a given application.

In addition to items in the above equation, the manufacturer usually provides the "maximum temperature" allowed for the junction. In many cases this temperature specifies the maximum temperature during storage in addition to the maximum operating junction temperature. If this maximum temperature is given, one can calculate the value of Θ by taking the difference in temperature $T - T_r$ divided by the power (P) at the reference temperature.

In any event, the maximum collector dissipation is a very important design consideration. The most direct effect of this power limitation upon the design of power amplifiers is that the product of the voltage and current of the operating point should never exceed the maximum power dissipation. We shall see the reason for this in a later section. For any transistor, then, we can draw a curve of constant power dissipation; that is, a curve on which the product of current and voltage at any point is equal to the allowable power dissipation. We shall see such a curve in the next section.

Power amplifiers

With regard to power dissipation, one must be particularly careful to avoid a condition known as "thermal runaway." This is a situation where, due to a small temperature increase, the power dissipation increases. This in turn may cause another temperature increase. If this cycle were to continue, the maximum junction temperature would be exceeded and the junction would be destroyed. Bias conditions to avoid this are treated in Chapter 11. An adequate heat sink can also prevent such thermal runaway.

POWER OUTPUT. At first the problem of obtaining a maximum output power may seem identical with the problem of obtaining an optimum power gain, as for the small-signal amplifiers. However, the voltage and current limitations specify that power gain be sacrificed for a maximum power output. A simple example will serve to illustrate this.

Figure 9-2 shows characteristics typical of a low voltage power transistor. On these characteristics the curved line is the power dissipation curve mentioned in the preceding section. The operating point should never be placed in the region to the right of this curve. Figure 9-2(a) also shows the maximum allowable current and voltage values for this transistor on the respective axes.

The *saturation region* and the *cutoff region* of the transistor can also be seen in Figure 9-2. The saturation region begins when the I_B curves blend together because there is not sufficient reverse voltage on the collector junction for normal transistor operation. The cutoff region starts at the $I_B = 0$ curve. This particular curve is also called the I_{CEO} curve. In Figure 9-2 the I_{CEO} value is so small that the curve coincides with the horizontal axis. These regions, along with the maximum current and voltage, limit the region of operation in transistors. The region of normal transistor action, it is remembered, is called the *active* region.

Referring to Chapter 7 for the construction of load lines, we see that if an operating point on the dissipation curve is used, the loads 1 and 2 can be used without exceeding the maximum values of current and voltage. These load lines correspond to the operating points Q_1 and Q_2 (for equal swings) and load resistances of 19 ohms and 3.6 ohms, respectively.

It was stated in the previous chapter that maximum power gain is realized if the load is matched to the output resistance. The tran-

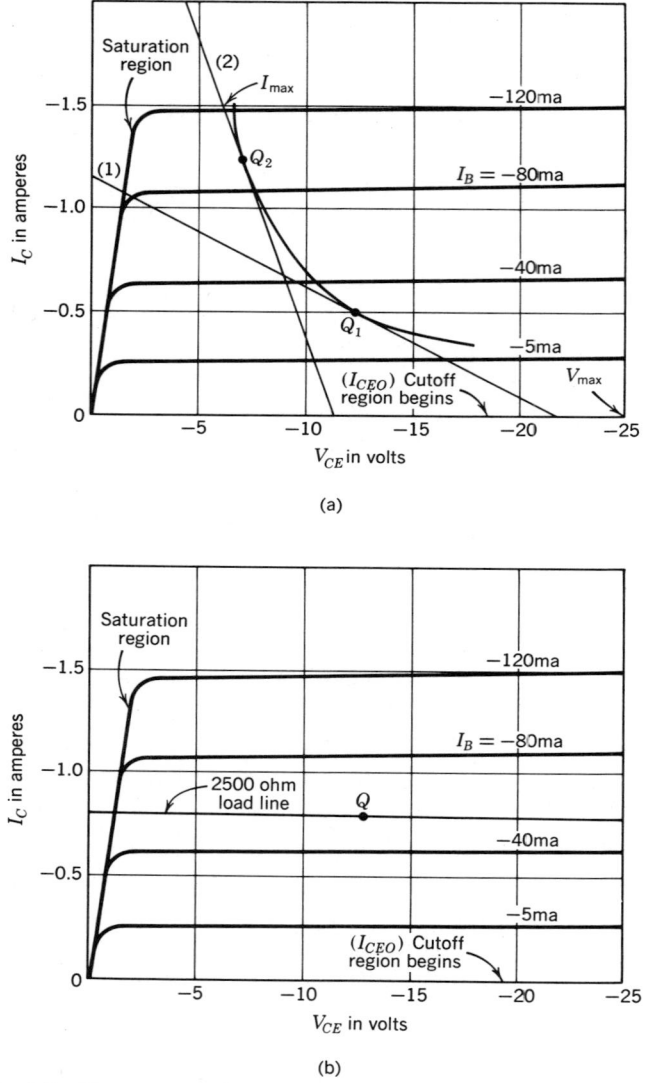

Fig. 9-2. Characteristics showing permissible load lines with current and voltage limitations.

sistor of Figure 9-2(a) has an output resistance of approximately 2500 ohms; the load line for a load resistance of 2500 ohms is shown in Figure 9-2(b).

By comparing Figures 9-2(a) and 9-2(b) we can see why power gain is sacrificed to obtain a maximum power output. Although

Power amplifiers

the power gain of Figure 9-2(b) is high, only an extremely small input base current swing is allowed before the transistor either saturates or exceeds the maximum allowed voltage. Therefore the power output of Figure 9-2(b) is much less than for either of the loads shown in Figure 9-2(a).

It is for this reason that power output, in addition to power gain, must be considered for large signal amplifiers. Usually one selects a load resistance that is a compromise between these two factors.

In large signal amplifiers another useful measure of performance is *collector efficiency*, which is defined as the ratio of the a-c output power to the d-c input power supplied by the battery.

$$\text{collector eff.} = \frac{\text{a-c output power}}{\text{battery input power}} \qquad (2)$$

A conclusion, then, is that for small-signal amplifiers and some driver stages a maximum power gain is the desirable goal, whereas for power amplifiers a maximum power output and collector efficiency is usually the goal. This is a design difference between the small-signal and power amplifiers.

DISTORTION. Whenever large signals are applied to electronic devices such as the transistor and the vacuum tube, the problem of distortion immediately arises because each of these devices is essentially nonlinear. We noted this in Chapter 7, when it was seen that the equivalent circuit parameters change for different points on the set of characteristics. If the transistor were perfectly linear, one set of parameters would be suitable for all regions on the characteristics.

Although some distortion is present even in small-signal amplifiers, its effect is much more severe for large-signal cases. This is the reason for taking up the issue here.

The result of distortion is that the output signal is not exactly like the input signal. Thus the amount of distortion present can be regarded as determining the "accuracy" of the electronic circuit. It is clear that an equivalent circuit analysis ignores distortion since the transistor is assumed to be linear for small variations about an operating point.

A common measure of distortion is the amount of *second harmonic distortion*. If a pure sine wave is applied to a power amplifier the distortion can be measured by noting the variation from the sine wave in the output. Since a nonsine wave can be considered the sum of a series of sine waves of different frequencies (Fourier analysis), the nonsine-wave output can be analyzed in this manner. The value of the second harmonic distortion (alone) is only a first approximation to the total distortion.

We shall briefly analyze the distortion values for the amplifiers considered here and also discuss the equations and methods.

CLASS A POWER AMPLIFIERS

Amplifiers are defined as Class A, Class B, or Class A-B depending upon where the bias point is placed with respect to the total swing of the signal. Class A operation occurs when the bias point is placed so that the signal swing does not carry the operation out of the region of normal transistor action, namely the active region. The small-signal amplifiers discussed in the preceding chapter were implicitly regarded as Class A.

Since the power amplifier is a large-signal device we shall use the method of graphical analysis to describe it; the concepts discussed in Chapter 7 will be relied upon. It was shown that the essential concept consists of superimposing the graph of the attached circuit on the graph of the transistor characteristics. Although both the common-base and the common-emitter connections are suitable for Class A amplifiers, the common emitter is used much more frequently than the common base.

Figure 9-3 shows the conventional common-emitter circuit and the graphical operation. This basic arrangement is often called "direct-coupled" since the *load* is directly connected to the transistor, without intervening capacitor or transformer. It is remembered from Chapter 7 that the load line for this case is determined by the collector battery and the value of the load resistance. The operating point occurs, on the load line, at the proper value of input (base) current. The total swing is then determined by the variation in input current produced by the signal.

This direct coupled case is usually not suitable for power amplifiers, since one usually must keep d-c current from flowing in the load. The load for the power amplifier is usually a magnetic transducer, such as a loudspeaker coil. Consequently, one needs a capacitor

Power amplifiers

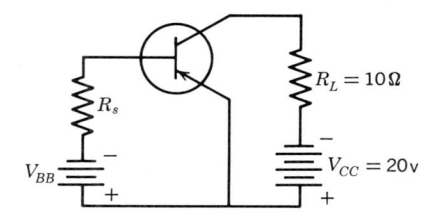

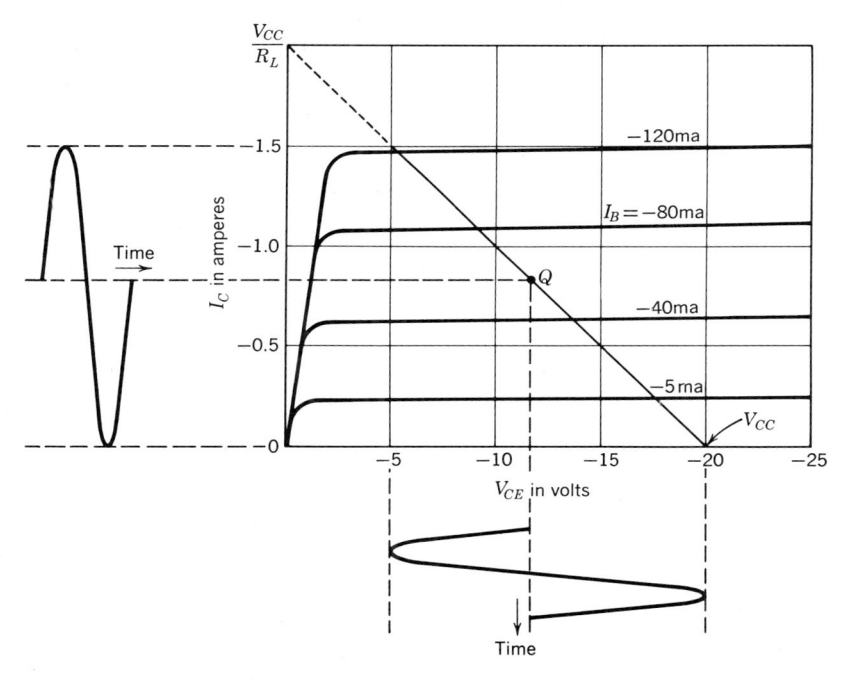

Fig. 9-3. Direct-coupled common-emitter circuit with its graphical operation.

coupling, a transformer coupling, or some circuit arrangement which presents d-c current in the load. The typical *RC* coupling, with its d-c load resistance (and its a-c one), is not suitable for Class A power amplifiers because large amounts of power are wasted in the d-c load resistance.

A circuit that would eliminate the d-c power losses is shown in Figure 9-4(a), and is called the *shunt-fed* circuit. An essential feature is that, for the output side, separate paths are provided for the a-c

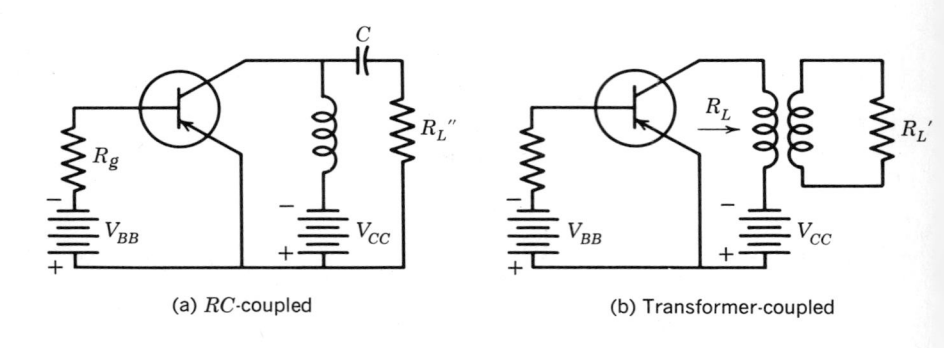

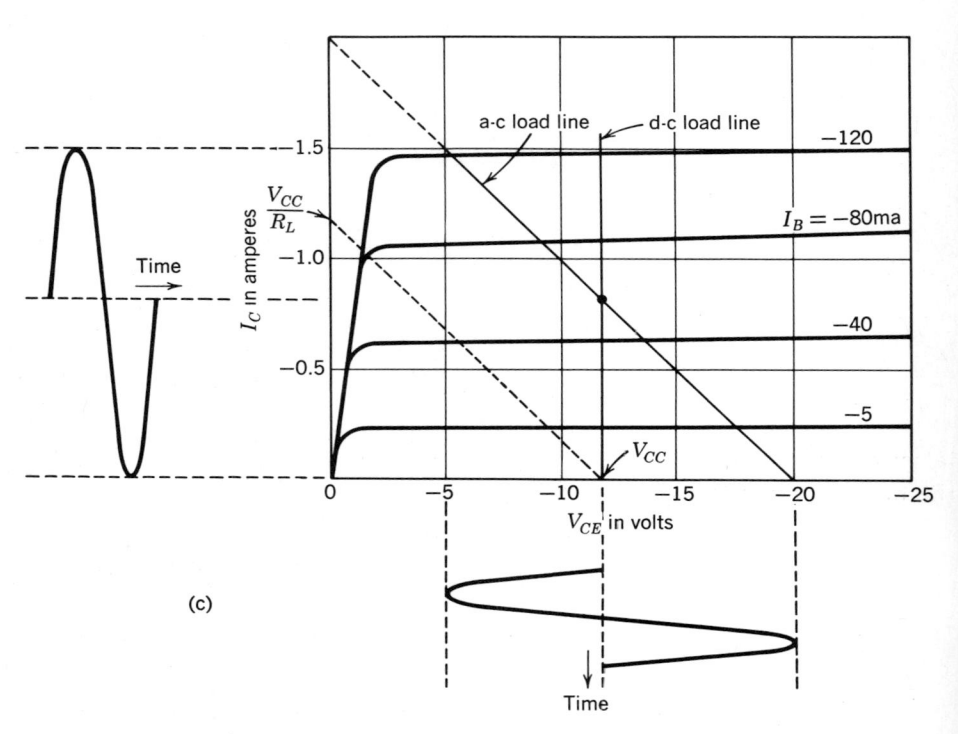

Fig. 9-4. (a) Shunt-fed emitter amplifier; (b) transformer-coupled emitter amplifier; (c) load lines for circuits of (a) and (b).

Power amplifiers

signal and the d-c bias currents. The inductor provides practically a zero resistance path for the biasing direct current. The d-c power losses are almost zero, while the inductor presents a high impedance to the a-c signal so that it flows through the load resistance. This circuit has the disadvantage of requiring both an inductive and a very large capacitive element.

A more frequent solution to the coupling problem for power amplifiers is the use of a transformer, as shown in Figure 9-4(b). This separates the a-c and the d-c paths in a manner similar to the above, except now the coupling to the load is inductive. An additional feature here is that any value of R'_L can be transformed to a suitable R_L by varying the turns-ratio of the transformer. Note that R_L, and not R'_L, is the load resistance used for the load line. This type of output circuit is very common for power amplifiers.

Since the a-c and the d-c loads of these circuits are not the same, we have to construct two separate load lines; one to find the d-c operating point and the other to depict the operation when an a-c signal is present. The first step is to construct the d-c load line in the manner reviewed above. Since the d-c resistance is smaller than the a-c, the d-c load line will be more vertical. If the d-c resistance is practically zero, the d-c load line appears vertical as shown in Figure 9-4(c). After the operating point is determined, the a-c load is constructed to pass through this point. This a-c load line may be constructed by momentarily assuming that the a-c load is the only one present. The resulting line must then be moved parallel to itself until it intercepts the operating point. Figure 9-4(c) suggests this process. This a-c load line, then, must be used to depict the a-c operation of the circuit.

It is important to stress that, for *any* circuit in which the a-c and the d-c load values are not the same, the two separate load lines must be constructed—the d-c load line to determine the operating point, and the a-c load line to find the a-c operation. This situation is very common and occurs whenever amplifiers are coupled by capacitors or transformers. Therefore, *for any large-signal analysis, the two load lines must be constantly kept in mind.*

In Figure 9-4 it is noted that, since the same value of a-c load resistance is used, the a-c operation is identical to that of Figure 9-3. The difference is that the circuits of Figure 9-3 and 9-4 need smaller batteries to achieve the same operating point, and their power efficiency is higher.

OPERATING POINT. For Class A amplifiers, the choice of operating point depends upon the total swing of the signal and the allowable power dissipation of the transistor. In general, the operating point may be placed at any point to the left of the *constant dissipation* curve. Usually it is placed about midway between the saturation and the cutoff region so that equal swings on either side of the bias point can occur without clipping.

The constant power dissipation curve, shown before in Figure 9-1, is calculated in the following manner: select a value of voltage on the V_{CE} axis; divide this voltage into the value of maximum power dissipation stated by the manufacturer—the result is the allowable collector current for the chosen value of voltage; finally, plot the resulting point on the graph. The above procedure can be defined by the equation

$$P_{\text{diss}} = V_{CE}I_C = \text{constant} \tag{3}$$

If this equation is used for the whole range of voltage values, the curve shown in Figure 9-1 will result.

It has been mentioned previously that the power dissipation curve, stated by the manufacturer, usually applies to either a case temperature or a room temperature of 25°C. If other temperatures are encountered, the allowable dissipation must be altered as described above.

If the maximum possible output of the transistor is required, the operating point should be placed on or near the dissipation curve. If less power output is required, any suitable point in the region to the left of the dissipation curve is permissible.

LOAD. With the operating point set, the next step is to decide upon the load resistance. The general idea is to select a load line that allows equal swings on either side of the operating point. This can be approximated graphically by placing a ruler on the bias point and rotating it.

Within the restriction of equal swings, it is generally best to use the higher values of load resistance that are suitable. Even though this may result in the same power output it will increase the power gain somewhat. Consequently, less power will be needed to drive the power amplifier to its full output.

Power amplifiers

PERFORMANCE EQUATIONS. We are interested here in calculating the power output, the collector efficiency, and the amount of distortion for sine-wave signals. Figure 9-5 shows the graphical operation obtained with either the direct-coupled or the transformer-coupled circuit provided that the same R_L is used for both.

Since the load is resistive we can calculate the a-c power output by multiplying the alternating voltage by the alternating current. This a-c power is independent of the bias conditions and depends only on the maximum and minimum values of output waves. Referring to Figure 9-5, the maximum value of the sine-wave output voltage is

$$V_m = \frac{V_{max} - V_{min}}{2} \tag{4}$$

Remembering that the rms value of a sine wave is determined by dividing V_m by $\sqrt{2}$:

$$V_{rms} = \frac{V_{max} - V_{min}}{2\sqrt{2}} \tag{5}$$

Performing the same operation for the current,

$$I_{rms} = \frac{I_{max} - I_{min}}{2\sqrt{2}} \tag{5a}$$

The a-c power output, consequently, is

$$P_{out} = V_{rms} I_{rms} = \frac{(V_{max} - V_{min})(I_{max} - I_{min})}{8} \tag{6}$$

To find the collector efficiency, we need to know the power supplied by the battery. Since the battery can supply only d-c power, the power must be the product of V_{CC} and I_C:

$$P_{battery} = V_{CC} I_C \tag{7}$$

Although the output alternating current may flow through the battery as in (a) of Figure 9-5, the battery itself supplies only I_C. It is useful to regard the total output current as an a-c sine wave superimposed on the d-c component I_C.

228   **Power amplifiers**

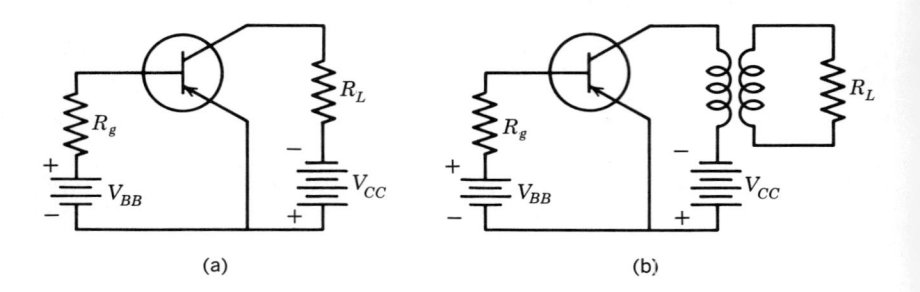

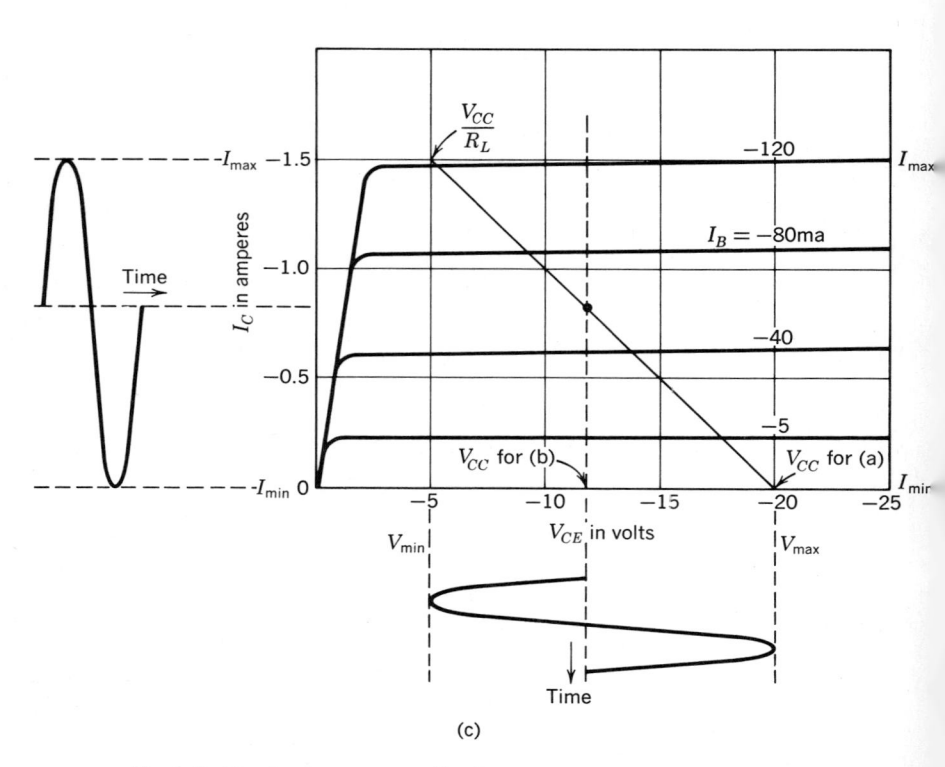

Fig. 9-5. Graphical operation of both conventional and transformer-coupled Class A, common-emitter operation.

Power amplifiers

The collector efficiency, then, is given by the ratio of Equation (6) to Equation (7).

$$\text{collector eff.} = \frac{P_{\text{output}}}{P_{\text{input}}} = \frac{(V_{\max} - V_{\min})(I_{\max} - I_{\min})}{8V_{cc}I_c} \quad (8)$$

Equation (8) tells us how much of the input battery power is converted to useful a-c output power. In this sense the transistor acts as a *convertor;* it converts d-c input power to a-c output power.

It is useful to find the "ideal" collector efficiencies for the circuits of Figure 9-5(a) and (b); that is, the collector efficiencies if the transistor were ideal. An ideal transistor in this sense would have both zero saturation resistance and an I_{CEO} of zero. The zero saturation resistance would mean that the I_B curves would extend linearly to the left and intersect the I_C axis. If I_{CEO} were zero, the $I_B = 0$ curve would lie on the horizontal (V_{CE}) axis. For the direct-coupled circuit of (a), the maximum possible voltage swing for an ideal transistor would be

$$V_{\max} - V_{\min} = V_{cc} \quad (9)$$

For this condition, the current swing would be

$$I_{\max} - I_{\min} = 2I_C \quad (10)$$

Substituting these two relations into Equation (8),

$$\text{ideal coll. eff.} = \frac{V_{cc}2I_c}{8V_{cc}I_c} = 25\% \quad (11)$$

Therefore the ideal collector efficiency for the direct-coupled circuit of Figure 9-5(a) is 25 per cent.

For the transformer-coupled circuit of (b), the fact that V_{CC} equals V_{CE} at the operating point results in maximum possible swings (for an ideal transistor) of

$$\begin{aligned} V_{\max} - V_{\min} &= 2V_{cc} \\ I_{\max} - I_{\min} &= 2I_c \end{aligned} \quad (12)$$

The ideal collector efficiency then is

$$\text{ideal coll. eff.} = \frac{(2V_{cc})(2I_c)}{8V_{cc}I_c} = 50\% \quad (13)$$

Consequently the ideal collector efficiency for the transformer-coupled circuit is 50 per cent. It is now clear why the transformer-coupled circuit may be desirable for Class A power amplifiers.

Although an ideal efficiency can never be reached since the transistor itself is never ideal, it can be closely approximated by a good design. Ideal efficiencies are useful for comparing the various connections and for making preliminary approximate calculations.

Making use of the above power relations, we may now find the dissipation power for the transistor. We have simply to write a power equation:

$$P_{in} = P_{output} + P_{losses} \tag{14}$$

Since any input power on the base (input) side is negligible compared with the powers on the collector side, the only essential input power is supplied by the collector battery. Then

$$P_{battery} = P_{output} + \text{d-c losses in load resistance} + P_{diss.\ of\ transistor} \tag{15}$$

This equation applies to both circuits (a) and (b) if it is remembered that, for any transformer-coupled circuit, the d-c load resistance losses are zero. We may write then

$$V_{cc}I_c = P_{output} + I_c^2 R_{Ldc} + P_{diss} \tag{16}$$

Solving for the P_{diss},

$$\begin{aligned} P_{diss} &= V_{cc}I_c - I_c^2 R_L - P_{output} \\ &= I_c(V_{cc} - I_c R_L) - P_{output} \end{aligned} \tag{17}$$

From the circuit of Figure 9-5(a), a simple d-c mesh equation will verify that $V_{CE} = V_{cc} - I_c R_L$; for the circuit (b), $V_{cc} \cong V_{CE}$ and $R_{L_{d-c}} = 0$. Therefore, for either case,

$$P_{diss} = V_{CE}I_c - P_{output} \tag{18}$$

Since $V_{CE}I_C$ is the operating point, *we now see why the operating point is restricted by the dissipation curve mentioned earlier.*

If there is no a-c power output, momentarily, Equation (18) tells us the transistor must dissipate a power equal to the product of V_{CE} and I_C. This is why it is necessary to calculate the power dissipation curve and keep the operating point to the left of this curve. Since an operating amplifier does not always have a signal present, the design

Power amplifiers

must be based on the worst condition; i.e., when no signal is present. Note that this applies to both direct-coupled and transformer-coupled circuits.

We can now find the relation between the required transistor power dissipation and the desired output power. For the transformer-coupled circuit the V_{cc} is practically equal to the V_{CE} (see Figure 9-5). Then the dissipation, for the worst condition of no signal, must be

$$P_{\text{diss}} = V_{cc}I_c = P_{\text{battery}} \tag{19}$$

Since the ideal collector efficiency, for the transformer-coupled case, is 50 per cent, the ideal power out is

$$(P_{\text{out}})_{\text{ideal}} = 0.50 P_{\text{battery}} \tag{20}$$

Then, using Equation (19), the dissipation capability required is

$$P_C > (P_{\text{diss}})_{\text{ideal}} = \frac{(P_{\text{out}})_{\text{ideal}}}{0.50} = 2(P_{\text{out}})_{\text{ideal}} \tag{21}$$

The allowed dissipation power for a given transistor is termed P_C, as discussed before. Above we have seen that the P_C must be at least twice the maximum sine-wave power output for Class A operation.

For the conventional circuit with a series load resistance, the V_{CE} is approximately $V_{cc}/2$ if an ideal full swing is used. Using the 25 per cent ideal efficiency of this circuit and performing the same operations as above, Equation (21) is found to hold for this circuit also.

Since an ideal efficiency is never achieved, the required dissipation will always be somewhat greater than that specified by Equation (21). Therefore, for any required output power in Class A operation, *the transistor must be capable of dissipating greater than twice the amount of output power.* This criterion is very useful for the initial selection of a transistor.

DISTORTION. The two most basic sources of distortion in Class A amplifiers are (1) nonequal spacing between constant-current curves along the load line (called output distortion), and (2) the nonlinear input resistance (called input distortion). Certain amounts of these distortions are inevitable and one must compromise to minimize the effects. Another possible source of distortion occurs when the operation moves either into the saturation or the cutoff region of the transistor. This happens when too large a signal is used for the given conditions, or if the bias point moves with temperature changes. These latter factors can, of course, be prevented with proper design.

Whereas the common-emitter characteristics have noticeable output distortion caused by nonequal spacing of the curves, the common-base characteristics are quite uniformly spaced, as mentioned in Chapter 7. In spite of this the common-emitter amplifier is overwhelmingly used as a power amplifier because one can use feedback (discussed in Chapter 12) to reduce the distortion of the common-emitter connection.

The nonlinear input resistance is the source of *input* distortion for transistor power amplifiers. By "nonlinear" we mean that the input resistance changes for different values of input current (or voltage). Figure 9-6 shows the general effect of applying a sine-wave voltage

(a) Sine-wave voltage (b) Nonlinear resistance (c) Resulting current

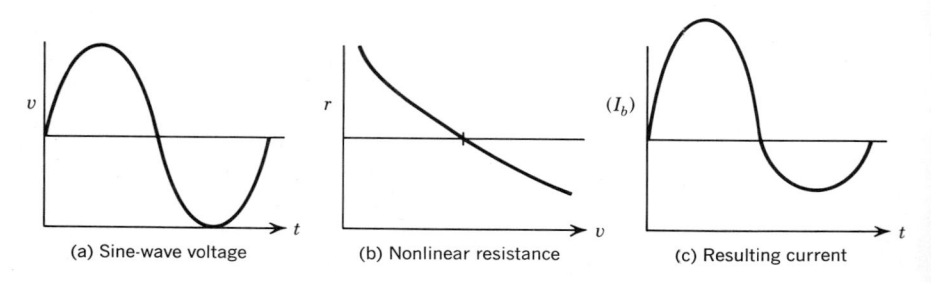

Fig. 9-6. Sketches showing current resulting from sine-wave voltage applied to a nonlinear resistance (input distortion).

to a nonlinear resistance. Part (b) shows that the nonlinear resistance decreases with increase in current, (a) shows the applied sine-wave voltage, and (c) indicates the resulting current. It is seen that the current is flattened on the bottom and exhibits a peak at the top. The action depicted here is grossly typical of the I that results if a low-impedance sine-wave source feeds a forward-biased P-N junction.

This is the current that would be amplified if a constant voltage source (or a source with a very low internal resistance) were used as the drive for the common-emitter transistor amplifier (causing input distortion).

If the stage were fed by a source with a very high internal impedance, it would appear as a constant-current source to the tran-

Power amplifiers

sistor and the input distortion would then be negligible. However, the output would be an amplified version of this input current, which would be exposed to the output distortion.

This output distortion, caused by the relative crowding of the constant I_B curves at high I_C values (which can be seen on most collector characteristics) causes the opposite effect to that shown in Figure 9-6. Thus, the upward current cycle is flattened, relative to the downward one. It is quickly seen that the input distortion and the output distortion are somewhat opposing. This factor creates a range of source resistances for which the total distortion is minimized. For the common-emitter stage typical values of source resistance vary from one to three times the normal input resistance.

Although the common emitter has inherently more distortion than the base connection, the common emitter is used almost entirely for power amplifiers because of the fact that the distortion can also be reduced by feedback. This is considered in Chapter 12.

Distortion caused by clipping occurs when the signal swings into the saturation or the cutoff regions (defined in Figure 9-1). Both saturation and cutoff would cause the output sine wave to be flat-topped. If the allowable power dissipation permits, the clipping may be remedied by moving the operating point farther from the origin (of the graph). If the operating point is already on the dissipation curve, the only remedy is either to change the load or to decrease the output signal.

If the signal operates close to the saturation and the cutoff region, distortion may be induced if the bias point is shifted because of a change in ambient temperature. The shift would allow the signal to move into either the saturation or the cutoff region. We remember, from the physics review in Chapter 2, that the properties of the transistor are temperature dependent. The most drastic effect, when temperature changes occur, is the shift in operating point. This can be remedied only by bias stabilization. This topic is considered in detail in Chapter 11. The methods described there can be used to eliminate this source of distortion.

Many times it is convenient to measure the distortion of an amplifier by the use of a harmonic analyzer. If we wish to calculate the amount of distortion, techniques making use of the graphical analysis are available. These techniques consist essentially of finding the coefficients of the various harmonics (in the Fourier series) that are present in the output signal. Although we shall not describe these methods here, one common first approximation of distortion is the amount of second harmonic present. Referring to the quantities of Figure 9-5, and assuming higher harmonics are negligible, the second harmonic component can be shown to be

$$\text{second harmonic} = \frac{1}{\sqrt{2}}\left(\frac{I_{\max} + I_{\min}}{4} - \frac{1}{2}I_C\right) \quad (22)$$

The per cent distortion is then found by dividing this value by the fundamental component of Equation 5(a):

% second harmonic distortion
$$= \frac{1/4(I_{\max} + I_{\min}) - 1/2I_C}{1/2(I_{\max} - I_{\min})} \times 100 \quad (23)$$

Using Equation (23), then, the per cent of second harmonic distortion can be used as a crude approximate measure of the total distortion. Note that this is a measure of output distortion only, unless some graphical method is used to note the distorted input (I_B) waveform.

COMMON-BASE CLASS A AMPLIFIER. All the methods and equations of the previous sections, illustrated for the common-emitter connection, apply equally well to the common-base case. The difference lies in using the common-base characteristics where the constant-current curves are for the emitter current I_E and the collector voltage is the voltage from collector to base V_{CB}. Also it may be noted in this case that the characteristic $I_E = 0$ is the cutoff current for the common-base connection. We called this curve the I_{CBO} curve.

Although the common-base connection has substantially less output distortion than the common-emitter case, nevertheless the common-emitter amplifier is still the most frequently used because the increased distortion can be reduced by feedback. It is generally better to apply negative feedback to the common-emitter circuits than to resort to the common-base configuration, which starts with a substantially smaller power gain.

For common-base circuits it is generally true that the source resistance is about twice the normal input resistance. This tends to minimize the distortion situation in the common-base case.

Power amplifiers 235

DESIGN EXAMPLE. Although each designer follows his own peculiar methods, and each design is different, the following is given as an example of the basic principles in the design of a Class A power amplifier.

It must be cautioned that the example here demonstrates the rather idealized considerations treated before. There are still a number of other considerations subsidiary to these most basic ones which must be considered in any practical design. Many of these factors will be studied in the following chapters. For a more complete design pattern it is recommended that the reader consult a more specialized source.

Problem. It is desired to design a single-stage, common-emitter transistor power amplifier that will supply 50 milliwatts of audio power to a loudspeaker with a voice coil impedance of 4.0 ohms.

Solution. The first step is to select a transistor, and the most essential criterion is the power-dissipating capability. From Equation (21) we know that the transistor must be able to dissipate at least twice the output power, or 100 milliwatts.

The 2N270 germanium P-N-P power transistor is selected because it will supply the required power (capable of 250 milliwatts dissipation). The characteristic curves for this transistor are shown in Figure 9-7(b) (for complete characteristics see Appendix III). In order to assure that the operating point will be placed within the dissipation limits, the dissipation curve is drawn for these characteristics.

For this design, the voice coil cannot be connected directly in the collector circuit for two reasons: (1) its resistance is too low to act as a suitable load for the transistor, and (2) the voice coil will not operate properly if the bias direct current flows through it. Therefore a transformer will be used on the output side. Note that the transformer also permits operating close to an ideal 50 per cent efficiency, which would not be possible for the directly connected case. The tentative circuit diagram, then, is shown in Figure 9-7(a).

The next step consists of selecting the operating point. Knowing that the transistor can dissipate 250 milliwatts and that nearly 50 per cent efficiency is possible with the transformer coupling, we note that the transistor could supply almost 125 milliwatts. Since we need only 50 milliwatts we do not have to operate directly on the maximum dissipation curve.

The available power supply should also be considered when

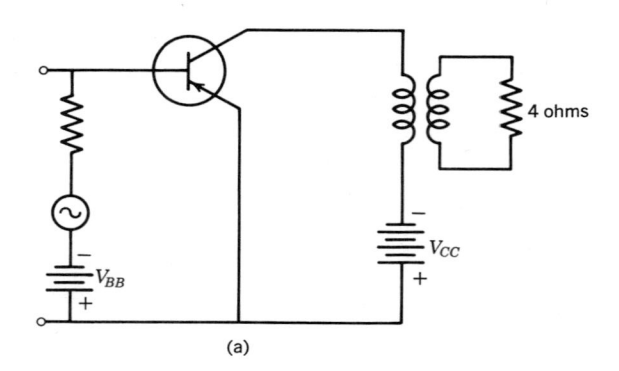

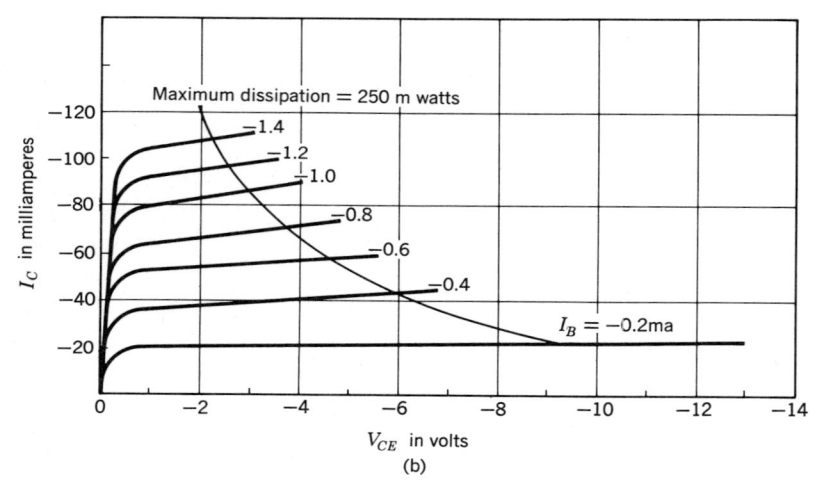

Fig. 9-7. Tentative circuit diagram and characteristics of 2N270.

deciding upon the operating point. The maximum transistor collector voltage is 40 volts, and we remember that the collector voltage has a maximum swing of twice the supply voltage in a Class A transformer connected circuit. Therefore the battery must be less than 20 volts. We will select a 6 volt battery. If a base current of 0.2 milliampere is selected, the power dissipation at the operating point is

$$P_\text{diss} = V_C I_C = 6 \times 20 = 120 \text{ milliwatts} \qquad (24)$$

This operating point Q is shown on Figure 9-8. By placing a ruler through this operating point and rotating it, an a-c load line is selected that has approximately equal current swings on both sides

Power amplifiers 237

of the operating point, while keeping the output distortion (due to unequal spacing) to a minimum. A load of 400 ohms will result in a proper load line. The resulting d-c and a-c load lines through the operating point are shown in Figure 9-8. The resulting maximum

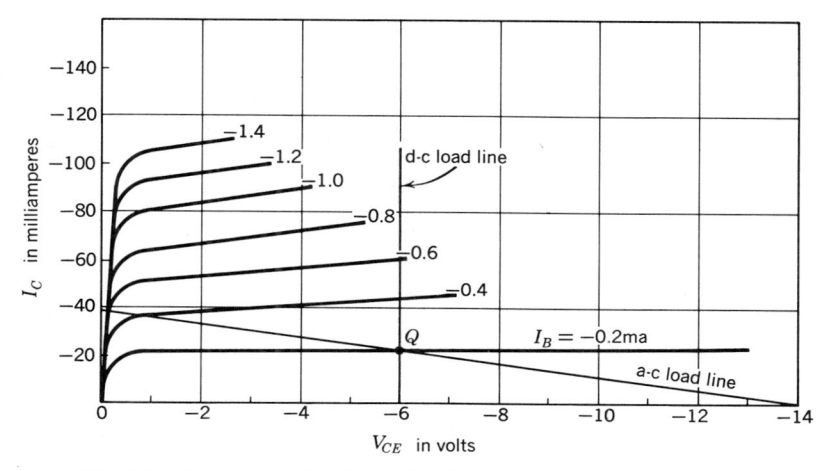

Fig. 9-8. A-c and d-c load lines for Class A, transformer-coupled amplifier of Fig. 9-7.

swings in collector current and voltage can be obtained from this figure:

$$V_{max} \cong 14 \text{ volts} \qquad I_{max} \cong 35 \text{ milliamperes}$$
$$V_{min} \cong 1 \text{ volt} \qquad I_{min} \cong 0 \text{ milliampere} \qquad (25)$$

These values correspond to a base current peak-to-peak swing of 0.4 milliampere, or 0.2 milliampere on either side of the operating point. The output power and collector efficiency under these maximum conditions are

$$P_o = \left(\frac{13}{2\sqrt{2}}\right)\left(\frac{35}{2\sqrt{2}}\right) = 57 \text{ milliwatts}$$
$$\text{eff.} = \frac{57}{120} \times 100 = 47.5\% \qquad (26)$$

Therefore the operating point and load resistance are satisfactory. The amplifier has a slightly higher output power available than required and is operating close to the maximum possible efficiency.

The remainder of the design consists of providing the correct base bias current, setting the transformer turns ratio, and checking the collector circuit distortion.

The base battery and series resistor can be found by writing a d-c equation for the input side. For this equation the emitter-to-base voltage may be neglected if the emitter battery is larger than a few volts. If, in addition, the signal source consists of the secondary of an input transformer, the d-c resistance of the source is essentially zero. Then, selecting a 4 volt battery,

$$R_s = \frac{V_{BB}}{I_B} = \frac{4 \text{ v}}{0.2 \text{ ma}} = 20K \text{ ohms} \tag{27}$$

The final circuit will then be as shown in Figure 9-9. The capacitor across R_s is used to bypass this resistance for alternating currents. The transformer must exhibit an impedance transformation of 400 to 4, so that the turns ratio is 10 to 1.

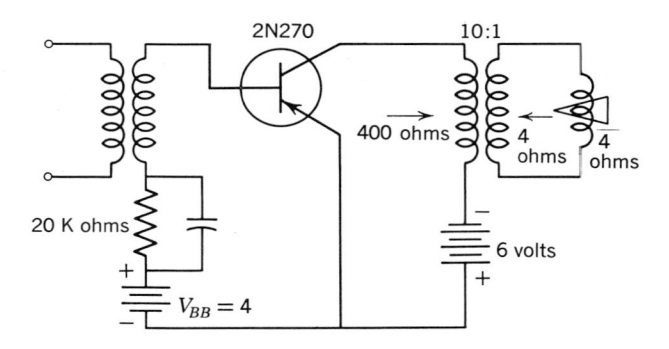

Fig. 9-9. Final common-emitter, Class A transistor power amplifier.

The second harmonic distortion of this circuit can be grossly approximated using Equation (23).

$$\begin{aligned}\left.\begin{array}{l}\text{second}\\\text{harmonic}\\\text{distortion}\end{array}\right\} &= \frac{1/4(I_{\max} + I_{\min}) - 1/2I_C}{1/2(I_{\max} - I_{\min})} \times 100 \\ &= \frac{1/4(35) - 1/2(20)}{1/2(35)} \times 100 = 7.1\%\end{aligned} \tag{28}$$

It should again be emphasized that the above example is intended to illustrate the rather idealized fundamentals portrayed before. Not

Power amplifiers

all aspects important to power amplifiers could be considered here; the object was to consider the most basic ones.

CLASS B POWER AMPLIFIERS

If Class B operation is used in a power amplifier, two transistors placed back to back are required and the two transistors work alternately. That is, if a sine-wave signal is applied, one transistor amplifies the upper half of the wave and the other transistor amplifies the lower half. Class B operation occurs when the bias point is located at cutoff; any signal swing above the bias point will be amplified normally by the transistor, and any signal below cutoff will not be operated on by the transistor. Thus, by placing two transistors back to back, operating Class B, one transistor can be made to amplify the positive signals and the other to amplify the negative signals. The use of this scheme (commonly called push-pull) permits a greater collector efficiency than is possible for the single-ended Class A type, and tends to cause the even harmonic distortion to cancel. However, other sources of distortion occur. Consequently the Class B power amplifier is very appropriate if a large power is required and the distortion limits are not too stringent.

The basic circuit of a Class B power amplifier, using the common-emitter connection, is shown in Figure 9-10. The essential operation

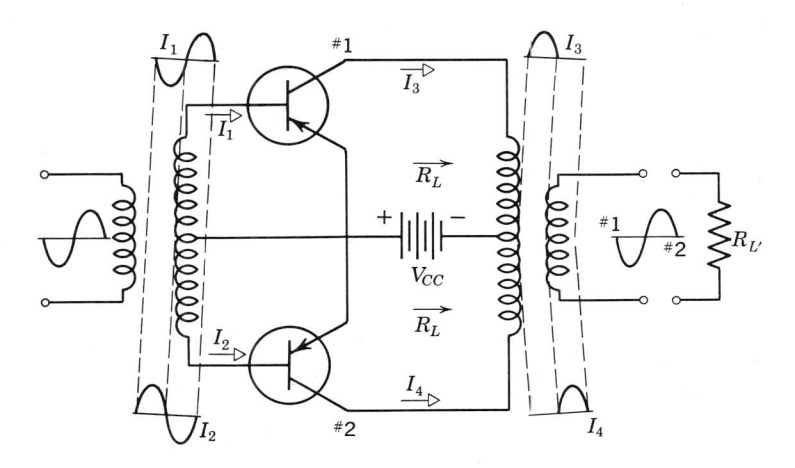

Fig. 9-10. Circuit diagram and waveforms showing basic operation of Class B power amplifiers.

of this circuit is described in the following way: considering a sine wave applied to the input terminals, a sine wave of like phase occurs in the upper half of the transformer secondary. Thus the input to transistor #1 is a sine wave whose phase is equal to that of the input. The lower half of the transformer secondary exhibits a current whose phase is opposite to that of the input; therefore transistor #2 receives a sine wave of opposite phase from that of transistor #1. It is seen that the center-tapped transformer acts as a phase inverter for the transistor input. Although other phase inverting circuits are available, the center-tapped transformer is one convenient way, and permits easy depiction of the phase inverting.

If both transistors are operating strictly Class B, they are biased at cutoff and will amplify only negative voltages. Referring to Figure 9-10, then, transistor #1 amplifies the first half of the input sine wave and stays in the cutoff condition for the other half. The half cycle amplified by this transistor is inverted in the collector lead because of the 180° phase shift of the common-emitter connection. Transistor #2, also amplifying only negative voltages, amplifies the second half of the input wave because its input phase is 180° from that of transistor #1. The currents appearing in the two collector leads are as shown in the figure.

The center-tapped output transformer now combines the two collector currents to form the sine-wave output in the secondary. It is the phase inversion property of the center-tapped transformer that causes the output of transistor #2 to be inverted in the secondary.

In any practical amplifier the two transistors are not operated strictly Class B, but are given a small bias to take them slightly out of the cutoff region. This is done to minimize *crossover distortion*, which will be considered later. Here we will ignore this factor in order to emphasize the fundamental properties of Class B amplifiers.

We can illustrate graphically the operation of the amplifier by joining the characteristics of the two transistors in the proper manner. In a push-pull circuit, transistors of the same type (and as nearly identical as possible) are used; therefore the two sets of characteristics will be the same. Figure 9-11 shows the back-to-back joining of the characteristics. It is seen that the characteristics of transistor #2 are inverted and joined to those of #1, much in the same manner that the transistors are actually electrically connected. *The two sets of characteristics are aligned at the value of V_{CC},* 10 volts in this case. In order for both transistors to be biased at cutoff, the operat-

Power amplifiers

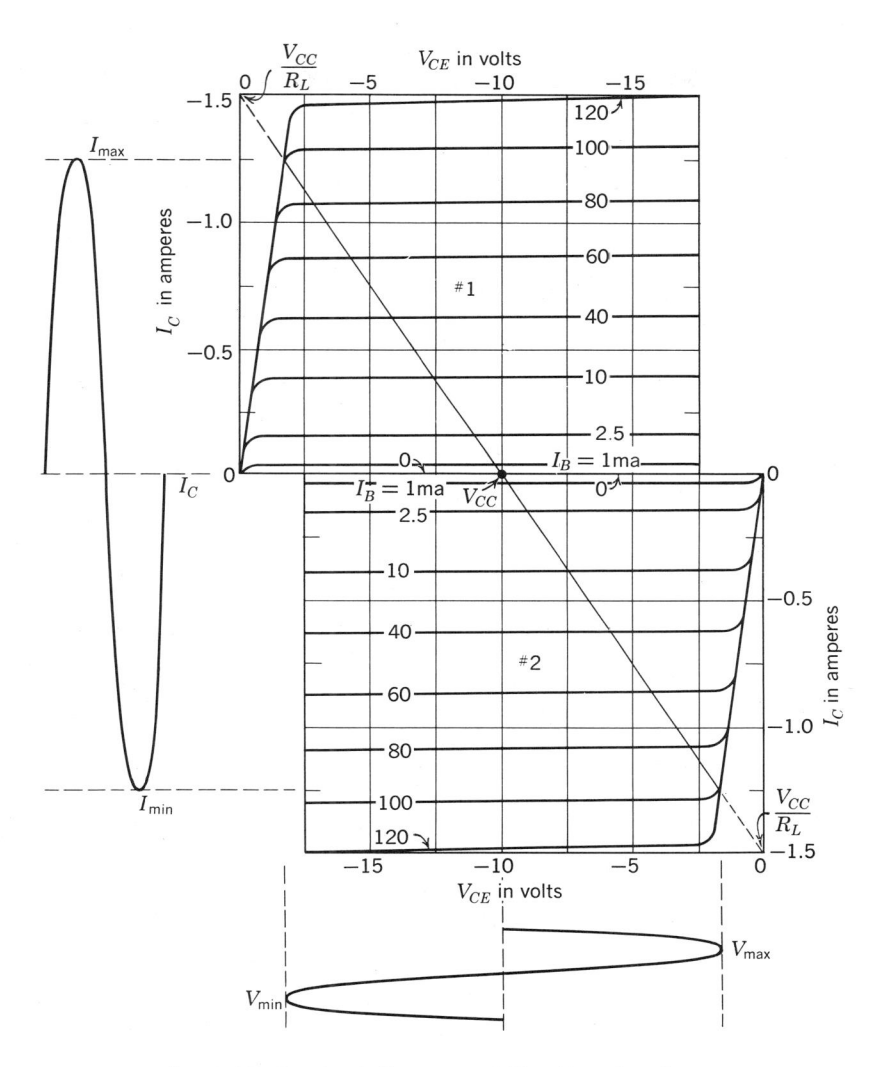

Fig. 9-11. Graphical illustration of Class B, push-pull operation.

ing point for each must be on the $I_B = 0$ line and appears as shown in the figure.

A proper load line is shown on the characteristics of Figure 9-11, and the resulting operation is depicted by the current and voltage waves. Now it is seen how transistor #1 deals with the upper half of the sine wave, and #2 deals with the lower half.

The important things to note on Figure 9-11, for the present, are: (1) the characteristics are aligned at the value of V_{CC}, since the collector battery is common to both transistors; (2) the load line is drawn for the a-c load resistance, that is, the R'_L transformed through one-half the output transformer; (3) the load line is obtained, for the R_L on both transistors, by the conventional method of noting V_{CC} and V_{CC}/R_L; and (4) the d-c load line would be a vertical line at the point $V_{CC} = 10$ since the output side is transformer coupled.

From the above comments it is clear that we could graphically analyze the push-pull circuit by considering only one stage and doubling the proper values. However, by using the total graph of Figure 9-11 we can easily visualize the basic operation.

PERFORMANCE CALCULATIONS. We shall refer to Figure 9-11 for finding the performance equations. Many of the calculations are similar to those for the Class A amplifier discussed earlier; therefore we shall treat in detail only that which is new.

The power output, for a sine-wave signal input, is:

$$P_{out} = V_{rms} I_{rms} = \frac{(V_{max} - V_{min})}{2\sqrt{2}} \times \frac{(I_{max} - I_{min})}{2\sqrt{2}}$$
$$= \frac{(V_{max} - V_{min})(I_{max} - I_{min})}{8} \quad (29)$$

Care must be used in reading the values of V_{max}, V_{min}, I_{max}, and I_{min}. It is noted in Figure 9-11 that the total current and voltage swings move from one set of characteristics to the other. Therefore we *add* the swing on the one characteristic to that of the other: i.e., $V_{max} - V_{min} = (17.5 + 1) - 1.5$ and $I_{max} - I_{min} = 1.25 - (-1.25) = 2.5$.

To find the collector efficiency we need to know the d-c power supplied by the battery. The battery power calculation is quite different from the Class A situation since here the one battery supplies both transistors, and each transistor operates fully over only one-half cycle. Consequently, the proper method is to calculate the d-c power required by one stage and then multiply it by two.

The direct voltage, of course, for either stage is simply the battery voltage, V_{CC}. We have, then, to find the direct current supplied to each transistor. Remembering that the transistor is conducting a sine-wave current for one-half cycle and is cut off for the other half

Power amplifiers

cycle, the current for one transistor will appear as in Figure 9-12. The current during the cutoff portion, although very small, is never quite zero; this current is exactly the back current of a reverse-biased diode in the common-emitter connection and is given by Equation (30):

$$I_{CEO} = \frac{I_{CO}}{1 + h_{fb}} = \frac{I_{CBO}}{1 + h_{fb}} = \frac{I_{CBO}}{1 - \alpha} \tag{30}$$

Part (b) of Figure 9-12 shows the currents of both transistors and exhibits how the total sine wave is preserved.

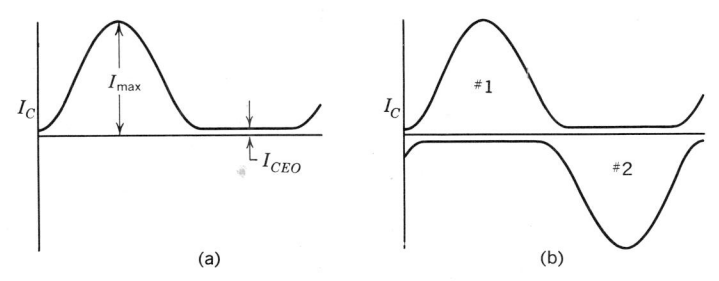

Fig. 9-12. Current waves for two transistors operating Class B.

The *average value* or d-c component of the wave of Figure 9-12(a) can be shown to be

$$I_{d\text{-}c} = \frac{I_{max} - I_{CEO}}{\pi} + I_{CEO} \tag{31}$$

Equation (31) is obtained by finding the d-c component of a sine wave over half a cycle, and then adding the I_{CEO} (a d-c value) of the remaining half cycle.

The total battery input power is then found by multiplying Equation (31) by V_{CC} and doubling to account for both transistors:

$$P_{\text{battery}} = 2V_{CC}\left(\frac{I_{max} - I_{CEO}}{\pi} + I_{CEO}\right) \tag{32}$$

The collector efficiency is found by dividing this quantity into Equation (29):

$$\text{collector eff.} = \frac{P_{\text{out}}}{P_{\text{battery}}} = \frac{(V_{max} - V_{min})(I_{max} - I_{min})}{16V_{CC}\left(\frac{I_{max} - I_{CEO}}{\pi} + I_{CEO}\right)} \tag{33}$$

Since, for any reasonable current swing, the I_{CEO} is negligible with respect to I_{max}, this can be written

$$\text{coll. eff.} = \frac{\pi(V_{max} - V_{min})(I_{max} - I_{min})}{16 V_{CC} I_{max}} \qquad (34)$$

As in the Class A case, it is useful to find the ideal collector efficiency, where "ideal" refers to conditions for an ideal transistor. If the transistor were thus ideal, the operation could swing out to the current axis (along the dashed lines of Figure 9-11). For such ideal conditions the following relations would be true (Figure 9-11):

$$V_{max} - V_{min} = 2V_{CC}$$
$$I_{max} - I_{min} = 2I_{max} = 2\frac{V_{CC}}{R_L} \qquad (35)$$

Substituting these relations into Equation (34), the result is found to be

$$\text{ideal coll. eff.} = \frac{\pi(2V_{CC})(2I_{max})}{16 V_{CC} I_{max}} = \frac{\pi}{4} = 78\% \qquad (36)$$

Remembering that the ideal Class A efficiency is 50 per cent, it is seen that the Class B push-pull amplifier is considerably better in this respect.

Using the relations of Equation (35), the *ideal* power output may be found by substituting into Equation (29):

$$P_{\text{out ideal}} = \frac{(2V_{CC})(2V_{CC}/R_L)}{8} = \frac{V_{CC}^2}{2R_L} \qquad (36a)$$

We can now deal with the matter of dissipation required of a Class B operated transistor. Since there are no d-c losses in the load resistor, the power equation for the collector side is

$$P_{in} = P_{output} + P_{losses}$$
$$P_{battery} = P_{output} + P_{diss} \qquad (37)$$

The P_{diss} of Equation (37) pertains to the pair of transistors; if the dissipation per transistor is desired, this result is divided by two. Also, in calculating the dissipation the assumption is made that I_{CEO} is small in comparison to any I_{max}, so that Equation (34) would hold.

Power amplifiers

$$P_{diss} = P_{battery} - P_{out}$$
$$= \frac{2V_{CC} I_{max}}{\pi} - \frac{(V_{max} - V_{min})(I_{max} - I_{min})}{8} \quad (38)$$

It is useful to rewrite this by recognizing that, from Figure 9-11,

$$I_{max} - I_{min} = 2I_{max} \quad (39)$$
$$V_{max} - V_{min} = 2(V_{CC} - V_{min}) = 2I_{max} R_L \quad (40)$$

The R_L here is the load corresponding to the load line, and consequently is the R'_L transformed through one-half of the output transformer. Equation (38) then is

$$P_{diss} = \frac{2V_{CC} I_{max}}{\pi} - \frac{I_{max}^2 R_L}{2} \quad (41)$$

The two important results of Equation (41) are: (1) *the permissible R_L is restricted by the transistor dissipation capability for a fixed V_{CC}*; and (2) *the maximum dissipation, for a particular V_{CC} and R_L varies with signal swing*.

Figure 9-13 shows a curve of required transistor dissipation versus I_{max}. Both the I_{max} and the dissipation power are referred to ideal

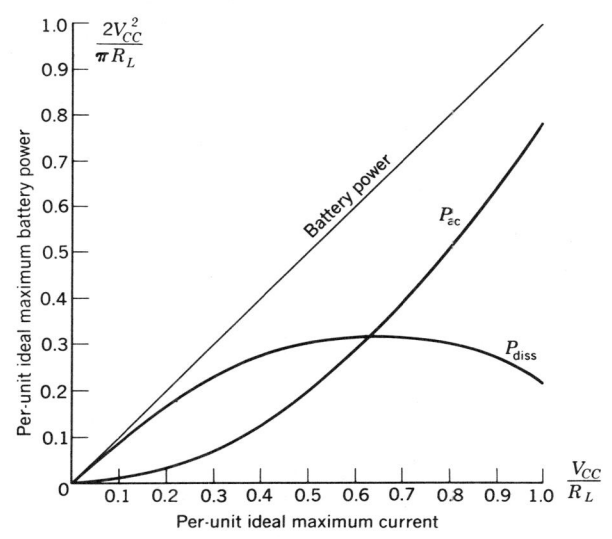

Fig. 9-13. Relation of output power and dissipation to ideal maximum current in Class B.

conditions; that is, the $I_{\max}$ is expressed as the portion of $I_{\max \text{ ideal}} = V_{CC}/R_L$ and the dissipation is expressed as the portion of total battery power under ideal conditions $= 2V_{CC}^2/\pi R_L$. The use of this procedure allows this curve to be used for any value of V_{CC} and R_L, and can thus be applied to any design situation.

Figure 9-13 also shows the battery power and the a-c power output versus $I_{\max}$. Both of these curves are referred to the ideal quantities stated above. Note that the maximum dissipation occurs where the difference between the battery power and the output power is greatest.

From the dissipation curve we see that maximum transistor dissipation is required when the signal causes an $I_{\max}$ of

$$I_{\max} = 0.637 I_{\max \text{ ideal}} = 0.637 \frac{V_{CC}}{R_L} \tag{42}$$

Since, in any design application, the signal may be of this value for a period of time, the transistor must be capable of dissipating the power required for this worst condition. As seen on the curve, the dissipation needed is

$$(P_{\text{diss}})_{\max} = 0.315 \frac{2V_{CC}^2}{\pi R_L} \tag{43}$$

Let us illustrate the foregoing by applying Equation (43) to the situation of Figure 9-11 where the $V_{CC} = 10$ and $R_L = 6.66$ ohms:

$$(P_{\text{diss}})_{\max} = 0.315 \frac{2 \times 100}{\pi 6.66} \cong 3 \text{ watts} \tag{44}$$

Since this includes the two transistors, each transistor must be able to dissipate 1.5 watts with the given V_{CC} and R_L. If the manufacturer's specification allows at least this amount, the transistor is suitable. Note that the degradation of capable power dissipation with increase in ambient temperature given in Equation (1) applies here also.

Given the value of $V_{CC} = 10$ and a dissipation capability, we could also use Equation (43) to find the *minimum* value of R_L that would assure that the dissipation is not exceeded.

Since the a-c power output also depends upon R_L and V_{CC}, we can find the relationship between a desired P_{out} and the required dissipation capability. From Figure 9-13 we see the maximum (ideal) P_{out} is $0.78 \times$ ideal battery drain; since the maximum dissipation is $0.315 \times$ ideal battery drain, it is found that

Power amplifiers

$$\frac{\text{dissipation}}{P_{\text{out}}} = \frac{0.315 \times \text{battery drain}}{0.78 \times \text{battery drain}} = 0.404 \quad (45)$$

Therefore for any desired power output, *the combined dissipation of the two transistors must be greater than 0.404 × the desired power.*

$$P_C = P_{\text{diss}} > 0.404 P_{\text{out}} \quad (46)$$

The value of 0.404 applies only in the case of ideal efficiency. Other cases can be estimated by using Figure 9-13. In any event, this means that each transistor must have a P_C of at least one-fifth the maximum sine-wave signal output. It is clear, then, that Equation (46) is useful in approximating the dissipation for purposes of selecting a transistor.

LOAD LINE. We have just seen that the choice of a load line for Class B operation is affected by the transistor dissipation capability. The dissipation defines the minimum value of R_L that is allowed for a certain V_{CC}.

The maximum value of R_L, on the other hand, is limited by the required output. If the R_L is increased, the load line of Figure 9-11 becomes more horizontal and less signal swing is available. Although the bias battery could be increased to compensate, this is limited also by the voltage maximum of the transistor.

As with the Class A amplifier, the best procedure is to study the characteristics carefully and then try tentative load lines with approximate calculations. Many times the availability of transformers and power supplies fixes the load line.

DISTORTION. The Class B power amplifier has the same sources of distortion as the Class A plus two additional sources: (1) *crossover* distortion, and (2) *mismatch* distortion. It is remembered that the distortion sources for Class A are: (1) nonequal spacing of constant current curves, (2) nonlinear input resistance, and (3) signal clipping due either to a large swing or possibly shift of bias point with temperature.

An important distortion source for Class B power amplifiers is the crossover point. This stems from the fact that the worst nonlinearity in input resistance occurs near the cutoff region of a transistor. Consequently, when two transistors are placed back to back as in the push-pull circuit, a serious distortion occurs when the operation moves from the cutoff region of one transistor to the cutoff region of the other. An exaggerated picture of the resulting distorted sine wave is shown in Figure 9-14.

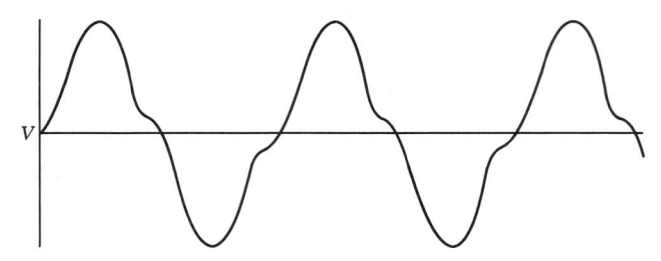

Fig. 9-14. Typical distortion resulting from "crossover" nonlinearity.

This effect can be alleviated by applying a small bias to take the transistor slightly out of the cutoff region. This permits a small collector current even when no signal is present; this bias current is called the *zero-signal d-c collector current*. The distortion can be further reduced by applying negative feedback (studied in Chapter 12).

Mismatch distortion refers to any unbalance between the two transistors used in the Class B arrangement. The major source of mismatch distortion is unequal current gains (h_{fe}). This produces large even-order harmonic distortion. In addition, unequal phase shift in the two transistors adds to the distortion.

Because some serious distortion occurs at crossover, the second harmonic distortion is not a good measure of the total distortion. Hence Equation (23) is not very useful for Class B operation. Probably the best means of evaluating the distortion is to measure it.

COMMON-BASE CLASS B AMPLIFIER. Although a common-emitter connection was used for the above Class B analysis, all the equations and graphical procedures apply also to the common-base connection. The characteristics, of course, would be I_C versus V_{CB} with emitter current as the variable.

Intrinsically, the common-base amplifiers have less distortion than common-emitter amplifiers. However, with negative feedback a common emitter will yield more power output for a given distortion

Power amplifiers

than the common base. This is because of the much higher gain of the emitter case.

DESIGN EXAMPLE. Again the purpose of this example is to illustrate the fundamentals just treated. This example does not represent a suitable design since features to be studied in later chapters are deleted here.

Problem. Design a 6 watt push-pull common-emitter amplifier to drive a 4 ohm voice coil. The driving stage has an output resistance of 5000 ohms.

Solution. From the use of Equation (46) we see the total dissipation required is at least

$$P_{\text{diss}} = 0.404 P_{\text{out}} = (0.404)(6 \text{ watts}) = 2.42 \text{ watts} \qquad (47)$$

Each transistor, then, must dissipate at least 1.21 watts; the actual dissipation will be higher since the ideal efficiency of 78 per cent can never be reached. A transistor having a dissipating capability (P_C) of 4 watts, is chosen. The tentative circuit diagram is shown in Figure 9-15.

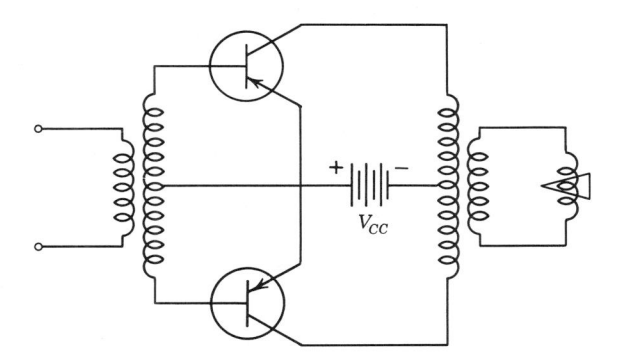

Fig. 9-15. Tentative common-emitter push-pull amplifier.

Assume that the maximum allowable voltage for this transistor is 25 volts. The maximum bias point is 12.5 volts due to the double swing incurred in Class B operation. A 12.5 volt battery is chosen.

Knowing the value of V_{CC}, we can now use Equation (43) to find the minimum value of load resistance with the 4 watts dissipation of this transistor. Since the pair of transistors will give 8 watts, the equation is

$$P_{\text{diss}} = 0.315 \frac{2V_{CC}^2}{\pi R_L} = 8 \text{ watts} \tag{48}$$

Solving for R_L gives

$$(R_L)_{\min} = \frac{0.315 \times 2V_{CC}^2}{8\pi} = \frac{0.630(12.5)^2}{8\pi} = 3.91 \text{ ohms} \tag{49}$$

This is the minimum load resistance, then, that can be used with 8 watts dissipation and a V_{CC} of 12.5 volts.

Since the required power output specifies the maximum value of load resistance, we can use the relation of Equation (36a):

$$(P_{\text{out}})_{\text{ideal}} = \frac{V_{CC}^2}{2R_L}$$

$$(R_L)_{\max} = \frac{V_{CC}^2}{2(P_{\text{out}})_{\text{ideal}}} = \frac{(12.5)^2}{(2)(6)} = 13 \text{ ohms} \tag{50}$$

Consequently the load resistance that we must use lies between 4 and 13 ohms. These values give only an approximation since they are based on the ideal case. In order to obtain 6 watts output we must use a resistor somewhat less than 13 ohms. Based upon the limiting values just calculated, and upon trying various loads on the graph, a load resistance of 8 ohms is selected.

The combined characteristics and the load line corresponding to 8 ohms is shown in Figure 9-16. From this graph the following values are read for a maximum swing:

$$\begin{aligned} V_{\max} &\cong 23.2 \text{ v} & I_{\max} &\cong 1.32 \text{ amp} \\ V_{\min} &\cong 1.8 \text{ v} & I_{\min} &\cong -1.32 \text{ amp} \end{aligned} \tag{51}$$

Using these values, the actual power output is

$$P_{\text{out}} = \frac{(23.2 - 1.8)(1.32 + 1.32)}{8} = 7.05 \text{ watts} \tag{52}$$

For the battery drain, Equation (32) specifies that

$$P_{\text{battery}} = 2V_{CC}\left(\frac{I_{\max} - I_{CEO}}{\pi} + I_{CEO}\right) \tag{53}$$

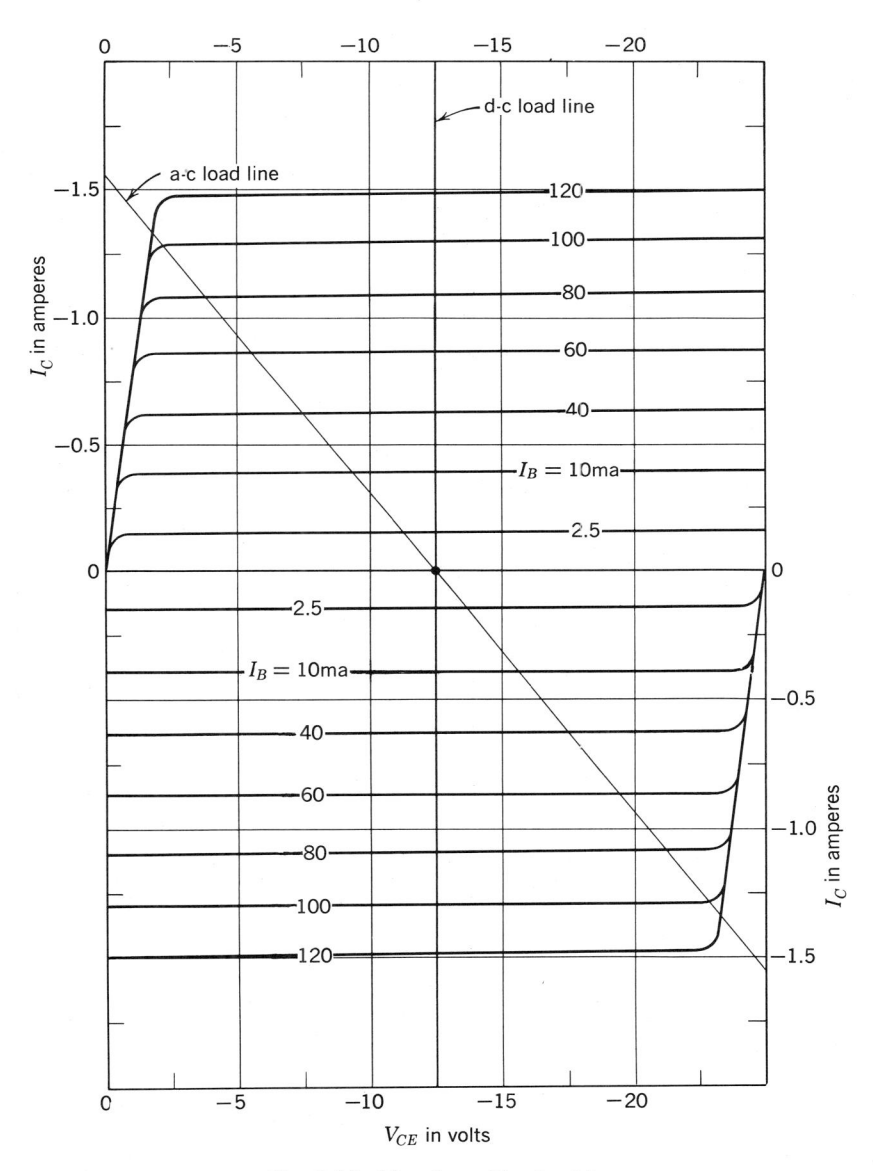

Fig. 9-16. Class B amplifier load line.

The value of I_{CEO}, too small to be read from the graph, is obtained from the manufacturer's specifications and is 0.004. Then

$$P_{\text{battery}} = (2)(12.5)\frac{1.32 - 0.004}{\pi} + 0.004 = 10.55 \quad (54)$$

Using the above results,

$$\text{coll. eff.} = \frac{P_{\text{out}}}{P_{\text{battery}}} = \frac{7.05}{10.55} \times 100 = 66.8\% \quad (55)$$

The total dissipation is

$$P_{\text{diss}} = P_{\text{battery}} - P_{\text{output}} = 10.55 - 7.05 = 3.50 \text{ watts} \quad (56)$$

This means that each transistor must dissipate 1.75 watts, and therefore this operation is suitable with this transistor.

Since each transistor is to see a load of 8 ohms, and the actual load (R'_L) is 4 ohms, each *half* of the center-tapped output transformer must have an impedance transformation of 8 to 4. We can consider each half of the center-tapped transformer as a separate unit, since only one transistor operates at a time. Therefore the turns ratio across one-half of the transformer must be

$$\left(\frac{N_1}{N_2}\right) = \sqrt{\frac{8}{4}} = \sqrt{2} \quad (57)$$

Since each half must have this ratio, considered one at a time, the total turns ratio must be

$$\frac{N_1}{N_2} = \sqrt{2} + \sqrt{2} = 2.83 \quad (58)$$

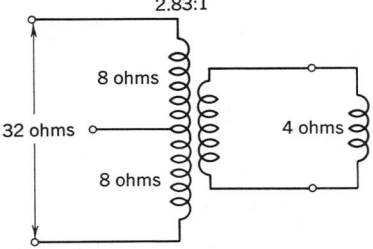

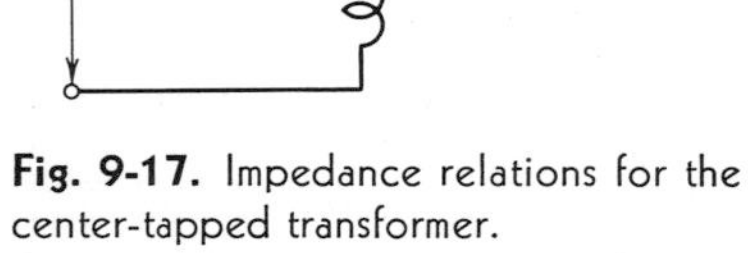

Fig. 9-17. Impedance relations for the center-tapped transformer.

The impedances will then appear as in Figure 9-17. When either half is considered alone, 8 ohms will appear as desired. If the entire transformer is considered, it is seen that 4 × the single-side impedance (4 × 8 = 32 ohms) appears from collector to collector. This is characteristic of all push-pull Class B operation.

The same procedure as above can be applied to the input transformer. The manufacturer specified that the average input impedance for the common-emitter connection of this transistor is

Power amplifiers 253

about 50 ohms. Since the driver impedance is 5000 ohms, the total transformer ratio is

$$\frac{N_1}{N_2} \cong \sqrt{\frac{5000}{4 \times 50}} = 5 \qquad (59)$$

The total circuit for this amplifier is then shown in Figure 9-18. This amplifier provides the required power output and its efficiency is good, 66.8 per cent compared with the ideal 78 per cent.

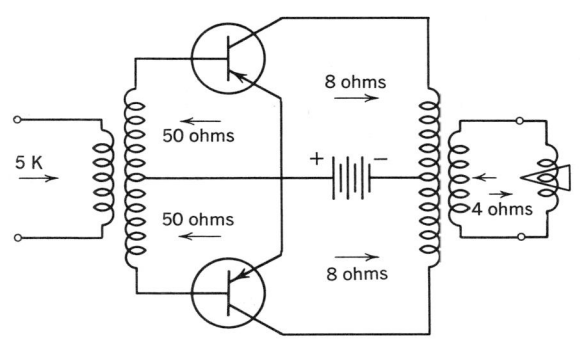

Fig. 9-18. Final circuit for Class B, common-emitter power amplifier.

For finding the power gain, the power input is

$$(P_{\text{a-c}})_{\text{input}} = \left[\frac{(I_B)_{\text{pk-to-pk}}}{2\sqrt{2}}\right]^2 R_{\text{in}} = \left(\frac{0.210}{2\sqrt{2}}\right)^2 \times 50 = 0.276 \text{ watts}$$

The power gain is then

$$A_p = 10 \log_{10} \frac{P_{\text{out}}}{P_{\text{in}}} = 10 \log_{10} \frac{7.05}{0.276} = 14.1 \text{ db}$$

OTHER POWER CIRCUITS

Although Class A and Class B are the basic modes of operation for transistor power amplifiers, there are other types that are worthy of mention here. These types are Class A push-pull, Class A-B, and complementary symmetry. It is our purpose here only to describe these various types briefly; the basic analysis procedures used in the preceding sections can be used, with modifications, for these other types.

Class A push-pull. The Class A push-pull amplifier consists essentially of two transistors connected back to back, with both transistors biased so as to operate Class A. The circuit connection for this amplifier is identical to that of the Class B except that here a bias battery is necessary in the input side to provide the Class A bias conditions. The chief advantage of this amplifier is that it exhibits an extremely low distortion compared with the other power amplifiers.

The circuit diagram of the Class A push-pull amplifier is shown in Figure 9-19. As in the case of the Class B amplifier, the input

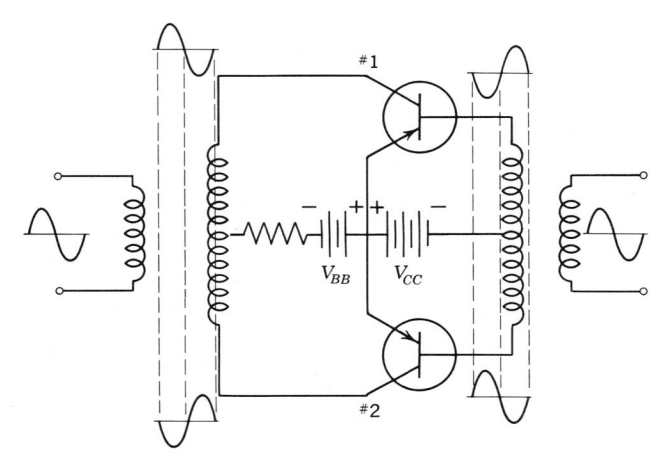

Fig. 9-19. Circuit diagram and waveforms showing basic operation of Class A, push-pull amplifier.

transformer acts as a phase inverter for the input signal. If a sine wave is applied to the input, transistor #1 receives a current wave that is in phase with the input wave, while transistor #2 receives a sine wave whose phase is 180° from that of the input. Since both transistors are operating Class A, the entire wave in each case is amplified by the respective transistor. With the 180° phase shift of the common-emitter connection, the entire sine wave for each transistor will appear in the collector lead. The phase of these two waves, however, will be opposing (180° apart) as shown in Figure 9-19.

Power amplifiers

The center-tapped output transformer then combines the two waves by acting as a phase inverter for the one wave. Consequently, the amplified output appears in the secondary of the output transformer.

Because of the action of the output transformer, all the even-order harmonics of the output sine wave will be eliminated in the output if the transistors used are well balanced. Since the second harmonic distortion is often the chief source, the distortion of this circuit can be made very low. Also, this circuit does not suffer from crossover distortion as does the Class B type. Compared with Class B, however, the power output is less and it operates less efficiently.

The power output from this circuit would, of course, be twice that obtainable from a single-transistor Class A amplifier.

If it is desired to analyze graphically the push-pull amplifier, the two transistor characteristics must be joined in the same manner as shown in Figure 9-11 for the Class B amplifier. The analysis differs somewhat from that of the Class B, however, since here both transistors are conducting at the same time. This can be handled by combining the characteristic curves for the two transistors to form a set of composite characteristics. This can be accomplished by subtracting the entire curve for x ma below the current bias value of transistor #2 from the entire curve of x ma above the bias value of transistor #1. For example, referring to Figure 9-11, let us assume that the I_B bias current is 40 ma for each transistor. One composite curve would be found by subtracting the $40 - 20 = 20$ ma curve of #2 from the $40 + 20 = 60$ ma curve of #1. This subtraction is performed by subtracting the I_C current values along any vertical line.

Since the characteristics of the junction transistor are essentially linear, the resulting composite characteristics will be linear lines displaced from the original characteristics. By the use of these characteristics and the load line, the graphical picture of push-pull operation can be depicted.

COMPLEMENTARY SYMMETRY. Complementary symmetry refers to a method of constructing Class B amplifiers without requiring the phase-inverting center-tapped transformers on the input and output. To do this, two transistors with similar characteristics are used, but one is an N-P-N type and the other a P-N-P. It was noted in Chapter 4 that these two types differ, electrically, in that the bias polarities are reversed; hence the common-emitter P-N-P transistor requires a negative base current drive and the N-P-N common-emitter transistor requires a positive drive. Therefore, if an N-P-N and a P-N-P are connected back to back and biased at cutoff in a push-pull circuit, the N-P-N unit will amplify the positive half signals and the P-N-P will operate on the negative signals. It is seen that the need for phase inversion has been eliminated.

Figure 9-20 shows the basic connection of a complementary sym-

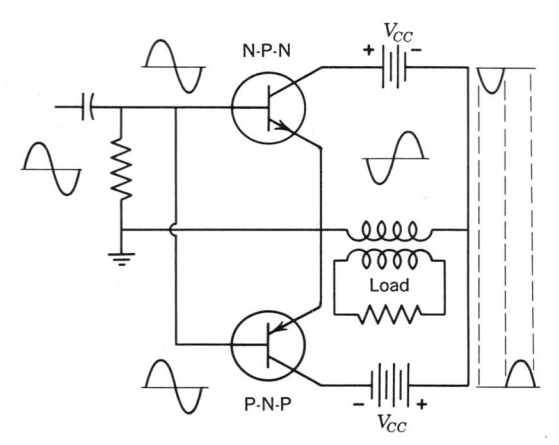

Fig. 9-20. Circuit diagram and waveforms of amplifier using complementary symmetry.

metry circuit. It is noted that a single battery will no longer suffice, since the two transistors require opposite polarities. (A single battery could be used if the point of battery connection could be off-ground.) Since there is no phase inversion here, the input sine wave feeds both transistors. The N-P-N unit operates only on the positive portion since it is biased at cutoff; the 180° phase shift of the common-emitter connection will cause the positive wave to be inverted in the output. The P-N-P unit amplifies the negative portion of the input wave, and with 180° phase shift a positive half cycle appears in its output. We now have a negative and a positive half cycle, so they may be added directly in the load; no output phase-inversion transformer is needed.

Figure 9-20 shows an output transformer (not center-tapped) that is usually required to transform the impedance of the load to a suitable transistor load.

If this circuit is to be illustrated graphically, the characteristics and load line of each transistor must be considered separately; the

Power amplifiers

characteristics cannot be combined as they were in Figure 9-11. It is noted that the load line for each transistor would consist of the actual load transformed by the complete turns ratio of the output transformer.

A stage of common-collector complementary symmetry may be added to the previous circuit to transform the impedance down so as to permit driving a low load resistance directly. This is advantageous from the viewpoint of obtaining some additional gain from the common-collector stage and also eliminating the output transformer. A circuit diagram is shown in Figure 9-21.

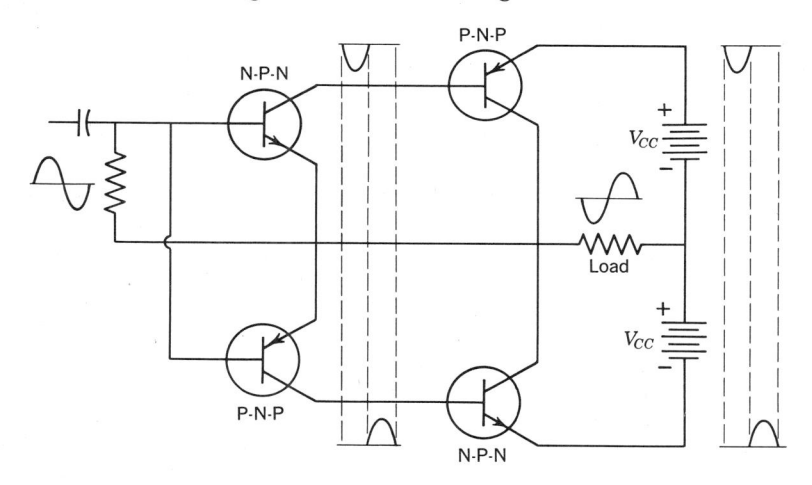

Fig. 9-21. Circuit diagram and waveforms of two-stage complementary symmetry amplifiers.

It is seen that a P-N-P follows the N-P-N transistor and an N-P-N follows the P-N-P. This is required since the common-emitter connection inverts the signal wave because of its phase shift. It is noted that the common-collector stage does not shift the phase of the signal. Since the output impedance of the collector stages are low, a low load resistance may be driven directly with this connection.

It should be noted, in Figure 9-21, that the common-emitter stages are *biased through the common-collector ones.* That is, the first N-P-N transistor obtains its collector-to-emitter bias through the emitter-to-base path of the P-N-P transistor. Since the emitter-to-base voltage is always small, the collector of the N-P-N receives practically the entire voltage of V_{CC}.

This method of biasing through another transistor is always a possibility in transistor circuits, and should be kept in mind when designing circuits.

SINGLE-ENDED CLASS B CIRCUITS. In addition to the expense and size of transformers, all power amplifiers that use transformers incur difficulty in providing a good low frequency response. For these

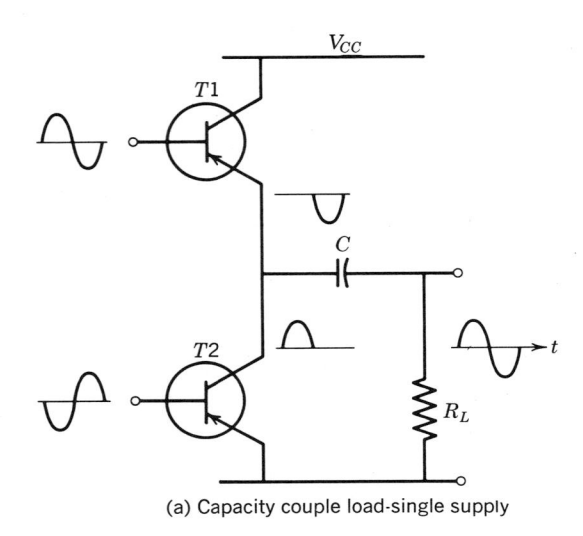

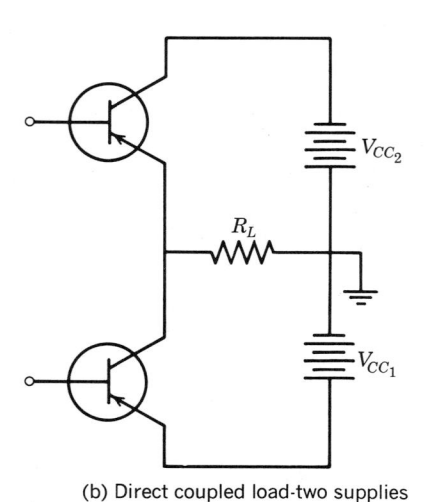

(a) Capacity couple load-single supply

(b) Direct coupled load-two supplies

Fig. 9-22. Basic single-ended Class B circuits, without input circuits.

(a) Transformer input

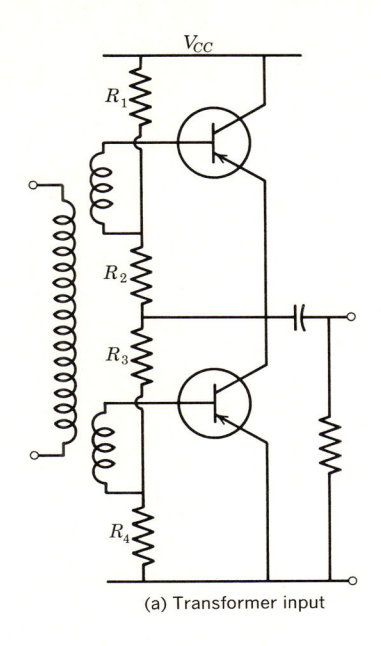

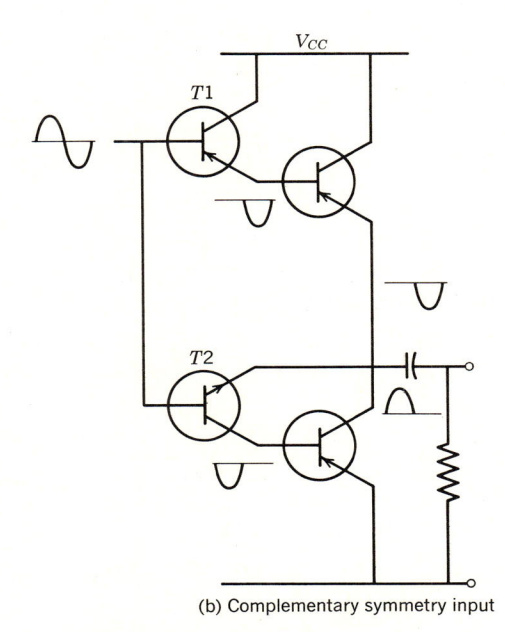

(b) Complementary symmetry input

Fig. 9-23. Two single-ended Class B circuits.

reasons there has always been a desire to develop and perfect power amplifiers without transformers. The successful development of ever larger power transistors has made this increasingly attractive. The single-ended Class B circuit allows one to obtain the advantages of Class B operation without the need for a transformer.

The essential action of the single-ended Class B operation, without biasing circuitry, is shown in Figure 9-22. Figure 9-22(a) shows an arrangement requiring only a single supply, but requiring capacity coupling. Part (b) indicates a direct-coupled arrangement—here two bias supplies are required. The basic push-pull action in these two circuits is identical. We will use part (b) to depict the essential action.

Essentially, the transistors are placed in series across the power supply. Phase inverted wave forms must be put onto the two respective bases. If the transistors are biased at cutoff, it can be seen that the wave forms depicted in Figure 9-22(a) will occur.

Consider the action of the top transistor. When the base signal goes positive $T1$ will cut off. When the negative base cycle appears, the upper transistor is turned on. Since the negative base signal on $T1$ is accompanied by a positive signal on $T2$, $T2$ is now cut off. $T1$ now behaves as a common collector circuit with a very high d-c resistance (cutoff $T2$) and the a-c resistance provided by R_L. Thus the emitter lead wave form of $T1$ is as shown.

Consider $T2$. When the first negative base cycle occurs, $T2$ is in the active region, and $T1$ is cut off. Now $T2$ behaves like a common-emitter amplifier with a very high d-c resistance (cutoff $T1$) and an a-c resistance provided by R_L. Thus the wave form in its collector lead will appear as shown. In this way the Class B push-pull operation is effected in the single-ended circuit.

Figure 9-23 shows two possible methods for obtaining the phase inverted inputs and the accompanying bias. Note that a center-tapped transformer (as in conventional Class B) cannot be used since the "common" a-c point has different d-c values. The resistors R_1-R_2 and R_3-R_4 bias the transistors slightly above cutoff to minimize the cross-over distortion (in the usual way). Note that eliminating the output transformer while retaining the input one is sensible, since the output requirements are much more stringent than the input ones.

Figure 9-23(b) shows a circuit which eliminates both transformers. Here a complementary symmetry circuit (treated above) is

Power amplifiers 261

used to form a transformerless phase inverter. The complementary symmetry part is operated in a Class B manner also, in a manner similar to that described in Figure 9-20. If the positive base cycle is put on the upper transistor $T1$, it cuts off. The lower transistor $T2$ passes this positive cycle, with a phase inversion. When the negative input cycle occurs, $T1$ operates (without phase inversion) and $T2$ cuts off. In this way the necessary phase-inverted inputs to the power transistors are effected.

Note that both circuits of Figure 9-23 could be used with a direct-coupled load. That is, if two supplies were used in the fashion of Figure 9-22(b), the load can be directly connected, without having d-c current flow through the load.

PROBLEMS

1. Assume that a transistor can dissipate 500 milliwatts at an ambient temperature of 25° centigrade. What power dissipation is safe at $T = 75°$ centigrade, if the Θ (junction to free air) is 0.25 degree/watt? Is a heat sink required to permit this dissipation?

2. Assume that a transistor has a permissible dissipation of 8 watts at an ambient temperature of 25° centigrade. The Θ_{jc} (junction to case) is 10 degrees/watt. What power can be dissipated at $T = 60°$ centigrade? Is a heat sink required to dissipate this power?

3. What power can be dissipated by the following transistors at an ambient temperature of 65° centigrade: 2N270; 2N3392; 2N3638; 2N1302? For the 2N3638, assume that a heat sink completely couples the case temperature to ambient; what power can now be dissipated at the 65° centigrade?

4. For the 2N270, what is the range of tolerable load resistance (assuming maximum swing) so that neither the maximum voltage, maximum current, or power dissipation (at 25° centigrade) is exceeded?

5. Find the range of tolerable load resistances, as in Problem 4, for the 2N1302; the 2N1097.

6. Assume that the 2N270 is used in the circuit shown in Figure 9-24. Let $V_{CC} = 6$ volts, $V_{BB} = 2.2$ volts, and $R_L = 400$ ohms. With the I_B of -0.2 milliampere, what is the I_C and power dissipation at the operating point? Neglect any d-c resistance of the primary. What is the maximum power out with this circuit? What is the

collector efficiency? Assuming an R_{in} of 400 ohms, what is the power gain of this circuit?

7. Assume the same basic circuit as shown in Figure 9-24, using the 2N1097. Let $V_{CC} = 10$ volts, $V_{BB} = 2.7$ volts, and $R_L = 450$ ohms. With the I_B of -0.25 milliampere, what is the I_C and power dissipation at the operating point (neglecting d-c resistance of primary)? What is the maximum power out with this circuit, and the collector efficiency?

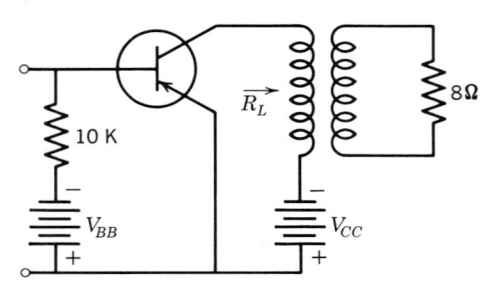

Fig. 9-24. Basic Class A amplifier.

8. Using the corrected h-parameters for the amplifier of Problem 7, calculate the input resistance and the power gain (extend curves).

9. Using Equation (23) as an estimate of distortion, calculate this distortion for the amplifier of Problem 7 (assuming a constant current sine wave is the input). Plot the output current (versus time), and note this "output distortion."

10. Assume that the amplifier of Problem 7 is driven by a voltage source V_s in series with an internal R_s. Determine the best source impedance for minimum distortion by proceeding in the following way. Start with the I_B versus V_{BE} curve. (Use the one curve given with the 2N270 data.) Using a given value of R_s, draw a load line (slope $= -1/R_s$). A series of such lines (all parallel) will permit finding the I_B (at the intersection of the curve and line) versus the V_s (the intersection of the load line on the abscissa). Then, using the output load line of Problem 7, find the I_C versus I_B curve. By combining these first two curves, a curve of I_C versus V_s can be formed. Note the curvature for given assumed values of R_s (source of distortion), and find the R_s providing the most linear I_C versus V_s.

11. Assume that the 2N270 transistor is used in the Class B basic circuit of Figure 9-10. Let the V_{CC} be -12 volts and the impedance per collector be 150 ohms. Assume that the collector current is zero if no signal is present. Draw the load line for one side, and cal-

Power amplifiers

culate the total maximum power output. Assume I_{CEO} can be neglected in the power calculations. What is the collector efficiency?

12. For the amplifier of Problem 11, what is the maximum dissipation power encountered? At what power output does this occur (refer to Figure 9-13)?

13. Compare the ratio of maximum power output-to-transistor dissipation for the two amplifiers: the Class A amplifier using the 2N270 (Problem 6), and the Class B one using the 2N270 (Problem 11).

14. For the 2N270 transistor, plot the crossover distortion by using the curves given (Appendix III) for I_C versus V_{BE}. Plot two curves back-to-back, with no overlap (one curve in first quadrant; one curve in third quadrant). Assume a sine wave voltage is applied to the V_{BE} axis; plot the resulting current.

    Indicate how crossover distortion is reduced by allowing the back-to-back curves to overlap, with a "sum" curve being drawn in the region of overlap.

15. Assume that 2N1097 is used in the Class B basic circuit of Figure 9-10. Let the $V_{CC} = -9$ volts and the impedance per collector be 225 ohms. Draw the load line for one side, and calculate the maximum power output. Assume the I_{CEO} is zero, in power calculations. What is the collector efficiency?

16. For the load line of Problem 15, plot the incremental current gain versus I_C by using, as the incremental base current, the distance between adjacent curves. Note how this produces output distortion.

17. Following the same procedure as in Problem 10, plot the I_C versus V_s for the amplifier of Problem 15. (Use the I_B versus V_{EB} curve given in the 2N270 data.) What is the value of source impedance R_s that provides the most linear curve, and hence the least distortion?

18. Design a Class A amplifier that will supply 100 milliwatts of audio power to a loudspeaker with a voice coil impedance of 4 ohms. Follow the general procedure described in the text design example. It is desirable, for convenience, to use a transistor whose characteristics appear in Appendix III.

19. Design a 600 milliwatt Class B push-pull common-emitter amplifier to drive a 4 ohm voice coil. Assume that the driving stage has an output resistance of 1000 ohms. Use the general procedure described in the design example and one of the transistors included in Appendix III.

20. For a Class B amplifier, show that the power output can be written

$$P_o = \frac{2\, V_{CE_o}^2}{R_{c\text{-}c}}$$

where V_{CE_o} is the collector-to-emitter voltage at no signal, and $R_{c\text{-}c}$ is the collector-to-collector load resistance.

21. Since in power amplifiers the load resistance is almost a short circuit compared to the transistor's output resistance, show that the power gain for the Class B amplifier can be written

$$\text{Power gain} = h_{FE}^2 \frac{R_{c\text{-}c}}{R_{b\text{-}b}}$$

where $R_{c\text{-}c}$ is the collector-to-collector load resistance and $R_{b\text{-}b}$ is the base-to-base input resistance.

22. Using Problems 20 and 21, show that for the Class B amplifier, power gain can be written

$$\text{Power gain} = \frac{2\, h_{FE}^2\, V_{CE_o}}{R_{b\text{-}b}\, P_{\text{out}}}$$

Compare this power gain to that found for the amplifier of Problem 15. Use the corrected small signal parameters as an estimate of the R_{in} for the amplifier of Problem 15.

23. Prove that in a Class A amplifier, if the a-c load line is drawn so that the operating point is at one-half the maximum V_{CE} and I_C (assuming an ideal transistor), that the power gain can be given by

$$\text{Power gain} = \frac{h_{FE}^2\, V_{CE}^2}{2\, R_{\text{in}}\, P_{\text{out}}}$$

where V_{CE} is the voltage at the operating point. Compare the value obtained using this with those values found for the amplifiers of Problems 6 and 7.

10

Cascade amplifiers

In Chapter 8 we considered the single-stage small-signal amplifier. The concentration there was upon finding the equations for the performance quantities of the transistor in small-signal applications. The equivalent circuit was used for the analysis and it was emphasized that any complex transistor network can be analyzed by considering the entire circuit on a stage-by-stage basis and using the performance equations derived there and listed in Tables 8-3 and 8-5.

Chapter 9 was devoted to the study of single-stage large-signal amplifiers, specifically power amplifiers. The graphical characteristics were used to aid in design decisions, and it was noted that the techniques applied to the power amplifiers apply to large-signal amplifiers in general. Basically, this chapter indicated the way in which graphical characteristics can be used to describe the operation of electronic circuits.

Thus we can consider the two previous chapters as dealing with the two fundamental methods of analyzing and designing transistor amplifier circuits: the equivalent circuit method for small-signal applications, and the use of graphical characteristics for large-signal conditions.

It is our purpose now to add to these two basic tools the factors that are encountered when transistor amplifiers are connected in cascade. These additional factors center around the interstage networks that are required for cascaded transistor stages.

The interstage networks between any electronic circuit devices are required for three reasons: (1) to provide the proper biases to the circuit device, (2) to separate the bias currents (or voltages) of one stage from that of another, and (3) to give better impedance match in the case of transformers only. Concerning (2), it is most often the case that the desired bias conditions in the output of one stage are not the same as those desired for the input of the next stage; therefore the bias currents must be separated. This amounts to providing separate paths for the alternating and direct currents between the electronic devices. As we have noted before, the two common means of accomplishing this separation is by the use of *RC* coupling or transformer coupling. Both of these separate the output of one stage, d-c wise, from the input of the next stage.

As would be expected, any type of interstage network affects the a-c operation of the cascaded amplifiers. The bias circuits tend to shunt out the a-c signal, and the coupling of the interstage affects frequency response. Even if the transistor were completely frequency independent, the interstage network would introduce a frequency dependency. We shall find that, for cascaded transistor amplifiers with *RC* coupling (and usually for transformer coupling), the low-frequency response is determined by the interstage, and the high-frequency action is specified by the transistor.

In this chapter, then, we first consider the various schemes available for providing proper transistor bias. The treatment here will portray the basic biasing methods, the reasons for their use, and the basic equations that apply. A more detailed analysis of these bias circuits is given in Chapter 11. Next, the effect of the complete interstage on the gain and the frequency response will be investigated. Since the transistor itself usually limits the high-frequency action, the frequency dependence of the transistor and the resulting effect will be considered. Finally, the concepts of gain and frequency response for cascaded amplifiers will be illustrated by a design example.

BIASING CIRCUITS

Thus far, when exhibiting the bias of a transistor, the simple method of inserting a suitable battery in each lead was used in order to allow concentration to be placed on the a-c analysis tools being considered. We wish here to examine the various available biasing schemes with approximate calculations to find a desired operating point.

It should be emphasized that when dealing with biasing circuits we are concerned with the d-c conditions of the circuit. As discussed previously in Chapter 7, one of the basic tools for analyzing and designing electronic circuits consists of treating the a-c and the d-c conditions separately. In Chapter 8, when working with the h parameters, we were dealing with the a-c properties. The values of these a-c h parameters *are not* valid for d-c conditions.

One of the most crucial aspects of transistor biasing is to maintain the desired bias point in the face of temperature changes and in the face of parameter changes from transistor substitution.

In the next chapter, when studying bias point stability, we shall examine bias equations in more detail and shall find that a d-c equivalent circuit can also be written that is very similar to the a-c h-parameter equivalent circuit used in Chapters 7 and 8. Of course, the h parameters will have d-c values that will be different from the corresponding a-c values.

Since the major goal here is to examine the biasing possibilities and note the effect of the bias circuits on the basic amplification process, it is useful to review the basic biasing conditions for a P-N-P transistor in the three possible connections, as given in Figure 10-1. For each of the connections, both an RC coupling and a transformer coupling are shown on the input side. The capacitor in the transformer-coupled circuits provides an a-c shunt across the bias resistor; if this were not present, the a-c signal would be decreased by the bias resistor. It should be noted that in all following circuits, the main bias resistor will be denoted by R_B.

It is remembered that biasing conditions in the *active* region are that the emitter junction be biased in the forward direction and the collector junction be biased in the reverse direction. For a P-N-P transistor this means that the emitter voltage will be slightly positive with respect to the base, and the collector is negative with respect to the base. With this criterion, it can be verified that the battery polarities of Figure 10-1 are correct. For an N-P-N transistor, the basic conditions would be reversed and hence all the battery polarities of this figure would be reversed.

The graphical characteristics of a transistor are useful for understanding the influence and role of the bias point and for visualizing the bias operation and the effects of various changes. It must be kept in mind, however, that these characteristics vary with temperature. Also, there may be variation among units of the same type. Therefore accuracy may demand measurement on each unit, rather than relying on the characteristics supplied by the manufacturer.

In general, the d-c calculations for a transistor can be handled by the same techniques as the a-c ones. Thus, we can use a d-c equivalent circuit for the transistor, and treat this equivalent circuit plus the attached circuitry as a composite electrical network. Applying the usual analysis techniques to this circuit enables writing the unknown currents (and voltages) in terms of both the transistor d-c parameters and the external circuit components.

On the other hand, the transistor characteristics can be used to analyze the entire d-c situation. The whole problem can be done this way if both input and output characteristics are used.

Both of these techniques suffer from having their transistor quantities vary with temperature and from unit to unit. In addition, the d-c equivalent circuit quantities vary with operating point. Nevertheless, the equivalent circuit method appears to be best suited for transistors. This is the method used in the next chapter when considering bias stability.

Because the introductory d-c analysis in this section treats the external circuitry separate from the transistor, the unknown currents are written in terms of the external components and the transistor voltages and currents. Thus here we will not delve inside the transistor. The major reason for doing this is to emphasize the role of the bias circuitry in establishing the bias point. In addition, this treatment is a sensible introduction to the more complex procedure of combining the external circuitry with the transistor equivalent circuit parameters.

As a beginning, then, we will calculate the input current in terms of circuit values and transistor voltages and currents. An implication here is that such an expression is useful for setting the *input* bias, while the transistor output characteristics may be used to help

Cascade amplifiers

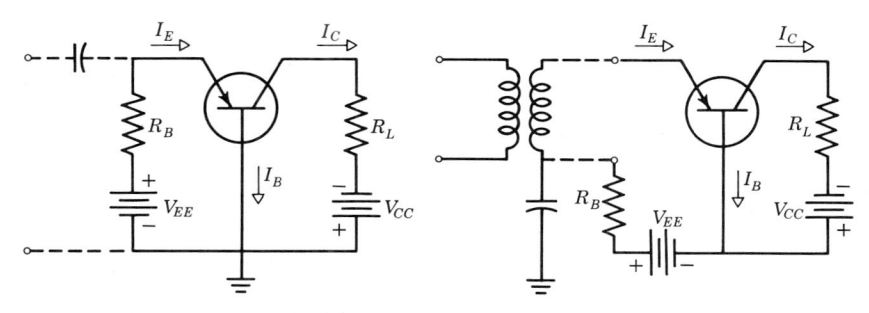

(a) Common-base connection

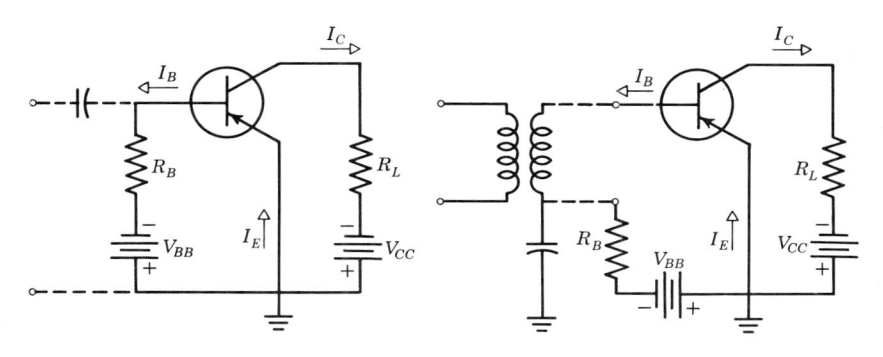

(b) Common-emitter connection

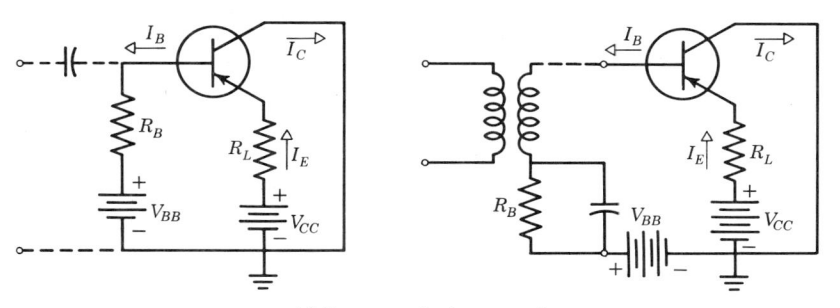

(c) Common-collector connection

Fig. 10-1. Basic battery polarities for the three connections using a P-N-P transistor and showing two types of coupling.

evaluate the output (V_C, I_C) conditions. It is remembered, of course, that the bias point will always lie at the intersection of the d-c load line and the input current value on the output characteristics. Note that we suggest the above method as a convenient way to assist in initially setting the bias point. The difficult problem of stabilizing (or retaining) the bias point when the temperature changes is the topic of the next chapter.

One of the factors that makes a separate treatment of the input and output reasonably accurate is that under normal conditions the transistor has little d-c feedback (from output to input). Thus changes in collector voltage, V_C, have only negligible effect on the input current.

In any d-c analysis it is also often true that the base-to-emitter voltage is small compared to the voltages in series with it; in those cases we can neglect this term. Germanium transistors have a V_{EB} of about 200 millivolts, while silicon ones have a V_{EB} of about 700 millivolts.

First we will write the basic input equations for the circuits of Figure 10-1. Although the circuits here are for P-N-P transistors, the same equations apply for the N-P-N. In the N-P-N case one simply reverses both the batteries and the current directions. If this procedure is used, the voltages and currents in the equations are always positive, for both P-N-P and N-P-N.[1] For the common-base connection the input current is I_E and is given by:

$$\text{(common base)} \quad I_E = \frac{V_{EE} - V_{EB}}{R_B} \tag{1}$$

The d-c equation for the common-emitter case, for both capacitor- and transformer-coupled, is

$$V_{BB} = I_B R_B + V_{EB} \tag{2}$$

[1] A comment on this matter of current direction is warranted. In providing information from the manufacturer to the user, an "absolute" convention is that all currents are positive *into* the terminals; therefore I_C, I_B are negative for a P-N-P transistor. However, in writing d-c circuit equations, such a convention is unwieldy. It is believed more natural and easier to let the current direction be the *actual* direction for the transistor. These directions, for both the P-N-P and the N-P-N transistor, are shown on the symbols sheet.

Cascade amplifiers

Solving for I_B, the result is

$$\text{(common emitter)} \quad I_B = \frac{V_{BB} - V_{EB}}{R_B} \quad (3)$$

For the common-collector case of Figure 10-1, the collector direct current must also be considered, since the R_L appears in the input loop. The equation is found to be

$$V_{CC} - V_{BB} = I_B(R_B + R_L) + V_{EB} + I_C R_L \quad (4)$$

Then solving for I_B:

$$\text{(common collector)} \quad I_B = \frac{V_{CC} - V_{BB} - V_{EB} - I_C R_L}{R_B + R_L} \quad (5)$$

It may be noted that the R_L in the common-collector case couples the input and output bias circuitry. For this reason both I_B and I_C appear in Equation (5). Such a coupling resistor will also appear in later bias circuits.

The bias situations depicted above are not useful in actual applications for two major reasons: (1) one desires to accomplish the biasing with a single power supply rather than two power supplies, and (2) if only these basic bias circuits were used, the transistor amplifier would be unsatisfactory due to unit-to-unit variation and results of temperature changes. Consequently more elaborate bias circuits have to be considered. Since the common-emitter connection is the most frequently used type, we will devote most of the bias circuit attention to this connection.

Figure 10-2 shows a common-emitter connection that is biased

(a) Capacitor coupling   (b) Transformer coupling

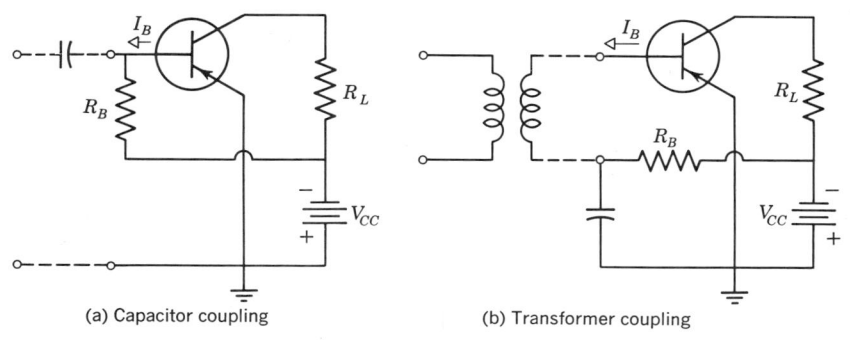

Fig. 10-2. One possibility for single-battery, common-emitter bias.

with only one battery. The circuit is shown for both capacitor and transformer coupling. By comparison with (b) of Figure 10-1, it may be seen that the right polarities are provided. The value of R_B must be high for two reasons: (1) to prevent loading down the a-c signal, and (2) to lower the emitter bias sufficiently from the value of V_{CC}. The d-c equation for the input current is

$$I_B = \frac{V_{CC} - V_{EB}}{R_B} \tag{6}$$

Although this biasing arrangement is the simplest possible for transistor circuits, it has the disadvantage that the operating point may vary with different transistors and with ambient temperature changes.

By far the most accepted biasing technique for the common-emitter amplifier is shown in Figure 10-3. The set of resistors R_1 and

(a) RC coupled (b) Transformer coupled

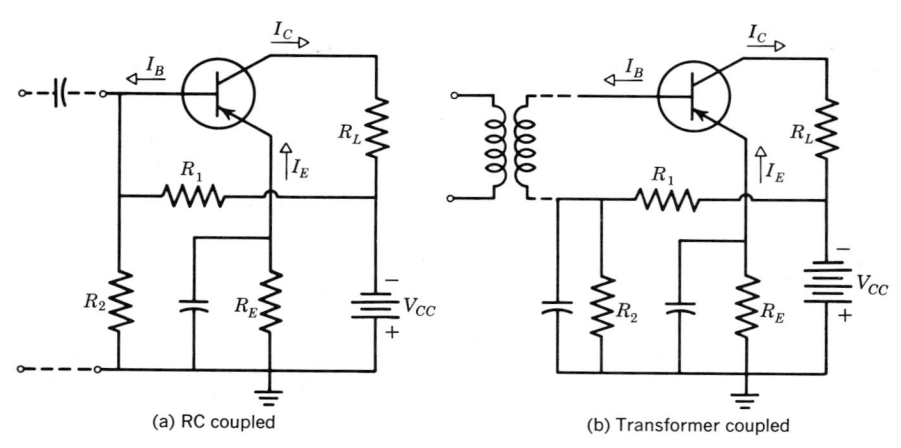

Fig. 10-3. A single battery, common-emitter bias circuit.

R_2 acts as a voltage divider to provide the base-to-emitter voltage. This arrangement makes the bias point less dependent on transistor changes, and the resistor R_E provides additional bias point stability. Note that this resistor is bypassed, so that for a-c conditions R_E is effectively shorted. The need for this resistor is explained in the next chapter.

In actual circuit diagrams, where many stages are cascaded, it is useful to rearrange the circuit for easier reading. The usual way of

Cascade amplifiers

treating an amplifier stage is shown in Figure 10-4, which is the identical circuit to that in Figure 10-3. This arrangement permits all the points that are connected to a given power supply to appear in a single horizontal line. Note that the arrangement of Figure 10-4 implies (but does not show) that the opposite side of the power supply is connected to ground. In the future we will use either arrangement, depending upon which is considered most suitable for the immediate purpose.

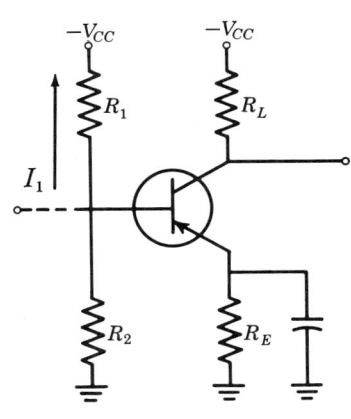

Fig. 10-4. Usual schematic arrangement for basic amplifier of Fig. 10-3.

In order to note the effect of the external elements on the bias point, we will again find the expression for the input current I_B of the amplifier of Figures 10-3 and 10-4 using the two assumptions noted before. The main point here is to emphasize that the d-c bias circuitry external to the transistor can be handled by the usual analysis methods. The R_E now couples the "input" circuit and the output (load line) circuit. Therefore, referring to Figure 10-3, it is seen that two d-c loop equations are required. We assume that I_C is chosen from the output load line analysis:

$$V_{CC} = (R_2 + R_1)I_1 - R_2 I_B$$
$$R_E I_C + V_{EB} = R_2 I_1 - (R_2 + R_E)I_B \tag{7}$$

Solving these for I_B, it is found that [1]

$$I_B = \frac{V_{CC}R_2 - I_C[R_2 R_E + R_1 R_E] - V_{EB}(R_1 + R_2)}{R_1 R_2 + R_E R_2 + R_1 R_E} \tag{8}$$

This equation is quite complex and can be simplified. Usually $R_1 \gg R_2$ so that a good approximation is

$$I_B \simeq \frac{V_{CC}R_2 - I_C R_E R_1 - V_{EB} R_1}{R_1 R_2 + R_1 R_E} \tag{9}$$

We will see, when considering bias stability, why the circuit of Figure 10-4 is the most stable of the three single-battery circuits.

[1] Note that finding I_B now involves consideration of I_C. If these equations are used, one must find commensurate values of I_B and I_C along the load line by trial and error. In most cases only a few trials are required. In Chapter 11 the bias equations will be written in terms of the h_{FE} and the I_{CBO} of the transistor.

At this point it should be noted that the bias circuitry of Figures 10-3 and 10-4 can also be employed to bias a common-base circuit. In this case the circuit would appear as shown in Figure 10-5. It may

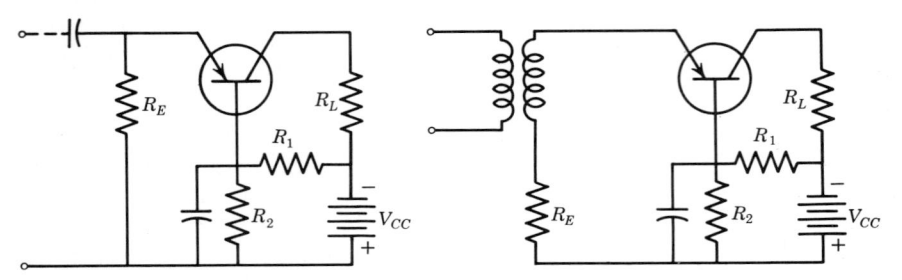

Fig. 10-5. Single-battery biasing circuit for common-base connection.

be verified that, d-c wise, this circuit is the same as Figure 10-3. Consequently, the equations written above also apply to this arrangement.

Another common-emitter bias connection which has stabilizing features is shown in Figure 10-6 (both the loop and the schematic

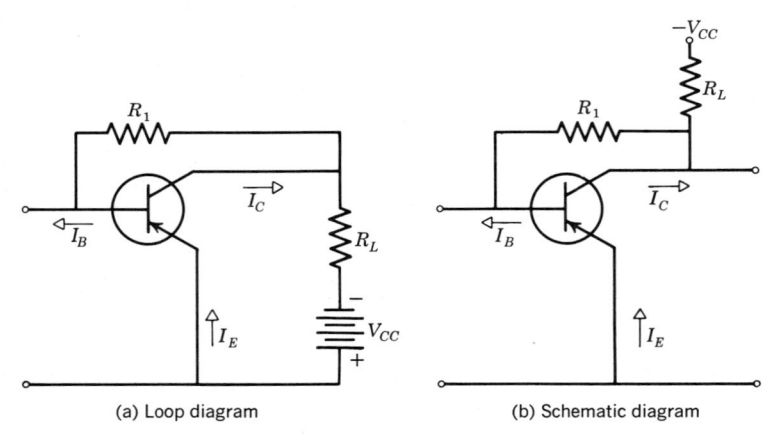

(a) Loop diagram (b) Schematic diagram

Fig. 10-6. Basic self-bias arrangement for common emitter.

representation are shown). This bias connection is often referred to as "self-bias," because of the way in which the bias varies with collector current I_C. The basic d-c input equation is

$$I_B = \frac{V_{CE} - V_{EB}}{R_1} \simeq \frac{V_{CE}}{R_1} \qquad (10)$$

Cascade amplifiers 275

Note that a resistor between the base and ground may be added to give additional stability.

This bias circuit has a disadvantage—it is not convenient to separate the d-c feedback conditions which stabilize the bias point from the a-c conditions. As it stands, the circuit of Figure 10-6 provides negative a-c feedback (studied in Chapter 12).

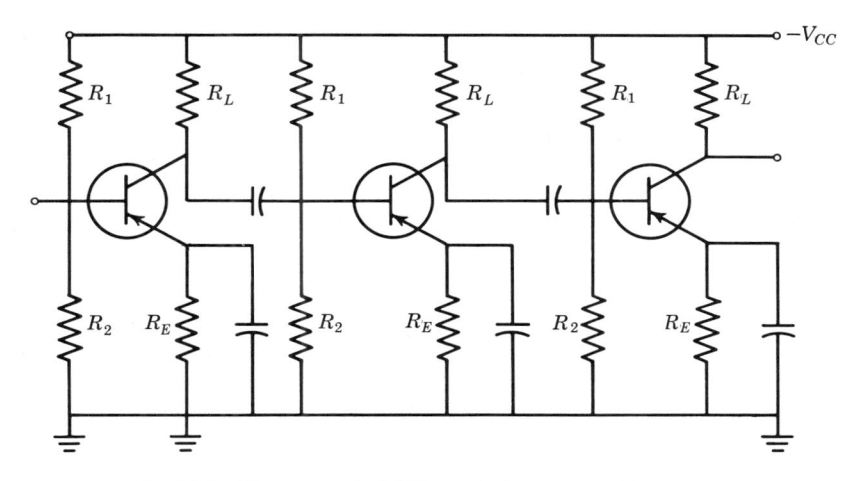

Fig. 10-7. Three cascaded, RC-coupled common-emitter stages.

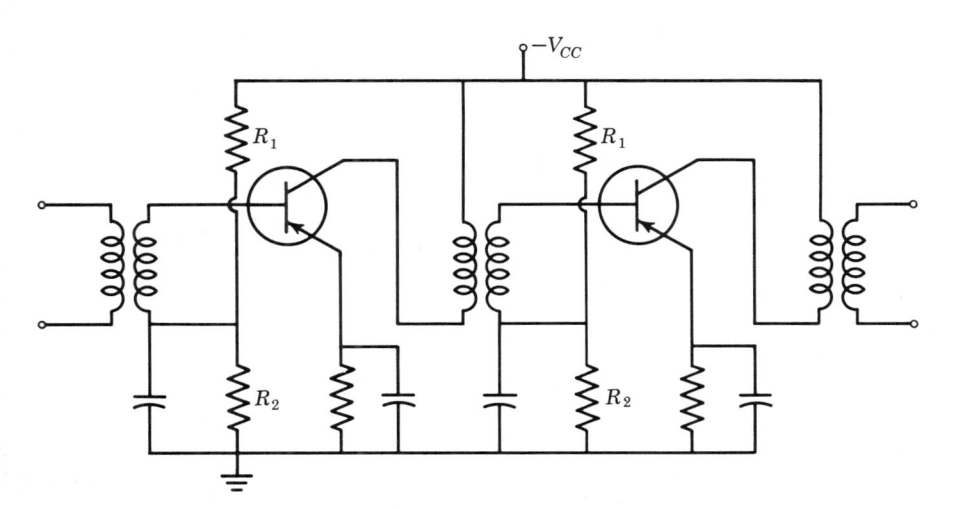

Fig. 10-8. Two cascaded, transformer-coupled common-emitter stages.

The biasing of cascaded stages can now be illustrated. Three cascaded stages, using the most frequently occurring emitter bias connection (of Figure 10-4), are shown in Figure 10-7. The operating point for each stage is depicted by Equation (8) or (9).

To illustrate the difference between the *RC*-coupled and the transformer-coupled stage, Figure 10-8 portrays a basic bias circuit for cascaded common-emitter stages. It is remembered that for the common-base stages, transformer coupling is required for impedance matching; if *RC* coupling were used, the power gain of the cascaded base circuit would be less than that for a single stage.

Here we have emphasized the methods of obtaining suitable bias, and methods of depicting the bias situation. The output graphical characteristics are useful for visualizing the setting of the bias point, along with d-c equations for the external circuitry as written above. It has been stated that the bias point is subject to severe change as a result of temperature changes and unit-to-unit variation, which makes the bias point *stability* a more difficult problem. The next chapter, devoted to this issue, indicates that the equivalent circuit method of analyzing bias point stability is superior to the use of characteristics.

FREQUENCY RESPONSE

In addition to calculating the gain of electronic circuits for a nominal frequency (as was done in Chapter 8), it is usually necessary to find the range of frequencies over which that value of gain is valid. The signals used in electronic circuits are usually nonsinusoidal, as opposed to the signals of power distribution systems, for example. By the use of the Fourier series concept, these nonsinusoidal signals can be treated as the sum of a series of sine-wave components of various frequencies. Because of this, the gain and phase versus frequency is very important for electronic circuits. If the electronic circuit does not amplify equally all frequency components of importance in the signal, the output signal will be distorted.

The frequency response of any electronic circuit depends upon both the electronic device itself and the attached circuitry. The low-frequency response will be determined by the coupling elements (capacitor or transformer) and the bypass capacitors. Here we will consider mainly the role of capacitive coupling. At the high-frequency end we shall find that the transistor itself provides a high-frequency limit to any transistor circuit (unless a circuit element provides a lower limit).

The electrical review in Chapter 6 showed that a basic way of treating the frequency response is to divide the circuit into three frequency areas: low-frequency, mid-frequency, and high-frequency. In addition, it was stated that for the stage-to-stage coupling circuits, the low-frequency circuit response is controlled by any series capacitors or parallel inductors, and the high-frequency circuit is controlled by parallel capacitors and series inductors. The mid-frequency circuit applies to the range of frequencies between the low and the high regions, and this circuit contains no reactances since it is independent of frequency.

When dealing with the three frequency areas, the usual procedure is to calculate first the gain for the mid-frequency case, and then find the *change in gain* (from the mid-value) that occurs in the low and the high regions. This is the procedure that will be followed in this chapter.

The central question, then, is: What factors cause the gain, in the low and high regions, to fall off from the mid-band value? We know that the capacitive or inductive coupling between stages is one cause of low-frequency decrease in gain. This is logical because the coupling elements are designed to block the bias direct current; hence the closer the signal frequency approaches direct current, the more the gain will be decreased by the coupling element. Another cause of low-frequency drop-off are the bypass capacitors, such as those which bypass R_E in Figures 10-4 and 10-7. We wish here to concentrate on the role of the coupling circuit.

In the high-frequency regions the transistor itself is usually the limiting factor. As in the case of vacuum tubes where the interelectrode capacitances become effective, the transistor exhibits reactances at the high frequencies. The situation for the transistor, however, is more complicated than for the vacuum tube. Typical high-frequency equivalent circuits (of the transistor) contain about ten elements, and these element values vary with operating point and with temperature (as do any parameters of the transistor).

For a general high-frequency analysis one can use either a matrix-type equivalent circuit (such as the h parameter circuit) and consider all the parameters to be complex, or one can use a circuit which ties the basic electrical parameters (R's and C's) to the physical structure. An example of the latter type of circuit is the "hybrid-π" equivalent circuit, which will be included in Chapter 16.

If one uses the complex matrix (h or y) parameters for a general high-frequency analysis, it is necessary to measure the complex parameters for the range of frequencies of interest. If one uses a physical-based equivalent circuit (such as the hybrid-π) a relatively complicated measurement procedure is required to find the correct parameter values. In addition, the parameter values of both approaches vary with operating point and temperature.

A standard amplifier design often does not require a general high-frequency analysis. It may be sufficient, from the design point of view, to only estimate where the gain drops off from its mid-frequency value. A reasonable approximation to establishing the gain drop-off point can be achieved by considering two important factors that limit the response of transistors at the higher frequencies: the current gain drop-off and the collector capacitance. For the general-purpose transistor, the manufacturer always supplies the frequency at which the short-circuit current gain of the transistor causes a 3 decibel gain drop-off from its mid-frequency value, and the value of the collector capacitance for a given operating point. As mentioned, these two items permit estimating the frequency at which the circuit gain is down by 3 db from the mid-band value.

The technique here, then, will be to use the low-frequency h parameter equivalent circuit and find the effect of h_{fe} drop-off and collector capacitance. A general high-frequency analysis, using both complex matrix parameters and the hybrid-π equivalent circuit, will be reserved for Chapter 16.

As stated, we will begin by calculating the mid-frequency gain and then find the *change in gain* brought about by certain basic factors in the high- and the low-frequency regions.

MID-FREQUENCY GAIN CALCULATIONS. Although we have attached the name mid-frequency here to distinguish from the low- and the high-frequency regions, we are dealing with the same quantities as were treated in Chapter 8 for the single stage. Consequently, we use the equivalent circuit and the methods treated in that chapter. It was emphasized there that the most profitable procedure when

Cascade amplifiers 279

cascaded stages are encountered is to analyze the circuit on a stage-by-stage basis. The other alternative would be to solve the entire circuit as an entity by the use of many simultaneous equations. Since solving the simultaneous equations involves much work, the stage-by-stage method is recommended. An example at the end of Chapter 8 was used to illustrate the technique of the stage-by-stage analysis.

We intend here to concentrate upon this analysis method and make one change from the former example: the gain will be expressed in terms of decibels rather than by number ratios. We will also show how the interstage networks influence the gain of the circuit.

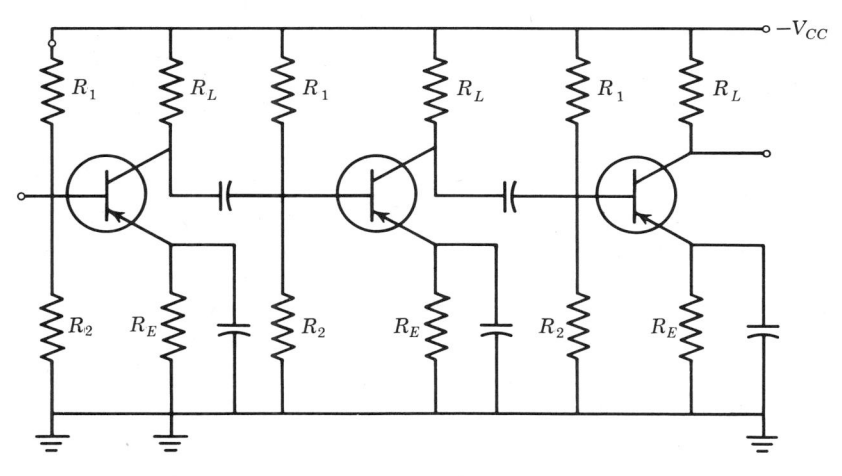

Fig. 10-9. Common-emitter transistor cascade amplifier.

Figure 10-9 represents a typical three-stage common-emitter circuit. This circuit is basically of the type shown in Figure 10-4, and is the same as the circuit of Figure 10-7.

The first step, when analyzing any electronic circuit, is to find the a-c mid-frequency circuit. This amounts to the following alterations of the original circuit: (1) all batteries (or d-c power supplies) are removed and replaced by their internal impedance; (2) all coupling capacitors are removed for the mid-frequency region; and (3) all bypassed resistors are short-circuited, since the bypass capacitors are assumed to short-circuit the resistance in the mid-frequency range. Performing these steps on the circuit of Figure 10-9, the resulting a-c equivalent is shown in Figure 10-10. Note

280 **Cascade amplifiers**

that the resistances connected to the base in Figure 10-10, called R_B, consist of the parallel combination of the R_1 and R_2 from Figure 10-9. Since the power supply represents an a-c short circuit, it is clear that these two resistors are in parallel between the base lead and ground.

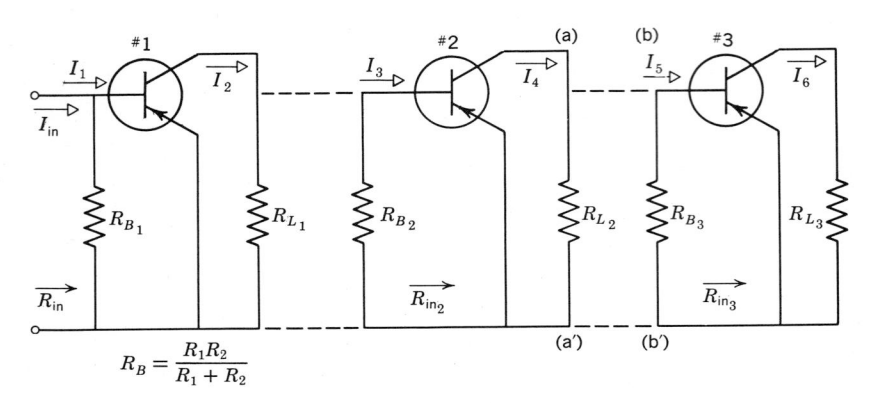

$$R_B = \frac{R_1 R_2}{R_1 + R_2}$$

Fig. 10-10. Mid-frequency a-c equivalent of Fig. 10-9.

Since the power gain is usually of chief interest for a transistor circuit, we will find the power gain of this circuit by using the stage-by-stage procedure. In the example of Chapter 8, we found the current gain of each transistor stage and each interstage, and then multiplied them to find the total current gain. This value was then used to find the total power gain by use of the equation

$$A_p = \frac{P_{\text{out}}}{P_{\text{in}}} = (A_i^2)_{\text{total}} \frac{R_L}{R_{\text{in}}} \tag{11}$$

In order to illustrate the effect of each stage, however, *we will here calculate the power gain of each transistor stage and each interstage.* We can then multiply all the power gains to find the total power gain, or we can change each gain value to db and then *add* the various gains to find the total power gain in decibels.

For the gain between the output and the input of the transistor, we use the equations derived in Chapter 8. The gain of the interstages is calculated by elementary circuit rules. It is also necessary to know the input resistance of each transistor input since this acts as part of the load for the previous stage.

It is remembered that, if we use the conventional equivalent circuit, we must begin with the last stage and proceed to the left because each stage acts as a load on the preceding one. If the greatly

Cascade amplifiers

simplified circuit of Figure 8-6 were used this would not be necessary. Here we will use the complete equivalent circuit in order to remain general and to emphasize the interrelated effects. For the various transistor stages we can use the equations developed in Chapter 8 and listed in Tables 8-4 and 8-5. Basic electrical laws will be used for the interstages. We will find the power gain in each case by applying Equation (11) to the individual stage.

THIRD STAGE. For the third stage the load is R_{L_3}. Using the relation in Table 8-5 for the current gain, we have

$$A_{i_3} = \frac{I_6}{I_5} = \frac{h_{fe}}{h_{oe}R_{L_3} + 1} \tag{12}$$

The h parameters in this equation are the common-emitter parameters for the third-stage transistor.

We need to know the input resistance both for calculating the power gain and for finding the load of the preceding stage. From Table 8-5,

$$R_{i_3} = \frac{\Delta^{he}R_{L_3} + h_{ie}}{h_{oe}R_{L_3} + 1} \tag{13}$$

The power gain for the third stage, then, is

$$A_{p_3} = \left(\frac{I_6}{I_5}\right)^2 \frac{R_{L_3}}{R_{i_3}} = (A_{i_3})^2 \frac{R_{L_3}}{R_{i_3}} \tag{14}$$

We can find the decibel value of Equation (14) by the following:

$$\text{Db}_3 = 10 \log_{10} \frac{P_{\text{out}}}{P_{\text{in}}} = 10 \log_{10} A_{p_3} \tag{15}$$

For denoting decibel power gain the symbol db will be used. Capital letters will be used for actual transistor gains, and lowercase letters will denote interstage gains.

PRECEDING INTERSTAGE. It is very important to remember that the relations developed in Chapter 8 and used above specify only the gain from the input to the output of the transistor. Since, in cascaded circuits, not all the output power reaches the next stage, we must find this interstage loss. We have merely to find the power gain of the interstage, and this can again be found by using Equa-

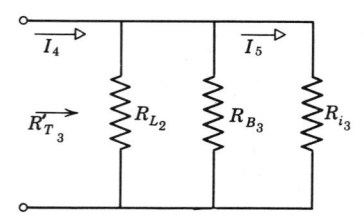

Fig. 10-11. Interstage circuit.

tion (11). The interstage appears as in Figure 10-11. The current gain, by the basic current-division law is

$$a_{i_3} = \frac{I_5}{I_4} = \frac{R_{L_2}R_{B_3}/(R_{L_2} + R_{B_3})}{R_{L_2}R_{B_3}/(R_{L_2} + R_{B_3}) + R_{i_3}} \quad (16)$$
$$= \frac{R_{L_2}R_{B_3}}{R_{L_2}R_{B_3} + R_{i_3}(R_{L_2} + R_{B_3})}$$

The load for the interstage is R_{i_3}, and the input resistance R'_T is given by the three parallel resistors.

$$R'_{T_3} = \frac{R_{L_2}R_{B_3}R_{i_3}}{R_{L_2}R_{B_3} + (R_{L_2} + R_{B_3})R_{i_3}} \quad (17)$$

The power gain (a_p) is then given by

$$a_{p_3} = \left(\frac{I_5}{I_4}\right)^2 \frac{R_{i_3}}{R'_{T_3}} \quad (18)$$

Again the decibel value may be found by the equation

$$db_3 = 10 \log_{10} a_{p_3} \quad (19)$$

Although the above method is suitable, we can simplify this interstage calculation. If Equation (18) is written out and simplified, it will be found that the a_p can be written directly as

$$a_{p_3} = \frac{R'_{T_3}}{R_{i_3}} \quad (20)$$

Cascade amplifiers

The decibel value, then, for an interstage is given by

$$db_3 = 10 \log_{10} \frac{R'_{T_3}}{R_{i_3}} \tag{21}$$

where R'_T = parallel combination of all resistors of the interstage,
R_i = load resistance of interstage, or input resistance to next stage.

The value of the interstage decibels will always be negative, since it is really a loss rather than a gain.

SECOND STAGE. The load for the second stage consists of the three parallel resistors of Figure 10-11; its value, therefore, is given by Equation (17). The current gain is then

$$A_{i_2} = \frac{I_4}{I_3} = \frac{h_{fe}}{h_{oe}R'_{T_3} + 1} \tag{22}$$

The input resistance of the second stage is

$$R_{i_2} = \frac{\Delta^{h^e} R'_{T_3} + h_{ie}}{h_{oe}R'_{T_3} + 1} \tag{23}$$

The power gain in decibels is then

$$Db_2 = 10 \log_{10} \left(A_{i_2}^2 \frac{R'_{T_3}}{R_{i_2}} \right) \tag{24}$$

Using the principles exhibited above, the remaining equations for the various power gains can be written. The procedure in each case consists of first finding the current gain, and then determining the load and the input resistance. Remember that all interstages must be accounted for; the equations of Table 8-5 deal only with the gain from the input to the output of the transistor. The interstage calculation above illustrates the procedure that may be used for any interstage.

After the power gain of each part of the circuit is calculated, and the decibel value is found, we have merely to add the separate decibel values to obtain the total power gain. Keeping in mind that db represents the interstages and Db refers to the transistor portion, the equation for the above circuit may be written

$$\left.\begin{array}{l}\text{total}\\ \text{decibel}\\ \text{power}\\ \text{gain}\end{array}\right\} = \text{Db}_{\text{total}} = \text{db}_1 + \text{Db}_1 + \text{db}_2 + \text{Db}_2 + \text{db}_3 + \text{Db}_3 \quad (25)$$

Since the values of interstage decibels are negative, they will actually be subtracted from the transistor gains.

Although there are a number of advantages in using decibels for electronic calculations, we see here one of the main advantages: it allows us to add directly quantities that would otherwise require multiplication. In the next section we will see further how the use of decibels simplifies matters.

For any cascaded circuit, then, we can find the a-c gain by using the stage-by-stage method illustrated above.

LOW-FREQUENCY GAIN CALCULATIONS. We now wish to find how the gain changes from the above calculations when the coupling capacitor determines the low-frequency response. As noted before, this coupling capacitor and the various bypass capacitors are responsible for low-frequency drop-off in *RC*-coupled stages. The coupling capacitor is discussed here to emphasize the frequency limiting aspect of the coupling circuit in any cascaded electronic amplifier stages. In an actual transistor circuit design the bypass capacitor across the emitter resistor (see Figure 10-4) may actually control the low-frequency drop-off before the coupling capacitor becomes influential. The influence of these bypass capacitors can be evaluated by the same methods as used here for the coupling capacitor. We will now evaluate the frequency dependence of the coupling capacitor. If we want an exact solution for the frequency dependence, we are again faced with the prospect of writing simultaneous equations for the entire network and solving them simultaneously. Since the objectives of a designer rarely warrant such effort, we will present an approximate solution for the low-frequency response.

The procedure to be used consists of, with the proper approximations, finding *the change in gain from the mid-band value*. Thus for any frequency in the low region, we will find the decibel value that must be subtracted from the mid-band gain. The derivation will result in a chart from which the proper loss can be read.

Since the low-frequency calculations are based on the mid-band

Cascade amplifiers

values, the first step is to redraw the mid-band interstage circuit. The third interstage circuit of Figure 10-10 is redrawn in slightly different form in Figure 10-12. This circuit is achieved by substituting

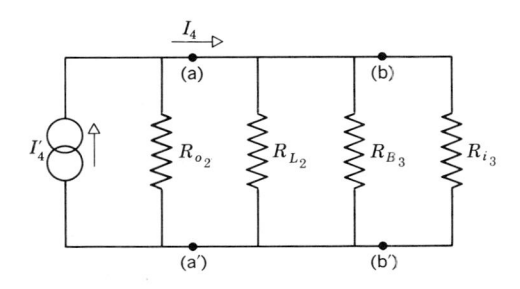

Fig. 10-12. One stage of Fig. 10-10.

equivalent circuits for the parts on either side of a-a' and b-b'. The value of the current generator must be of such a value that the I_4' of Figure 10-12 is identical to the I_4 of Figure 10-10. Although it is not important for our purpose, the value of I_4' is

$$I_4 = \frac{h_{fe}(R_{T_3}/R_{o_2} + 1)}{h_{oe}R_{T_3} + 1} I_3 \qquad (26)$$

where R_{T_3} = parallel resistance of all resistors in Figure 10-12,
h^e = parameters for preceding transistor.

With this value of I_4', then, the above circuit correctly represents the chosen portion of Figure 10-11 *for the mid-band conditions*. Note that the values of I_4', R_o, and R_i depend upon other circuit values; hence a given circuit of the type in Figure 10-12 applies only to a *particular* circuit and cannot be regarded as a general equivalent circuit.

If we now put the coupling capacitor between R_L and R_B, we can calculate the ratio of low-frequency gain to mid-band gain. This circuit is shown in Figure 10-13. Since all interstages appear similar to the one we are considering, we will drop the numerical subscripts in order to make the results general. If any concerned interstage does not have either an R_L or an R_B, the calculations will simply neglect this resistor.

We can now view the approximations made in this analysis since we shall regard all quantities of Figure 10-13 except X_c as being constant with frequency. In other words, *we are using the mid-frequency values of I', R_o, and R_i to find the low-frequency response.* In reality, the variation of X_c with frequency changes the value of Z_L and hence the values of I_4 and R_o. Similarly, the varying Z_L of the following stage actually varies R_i. Nevertheless, the stated approximations are neces-

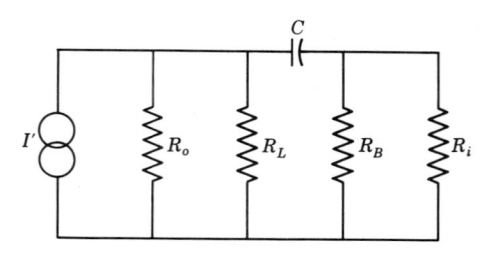

Fig. 10-13. Interstage circuit for low-frequency range.

sary if a practical solution is to be effected. These approximations are quite good for *RC*-coupled stages; if transformer coupling is used and matched conditions are achieved, only rough approximations result.

The object now is to find the frequency response of the circuit of Figure 10-13. We know that the series capacitor will act to decrease the gain as the frequency decreases. For convenience, the circuit of Figure 10-13 is redrawn in Figure 10-14(a); the only change is that

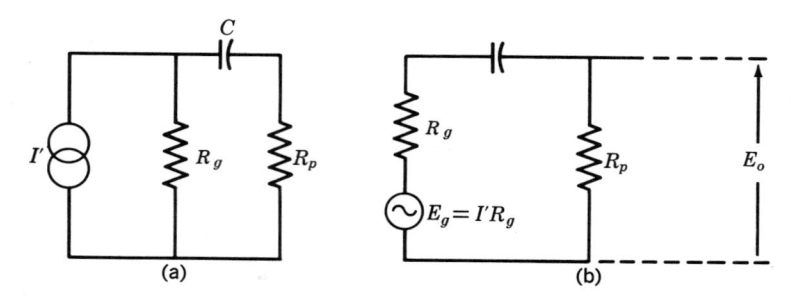

Fig. 10-14. Simplified circuits of Fig. 10-13.

the parallel resistors have been combined. It is noted that R_g and R_p are given by

$$R_g = \frac{R_o R_L}{R_o + R_L}, \qquad R_p = \frac{R_B R_i}{R_B + R_i} \tag{27}$$

Cascade amplifiers

Figure 10-14(b) shows the same circuit except that the current generator has been converted to a voltage source.

We can find the change in gain from the mid-band value by writing the equation for E_o/E_g for both low-frequency and mid-band cases. Referring to Chapter 6, the ratio of E_o/E_g for Figure 10-14(b) is

$$\left(\frac{E_o}{E_g}\right)_{\text{low}} = \frac{R_P}{\sqrt{(R_g + R_p)^2 + (1/\omega C)^2}} \qquad (28)$$

For the mid-band ratio, the capacitor is neglected and the ratio is simply

$$\left(\frac{E_o}{E_g}\right)_{\text{mid}} = \frac{R_p}{R_g + R_p} \qquad (29)$$

Since we want the *change* from the mid-band case, we take the ratio of Equation (28) to (29):

$$\frac{(E_o/E_g)_{\text{low}}}{(E_o/E_g)_{\text{mid}}} = \frac{(E_o)_{\text{low}}}{(E_o)_{\text{mid}}} = \frac{1}{\sqrt{1 + 1/[(R_g + R_p)C]^2\omega^2}} \qquad (30)$$

If for any given frequency we convert this voltage gain to power gain, and then find the decibel value, we can add the result to the mid-band decibel value of interstage gain. The final result will be the decibel gain of the interstage at any frequency. The power ratio of Equation (30) is found by squaring the voltage ratio, since the same R_i is assumed for both mid-band and low-frequency ranges.

$$\frac{(a_p)_{\text{low}}}{(a_p)_{\text{mid}}} = \frac{(E_o^2)_{\text{low}}/R_i}{(E_o^2)_{\text{mid}}/R_i} = \left[\frac{(E_o)_{\text{low}}}{(E_o)_{\text{mid}}}\right]^2 \qquad (31)$$

The change in decibels, then, from the mid-band value is given by

$$\text{change} = \text{db}_{\text{low}} = 10 \log_{10}\left[\frac{(E_o)_{\text{low}}}{(E_o)_{\text{mid}}}\right]^2 \qquad (32)$$

It is noted that the db_{low} is a function of frequency and would have to be calculated for each frequency of interest.

The gain for an interstage in the low-frequency range is now

$$\text{low-frequency db} = \text{db}_{\text{mid}} + \text{db}_{\text{low}} \qquad (33)$$

Since the signs of both quantities in this equation are negative, the equation says that the mid-band interstage loss plus the additional loss due to the coupling capacitor will be subtracted from the total gain of the transistor stages.

We can now note how Equation (25), the mid-band total gain, is altered by the low-frequency drop-off. The total gain now appears as

$$\begin{aligned}\text{total decibel} \atop \text{power gain}\Big\} &= (db_1 + db_{low_1}) + Db_1 + (db_2 + db_{low_2}) \\ &\quad + Db_2 + (db_3 + db_{low_3}) + Db_3 \\ &= \text{mid-band gain} + (db_{low_1} + db_{low_2} + db_{low_3})\end{aligned} \quad (34)$$

Hence, after having calculated the mid-band gain, we need merely add the loss given by each coupling capacitor. This equation may be used at any frequency in the low region.

Rather than calculating the loss at each frequency, it is more profitable to organize the information of Equation (30) so that a chart can be used to directly read the decrease in gain. This may be done by selecting a reference frequency for the gain decrease. *The most convenient reference is that frequency where the power gain is down 3 db.* From Chapter 6 it is remembered that this is also the half-power point, i.e., the power delivered to the following R_i is one-half that delivered at the mid-frequency. This occurs when the denominator of Equation (30) becomes $\sqrt{2}$. Therefore the following equation can be used to find the half-power frequency.

$$\frac{1}{[(R_g + R_p)C]^2 (2\pi f_L)^2} = 1, \qquad f_L = \frac{1}{2\pi(R_g + R_p)C} \quad (35)$$

Each interstage network, then, has a half-power frequency in the low end given by Equation (35).

Substituting Equation (35) back into Equation (30), we find

$$\boxed{\frac{(E_o)_{\text{low}}}{(E_o)_{\text{mid}}} = \frac{1}{\sqrt{1 + (f_L/f)^2}}} \quad (36)$$

Since we wish to work with decibel values, as in Equation (34), we can find the power decibel ratio of Equation (36). Remembering that the power ratio is determined by squaring the voltage ratio, it is found that

$$db_{\text{low}} = 10 \log_{10} \frac{1}{[1 + (f_L/f)^2]} \quad (37)$$

Cascade amplifiers

A chart showing the variation of Equation (36) or (37) versus the ratio f/f_L is given in Figure 10-15. Using the ratio f/f_L as the independent variable allows us to use this chart for any f_L *and hence for any design situation*. The decibel value read from this curve tells us the decibel loss from the mid-band decibel value. Hence for each interstage that contains a coupling capacitor, the decibel loss for any frequency, as shown on the chart, must be added to the total mid-band gain. (When using the chart, it is convenient to regard the process as subtraction since all losses are negative gains.)

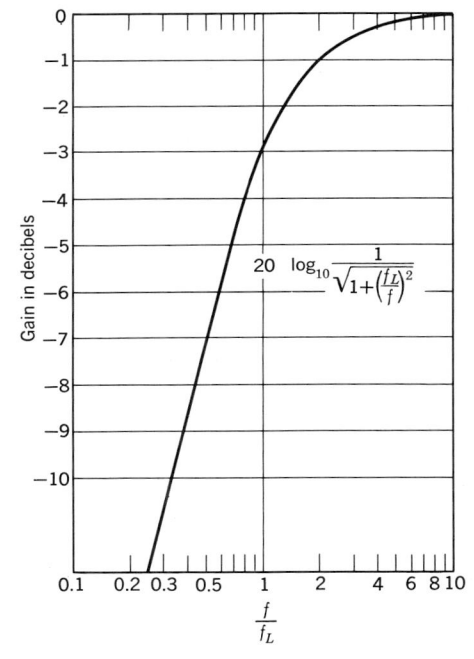

Plot of $20 \log_{10} \dfrac{1}{\sqrt{1+\left(\dfrac{f_L}{f}\right)^2}}$ versus f/f_L.

Fig. 10-15. Low-frequency response.

As an example of the use of the chart, let us assume that by Equation (35) we have an f_L of 500 cycles. Then the point 1 on the frequency scale corresponds to 500 cycles. At a frequency of 1000 cycles it is seen that the *additional loss* of the interstage is 1 db. Thus if three identical interstages would occur in a cascaded circuit under the above conditions, the total circuit would be down 3 db at 1000 cycles from the mid-band gain.

We can now summarize the procedure for calculating the gain change in the low-frequency range due to the coupling capacitor.

1. Find the mid-band power gain in decibels for the total circuit, including the interstage networks (Equation 25).

2. Find the necessary values of R_o and R_i for the circuit of Figure 10-13. These R_o and R_i values are based on mid-band conditions and the equations appear in Table 8-5.

3. Find the f_L of each interstage by use of Equation (35) and Equation (27).

4. For any given frequency, read the value of decibel loss associated with each interstage and based upon the f_L of that interstage from the chart.

5. Subtract the loss of each interstage from the total mid-band gain as found in (1).

The use of the chart will be further illustrated in the design example of this chapter. It is necessary to remember that the above procedure is not an exact analysis. The important approximations consist of assuming that the current gain and the output impedance of the preceding stage remain at their mid-band values, and also that the input impedance of the following stage remains fixed. These approximations are rather close for the RC-coupled cases where the permissible combinations are emitter-and-emitter, emitter-and-base, emitter-and-collector, or base-and-collector. The base-and-base, and the collector-and-collector combinations are never used with RC coupling since the resulting gain would always be less than that for a single stage.

For transformer coupling, the low-frequency response is determined almost solely by the frequency response of the transformer. If, in addition to the transformer, a capacitor is used to isolate the bias direct current, the above analysis will yield only a rough approximation since the assumptions are not so good when matched conditions are used.

Finally, note that the analysis here assumed that the bypass resistor across any R_E is sufficiently large so that the coupling capacitor controls the drop-off.

HIGH-FREQUENCY GAIN CALCULATIONS. In the previous section we examined one of the basic limitations of the low-frequency response: the effect of the coupling capacitor between stages. In this section we discuss the equivalent basic situations that determine the high-

Cascade amplifiers

frequency drop-off of the transistor amplifier. For many amplifier designs it is sufficient to estimate the frequency at which the gain drops by 3 db from its mid-band value. Here we will derive this estimate using the low-frequency h parameter circuit and find the effect of current-gain (h_{fe}) drop-off and collector capacitance. A general high-frequency analysis, considering both the matrix equivalent circuit with complex parameters and the hybrid-π equivalent circuit, will be reserved for Chapter 16.

The high-frequency gain decrease of a transistor amplifier is due to two basic effects. First the intrinsic current gain (h_{fe} or h_{fb}) decreases with frequency because of the time required for the carriers to pass across the base region. Secondly, the transistor output (shunt) capacitance causes a gain dropoff typical of any shunt capacitance. The major reason for examining separately these two effects (which warrant emphasis), before studying a general purpose high-frequency equivalent circuit is that such examination enables one to estimate the gain drop-off frequency from basic data always supplied by the manufacturer. In many design situations further complexity is not warranted. An additional reason for proceeding in this way is that an appreciation for the role of parallel capacitance in any electronic circuit is absolutely essential.

The h_{fe} drop-off is the more important factor since the output capacitance becomes less influential as R_L decreases. In many applications R_L is sufficiently low so that the capacitive effect is negligible.

For these high-frequency drop-off calculations a procedure similar to that used in the previous section will be used. The *change in gain* from the mid-band value will be sought. The same approximations as before will be made. They are: (1) the current gain and R_o of the preceding stage *do not vary with* Z_L; and (2), the input resistance of the next stage remains at its mid-band value. A distinct difference from the previous case is that here we have two effects to consider. This will be handled by again *separating the two effects*. The effect of the collector capacitance will be considered first, since the role of shunt capacitance is basic to any electrical circuit. In considering this capacitance, it will be assumed that the current gain does not vary with frequency; then the effect of the frequency variation of the current gain will be found with the capacitance removed.

Referring to Figure 10-10, the high-frequency equivalent circuit due to shunt capacitance for the interstage a-a' and b-b' is shown in

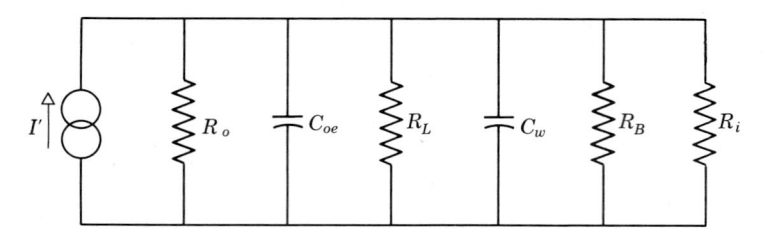

Fig. 10-16. Interstage circuit with collector capacity for high-frequency range.

Figure 10-16. The capacitor C_{oe} is the collector capacitance for the transistor preceding a-a'. The collector capacitance C_{ob} quoted by the manufacturer is usually given for the common-base connection. In the emitter connection the value of capacitance becomes

$$C_{oe} = \frac{C_{ob}}{1 + h_{fb}} \tag{38}$$

The value of h_{fb} is the common-base value of short-circuit current gain. Since h_{fb} is negative and close to 1 (see Table 8-4) it is seen that C_{oe} is substantially larger than C_{ob}. The ratio here is roughly the same as the ratio of h_{fe} to h_{fb} (β to α). The increase in capacitance can be described in terms of the Miller effect (see Chapter 16).

It is noted that an additional shunt capacitor C_W is inserted to account for the small value of wiring capacity found in each design.

Since all the elements are in parallel, the circuit of Figure 10-16 can be simplified by combining elements. In addition, for ease of calculation, the current generator may be changed to a voltage gen-

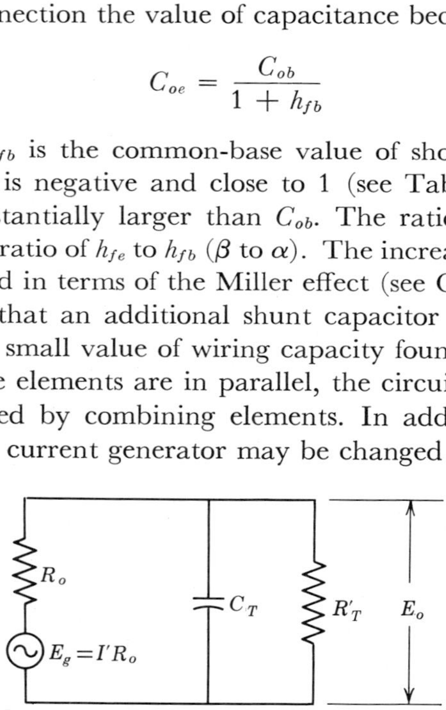

Fig. 10-17. Simplified circuit of Fig. 10-16.

erator. The result is the circuit of Figure 10-17. In this circuit the following relations hold:

$$C_T = C_{oe} + C_W, \qquad R'_T = \frac{R_L R_B R_i}{R_L R_B + R_i(R_L + R_B)} \tag{39}$$

Cascade amplifiers

As seen, R_T' consists of the parallel combination of the load resistance, the bias resistance, and the input resistance. *If the stage were transformer coupled, R_T' would consist only of the R_i transformed by the square of the turns ratio.*

As in the previous section, we need the ratio of E_o/E_g in the above circuit. That is, we are finding *how much the gain changes from the mid-band* value. From Chapter 6, the ratio of E_o/E_g is given by

$$\left(\frac{E_o}{E_g}\right)_{high} = \frac{R_T'}{\sqrt{(R_o R_T' \omega C_T)^2 + (R_o + R_T')^2}} \qquad (40)$$

For the mid-band gain, the result is identical to the previous case, given in Equation (29) as

$$\left(\frac{E_o}{E_g}\right)_{mid} = \frac{R_T'}{R_o + R_T'} \qquad (41)$$

The ratio then is

$$\frac{(E_o/E_g)_{high}}{(E_o/E_g)_{mid}} = \frac{(E_o)_{high}}{(E_o)_{mid}} = \frac{1}{\sqrt{1 + \left(\frac{R_o R_T' \omega C_T}{R_o + R_T'}\right)^2}} \qquad (42)$$

For the reference frequency at the 3-db point, we find

$$f_H = \frac{1}{2\pi \left(\frac{R_o R_T' C_T}{R_o + R_T'}\right)} = \frac{1}{2\pi R_T C_T} \qquad (43)$$

It may be seen that R_T is the parallel resistance of R_o and R_T', and hence equals the total parallel resistance of all the interstage resistors. From this equation we note a very important fact; *the cutoff frequency decreases with increase in R_T'*. We see here that the criteria of power gain and frequency response conflict; for maximum power gain R_T' should equal R_o. However, *the frequency response is improved as R_T' is made smaller.* Consequently, in any design situation, the two factors must be weighed against each other.

Substituting Equation (43) back into Equation (42), it is found that

$$\boxed{\frac{(E_o)_{high}}{(E_o)_{mid}} = \frac{1}{\sqrt{1 + (f/f_H)^2}}} \qquad (44)$$

Although we could use this result directly, similar to the low-frequency method, it is more profitable again to use a chart. The chart is drawn in terms of decibel loss from the mid-band value, and is plotted versus f/f_H. To find the decibel value of Equation (44) we can write

$$\text{decibel change} = 10 \log_{10} \frac{1}{1 + (f/f_H)^2} \tag{45}$$

The chart is shown in Figure 10-18 and we use it as we do the chart

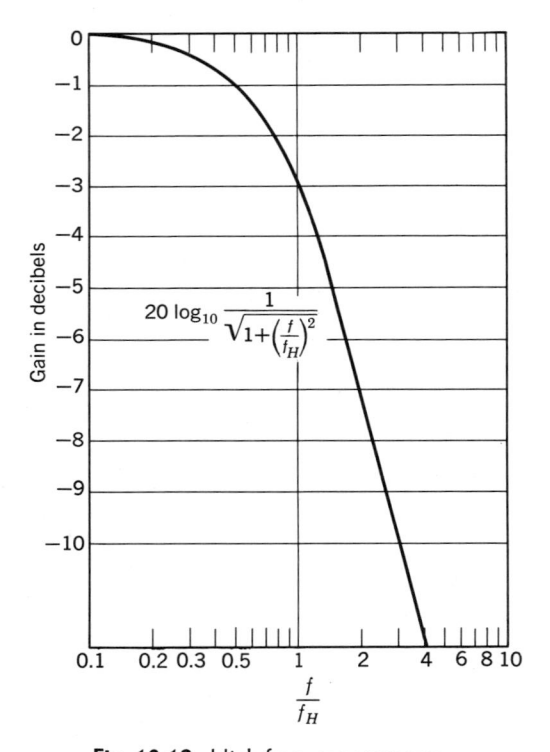

Fig. 10-18. High-frequency response.

for low-frequency response. That is, the first step is to find the f_H at each interstage by the use of Equation (43). This f_H corresponds to the point 1 on the frequency axis of the chart. For each interstage, then, *the value of additional loss due to collector capacitance* may be read directly from the chart at any frequency. The total losses from all the interstages must be subtracted from the total mid-band decibel

Cascade amplifiers

gain of the circuit. This, then, describes the role of transistor output capacitance in affecting the high-frequency response.

As mentioned, it is usually the h_{fe} drop-off which dominates the amplifier high-frequency drop-off. We are treating this as a separate problem, and hence the equivalent circuit will not contain the C_{oe}. If the variation of h_{fb} with frequency is measured, it is found that the resulting curve closely approximates the equation

$$(h_{fb})_{\text{high}} = \frac{h_{fb}}{1 + (f/f_{h_{fb}})^2} \tag{46}$$

where $f_{h_{fb}}$ = frequency where the value of h_{fb} has dropped to 0.707 of its low-frequency value. This corresponds to a 3-db change.

This equation may be used for the parameters of any connection, if the appropriate h parameters and the proper cutoff frequency are used. Thus the common-emitter relation is:

$$(h_{fe})_{\text{high}} = \frac{h_{fe}}{1 + (f/f_{h_{fe}})^2} \tag{46a}$$

where $f_{h_{fe}}$ = frequency where the value of h_{fe} has dropped to 0.707 of its low-frequency value.

Comparing this with Equation (44), it is seen that the approximate variation in current gain with frequency is the same as the variation in voltage gain caused by a shunt capacitor. As a matter of fact the current gain drop-off is represented by a capacitor in the hybrid-π equivalent circuit (see Chapter 16). Although the variation in Equation (44) is for a voltage ratio, and that of Equation (46) is for a current ratio, their effects will be the same because the input resistance to the next stage is assumed to remain at its mid-band value. Since power is given by I^2R, the decibel change in power caused by the h_{fe} variation is

$$\text{change in decibels} = \text{db}_{\text{high}} = 10 \log_{10} \frac{I_{\text{high}}^2 R_i}{I_{\text{mid}}^2 R_i}$$
$$= 10 \log_{10} \frac{1}{1 + (f/f_{h_{fe}})^2} \tag{47}$$

Since this equation is identical in form to that of Equation (45) *we can use the same chart as before (Figure 10-18) to find the decibel loss caused by the $h_{fe\ \text{high}}$ variation.*

Either the value of $f_{h_{fb}}$ or $h_{h_{fe}}$ is always stated by the manufacturer. The reference for the emitter case $f_{h_{fe}}$ may be found by the relation

$$f_{h_{fe}} = f_{h_{fb}}(1 + h_{fb}) \approx \frac{f_{h_{fb}}}{h_{fe}} \qquad (48)$$

where h_{fb} = common-base low-frequency current gain,
h_{fe} = common-emitter low-frequency current gain,
$f_{h_{fe}}$ = 3-db reference frequency for common-emitter case,
$f_{h_{fb}}$ = 3-db reference frequency for common-base (stated by manufacturer).

The right side of Equation (48) results from the fact that h_{fb} is approximately -1.

From this equation it is evident *that the cutoff frequency for the common emitter is less than that for the common base.*

The use of the chart, then, for the common-emitter situation is as follows: calculate the $f_{h_{fe}}$ by use of Equation (48) and then read the decibel power loss due to h_{fe} variation directly from the chart for any given frequency. The resulting decibel loss must then be subtracted, along with the loss due to the C_T found earlier, from the total mid-band decibel gain.

Although the common-emitter connection has been used throughout this section, the same methods can be used for the other connections. It is imperative, however, to use the proper parameters and capacitance values.

We can now summarize the procedure for finding the approximate high-frequency response, when considering both the collector capacitance and the h_{fe} variation. The steps are as follows:

1. After finding C_{oe} (or C_{ob}), use Equation (39) to find the quantities necessary for determining the f_H of Equation (43).

2. Referring this f_H to the chart, for each interstage, the decibel loss for each interstage may be determined for any frequency.

3. Add the losses of each interstage to determine the total loss due to collector capacitance.

4. Determine the value of $f_{h_{fe}}$ (or $f_{h_{fb}}$) from transistor data, and refer to chart.

5. Determine the loss due to decrease in h_{fe}, for each interstage, from the chart.

Cascade amplifiers

6. Add the decibel loss of each interstage to determine the total loss.

7. Add the loss in (3) to that in (6) and subtract this total from the mid-band decibel gain.

As in the low-frequency case, the approximations used in this analysis are usually valid for *RC*-coupled stages. If matched conditions are achieved with the use of transformers, this solution will yield only a rough approximation.

Comparing the common-emitter and the common-base connections, we have seen in this section that the common emitter has a lower f_H than the common base because of both an increased collector capacitance and a greatly decreased current gain cutoff. (This comparison is valid only if both connections have approximately equal matched or unmatched conditions at input and output.) Therefore a required frequency response could point to the use of the base connection (with transformers) in spite of the higher gain available with the emitter connection. However, other factors will usually contribute to selecting the common-emitter case.

The above procedures, then, can be used to examine the role of coupling capacitors and current gain drop-off as well as to estimate the points where low-frequency amplifiers begin to deviate from the mid-band values. As mentioned, a more general treatment of the high-frequency performance will be given in Chapter 16. There we will see that the high-frequency response can be written in closed form, as a function of frequency. However, this will require knowledge of the hybrid-π equivalent circuit parameters.

DESIGN CONSIDERATIONS

The first problem, when designing a cascaded transistor amplifier, consists of determining the number of required stages. The gain will probably be the criterion for the number of stages, although the subsequent frequency response may change this later. Consequently it is useful, after selection of a transistor based upon the general requirements, to find the maximum available gain for a single stage. Since the M.A.G. is a function of the transistor alone, no consideration of load and source is needed for this preliminary calculation. Based upon this M.A.G. and the total gain needed, the amount of required stages can be estimated. If transformer coupling is to be used, the

M.A.G. for each stage can be realized so that the minimum of stages is required; if *RC* coupling is used, the number of stages may be greater since M.A.G. cannot be achieved.

A next logical step is to estimate the high-frequency response; this will be fixed by the transistor, as shown in the previous section. The loss due to h_{fe} cutoff can be immediately found by using the chart and the manufacturer's data. The loss due to collector capacitance may be estimated by first performing the calculation for M.A.G. conditions. If the response of the two factors is not sufficient, an estimate of the amount of mismatch necessary is afforded by these calculations. Also, at this point it may be seen whether the chosen transistor is suitable.

After these preliminary calculations the various circuit elements can be fixed. For this, one must always begin with the last stage and proceed to the left since each stage acts as part of the load of the preceding stage. Many design factors are illustrated in the design example of the following section.

Regarding bias conditions, it is generally true that the operating point will be set at succeedingly higher value for the cascaded stages, since the signal level increases stage by stage from the input to the output. All stages may be set at the same operating point, however, if the point is high enough for the last stage. This is less efficient, in terms of d-c power, than the former since more d-c power is consumed by the higher operating points.

DESIGN EXAMPLE. The purpose of this design example, in addition to illustrating certain general design items, is to note the frequency response role of the items treated above in this chapter.

Problem. It is desired to design a preamplifier that will amplify a signal of −75 dbm to a 0 dbm power level. The source has an impedance of 150 ohms and the impedance of the load is 600 ohms. For frequency response, the amplification is allowed to be down 3 db at 100 and 5000 c. The power level of −75 dbm is sufficiently above the noise level of a transistor so that we will not consider noise here.

Solution. The power level of the signal throughout the amplifier is of such a magnitude that all the stages can be regarded as small-signal amplifiers. Hence the design can be carried out from the equivalent circuit techniques considered in this chapter.

Cascade amplifiers

The two criteria, in selecting a transistor for this design, are the power gain and the frequency response. For comparing the various available transistors, we may use the M.A.G. value and the frequency at which the h_{fb} is down 3 db. Let us assume a transistor which is recommended for "high-gain, low-to-medium power applications," that was used in Chapter 8, and which fits our category. Also assume that the M.A.G. of this transistor in the emitter connection is 40 db, and the h_{fb} cutoff frequency (f_{hfb}) is 1 megacycle with a C_{ob} of 40 pf. This transistor, then, is selected for this design.

Because of the greater power gain and the simpler bias circuitry, the common-emitter connection is chosen for all stages. We have next to choose whether RC or transformer coupling is to be used. It is clear from the above figure of M.A.G. that, for transformer coupling and matching conditions, only two stages are required. For the RC coupling the inevitable mismatch between stages will necessitate at least three stages. In order to show the various methods of design, we shall investigate both the transformer-coupled and the RC-coupled designs.

Transformer Coupled. As noted above, it should be possible to obtain the required 75 db gain from only two stages with transformer coupling. Note that this could be altered later if the resulting frequency response were not sufficient. Using two stages, then, and the simplest biasing circuit, the tentative circuit diagram is shown in Figure 10-19. If the transformer ratios are adjusted properly, we can obtain the full 40 db (the M.A.G.) from each of these stages, and hence can obtain 80 db. It is quite likely, however, that matched conditions will be undesirable in terms of frequency response. The first step, in dealing with the frequency response, is to determine the response under the M.A.G. conditions.

Remembering that two high-frequency factors of interest here are current gain cutoff and collector capacity, let us begin with the former. According to the specifications, the f_{hfb} is 1 megacycle; the cutoff value for the common-emitter connection is therefore

$$f_{hfe} = f_{hfb}(1 + h_{fb}) = (1 \times 10^6)(1 - 0.98) = 20{,}000 \text{ cps} \quad (49)$$

Using this value and referring to Figure 10-18, we find the decibel loss, at each interstage, due to the current gain cutoff. Since the response may be down 3 db at 5000 cps, we are always interested in the losses at this frequency. Using the chart, we find that the gain

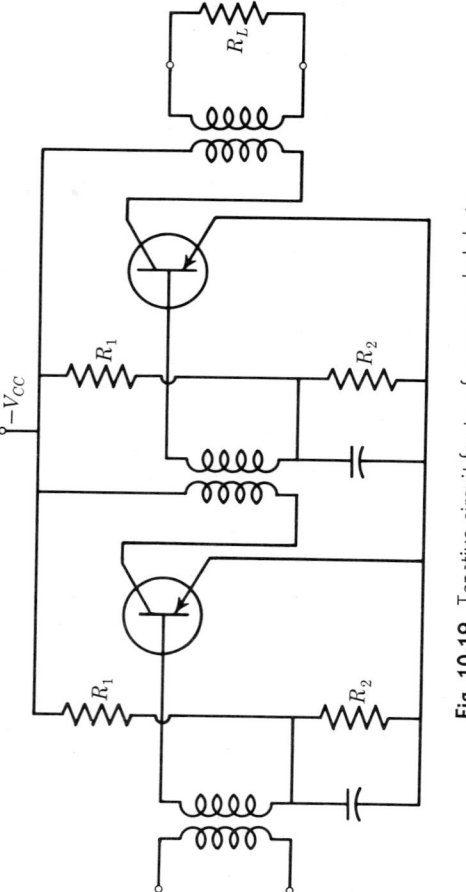

Fig. 10-19. Tenative circuit for transformer-coupled design.

Cascade amplifiers

loss is 0.28 db at 5 kc. For the two stages, then, the loss due to gain cutoff will be 0.56 db. This means that at 5 kc we can afford 3 − 0.56 = 2.44 db loss from the collector capacitance. We know that we can control the capacitance loss, somewhat, by altering the match conditions between stages.

Let us first find the capacitor loss at 5 kc if the stages are matched. From Equation (43) we see that the f_H due to collector capacitance depends upon the R_o for the transistor and the load facing this R_o; for matched conditions we want R'_T equal to R_o. We can calculate the matched load by use of Equation (69) of Chapter 8. (We will use the h parameter values given in Table 8-4.) We find that the matched load of this transistor in the emitter connection is approximately 40,000 ohms. It is noted that for the transformer-coupled case the R'_T consists only of the a-c resistance presented by the output transformer—assuming that the effective R_B is a-c shunted by capacitance. Note that the effective R_B in each stage of Figure 10-19 consists of R_1 in parallel with R_2. Thus for the moment we will consider that the R'_T of Equation (43) is equal to 40,000, which in turn is equal to the R_o; consequently, R_T equals 20,000 ohms. We need yet to find C_{oe}. Using equation (38) and the assumed manufacturer's value for C_{ob}, we find

$$C_{oe} = \frac{C_{ob}}{1 + h_{fb}} = \frac{40}{1 - 0.98} = 2000 \ \mu\mu\text{f} \tag{50}$$

We can now solve for the f_H:

$$f_H = \frac{1}{2\pi R_T C_T}$$

$$= \frac{1}{(2\pi)(2000 \times 10^{-12})(2 \times 10^4)} = 3980 \text{ cps} \tag{51}$$

Thus under matched conditions there is a 3 db loss from each stage due to collector capacitance at 3980 cps. This means that we cannot use matched conditions since we can afford only 2.44 db (or 1.22 db per stage) from the collector capacitance at 5000 cps.

Knowing that we cannot use matched conditions, let us find what degree of mismatch is needed. Referring to Figure 10-18 and setting the frequency where the loss is down 1.22 db at 5 kc, it is found that the f_H must be 9 kc; then the loss will be the allowable 1.22 db at

5 kc. We can now calculate what the R'_T should be to result in this f_H. Using Equation (43) again,

$$9000 = \frac{4 \times 10^4 + R'_T}{2\pi(4 \times 10^4 R'_T)(2000 \times 10^{-12})} \tag{52}$$

The resulting value of R'_T would be the maximum value of R'_T. Although the result is slightly greater than 10,000, we shall use the round figure of

$$R'_T = 10,000 \tag{53}$$

This means, then, that although the R_o of the transistor is about 40,000 ohms, we shall adjust the transformer ratio so that the transformer presents an impedance of 10,000 ohms to the transistor. Thus there will be a mismatch of about 4 to 1. (Note that the R_o of the final design will be different from 40,000 since it depends upon the source resistance.)

We now need a hasty check to determine whether with this mismatch the two stages will still provide sufficient gain. Using the equation and transistor h parameters from Table 8-2, the power gain, per stage, is found to be

$$\begin{aligned}A_p &= \frac{h_{fe}^2 R_L}{(1 + h_{oe} R_L)(h_{ie} + \Delta^{h_e} R_L)} \\ &= \frac{(49)^2(1 \times 10^4)}{[1 + (5 \times 10^{-5})(1 \times 10^4)][2 \times 10^3 + (2.16 \times 10^{-2})(1 \times 10^4)]} \\ &= 7240 = 38.6 \text{ db}\end{aligned} \tag{54}$$

Consequently we see that the two stages will still provide sufficient gain with the mismatch necessary to give the desired frequency response. The transformer ratios will be adjusted to provide a load impedance of 10,000 ohms for each stage; although this decreases the excess gain, this adjustment makes it possible to achieve the desired frequency response.

Having assured ourselves that there are sufficient frequency response and gain available, we can now calculate the a-c operation more thoroughly. We may note that, since we do not now have a matched load, the R_i for each transistor will change; consequently if we change the source resistance accordingly, the R_o for the tran-

Cascade amplifiers

sistor will change and its value will no longer be exactly 40,000 ohms as stated earlier. Using a load resistance of 10,000 ohms and the h^e parameters for this transistor, the equations of Table 8-5 can be used to find

$$R_i = \frac{\Delta^{he} R_L + h_{ie}}{h_{oe} R_L + 1} = 1470, \quad A_p = 7240 = 38.6 \text{ db} \quad (55)$$

This will apply to both stages since we are making the conditions the same. If we adjust the transformer turns ratio so that the source resistance equals the R_i, or 1470, it is found that the new R_o for the first stage is (the second stage calculation is similar)

$$R_o = \frac{h_{ie} + R_g}{\Delta^{he} + h_{oe} R_g} = 36{,}500 \quad (56)$$

We can now recalculate the frequency response, using the values stated above. For the total capacitance, the value of 100 $\mu\mu f$ is added to the transistor collector capacitance to account for the wiring capacitance. The actual f_H is then found to be

$$\begin{aligned} f_H &= \frac{1}{2\pi C_T R_T} \\ &= \frac{1}{(2\pi)(2000 \times 10^{-12} + 100 \times 10^{-12})(7850)} \quad (57) \\ &= 9660 \end{aligned}$$

where $R_T = R_o R'_T / (R_o + R'_T) = 7850$. Referring to Figure 10-18 again, we see that with this f_H the response is down 1.22 db at the frequency of 5.52 kc. Since this is above the required 5 kc, the calculations specify that the design is satisfactory. It must be remembered, however, that the frequency response calculations are only an analysis based on certain approximations. This is especially true if a matrix-type equivalent circuit (such as the h-parameter one) is used for these calculations. Therefore for any design, the frequency response calculations must be treated with some caution.

The transformer ratios, in each case, can be found by taking the square root of the desired impedance ratios, as shown in Chapter 6.

We have yet to determine the operating points, and the value of bias resistor to result in the chosen operating points.

The power level of 0 dbm at the output stage corresponds to a power of 1 mw, and we can use the graphical relationships of the previous chapter to suggest a suitable operating point. The chief criterion considered here is that the signal should not swing into either the cutoff or the saturation region. From the previous chapter, then, it can quickly be shown that the peak-to-peak current and voltage are

$$I_{pp} = \sqrt{\frac{8P_{out}}{R_L}} = \sqrt{\frac{8 \times 10^{-3}}{10,000}} = 0.894 \text{ ma} \tag{58}$$

$$E_{pp} = \sqrt{8P_{out}R_L} = \sqrt{8 \times 10^{-3} \times 10,000} = 8.94 \text{ v}$$

It must be emphasized that the factor of providing bias point stability, which is considered in the next chapter, is the most important factor in biasing transistor circuits. We will assume that the characteristics for our transistor appear as in Figure 10-22 or 10-23 below.

Due to the transformer, the d-c load line would appear as a vertical line (if no emitter resistance is inserted) and the battery voltage must be at least one-half the peak-to-peak swing. Hence the collector battery must be at least 4.47 volts. The collector current, at the operating point, must be at least equal to one-half of the maximum swing plus the value of I_{CEO}. The current may then be found by

$$I_C = \frac{I_{pp}}{2} + I_{CEO} = 0.447 \text{ ma} + 0.500 \text{ ma} = 0.947 \text{ ma} \tag{59}$$

where $I_{CEO} = I_{CO}/(1 + h_{fb})$. In order to provide some margin, the I_C will be set at 1.5 ma. Using the characteristics below, then, we will consider both a d-c and an a-c load line. We saw above that the a-c load is 10,000 ohms. For the d-c line, we will now insert an R_E of 1000 ohms to provide bias point stability (see Chapter 11). The d-c load line will be determined solely by this 1000 ohm R_E. From the characteristics, we choose a collector battery of 10 volts so as to assure staying out of the saturation region with the peak voltage swing. From the characteristics, then, the I_C of 1.5 ma occurs with an I_B of about 25 μa. Therefore, the biasing resistors R_1 and R_2 for the second stage, in conjunction with the 10.0 volt battery, must provide a current of 25 μa. The values of R_1 and R_2 can be found from the fol-

Cascade amplifiers

lowing diagram and equation. The emitter is at -1.5 volts since I_C is about 1.5 ma.

$$I_B = \frac{10 - 1.7}{R_1} - \frac{1.7}{R_2} \quad (60)$$

We will arbitrarily choose an R_1 of 1500 ohms. Using Equation (60), the R_2 is found to be about 310 ohms for an I_B of about 25 μa. Equation (8) of the text may be used to check the resulting value of I_B, using a V_{EB} of 0.2 volts (for germanium).

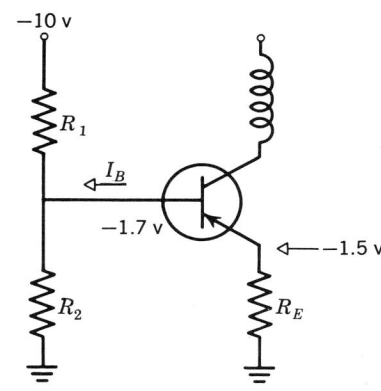

The value of C_2, the shunting capacitance for R_2, should be adjusted so that at 100 cps the capacitor provides a low shunt impedance. We shall use the criterion that the capacitor impedance should be equal to or less than one-tenth the a-c impedance of the input circuit. Remembering the a-c source impedance is 1500 ohms and the a-c input resistance of the transistor is also about 1500 ohms, the C may be found by

$$X_C = 0.1(R_i + R_g) = \frac{1}{2\pi f_L C}$$

$$C = \frac{1}{(0.1)(2940)(2\pi \times 100)} = 5.4 \times 10^{-6} \text{ f} \quad (61)$$

A capacitor of 10 μf will be selected. We will use a 50 μf capacitor to bypass the 1000 ohm R_E.

For the first stage, an identical operating point as above may be used. If it is desired, the same procedure can be used to find a lower operating point, since the power level of the first stage is smaller. This would result in a slightly better d-c power efficiency. However, distortion should also be considered when setting the operating point.

The final design, then, is shown in Figure 10-20.

RC-COUPLED AMPLIFIER. We will now design an *RC*-coupled amplifier to provide the required 75 db gain and the low and high 3 db points of 100 and 5000 cps. Because of the inherent mismatch of

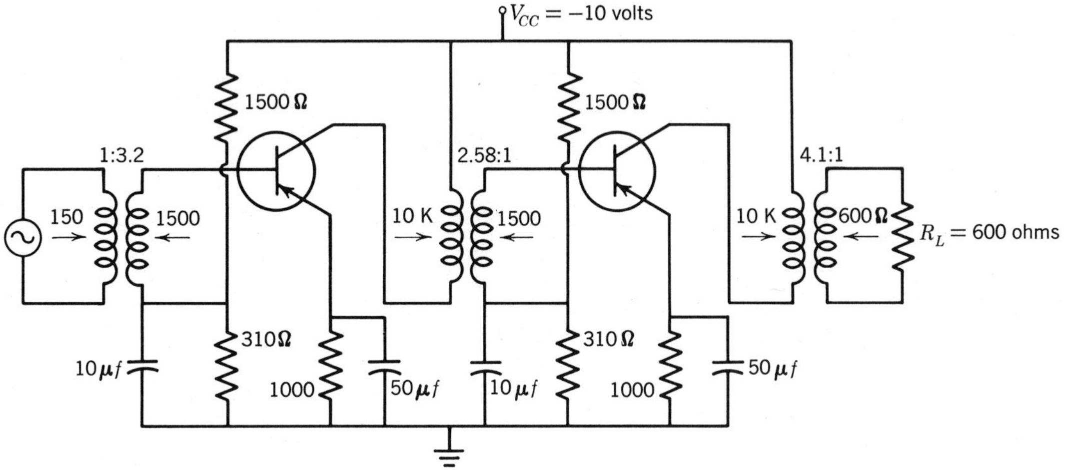

Fig. 10-20. Final transformer-coupled design.

Cascade amplifiers

RC-coupled stages, it was estimated earlier that at least three stages would be required. Although this will be checked after proper loads are assumed, we shall for the present assume that three stages are required. For biasing we will use the basic scheme shown in Figures 10-3 and 10-4. The tentative circuit diagram, then, is shown in Figure 10-21.

It may be noted that the biasing resistance R_1 and R_2, in parallel, form the R_B that was used previously in equivalent circuits.

In the *RC*-coupled case we cannot adjust the gain readily by altering the matching, since the load of any stage is mainly determined by the input resistance to the next stage. We can make a preliminary gain calculation by considering only the R_i of the next stage as the load on the transistor, and assuming the R_i has the nominal value given by the manufacturer (1000 ohms in this case),

$$A_p = \frac{(h_{fe})^2 R_L}{(1 + h_{oe} R_L)(\Delta^{h^e} R_L + h_{ie})} = 1130 \simeq 30 \text{ db} \qquad (62)$$

Based upon this preliminary calculation, it is seen that three stages is the correct number.

We can now estimate the frequency response for the three stages. First, it is remembered that the h_{fe} cutoff decreases the gain by 0.28 db at 5 kc for each stage. For three stages the loss due to this is then 0.84 db. This means that we can afford a total of $3 - 0.84$ db $= 2.16$ db, or 0.72 db per stage from the collector capacitance effect. Referring to the frequency chart of Figure 10-18, this results in requiring an f_H of at least 12.5 kc. This means that if the gain is down 3 db at 12.5 kc, the gain will be down 0.73 db at 5 kc, which is the allowable amount per stage.

Using Equation (43), then, we can find what the maximum value of R_T, the total parallel resistance at the interstage, may be.

$$f_H = \frac{1}{2\pi R_T C_T} = 12.5 \text{ kc}, \qquad R_T = 6.36 \times 10^3 \qquad (63)$$

where $C_T = 2000$ μμf = collector capacitance in common-emitter connection.

Equation (63) says that the parallel combination of R_o, R_L, R_B, and the R_i of the following stage may not be above 6360 ohms. Remember that R_B is made up of R_1 and R_2 in parallel. Since the

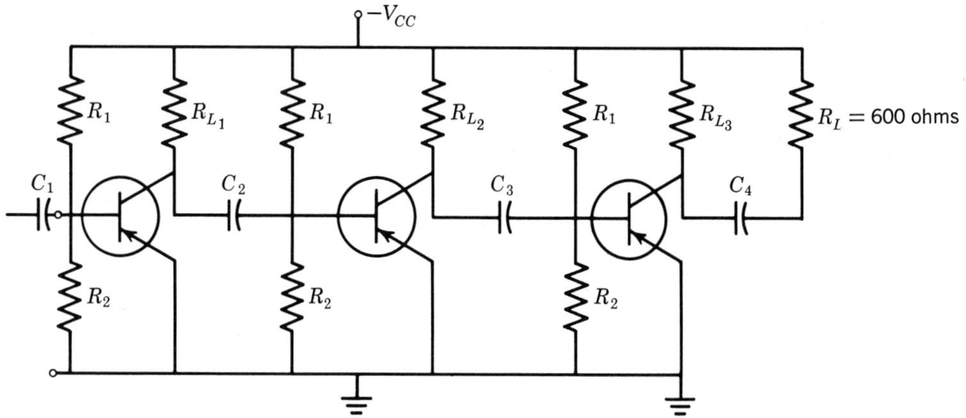

Fig. 10-21. Tenative RC-coupled design.

Cascade amplifiers

total resistance of a parallel combination is always less than the *lowest* resistance, the value of R_T will never be more than R_i. Furthermore, since the R_i is always of the order of 1000 to 2000 ohms for a common-emitter stage without feedback, Equation (63) tells us that *the collector capacitance will not limit the frequency response*. The mismatch is enough to cause the h_{fe} cutoff to affect the frequency response before the collector capacitance effect. Consequently, we need consider only the h_{fe} cutoff for the rest of this design.

We can now begin assigning proper values to the various resistors, based on the a-c operation. As in the case of analysis, we must start with the last stage. Referring to Figure 10-21, R_{L_3} should be much greater than R_L so that R_{L_3} does not shunt the a-c signal appreciably. However, a very large R_{L_3} would necessitate a large collector battery in order to obtain a suitable operating point. From considerations of the d-c load line, then, 10,000 ohms is selected for the value of R_{L_3}. The total load on the last stage, then, is 10,000 ohms in parallel with 600 ohms.

$$R'_{T_3} = \frac{R_L R_{L_3}}{R_{L_3} + R_L} = 566 \tag{64}$$

Using the equations of Table 8-5, we can find the following values:

$$R_{i_3} = 1960, \quad A_{p_3} = 655 = 28.14 \text{ db} \tag{65}$$

Since not all the power in the output of the transistor reaches the load resistor, we calculate the interstage loss by use of Equation (21).

$$\text{loss} = 10 \log_{10} \frac{R'_{T_3}}{R_L} = 10 \log_{10} \frac{566}{600} = -0.25 \text{ db} \tag{66}$$

The negative sign merely means that a loss is involved. The total power gain so far, then, is

$$\text{Db}_3 + \text{loss} = 28.14 \text{ db} + (-0.25) = 27.89 \text{ db} \tag{67}$$

For the resistors preceding stage three, R_{L_3} and R_{B_3}, we again wish to keep them much higher than the R_{i_3} so that they do not shunt the a-c signal appreciably. The R_{L_3} determines the d-c load line of the second stage, and hence the battery and operating point must be considered. Since the signal swing for the second stage is less than for the third, we can make R_{L_2} larger than R_{L_3} (for the same battery).

Consequently, the value of 30,000 ohms is chosen. For the R_{B_2}, we would desire to keep its value as high as 30,000 ohms. However, the bias stability is affected by this resistor combination (treated in next chapter), and therefore a value of 15,000 ohms is selected. The total a-c load on the second stage then is

$$R'_{T_2} = \frac{1}{1/30{,}000 + 1/15{,}000 + 1/1960} = 1640 \text{ ohms} \qquad (68)$$

Using this load resistance, the gain and the R_{i_2} for the second stage are

$$R_{i_2} = 1880, \qquad A_{p_2} = 1795 = 32.54 \text{ db} \qquad (69)$$

Subtracting the interstage loss, which is found by

$$\text{db}_3 = 10 \log_{10} \frac{1640}{1960} = -0.78 \text{ db} \qquad (70)$$

the net gain is

$$\text{Db}_2 + \text{db}_3 = 32.54 \text{ db} - 0.78 \text{ db} = 31.76 \text{ db} \qquad (71)$$

The same value of resistors for R_{L_1} and R_{B_2} will be selected as for R_{L_2} and R_{B_3}, respectively. It is then found that

$$R'_{T_1} = \frac{1}{1/30{,}000 + 1/15{,}000 + 1/1880} = 1590 \text{ ohms}$$
$$R_{i_1} = 1890 \text{ ohms} \qquad (72)$$
$$A_{p_1} = 1740 \text{ ohms}$$

The net gain, with the interstage loss subtracted, is

$$\text{Db}_1 + \text{db}_2 = 32.4 \text{ db} - 0.73 \text{ db} = 31.67 \text{ db} \qquad (73)$$

The only remaining gain calculation is for the interstage network preceding the first stage. If R_{B_1} is made equal to 15,000 ohms, the loss is

$$\text{loss} = 10 \log_{10} \frac{R'_T}{R_i} = 10 \log_{10} \frac{1680}{1890} = -0.492 \text{ db} \qquad (74)$$

The total gain is now found by adding all the decibel gains. The total is

Cascade amplifiers 311

$$\text{total gain} = 31.67 + 31.76 + 27.89 - 0.492 = 90.828 \quad (75)$$

Since the total gain is greater than required, a volume control may be placed in the circuit and will be shown in the final design.

The amplifier is now suitable for the a-c aspects. We have now to determine the proper d-c conditions. This is mainly a problem of setting the operating points of each stage so that the signal swing of each stage can be properly handled. Since from the above power calculations we know the maximum power out, we will begin with the last stage and work to the left.

The maximum power output will be 10 db above 1 mw. Let us assume that a volume control is inserted so the maximum power of 1 mw occurs. We will now indicate some aspects of selecting a suitable operating point and will here concentrate in particular on assuring that the peak signal swing can be handled. The next chapter treats of the important aspect of bias stability. To find a suitable operating point, then, we must find the peak-to-peak values of voltage and current.

Remembering that for a sine wave,

$$I_{\text{rms}} = 0.707 I_{\text{max}} \quad (76)$$

the following peak-to-peak values can be found by

$$I_{pp} = \sqrt{\frac{8P}{R_L}} = \sqrt{\frac{(8)(1 \times 10^{-3})}{566}} = 3.76 \text{ ma} \quad (77)$$

$$E_{pp} = \sqrt{8PR_L} = \sqrt{(8)(1 \times 10^{-3})(566)} = 2.13 \text{ v}$$

The minimum I_C, then, is given by

$$\text{min quiescent } I_C = \frac{I_{pp}}{2} + I_{CEO} = \frac{3.76}{2} + 0.5 = 2.38 \text{ ma} \quad (78)$$

As in the previous example, we will insert an R_E for bias point stability (treated in Chapter 11). The minimum collector battery can now be determined by adding the minimum allowable voltage $(2.13/2 = 1.06)$ to the voltage drop across the load resistor with the minimum quiescent current. Note that R_{L_3} in series with R_{E_3} forms the d-c load line. We will assume that R_E is a nominal 1000 ohms. Then the load line is formed by an 11,000 ohm load. The voltage, with the minimum allowable I_C, is

$$V_{R_{L_3}} = (I_C)(R_{L_3}) = (2.38)(1.1 \times 10^4) = 26.2 \text{ v}$$
$$\min V_{CC} = V_{CE} + I_C R_{L_3} = 1.064 + 26.2 = 27.26 \text{ v} \quad (79)$$

We will select a 30 volt battery. On the characteristics shown in Figure 10-22 we can now draw the a-c and the d-c load lines. An

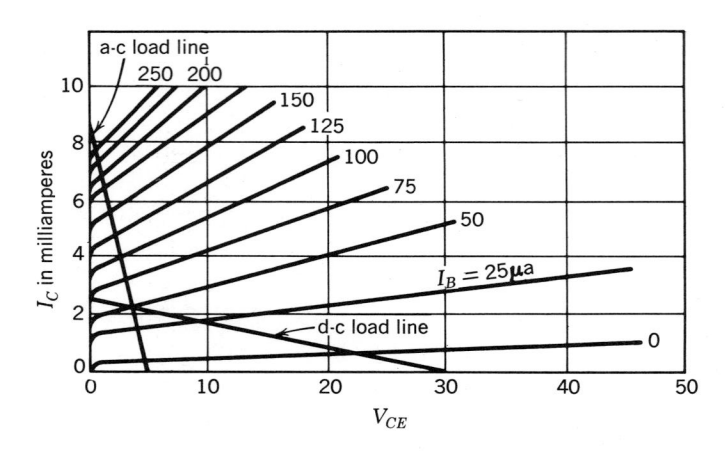

Fig. 10-22. A-c and d-c load lines for the third stage of assumed transistor.

operating point at $I_C = 2.4$ ma is selected, and this requires an I_B of about 50 µa. With an I_C of 2.4 ma, there is a 24 volt drop across the load resistor, a 3.6 volt V_{CE}, and a 2.4 volt drop across R_E. To find the proper values of R_1 and R_2 so that R_B is the assumed 15,000 ohms we will assume that V_{EB} is 0.2 volt. V_{EB} is often specified, at a given operating point, by the manufacturer.

The R_1 and R_2 can be found by solving the two simultaneous equations

$$50 \times 10^{-6} = \frac{27.4}{R_1} - \frac{2.6}{R_2}$$
$$66.6 \times 10^{-6} = \frac{1}{R_1} + \frac{1}{R_2} \quad (79a)$$

It can be shown that an R_1 of 134,800 ohms and an R_2 of 16,950 ohms produces a 15,000 ohms parallel resistance, and provides the approximate bias point specified above.

For the second stage the power output is about 28 db lower than 1 mw (about 2 µw). The I_{pp} and E_{pp} then are

Cascade amplifiers

$$I_{pp} = \sqrt{\frac{8P}{R_L}} = \sqrt{\frac{(8)(2 \times 10^{-6})}{1640}} = 0.0987 \text{ ma} \tag{80}$$

$$E_{pp} = \sqrt{8PR_L} = \sqrt{(8)(2 \times 10^{-6})(1640)} = 0.161$$

Although an I_C of 0.5494 ma would be sufficient, the value of 0.85 ma will be selected. It is noted that due to the required swing, only a 0.08 value for V_{CE} is required. Since this is down in the nonlinear region, we must make it greater than this. Since we wish to use a single battery, a V_{CC} equal to that of the third stage will be assumed (30 volts). The V_{CE} will then be, for an I_C of 0.85 ma,

$$V_{CE} = V_{CC} - I_C(R_L)_{\text{d-c}} = 30 - (0.85 \times 10^{-3})(3.1 \times 10^4) = 3.65 \text{ v} \tag{81}$$

This is satisfactory for V_{CE}.

From the characteristics we see that an I_B of about 10 μa is required. To provide an R_{B_2} of 15,000 again this time requires that R_1 be 375,400 and R_2 be 15,650. The a-c and d-c load lines for the second stage are shown in Figure 10-23.

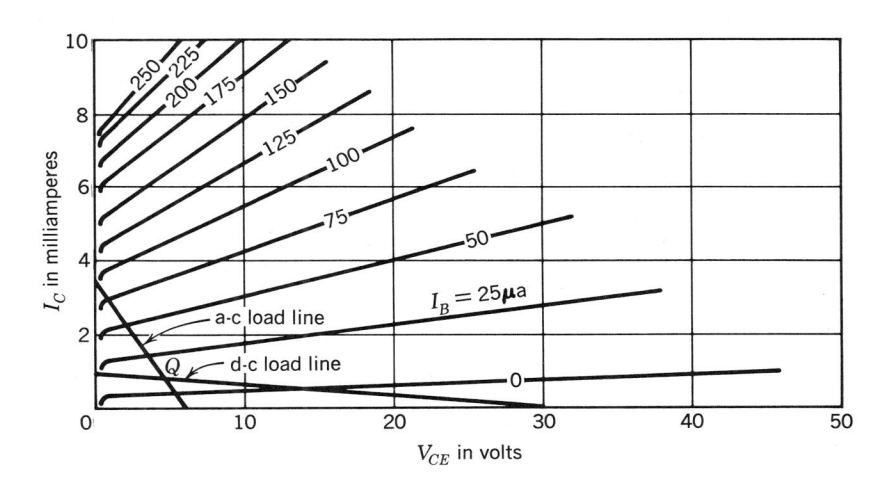

Fig. 10-23. A-c and d-c load lines for the second stage.

The operating point for the first stage is chosen identical to that of the second. Thus the load lines will be practically identical, as are the values of R_1 and R_2.

Since the coupling capacitors determine the low-frequency response, we must use Equations (35) and (27):

$$f_L = \frac{1}{2\pi(R_g + R_p)C} \tag{82}$$

where $R_g = \dfrac{R_o R_L}{R_o + R_L}$ and $R_p = \dfrac{R_B R_i}{R_B + R_i}$.

We will use this equation for each interstage. Since the values of R_o have not been previously calculated, we will first do this. By using the relations of Table 8-5,

$$(R_o)_{\text{1st stage}} = \frac{h_{ie} + R'_g}{\Delta^{he} + h_{oe}R'_g} = \frac{2000 + 148.5}{2.15 \times 10^{-2} + (5 \times 10^{-5})(148.5)}$$

$$= 74{,}400 \text{ ohms}$$

where R'_g = total resistance preceding the stage

$$= R_{B_1} \parallel R_{\text{source}} = 15{,}000 \parallel 150 \text{ ohms}.$$

$$(R_o)_{\text{2nd stage}} = \frac{2000 + 8820}{2.15 \times 10^{-2} + (5 \times 10^{-5})(8820)}$$

$$= 23{,}100 \text{ ohms} \tag{83}$$

$$R'_g = R_{B_2} \parallel R_{L_1} \parallel R_{o_1}$$

$$= 15{,}000 \parallel 30{,}000 \parallel 74{,}400 \text{ ohms}$$

$$(R_o)_{\text{3rd stage}} = \frac{2000 + 7000}{(2.15 \times 10^{-2}) + (5 \times 10^{-5})(7000)}$$

$$= 24{,}200 \text{ ohms}$$

$$R'_g = R_{B_3} \parallel R_{L_2} \parallel R_{o_2}$$

$$= 15{,}000 \parallel 30{,}000 \parallel 23{,}400 \text{ ohms}$$

Using these values, in combination with the previously calculated values of R_i in Equation (82), we can find the value of C if we know the proper f_L for each interstage. Since we are allowed a 3 db drop-off at 100 cps, and since there are four coupling capacitors, we can afford a 0.75 db loss in each interstage at 100 cps. Referring to the low-frequency chart of Figure 10-15, we find the f_L of 40 cps is proper. The value of the coupling capacitors may then be found to be

Cascade amplifiers

$$C_1 = \frac{1}{2\pi(R_{g_1} + R_{p_1})40} = \frac{1}{6.28(150 + 1680)40} = 2.17 \ \mu f$$

$$C_2 = \frac{1}{2\pi(R_{g_2} + R_{p_2})40} = \frac{1}{6.28(21{,}300 + 1670)40} = 0.173 \ \mu f$$

$$C_3 = \frac{1}{2\pi(R_{g_3} + R_{p_3})40} = \frac{1}{6.28(13{,}150 + 1735)40} = 0.268 \ \mu f \quad (84)$$

$$C_4 = \frac{1}{2\pi(R_{g_4} + R_{p_4})40} = \frac{1}{6.28(7100 + 600)40} = 0.386 \ \mu f$$

As in the transformer coupled design, we will use a 50 μf capacitor to bypass the R_E.

We can now exhibit the final design, and it is shown in Figure 10-24.

Although we estimated the high-frequency response in the beginning of this design, it was impossible to ascertain since the various components were not yet evaluated. It is useful, now, to check whether the high-frequency response is sufficient (3 db down at 5000 cps). We will first note the loss due to the collector capacitance in the emitter connection C_{oe}. Using Equations (39) and (43) at each interstage, and then referring to the chart of Figure 10-18 to determine the loss at 5000 cps, the calculations are

$$C_T = C_{oe} + C_W = \frac{C_{ob}}{1 + h_{fb}} + C_W$$

$$= \frac{40}{1 - 0.98} + 100 \ \mu\mu f = 2.1 \times 10^{-9} \ f \quad (85)$$

where a wiring capacity of 100 $\mu\mu f$ is assumed.

$$f_{H_3} = \frac{1}{2\pi R_T C_T} = \frac{1}{(6.28)(553)(2.1 \times 10^{-9})} = 128{,}000 \ c$$

db_3 (at 5000 c) $\cong 0$

$$f_{H_2} = \frac{1}{2\pi R_T C_T} = \frac{1}{(6.28)(1530)(2.1 \times 10^{-9})} = 49{,}500 \ c \quad (86)$$

db_2 (at 5000 c) $\cong 0$

$$f_{H_1} = \frac{1}{2\pi R_T C_T} = \frac{1}{(6.28)(1590)(2.1 \times 10^{-9})} = 48{,}500 \ c$$

db_1 (at 5000 c) $\cong 0$

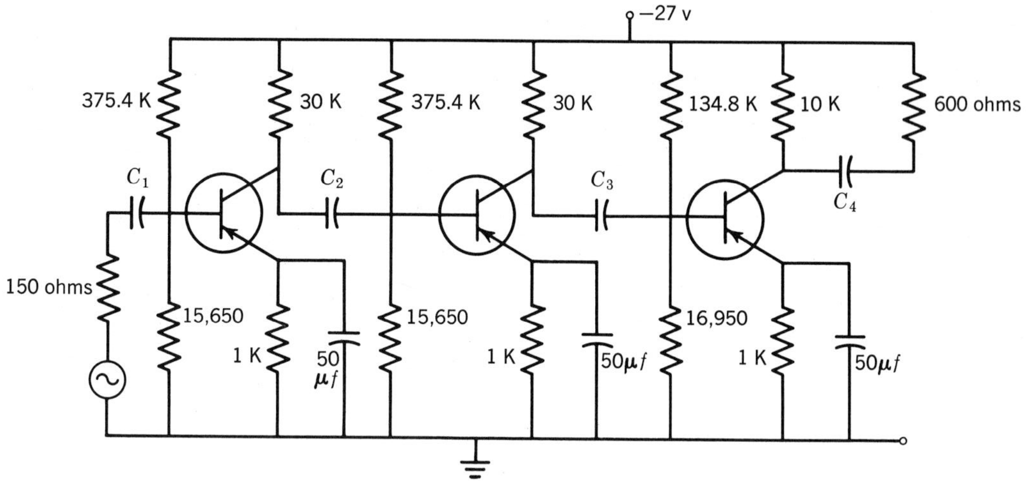

Fig. 10-24. Final design for RC-coupled amplifier.

Cascade amplifiers

These calculations agree with our former statement that the collector capacitance will not present a problem for the high-frequency drop-off. The calculations are shown here merely to illustrate the process.

For the drop-off due to h_{fe}, we note that the $f_{h_{fb}}$ is given by the manufacturer as 1 megacycle. Then $f_{h_{fe}}$ for the emitter connection is

$$f_{h_{fe}} = f_{h_{fb}}(1 + h_{fb}) = (1)(1 - 0.98) = 2 \times 10^4 = 20{,}000 \text{ cps}$$

From Figure 10-18 we see that the loss at 5000 cps is then 0.27 db per transistor. The total loss due to h_{fe} drop-off is then 0.81 db. Therefore at 5 kc, the high-frequency response exhibits only a 0.81 db drop-off and this is all due to the h_{fe} effect.

COMPARISON OF THE TWO DESIGNS

As noted, the transformer design required only two transistor stages, whereas the RC case required three. The choice of coupling rests with the cost and space considerations. Usually the RC case is chosen because the additional transistors cost less and require less space than the combination of transformers.

The two designs, depicted above, were carried by using the design center values for the transistor quantities. In order to certify that the amplifier is suitable with any transistors of the same type, the gain and frequency response should be checked under the worst possible conditions. For frequency response this would mean recalculation, using the maximum value of C_{oe} and the minimum value of $f_{h_{fb}}$; for gain, the minimum value of h_{fe} would be used. The manufacturer usually specifies the maximum and minimum quantities along with the design center quantities. This recalculation is left as an exercise for the student.

These two designs should not be construed as representing all aspects of transistor amplifier designing. In the next chapter we consider the stabilizing of the d-c operating points, and following this the use of feedback. The frequency response of the above amplifier, for example, could be improved by the use of feedback.

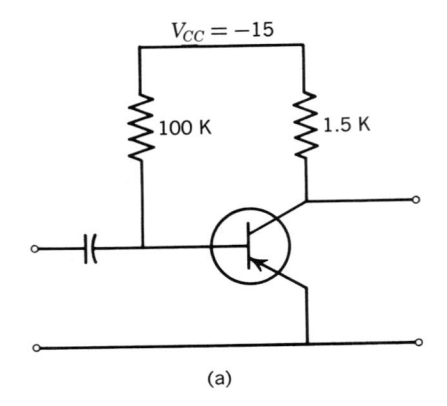

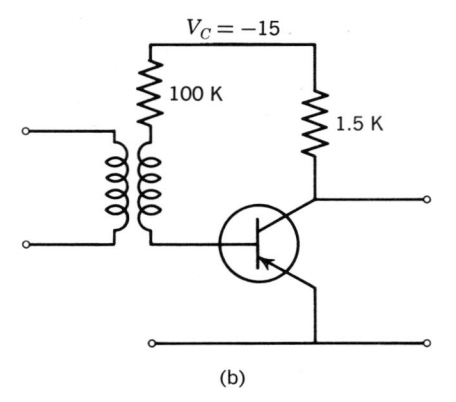

Fig. 10-25. Common-emitter amplifier.

Cascade amplifiers

PROBLEMS

1. What are the junction bias requirements (forward or reverse) for a transistor in the active (amplifying) region? With respect to ground, what must be the collector and base polarity of a common-emitter P-N-P transistor? Of an N-P-N transistor?

2. Using a line sketch of the transistor, indicate the direction of actual current flow for both the P-N-P and the N-P-N transistor.

3. Assume that the 2N1097 transistor is used in the amplifier of Figure 10-25 (a) and (b). What is the value of V_{CE} and I_C at the operating point for each of these circuits? Use the load line in combination with the input equation.

4. Assume that the 2N3638 transistor is used in the amplifier shown in Figure 10-26 (a). Let $V_{CC} = -15$; $R_1 = 22K$; $R_2 = 5K$; $R_L = 4K$; $R_E = 1K$; and $R_4 = 1K$. Find the operating point using the characteristics and input equation. Compare the result of Equation (8) with that of Equation (9). Draw the a-c load line and find maximum output power.

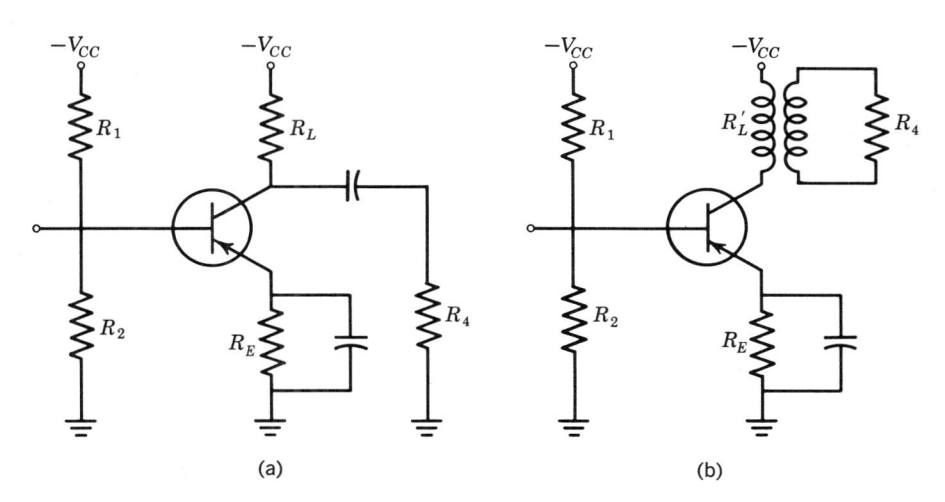

Fig. 10-26. Common-emitter amplifier.

5. Use the same circuit as is shown in Figure 10-26(b) with the 2N270 transistor. Let $V_{CC} = -9$; $R_1 = 15K$; $R_2 = 10K$; $R'_L = 400$ ohms; $R_E = 100$ ohms. What is the operating point, using the characteristics and the input equation? Compare the result of Equation (8) with that of Equation (9). Draw the a-c load line, and find the maximum output power.

6. Solve the d-c input equations for I_E in the common-base circuit of Figure 10-5. Do this by first writing equations similar to (7), but in terms of I_1 and I_E. Calculate the I_E of Problems 4 and 5. Check to see if the I_E determined in this way agrees with the I_E resulting by first calculating I_B.

7. Write the d-c input equations and solve for I_B for the circuit shown in Figure 10-27. Use the same general procedure as was used to determine Equations (7).

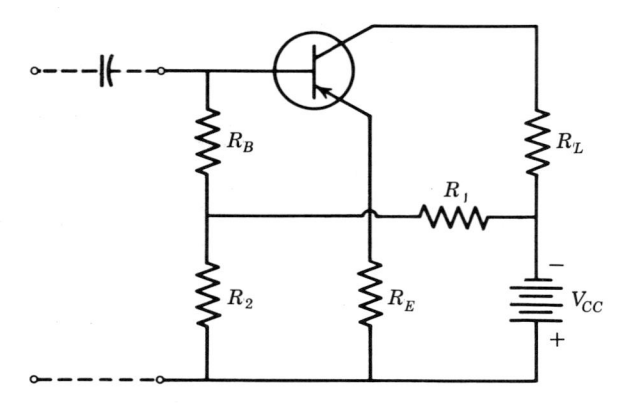

Fig. 10-27. Bias circuit for I_B calculation.

8. Follow both the RC and the RL design example calculations, using the simplified transistor equivalent circuit of Figure 8-6. Are the results more in agreement for the RC case than for the RL one?

9. Using the collector capacity of 50 pf (50×10^{-12}) and a f_{hfb} of 0.5 mc, determine whether the transformer coupled amplifier designed in the text would be satisfactory.

10. Using an h_{fe} of 32 for the transistor, check the mid-frequency gain of the transformer coupled design. Will this amplifier still give the required gain?

11. Using the conditions set forth in Problem 9, determine whether the RC coupled amplifier design will give the required frequency response.

12. Using the conditions of Problem 10 check the mid-frequency gain of the RC coupled amplifier. Is there still sufficient gain?

13. What is the mid-frequency loss through the interstages shown in Figure 10-28?

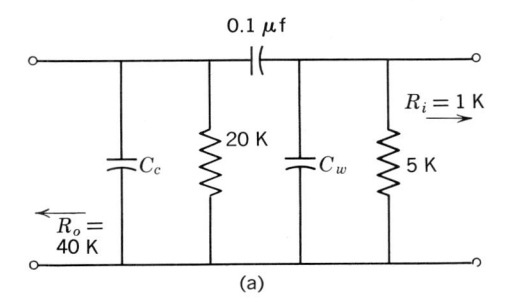

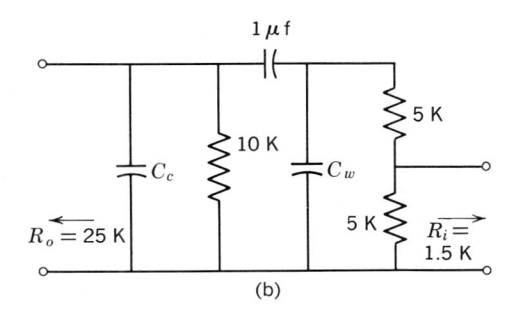

Fig. 10-28. Transistor interstages.

322 Cascade amplifiers

14. What are the upper and lower half-power frequencies for the interstages of Figure 10-28? Use a collector capacitance C_c of 2500 μμf and a wiring capacity C_W of 150 μμf.

15. If the upper cutoff frequency f_{hfb} of the transistors used with the interstages of Figure 10-28 is 10 mc and the common base short-circuit current gain h_{fb} is −0.96, what is the limiting factor in the high-frequency response? Use $C_c = 400$ pf and $C_W = 5$ pf.

16. What value of coupling capacitance would be required in the interstages of Figure 10-28 to improve the frequency response such that the low-frequency cutoff will be 20 c?

17. Assume that the 2N3638 is used in the single stage amplifier of Figure 10-29. First find the operating point by using the load line and input equations. Draw the a-c load line. Then, using the corrected h^e parameters, find the mid-frequency power gain for this amplifier. Assuming that the 5 μf coupling capacitors control the low-frequency drop-off (rather than the emitter bypass capacitors), find the low-frequency 3 db point. Find the high-frequency 3 db point, using an f_{hfb} of 10 mc and the C_{ob} of 12 pf, with the approximations used in this chapter.

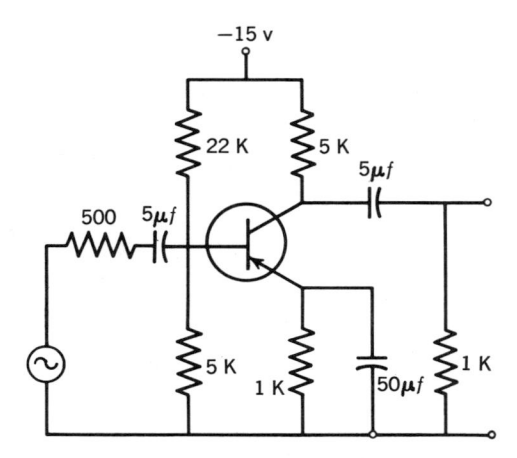

Fig. 10-29. Single stage common-emitter amplifier.

18. Assume that the 2N1097 is used in the two stage amplifier of Figure 10-30. Calculate the same quantities as in Problem 17.

Cascade amplifiers

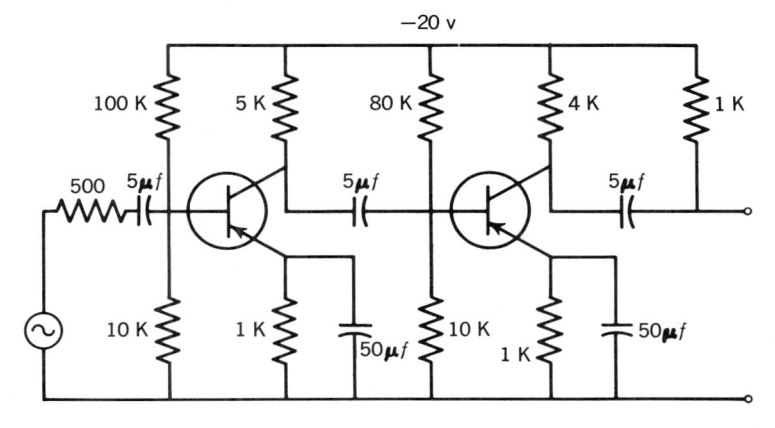

Fig. 10-30. Two-stage common-emitter amplifier.

19. Do Problems 17 and 18 using only the simplified transistor equivalent circuit of Figure 8-7. Compare results.

20. Find the transducer gain for the amplifiers of Problems 17 and 18.

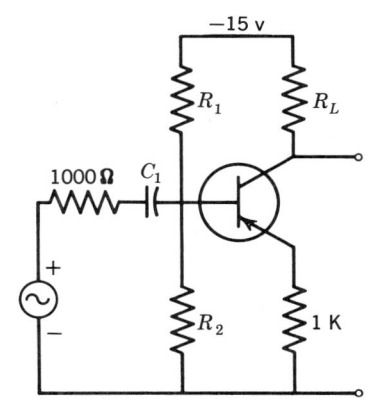

Fig. 10-31. Partially completed design.

21. Use reasonable assumptions, and complete the design of the circuit shown in Figure 10-31. Assume that the 2N1097 transistor is used. Determine the values of R_L, C_1, R_1, and R_2 so that: (1) a signal swing of ±2 volts is permissible without saturating or cutoff; (2) the magnitude of the gain is down 3 db at 200 cps. For the resulting values find the upper-frequency 3 db point using a C_{ob} of 18 pf. What is the transducer gain for this stage?

11
Bias equations and bias stability

When considering bias conditions for power amplifiers and cascaded amplifiers, methods for dealing with the d-c operating point were introduced. It was suggested that the collector characteristics are useful for visualizing the bias point, and for helping to set this point. It is now necessary to study the available measures for *retaining* the desired operating point under actual operating conditions—the most important aspect in biasing transistor circuits.

There are two major reasons for the difficulty in sustaining a desired operating point. First, as was noted in the physics review in Chapter 2, the characteristics of the transistor are temperature dependent. Although this affects both the a-c parameters and the d-c conditions, the latter are most important. Second, the characteristics of different transistors of the same type will vary from unit to unit. Consequently, when various transistors are placed in the same circuit, the operation will vary somewhat unless stabilizing measures are taken.

This chapter, then, treats of the various stabilizing measures and evaluates the resulting stabilized circuit. Since such an evaluation requires analyzing the complete d-c network, we will use a d-c equivalent circuit for the transistor and combine this with the external circuitry. Thus the bias analysis will be more complete than that done in the previous chapter, where a combination analytic and graphical technique was used. All the bias and stability consid-

ered
Bias equations and bias stability

erations will concern the common-emitter connection, since this is the most frequent amplifier connection. The same procedures may, of course, be used for the other two connections.

We will first consider the manner in which temperature and unit-to-unit variation affect the transistor. Next the d-c equivalent circuit of the transistor will be introduced. Using this equivalent circuit, the bias equations for the major circuit biasing methods will be calculated. The resulting set of bias equations can be used in setting the bias point. For purposes of evaluating bias stability for a given circuit, a stability factor S will be defined and explained. This stability factor will be evaluated for the biasing circuits. Since the problem of stability is very critical for d-c amplifiers, some basic d-c amplifier circuits and the resulting stability for such circuits, will be considered.

IMPORTANT FACTORS

We shall now consider the effect that temperature changes and unit-to-unit variation have on transistors.

TEMPERATURE VARIATION. The transistor characteristics specified by a manufacturer are actually valid only for a given junction temperature (usually 25°C). The actual junction temperature of a transistor (in a circuit) will depend upon both the power dissipated in the transistor and the means for removing heat from the transistor. In small-signal applications, where the dissipation power of the transistor is small, *we can regard the transistor junction temperature as being approximately equal to the temperature of the surrounding air*. As larger signals are encountered, however, the transistor power and its dissipating means must be considered in order to approximate the junction temperature. The method for doing this was described in Chapter 9, where power amplifiers were discussed.

Changes in temperature affect three transistor quantities: I_{CBO}, h_{FE},[1] and V_{EB}. In general the I_{CBO} and h_{FE} will rise as the temperature increases. The V_{EB} which is necessary to produce a given emitter current decreases as the temperature increases. Of these, the most serious variation is experienced by the I_{CBO} term. Consequently, here we will concentrate mainly on the variation of this parameter.

[1] Capital subscripts denote that a d-c quantity is being specified. Previously we have dealt solely with a-c parameters, where lower case subscripts were used.

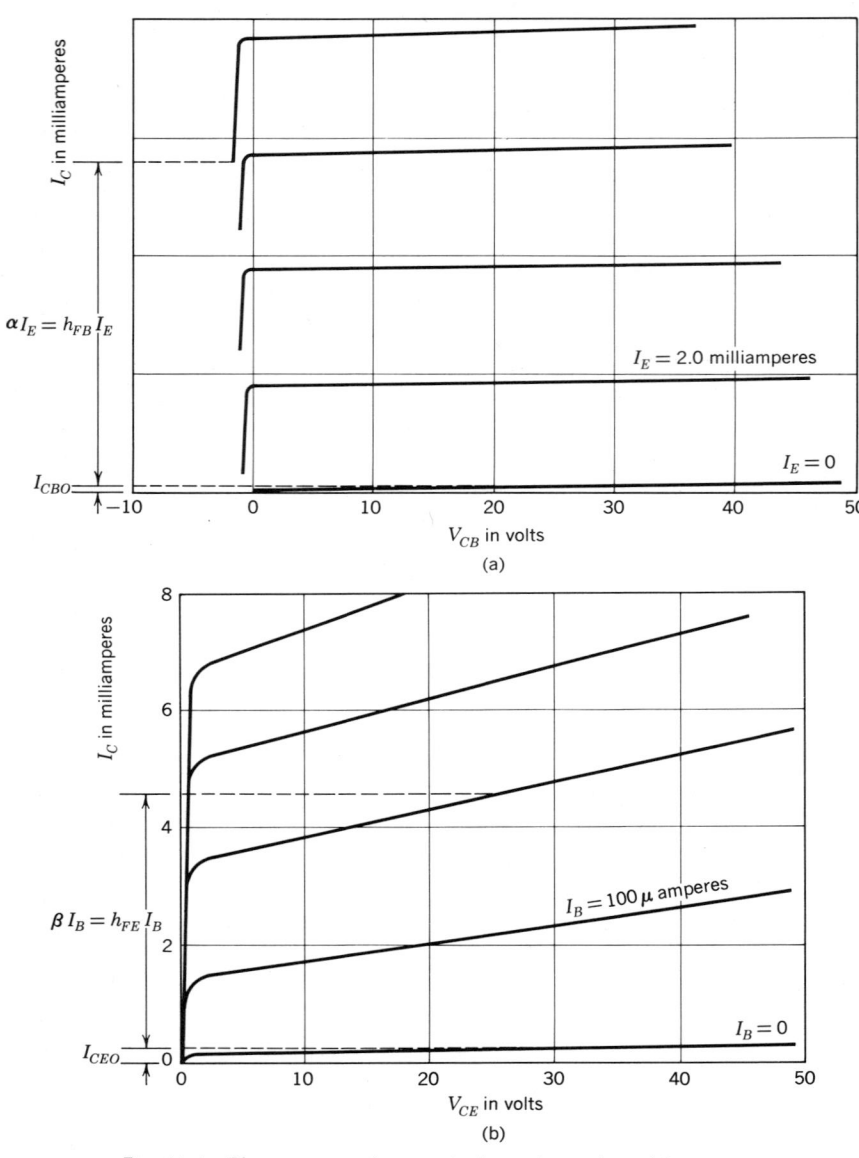

Fig. 11-1. Characteristics showing I_C, I_{CBO} relationships: (a) common-base; (b) common-emitter.

The effect of the variation of I_{CBO} with temperature, and the influence of h_{FE} can best be described by referring to the collector characteristics. When the temperature varies, the characteristics move upward from their original position. Figure 11-1 shows both the common-base and common-emitter collector characteristics. Any

326

Bias equations and bias stability

particular current I_C on the common-base characteristics can be written as[2,3]

$$I_C = I_{CBO} + \alpha I_E = I_{CBO} + h_{FB}I_E \qquad (1)$$

where I_{CBO} = collector cutoff current, with emitter open,
h_{FB} = d-c value of common-base current gain.

Note that this equation holds for *any* I_C, so long as the proper values of I_{CBO} and I_E are used.

As the temperature varies, the common-base characteristics move upward while essentially retaining their relative spacing. This situation is caused by the fact that the I_{CBO} for a transistor varies greatly with temperature while the α is fairly stable. It is remembered that the I_{CBO} is the bias current flowing through the reverse-bias collector junction (when the $I_E = 0$). This current is composed of the reverse-biased junction current due to thermal generation of electron-hole pairs and leakage currents across the junction. It is clear that the electron-hole pair current will be highly temperature sensitive. The d-c α (or h_{FB}) is the short-circuit d-c current amplification that is determined by the spacing between the curves. This is a d-c parameter (and not an a-c one), and this is the reason for using capital subscripts. Although the variation of α with temperature in the common-base case is overshadowed by the I_{CBO} variation, the α does vary somewhat with temperature. If the spacing between the curves remains essentially constant with temperature, Equation (1) tells us that the set of common-base curves will vary directly as I_{CBO} varies.

Figure 11-1(b) shows the relation of the reverse current and the current gain for the common-emitter connection. The equation here is

$$I_C = I_{CEO} + \beta I_B = I_{CEO} + h_{FE}I_B \qquad (2)$$

where I_{CEO} = collector cutoff current, with base open,
h_{FE} = d-c value of forward common-emitter current gain.

The emitter leakage current I_{CEO} is due to the base leakage current I_{CBO}. The leakage current I_{CEO} is larger than I_{CBO} in much the same

---

[2] We use the convention that both α and β may refer to *either* a-c or d-c quantities. Thus in this chapter we refer to d-c α and β, whereas in the past we dealt with a-c α and β.

[3] The convention regarding positive direction for the d-c currents will be the *actual* current direction, as in Chapter 10. Thus all the currents and the d-c parameters, h_{FB} and h_{FE}, will be positive. More is said about this later.

way that β is larger than α. In the common-emitter situation, both the I_{CEO} and the h_{FE} variation become important as temperature changes. The h_{FE} variation does this because, although the h_{FB} changes only slightly with temperature, the h_{FE} magnifies any such changes since they are related by

$$h_{FE} = \frac{\alpha}{1-\alpha} = \frac{h_{FB}}{1-h_{FB}} \tag{2a}$$

Since h_{FB} is close to 1, it is seen that any small change in h_{FB} creates a much larger change in h_{FE}.

The dependence of I_{CEO} on I_{CBO} is given by

$$I_{CEO} = \frac{I_{CBO}}{1-h_{FB}} = (1 + h_{FE})I_{CBO} \tag{3}$$

If we substitute both (2a) and (3) into Equation (2) we find

$$I_C = h_{FE}I_B + (h_{FE} + 1)I_{CBO} \tag{3a}$$

Here it is seen how changes in both h_{FE} and I_{CBO} with temperature will affect the I_C. It is seen that any changes in I_{CBO} cause a much greater change in I_{CEO}, since any changes are multiplied by the quantity $h_{FE} + 1$. It is this multiplication factor on the I_{CBO} term that causes the common-emitter connection to be less stable with temperature than the common-base connection. This is the main reason for wanting the d-c bias circuit to approach a common-base circuit while the a-c circuit approaches a common-emitter circuit.

The important situation, then, when temperature increases are encountered in the common-emitter case is depicted in Figure 11-2(a). The solid lines show the characteristics at 25°C, and the dashed lines portray the change when temperature increases. It is seen that not only do the characteristics in general move upward but the interval of change increases as I_B increases. The general upward movement reflects the change in I_{CBO} while the increased interval reflects the change in h_{FE}.

Although both germanium and silicon transistors experience the variation of I_{CBO}, the value of I_{CBO} is much less for the silicon than for the germanium transistor. Sometimes the I_{CBO} can be neglected for silicon transistors.

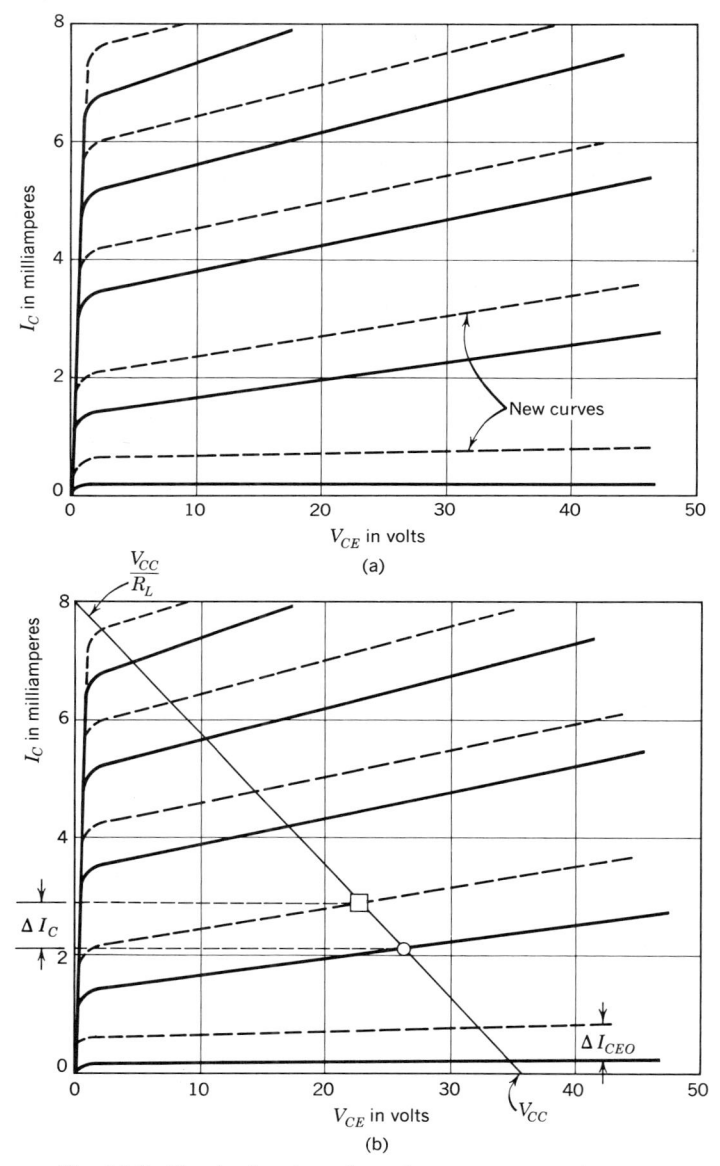

Fig. 11-2. Graphs showing effect of temperature on characteristics and operating point: (a) shift of characteristics with temperature; (b) shift of operating point with temperature.

If we now attach a circuit load line as shown in Figure 11-2(b), we may note the shift of operating point with temperature. Since the load line does not change with temperature, the operating point will shift along the stationary load line to the point where approximately

329

the same I_B is encountered as before. It is seen that, with the new operating point, the permissible swing on the upper half of the load line is reduced. If a relatively large signal is being used under the conditions of (b) above, the shifting operating point will induce clipping if the signal now moves into the saturation region.

If the temperature were to continue increasing, the action shown in Figure 11-2 would continue until finally the operating point would lie on the I_C axis. It is easily seen why it is necessary to stabilize the operating point for transistor amplifiers whenever a temperature variation is expected. The object of all stabilizing measures is to minimize the effect of the shift in characteristics shown above.

In addition to the change of I_{CBO} and h_{FE} with temperature, it is necessary to note still another effect. The base-to-emitter voltage (V_{EB}) necessary to produce an emitter current varies slightly with temperature. In many of the circuits that we deal with here it is good engineering practice to neglect the V_{EB} because it is so much smaller than the other series voltages. However, in switching circuits this change would become important.

Although the three quantities that vary with temperature are I_{CBO}, h_{FE}, and V_{EB}, for the usual amplifier applications only the I_{CBO} and h_{FE} need be considered. In addition, of these it is the I_{CBO} that is typically the more important.

UNIT-TO-UNIT VARIATION. When two transistors of the same type are manufactured, their characteristics are never identical. Again it is found that, although the a-c parameters vary somewhat, it is the I_{CBO} and h_{FE} that show the chief deviation. The I_{CBO} deviation will again be magnified, in the common-emitter connection, according to Equation (3). Therefore *unit-to-unit variation, in the same circuit, produces the same general effect as temperature variation.* Consequently, the measures suitable for stabilizing the temperature dependence will also serve to stabilize the unit-to-unit variation.

D-C EQUIVALENT CIRCUIT

In order to treat and analyze the various factors treated above to obtain bias stability, we need to consider the d-c aspects of the transistor. Thus far in Chapters 7 through 10 we have concentrated

Bias equations and bias stability

on the a-c operation of the transistor, since it seemed better to deal with this first. Here we focus on d-c aspects and certain differences that must be noted. We will first portray a d-c equivalent circuit of the transistor and then combine this equivalent circuit with the external circuitry to write the complete bias equations for the transistor circuit. These equations will permit d-c analysis in general, and may be used to analyze the bias situation with respect to the varying characteristics. In particular we will introduce a stability factor and study the movement of bias point with respect to changes in I_{CBO}. It should be emphasized that the bias equations can be used for studying both bias setting and bias changes with respect to any variable.

In seeking a d-c equivalent circuit for a transistor, there is again a variety of choices possible,[3] as was the case for the a-c equivalent circuit. However, since we have been using the h-parameter equivalent circuit for the a-c case, it is desirable to use the basic h parameters for the d-c equivalent circuit.

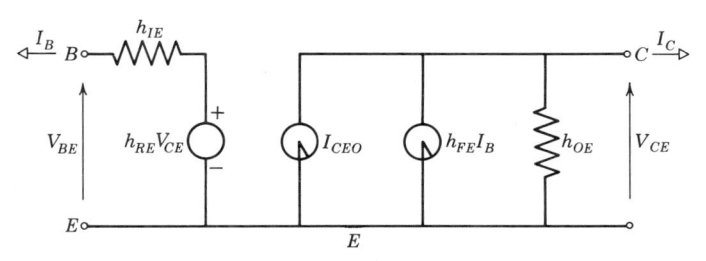

Fig. 11-3. A d-c equivalent circuit of the transistor.

Figure 11-3 shows an h parameter d-c equivalent circuit of a transistor. We note two important changes from the a-c equivalent circuit treated before:

1. The subscripts appear as capital letters in order to denote that now the d-c quantities are meant rather than the a-c incremental quantities.

2. The output side has an additional current source of I_{CEO}, which is the leakage current in the common-emitter connection.

In general the quantity h_{OE} is much smaller than parallel con-

---

[3] For example, the Ebers-Moll equations described in Chapter 15 form a d-c equivalent circuit. These equations are more detailed than is necessary for the usual biasing situation, and the parameters required are not usually given by the manufacturer.

ductances so that it may usually be neglected. Also, generally h_{RE} is negligible at the lower frequencies, and the h_{IE} may be replaced by a voltage drop V_{EB} across a diode (assumed ideal) to represent the base-to-emitter input characteristic. Note that neglecting h_{OE} and h_{RE} means one can assume that the collector-to-emitter voltage has negligible effect upon the collector current.

In any case, for many applications the d-c equivalent circuit can be considered as shown in Figure 11-4.

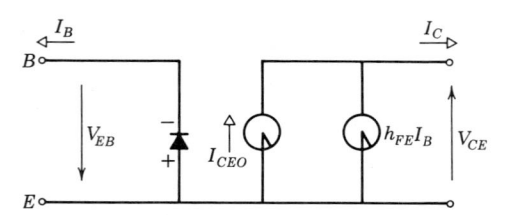

Fig. 11-4. Simplified d-c equivalent circuit for P-N-P transistor.

As in Chapter 10, it is necessary to be cautious regarding the convention of current and voltage direction when writing d-c equations. We assign directions based on the actual directions of the current and voltage for the (P-N-P or N-P-N) transistor (noted on the symbols sheet). It can be seen that Figure 11-4 has the correct current directions for a P-N-P transistor. With this convention, any d-c equations remain valid for P-N-P and N-P-N; in changing from one to the other, one simply reverses the currents, bias sources, and emitter-base diode. This system has the advantage that the source quantities (V_{BB}, V_{CC}, etc.) always have a positive value when used in the equations. The emitter-to-base voltage should always be positive with this convention: V_{EB} is positive for P-N-P equations while V_{BE} is positive for N-P-N equations.

Although all our equations (and directions) are written for the P-N-P case, it must be emphasized that they apply without change to the N-P-N if the above convention is used.

Note that in Figure 11-4 use of a diode to represent the V_{EB} reminds us of the true nature of the junction, and also specifies the direction of forward bias. Also, it may be emphasized that an important factor is the presence of the I_{CEO} current, and that the d-c h_{FE} differs in value from the a-c h_{fe}. We will later use this d-c equivalent circuit to write the general bias equations and to analyze the I_{CBO} stability factor of transistor circuits. We now introduce this stability factor.

Bias equations and bias stability

STABILITY FACTOR

As we saw before, the variation of I_{CBO} is the most important effect of temperature variations. It has become the practice to measure the bias stability of a transistor circuit by investigating the change in collector current with respect to the change in I_{CBO}. A stability factor S is defined as the change in collector current I_C per change in cutoff current I_{CBO}

$$S = \frac{\Delta I_C}{\Delta I_{CBO}} \tag{4}$$

where I_{CBO} = cutoff current in the common-base connection.

It may be noted that one can also define a stability factor of change in collector current with respect to change in h_{FE}. However, because any measures taken to correct for changes in I_{CBO} also correct the h_{FE} situation, it makes the stability factor here most important.

The Δ in Equation (4) stands for a small change in the quantity which it precedes. Equation (4) thus states that for the small change in $I_{CBO}(\Delta I_{CBO})$ a resulting change in $I_C(\Delta I_C)$ results and the ratio of these two changes is the stability factor S.

We can see why this method of measuring stability is useful by referring to Figure 11-2. There we note that the change in I_C is the measure of how much the operating point moves. Also, it is remembered that it is the I_{CBO} that varies most with temperature and various transistors. By referring to Equations (2) and (3) we can quickly note the *stability factor of an unstabilized common-emitter circuit*. From Equation (2) we see that $\Delta I_C = \Delta I_{CEO}$ since S involves only the relation between I_C and I_{CBO}. From Equation (3), then, the stability is

$$S = \frac{\Delta I_C}{\Delta I_{CBO}} = \frac{\Delta I_{CEO}}{\Delta I_{CBO}} = \frac{1}{1 - h_{FB}} = 1 + h_{FE} \tag{5}$$

where h_{FB} = common-base short-circuit current amplification.

Thus the stability factor of the unstabilized emitter circuit approximately equals the circuit current gain. We will see below how this value is improved by the various stabilizing schemes.

The optimum value of S would be 1. If this were the case, the ΔI_C would always equal the ΔI_{CBO}. This is an idealized objective and is not realizable with ordinary measures; the value of S is always greater than 1 for the common-emitter configuration. However, it should be remembered that the closer the value of S is to 1, the better.

The stability factor then should be taken into consideration whenever a temperature variation is expected or when transistor replacement is necessary. If an a-c amplifier consists of cascaded stages, the S is considered separately for each stage because in the a-c amplifier, with coupling capacitors (or transformers) between the stages, the I_C change (d-c) of any one stage does not affect the other stages. For d-c amplifiers any change in I_C *will* affect all succeeding stages; therefore other considerations are involved, and these will be considered later in this chapter.

The primary use of S is as a comparison figure among circuits. Usually the circuit values determining stability must be a compromise because the d-c stability usually conflicts with optimum a-c conditions. Typically one would adjust the circuit components according to the a-c considerations, as was done in the previous design examples, and then check the S of the resulting circuit. If the ensuing S is not low enough, the proper circuit values may be changed, always keeping in mind the a-c considerations, to obtain a suitable S.

In order to illustrate the use of the stability factor, let us consider the following example:

Assume that a temperature range of 50°C is encountered, and that the I_{CBO} varies by 20 μa in this range. Assume also that the given circuit exhibits a stability of $S = 5$. The I_C will then vary by

$$\Delta I_C = S \Delta I_{CBO} = 100 \ \mu a \quad (5a)$$

The next step would consist of estimating the total swing of the circuit. Using this swing in conjunction with the load line, it may be determined whether the ΔI_C is tolerable. If not, the circuit must be altered so as to provide a *lower* value of S.

As mentioned before, those measures that provide a suitable S in terms of varying I_{CBO} are also suitable for accompanying changes in h_{FE}. If the h_{FE} changes alone, due to unit-to-unit change, it may be necessary to consider a stability factor in terms of h_{FE}. Also in some cases the V_{EB} variation must be considered; many of the same techniques used here can be applied to analyze this variation.

STABILIZED BIAS CIRCUITS AND EQUATIONS

There are, in general, four methods of stabilizing the operating point of transistor amplifiers: (1) direct current feedback; (2) direct voltage feedback; (3) use of temperature-sensitive circuit elements; and (4) particular tandem connections.

In this section we will write the detailed bias equations and stability factor for various bias circuits that achieve current and voltage feedback.

D-C CURRENT FEEDBACK. Feedback can be defined generally as the condition where part of the output is applied to the input circuit. For stabilizing purposes we are interested in inverse feedback, that is, if the output increases, the part fed back to the input serves to decrease the output. In current feedback the amount of signal fed back to the input depends upon a current flowing in the output circuit.

For the common-emitter connection, current feedback is achieved by simply placing a resistor R_E in the emitter lead. We can examine how this serves to stabilize the operating point, intuitively, by noting Figure 11-5. Part (a) of this figure shows the circuit in usual schematic form, while part (b) is the "loop" illustration. Note that V_{BB} may equal V_{CC} in single-battery operation. We will use this basic

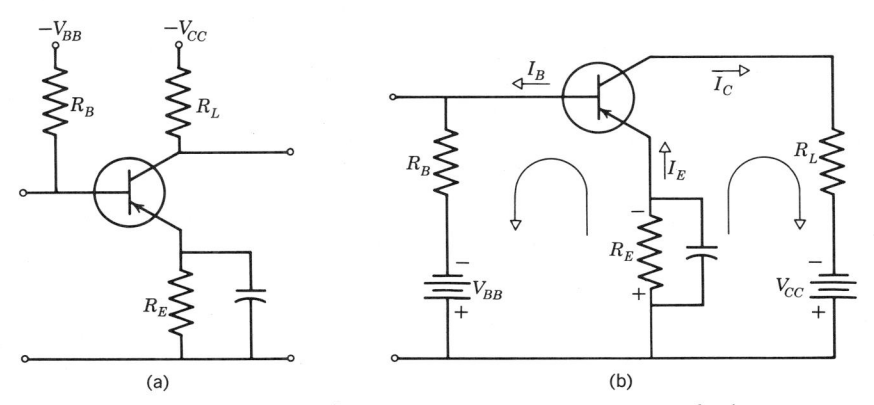

Fig. 11-5. Conventional common-emitter circuit using current feedback: (a) schematic diagram; (b) loop illustration.

circuit to first study the influence of R_E. Later we will examine several circuits that use such an R_E.

In Figure 11-5 the bypass capacitor across R_E is used to prevent the resistor from also providing a-c feedback; this capacitor will be used on all the current-feedback circuits. Let us assume that, due to an increase in temperature, the characteristics as shown in Figure 11-2 are moved upward. Regarding the I_B as being constant, momentarily, this means that the I_C would increase. When the I_C increases, an additional voltage will appear across R_E in the direction shown. It is seen that this voltage opposes the input bias voltage; hence the I_B will be reduced. Referring to Figure 11-2 again, it is seen that this tends to return the operating point to its original position. Thus, although the characteristics of the transistor itself have moved, the operating point attempts to stay in the same position with respect to the axis. In addition, if R_E is considered part of the transistor, the characteristics of the combination are stabilized so that their shift with temperature is not so great as the shift for the transistor alone. It is in this manner, then, that the current-feedback resistor R_E counteracts the effect of temperature and unit-to-unit variation. When the temperature acts to raise the set of transistor characteristics, the voltage developed across R_E acts to restrict the shift of the effective characteristics of the transistor R_E combination.

The bias equations and the stability factor of this circuit can now be calculated by inserting the d-c equivalent circuit of Figure 11-4 into Figure 11-5. We can use the simplified d-c equivalent circuit of Figure 11-4 since both h_{oE} and h_{rE} can usually be neglected.

Using this d-c circuit, then, the entire circuit appears as in Figure 11-6. We can now use the equivalent circuit with its attached external circuitry to analyze entirely the bias equations. This constitutes the complete analysis since it involves the parameters of the transistor, in addition to the components of the external circuit. In the bias section of the preceding chapter we wrote the equations in terms of the external circuit components, and in terms of the transistor voltages and currents. Thus, we did not use the transistor parameters. Consequently, the bias equations here are more complete and detailed than the ones written previously. The material in Chapter 10 served as an introduction to the more complete analysis here. It is always recommended that the least detailed procedure be used wherever possible. When setting a bias point one may or may not need to write the entire equations for the bias circuit.

Bias equations and bias stability

Our first goal, then, is to find the general bias equations; this entails solving the circuit for both I_B and I_C (input current and output current). Following this, we will calculate the stability factor for this circuit.

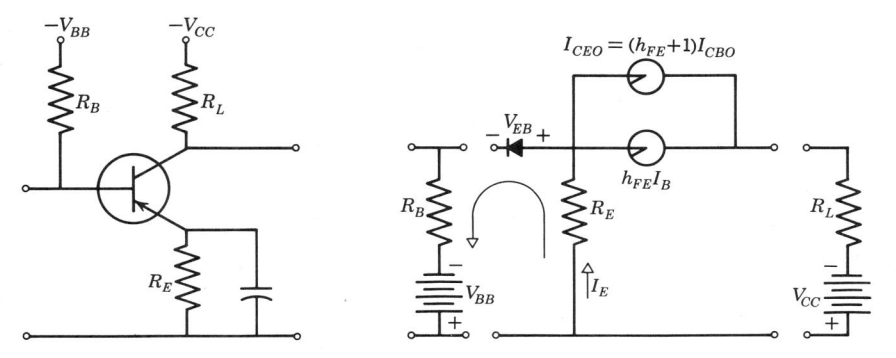

Fig. 11-6. D-c equivalent circuit of Fig. 11-3.

Note that in Figure 11-6 the diode is assumed ideal so that its influence is entirely accounted for by V_{EB}. At first glance, it would appear that two mesh equations would be appropriate. However, this would not permit us to write the equations solely in terms of I_B and I_C. Another unknown, V_{CE}, would be introduced in the output mesh equation.

Since the current sources are in the output side, it is appropriate to write a mesh input equation, and a nodal equation for the output side. The nodal equation will appear as

$$I_E = I_C + I_B \tag{6}$$

This can be written in terms of I_B and I_{CBO}.

$$I_C = h_{FE}I_B + (h_{FE} + 1)I_{CBO} \tag{6a}$$

Note that our objective is to let the unknowns be I_C and I_B. We will write any other currents that occur in terms of these.

It now remains to write the input mesh equation. This is

$$V_{BB} = R_E I_E + R_B I_B + V_{EB} \tag{6b}$$

Therefore

$$I_E = \frac{V_{BB}}{R_E} - \frac{V_{EB}}{R_E} - \frac{R_B}{R_E} I_B$$

Using Equation (6) to write I_E in terms of I_C and I_B, and using Equation (6a) the two equations for the d-c circuit are

$$I_{CBO} = \frac{1}{h_{FE}+1} I_C - \frac{h_{FE}}{h_{FE}+1} I_B \quad (6c)$$

$$V_{BB} - V_{EB} = R_E I_C + (R_B + R_E) I_B$$

We can now use these equations to find the bias equations for the input current I_B and the output current I_C. Solving these equations for I_C via simultaneous equation we obtain

$$I_C = \frac{(R_B + R_E)(h_{FE}+1)}{R_B + R_E + h_{FE} R_E} I_{CBO} + \frac{h_{FE}(V_{BB} - V_{EB})}{R_B + R_E + h_{FE} R_E} \quad (6d)$$

The other desired quantity is I_B. This is shown in Equation (6e).

$$I_B = \frac{V_{BB} - V_{EB} - R_E(h_{FE}+1) I_{CBO}}{R_B + R_E + h_{FE} R_E} \approx \frac{V_{BB} - V_{EB}}{R_B + R_E + h_{FE} R_E} \quad (6e)$$

If desired, one could now solve for the V_{CE} by using the output mesh equation

$$V_{CC} - V_{CE} = R_E I_B + (R_E + R_L) I_C \quad (6f)$$

In the above equations, the voltages and currents will always have a positive value. Thus V_{EB} and V_{CE} will both be positive. Again it must be emphasized that we are here writing the *d-c equations*; in the network analysis of Chapter 8, we were mainly interested in the a-c conditions. It is remembered that, for electronic circuits in general, the a-c and the d-c conditions are treated separately.

We have now found the bias equations for the circuit of Figure 11-5. It will be noted that these equations are in terms of the transistor parameters and the external components.

We can now use the above I_C equation to find the stability factor for this circuit. Since stability is defined as a change in I_C when I_{CBO} varies, and if the changes in h_{FE} and V_{EB} are ignored, only the first term of Equation (6d) will affect the stability. Therefore S will be given by

$$S = \frac{\Delta I_C}{\Delta I_{CBO}} = \frac{(R_B + R_E)(h_{FE}+1)}{R_B + (1 + h_{FE}) R_E} \quad (7)$$

Equation (7) states how the I_C, and hence the operating point, will vary with the given change in I_{CBO}. The stability, it is noted, is

Bias equations and bias stability

affected by R_E, R_B, and the h_{FE} of the transistor. Note that the stability does not depend on the R_L; this is reasonable when it is remembered that I_C is independent of V_C, which was assumed when choosing the transistor equivalent circuit.

We can compare the results of Equation (7) with that of the unstabilized circuit by simply letting R_E equal zero [given in Equation (5)].

It may be seen that if R_B were to approach zero, the S would approach one. Clearly for stability one would like to make R_E high and R_B low. One cannot make R_E larger and R_B smaller indefinitely, however; even though R_E can be a-c bypassed by a capacitor, the input bias battery must be made larger as R_E is increased. For R_B a lower limit is set by the shunting effect on the a-c signal if the stage is capacitance-coupled; if it is transformer-coupled the lower limit on R_B is set only by the small size of the input battery.

For low power stages, with the temperature rise moderate, an S of about 10 can often be tolerated. For a typical value of h_{FE} of about 50 this requires an R_B/R_E of about 10.

As an example of the use of the stability factor let us assume the following component values:

$$R_E = 1000, \quad R_B = 10{,}000, \quad h_{FE} = 50 \tag{8}$$

The S is then

$$S = (h_{FE} + 1) \frac{1}{1 + h_{FE}R_E/(R_B + R_E)} = 9.2 \tag{9}$$

Let us also assume that, either from manufacturer's data or from experimental tests, we will experience an I_{CBO} variation of 5 μa to 25 μa due to temperature change or unit-to-unit variation. Equation (9) then tells us that when I_{CBO} varies by 20 μa the I_C will vary by 180 μa instead of by 1000 μa for the unstabilized case.

Following such a calculation one would determine whether the I_C variation is permissible, in terms of signal swing, permissible power dissipation, or conditions for thermal runaway. If not, the R_E must be raised or the R_B lowered until a suitable condition is found.

We have used the basic biasing circuit of Figure 11-5 to study the effect of the d-c current feedback, and noted how to handle the d-c equations. The most frequently used biasing circuit is shown in

Figure 11-7 where an additional resistor is added. Part (a) shows the usual schematic arrangement, while (b) shows the loop illustration which aids in writing equations.

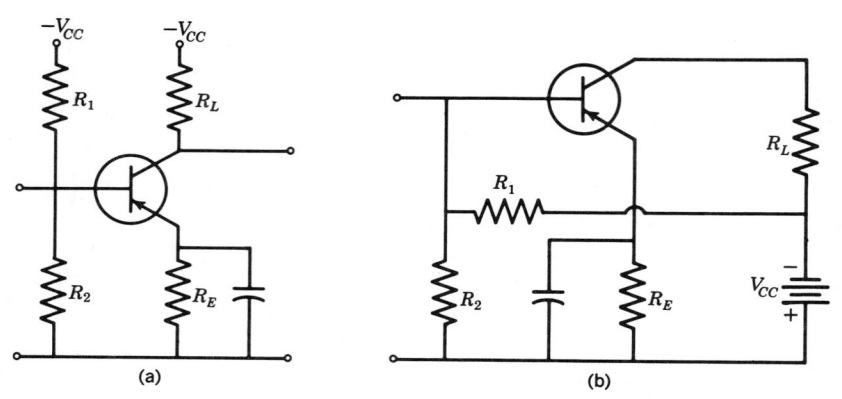

Fig. 11-7. Frequently used common-emitter biasing circuit: (a) schematic diagram; (b) loop arrangement.

The bias equation for I_C and I_B for this slightly altered circuit may be found from the equations above by simply noting that now

$$V_{BB} = \frac{V_{cc}R_2}{R_1 + R_2}$$

and

$$R_B = \frac{R_1 R_2}{R_1 + R_2}$$

The I_C is given by [1]

$$I_C = \frac{[R_1 R_2 + R_E(R_1 + R_2)](h_{FE} + 1)}{R_1 R_2 + R_E(1 + h_{FE})(R_1 + R_2)} \times I_{CBO}$$
$$+ \frac{h_{FE}[V_{cc}R_2 - V_{EB}(R_1 + R_2)]}{R_1 R_2 + R_E(1 + h_{FE})(R_1 + R_2)} \quad (10)$$

The I_B is given by

$$I_B = \frac{V_{cc}R_2 - V_{EB}(R_1 + R_2) - R_E(h_{FE} + 1)(R_1 + R_2)I_{CBO}}{R_1 R_2 + R_E(1 + h_{FE})(R_1 + R_2)} \quad (11)$$

Usually R_1 is much higher than R_2 so that in effect R_2 acts as R_B did in Equation (7). In this case

---

[1] Under normal conditions and at temperatures about 25°C, the second part of Equation (10) will be considerably larger than the first part. Consequently the first part can oftentimes be neglected except when increased temperatures with germanium transistors are encountered.

$$S = \frac{(R_2 + R_E)(h_{FE} + 1)}{R_2 + (1 + h_{FE})R_E} \quad \text{if } R_1 \gg R_2 \tag{12}$$

The circuit of Figure 11-6, where two batteries are implied, could use a low R_B by using a low V_{BB}. If Figure 11-6 were used in a single battery configuration ($V_{BB} = V_{CC}$), R_B would make S quite large $[\approx (h_{FE} + 1)]$.

An advantage of the circuit of Figure 11-7 is that it permits the single-battery operation while allowing a small effective R_B. This in turn provides the possibility of a reasonable stability.

The influence on stability of R_E and the effective R_B for this circuit are the same as previously:

$$\text{if } R_E \to 0, \quad S \to h_{FE} + 1$$
$$\text{if } R_B \to 0, \quad S \to 1$$

With no current feedback, the stability is the same as an unstabilized circuit. When R_B is zero and R_E is finite, the d-c circuit becomes a common-base circuit. Thus, for good bias stability, *the bias circuit should approximate that of a common-base circuit.* This is an important fundamental in biasing circuits. The a-c circuit would of course remain common emitter since a capacitor bypasses the emitter resistance.

D-C VOLTAGE FEEDBACK. Another general method for stabilizing the operating points of transistor amplifiers consists of using direct-voltage feedback. Voltage feedback is defined as that situation when the amount of signal fed back to the input (from the output) depends upon a voltage in the output circuit.

The simplest type of circuit using voltage feedback is shown in Figure 11-8. Whenever a voltage appears across the load resistor R_L, a part of this voltage is fed back to the input through R_F. Note that the R_F also applies the correct sign for bias voltage to the input side. It should be realized that the circuit of Figure 11-8 will provide a-c feedback also (discussed in the next chapter) unless the R_F is broken up according to the manner of Figure 11-10.

The basic d-c equations for this circuit can again be found by

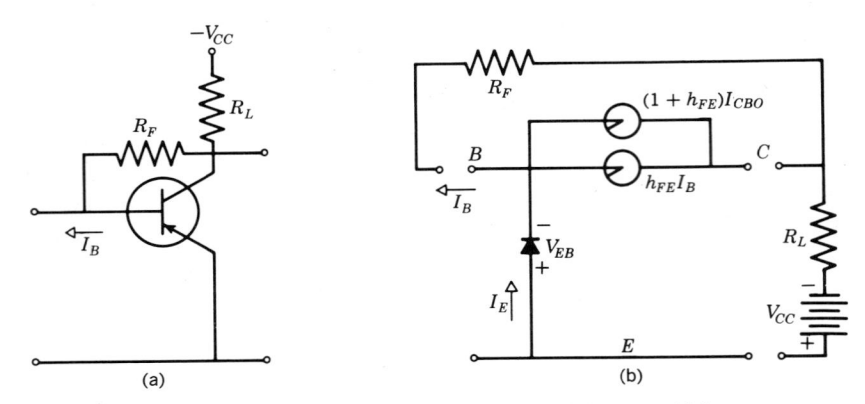

Fig. 11-8. Circuit using voltage feedback for stabilization: (a) basic circuit; (b) d-c equivalent circuit.

using the equivalent circuit shown in Figure 11-8. Again it helps to separate the transistor circuit from that of the external circuitry. The resulting d-c equations are first the transistor circuit equation and then the mesh equation for the circuit.

$$I_C = h_{FE}I_B + (h_{FE} + 1)I_{CBO}$$
$$V_{CC} = V_{EB} + I_B R_F + (I_B + I_C)R_L \qquad (13)$$

As before we will let the unknowns be I_C and I_B, since I_B is the input and the I_C is the output current. Both of these together completely specify the bias point. Rearranging the above equations, they appear as

$$(h_{FE} + 1)I_{CBO} = I_C - h_{FE}I_B$$
$$V_{CC} - V_{EB} = R_L I_C + (R_F + R_L)I_B \qquad (14)$$

Using determinants to solve first for I_C we find

$$I_C = \frac{(R_F + R_L)(h_{FE} + 1)}{R_F + R_L(1 + h_{FE})} I_{CBO} + \frac{h_{FE}(V_{CC} - V_{EB})}{R_F + R_L(1 + h_{FE})} \qquad (15)$$

In usual cases the R_F is much greater than R_L so that the I_C is approximately

$$I_C \approx \frac{h_{FE}(V_{CC} + I_{CBO}R_F)}{R_F + h_{FE}R_L} \qquad \begin{array}{c}(R_F \gg R_L)\\(h_{FE} \gg 1)\end{array} \qquad (16)$$

Bias equations and bias stability

Using the same set of equations and solving for I_B, the result is found to be

$$I_B = \frac{V_{CC} - V_{EB} - R_L(h_{FE} + 1) I_{CBO}}{R_F + R_L(1 + h_{FE})} \approx \frac{V_{CC}}{R_F + R_L(1 + h_{FE})} \qquad (17)$$

To find the stability we can use Equation (15)

$$S = \frac{\Delta I_C}{\Delta I_{CBO}} = \frac{(R_F + R_L)(h_{FE} + 1)}{R_F + R_L(1 + h_{FE})} \qquad (18)$$

We can test the limits; if R_F is much greater than $R_L(1 + h_{FE})$

$$S = \frac{R_F(h_{FE} + 1)}{R_F} = h_{FE} + 1 \quad \text{if } R_F \gg R_L(1 + h_{FE}) \qquad (19)$$

At the lower value:

$$S = \frac{(R_F + R_L)(h_{FE} + 1)}{R_L(h_{FE} + 1)} = 1 + \frac{R_F}{R_L} \quad \text{if } R_L \ll R_L(1 + h_{FE}) \qquad (20)$$

Clearly R_F should be kept of the same order of magnitude as R_L for reasonable stability.

Another circuit that uses voltage feedback is shown in Figure 11-9(a). In this case the resistor R_B is added. This additional resistor

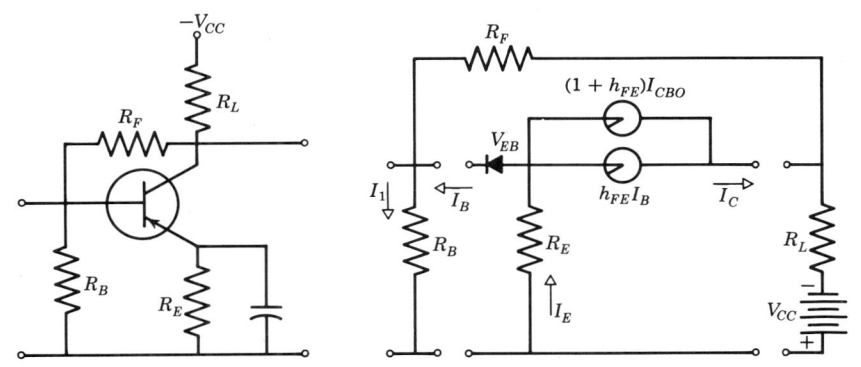

Fig. 11-9. Use of voltage feedback with current feedback: (a) connection; (b) equivalent circuit.

serves to provide more stability than Figure 11-7 but there is slightly less gain. We have noted, of course, that with the feedback resistor as shown, the bias circumstances and the a-c feedback circumstances are interrelated. These can be somewhat separated by breaking up the feedback resistor (as will be seen later).

We will now move to the most general case where the voltage feedback is combined with current feedback. This circuit is shown in Figure 11-9. Notice that this circuit includes all possible resistors and can be made to cover the preceding case, which involved voltage feedback only. The equations for this general circuit are done as before. Figure 11-9(b) shows the d-c equivalent circuit, where the technique of dividing the transistor part from the external part is used. Three equations are required for this circuit: the first equation is a nodal equation taking care of the output loop which contains the current sources. This equation is simply the transistor current relation. The next equation is taken by writing a mesh around the outside loop, and the final equation is by making a mesh around the left-hand loop. The equations then appear as

$$I_C = h_{FE}I_B + (h_{FE} + 1)I_{CBO} + 0I_1$$
$$V_{CC} = -I_1R_B + (I_B - I_1)R_F + (I_C + I_B - I_1)R_L \qquad (21)$$
$$0 = I_1R_B + (I_B + I_C)R_E + V_{EB}$$

We can use these equations now to solve for both I_C and I_B. The I_C is found to be

$$I_C = \frac{h_{FE}[V_{CC}R_B - V_{EB}(R_L + R_F + R_B)] + (1 + h_{FE})[R_E(R_L + R_F + R_B) + R_BR_L + R_BR_F]I_{CBO}}{R_BR_F + (1 + h_{FE})[R_E(R_L + R_F + R_B) + R_BR_L]} \qquad (22)$$

The I_B is found to be

$$I_B = \frac{V_{CC}R_B - V_{EB}(R_L + R_F + R_B) - I_{CBO}(1 + h_{FE})[R_E(R_L + R_F + R_B) + R_BR_L]}{R_BR_F + (1 + h_{FE})[R_E(R_L + R_F + R_B) + R_BR_L]} \qquad (23)$$

We can use Equation (22) for I_C to find the stability S for this general case. The stability S is given by

$$S = \frac{(1 + h_{FE})[R_E(R_L + R_F + R_B) + R_BR_L + R_BR_F]}{R_BR_F + (1 + h_{FE})[R_E(R_L + R_F + R_B) + R_BR_L]} \qquad (24)$$

If R_B were removed from the circuit, the stability would be

$$S = \frac{(1 + h_{FE})[R_E + R_L + R_F]}{R_F + (1 + h_{FE})[R_E + R_L]} \quad \text{if } R_B \to \infty \qquad (25)$$

Bias equations and bias stability 345

With R_B thus removed, the limiting behavior of S with respect to extreme R_F values is

$$S \to 1 \quad \text{if } R_B \to \infty, \text{ and } R_F \gg (h_{FE} + 1)(R_E + R_L)$$
$$S \to 1 + \frac{R_F}{R_E + R_L} \quad \text{if } R_B \to \infty, \text{ and } R_F \ll (h_{FE} + 1)(R_E + R_L) \tag{25a}$$

For voltage feedback we notice that the effect of a given R_F on stability depends not only on R_F, but on the ratio of this factor to $(R_E + R_L)$. The influence of the feedback for a given R_F increases as R_L increases. If R_L were zero, the resistor would effectively be tied back to the collector and there would be no feedback.

As mentioned previously, the R_F of the voltage feedback case will provide a-c feedback also since it cannot be directly bypassed. The a-c voltage can be reduced greatly by splitting the feedback resistor and bypassing the junction point to ground, as shown in Figure 11-10.

Each of the circuits using voltage feedback can make use of the "no a-c feedback" scheme shown in Figure 11-10. The issue here is that by this process the a-c feedback is reduced but the d-c situation is not altered appreciably. All the above equations apply directly but the R_F is always the sum of R_{FB} and R_{FC}.

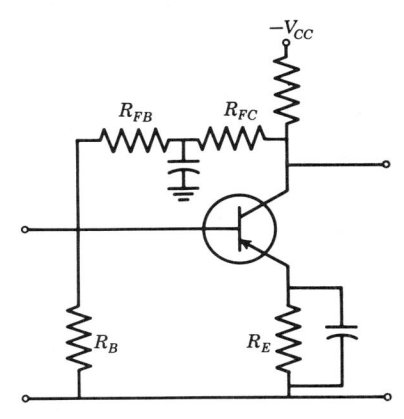

Fig. 11-10. Circuit of Fig. 11-9 with reduced a-c feedback.

These, then, are the stabilizing schemes and equations for the voltage feedback case. The choice between voltage and current feedback is largely determined by the size of the d-c load resistance. If the d-c R_L is large, as is usually the case for RC-coupled cases, the voltage feedback is as effective as the current type. For transformer coupling, where the d-c R_L is low, current feedback is much more effective than the other.

Although we have concentrated on the I_{CBO} variation in the entire bias analysis, it should be remembered that h_{FE} and V_{EB} may also need attention. Many of the same techniques can be applied to the analysis of these two factors.

The above general methods, then, can be used in the given design situation. The bias equations in general can be consulted for their dependence on any characteristics both in the internal transistor and in the external circuit. As a rule it will be found that rather than use the detailed equations to solve for bias points, one will make crude approximations and then settle on the final bias point by trial and error. This procedure is necessary to some degree in practice.

Remember that although all the d-c equations in this chapter were written for a P-N-P transistor, they apply to the N-P-N case without change. One simply must reverse (in the circuit diagram) the directions of the currents, bias sources, and emitter-base diode.

The other issue is the matter of stability factor in design considerations. Two general procedures are available for incorporating the S in any design situation: (1) determine the appropriate S value and then use the various d-c equations to fix the circuit component values which will give this S; or (2) decide upon the component values by the usual a-c considerations and then check the resulting S.

Many times the designer will prefer to avoid the lengthy calculations of the first method and use the system whereby all circuit components are selected on the basis of the a-c considerations. After this is done, the stability may be checked and suitable alterations made to improve the stability if necessary. It is recommended that, after some experience is achieved, this latter method be employed.

ADDITIONAL STABILIZING TECHNIQUES

Here we will consider qualitatively two additional techniques for improving bias stability.

TEMPERATURE-SENSITIVE ELEMENTS. When using temperature-sensitive elements for stability, the idea is to cause the circuit conditions to change with temperature so that the changes effected by the transistor are compensated.

It is remembered that the basic change in transistors, when temperature changes occur, consists of the entire set of characteristics moving with respect to the axis. This, in turn, happens because the collector junction is biased in the reverse direction and the ensuing reverse current is a function of the existing temperature. One tem-

Bias equations and bias stability

perature-sensitive element, then, would be a junction diode whose temperature properties are similar to that of the collector junction in the transistor. Thermistors, varistors, and special types of resistors may also be used as the temperature-sensitive elements.

Figure 11-11 shows a stabilized circuit in which a junction diode is used as the stabilizing means. The current flowing through the resistance R_1 and the diode D_1 furnishes the biasing voltage for the input of the transistor. We can describe the operation of this circuit generally by momentarily assuming that the diode is not temperature sensitive. When the temperature increases, the characteristics and the operating point will move upward according to the illustration of Figure 11-2. In order to return the operating point (and effectively the entire characteristics) to the original position it is necessary to reduce the I_B.

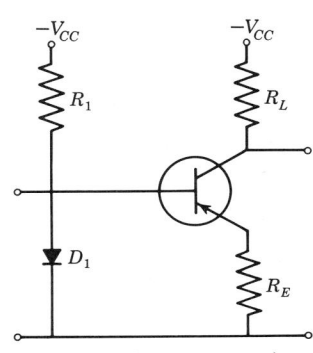

Fig. 11-11. Biasing network stabilized by a diode.

The presence of the temperature-sensitive diodes accomplishes this I_B reduction in two ways. First, the decreased forward resistance of the diode (with temperature) makes the stabilizing resistor R_3 more effective, as will be remembered from the previous section on current feedback. Second, the reduced resistance of the diode means that a smaller bias voltage is supplied to the base by the voltage-dividing network of $R_1 - D_1$. With the I_B properly reduced, the displaced characteristics of the transistor are effectively returned toward their original positions.

There are many special ways in which diodes and other temperature-sensitive elements can be used to stabilize a transistor circuit. We will not treat these special cases here, but refer the student to the literature for additional information.

Since the temperature dependence of diodes is a nonlinear phenomenon, it is not possible to calculate a stability factor for such circuits in any simple manner. Therefore the only method recommended for finding the S is by experiments with the circuit. The operation of the diode may be altered to suit the designer by adding ordinary series and shunt resistors. By a process of trial and error the circuit may be adjusted for a suitable stability factor.

The choice of using either feedback elements such as described before or bias compensation as described here depends primarily on whether one can afford to lose the gain at low frequencies which accompany the feedback methods. It is clear, of course, that the d-c feedback stabilization methods reduce the d-c gain of the circuit.

TANDEM OPERATION. Another stabilizing method consists of appropriately connecting two or more transistors directly in cascade. By the use of special connections the circuit may be made stable with respect to temperature changes.

One such method consists of using two transistors of different types; i.e., an N-P-N followed by a P-N-P. This is done because the direction of collector current increase, when the temperature rises, is opposite for the two transistors. Thus the variation in one transistor tends to cancel that in the other. This is suitable only if the transistors are directly connected without a coupling capacitor or transformer. Assuming that the variation with temperature is approximately equal for both transistors, the first transistor would have to be stabilized by some other means, since the second transistor amplifies any temperature-induced variations. Since the alternative to this would be to stabilize each transistor by one of the methods discussed previously, it is worthwhile to consider using this method. A small saving in efficiency is achieved, since the second transistor would not require any explicit stabilizing.

Another way to utilize tandem operation in improving the stability is to use the first transistor as a constant-current source for the second transistor. The first transistor, of course, would still provide amplification. If the I_E of the second transistor, for example, is held relatively fixed, the sum of I_B and I_C will have to adjust so as to remain constant.

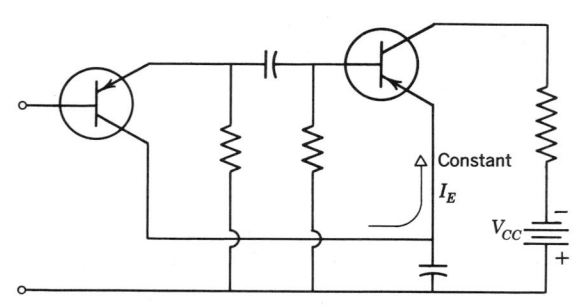

Fig. 11-12. An example of the use of tandem operation to obtain stabilization.

Bias equations and bias stability

In this way the I_B will be caused to decrease (the desired effect when the I_C increases due to temperature changes).

Figure 11-12 shows one application of this scheme. The fact that the I_E of the second transistor passes through the high-resistance collector junction of the first guarantees that it will be relatively constant if the first transistor is stabilized. Thus here again the net saving comes from the fact that only one of the two transistors must be stabilized to obtain a two-stage stabilized circuit.

COMMENT ON COMMON-BASE STABILIZED CIRCUITS. All the previous stability considerations were devoted to the common-emitter connection because: (1) this is the most suitable connection for amplifiers; and (2) the stability problem is more critical for this connection. It is worthwhile, however, to make some comment about the common-base case.

The use of negative feedback for the common-base connection is not possible unless transformers (for phase shifting) are used and these will not work for d-c conditions. Therefore the simple method of shunt and series resistors, shown above for the emitter case, is not applicable here. For example, if a resistor is placed in the base lead of a common-base connection, the circuit has positive feedback and the stability is *reduced* (S increased). This is also true for a shunt resistor connected from collector to emitter.

One simple method of stabilizing the base connection is to insert a resistor in series with the emitter (input) lead, thus driving with a constant-current source. This would be bypassed, of course, to avoid attenuating the a-c signal. This is still a relatively costly solution, however, since the large I_E (compared to I_B) causes an appreciable d-c power loss in the stabilizing resistor.

The use of temperature-sensitive elements and tandem operation are also applicable to the common-base case.

D-C AMPLIFIER

Although it is usually the case that electronic amplifiers are designed to amplify alternating voltage or power it is sometimes necessary to construct amplifiers that will amplify a change in a direct potential or power. The essential difference between a d-c and an a-c amplifier is that, in the d-c case, a capacitor (or transformer) cannot be used as a coupling element between the stages. This, of course, changes the biasing conditions for the d-c amplifier. From the previous study of maintaining a stable bias point, it is evident that building stable d-c amplifiers in the face of varying temperatures is a sizable problem. In general, one can tackle the problem straightforwardly by directly connecting transistor stages and paying good attention to stabilizing all the stages, or one can circumvent the d-c amplifier by using a chopping method. In this method an a-c signal is formed whose magnitude is proportional to the d-c signal being amplified, and the resulting a-c signal is then amplified by the conventional method. After sufficient amplification is acquired, the signal is then converted to direct current by a filtering process.

In order to illustrate the stability problems of the d-c amplifier we shall show some basic d-c amplifier circuits. Figure 11-13 shows the simplest type of common-emitter d-c amplifier. Here it is seen how the absence of any coupling element alters the biasing situation. The battery V_{CC} provides both the collector bias for the first transistor and the base bias for the second transistor.

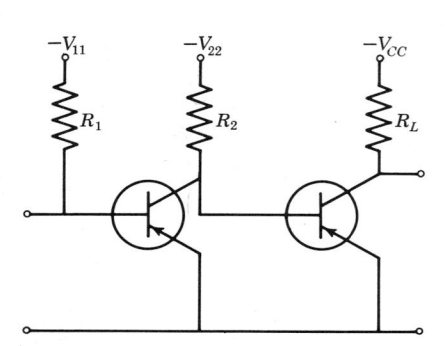

Fig. 11-13. A basic d-c amplifier circuit using a common-emitter connection.

The scheme of Figure 11-13 cannot be carried out to many stages since each succeeding battery must be larger than the previous one in order to provide a negative collector-to-base voltage for each transistor.

Still another basic circuit utilizing a common-base and a common-emitter connection is shown in Figure 11-14. Here the input of the second transistor acts as the only load on the first stage. Note that the collector bias for the first transistor is obtained *through* the collector-to-base junction of the second transistor. This biasing through another transistor, not possible with vacuum tubes, should always be kept in mind as a possibility when devising transistor circuits.

Although each of these amplifiers provides the desired d-c amplification, it is very difficult to maintain a stable operation with them. We can readily see the reason for this. If the I_C of the first transistor, in either of the cases, changes because of temperature variation, the

Bias equations and bias stability 351

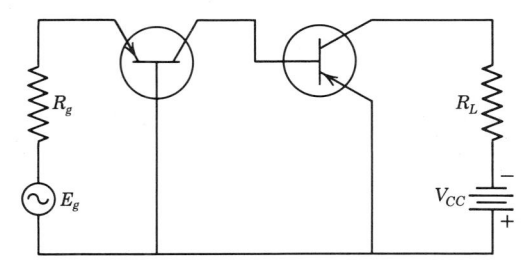

Fig. 11-14. D-c amplifier using common-base to common-emitter connection.

second transistor will *amplify* this change and will also add its own temperature variation. Thus due to the amplification of any changes in the previous stages, the operating point stability is very low for d-c amplifiers (S high). Note that, for a-c amplifiers, the d-c conditions of each stage are separated by the coupling element and hence the cumulative condition is not encountered.

The stability situation can be improved, somewhat, by applying the stabilizing measures discussed in the previous section. The basic circuit of Figure 11-13, with both series and shunt resistors added for stabilization, is shown in Figure 11-15. The gain of this circuit will,

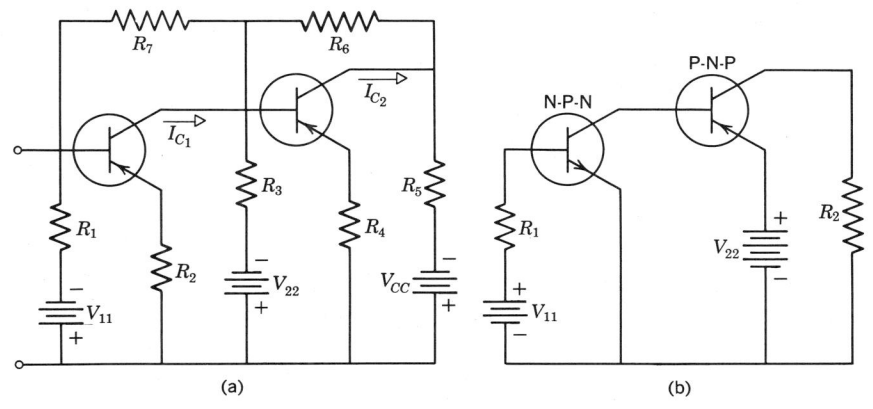

Fig. 11-15. D-c amplifiers with stabilizing measures: (a) stabilizing by current and voltage feedback; (b) stabilization by tandem operation.

of course, be less than that for the unstabilized circuit; for here it is undesirable to by-pass the d-c feedback resistors. Therefore the stabilizing resistors will provide d-c as well as a-c feedback.

Figure 11-15(b) shows another application of a stabilizing method to d-c amplifiers. Here use is made of tandem operation, where one transistor is of the N-P-N type and the other is of the P-N-P type. As noted in the previous section, the stabilizing action stems from the fact that the direction of I_C change with temperature is opposing for the two transistors. Note that here again, in the biasing circuit, the collector bias for the first transistor is obtained *through* the second transistor.

In order to illustrate the stability calculation for d-c amplifiers, and compare it to the a-c case, we will calculate the stability of the circuit in Figure 11-13. If the temperature changes so as to vary the I_{CBO}, the variation in I_{C_2} will be

$$\Delta I_{C_2 T} = A_{i2}\Delta I_{C_1} + \Delta I_{C_2} = A_{i2}S_1\Delta I_{CBO_1} + S_2\Delta I_{CBO_2} \tag{30}$$

where A_{i2} = current gain of the second stage,
$S_1 = \Delta I_{C_1}/\Delta I_{CBO_1}$,
$S_2 = \Delta I_{C_2}/\Delta I_{CBO_2}$.

If the I_{CO} change with temperature is approximately the same for both transistors, then

$$\Delta I_{CBO_1} \cong \Delta I_{CBO_2} \tag{31}$$

and Equation (30) may be written

$$S_{\text{total}} = \frac{\Delta I_{C_2 T}}{\Delta I_{CBO}} = A_{i2}S_1 + S_2 \tag{32}$$

We can now see why the stabilizing problem is more difficult for d-c than for a-c amplifiers. In a-c amplifiers, when each stage is isolated from the others will regard to d-c, a stability factor applies to only one stage and affects only the operation of that one stage. In Equation (32), however, we note that the current gain multiplies the first stage stability. This exhibits, mathematically, the statement that the I_C variation is cumulative in d-c amplifiers.

Using Equation (32) we can now find the stability of Figure 11-13. It has been shown previously that, for the unstabilized condition

$$S_1 = 1 + h_{FE_1} \qquad S_2 = 1 + h_{FE_2}$$

For finding the A_{i2} we can use the a-c relation for current gain as given by Table 8-5.

$$S_{\text{total}} = \frac{h_{FE}}{R_L h_{oe} + 1}(1 + h_{FE_1}) + (1 + h_{FE_2})$$

Bias equations and bias stability

Although the stability calculation for d-c amplifiers is distinctly different from that of the a-c case, the other performance quantities are calculated in an identical manner. Therefore *the equations of Table 8-5 are used to calculate the performance quantities of d-c amplifiers*, using the d-c parameters.

In addition to the I_{CBO} variation, the V_{EB} variation is often an issue in d-c amplifiers. The combined I_{CBO} variation and V_{EB} variation are referred to as "drift." The measures suitable to reduce the drift in a d-c amplifier differ from those suitable for stabilizing a bias point of a single stage. When stabilizing the bias point we could use either resistive feedback or compensation devices. Since the resistive feedback elements all decrease the gain at d-c, it is clear that these techniques are more or less ruled out for d-c amplifiers (for a-c amplifiers bypass capacitors prevent gain decrease except at the very low frequencies). Consequently, if one wishes to build d-c amplifiers and give excellent stabilization to single stage units, one must do it with bias compensation using thermistors, junction diodes, or various multistage techniques.

For this purpose there are a variety of relatively ingenious multistage connections, which can afford successful d-c amplifiers. They will not be discussed in detail here because they represent a more or less specialized area of study deserving of fuller treatment.

One relatively successful technique, however, is of sufficient importance to be mentioned here. This consists of using a balanced- or differential-type direct connection to form a d-c amplifier. This connection, shown in Figure 11-16 is useful not only as a d-c amplifier but also as a general difference amplifier.

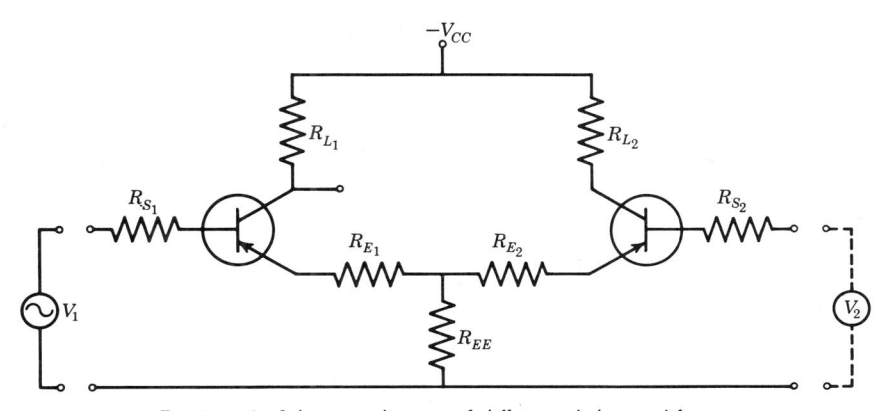

Fig. 11-16. Schematic diagram of differential d-c amplifier.

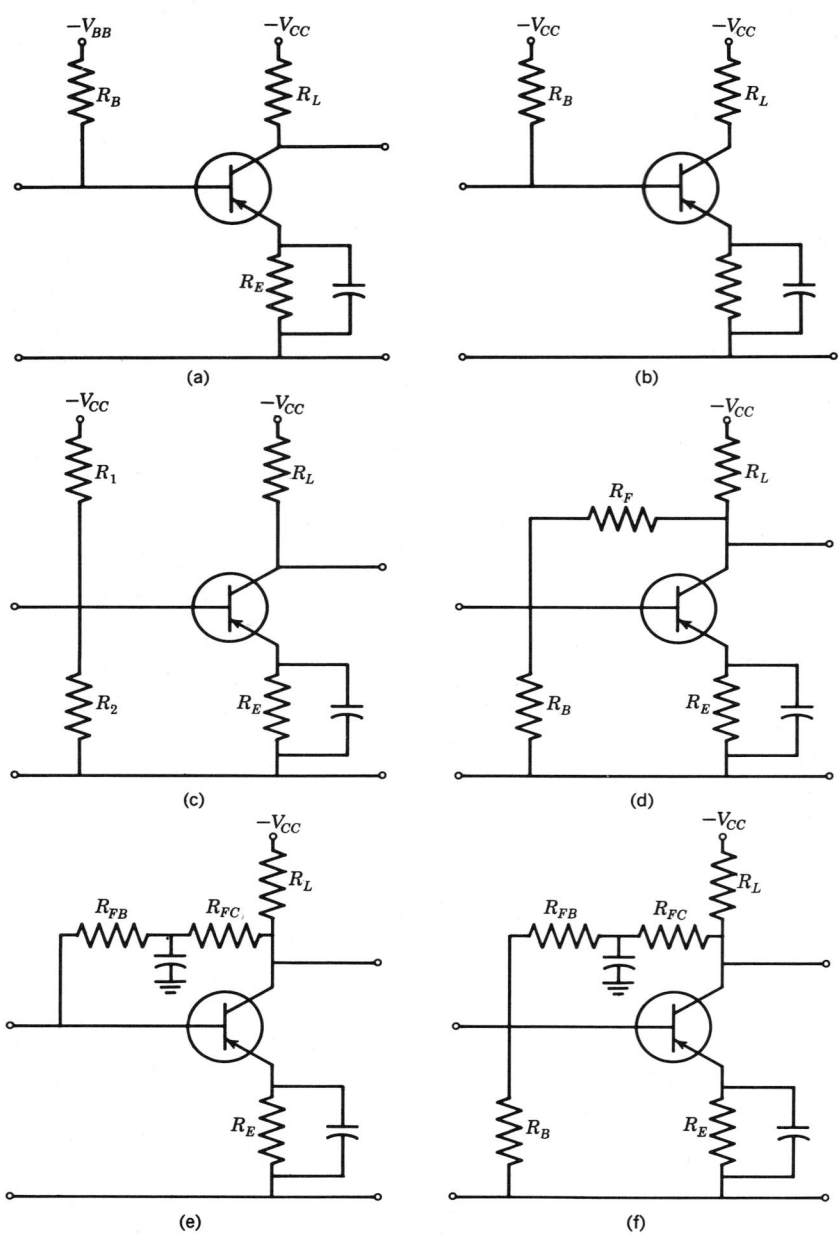

Fig. 11-17. Typical bias stability circuits. (a) $R_B = 10K$, $R_E = 500\Omega$, $R_L = 20K$; (b) $R_B = 30K$, $R_E = 1K$, $R_L = 40K$; (c) $R_L = 10K$, $R_E = 100\Omega$, $R_1 = 50K$, $R_2 = 5K$; (d) $R_F = 30K$, $R_B = 20K$, $R_L = 20K$, $R_E = 1K$; (e) $R_{FB} = 20K$, $R_{FC} = 80K$, $R_E = 1K$, $R_L = 20K$; (f) $R_B = 5K$, $R_E = 1K$, $R_L = 20K$, $R_{FB} = 10K$, $R_{FC} = 50K$.

Bias equations and bias stability

The difference-type amplifier is applicable for a d-c amplifier because it has been possible to construct two transistors on the same substrate; consequently their temperature characteristics are exceedingly well-matched. This allows the use of the difference amplifier concept to work exceedingly well in the presence of parameter change.

The circuit shown will amplify faithfully the "difference" between V_1 and V_2. If a single-ended d-c amplifier is desired, one can ground V_2 (or establish some other reliable reference). The output from R_{L_1} will accurately deal with V_1, since the differential circuit arrangement will effectively handle bias changes.

PROBLEMS

1. Assume that a circuit containing the 2N1097 transistor experiences a temperature change that moves from 25°C to 65°C. Using an I_{CBO} stability factor of 5, what is the change in collector current due to the I_{CBO} variation? Use the curves given for the 2N1097.

2. What are the stability factors of the circuits shown in Figure 11-17, given that h_{FE} is 100?

3. What should the values of R_E be in Figure 11-17 [(a), (b)] for a stability factor S of 10, leaving the other components the same?

4. What effect does an increase in R_L have upon the stability factor S of Figure 11-17 [(e), (f)]?

5. Refer to Problem 3 of Chapter 10. Note the operating point found there. (Amplifier is repeated in Figure 11-18.) Assume that the temperature changes from 25°C to 65°C. Using the I_{CBO} curve given for the 2N1097 germanium transistor and the I_{CBO} stability factor for this amplifier, estimate the operating point at 65°C. Find first the I_C, and then the V_{CE} with a load line equation. Use the mean h_{FE} value (over the temperature range), since it also varies.

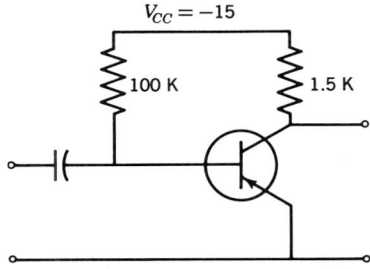

Fig. 11-18. Common-emitter amplifier.

6. Again assume the amplifier of Problem 5 above; use the silicon 2N3638 transistor, and first find the operating point at 25°C. Assume that the temperature changes to 65°C. Find the new I_C and V_{CE} as in Problem 5 above. Assume that I_{CES} approximates I_{CEO}. Compare the behavior of a germanium transistor in this circuit (Problem 5) with the silicon one used here.

7. Assume that the germanium 2N1302 transistor is used in the amplifier which is described in Figure 11-19. Assume the following values: $V_{CC} = 15$; $R_1 = 22K$; $R_2 = 5K$; $R_L = 4K$; $R_E = 1K$; and $R_4 = 1K$. First find the operating point at the normal 25°C. Now assume that the temperature rises to 65°C. Using the stability factor derived in this chapter, find the I_C increment resulting from this change. Then find the new V_{CE} from an output equation. Use the mean h_{FE} over the temperature range.

8. Use the silicon 2N3392 transistor in the same amplifier as described in Figure 11-19 and Problem 7. Assume that the 25°C to 65°C temperature range is encountered. After finding the original operating point, find the new bias point, using the mean h_{FE} over the range. Compare the action with this silicon transistor to that of the germanium one in Problem 7.

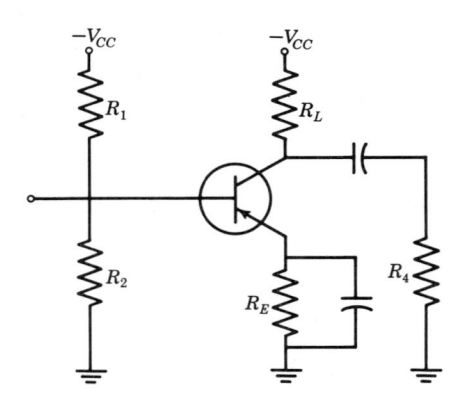

Fig. 11-19. Common-emitter amplifier.

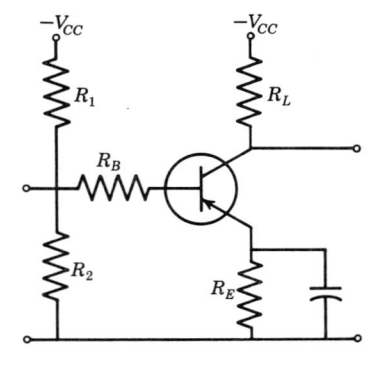

Fig. 11-20. Common-emitter amplifier with series R_B.

9. Using the same methods as used in this chapter, derive the stability factor for the circuit shown in Figure 11-20. Check your result by letting R_B approach zero, and see if S equals the expression calculated from Equation (10) of this chapter.

Bias equations and bias stability

10. Assume the d-c equivalent circuit (with its current and voltage directions) for an N-P-N transistor. Using the circuit of Figure 11-7(a), with the general d-c bias equations for this situation, calculate I_C, and the ensuing stability factor. Compare your result to Equation (10).

11. For the circuit of Figure 11-7, assume that $R_1 \gg R_2$. Assume that the one is given the S, V_{CC}, R_L, I_C, I_{CBO}, and R_2 in terms of these quantities. Start first with the R_E. Then derive R_1. R_2 can be written in terms of R_E and R_1, plus the above qualities. If desired, one could specify the S and other qualities required, and use these derived equations to determine the three resistors.

12. For the circuit of Figure 11-7, find the ratio expressing the variation of I_C with changes in h_{FE}. Do this both with and without the assumption that $R_1 \gg R_2$.

13. For the circuit of Figure 11-7, find the ratio expressing the variation of I_C with respect to changes in V_{EB}. Do this both with and without the assumption that $R_1 \gg R_2$.

14. Assume that the circuit of Figure 11-21 is used with the 2N1097 transistor. First find the operating point at 25°C. Then, using the mean value of h_{FE} over the range, find the ensuing operating point at 75°C.

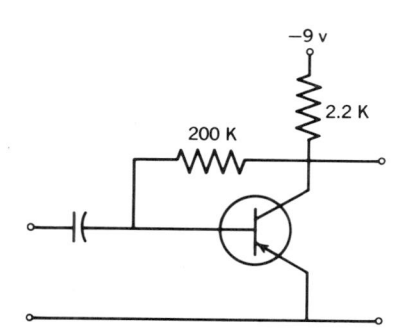

Fig. 11-21. Single stage with voltage feedback.

15. Assume that in the amplifier of Figure 11-21, an a-c current peak of ±1.15 ma must be amplified linearly. What is the maximum temperature that this stage can tolerate, using only I_{CBO} variation?

16. In the amplifier of both Problems 7 and 8, compare the change in I_C, with the 25°C to 65°C change in temperature, from that due to I_{CBO} change (using a mean h_{FE}) and the change caused by the variation of h_{FE}.

17. For the amplifier of Problem 5, assume that a peak current of 50 μa must be linearly amplified. Under the conditions given (at 25°C), what is the maximum temperature that can be tolerated?

18. For the amplifier of Problem 6, assume that a peak current of 75 μa must be linearly amplified. Under the conditions given (at 25°C), what is the maximum temperature that can be tolerated?

19. For the bias stabilizing circuit of Figure 11-11, write the equation for I_C in terms of the R_1 current, the diode reverse current, the h_{FE}, and the I_{CBO}. What would be the stability of this circuit if the diode reverse current exactly equaled the I_{CBO}?

20. Using the d-c equivalent circuit for the transistor, write the basic d-c equations for Figure 11-16. Assume that $V_2 = 0$; derive the output voltage at R_{L_1} in terms of the input voltage V_1. Note the role of I_{CEO_1} and I_{CEO_2}; assume that they are equal for all temperatures since they occur on the same substrate.

12
Feedback

The application of feedback to an electronic circuit consists essentially of adding additional elements (usually passive) to the basic circuit in order to favorably change the performance quantities. Feedback, then, represents a general method by which we may alter either the a-c or the d-c performance quantities of the transistor. In the previous chapter, d-c feedback was considered as a means of stabilizing the operating point. In this chapter we are interested in a-c feedback, where the a-c performance quantities are influenced.

If we are dealing with a circuit in which an input and an output can be isolated and identified, as is true for all active circuits, then any element that couples the output to the input is a feedback element. For a passive circuit this means that the element appears in both the output and the input portions; for an active circuit it means that either a voltage source in the input depends upon a current or voltage in the output, or a passive element may directly couple the input to the output. It is interesting to note that the transistor itself contains a feedback element; the h_{12} term of the equivalent circuits (Chapter 8) couples the output circuit to the input circuit. This is distinctly different from the vacuum tube where the output is normally isolated from the input circuit.

In this chapter our purpose will be to consider the effects and methods of treating externally added feedback elements in transistor amplifiers. We will begin by noting the qualitative effect of feedback upon each of the a-c performance quantities. A simplified feedback theory will be used to illustrate these effects in a general way. Following this, the usual circuit analysis techniques will be used to evaluate the effect of feedback on the performance quantities. The conventional transistor feedback circuits will be portrayed, and simplified equations presented to facilitate the quick determination of a given feedback upon the amplifier performance.

In the presentation of the fundamentals concerning feedback, single-stage feedback circuits are our major concern. It is assumed that the transistor is operating in the mid-frequency range, i.e., the transistor parameters are all assumed to be resistive and the h_{21} is regarded as constant. Finally, the feedback theory described here is limited to small-signal analysis where the equivalent circuit representation is valid.

EFFECTS OF USING FEEDBACK

In order to show the over-all effect of feedback on the gain and various other performance quantities, a simplified and elementary treatment of feedback is useful.

To illustrate this simplified theory, consider a general current amplifier as depicted in Figure 12-1(a). We will label the current

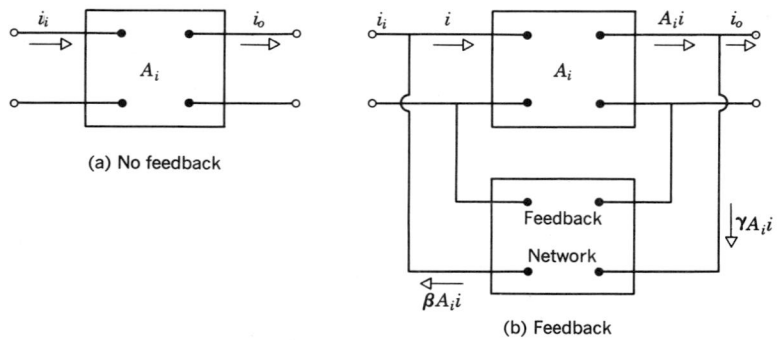

Fig. 12-1. Block diagram illustrating effect of feedback on amplifier gain.

amplification A_i. This value would be determined, for any particular amplifier, by the amplifier parameters and the load conditions as

Feedback

described in Chapter 8. For any value of input current i_i, then, the output current will appear as

$$i_o = A_i i \tag{1}$$

If feedback is applied to this general amplifier, the resulting circuit can be represented as in Figure 12-1(b). The input and output currents are still i_i and i_o, respectively; however, the currents associated with the active amplifier are now i and $A_i i$. The symbol γ is used *to represent the fraction of $A_i i$ that flows to the feedback network* (it may be only a single element). Hence the current flowing to the network is $\gamma A_i i$. That portion of $A_i i$ that flows out of the feedback network to the amplifier input is labeled $\beta A_i i$. Thus β *is the fraction of $A_i i$ that is sent back to the input*.[1] The relation between β and γ is determined by the feedback network in conjunction with the input to the amplifier. With these defining quantities, then, the various currents appear as shown in the block diagram of Figure 12-1(b).

We now wish to find the current gain for the feedback case. Referring to the figure, the following equations may be intuitively verified:

$$\begin{aligned} i_o &= A_i i - \gamma A_i i = i A_i (1 - \gamma) \\ i_i &= i - \beta A_i i = i(1 - \beta A_i) \end{aligned} \tag{2}$$

The ratio of i_o to i_i then is

$$A_{if} = \frac{i_o}{i_i} = \frac{A_i(1 - \gamma)}{1 - \beta A_i} \tag{3}$$

where A_{if} = current gain with feedback applied.

For many cases the feedback network consists of a single series element, usually a resistor. For these cases the γ equals β, and Equation (3) appears

$$A_{if} = \frac{i_o}{i_i} = \frac{A_i(1 - \beta)}{1 - \beta A_i} \tag{4}$$

Comparing this with Equation (1), it is noted that the current gain has been changed by a factor of $(1 - \beta)/(1 - \beta A_i)$. The feedback gain can be written as the product of the nonfeedback gain and the above factor:

$$A_{if} = A_i \frac{1 - \beta}{1 - \beta A_i} \approx A_i \frac{1}{1 - \beta A_i} \tag{5}$$

[1] The β here is the traditional feedback term and should not be confused with the transistor common emitter current gain. Since h_{fe} or h_{FE} is now predominantly used for the latter, it was judged permissible to retain β also for the feedback ratio here. The two usages are sufficiently different that confusion is unlikely.

For most feedback circuits the β is small compared with unity so that a further simplification may be made by neglecting the β term in the numerator. The expression we are interested in, then, is given by the right side of Equation (5).

Under the conditions assumed in this development, Equation (5) states that when feedback is added to a single-stage amplifier, the current gain is altered by the factor of $1/(1 - \beta A_i)$. If the quantity βA_i is real and negative, the gain will be reduced and this is called *negative* or *inverse* feedback. If the sign of βA_i is real and positive, the situation is termed *positive* feedback. The sign of this quantity, of course, depends upon the sign of both β and A_i. Actually βA_i is a phasor and can take on any angle from 0 to 360°. For simplicity we have referred to two possibilities only.

The sign of A_i in turn depends upon the basic amplifier circuit; we noted in Chapter 8 that A_i is positive for common-base and common-collector connections, and negative for common-emitter connections. The feedback network is often made up of only resistors; then its sign will be positive since this means that the current flows through the feedback network without changing its direction. With a resistive feedback, then, the $A_i\beta$ term will be negative for common-emitter connections and positive for both common-collector and common-base connections. This, in turn, means that *the common emitter will have negative feedback and the other two connections will experience positive feedback*. A simple method of reversing the feedback sign consists of using a transformer. This is usually undesirable, however, in terms of cost and space consumption.

For most purposes negative feedback is desired. We shall see below that, although the gain is reduced with negative feedback, the circuit stability, frequency response, and distortion are all improved. Positive feedback, where the gain is increased, is used where the absolute maximum gain is required at the sacrifice of the other quantities. The regenerative radio receiver, where a sufficient sensitivity is achieved with only a minimum of circuitry, is an example of positive feedback.

It is interesting to note here that if the sign of $A_i\beta$ is positive and exactly equal to 1, the denominator of Equation (5) goes to zero. This would imply that the current gain is now infinite. The circuit under these conditions will not operate as an amplifier because $A_i\beta$ equal to 1 defines one of the conditions necessary for an oscillator. *Thus any oscillator can be regarded as a feedback amplifier whose value of*

Feedback

$A_i\beta$ equals 1. We will see later in the chapter that with any feedback amplifier one must always assure that the conditions necessary for oscillation cannot occur at any frequency.

Since negative feedback is the one usually utilized, we shall consider this type in the present chapter. We wish to see, then, how negative feedback affects the gain, the frequency response, the distortion, and the input and output impedances of a single-stage amplifier. Equation (5) is used to exhibit the general effect of feedback, while the usual circuit analysis methods are used to find the effect of specific feedback connections.

GAIN. It has been seen above that the current gain of the amplifier is reduced by the factor $1/(1 - A_i\beta)$ when negative feedback is applied. Since the power gain is proportional to the square of the current gain, this quantity will be reduced by the square of the $1/(1 - A_i\beta)$ term.

GAIN STABILITY. The stability of the d-c operating point was considered in the previous chapter. It was mentioned there that although of less consequence than the operating point change, the a-c parameters do tend to change with temperature. In addition, these a-c parameters vary from transistor to transistor and with aging. Therefore if an amplifier is to be completely stable it may be necessary to consider stabilizing the effect of the a-c parameter variation. We will see here that negative feedback acts to stabilize the effect of variations in the a-c performance quantities.

Referring to Equation (5), it is easily seen that if the quantity $A_i\beta$ is large with respect to 1, then the equation will reduce to

$$A_i \approx \frac{A_i}{\beta A_i} = \frac{1}{\beta} \tag{6}$$

It is noted that the gain now depends only upon the β feedback term. If sufficient gain remains, this is a very desirable condition for electronic amplifiers since the β is determined almost entirely by the feedback network. It, in turn, is usually very stable with temperature and aging changes since it is usually composed of resistors, capacitors, and inductors.

Although it may not always be desirable to apply feedback to the extent depicted in Equation (6), any negative feedback has the general effect of tending to stabilize variations in the active amplifier circuit. Positive feedback, on the other hand, tends to accentuate any circuit changes.

FREQUENCY RESPONSE. It is remembered that the frequency bandpass of an amplifier is defined by the two points where the response is down 3 db from its mid-band value. In the usual notation used, f_L is the low-frequency and f_H is the high-frequency 3-db down point.

If Equation (5) is taken to be the relation between the feedback and no-feedback current gain, and if in addition the β network has no frequency-dependent quantities (capacitors or inductors), then the 3-db points of the amplifier will be changed to

$$f_{Hf} = (1 - A_i\beta)f_H; \qquad f_{Lf} = \frac{f_L}{(1 - A_i\beta)} \qquad (7)$$

where f_{Hf} = upper 3-db down point with feedback,
f_{Lf} = lower 3-db down point with feedback.

It is seen that the upper limit is increased by the factor $(1 - A_i\beta)$ and the lower limit is decreased by the same factor. The negative feedback therefore improves the frequency response of the basic amplifier by affecting both 3-db down points. The combination of decreased gain and increased frequency response is illustrated by the gain versus frequency curves in Figure 12-2. One curve applies to

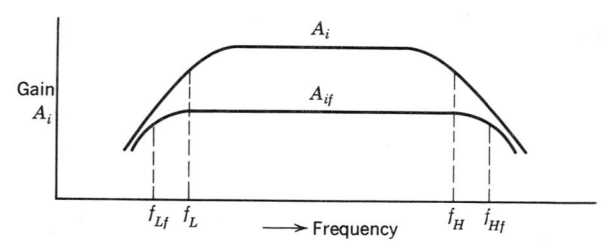

Fig. 12-2. Sketch illustrating the effect of negative feedback on gain versus frequency characteristic.

the basic amplifier and the other depicts the use of the negative feedback.

Feedback

INPUT AND OUTPUT IMPEDANCES. The application of feedback affects both the input and the output impedances of the resulting amplifier. Whether the impedances are increased or decreased depends upon the manner in which the negative feedback is achieved. We will show how the impedances are affected when considering the analysis of transistor feedback circuits later in this chapter.

NONLINEAR DISTORTION. Feedback improves an amplifier from the standpoint of distortion. Distortion can be considered a change in the signal produced by the amplifier. The change in the signal is applied back at the input of the amplifier by the feedback network and if the feedback is negative, at the opposite sign. Thus the distortion is effectively reduced. If the distortion is equivalent to an input current of i_d before feedback is used, the distortion output is

$$i_{od} = \text{distortion output current} = i_d A_i \tag{8}$$

After feedback is applied the output from Equation (5) is

$$i_{odf} = \text{distortion output current with feedback}$$
$$= \frac{A_i i_d}{1 - A_i \beta} \tag{9}$$

The ratio of i_{odf} to i_{od} is

$$\frac{i_{odf}}{i_{od}} = \frac{A_i i_d / (1 - A\beta)}{A_i i_d} = \frac{1}{1 - A_i \beta} \tag{10}$$

From Equation (10) it is seen that the distortion may be reduced considerably with negative feedback.

We will now see how the above general effects of a-c feedback are implemented by specific circuit connections.

METHODS OF TREATING FEEDBACK IN TRANSISTORS

In the foregoing section the effects of feedback were illustrated by using an approach that resulted in

$$A_{if} = A_i \frac{1}{1 - \beta A_i} \tag{11}$$

where A_{if} = current gain with feedback,
A_i = current gain without feedback,
β = fraction of current sent back to input.

For those schooled in vacuum tubes the above will be a familiar representation of the feedback case; there, however, the voltage gain is used instead of the current gain of Equation (11). For transistors a word of caution with regard to analyzing Equation (11) is in order.

Equation (11) is especially convenient to analyze the effects of feedback if A_i and β can be determined separately and independently. In transistors, however, the input side of a transistor may be affected by the loading conditions on the output. Therefore it is often true that the A_i varies with changes in β. Furthermore, the feedback elements are usually not clearly separable from the remaining circuitry. For this reason the usual circuit methods will be used here to evaluate the effect of feedback.

A TRANSISTOR CONNECTION USING CURRENT FEEDBACK

In this section we will apply the principles discussed in the foregoing section to a frequently used feedback connection. Figure 12-3 shows a common-emitter connection to which a resistor R_E has been added. It can easily be shown that this resistor affords *current feedback;* that is, the signal fed back to the input is proportional to the *current* flowing in the output side. This type of feedback is often termed *series* feedback.

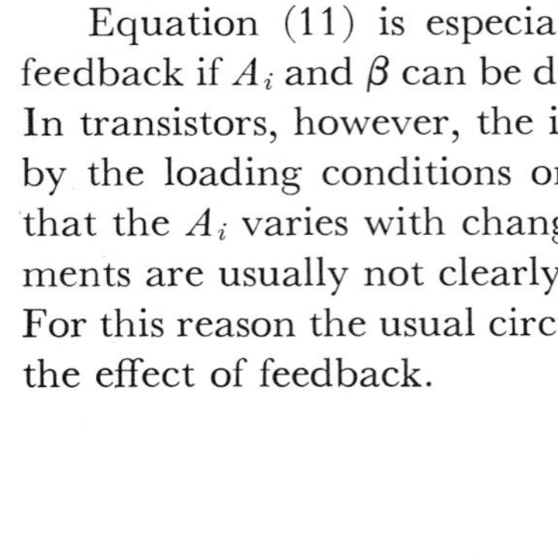

It is remembered from the previous chapter that this circuit was used to stabilize the d-c operating point; there, however, a bypass capacitor was used to produce only a d-c feedback. The only change, then, is that the bypass capacitor is removed so that a-c feedback is now achieved.

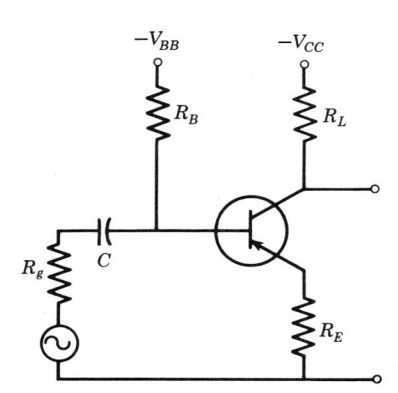

Fig. 12-3. Transistor circuit using current or series feedback.

From the material in the beginning of this chapter it can be seen that the current feedback of this circuit is of the negative type. When a positive signal is applied, for example, the amplified current appears

Feedback

in the output side in the direction shown. This current causes a positive voltage to appear across the R_E, which is in a direction to oppose the input signal. The greater the input signal, the greater the feedback voltage, etc. In this manner, then, the circuit provides negative current feedback.

It may be noted here that if such a series resistor were used in the common-base or the common-collector connection, the resulting feedback would be positive. This is because these connections do not exhibit a 180° phase shift as does the common-emitter connection.

We will now evaluate the performance quantities for this series-feedback stage. We will first do this by using the simple transistor equivalent circuit of Figure 8-6, and writing mesh equations. Later we will indicate that an alternative technique is to calculate new h parameters (including the feedback) and use these in the usual performance equations of Chapter 8.

Using the equivalent circuit of Figure 12-4(a),[1] we add the feed-

(a) Transistor equivalent circuit

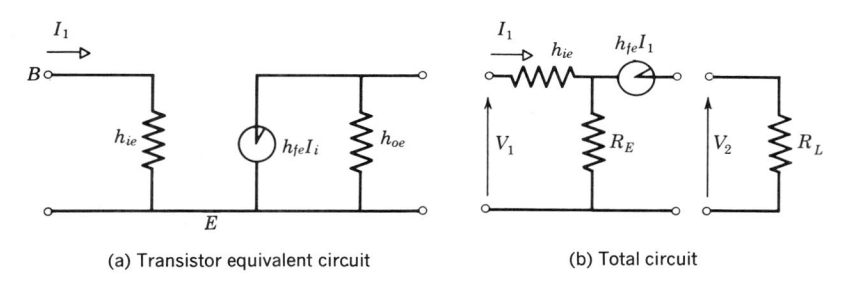

(b) Total circuit

Fig. 12-4. Common-emitter circuit with series or current feedback.

back resistor R_E and the load resistor to permit calculation of R_{in} and A_v. Note that the equivalent circuit of Figure 12-4(a) assumes that h_{re} is negligible. Also, for the calculations in which the R_L is connected, we will neglect the h_{oe} term. (h_{oe} will be used below when calculating output impedance.)

The equations for Figure 12-4(b) are

$$V_1 = I_1(h_{ie} + R_E) + h_{fe}I_1 R_E$$
$$V_2 = I_1 h_{fe} R_L \qquad (12)$$

[1] The reader is reminded that, whereas the previous chapter dealt with d-c equivalent circuits, we are here returning to the a-c circuit. Note that the lower case subscripts denote a-c quantities.

From this it is easily seen that the input impedance R_i equals

$$R_{in} = \frac{V_1}{I_1} = h_{ie} + R_E(1 + h_{fe}) \tag{13}$$

The current gain in Figure 12-4(b) is simply h_{fe}; the voltage gain is given by

$$A_v = \frac{V_2}{V_1} = \frac{h_{fe}R_L}{h_{ie} + R_E(1 + h_{fe})}$$
$$A_v \approx \frac{R_L}{R_E} \quad \text{if } h_{fe} \gg 1, \text{ and } h_{fe} \gg \frac{h_{ie}}{R_E} \tag{14}$$

To calculate the output impedance R_o we need to use the circuit shown in Figure 12-5.

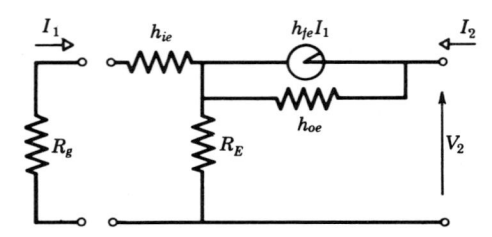

Fig. 12-5. Common-emitter series-feedback circuit for calculating R_o.

The two mesh equations for this circuit are

$$0 = (R_g I_1 + h_{ie} + R_E) + R_E I_2$$
$$V_2 = (R_E - h_{fe}/h_{oe})I_1 + (R_E + 1/h_{oe})I_2 \tag{15}$$

Solving for R_o, the result is

$$R_o = \frac{E_2}{I_2} = R_E + \frac{1}{h_{oe}}\left[1 + \frac{R_E(h_{fe} - R_E h_{oe})}{R_g + h_{ie} + R_E}\right] \tag{16}$$

Since $R_E h_{oe} \ll h_{fe}$:

$$\approx R_E + \frac{1}{h_{oe}}\left[1 + \frac{h_{fe}R_E}{R_g + h_{ie} + R_E}\right] \tag{17}$$

It is almost always true that $R_E \ll 1/h_{oe}$; also, if the preceding stage is a common-emitter one, the R_g will be much greater than either h_{ie} or R_E. Then

Feedback

$$R_o \cong \frac{1}{h_{oe}}\left[1 + h_{fe}\frac{R_E}{R_g}\right] \quad \text{if} \begin{cases} R_E \ll 1/h_{oe} \\ R_g \gg h_{ie},\ R_E \end{cases} \tag{18}$$

It is seen that the output resistance is increased by the factor $[1 + h_{fe}R_E/R_g]$. It can be shown that the upper frequency limit is also increased by this same factor. These, then, are the effects of the series (current) feedback on the performance quantities.

We used ordinary network equations to evaluate these effects. However, these equations quickly become tedious if one is not able to make approximations such as shown above. An alternative method of analysis is to calculate new h parameters for the transistor-plus-R_E.

With this alternative method we will use the complete equivalent circuit of the transistor, as in Chapter 8, and add the feedback element to this circuit. Then, proceeding as before, we can write the mesh equations to find the new h^{e^*} parameters in terms of the transistor h^e parameters and the feedback element. Since the principle of finding the proper equations was fully covered in Chapter 8, it will not be repeated here.

The results can be shown to be

$$\begin{aligned} h_{ie}^* &= \frac{h_{ie} + R_E(1 + h_{fe} + \Delta^{h^e} - h_{re})}{1 + R_E h_{oe}} \\ h_{re}^* &= \frac{h_{re} + R_E h_{oe}}{1 + R_E h_{oe}} \\ h_{fe}^* &= \frac{h_{fe} - R_E h_{oe}}{1 + R_E h_{oe}} \\ h_{oe}^* &= \frac{h_{oe}}{1 + R_E h_{oe}} \end{aligned} \tag{19}$$

Note that the feedback parameters are expressed in terms of the transistor common-emitter parameters. Thus the analysis steps for this more detailed method can be summarized:

1. Find the transistor common-emitter parameters by use of the manufacturer's data.

2. Use the above equations to determine the feedback parameters for the R_E used.

3. Use these resultant parameters, then, in the same manner as described in Chapter 8. In other words, any cascaded circuit can be analyzed on a stage-by-stage basis using the feedback parameters for each stage that incorporates a feedback element. If any stage has

no feedback, of course, the proper h parameters are used directly. Thus one can proceed by calculating the new h parameters and then substituting them into the performance equations of Chapter 8.

Either of the above methods, then, can be used to evaluate the effect of current feedback on a single stage.

A TRANSISTOR CONNECTION USING VOLTAGE FEEDBACK

Another common-emitter feedback circuit that is frequently used is shown in Figure 12-6. Here a resistor R_F is connected from the collector to the base input. In this way, by feeding part of the output signal back through the resistor to the input, a *voltage* feedback is achieved. Voltage feedback occurs when the signal fed back to the input is proportional to a voltage on the output side. This type of feedback is also termed "shunt feedback."

Assume for a moment that positive input signal is applied; due to the current amplification an amplified current appears in the output. This increase in output current causes a greater voltage drop across the load resistor and hence the collector voltage decreases. Thus the voltage fed back to the input opposes the positive input signal and consequently negative feedback is provided.

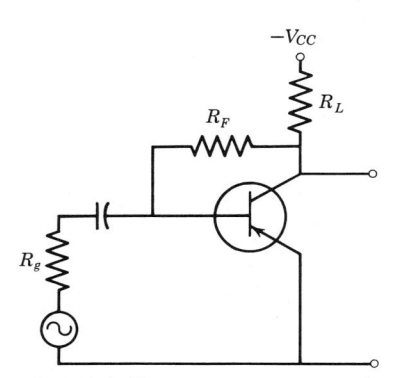

Fig. 12-6. Transistor circuit using voltage or shunt feedback.

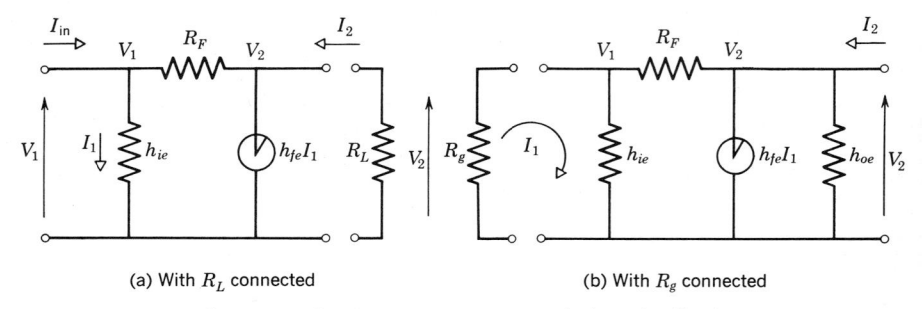

(a) With R_L connected

(b) With R_g connected

Fig. 12-7. Common-emitter circuit with shunt feedback.

Feedback

Again we will use the simplified transistor equivalent circuit and note the effect of the feedback resistor on the performance quantities directly. In general, with this feedback, we will find that the current gain is reduced and that both the input and the output resistance are reduced.

To find the current gain and input resistance we will use the circuit shown in Figure 12-7(a). If we use two nodal equations and write in terms of V_1 and V_2, it can be shown that the following two equations apply to this circuit.

$$I_{in} = I_1\left(1 + \frac{h_{ie}}{R_F}\right) + I_2 R_L/R_F \quad (20)$$
$$0 = I_1(h_{fe} - h_{ie}/R_F) - I_2(1 + R_L/R_F)$$

Solving these equations for A_i

$$A_i = \frac{I_2}{I_{in}} = \frac{R_F h_{fe} - h_{ie}}{(R_F + h_{ie})(1 + R_L/R_F) + R_L h_{fe} - R_L(h_{ie}/R_F)} \quad (21)$$

$$A_i \approx \frac{h_{fe}}{1 + h_{fe} R_L/R_F} \quad \text{since } h_{ie} \ll R_F$$

Consequently it is seen that the current gain is reduced by the factor $[1 + h_{fe} R_L/R_F]$. If $h_{fe} \times R_L/R_F$ is much greater than 1, then the A_i is given by

$$A_i \approx \frac{R_F}{R_L} \quad (22)$$

Solving for R_i it is found that

$$R_{in} = \frac{V_1}{I_{in}} = \frac{h_{ie} R_F (R_F + R_L)}{(h_{ie} + R_F)(R_F + R_L) + (h_{fe} R_F - h_{ie}) R_L} \quad (23)$$

$$R_{in} \approx h_{ie} \times \frac{1}{1 + h_{fe}(R_L/R_F + R_L)} \quad \text{since } h_{ie} \ll R_F$$

The above simplification is based on transistor parameters. It may be further noted that a reasonable A_i requires that R_F be much larger than R_L; then R_i further simplifies to

$$\boxed{R_{in} \approx h_{ie} \times \frac{1}{1 + h_{fe} R_L/R_F}} \quad (24)$$

For the output impedance calculation the equivalent circuit appears as in Figure 12-7(b). If we write nodal equations for the two voltages V_1 and V_2 in terms of I_1 and I_2 the result is

$$\frac{V_2}{R_F} = 0I_2 + \left[\frac{h_{ie}}{R_g} + 1 + \frac{h_{ie}}{R_F}\right]I_1$$
$$V_2\left[h_{oe} + \frac{1}{R_F}\right] = I_2 + \left[\frac{h_{ie}}{R_F} - h_{fe}\right]I_1 \qquad (25)$$

This can be solved for R_o by using the following measures:

$$h_{ie}/R_g < h_{fe}; \quad h_{oe} \ll 1/R_F; \quad h_{ie}/R_g \ll 1$$

The R_o will then be given by

$$\boxed{R_o \cong \frac{R_F}{h_{fe} + 1} \approx \frac{R_F}{h_{fe}}} \qquad (26)$$

This value of R_o, of course, will be less than the normal output resistance, $1/h_{oe}$.

The voltage gain with the shunt feedback can be shown to be relatively constant because R_L is typically much lower than R_F. Consequently the voltage gain remains as before—about $h_{fe}R_L/h_{ie}$.

Again one can do a more complete analysis by devising new (total) h parameters ($h^{e'}$) for the transistor-plus-R_F. These new parameters can then be used in the performance equation of Chapter 8.

The $h^{e'}$ parameters of this transistor circuit-plus-feedback can be found by adding the feedback resistor to the equivalent circuit of the transistor and then writing the mesh (or nodal) equations to determine the parameters. It is convenient to express these resultant $h^{e'}$ parameters in terms of the usual h^e parameters for the transistor part of the circuit and the resistor R_F. The parameters can be shown to be

$$h'_{ie} = \frac{h_{ie}R_F}{R_F + h_{ie}}$$
$$h'_{re} = \frac{R_F h_{re} + h_{ie}}{R_F + h_{ie}}$$
$$h'_{fe} = \frac{R_F h_{fe} - h_{ie}}{R_F + h_{ie}} \qquad (27)$$
$$h'_{oe} = \frac{R_F h_{oe} + (1 + h_{fe} + \Delta^{h^e} - h_{re})}{R_F + h_{ie}}$$

One can use these modified h parameters in the performance quantities equations of Chapter 8, as suggested previously. It should be noted that these equations can be used for both common-base and common-collector connections. However, remember that in these cases the resulting feedback is positive unless some means is taken to shift the phase of the feedback signal.

The effect of shunt feedback can be evaluated by the above method.

MULTISTAGE FEEDBACK

In the previous sections we have discussed the use of feedback on a single transistor stage. The object was to examine the effects of feedback in its most basic form, so as to easily grasp its effect. Also note that d-c feedback for bias stability is usually a single-stage proposition.

Very often transistor circuitry employs feedback around more than one stage. It can be shown that feedback around more than one stage is more effective than feedback around a single stage. In other words, for a given "stabilizing effect," feedback around multiple stages will provide this stability with less sacrifice in gain than if it were done around each individual stage. Many times feedback is employed simultaneously around single stages and around a multistage.

Since one usually desires negative feedback, and since the common-emitter amplifier has an 180° phase shift, it is true that the multiple stages for the common-emitter amplifiers (with conventienal feedback) are limited to odd number of stages. Two frequently used three-stage amplifier configurations are indicated in Figures 12-8 and 12-9.

In analyzing the effects of feedback, the loop or $A\beta$ concept is more appropriate for the multistage case than for the single-stage case for two reasons: (1) the increased complexity of the multistage case makes the $A\beta$ concept a more potent and necessary simplification, and (2) the loading assumptions and role of forward transmission is better met in the multistage case. The general results for the multistage feedback case are analogous to those of the single-stage case. For example, with the shunt feedback of Figure 12-8, the current gain and input and output resistance are reduced whereas the voltage

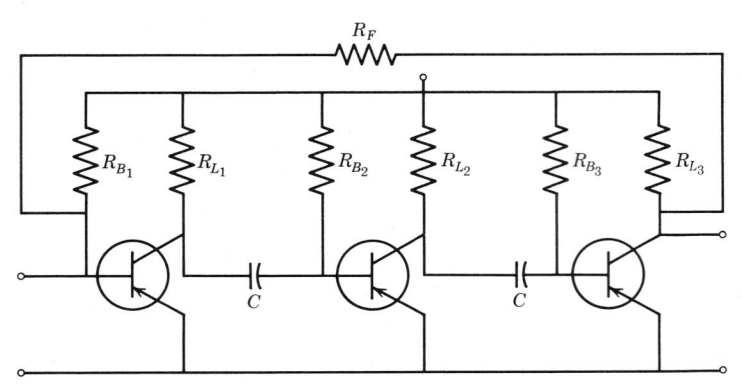

Fig. 12-8. Multistage using shunt feedback.

gain is relatively unaffected. Since it can be shown that all the assumptions used in the single-stage derivation are easily met here it can be seen that the new current gain is given by

$$A_i^* = \frac{A_i}{1 - A_i R_L/R_F} \qquad (28)$$

where A_i = current gain of multistage circuit without feedback
A_i^* = current gain with feedback.

Although the $A\beta$ product is actually a phasor, its real part will be negative for an odd number of stages.

In a manner analogous to the single-stage case, the R_i can be shown to be

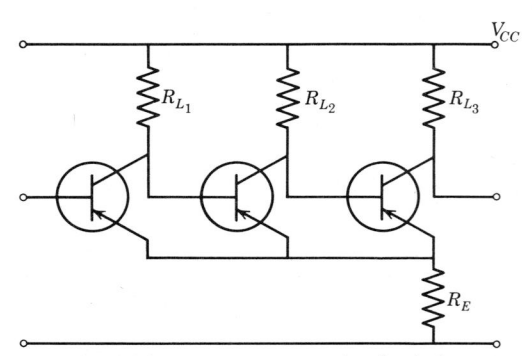

Fig. 12-9. Multistage using series feedback (bias circuit not shown).

Feedback

$$R_i^* = \frac{R_i}{1 - A_i R_L/R_F} \tag{29}$$

For the series feedback circuit Figure 12-9, it can be shown by analogy with the single-stage circuit, that the voltage gain is given by

$$A_v^* = \frac{A_v}{1 - A_v R_E/R_L} \tag{30}$$

Furthermore, the input impedance is changed by

$$\begin{aligned} R_i^* &= R_i(1 - A_v R_E/R_L) \\ &= R_i + R_E(1 + A_i) \end{aligned} \tag{31}$$

It is remembered that for the series case the current gain is not appreciably changed.

In the above procedure we have used the concept of lumping the total gain of the multistage amplifier and treating it as a single-stage amplification. Then we can employ the previous single-stage calculation in noting the changes. It should be realized that one can rigorously pursue the analysis of such a circuit by using matrix-combining methods for the individual stages, and then in addition follow a matrix method for accounting for the feedback. Although this would be more precise, for most purposes the techniques shown here will suffice.

We will now briefly consider the stability of feedback amplifiers. Although stability is usually not a problem for a single-stage feedback amplifier, it is very important for multistage amplifiers, where the gains become high. The entire issue is that a feedback amplifier which is stable at mid-band frequencies may oscillate at much higher frequencies. Such an amplifier will be unstable since many sporadic disturbances could instigate the oscillation at the higher frequencies. Referring to Equation (11) one can talk about the stability in terms of the criterion based on the forward amplification A and the feedback quantity β.

As we saw above, any feedback amplifier typically is designed so that the $A\beta$ product at mid-band frequencies is negative and real. In Chapter 6 it was seen that any inductors and capacitors in the circuit cause the $A\beta$ product to be a phasor whose amplitude and angle change with frequency. It is remembered also that a transistor exhibits capacitance as frequency increases. This subject will be treated further in a later section on high frequency.

To begin, then, one usually thinks of a feedback amplifier design in terms of the center frequency situation. Assume that the parameters here are resistive—both the transistor parameters and the feedback circuit parameters. In this case the problem of stability mainly concerns the presence of any frequencies at which the phasor product $A\beta$ could cause possible oscillation. The criterion for preventing oscillation (at any conceivable frequency) can be stated in terms of the $A\beta$ product. The following are the two criteria for preventing oscillation at any conceivable frequency:

1. When the loop gain ($A\beta$) is greater than 1, the total loop phase shift must be less than 360°.
2. When the loop phase shift is 360°, the loop gain must be less than 1.

In design descriptions the terms "phase margin" and "gain margin" are often used. The phase margin is that amount by which the phase shift is less than 360° at the unity gain frequency. The gain margin is that amount of gain less than 1 at that frequency where the phase shift is 360°.

It must always be remembered then, especially when building multistage feedback amplifiers, that assuring absolute stability of the amplifier is a very important part of design. Very often a "shaping" of the frequency response for the transfer function between stages is required in order to provide absolute stability of the feedback amplifier.

PROBLEMS

1. Assume that one uses the 2N3638 transistor in the circuit shown in Figure 12-10. First find the operating point. Draw both the d-c and the a-c load line. Using the h parameters corrected for bias point, find the R_{in}, the A_i, the A_v, the A_p, and the R_o for this stage. For each performance quantity, use both the accurate equations and the approximations. Compare the results in each case.

2. Using the corrected h parameters for the amplifier (and its operating point) of Problem 1, calculate the five performance quantities if the 100 ohm emitter resistor is set to zero. Compare each of these results with those of Problem 1.

Feedback

3. For current feedback of Fig. 12-3, plot the R_{in} and R_o versus R_E, using the uncorrected h parameters for the 2N3392 (at $V_{CE} = 10$ v, $I_C = 1$ ma).

4. Using the amplifier of Problem 1, calculate the new h^{e*} parameters. Calculate the performance quantities using these parameters, and compare the results with those of Problem 1.

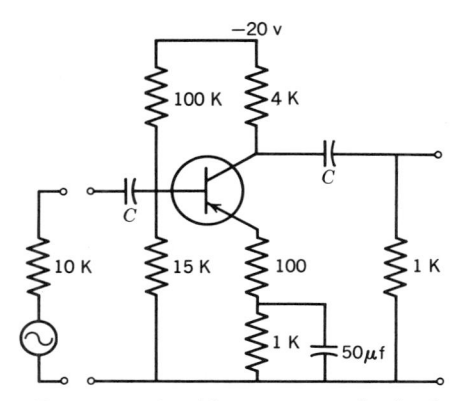

Fig. 12-10. Amplifier using series feedback.

5. Use the 2N1097 in the amplifier of Figure 12-10. Draw the new d-c and a-c load line. Knowing the effect of increases in R_E, calculate, for increasingly lower frequencies, the increase in total R_E of this circuit. Then draw the power gain as a function of frequency at this low end.

6. Derive a decibel equation so that the decrease in gain, at low frequencies, due to increase in (bypass) capacitor reactance can be added to that due to coupling capacitance, as was derived in Chapter 10.

7. For the amplifier in Figure 12-11, assume a 2N1302 transistor is used. First find the operating point, and draw the a-c and d-c load line. Using the parameters corrected for operating point, find the R_{in}, R_o, A_i, A_v, and A_p for this stage. For each performance quantity, compare the accuracy of the approximations suggested in the text.

8. Using the amplifier of Problem 7, calculate the new h'_{ie} parameters. Calculate the five performance quantities (R_{in}, R_o, A_i, A_v, and A_p) for the parameters. Compare the results to those of Problem 7.

9. Assume that Figure 12-11 is modified in the way shown in Figure 12-12. Draw the a-c equivalent circuit, and calculate the performance quantities for this amplifier, using the same characteristics as in Problem 7. Compare the results to those of Problem 7.

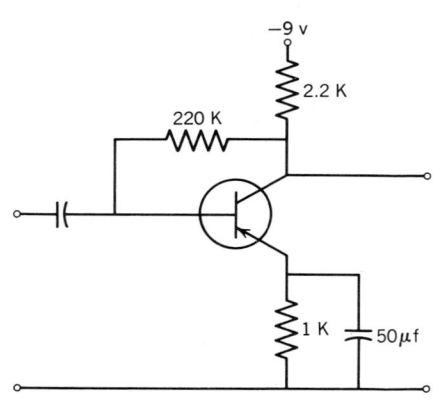

Fig. 12-11. Amplifier using shunt or voltage feedback.

10. For an amplifier, such as given in Figure 12-12, derive the current gain and power gain as a function of frequency at the low end. Use the a-c equivalent circuit, with capacitors attached, showing the low frequency response.

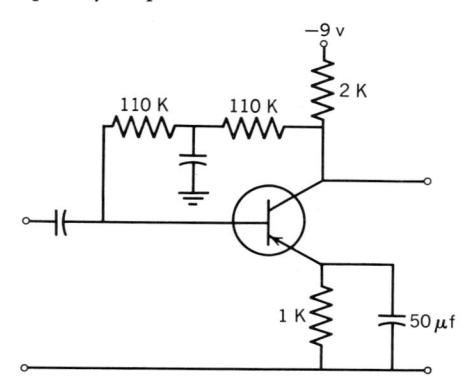

Fig. 12-12. Amplifier with modified feedback.

11. Derive the set h^{e*} parameters for series feedback in terms of the h^e parameters (given in Equation 19). Use the basic definition of each of the h parameters (see Chapter 6, 7, or 8) and the a-c equivalent circuit with the usual equations.

Feedback

12. Derive the set of h'^e parameters for shunt feedback, given in Equation (27).

13. Using reasonable assumptions, derive both Equations (28) and (29) for the multistage shunt feedback case. Under what conditions are these equations accurate?

14. Using reasonable assumptions, derive Equation (31), for the multistage series feedback.

15. Tabulate, in a table, the effect of both shunt and series feedback on all the performance quantities. Use the categories (1) increase, (2) decrease, (3) no change.

13
Noise

Whenever an amplifying device is dealing with extremely small signals it is necessary to consider the *noise* aspects of the devices. The noise of the amplifying device, in conjunction with the inherent noisiness of the signal source, determines the smallest signal that can usefully be handled by the device.

We are all familiar with the situation where a distant radio or television station provides such a small signal that the sound or picture is buried in noise. For both radio and television the noise comes both from atmospheric disturbances between the transmitter and the receiver and internal noises within the receiver itself. In radio and the audio part of television this manifests itself as static or background noise; the television picture has a "snowy" appearance in the presence of severe noise. Many times the signal versus noise problem becomes very critical in radar sets; here an operator must determine the presence or absence of a target among the various noises—often a delicate choice indeed. Much research has been devoted to improving this situation in the radar area. Since the topic of noise is a rather profound subject, we can do little more than present the fundamental ideas and apply them to transistors in this chapter.

One of the data supplied by the manufacturer of a transistor is a *noise figure*. Hence, it may be considered that the foremost object of this chapter is to note how this noise figure can be used to evaluate the noisiness of any amplifier we build with a transistor. First, however, it is necessary to consider the basic concepts of noise and noise figure.

We will begin by describing noise in very general terms in order to note the fundamental aspects. *Thermal noise* will be introduced as the basic noise phenomenon, and the equivalent circuit of a noise source will be treated. Following this, the sources of noise in a transistor are described and their effects are noted by placing fictitious noise sources in the transistor equivalent circuit.

The concept of noise figure is then introduced and its significance is noted. The chapter is concluded with consideration of the consequence of a given amplifier noise figure.

GENERAL NOISE CONSIDERATIONS

In the broadest possible definition, noise can be defined as *any undesired signal*, and can be divided into two categories: externally induced noise, and internally generated noise. *External noise*, as the name implies, includes those disturbances that appear in the system as a result of an action outside the system. Two examples of external noise are hum pickup from the 60-cycle power lines, and radio static caused by electric storms. *Internal noise*, on the other hand, includes all those noises that are generated within the system itself. It is now well known that every resistor produces a discernible noise voltage and also every electronic device (the vacuum tube and the transistor) has internal sources of noise. This internal noise can be thought of as an ever-present limit to the smallest signal that can be handled by the system.

In this chapter we will consider only the effect and sources of *internal* noise. The external noise considerations are well established and many references to this can be found. Usually these external noises can be eliminated by proper shielding of the equipment.

As mentioned in the introduction, internal noise needs to be considered only when the signals are very small. Although the noise is still present with large signals, the noise is masked by the signal in this case, and need not be considered. Because of this we would expect that noise is important only in the initial stages of a cascaded set of amplifiers. Since the signal is amplified with each succeeding stage, the noise of all except the first few stages will be completely masked. Usually, then, the first stage, and at the most the first and second stages, determine the noise properties of an entire set of amplifiers.

DESCRIPTION OF NOISE. The first thing to note about noise is that it cannot be described in the same manner as the usual electric voltages and currents. It is common for us to think of a current or voltage in terms of its behavior with time. For example, we think of a sine wave as periodically varying with time, a direct current as being constant with time, etc. Now, if we look at the *noise* output of any electric circuit as a function of time it will be found that the result is completely erratic; that is, we cannot predict what the amplitude of the output will be at any specific instant. Also, there would be no indication of regularity in the wave. When completely unpredictable conditions such as this exist, the situation is described as *random*.

The internal noise being considered here is characterized, then, as *random noise*. If we were to look at an oscilloscopic trace of random noise, it would appear as shown in Figure 13-1.

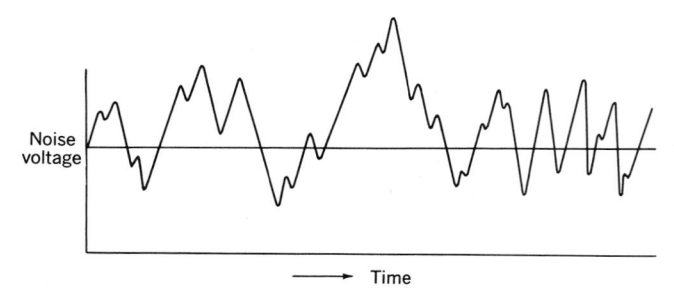

Fig. 13-1. General appearance of a random noise voltage.

Because the noise is random, it is impossible to specify the noise voltage (or current) as a function of time, as we do for the sine wave, for example. In order to gain useful knowledge about the action of a random noise one has to utilize the concepts of probability. We shall not, of course, discuss probability theory here but will consider the important results of such an analysis.

By using highly specialized probability theory it can be shown that there are two things that can be determined about random noise: (1) the *average energy* (or power) produced by the noise; and (2) the average frequency distribution of this energy—commonly called *power spectrum*. The average power can be thought of as the net effect of the many actions in the random phenomenon. In a sense, this average power is analogous to the square of the root-mean-square (rms) value of any a-c wave. When one speaks about the rms value of a sine wave, for example, one refers to the *average* effect without considering the time behavior. Therefore this average effect should not be entirely unfamiliar.

The concept of power spectrum, although strange on first encounter, is very important and very basic to noise considerations. The power spectrum refers to the amount of power in a small band of frequencies, and to the variation in this power density as the small band varies over a whole range of frequencies. A pure sine wave, for example, has a power spectrum that has a value for one frequency (the frequency of the sine wave) and is zero everywhere else. If we have a complex wave that is periodic we can regard it as the sum of a number of sine waves of different frequencies; the power spectrum then would consist of finite values at each of the frequencies of the component waves and would be zero at all other frequencies. The power spectrum of a random noise is an extension of this idea to the case where the wave is purely random. When specifying the power spectrum of a random wave, we are doing the equivalent of specifying the *frequency* of a sine wave or of a group of sine waves.

Of the many possible power spectrums of random waves there are two types that will be of interest to us: a power spectrum that is "flat"—that is, the power density at all frequencies is equal; and a power spectrum that varies (with frequency) as the inverse of the frequency $(1/f)$. We shall find in the next section that the most basic type of noise, thermal noise, has a flat frequency spectrum and this type is called *white noise*. Later we shall see that the most important noise within the transistor has a $1/f$ spectrum.

In conclusion, then, we cannot speak about random quantities in terms of their behavior as a function of time, as we would for a sine wave, but must describe them in terms of the average effect they produce and how this average effect varies over the frequency spectrum.

THERMAL NOISE. The most basic type of noise, and one that can never be evaded, is thermal noise. Thermal noise is present in every electric conductor (whether or not it is connected) and hence is present in every electric circuit. This noise is pictured as being due to the random motion of free electrons (the current carriers) from thermal energy. Because of this thermal agitation the electrons fly about in a random fashion and the resulting current due to these moving charges produces a voltage across the ends of the conductor. Thus, even when no current flows, this thermal noise may be observed. When current does flow, the random motion is still present, but now the noise phenomenon is superimposed on the flowing current.

In 1928 H. Nyquist showed that the average noise power *available* from any conductor is

$$\text{available noise power} = kTB \tag{1}$$

where T = temperature of conductor in degrees Kelvin (273.1 + centigrade),
k = Boltzmann's constant = 1.38×10^{-23} watt-sec/deg,
B = bandwidth of measuring system in cycles per second = $f_H - f_L$.

Note first that this is *available power*. From Chapter 8, Equation (65), it is remembered that available power is obtained if the load is matched to the source. Suppose, then, that a given conductor has a resistance R; Equation (1) says that, if a noiseless resistance of R were connected to the noise resistance, the load R would absorb kTB watts of power. This example is only illustrative since it is impossible to produce a noiseless resistance; we noted above that every conductor has thermal noise.

We can now find what noise voltage appears across the conductor of resistance R. Since available power can always be expressed as $E^2/4R$, we can write

$$\frac{\overline{E_n^2}}{4R} = kTB \quad \therefore \quad \boxed{\overline{E_n^2} = 4RkTB} \tag{2}$$

where $\overline{E_n^2}$ = rms value of noise voltage squared,
R = resistance (or the real part of a complex impedance).

Equation (2) specifies the value of rms noise voltage that appears across any resistor R. This voltage could be read on a high-impedance voltmeter if precaution is taken to find the rms value of the random wave. Note that expressing the rms voltage in terms of its square cor-

Noise

responds to expressing the average power, as discussed in the preceding section. We can always find the square root of Equation (2) and thus have the rms voltage. However, for random waves, it is usually left in the squared form.

There are two important things to observe from Equation (2). First, the noise voltage-squared is proportional to the value of resistance. Secondly, the noise voltage-squared is proportional to bandwidth, *no matter where the $f_H - f_L$ occurs*. This means that *the power spectrum of thermal noise is flat*. For example, the noise power between 0 and 1000 cycles is the same as the power between 1,000,000 and 1,001,000 cycles. Whenever noise has a flat power spectrum it can be regarded as containing components of all frequencies and is usually called *white noise*.

Although thermal noise theoretically possesses power at all frequencies, as seen above, any electric system that we connect to a resistor has a finite bandwidth. If our object is to measure the noise, the measuring instrument itself would have a finite bandwidth and this bandwidth would determine the amount of noise power that the instrument would accept. If we have an amplifying system connected to a resistor, the bandwidth[1] of the system will determine the amount of thermal noise that is accepted. Thus we can think of the thermal noise source (the resistor) as supplying power at all frequencies possible, but when we use the resistor in any electric circuit the bandwidth of the circuit selects only a part of the total possible power—that part that corresponds to the bandwidth of the circuit.

OTHER THERMAL-TYPE NOISES. It was stated in the previous section that thermal noise is the most basic type of noise encountered in electric circuits. It is also true that, in electronic devices, there are a number of noises present that, although not strictly thermal in nature, behave much like a thermal noise. Examples of this type of noise are the shot effect and the induced grid noise of vacuum tubes. Although both of these noises arise from physical sources within the tube, we can treat the noises *as though they were due to a fictitious resistor*. This is the basis for using an equivalent resistance in the grid circuit of a

[1] For noise considerations the bandwidth refers to an ideal, straight-sided bandpass characteristic. For any system having a reasonably flat characteristic between half-power points, however, the half-power points may be taken to define the bandwidth. [Chapter 6, Equation (83).]

vacuum tube to account for the shot and the induced grid noise. Although we are not interested in vacuum tube noises here, the above was included as an example since the concept of using the noise equivalent resistance of a vacuum tube is familiar to most electronics designers.

We shall find that an analogous situation holds for one type of transistor noise. The shot noise or *diffusion recombination* noise of a transistor is a noise that acts essentially like a thermal noise. Its power spectrum is flat and hence it can be called white noise.

EQUIVALENT CIRCUIT OF A NOISE SOURCE. When we wish to take account of the various noise sources in a given circuit, it is useful to have an equivalent circuit of the source itself so that we may treat the noise in a manner similar to the usual voltage source.

In the case of thermal noise it is noted that the noise voltage appearing across a resistor is always given by Equation (2). We may say, then, that the equivalent circuit of any resistor (noisewise) is given by a fictitious noise generator in series with the given resistance.[2] This is depicted in Figure 13-2. To account for all thermal noise sources, then, we would replace every resistor by its equivalent circuit; as noted earlier, however, only those thermal sources in the *first stages* of an electronic amplifying circuit need be considered.

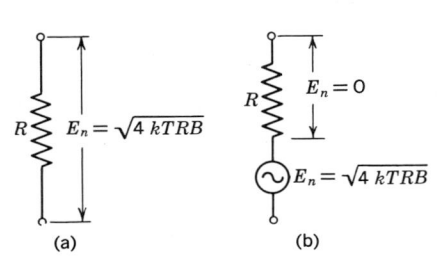

Fig. 13-2. The noise voltage of a resistor and its equivalent circuit: (a) thermal noise across resistor; (b) equivalent circuit of the resistor.

If we have noise sources within the transistor that are not strictly thermal in physical nature, but act as though they were thermal noises, we can again use a fictitious generator to represent this source of noise. To do this, we need to know the value of the fictitious resistance in order to assign the proper voltage to the source, as given by Equation (2). Note that in this case *the equivalent noise source does not contain a series resistor;* the value of the noise voltage is determined

---

[2] Note that Norton's equivalent circuit is also acceptable and is found in the usual way. The result is a current generator $I^2 = \dfrac{4KTB}{R}$ in parallel with a resistance R.

by the value of a fictitious resistance, but this resistance does not appear in series with the voltage source.

If we encounter a noise source that is not like a thermal source (it does not have a flat power spectrum) we may still represent it by an equivalent voltage source. It must always be kept in mind, however, that the power spectrum is not flat. Again, no equivalent resistance will appear in series with the fictitious source.

TRANSISTOR NOISE SOURCES

The important noise sources of a semiconductor device, such as the transistor, fall into two categories: the *shot noise* or *diffusion recombination noise* makes up one type, and the *surface noise* and *leakage noise* make up the other. The physical phenomenon that acts to create these noises is not well understood and we shall not attempt to describe it here. The important properties of the noises, however, have been measured and it is these that interest us.

The *diffusion recombination noise* (shot noise) is similar to thermal noise in its action. Its power spectrum is flat with frequency and its voltage-square value is given by Equation (2). This means that we can assign a fictitious resistance to this noise, for any particular transistor, and use a voltage source to account for the noise. Again, it must be remembered that the fictitious resistor will not appear in series with the noise source.

The other types of transistor noise, surface noise and leakage noise, both exhibit a phenomenon that is common to all semiconductors. This noise is distinguished by the fact that it exhibits a $1/f$ power spectrum. This means that if the frequency is increased the noise decreases for a given bandwidth. These two noises are commonly grouped together and called *semiconductor* or *1/f noise*.

The two types of noises encountered in transistors then are *white noise* and *semiconductor noise*. Since the semiconductor noise decreases as the frequency goes up, we may expect that at some frequency this noise will become less than the white noise.

Let us consider how these sources of noise can be accounted for in a transistor circuit. The most fundamental circuit to include noise sources would have the noise sources appearing at the appropriate places within the transistor equivalent circuit and identified with the physical phenomenon that produces the noise. The result would be an equivalent circuit such as the h-parameter circuit or the T-equivalent circuit, and would incorporate a number of noise generators. Such a circuit could then be analyzed on the same basis as other electrical circuits.

However, this method is too complex and too detailed for the usual design problem. It is much more practical to lump all the internal noise generators for the transistor. Then the basic idea will be to use an equivalent noise generator at the input of the transistor. Thus this equivalent input, going through a theoretically noiseless transistor, will produce at the output of the transistor the same noise as the actual internal noise sources. This is a much more convenient and effective way to proceed for design purposes. On the other hand, if one is trying to produce low-noise transistors one would be interested in relating the noise sources to the actual physical phenomenon in the transistor.

The noise properties of a basic transistor circuit, then, can be treated as shown in Figure 13-3. Although in theory only one gen-

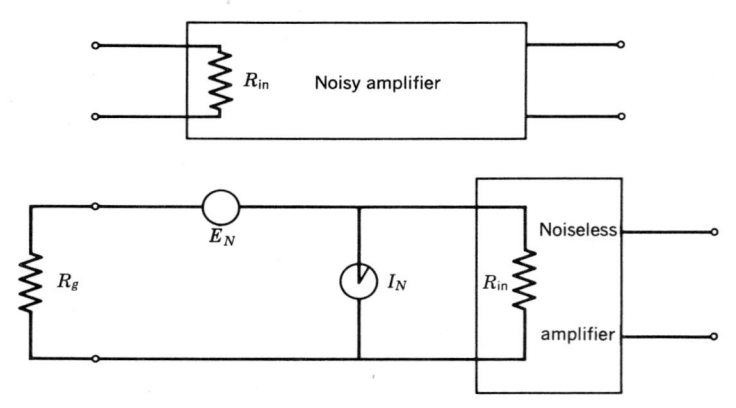

Fig. 13-3. Basic method of treating noise in transistor amplifiers.

erator to represent the noise would be needed, two are necessary in order to be able to measure the total noise contribution. This measurement will be depicted later. All the noise from within the transistor, then, can be treated by using the separate generators shown in Figure 13-3.

Having dealt with the subject of transistor noise sources, we are now ready to consider the practical effect of noise in a given circuit. It is the noise figure that is universally used to evaluate the effect of noise in electronic circuits.

NOISE FIGURE

It is clearly evident that whenever extremely small signals are encountered in any amplifying circuit, the noise quality of the circuit must be considered. In the past, various measures of this noise quality have been used. The most important is that of noise figure.

The aim of defining a quantity such as the noise figure is to provide a basis of comparison between similar electronic circuits (or devices) and also to provide a method whereby the noisiness of the component parts of a circuit may be related to the noisiness of the complete circuit. In transistors, for example, the manufacturer always specifies a noise figure for the transistor; with this value the noise figure of an amplifier in which that transistor is used may be found. From such a resultant noise figure the smallest signal that can be accepted for specified conditions can be calculated.

The noise figure is the decibel value of the noise factor (F). The noise factor is defined as "the ratio of the total noise power appearing in the load to the noise power in the load due to amplified thermal noise from the source resistance R_g." The source resistance may be an antenna resistance, an actual voltage source resistance, or the output impedance of a previous stage.

$$\text{noise factor} = F = \frac{\text{total noise power in load}}{\text{load noise from source resistance}} \quad (3)$$

The *noise figure*, then, is the decibel value of F

$$\text{noise figure} = NF = 10 \log_{10} F \quad (3a)$$

When stating the noise quality of a circuit or a transistor, one usually deals with the noise figure in decibels. For derivations and manipulations (as in this chapter), however, one often deals directly with the F.

It is of great importance to note that the noise figure is independent of the load resistance. In the definition above this comes about because, when taking the ratio of the two noise powers, the R_L cancels out. It is equally important to observe that the noise figure does depend upon the source resistance R_g.

It is useful to discuss the concept of noise figure before proceeding with the calculations. Although we refer to the transistor here, the noise figure concept can be applied to any two-terminal network. First, it is noted that the noise figure gives the measure of *how much noise is added by the transistor*. If the transistor were completely noiseless the numerator of Equation (3) would equal the denominator, i.e., the total noise power appearing in the load would consist of only the amplified source resistance noise power. Thus it is seen that the most desirable value of F is 1, a noise figure of 0 db. For any noise contributed by the transistor the NF will increase correspondingly from 0 db. In general, then, the closer NF is to zero, the better.

This can be looked at in still another way. We know that the *least* amount of noise that can be achieved in a circuit is the thermal noise of the resistances. Therefore if we connect any electronic amplifying device to a source, the ideal minimum amount of noise in the output will be the amplified thermal noise of the source resistance. Achieving only this amount of noise in the output can be regarded as being the *ideal* condition. The noise figure as defined above, then, gives us a measure of how far from the ideal we are. If we have a noise figure of 3 db, for example, ($F = 2$), this means that the transistor is providing a noise power (in the output) equal to the thermal source resistance noise power. The output noise power is twice the *ideal* value. It is useful, then, to rewrite the F in the following manner:

$$F = \frac{\text{thermal noise power} + \text{transistor noise power}}{\text{thermal noise power}}$$

$$= \frac{P'_{RN} + P'_{TN}}{P'_{RN}} = 1 + \frac{P'_{TN}}{P'_{RN}} \qquad (4)$$

where P'_{RN} = thermal noise power in load,
P'_{TN} = transistor noise power in load.

An equivalent definition of F can be stated in terms of signal-to-noise ratio. The F appears as

$$F = \frac{\left(\dfrac{S}{N}\right)_{in}}{\left(\dfrac{S}{N}\right)_{out}} \qquad (5)$$

where $\left(\dfrac{S}{N}\right)_{in}$ = input signal-to-noise ratio

$\left(\dfrac{S}{N}\right)_{out}$ = output signal-to-noise ratio.

Noise

It is not difficult to show the equivalence of Equation (5) to Equation (4). We will use this definition as one means of measuring the F for a transistor circuit.

As a final thought, it should be emphasized that the noise figure is a function of the source resistance. Hence the F may be regarded, basically, as a means of comparing the noise properties of different amplifying devices (or circuits) *used with a given source*.

We can now examine the behavior of the noise figure with respect to frequency. Figure 13-4 shows that the NF is flat in a middle range

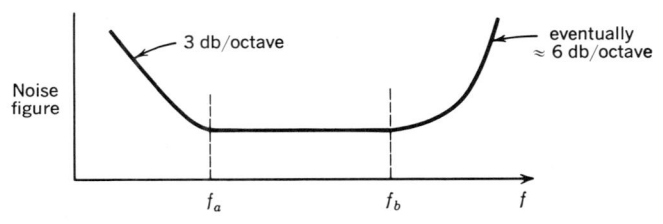

Fig. 13-4. Noise figure as a function of frequency.

(from about 1 Kc to 100 Kc or more) and rises on either side. At the low end the rise is due to the $1/f$ semiconductor noise as discussed before. As frequency decreases, the noise increases at the rate of about 3 db per octave. In the middle region thermal and shot noise are the chief contributors; the $1/f$ noise can be neglected in this region. At the high end the NF rises due to the fact that the transistor gain drops off at the high frequencies. The predominant noise source is still thermal and shot noise. The slope eventually reaches 6 db per octave at this high end.

There are two basic ways in which the noise figure can be used by the circuit designer: (1) in the *spot noise figure* sense, or (2) in the *integrated noise figure* sense. The spot noise figure refers to measuring the noise figure at a given (single) frequency. The integrated noise figure refers to a noise measurement that is taken over a given bandwidth of frequencies.

The integrated noise figure must usually be done for a given amplifier, since each amplifier will have its own particular bandpass characteristic. The spot noise figure can serve as a reference value which possibly can be used to estimate the total NF of a given amplifier.

The manufacturer usually specifies a spot noise figure at 1000 cps. Sometimes an integrated NF, over a stated flat bandpass, is also given. In practice one has the option of two methods with regard to noise figure. One can directly measure the total (integrated) noise figure for the particular amplifier (bandpass) being considered, or one can use the manufacturer's measured values to estimate the noise figure. Each of these techniques will be discussed in the following two sections.

METHODS OF MEASURING NOISE FIGURE

We will briefly describe two methods of measuring the noise figure directly. These methods can be applied to any particular amplifier. They can be used to obtain either a spot noise figure (at a single frequency) or an integrated noise figure for the total bandpass of the amplifier.

TWO-GENERATOR METHOD. The two-generator method for measuring the noise figure utilized the voltage and current input noise sources described in Figure 13-3. In general, the noise aspects of any linear two-terminal network can be characterized by a series noise voltage and a parallel noise current generator at the input. One can measure the contribution from these two sources by conducting an "open-circuit" and a "short-circuit" test. Since the item here is (random) noise, one must also measure the correlation (γ) between two sources.

To begin, one can measure e_N by conducting a short-circuit test. The shorting resistance (R_short) must fulfill the following:

$$R_\text{short} \ll R_\text{in}$$

$$\frac{i_N R_\text{short}}{R_\text{in} + R_\text{short}} \ll \frac{e_N}{R_\text{in} + R_\text{short}} \tag{6}$$

The first condition is necessary to assure that all the generator voltage e_N will appear across the amplifier input; the second requirement keeps the contribution from i_N negligible. Under these conditions the output voltage can be measured with a true reading rms voltmeter. Dividing this value by the amplifier gain results in the value for e_N.

Noise

The contribution of i_N can be measured with an open circuit test in which

$$R_{\text{open}} \gg R_{\text{in}}$$

$$\frac{i_N R_{\text{open}}}{R_{\text{in}} + R_{\text{open}}} \gg \frac{e_N}{R_{\text{in}} + R_{\text{open}}} \qquad (7)$$

If the e_N and i_N are known, the noise figure can then be calculated by

$$NF = 1 + \frac{1}{4kT\Delta F}\left(i_N^2 R_g + \frac{e_N^2}{R_g} + 2\gamma e_N i_N\right) \qquad (8)$$

where K = Boltzmann's constant,
T = temperature in degrees Kelvin,
ΔF = noise power bandwidth,
γ = correlation coefficient,
$4kT$ = 1.66 × 10^{-20} watt-sec at 25°C.

It is clearly seen that the noise figure is a function of the source resistance R_g. Also, one must know the value of the correlation coefficient (γ). Since γ is between zero and one, a gross result can be achieved by finding the two NF values for these two values of γ. A more accurate γ must be found by measurement or using theoretical information. At low emitter currents the γ can be estimated to be

$$\gamma \cong \frac{1}{\sqrt{h_{FE}}} \qquad (9)$$

Equation (8) can be used to find an optimum value for R_g. It can be shown that the optimum is

$$R_{g_{\text{opt}}} = \frac{e_N}{i_N} \qquad (10)$$

With this R_g then the resulting optimum noise figure (optimum with respect solely to source resistance) is shown to be

$$F_{\text{opt}} = 1 + (1 + \gamma)\frac{e_N i_N}{2kT\Delta F} \qquad (11)$$

The above, then, is a basic method in which any given transistor amplifier can be measured to ascertain its noise figure. This method can be used to obtain either a spot noise figure or an integrated noise figure. Some manufacturers give curves of e_N and i_N versus I_E for three spot frequencies. The lowest frequency should be within the $1/f$ region, while the highest frequency should be in the flat region. The intervening frequency should be near the "knee" of the curve.

DIRECT NOISE FIGURE MEASUREMENT. The direct noise figure measurement is based on the basic definition of noise factor as given in Equation (5). The basic idea in this method is to insert a specified amount of signal power and measure the corresponding output. When this input power is removed, the resulting output must be due to noise alone. It is necessary to assure that when the signal is present the ever-present noise is negligible. The method can be described by writing Equation (5) in the form:

$$NF = 20 \log \frac{S_{\text{in}}}{N_{\text{in}}} - 20 \log_{10} \frac{S_o}{N_o} \qquad (12)$$

where S_{in} = input signal voltage,
N_{in} = input noise voltage,
S_o = output signal voltage,
N_o = output noise voltage.

First the (nontransistor) input noise can be determined by using R_g in Equation (2) and taking the square root.

$$N_{\text{in}} = \sqrt{4kT \text{ of } R_g} \qquad (13)$$

If the input signal is now made ten times greater than this theoretical noise voltage, Equation (12) can be written

$$NF = 20 \text{ db} - 20 \log_{10} \frac{S_o}{N_o} \qquad (14)$$

One then observes the output S_o with this given input and then the *change* in the output when the input signal is set to zero. This change is the measure of $20 \log_{10} (S_o/N_o)$.

If this change (in db) is subtracted from 20 db [as in Equation (14)], the result is a direct measurement of the noise figure.

A source of error in this method is that the S_o measurement is actually $S_o + N_o$. Consequently, one should have a sufficiently high

Noise

signal so that the noise during the signal measurement is insignificant.

Although this method of measuring the noise figure is direct, there is very little information in this method as to how to improve the *NF* except by experimenting. For example, there is no indication of the optimum source resistance R_g or the resulting optimum noise figure. However, this method does provide a straightforward way to measure the noise figure.

Both of the above methods can be applied to whatever spectrum the particular transistor circuit has. It must also be remembered that any results of noise measurements are dependent on the bias point and the temperature, in addition to the R_g. Hence, any specification of noise figure must specify all these items.

The alternative to measuring noise figure is to estimate the noise figure, for any particular amplifier, by applying the spot noise figure usually provided by the manufacturer. This is possible only because the behavior of the noise figure versus frequency is pretty straightforward, as indicated by Figure 13-4. The crucial issue, however, is that one must know the location, on this frequency diagram, of this spot noise figure.

We will now discuss using the quoted spot noise figure in estimating the noise figure for any particular amplifier.

USE OF MANUFACTURER'S STATED NOISE FIGURE

One of the data supplied by the manufacturer of transistors is a noise figure *NF*, stated under specified conditions. It is our object, in this section, to determine how to use this information to estimate a relatively wideband noise figure of a given transistor application. We will do this by taking advantage of the fact that the noise sources either vary as $1/f$ (at the low end) or are flat with frequency. We will assume that we do not go above f_b in Figure 13-4.

At present, if only a single-frequency value is given, the noise figure *NF*, stated by the manufacturer, usually applies to a noise measurement at a frequency of 1000 c and for a bandwidth of 1 c. The value of source resistance (R_g) used in the measurement is usually given since the noise figure depends upon its value.

We can use this spot noise figure and its corresponding noise factor F_o ($NF = 10 \log F_o$) to estimate an integrated noise figure for our amplifier if (1) we know the frequency at which the $1/f$ region ends (f_a), and (2) our amplifier gain characteristic is fairly flat within the bandpass.

We will assume that the f_a is greater than 1000 cps so that the stated NF lies in the $1/f$ region.

The question we then deal with is "How is the F_o, measured for a 1-c bandwidth, related to a given bandwidth we may encounter?"

First, we consider the case where our bandwidth lies wholly in the $1/f$ region (to the left of f_a in Figure 13-4). In addition, for this first case we will consider the bandwidth as being small.

In this region the $1/f$ noise is much larger than the white noise. If the noise power varies as $1/f$, then it can be shown that the total power available in a given bandwidth between f_H and f_L is given by

$$1/f \text{ noise power} = C \ln \frac{f_H}{f_L} \tag{15}$$

where f_H = upper limit of bandwidth
f_L = lower limit of bandwidth

This results from simply integrating $1/f$ with respect to f.

If this equation is substituted into the NF Equation (4) it is found that

$$F = 1 + \frac{K \ln (f_H/f_L)}{4kTR_g B} \tag{16}$$

Now, if the bandwidth is small $[(f_H - f_L) \ll f_L]$, we can make the following approximation:

$$\ln \frac{f_H}{f_L} \simeq \frac{f_H - f_L}{f_L} \tag{17}$$

The F may then be written

$$\boxed{F = 1 + \frac{K'}{f_L}} \tag{18}$$

where $K' = \dfrac{K}{4kTR_g}$.

If, at a frequency of 1 c, a value of F_o is measured, it must be true that

Noise

$$F_o = 1 + \frac{K'}{1000}; \quad K' = 1000(F_o - 1) \quad (19)$$

Substituting this K' into Equation (14), we have the important result:

$$F = 1 + \frac{1000(F_o - 1)}{f_L} \quad \text{if} \begin{Bmatrix} (f_H - f_L) \ll f_L \\ f_a < f_L < f_b \end{Bmatrix} \quad (20)$$

where F_o = noise figure measured at 1000 c.

Equation (20) enables us to calculate the noise figure for an amplifier with any center frequency in terms of the noise figure at 1000 c (F_o). The restrictions on Equation (20) are that the f_L lie in the $1/f$ region, the bandwidth be small, and the measured F_o lie in the F_o region. *Also, the F given by this equation will result only if we are using an R_g close to the value used to measure F_o.* This is usually the case because we generally operate the transistor with circuit values close to the recommended ones. However, if this R_g criterion is not filled, it simply means that the F_o data do not apply. We would then have to measure the noise figure to obtain any accuracy.

Next, we consider the case where the $f_H - f_L$ occurs wholly within the $1/f$ region, but the bandwidth (of our amplifier) is not small. This means that we cannot use the approximation given in Equation (17). However, the approximation does still apply to the F_o measurement (supplied by the manufacturer) so that Equation (19) holds. Substituting this value of K' in Equation (16) we find

$$F = 1 + \frac{(F_o - 1)1000 \ln (f_H/f_L)}{f_H - f_L} \quad \text{for } f_a < f_H, f_L < f_b \quad (21)$$

Equation (21) then is the more general equation that applies when the pass band is within the $1/f$ region, but the bandwidth is not small. At first thought it may appear that the noise figure of the circuit with the greater bandwidth will be the higher since the greater bandwidth allows more $1/f$ noise. However, the larger bandwidth also allows more source resistance thermal noise to be present, so that the F in the application of Equation (21) may well be less than for the case where Equation (20) applies.

Now suppose the measured F_o (1000 cps) lies in the flat shot noise region of the spectrum. Then the noise figure is immediately available for any amplifier whose bandwidth is also entirely in the flat region.

If now the amplifier bandwidth includes a substantial part of the $1/f$ region we want to account for both $1/f$ and shot noise. By applying Equation (4) and the previous material, it can be shown that

$$F = \frac{1 + (F_o - 1)[1000 \ln f_a/f_L + (f_H - f_a)]}{f_H - f_L} \qquad (22)$$

The above relations provide a means to estimate an integrated noise figure for any given transistor amplifier in terms of the manufacturer's stated spot measurement at 1000 cps.

One important restriction must be repeated: in order to use the manufacturer's value of F_o with reasonable accuracy, it is necessary that the given amplifier have a source resistance close to the R_g used in evaluating F_o.

These, then, are the methods in which noise figures can be handled in transistor circuits: the two-generator and the direct measurement method. In the above we described a way of estimating the amplifier NF from the manufacturer's transistor data.

It must be kept in mind that the noise figure varies with the source resistance (R_g), the bias currents I_c and I_e, the frequency, and the temperature. Generally speaking, the best R_g's are in the range of 100 to 1000 ohms and relatively low I_E and V_{CE}'s are beneficial to low noise figures.

USE OF THE NOISE FIGURE

Having now explored the meaning and the method of calculating the noise figure of transistor amplifiers, it follows to see what information this gives us.

In the first place the F_o data of a transistor allow us to compare the noisiness of one transistor versus another. The transistor with the lowest noise figure, of course, is the most desirable from the noise standpoint. Remember that comparing F_o's is only valid if the same source resistances are involved.

This means, then, that if we are comparing different transistors for use in a given amplifier (given R_g and bandwidth) that transistor with the lowest F_o will provide the lowest F for the amplifier.

Noise

As indicated in the introduction, we need only consider the noise figure of the first stage—or at most the first and the second stage of a string of cascaded amplifiers. After the first few stages the signal has been amplified to the extent that the noise in the following stages is completely negligible. Therefore the noise figure of the first few stages may be regarded as being the noise figure of the entire set of cascaded circuits.

Many times it is necessary to know the smallest signal that can be handled by an amplifier or a set of amplifiers. We can use the noise figure to calculate this. Suppose that it is agreed that the signal is recognizable if the signal-to-noise ratio at the output is equal to 1. Given that our circuit has a noise figure F and a source resistance R_g, and remembering that the noise figure gives the ratio of total output noise to thermal noise in output, we can write

$$\frac{P_{\text{noise}}}{P_{\text{signal}}} = 1 \qquad (23)$$

$$P_{\text{noise}} = P_{\text{signal}} = F \times P_{\text{thermal}} = F \times 4kTR_g B$$

We may regard the signal power of Equation (21) as a *minimum detectable signal* for a signal-to-noise ratio of 1. In this way we can determine the smallest signal that can be handled by the given amplifier.

REFERENCES

1. Cooke, H. F., "On the Two-Generator Method of Noise Characterization," *Proc. I.R.E.*, **50** (December, 1962), p. 2520.
2. Crawford, B., "Low Noise Devices and Circuits," *Texas Instruments Seminar Paper* (July, 1963).
3. Friis, H. T., "Noise Figures of Radio Receivers," *Proc. I.R.E.*, **32** (July, 1944), p. 419.
4. Goldberg, H., "Some Notes on Noise Figures," *Proc. I.R.E.*, **36** (October, 1948), p. 1205.
5. Neilson, E. G., "Behavior of Noise Figures in Junction Transistors," *Proc. I.R.E.*, **45** (July 1957), p. 957.
6. van der Ziel, A., *Noise* (Englewood Cliffs, N. J.: Prentice-Hall, Inc., 1954).

PROBLEMS

1. Show that Equation (4) is equivalent to Equation (5).
2. Assume that the 2N3392 is used at an I_E of 1 ma. Using Equation (8), find the spot noise figure at 100 cps, 1 kc, and 10 kc for a temperature of 25°C. The ΔF is 1 cps, and let $R_g = 1000$ ohms.
3. Using the 2N3392 at an I_E of 2 ma, and 25°C, find the value of $R_{g\,\text{opt}}$ for minimum noise figure. Also, find the optimum noise factor F and noise figure NF. Do this for all three frequencies: 100 cps, 1 kc, and 10 kc.
4. What would be the noise figure of an amplifier employing a 2N1302 transistor if the bandpass of the amplifier were 100 to 10 kc? See characteristics of the transistor in Appendix III. Assume that the bandpass lies wholly within the $1/f$ noise region.
5. If the noise figure of a transistor in the white region is 10 and the noise figure measured at 1 kc is 100, at what frequency (f_b) will the noise due to the $1/f$ contribution be equal to that of the white noise?
6. What would be the over-all noise figure of the transistor of Problem 5 over a frequency bandpass of 100 c to 100 kc?
7. If the 2N3392 is used in place of the 2N1302 of Problem 4, what would the noise figure be?
8. What would be the minimum detectable signal for the amplifiers in Problems 4, 6, and 7 if the generator resistance in all cases were 1000 ohms?
9. Given that an amplifier using the 2N3392 has a bandwidth extending from 100 cps to 100 kc. Estimate the integrated noise figure, using the spot noise figure values given for the 2N3392 at an I_E of 1 ma, $T = 25°C$, and the $R_{g\,\text{opt}}$ at 1 kc.

14

Transistor oscillators and negative impedance devices

In addition to amplifiers, oscillators are electronic circuits common to most communications equipment. Their basic function is to generate the sine-wave or other periodic currents and voltages utilized in these equipments. Consequently, we can regard the oscillator as the electronic equivalent of a power generator that supplies the low-frequency sine-wave power to our homes. As an example of an oscillator we may note that every modern radio has a local oscillator and it is the frequency of this oscillator that is adjusted when we turn the dial. The power output of this oscillator is combined with the incoming signal to form a *beat frequency* signal and this is then further amplified.

In performing the function of sine-wave generator, the oscillator circuit acts essentially as a *converter*. It converts power from the d-c plate supply to a-c power whose wave shape is a sine wave, and whose frequency is determined by the reactive components of the circuit.

Here it is important to stress a basic difference between the considerations of this chapter and of the entire preceding material. Thus far we have concentrated upon the operation of the transistor in its active region, i.e., the region wherein it serves as an amplifier.

Although this active region is still of prime importance in oscillators, both the saturation and the cutoff regions are also involved. Hence we shall have to take account of the transistor in all three regions when dealing with oscillators.

This chapter, then, deals primarily with transistor *feedback oscillators*. However, since oscillators can also be viewed in terms of a negative impedance, the concepts and methods of negative impedance are also described.

GENERAL DESCRIPTION OF OSCILLATORS

We may observe first that the process of amplification is very basic to an oscillator. Certainly, most oscillators involve an amplifying element such as a transistor or a vacuum tube. We may regard the oscillations as representing an unstable amplifying condition; it is also implied that the instability is regulated so that a constant amplitude sine wave results.

We remember from Chapter 11 that if positive feedback is applied to an amplifier circuit, the circuit may become unstable. This, then, represents *one* fundamental way to achieve an oscillator: apply sufficient positive feedback to an amplifier circuit.

In any unstable circuit we will need a *frequency-determining* circuit if we wish to control the frequency of oscillation. This, of course, means the use of either a series or a parallel resonant circuit. A *feedback oscillator*, then, is the combination of an unstable amplifying circuit and a frequency-determining circuit.

Such a feedback oscillator can be viewed as a tuned feedback amplifier which requires no additional input; in other words, part of the output serves as the input to (in turn) sustain the output. The most basic block diagram of a feedback oscillator is as depicted in Figure 14-1; note the similarity of this to Figure 12-1 in Chapter 12 where feedback was discussed. In that chapter we were interested in *negative* feedback, since it was desired to improve the various per-

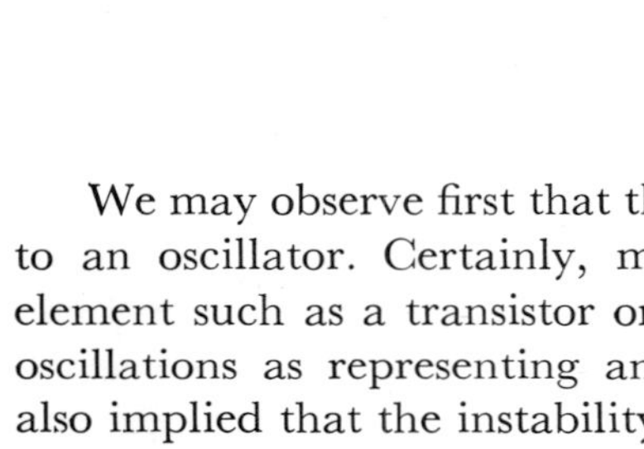

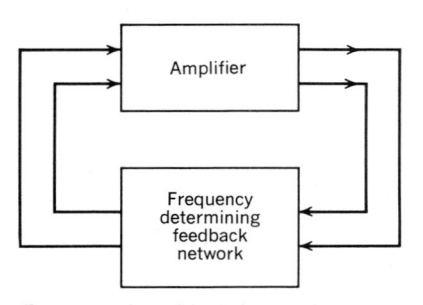

Fig. 14-1. Basic block diagram for a feedback oscillator.

Transistor oscillators and negative impedance devices

formance quantities of the total amplifier. Here the feedback is *positive* so that the "amplified output" is sufficient to serve as its input. In this way, basically, the total amplifier serves to convert energy from the d-c power supply to oscillating energy at the desired frequency.

The frequency-determining element in an oscillator is either an *LC* circuit, an *RC* circuit, or a crystal. The above, then, is a general description of the feedback oscillator.

An interesting way of viewing oscillators is to regard them as a combination of a resonant circuit and a negative impedance. In fact, if a two-terminal circuit can by itself be made to exhibit a negative impedance over some region of operation, then an oscillator formed by joining this negative impedance to a resonant circuit is termed a *negative impedance oscillator*.

It should be noted that the point contact transistor oscillators (which preceded the junction type) were of the negative-resistance type. This was primarily due to the fact that the h_{fb} was greater than 1 in the now obsolete point contact transistor. A device used at present—the tunnel diode—can be employed to form a negative-resistance oscillator; this subject is briefly discussed later in this chapter. The unijunction transistor also has a negative input impedance region.

The feedback oscillator can also be thought of in terms of a negative impedance coupled to a resonant circuit. In a sense, then, the basic circuits of Figure 14-2 can be considered as an equivalent

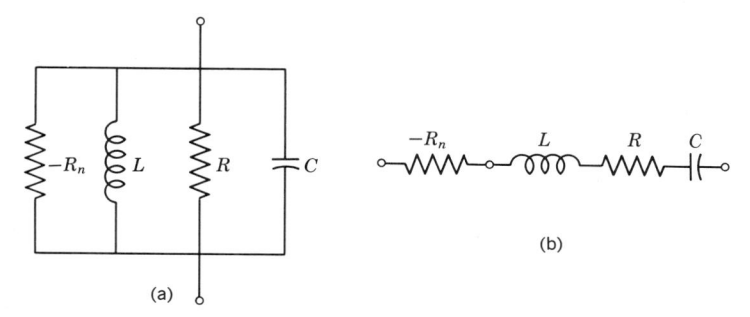

Fig. 14-2. Basic equivalent circuits of an oscillator: (a) parallel resonant circuit oscillator; (b) series resonant circuit oscillator.

circuit of an oscillator. This concept may be helpful when qualitatively viewing an oscillator. In a feedback oscillator the negative impedance part is not separable; the resonant circuit itself is needed to complete the requirement for a negative impedance within the circuit. Nevertheless, the general concept should prove useful.

In the following we will first treat the transistor feedback oscillator. Later we will briefly treat the negative impedance type of oscillator.

FEEDBACK OSCILLATORS

Feedback oscillators are those oscillators that are formed basically by adding a frequency-determining network with regenerative feedback to a basic transistor amplifier circuit. It is fundamental with feedback oscillators that *any amplifying device can be made into an oscillator*.

In this section we will investigate the factors that determine the frequency and the basic criteria required for a given circuit to oscillate. In general, the frequency of oscillation is determined approximately by the resonant frequency of the frequency-determining part of the circuit; but this must be modified by the effect that the rest of the circuit has on this resonant circuit.

The first requirement for oscillation is that the circuit have unity gain around the feedback loop (so that its amplitude is sufficient to supply its own input). Second, the phase shift of the active circuit plus the feedback network must be zero—so that the output is of the proper phase to serve as the input.

How the oscillator circuit establishes its equilibrium condition is of interest. If the gain around the loop is less than unity, no oscillation can be sustained. If the gain is greater than unity, the output will increase (from zero) until unity gain is achieved; the gain will inevitably drop as output increases because of limiting (or saturation) that always occurs. If the phase shift were not proper, the frequency of oscillation would shift until proper phase (0) is achieved.

It is seen that oscillating circuits are somewhat self-regulating. Since the amplitude of oscillation is controlled by the nonlinear characteristics (limiting effects), oscillators are very difficult to analyze. Here we will consider only a linear analysis, which will permit evaluating the frequency of oscillation as well as circuit conditions that relate transistor parameters to external circuit values (to permit oscillation).

Two types of oscillator circuits frequently used are the trans-

Transistor oscillators and negative impedance devices 405

istorized versions of the Hartley and the Colpitts circuits that are quite familiar to the vacuum tube fields. We will treat only these two basic circuits, since the fundamentals involved here can be applied to various other circuits with little difficulty.

The basic Hartley circuit, without the biasing network, is shown in Figure 14-3(b). We have omitted the bias circuitry at first to

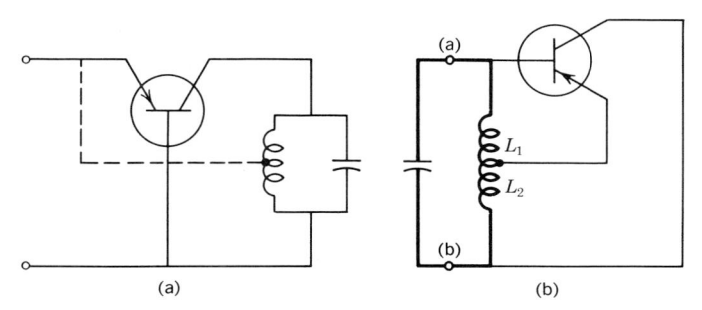

Fig. 14-3. The a-c equivalent of a Hartley oscillator: (a) an amplifier with feedback; (b) the Hartley circuit.

emphasize the a-c oscillating action; the entire circuit will be pictured later. In order to gain some concept of how the feedback oscillators perform, consider for a minute the circuit of Figure 14-3(a). Although drawn to suggest a common-base amplifier having a tuned collector load, the feedback is from collector to base so that it is actually a common-emitter connection. If we now consider driving this circuit with a source at a varying frequency, it is clear that we will obtain a maximum amplification only at the resonant frequency of the tuned circuit. As a matter of fact, the amplification on either side of this frequency will drop off sharply if the circuit has a high Q; this is simply because the effective load impedance drops to a low value at frequencies different from resonance. It should be noted that we are considering a junction transistor here; although the current gain is less than 1, there is a substantial voltage and power gain (Chapter 8).

Consider now that we connect a lead as shown by the dashed line in (a). We first note that the current fed back to the input is in *phase* with the input driving current. Since the phase is proper, it can be seen that if the amplification is sufficient, the power fed back to the input may be *equal* to the power being supplied by the external source. If this is the case, we can consider the circuit to be *supplying itself*, and of course this represents an oscillator. The basic idea here is that we have essentially an amplifier that is providing its own input. The actual source of power, then, comes from the bias battery; the circuit acts as a converter in that it converts d-c power from the bias battery into a-c power of a sine-wave shape.

The two conditions to be fulfilled for an amplifier of this type are: (1) that the *amplitude* of current fed back to the input be the correct value to obtain the corresponding output, and (2) the *phase* of the fed-back current be in phase with the output, hence giving positive feedback.

The Hartley oscillator of Figure 14-3(b) is exactly the type of circuit we have described. Part (b) of the figure is obtained by merely rearranging the diagram. For feedback oscillators in general, it is profitable always to emphasize the tank circuit; for this reason the heavy lines are used in part (b).

It should be noted that, although we have used a feedback description here, any feedback oscillator can be described in terms of a negative resistance property. The essential difference is that this circuit *cannot be separated into its negative resistance portion and its tank circuit*. The reason for this is that the tank circuit is required to form the negative resistance condition. In short, the negative resistance (discussed later in this chapter) occurs in the *dynamic* characteristic of the circuit, rather than in the static characteristic.

Nevertheless, it is still useful to note that an effective negative resistance occurs across the tank circuit when the circuit is oscillating. Hence in Figure 14-3(b) a negative resistance occurs across the points *a-b*.

MATHEMATICAL ANALYSIS OF OSCILLATORS. Having gained some insight into how an oscillator works in general, we now deal with the appropriate mathematical analysis.

The type of mathematical analysis implied here refers only to the *linear* considerations of the circuits. Because nonlinear calculations are quite involved, we shall not use this method here. Nevertheless, we remember that the amplitude of oscillations depends upon the fact that the input characteristic is nonlinear. It is so nonlinear, in fact, that it changes from a region of positive to a region of negative resistance. In spite of the limitation of not being able to predict the amplitude of oscillation from a linear analysis, we can predict the frequency and the circuit conditions necessary for oscillation. We

Transistor oscillators and negative impedance devices

proceed then to the analysis that involves only the linear considerations.

The general analysis of oscillators is based upon the ordinary mesh (or nodal) equation used throughout this book. For a circuit to be in a state of stable oscillation, it is required, mathematically, that the solutions to the mesh equations be *indeterminate*. This means that if the solution involves both a numerator and a denominator, they both equal zero (zero over zero is an indeterminate solution). Now, let us consider the case when we write a set of mesh equations. To solve them for any of the currents, we obtain essentially one determinant as the numerator and one determinant as the denominator. Now the numerator determinant will automatically be zero since the oscillator is a completely closed loop situation; all the mesh voltages will total to zero.

The criterion remaining, then, is that the denominator determinant be zero. However, the denominator consists of the determinant of the circuit impedances; hence the linear criterion for any oscillator is that *the determinant of the mesh equations be equal to zero.*

This determinant, if expanded, will contain both a resistive and a reactive part, since every oscillator contains reactive elements.

The linear analysis, then, consists of setting the resistive part of the circuit determinant to zero to find the circuit requirements, and setting the reactive part to zero to find the frequency. Although we could follow this procedure in the analysis for a general circuit, we

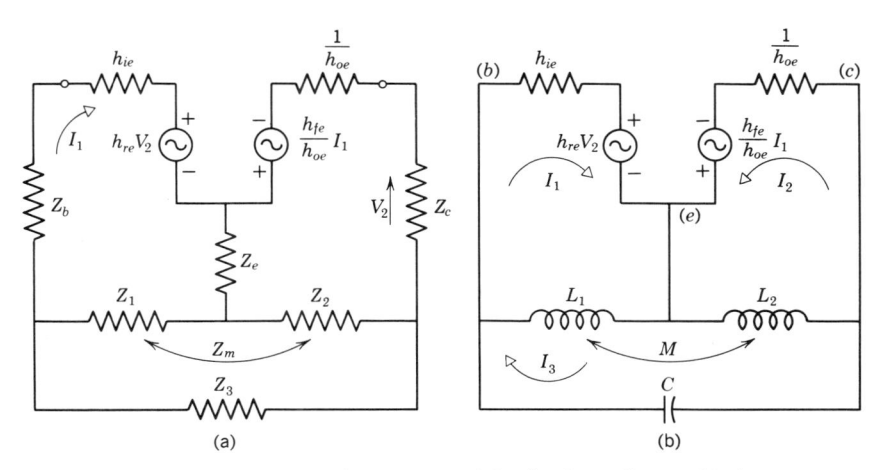

Fig. 14-4. A-c equivalent circuits of feedback oscillators: (a) the general equivalent circuit; (b) the Hartley circuit.

restrict it to more specific circuits since it would be too complex for the general circuit.

In order to achieve some uniformity in writing the mesh equations (to find the determinant) it is profitable to always consider the feedback oscillator in terms of the general circuit of Figure 14-4(a). Note that the *common-emitter parameters* are used since the transistor is connected in the common-emitter manner. The terms Z_1, Z_2, and Z_3 are the components of the resonant circuit, and the Z_m represents the mutual impedance between Z_1 and Z_2 (if any). In the case of the Hartley oscillator this Z_m is the mutual impedance between L_1 and L_2. Also, this general circuit contains the terms Z_b, Z_e, and Z_c. In many oscillators these impedances are frequency-stabilizing elements, but they shall be considered zero for our cases. Figure 14-4(b) shows the linear equivalent circuit of the Hartley oscillator.

To find the determinant for this Hartley oscillator, we first write the three mesh equations. They are

$$I_1(h_{ie} + jX_{L_1}) + I_2(-jX_M) + I_3(-jX_{L_1} - X_M) = -h_{re}V_2$$

$$I_1(-jX_M) + I_2\left(\frac{1}{h_{oe}} + jX_{L_2}\right) + I_3(jX_{L_2} + jX_M) = +\frac{h_{fe}}{h_{oe}}I_1 \quad (1)$$

$$I_1(-jX_{L_1} - jX_M) + I_2(jX_{L_2} + jX_M)$$
$$+ I_3(jX_{L_1} + jX_{L_2} - jX_C + 2jX_M) = 0$$

Using the fact that V_2 is equal to $I_2/h_{oe} - h_{fe}I_1/h_{oe}$, the equations can be written

$$I_1\left(h_{ie} + jX_{L_1} - \frac{h_{re}h_{fe}}{h_{oe}}\right) + I_2\left(\frac{h_{re}}{h_{oe}} - jX_M\right) + I_3(-jX_{L_1} - jX_M) = 0$$

$$I_1\left(-jX_M - \frac{h_{fe}}{h_{oe}}\right) + I_2\left(\frac{1}{h_{oe}} + jX_{L_2}\right) + I_3(jX_{L_2} + jX_M) = 0 \quad (2)$$

$$I_1(-jX_{L_1} - jX_M) + I_2(jX_{L_2} + jX_M)$$
$$+ I_3(jX_{L_1} + jX_{L_2} - jX_C + 2jX_M) = 0$$

Since the determinant of these equations is extremely complex, we look for some simplifications. It may be noted that, at the resonant frequency, the series reactance of the tank circuit is practically zero (this assumes that the frequency of oscillations is close to the resonant frequency). With this approximation, the coefficient of I_3 in the third equation is zero. The resulting determinant then is

Transistor oscillators and negative impedance devices

$$\Delta = \left(\frac{h_{re}}{h_{oe}} - jX_M\right)(jX_{L_2} + jX_M)(-jX_{L_1} - jX_M)$$

$$+ (-jX_{L_1} - jX_M)\left(-jX_M - \frac{h_{fe}}{h_{oe}}\right)(jX_{L_2} + jX_M)$$

$$- (-jX_{L_1} - jX_M)\left(\frac{1}{h_{oe}} + jX_{L_2}\right)(-jX_{L_1} - jX_M) \quad (3)$$

$$- (jX_{L_2} + jX_M)(jX_{L_2} + jX_M)\left(h_{ie} + jX_{L_1} - \frac{h_{re}h_{fe}}{h_{oe}}\right)$$

Solving for the real part of this equation,

$$0 = \left(\frac{h_{re}}{h_{oe}} - \frac{h_{fe}}{h_{oe}}\right)(X_{L_1} + X_M)(X_{L_2} + X_M) + \frac{1}{h_{oe}}(X_{L_1} + X_M)^2$$

$$+ \left(h_{ie} - \frac{h_{re}h_{fe}}{h_{oe}}\right)(X_{L_2} + X_M)^2 \quad (4)$$

In this equation we solve for h_{fe}, using the fact that h_{re} is very much less than h_{fe}; solving for the real part less than or equal to zero,

$$h_{fe} \gtreqless \left(\frac{X_{L_1} + X_M}{X_{L_2} + X_M}\right) + \Delta_{h^e}\left(\frac{X_{L_2} + X_M}{X_{L_1} + X_M}\right)$$

or

$$h_{fe} \gtreqless \left(\frac{L_1 + M}{L_2 + M}\right) + \Delta_{h^e}\left(\frac{L_2 + M}{L_1 + M}\right) \quad (5)$$

Equation (5), then, gives the relation between the circuit components and the transistor parameters that are required if the circuit is to function as an oscillator. This equation can be reduced by regarding either ratio on the right side as a variable and solving the resulting quadratic equation. Using the fact that $h_{fe}^2 \ll 4\Delta_{h^e}$,

$$\frac{L_2 + M}{L_1 + M} < \frac{h_{fe}}{\Delta_{h^e}} \quad (6)$$

This is the result, then, of equating the resistive part of the determinant to zero; it states the circuit conditions necessary to cause oscillation for the Hartley circuit.

To find the frequency of oscillation we need to set the reactive part of the determinant to zero. Using Equation (3) the reactive part is found to be

$$(X_C X_{L_2} X_{L_1} - X_C X_M^2) + \frac{h_{oe}}{h_{ie}} (X_{L_1} + X_{L_2} - X_C + 2X_M) = 0 \quad (7)$$

Solving this relation for frequency,

$$f = \frac{1}{2\pi \sqrt{C(L_1 + L_2 + 2M) + \frac{h_{oe}}{h_{ie}} (L_1 L_2 - M^2)}} \quad (8)$$

Figure 14-5 shows the complete Hartley oscillator with its bias circuitry. The resistor R_B is connected from collector to base in order

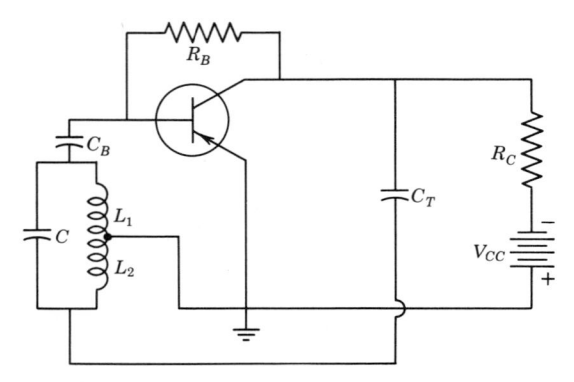

Fig. 14-5. The Hartley oscillator complete with bias circuitry.

to achieve a proper d-c bias on the base (the emitter is grounded). A proper bias point may be considered as being the center of the active region (on the collector characteristics) when the d-c load line corresponding to V_{CC} and R_C is constructed. It is evident that the capacitor C_B is necessary to block the direct current from base emitter, since otherwise they would be d-c short-circuited through the inductor winding. Likewise C_T prevents the collector from being d-c short-circuited to ground through the L_2 winding.

The addition of these components, if properly designed, will not influence the a-c analysis shown previously. The components simply provide the proper d-c operating point to the circuit.

The other basic type of feedback oscillator is the Colpitts, and its a-c circuitry is shown in Figure 14-6. As seen, the operation is very similar to the previous case except that now the capacitance is split to provide the necessary feedback, rather than the inductance. Its physical operation can be described in a completely analogous way to the operation of the Hartley circuit. If the three mesh equations are written for this circuit, and the resistive part of the determinant set equal to zero, it is found that the necessary condition for oscillation is

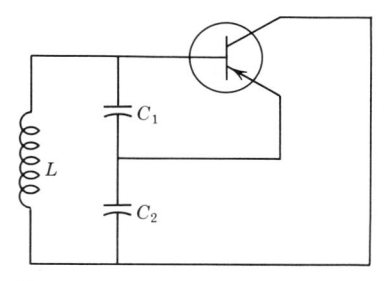

$$\frac{C_1}{C_2} \geq \frac{h_{fe}}{\Delta_{h_e}} \qquad (9)$$

Fig. 14-6. A-c circuit for the Colpitts oscillator.

A suggested exercise for the student is to show this in a manner identical to that used to find Equation (5). Also, solving the reactive part of the equation for the frequency is left as a problem. If the effect of the transistor on the tank circuit can be neglected, the frequency, of course, is given by

$$f = \frac{1}{2\pi\sqrt{LC_T}} \qquad \text{where } C_T = \frac{C_1 C_2}{C_1 + C_2}. \qquad (9a)$$

The above, then, is the most fundamental treatment of two common transistor oscillators. Here we have considered only two representative forms of single-transistor oscillators. The analysis was linear, which permits the approximate frequency determination and circuit conditions for oscillation.

In many respects oscillator design is an art rather than a science, especially since it involves many nonlinear considerations as well. The study of these warrant more specialized treatises and notes on application.

It should be noted that often more than one transistor will be used. The frequency-determining circuit is usually an RC or an LC. The oscillator is built with crystals where extreme frequency stability is required. If a crystal is in a circuit, then of course the crystal can be replaced by an equivalent circuit and the same sort of analysis as above can be applied.

NEGATIVE IMPEDANCE CONSIDERATIONS

It was mentioned previously that oscillators can be either the feedback oscillator type (as just discussed) or of the negative impedance type, and that the feedback oscillators can be interpreted or modeled in terms of negative impedance. In this section this negative impedance situation is discussed in detail.

The negative impedance concept is best visualized in terms of the basic diagram treated in Figure 14-7. In this diagram the frequency-determining circuit and negative resistance part of the circuit can be separated. Although this situation need not exist, it is the one easiest to understand. Consequently, we will begin with this. However, before dealing with the negative resistance characteristic in this situation, and although we are interested in those input characteristics that give us a negative resistance in some region, we must first treat input characteristics in general.

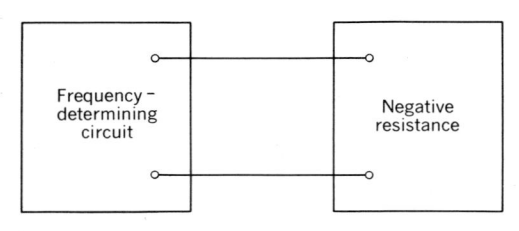

Fig. 14-7. General equivalent circuit for a negative impedance oscillator.

When considering the transistor as an active circuit element in the previous chapters, we considered the two major methods of treating the circuit as (1) the equivalent circuit method, and (2) the graphical analysis method. Now, when considering the total three regions of operation of the transistor, we shall introduce another method: this method consists essentially of obtaining the input characteristic of the transistor connection. The input may be at either the emitter, the collector, or the base terminals. After obtaining the input characteristic, the d-c circuitry attached to the input terminals forms a load line to the input.

The usefulness of this method, for oscillators and multivibrators, lies not in its ability to permit quantitative analysis, but rather in its ability to provide a picture of the operation of these devices. The mathematical analysis itself is a rather simple technique that gives us no insight into the physical operation.

USE OF THE INPUT CHARACTERISTIC. The basic idea of the input characteristic consists essentially of selecting two terminals of the

Transistor oscillators and negative impedance devices

transistor as the input, and then plotting the voltage versus current for this input. Note that it is assumed that some circuitry is attached to the other set of terminals.

For example, let us consider that we have a junction transistor connected in the common-base connection, and the input terminals we choose are those of the emitter to base. If now we vary the d-c input current and note the resulting voltage at each point, the curve will appear as shown in Figure 14-8. We note that three different

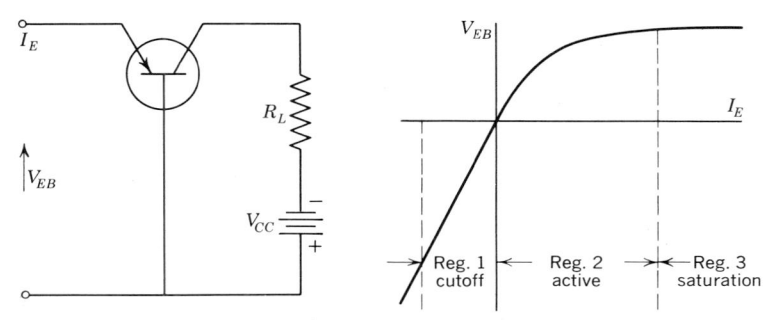

Fig. 14-8. Input characteristic of emitter terminals for three different regions.

regions are apparent: the cutoff region, the active region, and the saturation region. Since the input resistance *for a-c varying signals* is given by the slope of the curve, we can justify the general shape of this curve for the three regions.

In region 1, the cutoff region, a negative voltage must be applied to the emitter junction, as shown on the curve. This means that the emitter junction is reverse biased. Consequently, in the cutoff region both the emitter and the collector junction are back biased. With this back bias of the emitter junction we would expect the input resistance to be very high, and hence the steep slope of the curve in this region.

In the active region the transistor is biased as described earlier. The emitter junction is forward biased and the collector junction is reverse biased—this is the region of normal amplification treated thus far in this book. As we remember, the input resistance in this region varies with the input current; as shown in the curve, the input resistance decreases as the current increases. It is this varying resistance, in the active region, that accounts for the nonlinear input resistance as discussed in Chapter 9.

In the saturation region the input voltage is high enough to cause the collector junction to become forward biased; hence in this region both the emitter and the collector junction are *forward biased*. As would be expected for this condition, the curve shows that the input resistance is very low for this region.

The important consequence of this characteristic is that now we can consider any d-c circuitry attached to the input terminals *in terms of a load line on the input graph*. This concept is perfectly analogous to the concept of drawing a load line on a set of collector characteristics, as is done for the usual graphical analysis. The graphical analysis was treated in Chapter 7, Figure 7-4. There the load line portrayed a graphical simultaneous solution of the circuit to the left and to the right of the breaking point. In Figure 14-9 we consider that the cir-

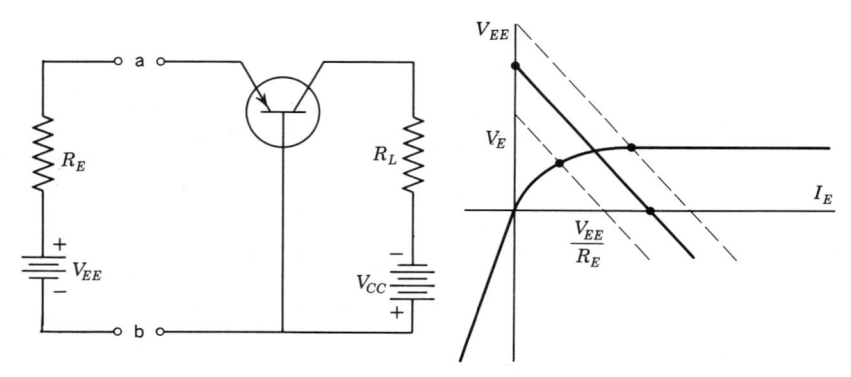

Fig. 14-9. Illustrating use of d-c load line on input characteristic.

cuit is broken at *a-b*; consequently, the input characteristic portrays the circuit to the right of these points; the load line the circuit to the left. As previously, the voltage intercept of the load line equals the open-circuit voltage of the circuitry, and the current intercept is the short-circuit current. This is illustrated in Figure 14-9. If we had a signal alternating voltage placed in the load circuit, we could envisage the operation on this figure in terms of moving the load line up and down. Remember that we can draw a simple load line only for resistive loads; if reactance forms part of the load, the load line concept is not nearly so useful.

Having noted the load line concept, we can now see how the input characteristic is obtained experimentally. One merely attaches a

Transistor oscillators and negative impedance devices

proper load resistance (R_E) with a variable direct voltage. Then as the voltage is varied, the respective currents and voltages will be given by the intersection, as shown by the dashed lines on Figure 14-9. By using a large enough voltage swing, including negative emitter voltages (for P-N-P), the entire characteristic in the three regions can be scanned.

Before leaving this topic of general input characteristic, it is worthwhile to emphasize the difference from the input characteristics as depicted by Figure 7-3. There the characteristics, and there are a number of them, give the transistor V_E versus I_E with various constant collector currents, i.e., this is information about the transistor alone. If we attach an emitter load line to these characteristics, we have to know, in addition, the swing of the collector current if we are to depict the operation. The input characteristic, on the other hand, is a single curve that specifies information about the transistor *and the associated circuitry*. Here the collector current is not constant, but varies according to the collector circuitry (battery and resistor) and the input current. A different input characteristic will result if either the transistor, the collector battery, or the resistor is changed.

Although we have here regarded the emitter-to-base terminals as the input, it is clear that we can obtain an input characteristic for any two terminals, with the other pair attached to a given circuitry.

NEGATIVE RESISTANCE INPUT CHARACTERISTICS. As mentioned previously, any oscillator can be considered in terms of a resonant circuit and a negative resistance. Using the above concepts, we can now show how a negative resistance is obtained at the input of certain transistor connections.

If we had a circuit that exhibited a negative resistance over a portion of its operating range, we could, then, form an oscillator and attach a load line by using the methods described above. If we had a single device that would offer such a negative resistance, we would need only that single device. For example, a tunnel diode is a two-terminal device that has a negative resistance region and can be used in the fashion to be described. In the past, point contact transistors (before they were outmoded because of better fabrication techniques and better performance with junction units) were a source of nonlinear operating characteristics because their h_{fb} was greater than 1. A nonlinear resistance characteristic can be obtained with two cascaded junction transistors with the circuit shown in Figure 14-10. The V_B versus I_B input characteristic of this circuit is shown

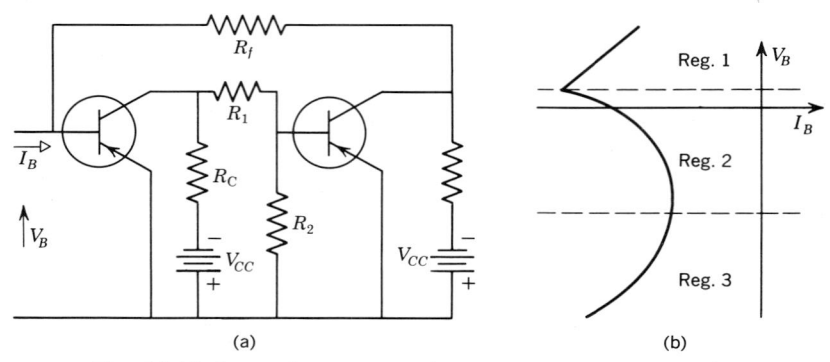

Fig. 14-10. Input characteristic of two junction transistors, d-c coupled and with positive feedback.

in Figure 14-10(b). If a tank circuit or a resonant circuit were attached to this input circuitry and proper bias conditions obtained, this circuit could be used to obtain an oscillator (although it would not be the most efficient way).

Referring to Figure 14-10, if we now determine the input characteristics, we will find they are as shown in (b). Here we see that in region 2, or the active region, *the slope of the curve is negative*. This means that with regard to a-c a negative resistance is exhibited. Note that the two junction transistors are direct coupled. In effect, this two-transistor unit could be considered as the equivalent of a single unit (with its power gain) with a feedback as shown, which affords the possibility of oscillation. Since this circuit can form a flip-flop, it constitutes one way of considering the flip-flop phenomenon (see Chapter 15).

Another type of nonlinear negative resistance characteristic can be obtained from the tunnel diode. Assuming a negative resistance characteristic is available, we can form an oscillator by connecting either a series or a parallel resonant circuit to the input terminals. Also, we must connect a bias source and a load line to these terminals in order to establish the d-c operating point.

To form an oscillator, we want the d-c operating point to *appear in the negative resistance region of the input characteristic*. In addition, this

Transistor oscillators and negative impedance devices

operating point must be unstable. If the operating point is unstable the circuit action cannot remain at that point, but will move away from it. An unstable operating point in conjunction with a frequency-determining circuit will form a basic oscillator. The circuit action never rests at the operating point, but oscillates *about* this point. The path and speed of the action is determined by the frequency-determining circuit; this circuit forms an effective a-c load line, which could also appear on the input characteristic.

The condition on the a-c load, the frequency-determining network, is that the resonance shall appear at the desired frequency, and also that the impedance of the resonant circuit shall not load the d-c condition so as to move the operating point out of the negative resistance region.

There are basically two types of negative resistance input characteristics: *voltage-controlled* and *current-controlled*. Figure 14-11 shows the two types of characteristics with unstable load lines. The voltage-controlled curve is single-valued with respect to voltage, while the current-controlled case is single valued with respect to current.

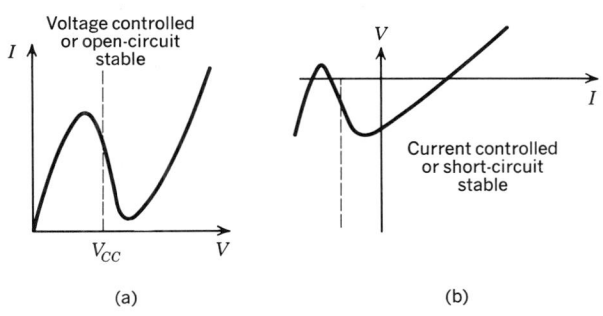

Fig. 14-11. Negative resistance characteristics: (a) voltage-controlled; (b) current-controlled.

Any intersection of a V-I characteristic and the load line represents a possible operating point. In regions where the input characteristic is positive, the intersection is *stable* and is an operating point. In negative resistance regions, however, the intersection may be either stable or unstable.

Let us consider the matter of stability in the negative resistance region. The voltage-controlled case can have a stable operating point if the static "load" resistance is *greater* than the magnitude of the negative resistance. For this reason the voltage-controlled case is often called "open circuit stable." In other words, an infinite static load resistance would guarantee stability in the negative resistance region.

The current-controlled case can have a stable operating point in the negative resistance region if the static load resistance is *less* than the negative resistance magnitude. Thus it is often termed "short circuit stable."

Based on this, it is seen that the load lines in Figure 14-11 would provide unstable operating points for the two cases, which are the type required to form an oscillator. An infinite load resistance is shown for the short-circuit stable case, while a zero static load is shown for the open-circuit stable case.

We may note that a negative resistance curve such as is shown in Figure 14-11(a) or (b) may occur either from a single element or from a circuit containing more than one active element. For example, the tunnel diode furnishes a circuit by itself very similar to that shown in Figure 14-11(a). On the other hand, a circuit such as Figure 14-11(b) will be provided by an emitter-coupled monostable multivibrator, discussed in the next chapter. There are a number of single devices (such as the unijunction transistor and the p-n-p-n diode) that provide a current controlled characteristic.

The negative resistance viewpoint, then, should be considered as one possible way to look at certain types of oscillators (the negative impedance type); in addition, it would be helpful to use such circuits as astable multivibrators (see Chapter 15). In general, the value of the input characteristic is in that it serves as an additional tool for the analysis of circuit operations.

We can now gain some insight into how an oscillator operates. Assume first that the oscillations have begun. Then the current is periodically varying as a sine wave. This would normally damp out due to the inevitable resistance of the coil. However, the transistor input terminals exhibit an a-c negative resistance; this means that if the current increases slightly, the transistor makes it increase still more. Thus pictorially we can consider the transistor operation as proceeding back and forth along the input characteristic, about the d-c operating point.

We can see how the *amplitude* of the oscillations is governed in this type of oscillator. As the amplitude of swing increases, the positive resistance region will eventually be reached. When the operation

Transistor oscillators and negative impedance devices

swings into the region where the negative resistance no longer balances out the coil resistance the amplitude rise will be stopped. This is the reason for labeling the oscillator a nonlinear circuit. It is the nonlinearities that limit the amplitude of oscillation.

In a sense we can regard this type of oscillator as a circuit that has a stable operating point but which is never allowed to stay at this operating point because of the unstable a-c conditions effective in this region. It is in this way that the very simple representation of Figure 14-2 is achieved.

The mathematical analysis associated with a negative impedance type oscillator is similar to that for the feedback oscillator described before. That is, it is based primarily on the ordinary mesh (or nodal) equation method. For a circuit to fulfill the conditions of an oscillator it is required that the solutions to the mesh equations be indeterminant. This means that if the solution involved both a numerator and a denominator, they both equal zero. As shown before, this reduces to the criterion that the denominator determinant must be zero.

The mathematical method for a negative impedance type oscillator, where the frequency determining part of the circuit and the other part of the circuit are separable, can be illustrated by the following example. Suppose that the nonfrequency-affected part of the circuit is described in terms of its h parameters (note that if an oscillator is to be formed, the h parameters will have to include more than a single transistor since the h_{fb} is not equal to 1; therefore to be separable an additional circuitry is required). Nevertheless, the circuit can be evaluated on this basis. We will use the general h parameters to indicate that we mean the parameters for a total circuit, and not just for a single transistor.

The frequency of oscillation of this type of circuit will be given approximately by the resonant frequency of the coil and capacitor combination. The circuit determinant will contain both a resistive and a reactive part. To extract the necessary information we separate the resistive and the reactive part. Then by setting the resistive part of the determinant equal to zero we find the necessary condition for oscillation, i.e., the necessary conditions to obtain a negative resistance region. Further, by setting the reactive part equal to zero, we can find the frequency at which the circuit will oscillate.

For the circuits treated thus far, this last part is trivial since we already know the approximate oscillation frequency from the resonant circuit. However, this maneuver is perfectly general and we shall see in the next section that this procedure may be necessary to find the frequency.

The circuit determinant for all three of the isolated oscillators can be written generally. We first write the general mesh equations based upon the equivalent circuit in Figure 14-12. Note that in the equiv-

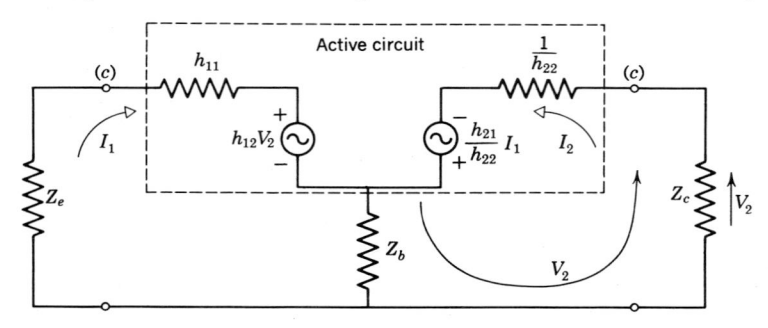

Fig. 14-12. General linear equivalent circuit of a two-terminal oscillator.

alent circuit of the transistor we have used Thevenin's theorem on the output side to obtain a voltage generator. The Z_e, Z_b, and Z_c represent the entire external impedances that appear at the respective terminals. The two mesh equations are

$$I_1(Z_e + Z_b + h_{11}) + I_2(Z_b) = -h_{12}V_2$$
$$I_1(Z_b) + I_2\left(Z_b + \frac{1}{h_{22}} + Z_c\right) = +\frac{h_{21}}{h_{22}}I_1 \qquad (10)$$

where V_2 = voltage across output of transistor (shown in the diagram).

Using the fact that V_2 is found to be

$$V_2 = -I_2 Z_c - (I_1 + I_2)Z_b \qquad (11)$$

the equations can be written

$$I_1[Z_e + h_{11} + Z_b(1 - h_{12})] + I_2[Z_b(1 - h_{12}) - h_{12}Z_c] = 0$$
$$I_1\left(Z_b - \frac{h_{21}}{h_{22}}\right) + I_2\left(Z_b + \frac{1}{h_{22}} + Z_c\right) = 0 \qquad (12)$$

The determinant for these two equations, after expansion, is

Transistor oscillators and negative impedance devices

$$\Delta \equiv Z_e Z_b + Z_e \frac{1}{h_{22}} + Z_e Z_c + \frac{Z_b(1 - h_{12})}{h_{22}} + Z_c Z_b + h_{11} Z_b$$
$$+ \frac{h_{11}}{h_{22}} + h_{11} Z_c + Z_b(1 - h_{12}) \frac{h_{21}}{h_{22}} - \frac{h_{12} h_{21}}{h_{22}} Z_c = 0 \quad (13)$$

Using the fact that

$$h_{12} \ll 1, \qquad h_{11} \ll \frac{1}{h_{22}} \quad (14)$$

the determinant simplifies to

$$\Delta \approx Z_e Z_b + Z_e \frac{1}{h_{22}} + Z_e Z_c + Z_b \left(\frac{1 + h_{21}}{h_{22}} \right) + Z_c Z_b + \frac{h_{11}}{h_{22}}$$
$$+ h_{11} Z_c - \frac{h_{12} h_{21}}{h_{22}} Z_c \leqq 0 \quad (15)$$

We can use this equation, then, to find the conditions for oscillation and the frequency for any of the oscillators treated in this section.[1]

Equation (15) specifies the relation between the transistor parameters and the other circuit quantities that will permit a negative resistance to be realized.

To find the frequency, we set the reactive part of Equation (15) to zero. Assume Z_e is purely imaginary, then the equation is

$$Z_e \left(Z_b + \frac{1}{h_{22}} + Z_c \right) = 0 \quad (16)$$

To fulfill this equation, either of the terms may be set to zero. Since the term in parentheses cannot possibly be zero, we must set $Z_e = 0$. But Z_e is given by

$$Z_e = j\omega L + \frac{1}{j\omega C} = 0$$
$$\omega = \frac{1}{\sqrt{LC}}; \qquad f = \frac{1}{2\pi \sqrt{LC}} \quad (17)$$

Hence we have shown that the frequency is given by the resonant frequency of the tuned circuit, which we knew beforehand, of course.

[1] The h parameters here refer specifically to a general active circuit and not to a particular transistor connection.

This, then, is the manner in which the linear considerations of an oscillator are handled. For any oscillator of the type considered in this section, that is, where the negative resistance and the frequency-determining portion of the circuit can be separated, Equation (15) may be used.

TUNNEL DIODE AS AN EXAMPLE OF A NEGATIVE IMPEDANCE DEVICE

The tunnel diode is an example of a two-terminal negative impedance device that is useful in a variety of functions. It has a general voltage versus current characteristic as depicted in Figure 14-11(a). We will discuss this device as an example of a single two-terminal device that exhibits a negative resistance.

As seen in Chapter 5, the tunnel diode is basically a small P-N junction in which a very high concentration of impurities is used in both the P and the N regions. This very high impurity density causes the junction depletion region, also called the space charge region, to be sufficiently narrow so that both holes and electrons can transfer across the junction by quantum mechanical action called tunneling.

The current variation near the origin is determined by the quantum mechanical tunneling effect of the electrons. The furthermost right portion of the curve is the ordinary forward-biased diode portion of the curve. Near the origin, as the voltage is increased, the current first increases due to the tunneling effect. However,

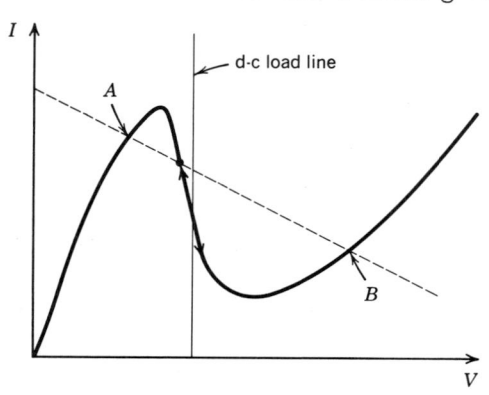

Fig. 14-13. Tunnel diode characteristic and load lines.

after a certain voltage is reached the current begins to decrease toward zero. This decreasing current, while the voltage is increasing, of course causes the negative resistance portion of the device. The result is the curve shown in Figure 14-13.

To form either an oscillator or an amplifier the operating point must occur in the negative resistance region. Since this characteristic is open-circuit stable, the d-c load resistance must be low enough (vertical enough) so that the curve is intersected at only one point.

An oscillator would have an *a-c load line* similar to the dashed line connecting A and B. The a-c load line for an amplifier would be similar to the d-c load line—having only one intersection with the characteristic.

A basic "switch" can be formed by using a load line which intersects the characteristic at three points, as shown in Figure 14-13. Only the points A and B are stable points. Assume the operation is initially at point A. Then a current trigger can switch operation to point B. From there a negative step can return the operation to point A.

The use of the negative resistance characteristic, with both d-c and a-c load lines, is valuable in understanding a variety of tunnel diode circuits. The outstanding feature of the tunnel diode is its high (switching) speed.

PROBLEMS

1. In Figure 4-12 let Z_c be a 2 K ohm resistance and Z_e be a parallel tuned circuit composed of a 0.1 µf capacitor and a 1 millihenry inductor. Let the parameters of the entire circuit be

$$h_{11} = 100 \text{ ohms} \qquad h_{21} = -3$$
$$h_{12} = .01 \qquad h_{22} = .0003 \text{ mh}$$

   a) Determine the range of the resistance Z_b for which oscillations will exist.
   b) What is the frequency of oscillation?

2. Derive the inequality relation for the starting condition of the Colpitts oscillator, stated in Equation (9). Write three mesh equations for the circuit, and set the real part of the circuit determinant to zero.

424   **Transistor oscillators and negative impedance devices**

3. Using the same equations as developed in Problem 2, set the reactive part of the circuit determinant to zero. Solve for the frequency of oscillation of the Colpitts oscillator. Under what conditions is the approximation of Equation (9a) correct?

4. Using the 2N3638 characteristics given in Appendix III, determine whether the circuit shown in Figure 14-14 will oscillate. Use the h parameters at the $V_{CE} = -10$, $I_C = 10$ ma, operating point.

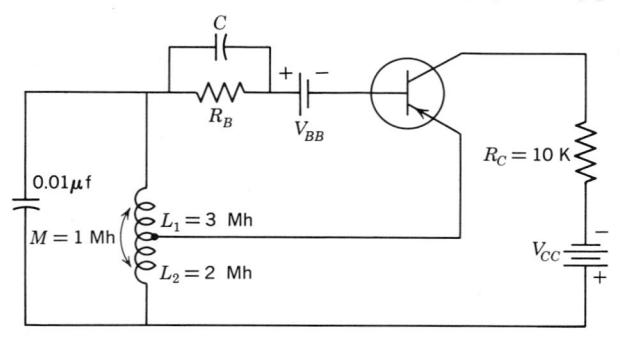

Fig. 14-14. Hartley oscillator.

5. Would the oscillator of Problem 4 operate if $L_1 = 100$ mh, $L_2 = 1$ mh, and $M = 4$ mh?

6. In Problem 5, what value of M will cause the oscillator to operate correctly if it does not operate with the value of M given?

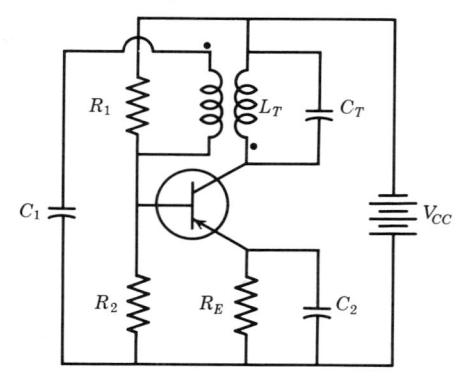

Fig. 14-15. Feedback oscillator.

7. In the feedback oscillator of Figure 14-15, L_T and C_T form a tuned circuit. L_T is transformer-coupled to the base circuit, C_1 and C_2 are large bypass capacitors, and R_1, R_2, and R_E provide the necessary d-c bias.

Transistor oscillators and negative impedance devices

a) Qualitatively explain how this oscillator operates in light of the basic block diagram shown in Figure 14-1.
b) What is the frequency of oscillation?
c) Draw the linear a-c equivalent circuit and determine the circuit equations.

8. Assume that the 2N1097 transistor is used in the circuit of Figure 14-15. Find the operating point if $R_1 = 100$ K, $R_2 = 10$ K, $R_E = 1$ K, and $V_{CC} = -12$ v. Based on this, and using the characteristics, sketch the I_B and I_C current waveforms.

9. Using the a-c equivalent circuit of Figure 14-4, find the conditions necessary for starting oscillation by applying the Barkhausen condition of unity gain to the circuit. Compare your result with that of Equation (6).

10. In the common emitter amplifier connection the output voltage is 180° out of phase from the input voltage. It is possible to obtain an additional 180° of phase shift from three cascaded RC filters. It follows that the circuit shown in Figure 14-16 can be made to

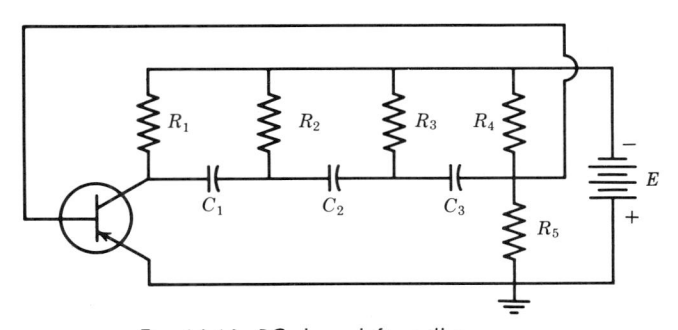

Fig. 14-16. RC phase shift oscillator.

oscillate. An a-c equivalent circuit for this oscillator has the form with node voltages $e_1 - e_4$ and currents $i_1 - i_4$ and i_b as indicated in Figure 14-17. To simplify the analysis without materially reduc-

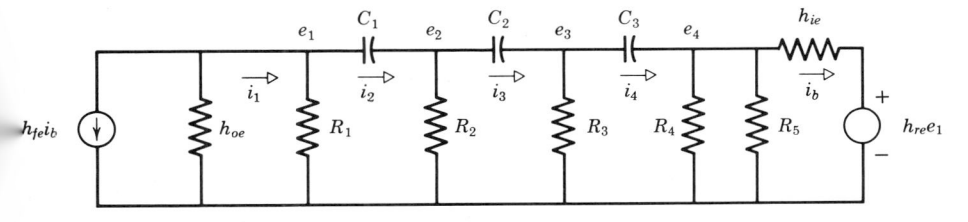

Fig. 14-17. Equivalent circuit for Fig. 14-16.

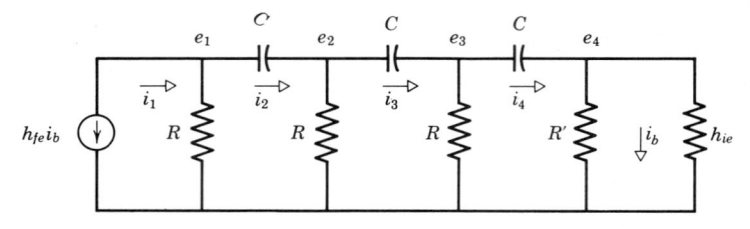

Fig. 14-18

ing the generality of the results, the following assumptions will be made. The transistor parameters h_{re} and h_{oe} will be considered equal to zero. All of the capacitors will have the same value, C. The resistors R_1, R_2, R_3, and the parallel combination of R_4, R_5 and h_{ie} will all have the value R. (*Note:* The division of resistance between R_4 and R_5 is selected so as to provide the proper d-c bias conditions.) The equivalent circuit now has the form of Figure 14-18 where $R' = R_3 R_4 / R_3 + R_4$, and by the above assumptions

$$R = R' h_{ie}/R' + h_{ie}.$$

Recall that the conditions for oscillation require that the total phase shift must be zero (or 360, etc.) degrees and loop gain must exceed unity. Apply these conditions to this circuit and determine minimum value of R that will support oscillations in terms of the two transistor parameters. Determine the value of C from the desired frequency of operation and the value of R found above. *Hint:* Assume the voltage e_4 equals e. Thus $i_b = e/h_{ie}$. Next find i_4 in terms of e and R. Proceed by calculating e_3 from i_4 and e at an assumed frequency of oscillation. In this way i_1 can be found in terms of R, C, f (the assumed frequency of oscillation), and e.

11. Using the negative resistance characteristic for a tunnel diode as sketched in Figure 14-13, describe and sketch the operation of the monostable switching circuit shown in Figure 14-19. Assume that

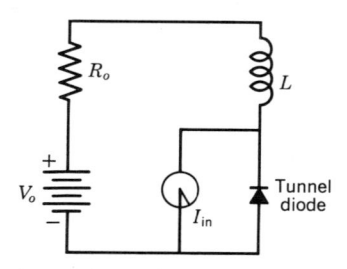

Fig. 14-19. Monostable switching circuit.

V_o and R_o are such that the d-c load line is steep and intersects the characteristic at one point at a time. Assume operation starts at point A of Figure 14-13. Using the fact that, in an inductor, the current cannot change instantaneously (but the voltage can), describe the monostable operation of this circuit. Assume that the L/R time constant is much greater than any switching time.

15

Digital switching circuits

Thus far this book has considered those factors that mainly affect analog transistor amplifiers and oscillators. Both amplifiers and oscillators are *analog* in nature. By this we mean that a continuous range of stable parameter values (current and voltage) exists at the input and the output. Consequently, one can typically use linear circuits methods for most parts of the circuit analysis.

The circuits in this chapter are *digital*, rather than analog. A digital circuit has only a finite, discrete number of stable states. Thus, no matter what the input, the output will have only a few discrete states. Such circuits involve some nonlinear action, as will be seen.

If a digital circuit has two stable states it is called a *binary* or a *bistable* digital circuit. If it has only a single stable state it is called a *monostable* digital circuit. The most common and frequent example of a digital circuit is the binary flip-flop (discussed later).

The most basic unit of all digital circuits is the "transistor switch." That is, most digital circuits are formed by combinations of transistor switches. The transistor switch is simply a single transistor stage that is caused to be ON (full collector current flowing) or OFF (essen-

Digital switching circuits

tially no collector current flowing). This action is clearly analogous to that of a mechanical switch.

As mentioned, digital switching circuits are formed by combining transistor switches in various ways. There are a number of areas where digital switching circuits are required, but by far the most extensive application is in digital computers. Practically all the circuits in such computers are switching circuits; of these the leading one is the flip-flop.

The previous chapters concentrated primarily on the active (or amplifying) region of the transistor. In digital switching circuits the active region is traversed while the circuit changes from one stable state to another. For this reason it is called the *transition* region for switching circuits.

We will begin by studying the basic transistor switch. Next we consider those switching circuits that are controlled by an external trigger—called triggered switching circuits. This will include bistable multivibrators (flip-flops), monostable multivibrators, astable multivibrators, and Schmitt triggers.

Finally, the basic circuits used to perform digital logic—called logical gating circuits—will be considered. This will emphasize the basic AND- and OR-circuits.

BASIC TRANSISTOR SWITCH

Almost all the digital switching circuits are formed out of combinations of the basic transistor *switch*. The fundamental idea here is to allow only two operating points: (1) an OFF condition, which corresponds to operating the transistor in the cutoff region with almost zero collector current; and (2) the ON condition, which corresponds to operating the transistor either in or near saturation (heavy collector current).

Consider for a moment an ideal mechanical switch. When the switch is open (OFF) its resistance is infinite; no current flows and the voltage is determined by the attached circuitry. When the switch is closed (ON), its resistance is zero; the voltage across it is zero while the current is determined by the attached circuitry. Any electronic switch should have the gross characteristics of the mechanical one.

In Chapter 7 it was noted that the transistor can be thought of as having three distinct regions of operation: (1) the active region, (2) the saturation region, and (3) the cutoff region. The three regions are shown again on the characteristic curve depicted in Figure 15-1.

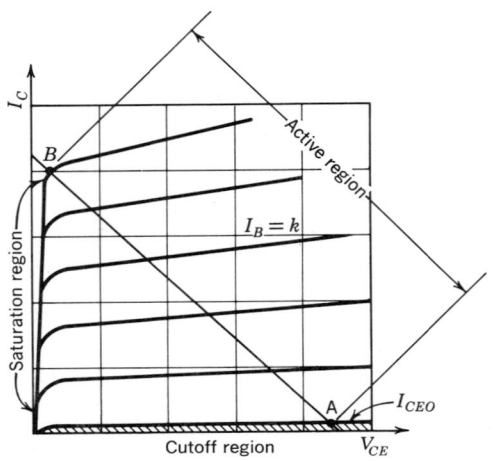

Fig. 15-1. Three regions for a transistor.

For the load line shown there, point A would be in the cutoff region, points between A and B would be in the active region, and point B would be in the saturation region.

When the transistor is in the cutoff region its collector current is very small and the voltage across it is dependent on attached circuitry (until breakdown voltage is reached). Hence its OFF resistance is quite high. If a transistor is saturated, the V_{CE} voltage is low (see Figure 15-1) and the current is determined by circuitry (until maximum specified current or power is reached). Therefore its ON resistance is quite low, as desired. Consequently, the transistor is a fairly natural switch.

It is worthwhile to review the status of the transistor junctions for each of the regions. It will be remembered that, in the *active* (amplifier) region the emitter-to-base junction is forward biased, whereas the collector-to-base junction is reversed biased. In the *cutoff* region both of the junctions are reverse biased. In the saturation region both of the junctions are forward biased.

The basic common-emitter transistor switch is shown in Figure 15-2. We will discuss the transistor switch in terms of this circuit. It must be remembered that one could form a transistor switch out of both the common-base and the common-collector connections.

Digital switching circuits

However, as with most other transistor circuits, the higher gain of the common-emitter connection makes it the more useful. Also, the 180° phase shift (or inverting) of the emitter connection is especially useful in digital circuits. For these reasons the common-emitter circuit is almost the only circuit used as a switch.

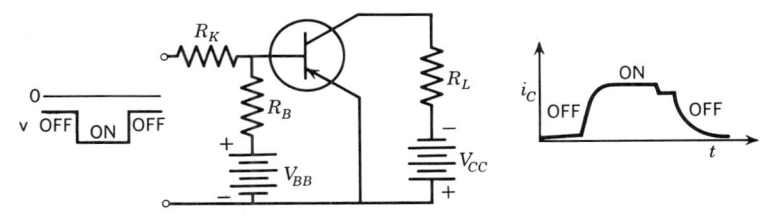

Fig. 15-2. Basic common-emitter transistor switch.

Very often in switching circuits a resistor occurs between the transistors of the circuit (i.e., resistor-transistor logic). The series R_K in Figure 15-2 represents such a coupling resistor. It also has the effect of making the input voltage source appear as an approximate current source to the transistor.

The most basic issue in dealing with a transistor switch is to assure that the stable circuit conditions are proper to establish both the ON and the OFF state. Before discussing this issue, a comment on conventions of current and voltage direction is needed. As before, we will assume as positive those transistor current directions which correspond to the *actual* current directions in the *normal* region. Thus the bias batteries and current directions would be reversed when changing from P-N-P to N-P-N. This convention has the advantage that all the current equations are valid for both the P-N-P and the N-P-N transistor. Any voltage equations will of course be reversed in sign when changing from N-P-N to P-N-P.

In the ensuing material a P-N-P transistor is used, both for the equations and in the descriptive material. This should be immediately convertible to the N-P-N case using the above conventions.

OFF CONDITION. First consider the OFF point, where the transistor in the cutoff region. As stated, the emitter junction is also reverse biased in the cutoff region. When this is true

$$I_C = I_{CBO} \quad \text{if } V_{BE} \gg 0 \quad \text{(P-N-P)} \tag{1}$$

This, then, is the leakage current for the common-base connection—the common-emitter leakage current cannot be reduced below this. A reverse bias is needed to accomplish the I_{CBO} value.

It is of interest to note the collector currents near cutoff. If the base were shorted to the emitter ($V_{BE} = 0$) then the current would be

$$I_C = I_{CES} \quad \text{if } V_{BE} = 0$$
$$I_{CES} > I_{CBO} \tag{2}$$

If the base connection were left open ($I_B = 0$), the current would be the usual I_{CEO}:

$$I_C = I_{CEO} \quad \text{if } I_B = 0$$
$$I_{CEO} > I_{CES} > I_{CBO} \tag{3}$$

Equation (3) indicates that I_{CEO} is the largest and I_{CBO} the smallest current. Usually a transistor switch in the OFF condition involves a slight reverse bias so that the I_{CBO} current can be approximated. The manufacturer usually gives I_{CBO} at a stated collector voltage and temperature.

When designing a switch, then, one must ascertain that a slight reverse bias is applied to the emitter junction for the cutoff condition:

$$\text{OFF condition} \quad V_{BE} > 0 \quad \text{(P-N-P)}$$
$$V_{BE} < 0 \quad \text{(N-P-N)} \tag{4}$$

Usually the approximations described above are sufficient to aid in designing transistor switches. However, whenever more accuracy is required, one can make use of the Ebers-Moll equations. These equations allow calculation of the voltages in terms of the currents and various transistor parameters and are valid for all three transistor regions. Because such accuracy is usually unnecessary, and because the manufacturer does not specify the needed parameters, these equations are not described at this point but in the last section of this chapter.

ON CONDITION. When a transistor switch is in the ON condition the transistor is either saturated or at least has a relatively high collector current. If the circuit is operated short of saturation (in the

Digital switching circuits

active region), the usual considerations with load lines would apply. If the switch is allowed to go into saturation, then the I_C is given by

$$I_{C_{sat}} \approx \frac{V_{CC}}{R_L} \quad (V_{CE} = I_{C_{sat}} R_{CS} < 1 \text{ volt}) \quad (5)$$

Often, when characteristic curves are not available, the manufacturer will specify the "maximum saturation resistance." The saturation resistance is given by:

$$R_{CS} = \frac{V_{CE}}{I_C} \text{ in saturation region} \quad (6)$$

Since the I_B curves in a saturation region (see Figure 15-1) are all collapsed on top of each other, the curves do not show what I_B will cause saturation. An approximate way of finding the $I_{B_{sat}}$ is by the equation

$$I_{B_{sat}} \geq \frac{I_{C_{sat}}}{h_{FE}} \quad (7)$$

Again, the saturated collector voltage $V_{CE_{sat}}$ is usually less than one volt. Since this is much smaller than the voltages in series with it, it is usually taken to be zero:

$$V_{CE} \approx 0 \quad (8)$$

Again, more accurate results for the saturation region can be obtained by using the Ebers-Moll equations. These allow calculation of the voltages in terms of the currents, or vice versa.

TRANSIENT CONDITIONS. In addition to the ON-OFF character of any switch, another item of interest in any switching circuit is the *switching time;* i.e., the time required to switch from one state to the other. There are two basic reasons why the transistor cannot immediately switch from one state to the other: (1) the diffusion time of the minority carriers in the base region and (2) the junction capacitances. These two factors will prevent the output from following accurately an input signal that changes instantaneously. The response of any circuit to a *step* or *pulse* input is called the *transient response*. The transient response determines the maximum speed at which switching circuits can be operated.

The typical relation between an input pulse (v_{in}) and the ensuing I_B and I_C output pulse for a transistor switch is shown in Figure 15-3. We will discuss the transient response of the transistor switch in terms of the diagram.[1]

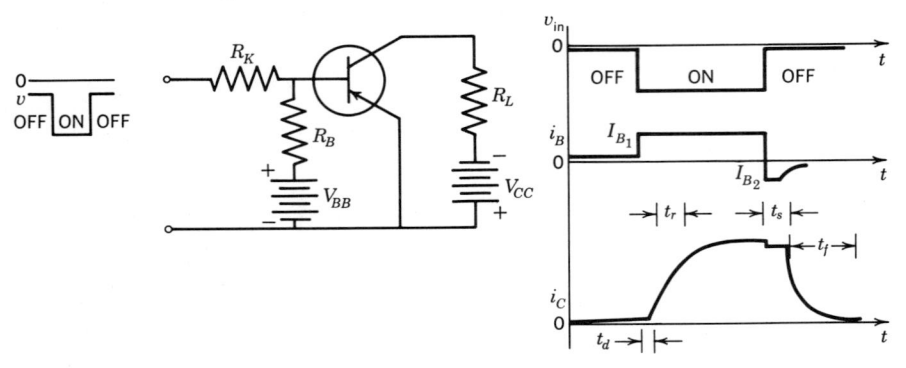

Fig. 15-3. Input and output waveforms plus terminology for basic switch.

As noted, the circuit is first in the OFF state. Remember that in the OFF state the emitter junction is reversed biased, as well as the collector junction. The exact amount of collector current flowing in the cutoff region is dependent upon the actual input conditions, as discussed above.

If a square wave negative step is applied as shown in Figure 15-3, the transistor will attempt to go from point A to point B in Figure 15-1. It cannot do so immediately, however, because of the "delay time" and the "rise time."

Delay time t_d is the length of time that the transistor remains cut off after the input pulse is applied. During this delay time two things occur: the base-to-emitter junction capacitance has to first discharge from the negative value and then charge to the forward voltage; and the emitter current begins to diffuse across the base region.

Rise time t_r is that time that is required for the leading edge of the pulse to increase in amplitude from 10 per cent to 90 per cent of its maximum value. The predominant action during the rise time is the diffusion of the carriers across the base region.

---

[1] Note that, in Figure 15-3, we use lower case symbols with capital subscripts to indicate total instantaneous values. Thus in digital circuits we cannot consider a d-c value plus an incremental one (as we did for amplifiers) but must consider the total waveform.

Digital switching circuits

Although the manufacturer often gives the maximum rise time under given conditions, the rise time can be related to the parameters of the transistor and operating currents by the equation:[2]

$$t_r = \tau_r h_{FE} \ln \frac{1}{1 - 0.9 \frac{I_C}{h_{FE} I_{B1}}} \tag{9}$$

where

$$\tau_r = \frac{1}{w_t} + 1.7\, R_L C_{TC}$$

C_{TC} = collector-base junction capacitance = C_{bc},
I_{B1} = turn-ON base current, see Fig. 15-3,
w_t = radian frequency at which $|h_{fe}| = 1$,
I_C = full-ON collector current.

Note that the rise time is most directly related to the frequency response of the transistor through the parameter w_t. Note also that the rise time decreases with increase in Turn-ON base current. Consequently overdrive on the Turn-ON base current is desirable from the standpoint of rise time; however, only small amounts of overdrive are useful because overdrive increases the storage time (see below).

When the transistor has reached the ON state it may be either in saturation or the active region depending on the particular design. The basic transistor switch, without other components attached, is usually driven into the saturation region in the ON state. Later we will discuss adding clamping diodes to stop the action short of the saturation region so that storage time is reduced. However, for the moment let us consider that the transistor is driven into saturation.

As we noted before both the collector and the emitter junctions are forward biased in the saturation region. Thus both junctions are supplying minority carriers to the base region and the transistor is behaving very similar to a short circuit between the collector and emitter junction. The Turn-OFF time for the transistor is determined by the sum of the storage time and the fall time.

Storage time t_s is the length of time that the output current i_C remains at or near its maximum value after the input current i_B is reversed. The main action during the storage time is that the minority carriers

---

[2] Transient equations of the type given in Equations (9), (10), and (11) appear throughout the literature. The terminology followed here is taken from A. B. Phillips, *Transistor Engineering*, New York: McGraw-Hill Book Company, 1962.

in the base region from both the emitter and the collector regions must be swept out before the collector current can decrease toward zero.

The storage time can be related to the transistor parameters and Turn-OFF current I_{B2} by the following equation:

$$t_s = \tau_s \ln \frac{\frac{I_{B1}}{I_{B2}} - 1}{\frac{I_C}{h_{FE}I_{B2}} - 1} \qquad (10)$$

where τ_s = storage-time constant
I_{B1} = turn-on base current
I_{B2} = transient turn-off base current (negative), see Fig. 15-3

It is seen the storage time is a function of both the Turn-ON and Turn-OFF currents and the h_{FE}. High h_{FE} and large Turn-ON currents increase the storage time; large Turn-OFF drives (I_{B2}) decrease the storage time.

Fall time t_f or decay time is the time required for the trailing edge to decrease in amplitude from 90 per cent to 10 per cent of its maximum value. The significant action during the decay time is that now the collector junction is reversed biased and the minority carriers are diffusing out of the base region.

The fall time can be related to the transistor parameters and drive currents by

$$t_f = \tau_f h_{FE} \ln \frac{\frac{I_C}{h_{FE}I_{B2}} - 1}{0.1 \frac{I_C}{h_{FE}I_{B2}} - 1} \qquad (11)$$

where $\tau_f = \tau_r$

It is evident that for rapid transistor switching all the transient times treated above should be as short as possible. One way to decrease both the rise time and the fall time is to place a "speedup" capacitor across the input resistor R_K. This capacitor has the effect of initially putting a large current into the base (on Turn-ON conditions) and reverse current on the Turn-OFF conditions. Such speedup capacitors are often used in transistor switch circuits, and the circuits formed from them.

Another standard technique to increase switching speed capability is to prevent the circuit from going into saturation and also from going into cutoff. One can eliminate the storage time if the circuit is prevented from going into saturation. On the other hand, one can

Digital switching circuits

partly eliminate the delay time if one does not go into the cutoff region. In effect, then, one would limit oneself to operating between the boundaries of the active region for switches of this sort. Such action can be accomplished in a straightforward way by the clamping diodes such as is shown in Figure 15-4. A suggested exercise is to justify how the load line depicted in Figure 15-4 is realized by these diodes.

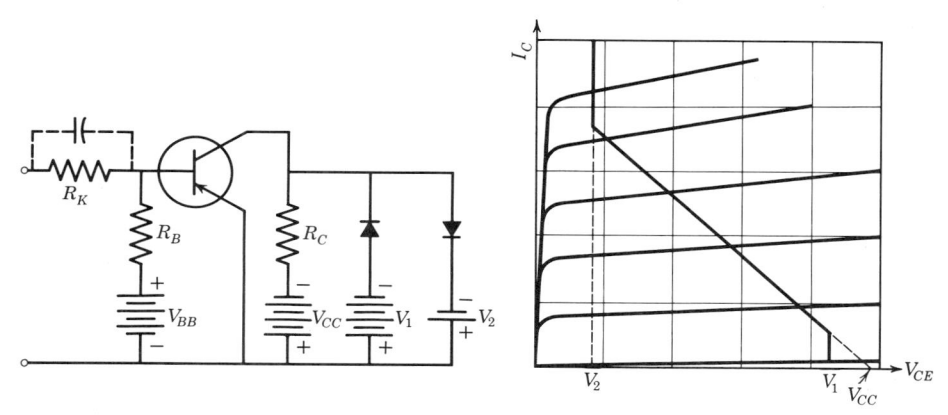

Fig. 15-4. Clamping method to prevent saturation.

If the basic transistor switch is allowed to go into saturation, any circuitry formed out of the transistor switch is said to operate in the *saturation mode*. If saturation is prevented by the above scheme or any other, the circuitry formed out of the basic transistor switch is said to operate in the *current mode*.

Before concluding this section we should also note that the basic *common-emitter* switch studied here is often called an "inverter" in computer language. This is simply because voltage or current changes in the input are opposite those in the output for the common-emitter circuit (because of 180° phase shift). Thus this common-emitter switch automatically performs inversion in the logic sense. The inverter is considered to be one of the basic logic functions required for computer circuitry.

This concludes the discussion of the basic transistor switch. We will now consider those circuits that use transistor switches to form trigger digital circuits.

TRIGGERED DIGITAL CIRCUITS

In this section we will describe bistable multivibrators (flip-flops), astable multivibrators, monostable multivibrators, and the Schmitt trigger. We will consider all of these as triggered digital circuits. As the name implies, triggered digital circuits have an external input (or trigger) that controls the digital switching.

The next section will consider "logical gated" circuits, as opposed to the triggered digital circuits. Both types make use of various combinations of basic switching circuits to form desired digital operations. The chief difference between the two types of circuits is the presence of the trigger in the triggered digital circuits. In addition we will see that the triggered circuits are highly developed (special) digital circuits, whereas the "logical circuits" refer to general combinations of digital switches.

Essentially, then, the triggered digital circuits considered here are combinations of basic switching circuits that involve the use of an external trigger to either coordinate or control their switching.

For each circuit considered below we will first describe the switching action qualitatively. Then the most basic quantitative relations for that circuit will be depicted.

FLIP-FLOPS (BISTABLE MULTIVIBRATORS). In digital circuitry the most frequently occurring circuit is the flip-flop, or the bistable multivibrator. Basically the flip-flop has two stable states; application of a trigger causes the flip-flop to change state. Since every application of two triggers returns the flip-flop to its original state, it is a basic binary circuit. This circuit serves as the basic "storage" circuit for binary digits in a digital computer, and is the basic unit in counters, shift registers, and many other devices that operate in a binary fashion.

With regard to the circuit the flip-flop is a combination of two basic switches, which are coupled so that when one is in the OFF condition the other *must* be in the ON condition, and vice versa. If the switches are allowed to go into saturation, the flip-flop is said to operate in the *saturation mode*. If the switch operation is restricted to the borders of the active region, the flip-flop operates in the *current*

Digital switching circuits

mode. The saturation mode circuit is simpler, and more basic. For this reason we will concentrate mainly on the saturated flip-flop.

The basic flip-flop is shown in Figure 15-5. This should be looked at as two coupled common-emitter switches. The output can be taken from either collector; we show it as taken from the right-side collector. The trigger for a flip-flop is usually made to either turn the ON transistor OFF (positive pulses), or turn the OFF transistor ON (negative pulses). Thus a "steering network" is usually required, which steers the pulses to the correct base. Figure 15-5 simply shows that a trigger can be placed onto either base.

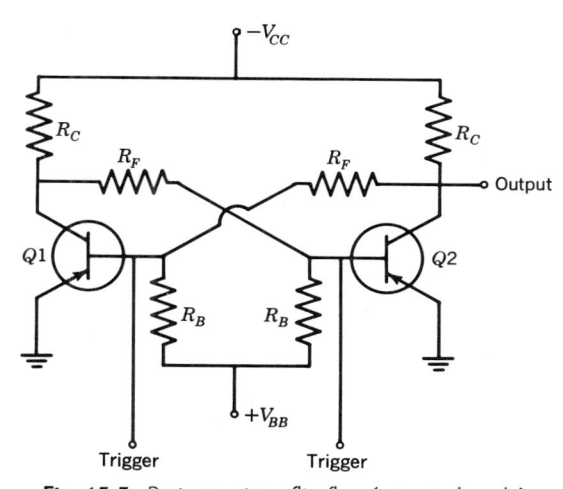

Fig. 15-5. Basic transistor flip-flop (saturated mode).

Before noting the basic action of this circuit, let us quickly review the approximate circuit conditions for both the ON and the OFF condition. The approximate voltage and current values are as follows:

(ON) *Saturation Conditions*   (OFF) *Cutoff Conditions*

$$V_{CE} \approx 0 \quad \text{(P-N-P)} \quad V_{CE} \approx \frac{-V_{cc}R_F}{R_F + R_C}$$

$$I_C \approx \frac{V_{cc}}{R_C} \quad\quad\quad I_C \approx 0 \tag{12}$$

$$V_{BE} = (0^-) \quad \text{(P-N-P)} \quad V_{BE} = (0^+)$$

$$I_B > \frac{I_{C_{\text{sat}}}}{h_{FE}} \quad\quad\quad I_B \approx 0$$

The basic circuit action of this flip-flop can now be reviewed as follows:

1. Assume that $Q1$ is ON; then $Q2$ is OFF if the flip-flop is designed correctly. Note that V_{BE_1} is slightly less than zero.

2. Now assume that a positive trigger pulse is placed on the base of the ON transistor ($Q1$). Assume that this trigger is sufficient (through a regenerative action) to turn $Q1$ OFF.

3. When $Q1$ turns OFF, the collector voltage of $Q1$ goes from 0 volts to a negative V_{CC}. Thus there is a negative "step" occurring at the collector voltage.

4. This negative step voltage is coupled to the base of $Q2$ by the resistor (voltage) division network $R_F - R_B$. Since a negative signal applied to the base is in the direction to produce forward bias, $Q2$ will be turned ON.

5. Consequently, we now have $Q2$ ON and $Q1$ OFF, which is a change of state from the starting point. If a positive pulse is now placed on the base of $Q2$ the above sequence of steps will again take place and the circuit will return to its original state. This is the basic way in which a flip-flop works.

Each of the transistor actions could be viewed on the load diagram, as depicted in Figure 15-1. For example, $Q1$ was moved from point B to point A, whereas $Q2$ was moved from A to B. During the time that the circuit is traversing the active region (between A and B) the gain of each transistor switch is effective in determining the switching time. With transistors connected in this way, a regenerative (positive) feedback occurs during the switching. Thus, although one starts the action externally with the trigger applied to the base, regeneration occurs when the circuit begins to switch and in effect the circuit continues to switch itself. This regenerative action during the switching time has often been called "multivibrator action."

We will now consider the fundamental equations that apply to this basic saturated flip-flop circuit. This will not be an attempt to describe a design procedure, which is best dealt with either in manufacturer's application notes or in more specialized treatises. The objective here is to look at the most basic equations which apply, so that more complicated procedures can be followed with understanding.

In flip-flop circuit design, the essential requirement is to assure that the circuit conditions (biases and resistors) are such as to require

Digital switching circuits

either saturation or cutoff. We will now write the basic steady state equations which must be fulfilled in order to assure that the transistor be either in saturation or in cutoff. Consider the extracted part of the circuit shown in Figure 15-6(a). This diagram shows the

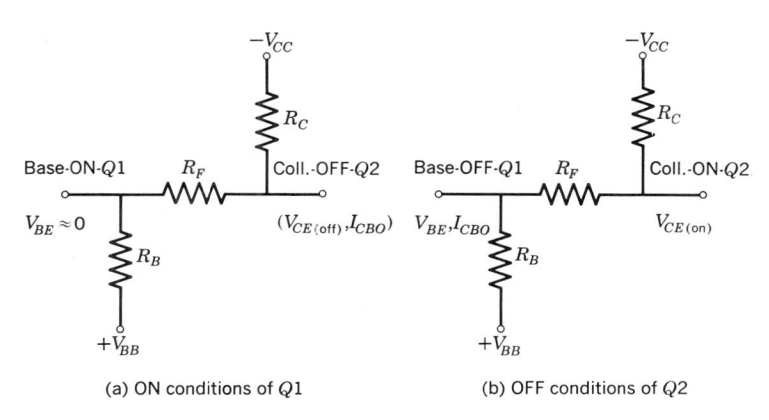

Fig. 15-6. Circuit analysis for flip-flop.

(a) ON conditions of Q1

(b) OFF conditions of Q2

crucial part of the circuitry, and the voltage conditions, when $Q1$ is ON. $Q1$ will be in saturation only if its current exceeds the minimum saturation current; using Equations (5) and (7) this is shown to be

$$I_{B1\min} > \frac{V_{CC}}{h_{FE} R_C}$$

$$\frac{V_{CC}}{R_F + R_C} - \frac{V_{BB}}{R_B} > \frac{V_{CC}}{h_{FE} R_C} \quad \begin{pmatrix} V_{BE(\text{sat})} = 0 \\ I_{CBO} = 0 \end{pmatrix} \quad (13)$$

Thus, Equation (13) must be met in order to assure that the transistor will go fully into the ON (saturated) state.

For the cutoff condition one can use the extracted part of the circuit shown in Figure 15-6(b). Since the collector for the ON transistor is at approximately 0 volts, it is seen that the V_{BE} can be written as

$$V_{BE} = \frac{V_{BB}}{R_B + R_F} \times R_F \geq 0 \qquad (V_{CE} = 0) \qquad (14)$$

Note that V_{BE} is a positive voltage, and the voltage value equals the reverse bias on the emitter junction. There is some latitude in the degree of reverse bias used. The greater V_{BE} is made the more protection there is against noise accidentally triggering the circuit. However, it would also require a larger trigger signal to trigger the circuit.

Although Equations (13) and (14) give a straightforward picture of the requirements for switch operation, a typical design will usually require further calculation. Since transistor parameters change (with age, temperature, and unit-to-unit) one must consider the effect of such changes on the switching requirements. One method of treatment is to assume that all the changes adversely affect the switching requirement. This produces a reliable, although conservative design. As an example, let us account for all the voltages and currents in the flip-flop segments of Figure 15-6, and then find the R_B tolerance based on the tolerances of the individual parameter. Assume that h_{FE}, $V_{BE(\text{on})}$, $V_{CE(\text{sat})}$, and I_{CBO} are all transistor parameters subject to some variation (above all these except h_{FE} were approximated to be zero). From Equation (13) we see that the minimum $R_B(\underline{R}_B)$ is defined by the ON requirement; from Equation (14), the maximum $R_B(\overline{R}_B)$ is set by the OFF requirement. We can now use Figure 15-6(a) to evaluate the minimum R_B to assure saturation. This is done by writing the complete equation [similar to (13)], accounting for all voltages and the I_{CBO} of the opposite OFF transistor. Figure 15-6(b) can be used in the same way for the maximum R_B to assure cut-off. We will evaluate both $\overline{R}_B$ and $\underline{R}_B$ in terms of the maximum and minimum transistor parameters. Referring to Figure 15-6:

$$\text{ON:} \quad R_B > \underline{R}_B = \frac{V_{BB} + V_{BE(\text{on})}}{\dfrac{V_{CC} - R_C \overline{I}_{CBO} - \overline{V}_{BE(\text{on})}}{R_F + R_C} - \dfrac{1}{h_{FE}}\left(\dfrac{V_{CC} - \underline{V}_{CE(\text{sat})}}{R_C} - \dfrac{\underline{V}_{BE(\text{off})} + \underline{V}_{CE(\text{sat})}}{R_F}\right)}$$

$$\text{OFF:} \quad R_B < \overline{R}_B = \frac{V_{BB} - V_{BE(\text{off})}}{\dfrac{\overline{V}_{BE(\text{off})} + \overline{V}_{CE(\text{sat})}}{R_F} + \overline{I}_{CBO}} \tag{15}$$

Note that an "underline" indicates a minimum value, while an "overline" indicates a maximum one. Often the manufacturer provides the maximum and minimum values used in Equation (15). Even if the maximum and minimum values are not used, Equation (15) serves as a more accurate definition of the switching requirements than Equations (13) and (14). Note that these equations apply to both P-N-P and N-P-N transistors.

Digital switching circuits

Again it should be noted that one can ascertain more accurately the actual cutoff and saturation conditions (such as V_{sat} and V_{off}) by using the Ebers-Moll equations (discussed later). However, such accuracy is usually not necessary for most design situations. Our objective here is to concentrate on the main items, and avoid losing these items in the detail.

Having now noted the basic qualitative operation and basic quantitative situation for saturated flip-flop, we consider some auxiliary factors. First of all, saturated flip-flops have their repetition speed limited by the storage time of the transistor. Consequently, very often one will build a nonsaturated flip-flop. This can be accomplished by incorporating clamping diodes on each transistor in a manner similar to those in Figure 15-4. The clamping diodes may be placed either in the collector circuit or the emitter circuit. Flip-flops operating in this manner are said to operate in the "current mode," rather than the saturation mode.

Finally, the trigger circuits of flip-flops deserve some mention. If one wishes to operate with a single-polarity pulse, one must alternate the trigger from Q1, then Q2, etc. Various "steering circuits" have been evolved to accomplish this. Figure 15-7 shows the flip-

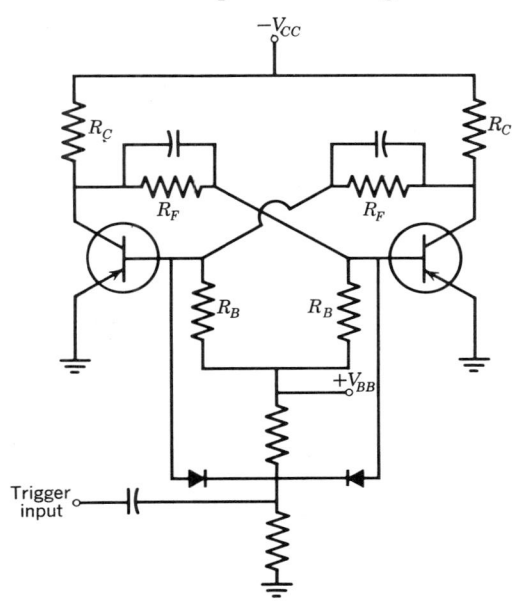

Fig. 15-7. Transistor flip-flop including speed-up capacitors and trigger steering circuit.

flop circuit used previously with the addition of a basic steering circuit. As an exercise, the reader could analyze how this circuit puts a negative pulse alternately on the base of that transistor which is OFF.

Figure 15-7 also shows the addition of "speed-up capacitors" across the coupling resistors R_K. These play the same role as the speed-up capacitors discussed before for the basic switch.

ASTABLE MULTIVIBRATORS. The astable multivibrator is a type of nonsinusoidal oscillator; it has no stable state and hence constantly "oscillates." Often its oscillating or "multivibrating" is coordinated with other circuitry by a trigger. The astable multivibrator consists of two coupled switches similar to the flip-flop; however, the coupling now is via capacitors. It is the energy storage capability of these coupling capacitors that cause constant dynamic action with no stable quiescent point of operation.

As in the flip-flop, a basic property is that the transistor will either be fully ON or fully OFF, except during the switching time. Also, a transistor being in one state means that the other transistor must be in the other state. However, whenever any one combination exists, the opposite combination is always building up, so that a reversal will take place. This is in contrast to the previous flip-flop where an overt external trigger was required to change state. Although no external trigger is actually used for changing the state in the multivibrator, the trigger may be used to synchronize the oscillations with other circuitry.

The basic circuit diagram of a saturated astable multivibrator is shown in Figure 15-8. This basic diagram is very similar to that of the flip-flop shown before in Figure 15-5, except that the coupling element is now a capacitor between the collector and the opposite base in both cases.

The self-sustaining action of this multivibrator is caused by the energy storage of these capacitors. In general, when a transistor turns from the OFF to the ON state, it, in effect, puts a step voltage input into the coupling capacitor. Since this coupling capacitor cannot change voltage instantaneously it produces a large step voltage at the opposite base, which then begins an elementary RC decay time (see Chapter 6). When the decaying voltage reaches a transition point, the circuit will "reflip" and go to the opposite state. This

Digital switching circuits

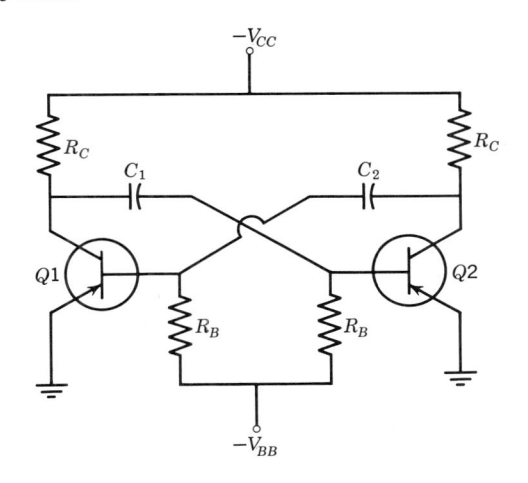

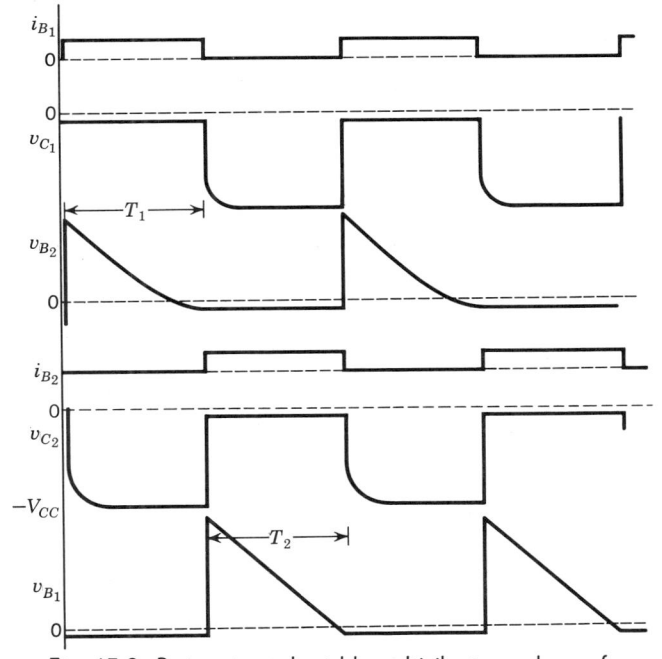

Fig. 15-8. Basic saturated astable multivibrator and waveforms.

action will keep repeating itself, since one or the other of the capacitors will be thus discharging.

Let us describe the operation by referring to the waveforms shown in Figure 15-8. Since we are here dealing with a continuous process we must interrupt the process at some (assumed) starting point to begin tracing the action. This is more difficult than in the flip-flop where the two stable states existed.

The qualitative action of the multivibrator can be portrayed as follows:

1. Assume that we begin at that point at which $Q1$ has just turned ON. Just prior to $Q1$'s turning ON, the capacitor $C1$ was charged because its right side was at 0 volts (the base voltage of the ON transistor) while the left side was at $-V_{CC}$ (collector of OFF transistor).

2. When the transistor $Q1$ turns ON, this stored charge on the capacitor causes the coupling circuit to act as though a positive step input of voltages has been applied to a series CR circuit. This puts a positive step voltage onto the base of $Q2$, as shown in Figure 15-8.

3. This positive voltage on the base of $Q2$ immediately cuts off this transistor. Thus the switching action is effected; when one transistor turns ON the other must turn OFF.

4. The next action is that the stored charge that was responsible for the positive step voltage on the base of $Q2$ now decays, with its decay path being through R_B and back through the ON transistor. This time constant is relatively large (compared to the "charging time constant" to be discussed). In any case, the $Q2$ base voltage waveform (v_{B2}) decays as shown in Figure 15-8.

5. When the base voltage crosses 0 volts it will turn $Q2$ ON again. Now the $Q1$ base voltage will experience the decaying voltage from $C2$'s discharge.

6. When $Q1$ is turned OFF, as a result of $Q2$ coming ON, the capacitor will *charge* via the R_C-C_1 path and through the $Q2$ ON transistor. This time constant is much shorter than the discharge time constant (R_B-C_1). Thus for each side, it is the discharging time constant that controls the time between reversals.

The above, then, is the qualitative action of the astable multivibrator.

It is again possible to obtain the basic quantitative evaluation of the circuit by extracting pertinent parts of the circuit and considering the behavior at certain times. Consider the circuit in Figure

Digital switching circuits

15-9(a) and (b). Figure 15-9(a) demonstrates the action just after $Q1$ is turned ON. We are interested in writing the basic equation for the voltage of this circuit.

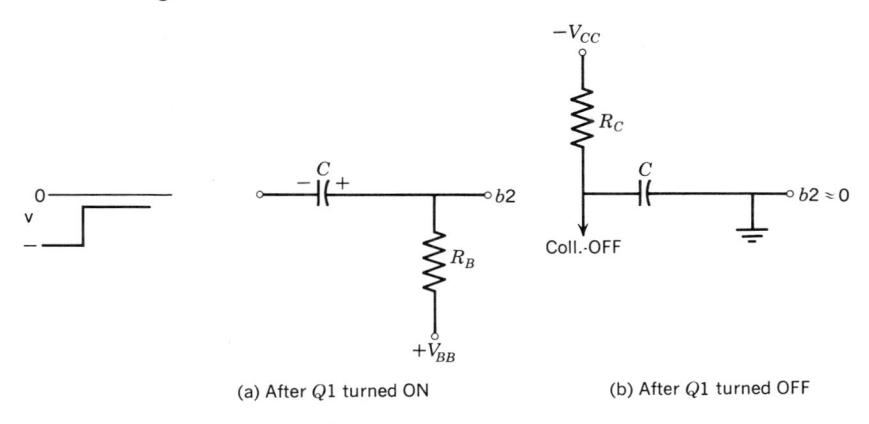

(a) After $Q1$ turned ON   **(b) After $Q1$ turned OFF**

Fig. 15-9. Circuit analysis for multivibrator.

The action just after $Q1$ is turned ON can be construed as applying a positive step voltage (of value V_{CC}) to the RC circuit depicted in Figure 15-9(a). For any step voltage applied to such an RC circuit the output is always given as

$$e_{\text{out}} = B_1 + B_2 e^{-t/RC} \tag{16}$$

The unknown constants B_1 and B_2 can be found by evaluating Equation (16) at the terminal times ($t = 0$ and $t = \infty$). For the conditions here we know that at $t = 0$ (immediately after $Q1$ is turned ON) $v_{B2} = +V_{CC}$ since the collector experienced a positive step of V_{CC} and this must be passed onto the base because the voltage cannot change instantaneously across the capacitor. At $t = \infty$ the v_{b2} would equal $-V_{BB}$ (if it were allowed to proceed that far). We shall see that it will stop short of $-V_{BB}$ since $Q2$ turns ON when it reaches zero. Equation (17) shows the conditions that determine B_1 and B_2, and the resulting values. The voltage v_{b2}, then, caused by the decaying

$$\text{at } t = \infty, \quad v_{B2} = -V_{BB} \left(\begin{smallmatrix}\text{unless}\\\text{interrupted}\end{smallmatrix}\right) \quad \therefore B_1 = -V_{BB} \tag{17}$$
$$\text{at } t = 0, \quad v_{B2} = +V_{CC} \quad \therefore B_2 = V_{BB} + V_{CC}$$

Discharge current from capacitor (just after cutoff) is given by

$$v_{B2} = (V_{BB} + V_{CC})e^{-t/R_B C} - V_{BB} \tag{18}$$

Although this is the "discharge curve," it will not complete the discharge all the way to $-V_{BB}$ because Q2 will turn ON when the voltage crosses zero. Therefore we can solve for time T_1, the discharge cycle time for C_1, by setting v_{B2} to zero:

$$0 = (V_{BB} + V_{CC})e^{-T_1/Rc} - V_{BB}$$

$$\therefore T_1 = R_B C \ln \frac{V_{BB} + V_{CC}}{V_{BB}} \tag{19}$$

where T_1 = one side of the cycle time for multivibrator.

A similar equation would apply to the "opposite cycle"—that is, the cycle in which the opposite capacitor is discharging and at the end of which discharge Q1 would turn ON. We need not go through this derivation again; if the T_2 time constant (for C_2) is different one would have to substitute the proper values. These time constants are shown on Figure 15-8.

The remaining action to consider is the capacitor charge time, which occurs directly after the associated transistor is turned OFF. In typical multivibrator circuits this time constant is made very short. The extracted circuit diagram applying to this charge time is shown in Figure 15-9(b). When the transistor is turned OFF this amounts to putting a negative step of $-V_{CC}$ volts on the resistor-capacitor series circuit. (The capacitor has essentially zero charge at this point since both the connected collector and base are near 0 volts.) In response to the applied step, the voltage across the capacitor will build up according to the equation

$$v_{C1} = -V_{CC}(1 - e^{-t/R_C C}) \tag{20}$$

This time behavior is indicated in the collector voltage diagrams of Figure 15-8. Usually the time constant $R_C \times C$ is made much less than the time constant $R_B \times C$. This means that the *discharging* time constant of Equation (19) controls the half-cycle time. The frequency of "oscillation" of the circuit, then, is given by

$$f = \frac{1}{T_1 + T_2} \tag{21}$$

Consequently, the rise time (or charge time) for the condenser will

Digital switching circuits 449

be quite rapid and this is indicated in Figure 15-8. Based on the foregoing, then, all the waveforms shown in Figure 15-8 can be justified. At this point it is helpful to trace carefully through these waveforms for a clearer understanding of this action.

The requirements for the d-c conditions of this multivibrator are similar to those for the flip-flop. Since there are no R_F in this circuit, substituting $R_F = \infty$ into the previous d-c equations yields

$$\text{ON:} \quad R_B \leq \frac{(V_{BB} - V_{BE(\text{on})})}{V_{CC} - V_{CE(\text{sat})}} R_C$$

$$\text{OFF:} \quad R_B \geq \frac{V_{BB} - V_{BE(\text{off})}}{I_{CBO}} \tag{22}$$

The ON equation will be the more important in restricting R_B.

Note again that we have described here a saturated astable multivibrator. One can operate in the current mode so that saturation is avoided. However, we will leave these complexities to further study.

It should be remembered that the multivibrator is in many respects similar to an oscillator of the feedback type. Its cycling is self-sustaining. One could obtain sinusoidal oscillations out of it if one were to use a resonant circuit as the load.

MONOSTABLE MULTIVIBRATORS. The next triggered digital circuit that we will consider is the monostable multivibrator. For this multivibrator application of a small "trigger" input pulse causes a much larger output pulse whose width is the critical factor. One major application of a monostable multivibrator is in providing a given desired *delay*. Thus the monostable multivibrator has an output pulse whose width is controlled by the designer. Monostable multivibrators are typically called "one-shots" by circuit designers.

As the name implies, the monostable multivibrator has only a single stable state. The basic action is that an input pulse (or trigger) temporarily moves the circuit from its stable state. The circuit remains thus "moved" for a prearranged amount of time, and then returns to its stable state.

As in previous digital circuits, the monostable multivibrator is made up of two coupled basic switches. In this case, as shown in Figure 15-10, the one coupling element is a capacitor (as in the a stable multivibrator) and the other is a resistor (as in the flip-flop). Note that the resistor R_{B_2} is often connected to the collector bias source; then $V_{BB_2} = V_{CC}$. As in previous circuits, if one transistor is in one state, the other transistor must be in the other state. The waveform of Figure 15-10 shows that the pulse width is determined by the decay curve of v_{B2}, similar to the controlling factor in the

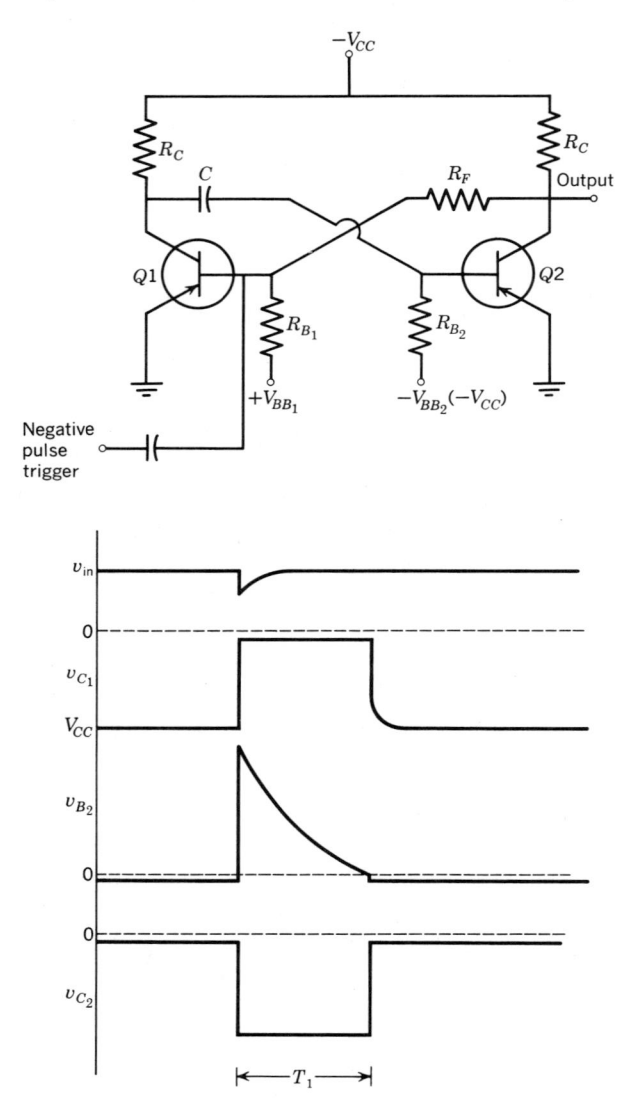

Fig. 15-10. Monostable multivibrator and waveforms.

Digital switching circuits   451

astable multivibrator. As a matter of fact, the action here is similar to a one-half cycle of astable multivibrator action. Typically the "delay interval" is determined by the discharge time of the capacitor when the associated transistor is cut off. By doing this the time constant can be made independent of the transistor parameters, and is dependent only upon the circuitry.

The d-c conditions for the multivibrator can be determined in a fashion similar to those for the flip-flop. Thus Equation (15) will apply to the $Q1$ circuit design, whereas Equation (22) will apply to the $Q2$ circuit design.

The qualitative circuit action can be described as follows:

    1. Assume that the transistor $Q1$ is normally OFF and transistor $Q2$ is ON. With $Q2$ being normally ON, the capacitor C is charged, having voltage $-V_{CC}$ on its left-hand plate and about zero on the right-hand plate.

    2. If a negative trigger on the base of $Q1$ now turns $Q1$ ON, its collector (v_{C1}) will increase from $-V_{CC}$ to approximately zero. This puts a positive step voltage onto the R_B-C circuit, which drives the base of $Q2$ upward.

    3. This upward positive voltage on the base of $Q2$ turns $Q2$ OFF. Now the important "width-determining" action of the monostable multivibrator comes into play. The time at which the circuit will reset itself is determined by the decay curve of the discharging capacitor. (This is similar to the astable operation.)

    4. When the voltage v_{B2} has decayed to zero, the circuit will

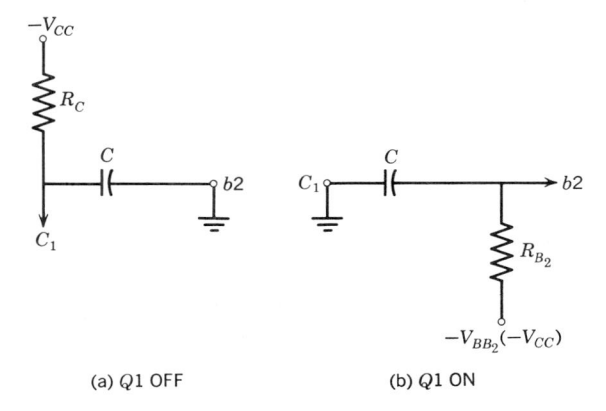

(a) $Q1$ OFF   (b) $Q1$ ON

Fig. 15-11. Circuit analysis for monostable multivibrator.

reset itself and the one-shot output pulse will have been accomplished. The output waveform (v_{C2}) would appear as shown in Figure 15-10.

We will not go into much detail in the quantitative analysis here because the analysis is similar to the astable multivibrator case. We will, however, indicate the results by referring to Figure 15-11. In part (a) of this figure it is seen that when Q1 is OFF, the capacitor will attain a voltage of $-V_{CC}$. This charge curve for this voltage is quite short compared to the decay curve, as indicated in the Figure 15-10 waveform. Assume Q1 is triggered ON by an input trigger; then, by reasoning analogous to that for the astable multivibrator, the v_{B2} can be written as

$$v_{B2} = (V_{CC} + V_{BB})(1 - e^{-t/R_{B_2}C}) - V_{CC} \qquad (23)$$

Solving for the time at which the waveform reaches zero (which is the time at which it will reset itself), the pulse width, or the delay time of the output pulse, is given by

$$\begin{aligned} T_1 &= R_{B_2}C \ln \frac{V_{CC} + V_{BB_2}}{V_{BB_2}} \\ &= R_{B_2}C \ln 2 \quad \text{if } V_{BB_2} = V_{CC} \end{aligned} \qquad (24)$$

Many times V_{BB_2} is made equal to V_{CC}; Equation (24) shows the result for this case.

In summary, the monostable multivibrator can be considered as a circuit having a single stable state. When moved out of that state it will return in a predesigned time.

SCHMITT TRIGGER. Another multivibrator that is extremely useful in digital circuits is the Schmitt trigger. Basically the Schmitt trigger converts any input waveform into a square-wave output. It does this by switching in one direction whenever the input reaches a given positive level, and switching in the other direction for a given negative level. Frequently the positive and negative input "trigger levels" are incrementally close to zero; in such cases the Schmitt trigger switches essentially at the zero-crossings of the input waveform. In fact, one of the main uses of the Schmitt trigger is as a zero-crossing detector.

Digital switching circuits

In general, they are used as "decision circuits" for determining when an input waveform crosses a predetermined level.

The Schmitt trigger is a type of multivibrator; it has the basic multivibrator action of having one transistor change from the ON to the OFF state while the other transistor changes from the OFF to the ON state. The coupling that is used for the Schmitt trigger is as is shown in Figure 15-12. This circuit may be compared to that of a

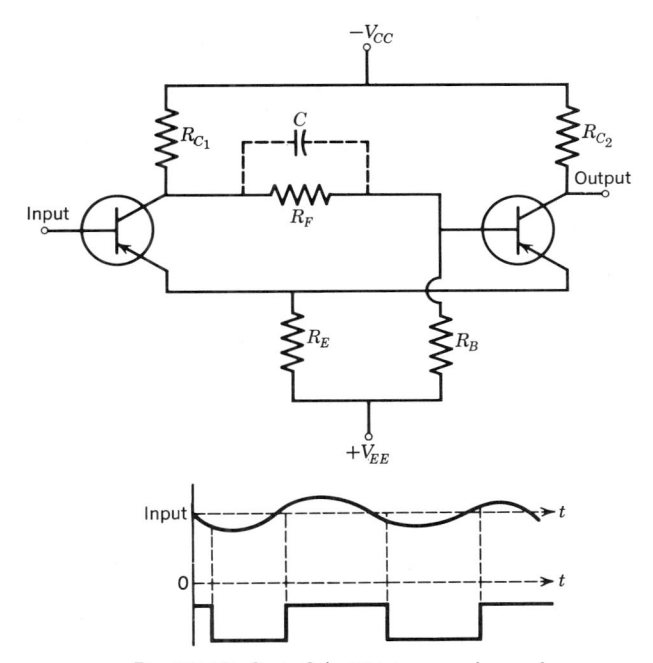

Fig. 15-12. Basic Schmitt trigger and waveforms.

basic flip-flop. It is apparent that one side of the coupling is similar to that of a typical flip-flop. The other side of the coupling is formed by having the two transistors share a resistor in their emitter leads (R_E). It will be seen that this resistor forms an additional regeneration action during the multivibrating action, so that this circuit changes states faster than flip-flops.

The "trigger" for this circuit would of course be the input waveform, as depicted in Figure 15-12. This circuit would remain in its given state except in response to the input waveform or trigger.

The circuit description of this can be stated as follows:
   1. Assume that $Q1$ is originally OFF and $Q2$ is ON.

2. Now assume that the input voltage crosses a given negative value so that it turns $Q1$ ON.

3. The turning ON of $Q1$ will immediately raise the $Q1$ collector voltage from $-V_{CC}$ to approximately zero. This is directly coupled to the base of $Q2$ and will start to turn $Q2$ OFF by raising the base voltage.

4. In addition to this action on the base, the emitter of $Q2$ is being decreased; when $Q1$ is turned from OFF to ON, the emitter potential is reduced toward zero. Consequently, the base is raised and the emitter is lowered in the same regenerative action; this accounts for the great speed of the Schmitt trigger.

5. When the waveform crosses a positive reference voltage, the reverse action happens and the transistors are put back in their initial state.

Note that there is no capacitive charging action here since the transistors are resistively coupled. The d-c conditions for this case can be evaluated by applying the cutoff and saturation conditions, as was done for the flip-flop.

LOGICAL GATING CIRCUITS

In the above section we considered triggered digital switching circuits. These essentially were combinations of basic transistor switches (discussed in the first section) that usually required an associated external trigger. Another basic issue in those triggered circuits was that these particular combinations of basic digital switches are so widely used and are the basic components for so many circuits that special attention is given to them and to their particular design procedures (flip-flops, and multivibrator).

The logical gating circuits considered here are also formed by combining basic switches. The issue here is that these circuits represent particular combinations of basic switches that perform certain "logic" functions. These logic circuits, in combination with the triggered digital circuits make up the bulk of the digital circuitry both in computers and in other functions.

By logical gating circuits we mean simply those combinations of basic digital switches that form the fundamental logical operation

Digital switching circuits   455

of AND, OR, and their inversions NOT-AND (NAND) and NOT-OR (NOR).

We will see that the particular coupling method is an important feature in logical operations. Whereas the digital triggered circuits considered before usually had one single input and one single output, the logical circuits here have many inputs and one output (but this one output may have to feed many stages).

The basic idea of these circuits is that they evaluate a set of input conditions and provide a prearranged output. Thus, the AND-gate will produce an "output" only if *all* the parallel inputs have voltages present. The OR-gate will operate if *either* or all of a number of inputs are present.

Logic circuits are often identified by the coupling that is used between the various logic stages. Thus "resistor-transistor logic" implies that the coupling elements are resistors. In "direct-coupled logic" the transistors are coupled directly to each other, without intervening elements.

We will discuss the basic logic circuits for both of these cases.

RESISTOR-TRANSISTOR LOGIC (RTL). The basic idea in resistor-transistor logic consists of forming a current-summing network and causing a switching transistor to supply the current to this network. This is shown in Figure 15-13. Either an AND-circuit or an OR-

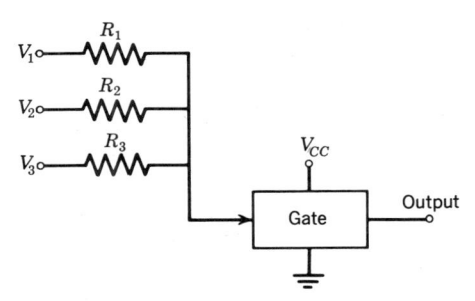

Fig. 15-13. Fundamental AND- or OR-circuit.

circuit (or the NAND and NOR) can be formed with this basic idea. Consider that the gate is initially in the ON state (the saturated state). If the transistor is normally saturated, then all the voltages would have to be turned OFF in order to turn the gate OFF, since any one (or all) of the sources can supply the current necessary to keep the transistor ON. This, then, would form a basic AND function. On the other hand, consider biasing the switching transistor so that it is normally OFF. Then any single one of the voltages V_1, V_2, or V_3 could turn the transistor ON; in that case the OR function would be formed. It is seen that the basic resistor-transistor logic circuit can form either the AND or the OR function by simply changing the quiescent condition.

There are two fundamentals involved in the above description:
1. All inputs must be OFF in order to turn an ON switch OFF.
2. Any one input can turn an OFF switch ON.

These are the two aspects fundamental to resistor-transistor logic. The circuits that show the transistor are given in Figure 15-14.

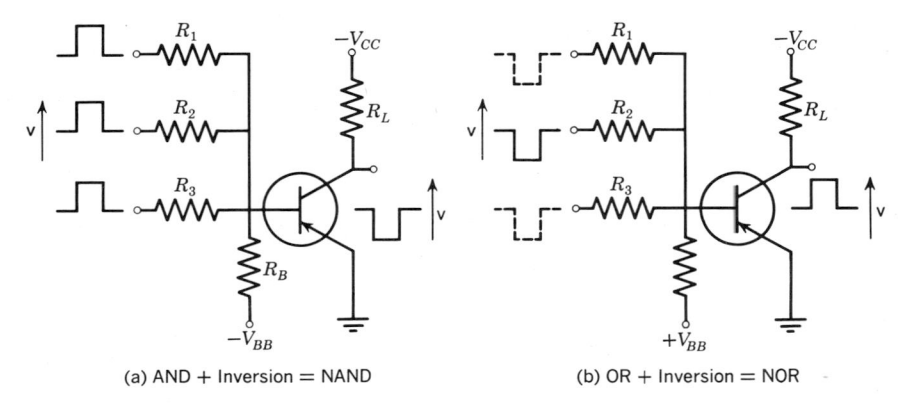

(a) AND + Inversion = NAND (b) OR + Inversion = NOR

Fig. 15-14. Basic resistor-transistor logic (RTL) circuits.

Note that Figure 14(a) shows the basic AND-circuit and Figure 14(b) the basic OR-circuit. The circuits are identical in appearance except for the sign of V_{BB}. The AND-circuit is biased to be normally ON, and positive pulses are required at the inputs. The OR-circuit is biased to be OFF, and negative pulses are required at its input. Note that since the common emitter automatically has the inversion function (the output pulses negative of the input pulses), one actually obtains the NAND and the NOR rather than the AND and the OR. One could use common-base switch circuits to obtain the basic AND and OR function. However, this is usually not necessary. Typically one arranges a logic circuit so that the AND and OR functions are alternated. In such cases the phase reversal (inversion) of the common-emitter gate is appropriate, since the inputs must alternate in sign [compare Figure 15-14(a) with 15-14(b)]. Then

Digital switching circuits

one can just as well operate basically with the NAND and NOR function. The above, then, are the basic logic functions using resistor-transistor logic.

To determine the d-c conditions one must apply the basic ideas depicted before (in studying flip-flops) to the circuit conditions here. For example, consider the AND-circuit of Figure 15-14(a). This transistor is normally ON, and will be turned OFF only if all inputs are present. To effect the OFF condition, then, note that the current would be given by

$$I = \frac{V_1 - V_{BE(\text{off})}}{R_1} + \frac{V_2 - V_{BE(\text{off})}}{R_2} \ldots, \text{etc.} \qquad (25)$$

If this equation is applied to determining the maximum R_B for assuring cutoff, it can be shown that:

$$R_B < \overline{R}_B = \frac{V_{BB} + V_{BE(\text{off})}}{M\dfrac{(V_K - V_{BE(\text{off})})}{R_K} - I_{CBO}} \qquad (26)$$

where R_K = respective input resistors (all have same value),
M = number of inputs.

The same technique can be used to find limiting value of R_B for the ON condition, which can be applied to any single input of the AND-circuit (any single input must be able to turn the transistor ON). Since this equation is rather lengthy, we have not derived it here.

DIRECT-COUPLED TRANSISTOR LOGIC. Another basic method is available for obtaining the AND and the OR function. This method vies in popularity with the system discussed above. In this process the transistors are connected directly without the resistor intervening. This is probably examined best by considering the basic diagrams shown in Figure 15-15. Figure 15-15(a) shows a way to obtain an AND-circuit, and Figure 15-15(b) a way to obtain an OR-circuit. Here the basic logic is performed by the "switching of the inputs," rather than by the resistor-summing network as before. Here the limit is set by the ability to obtain proper drivers.

It is interesting that, prior to the advent of transistors, logic functions were usually handled by the diode method shown in Figure 15-15. However, with the power gain available in transistors, they have largely replaced diodes in logic circuits.

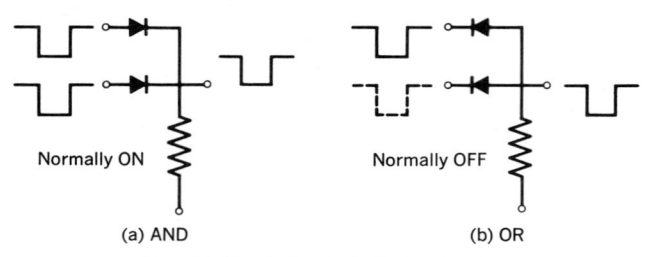

Fig. 15-15. Basic diode logic circuits.

In any case, note that the AND function is achieved by biasing the switches (or diodes) so that they are normally ON. Then it requires that one turn all of them OFF before the output will experience its change as depicted in the diagram. On the other hand, on the OR-circuit the diodes or switches are normally OFF, and either one of them turning ON will fulfill the "change" conditions. In this basic way, then, logic can be performed. Transistors can suitably be used in a similar fashion by operating as shown in Figure 15-16.

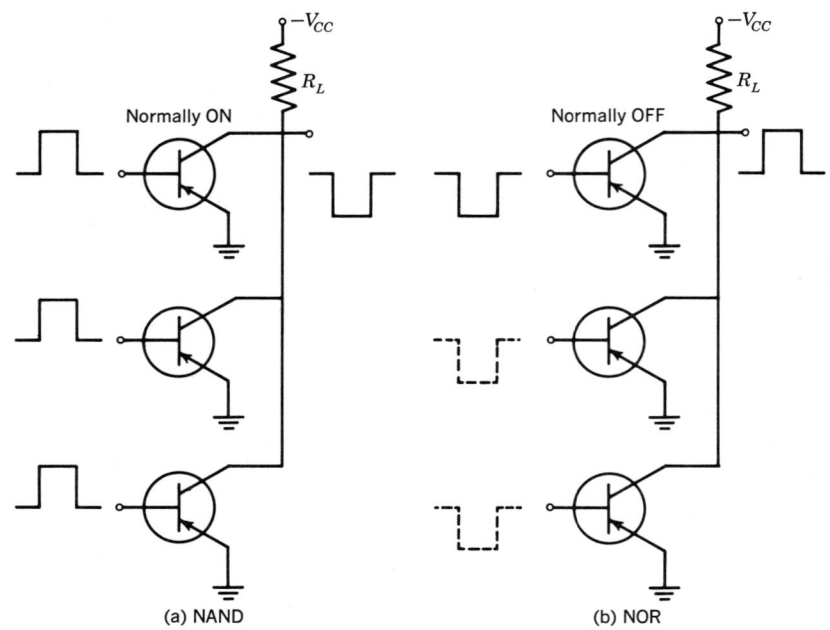

Fig. 15-16. Direct-coupled (parallel) transistor logic (DCTL).

Digital switching circuits

It is seen that the basic idea is exactly as shown before in Figure 15-15 with the diode method. For the AND-circuit the transistors are normally ON (usually saturated) and a positive pulse is required to cut them off. Therefore all inputs must be cut off before the change is noted in the output. In the OR function the transistors are normally cut off and negative pulse is required to turn them ON. Any one of the inputs turned ON will fulfill the conditions for driving the voltage up.

Again it is seen that the same basic circuit serves for both the AND and the OR function. They differ in that the input transistors are normally ON for the AND-circuit, whereas they are normally OFF for the OR-circuit. Also, a given circuit will require positive pulses in the AND condition and negative ones for the OR-circuit.

Referring to Figure 15-16 a very important fact should be noted. Since the process of inversion is always involved with these common-emitter transistor amplifiers, it is again found that in logic circuits one wishes to alternate AND and OR logics. This makes for a very convenient implementation situation. Since it can usually be done for almost any logic functions, this is typically the way circuits will be designed. If this method is impossible in a particular case, of course, a simple inversion stage with a single common-emitter amplifier would have to be inserted.

In the above manner, then, both the NAND and the NOR function can be obtained with the direct-coupling logic. In general, the resistor-transistor logic requires the fewest active elements and permits a high fan-out but is relatively slow. The direct-coupled logic, on the other hand, offers a much higher speed capability but requires many active elements (transistors), and the transistor parameters are critical.

There is still another form of combining transistors in direct-coupled logic, which should be mentioned here. That is, transistors can be added in series (at least up to a certain amount) as shown in Figure 15-17. This circuit can serve as an AND-gate for negative input signals and an OR-gate for positive signals. If the transistors are turned ON, the voltage across the base-to-emitter is

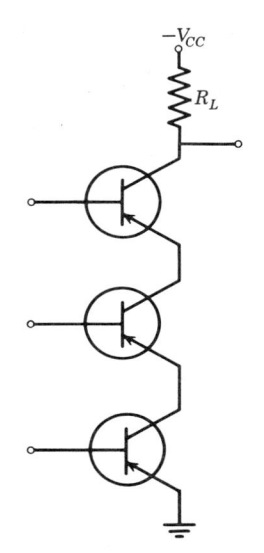

Fig. 15-17. Direct-coupled (series) transistor logic.

so low that each driver stage of the series can be connected to ground with little effect. However, there is a limit to the amount of stages that can be stacked in this way. In addition, the transistors in series for a given load current require more base drive in the ON state than do transistors in parallel gates.

The basic logic functions we have considered, then, can be combined with any number of inputs (fan-in) and outputs (fan-out). Various logical operations within computers and other specialized equipment are formed with just such special building blocks. As we noted, these basic logic elements and other possible combinations are combined with other digital switching circuits to form various computing and digital circuits.

Besides the coupling methods described here, there are other coupling methods possible. However, we cannot pursue these in any detail and refer the reader to more specialized sources on digital circuits. In addition to these methods, chosen because they are the most popular and seem to be the most basic, a form of logic that uses RC transistor-coupled logic is widely used. However, note that the coupling methods we considered here could also be applied to the triggered digital circuits.

ANALYTICAL EXPRESSIONS FOR THE TRANSISTOR

In the previous sections we have seen that the voltage values in the saturation and cutoff regions ($V_{CE(\text{sat})}$, $V_{BE(\text{off})}$, etc.) are of substantial interest in digital circuits. For most purposes we assumed these voltages to be approximately zero (in light of other circuit considerations) or relied on values given by the manufacturer.

Here we wish to note that the relation between currents and voltages in all three regions of transistor operation are possible, given certain measured parameters. First let us review the information given by the characteristics.

Since the transistor graphical characteristics depict the operation of the transistor in all three regions of operation (see Chapter 7), we might expect that any calculations in either the saturation or the cutoff region would have to be done with the use of these characteristics. The difficulty, however, is that the characteristics are usually not accurate in these regions. For example, if we wish to read a V_{CE}

Digital switching circuits

from a set of collector curves for an I_B in the saturation region, the reader will quickly agree (see Figure 7-7) that it is practically impossible to achieve an accurate result. To remedy this situation one could always provide a number of detailed sets of characteristics.

A more reasonable solution, however, is to find a set of mathematical expressions that give the operation in any of the three regions. Such a set of equations was published by Ebers and Moll in December, 1954 (*Proc. I.R.E.*, page 1761). These equations, then, enable us to find the expressions for the entire set of characteristics; hence they describe the action of the transistor in all three regions. In effect these equations define a large signal equivalent circuit.

As already mentioned, these equations have great practical value, among other uses, in finding the operating conditions in the saturation and the cutoff regions. Although the topics covered in this book did not require accurate calculations in these regions, one may need such relations when using detailed design procedures for digital circuits. As was explained, the two major items in pulse circuit analysis and design are the transient response of the circuit and the fixing of the stable states; many times the stable states occur in either the saturation or the cutoff region.

We are not studying the Ebers-Moll equations in detail here for the reasons given. However, the reader should be aware of their existence and is referred to the original source (or text on transistor pulse circuits) for a complete treatment. Nevertheless, it is essential to specify what these equations say, and how this relates to the material that we have covered.

In Chapter 7 it was stressed that the graphical characteristics depict the operation in its entirety whereas the equivalent circuit is accurate only for a small region about a given bias point. When we have the equivalent circuit, of course, we also have mathematical expressions for the given region. It is also true that the a-c equivalent circuit always lies in the *active* region; i.e., the region where the transistor acts as an amplifier. It will be remembered that the a-c equivalent circuit (with h parameters) was used for the small-signal amplifiers, feedback, noise, and for the linear analysis of oscillators and multivibrators.

The Ebers-Moll equations represent an alternative, in a sense, to the use of the characteristics. They, too, deal with the operation of the transistor in all three regions. In fact, the transistor characteristics can be derived from the use of the Ebers-Moll equations. Also, since the mathematical expressions do exist, we have available, in effect, an equivalent circuit of the transistor that is valid in all regions. Since such an equivalent circuit is nonlinear it is of little practical value except in some special cases, and it certainly does not supplant the a-c linear equivalent circuit that we have dealt with.

Although the Ebers-Moll equations give the same sort of information as the characteristics, it should not be construed that they replace these characteristics; it would be very tedious and impractical to use these equations for every purpose to which the characteristics have been put. In the saturation and the cutoff regions, however, these equations do have significant practical value as noted before.

In using the Ebers-Moll equations the essential idea is to measure certain quantities of the transistor and then insert these measured values into the given expressions. If any two of the four variables (two currents and two voltages) are given, the remaining two may then be found by the use of the expressions.

Without any derivation, the Ebers-Moll equations are shown in Equation (27). In this form the unknown currents are written in terms of the unknown voltages. All quantities in these two equations should be regarded as measured constants except V_E, V_C, I_C, and I_E.

$$I_E = \frac{I_{EO}}{1 - \alpha_N \alpha_I}(e^{qV_E/kT} - 1) - \frac{\alpha_N I_{EO}}{1 - \alpha_N \alpha_I}(e^{qV_C/kT} - 1)$$
$$I_C = \frac{\alpha_I I_{CO}}{1 - \alpha_N \alpha_I}(e^{qV_E/kT} - 1) + \frac{I_{CO}}{1 - \alpha_N \alpha_I}(e^{qV_C/kT} - 1)$$
(27)

where V_E = voltage across emitter-base junction,
V_C = voltage across collector-base junction,
I_{EO} = emitter current when collector current is zero and with emitter junction reverse-biased,
I_{CO} = collector current when emitter current is zero and with collector junction reverse-biased,
α_N = normal transistor current gain, corresponding to $-h_{fb}$,
α_I = inverse transistor current gain; the equivalent of $-h_{fb}$ if the emitter is made to serve as a collector and vice versa.

The reader is warned that the voltages appearing in Equation (27) refer only to the junction itself, and not to terminal-to-terminal points. This means that the bulk resistance of the three regions

Digital switching circuits

must be taken into account; usually only the base resistance need be considered.

When using the Ebers-Moll equations one usually starts by estimating the apparent quantities—such as the forward-biased junction voltage, the reverse-biased current, or the ON saturation current. Then one can solve for the other quantities. Using these calculated quantities, the original estimated quantities should then be calculated for correction.

Given all the measured quantities and two of the unknown variables, then, these equations can be used to find the remaining two variables for all three regions of transistor operation.

These are the equations, then, that enable us to accurately find the d-c conditions in the saturation and the cutoff region. As noted, this is vital when dealing with pulse circuits. Again, it is suggested that for further study of these important equations, the original source as well as other available material be consulted. Oftentimes detailed transistor characteristics, such as rise time, are expressed in terms of the parameters of the Ebers-Moll equations.

PROBLEMS

1. Consider the transistor switch (inverter) shown in Figure 15-18. The 1K ohm resistor represents the loading (input impedance) of the following circuitry.

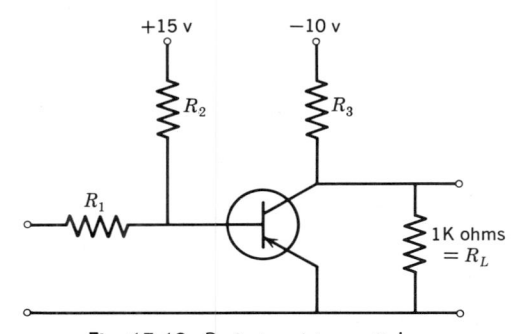

Fig. 15-18. Basic transistor switch.

a) Determine the Thevenin equivalent circuit seen by the collector. This transforms the above circuit into that of Figure 15-2.
b) Assume that $I_{CBO} = 0$. When $V_{BE} > 0$, determine the value of

R_3 such that $V_{CE} = -4$ volts in this OFF condition. Show that if $I_{CBO} = -10$ ma, the value of R_3 just calculated is reduced by only approximately one half of one per cent.

c) Calculate the ON condition transistor collector current, $I_{C(\text{sat})}$, for the value of R_3 found in Part b), given that $V_{CE} = I_{C(\text{sat})}R_{CS} = -0.5$ volts. What is the value of the saturation resistance for this value of $I_{C(\text{sat})}$? What is the percentage error due to neglecting the collector saturation voltage, i.e., assuming it to be zero?

d) Given that the transistor has a h_{FE} of 100, what is the minimum base current needed to supply the $I_{C(\text{sat})}$ calculated in Part c)?

e) Let the input voltage applied to R_1 for the OFF and ON conditions be respectively 0 and -4 volts. Determine the values of R_1 and R_2 such that V_{BE} will be reversed biased to plus 1 volt when the transistor is in the OFF condition (assume that the base current is zero) and that I_B equals twice the value found in Part d) when the transistor is in the ON condition (assume that V_{BE} will be -0.5 volts). The reason for choosing twice the minimum necessary base saturation current is to insure that the transistor is well into the saturation region.

2. a) For the circuit in Figure 15-18 with $R_3 = 1.5$K ohms, plot the OFF condition collector voltage as a function of R_L for values of R_L between 500 ohms and 5K ohms.

b) To maintain a constant OFF condition collector voltage over a wide range of load resistance values, a diode clamp may be added to the circuit shown in Figure 15-18. The cathode of the diode is connected to the transistor collector. The diode anode is connected to a reference voltage supply. Repeat Part a) for this clamped circuit when the reference source is -4 volts. What minimum load resistance would you recommend to a user of this circuit? What effect, if any, does the addition of the diode do to the ON condition?

3. Referring to Figure 15-4, show that the clamping diodes give the three load line segments depicted in the Figure 15-4.

4. a) Add to the basic transistor flip-flop circuit shown in Figure 15-5 a 1K ohm load resistance from each transistor collector to ground. Given that $V_{BB} = +12$ volts, $-V_{CC} = -12$ volts, and $h_{FE} = 100$ for each transistor, determine the values of R_B, R_C, and R_F such that the voltage across the load resistors is alternately 0 and -8 volts. Further require that $I_{B(\text{sat})} = 2\,I_{C(\text{sat})}/h_{FE}$ for the ON condition transistor (assume that $V_{CE} = V_{BE} = 0$), and $V_{BE} = +1$ volt for the OFF condition transistor (assume that $I_C = I_B = 0$).

Digital switching circuits

Calculate the maximum power dissipated in each of the resistors.

b) Demonstrate for the values of R_B, R_C, and R_F calculated in Part a) that the flip-flop will operate satisfactorily when the load resistors are removed. What will the output voltages (V_{CE}) be in this case?

c) Find, for the values of R_B, R_C, and R_F calculated in Part a) the minimum value of load resistance that still maintains the ON transistor in saturation.

5. For the circuit of Figure 15-7, describe how the steering circuit puts a pulse alternately on the base of that transistor which is OFF.

6. a) For the basic saturated astable multivibrator circuit shown in Figure 15-8, calculate the component values given that:
   (1) $-V_{CC} = -V_{BB} = -10$ volts
   (2) A 10 KC operating frequency is required
   (3) Equal "half" cycle times are required
   (4) The discharge time constant is ten times greater than the charge time constant
   (5) The ON condition collector current must be 10 ma (assume $V_{CE(sat)} = 0$).

   b) Assume that the transistors turn on when V_{BE} reaches $-.5$ volts. Sketch carefully the collector and base voltage waveforms for the component values found in Part a).

   c) Find the values for C_1 and C_2 such that one "half" cycle is one-third the other. Use the resistance values found in Part a) and assume that the 10 KC operating frequency is still required.

   d) What is the minimum value of h_{FE} required by the transistors in the circuit designed in Part a)? Will the requirement be altered for the circuit in Part c)?

7. a) Draw a monostable multivibrator circuit with N-P-N transistors analogous to the one shown in Figure 15-10 with P-N-P transistors. Use only one positive and one negative power supply voltage.

   b) Draw the corresponding voltage waveforms for the above N-P-N circuit (see Figure 15-10).

   c) Calculate the resistance for the circuit in Part a) required to provide a delay of 10 milliseconds if $C = 1\mu f$.

8. For the NAND circuit shown in Figure 15-14(a) let $-V_{BB} = -10$ volts and $R_B = 10K$ ohms. If the input voltage levels to each of four equal input resistors, R, are either 0 or V volts, determine the values of V and R such that:
   (1) When all inputs are equal to V the transistor is OFF and $V_{BE(off)} = 0.5$ volt. Assume no base current flows.

(2) When any one input is zero volt and the other three are equal to V the transistor is ON with $V_{BE(\text{on})} = -0.5$ volt. Assume a base current of 10 μamps.

9. For the values found in Problem 8 determine the base to emitter voltage when all four inputs are at zero volt. Assume that the base current increases linearly with base voltage, i.e., $I_B = 20$ μamps/volt $\times V_{BE}$. What is the significance of this answer?

10. Derive the limiting value of R_B for the ON condition, similar to that which was found for the OFF condition in Equation (26).

11. The mathematical tool used with logical gating circuits is Boolean algebra. Arithmetic operations in Boolean algebra relate only the binary numbers 0 and 1. In particular, addition is assigned the meaning of "or" and multiplication the meaning of "and." The results obtained when "adding" and "multiplying" the various combinations of 0's and 1's are:

Addition (or)	Multiplication (and)
$0 + 0 = 0$	$0 \times 0 = 0$
$0 + 1 = 1$	$0 \times 1 = 0$
$1 + 1 = 1$	$1 \times 1 = 1$

Draw both RTL and $DCTL$ implementation of the above operations.

16

High-frequency description of transistors

In this chapter we will consider alternate ways of describing the transistor at high frequencies. Previously we have limited the considerations in this book to low frequencies, except for the 3 db down gain estimates of Chapter 10. The techniques used here allow one to study the circuit behavior precisely over the entire range of frequencies.

In a gross way the high-frequency effects of a transistor can be characterized in the manner shown in Figure 16-1(a). The emitter capacitor $C_{b'e}$ is primarily a *diffusion* capacitance, related to the current flowing through the junction depletion region. $C_{b'c}$ is primarily a *transition* capacitance, due to the electric field across the (reverse-biased) collector junction depletion region. The bulk resistance for each region is depicted as $r_{b'}$, $r_{e'}$, and $r_{c'}$, respectively. Thus it is seen that the frequency dependence of the transistor can be considered in terms of capacitances. The decrease of h_{fe} (considered in Chapter 10) will be approximated by these capacitances.

Figure 16-1 shows an electrical equivalent circuit which approximates the physical structure of the transistor, and exhibits the capacitors of interest. This equivalent circuit is frequently used in the high-frequency area, and will be discussed later.

As was noted in Chapter 10, the low-frequency response of the typical *RC* coupled transistor circuit is determined by interstage coupling capacitors and bypass capacitors of the emitter resistors. The high-frequency response, on the other hand, is determined by the transistor itself. From Figure 16-1 it is seen that the frequency dependence can be approximated by capacitors.

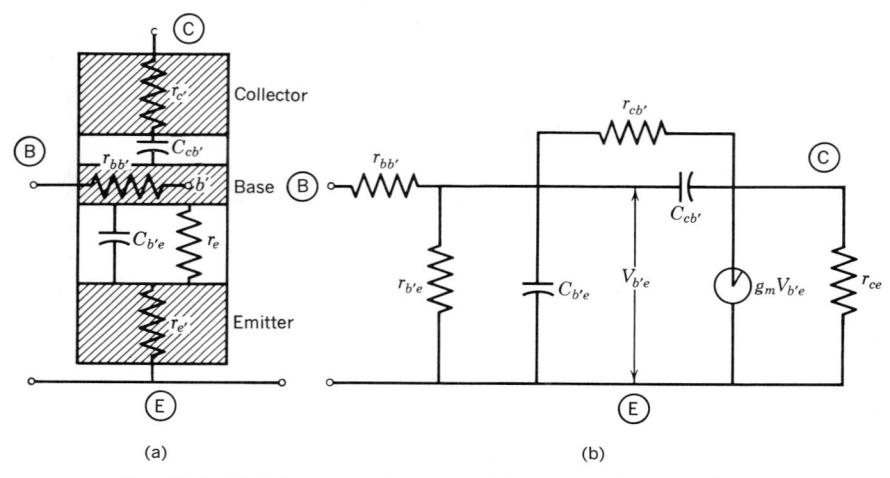

Fig. 16-1. High-frequency description of transistor: (a) gross effects; (b) equivalent circuit.

Our objective in this chapter then is to consider the various ways of describing the transistor, for circuit-design purposes, in the region where these capacitances need to be considered. We will be doing this in a more general way than was done in Chapter 10, where only the 3 db point was to be estimated.

There are two basic approaches to dealing with the circuit aspects of transistors in the high-frequency area. One method consists of using the conventional matrix parameters (such as the h or y), and recognizing that they become complex at the high frequencies. The other method is to use an equivalent circuit closely related to the physical structure of the device (such as Figure 16-1), which will directly reflect the frequency dependence of the device.

If one uses the matrix parameters (either h or y) one must know both the real and the imaginary part of each parameter, at the frequency of interest, in order to calculate the transistor behavior at the given (high) frequency. On the other hand, if one had accurate

High-frequency description of transistors

values of a physical equivalent circuit [such as is shown in Figure 16-1(b)] one does not need to do any more measuring, but can calculate the frequency response at any frequency. However, the latter will always be a relatively complicated calculation; in addition, it is difficult to get parameters so accurate that they hold over the entire frequency region.

For the circuit designer's functions, the matrix parameter method is probably more efficient and precise. If the transistors are specifically designed for high-frequency use, the manufacturer usually specifies the behavior of the y parameters as a function of frequency. The circuit designer can of course measure the particular parameters of interest to him on the particular transistor. In any case, use of matrix parameters allows a precise determination of the circuit behavior from the designer's point of view. Its disadvantage is that the parameter behavior has no resemblance to the physical phenomenon which is causing the frequency dependence of the transistor. The physical equivalent circuit method is necessary for any calculation where one must know the solution as a (closed form) function of frequency. Thus the circuit designer will use this method in derivations, which need only be done once and then can be reused. For example, if one wishes to write a closed equation for the circuit behavior as a function of frequency one must use the physical equivalent circuit method. Any derivations of the transient response also require this method. Manufacturers of the devices find the physical equivalent circuit necessary since it tells them what device alterations would be required to effect a desired response. In this chapter we will consider the essentials of both the matrix and the physical circuit points of view.

We begin by considering the h parameter matrix representation, where the h parameters are complex. The main point in this h parameter treatment will be to emphasize that some of the h parameter equations developed in Chapter 8 are valid in the high-frequency region if the complex parameter values are used.

Next we will develop briefly the y parameter equivalent circuit. This is an appropriate matrix circuit for high-frequency cases. Finally, we will write the basic equations using the physical equivalent circuit depicted in Figure 16-1(b) (called the hybrid-π model). We will illustrate the use of this type of equivalent circuit and compare its use to that of the matrix type.

High-frequency description of transistors

h PARAMETER DESCRIPTION. Figure 16-2 again shows the *h* parameter equivalent circuit that we have used throughout this book. We wish here to emphasize that this equivalent circuit is valid in any frequency region so long as the correct parameters are used. Thus, as frequencies increase, all the *h* parameters become complex and of course change with frequency. (It may be advisable for the reader to review complex quantities and vectors in Chapter 6.)

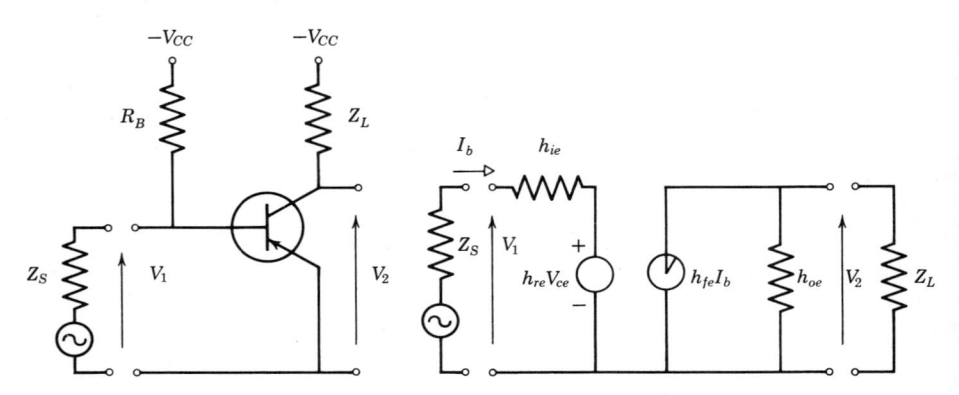

Fig. 16-2. *h* parameter equivalent circuit in high-frequency region.

We can use the *h* parameter derivations of Chapter 8 for most of the performance equations here. For example, the R_i of Equation (11) in Chapter 8 can be written as a complex input impedance:

$$Z_{\text{in}} = h_{ie} - \frac{h_{fe} h_{re} Z_L}{1 + h_o Z_L} \tag{1}$$

All the quantities of Equation (1) are presumably complex. Although we are going to write all the equations in terms of the common-emitter parameters (because these are the most frequently used), it should be emphasized that one can evaluate any of the other connections simply by using the corresponding matrix parameters. This will also be true of all equations in this chapter.

Using Equation (23) of Chapter 8 we can write the output admittance (the inverse of the impedance) as

$$Y_{\text{out}} = h_{oe} - \frac{h_{fe} h_{re}}{h_{ie} + Z_S} \tag{2}$$

High-frequency description of transistors

The A_i in Equation (17) of Chapter 8 can be written as

$$A_i = \frac{h_{fe}}{1 + h_{oe}Z_L} \tag{3}$$

The voltage gain of Equation (15), Chapter 8, appears as

$$A_v = \frac{1}{h_{re} - \frac{h_{ie}}{Z_L}\left(\frac{1 + h_{oe}Z_L}{h_{fe}}\right)} \tag{4}$$

One must be cautious in applying the power gain equation of Chapter 8 to the complex case. It is remembered from Chapter 6 that one method of calculating power is to use

$$P = VI \cos \theta \tag{5}$$

where θ = impedance angle: angle between voltage and current vector

Another method is to use the $P = I^2R$ approach. Using this latter, the A_p can be written

$$A_p = \left|\frac{h_{fe}}{1 + h_{oe}Z_L}\right|^2 \times \frac{Re[Z_L]}{Re[Z_{in}]} \tag{6}$$

where: Re = "real part of."

If the Z_L is much smaller than the $1/h_{oe}$ (as is usually the case for cascaded common-emitter stages) the power gain equation simplifies to

$$A_p = |h_{fe}|^2 \frac{R_L}{R_{in}} \tag{7}$$

From many standpoints the variation of h_{fe} with frequency is the most influential h parameter at high frequencies. In cascaded common-emitter connections the h_{fe} approximates the A_i, and h_{fe} directly controls the power gain [Equation (7)]. As noted in Chapter 10, the variation of h_{fe} with frequency can be written

$$h_{fe} = \frac{h_{feo}}{1 + jf/f_{hfe}} \tag{8}$$

where h_{feo} = low-frequency value of h_{fe}
f_{hfe} = frequency at which h_{fe} falls to 0.707 of its low frequency value

Thus, above f_{hfe}, the $|h_{fe}|^2$ drops at a constant rate of 6 db per octave. Consequently, knowing f_{hfe} alone permits one to find the frequency behavior of h_{fe}.

Usually the upper frequency for a given transistor amplifier is chosen to be somewhere in the 6 db/octave region (i.e., above the f_{hfe}), by using feedback or an input circuit which *reduces* the gain in the low-frequency region. By this means, one can extend the range over which the gain drops less than 3 db beyond the f_{hfe}. Thus, it is the *gain-bandwidth* product that is most important.

The role of the gain-bandwidth is as follows: assume that the frequency is about a factor of 5 above the f_{hfe} value. This is solidly in the 6 db/octave region. In this region the product of $|h_{fe}|$ and the corresponding frequency is a constant. The gain-bandwidth product is equal to the frequency at which $|h_{fe}|$ equals 1. The relation can be written

$$f_t = h_{feo} \times f_{hfe} \qquad (9)$$

where f_t = gain bandwidth product of common emitter connection, and equals the frequency at which $|h_{fe}|$ reduces to 1

It should be emphasized that the f_t can be used anywhere in the 6 db/octave region.

Another item serving as a figure of merit is the maximum available gain (M.A.G.). This is the power gain that would be realized if the source admittance is the conjugate of the input admittance (at each frequency) and the load admittance is the conjugate of the output admittance. The M.A.G. is directly related to $|h_{fe}|^2$, and therefore also drops at a 6 db/octave rate; the breakpoint is also f_{hfe}.

In the above, then, we have learned that the complex h parameters can be used at high frequencies. Also, for many cases the high frequency response can be related to the behavior of h_{fe} with frequency.

y PARAMETER DESCRIPTION. The h parameters are the most suitable matrix parameters at the low frequencies. As the frequencies increase, however, it becomes more difficult to meet the conditions for accurate h parameter measurements. For high-frequency matrix parameters, the *y* parameters are easier to find and have traditionally been used to indicate the transistor parameters. An additional reason for considering *y* parameters is the frequent use of shunt feedback at the high frequencies. A shunt connection is easily handled with *y* parameters since one merely adds the admittances.

Whereas the h parameter circuit involves a mesh equation on the input side and a nodal equation on the output side, the *y* parameter

High-frequency description of transistors

circuit uses a nodal equation on both the input and the output sides. Thus first the output and then the input must be short-circuited to measure the y parameters.

The basic equations and definitions for the y parameters are as given by

$$I_1 = y_{11}V_1 + y_{12}V_2$$
$$I_2 = y_{21}V_1 + y_{22}V_2$$

where $y_{11} = \dfrac{I_1}{V_1}\bigg|_{V_2=0}$ = input admittance

$y_{21} = \dfrac{I_2}{V_1}\bigg|_{V_2=0}$ = forward transfer admittance (10)

$y_{12} = \dfrac{I_1}{V_2}\bigg|_{V_1=0}$ = reverse transfer admittance

$y_{22} = \dfrac{I_2}{V_2}\bigg|_{V_1=0}$ = output admittance

Note that the unit for each of the y parameters is the reciprocal of resistance, *mhos*.

As before, we will write the equations in terms of the common-emitter parameters, although any connection could be described by its corresponding parameters. The common-emitter y parameter circuit representation is shown in Figure 16-3. Directly below the circuit

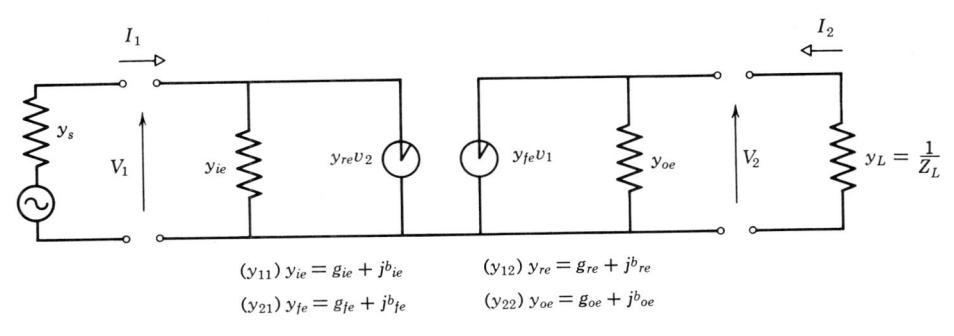

$(y_{11})\ y_{ie} = g_{ie} + jb_{ie}$ $(y_{12})\ y_{re} = g_{re} + jb_{re}$
$(y_{21})\ y_{fe} = g_{fe} + jb_{fe}$ $(y_{22})\ y_{oe} = g_{oe} + jb_{oe}$

Fig. 16-3. y parameter circuit for common-emitter case.

the common-emitter y parameters are expressed in terms of their real and imaginary parts.

An important quantity in any equivalent circuit is the "forward transfer" function. In the h parameter case it was the h_{fe}; here it is y_{fe}. Note that y_{fe} equals the output current over input voltage (with output a-c short-circuited). At low frequencies the y_{fe} is related (by a constant) to the g_m factor (mutual transconductance). The g_m relation will appear in the next section, and will also occur in Chapter 17, on field effect transistors. In any case, the y_{fe} (or g_{fe}) specification should be regarded as an alternative to specifying the h_{fe}. At low frequencies the h_{fe} is most appropriate; at high frequencies (and in field effects) the g_m version is appropriate.

The performance quantities can be calculated in the usual way. For example, to find y_{in} $(1/R_{\text{in}})$, the load is attached and the two (nodal) equations appear as

$$I_1 = y_{ie}V_1 + y_{re}V_2$$
$$0 = y_{fe}V_1 + (y_{oe} + y_L)V_2 \tag{11}$$

Solving for V_1, and then taking the ratio I_1/V_1, we find

$$y_{\text{in}} = \frac{I_1}{V_1} = \frac{y_{ie}(y_{oe} + y_L) - y_{re}y_{fe}}{(y_{oe} + y_L)} = y_{ie} - \frac{y_{re}y_{fe}}{y_{oe} + y_L} \tag{12}$$

Using a similar matrix analysis, one can readily derive the following performance equations:

$$y_{\text{out}} = y_{oe} - \frac{y_{fe}y_{re}}{y_{ie} + y_s}$$

$$A_i = \frac{y_{fe}y_L}{y_{ie}(y_{oe} + y_L) - y_{fe}y_{re}} \tag{13}$$

$$A_v = \frac{-y_{fe}}{y_L + y_{oe}}$$

The power gain can be shown to be

$$A_p = \left|\frac{y_{fe}}{y_{oe} + y_L}\right|^2 \frac{g_L}{g_{\text{in}}} \tag{14}$$

where g_L = real part of load admittance y_L
g_{in} = real part of input admittance y_{in}

In summary, the y parameter treatment is an alternative to the h parameter method at high frequencies. Both these methods are "matrix" methods, as opposed to the physical equivalent circuit approach of the next section.

The above matrix treatments can be used in a conventional stage-by-stage fashion. Thus the action (at the given frequency) of such things as the interstage would have to be calculated and combined with the single-stage analysis here in exactly the fashion as in previous low-frequency studies.

High-frequency description of transistors

THE HYBRID-π EQUIVALENT CIRCUIT. The hybrid-π equivalent circuit treatment enables the designer to study the action of the circuit as a function of frequency. Thus it permits many derivations in which the frequency effects of various components and parameters can be determined. Transient response evaluations also require use of a physical equivalent circuit approach.

The hybrid-π circuit which is widely used at high frequencies is shown in Figure 16-4. This equivalent circuit is essentially that of

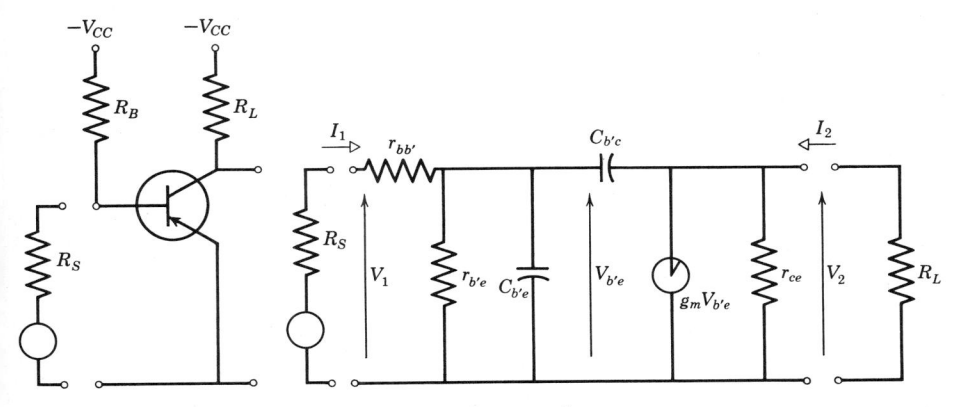

Fig. 16-4. Hybrid-π equivalent circuit.

Figure 16-1(b) except that the $r_{cb'}$ has been neglected. As mentioned, one of the chief aspects of this type of equivalent circuit is that it is directly related to the actual physical phenomenon involved in the transistor.

Before dealing with the circuit of Figure 16-4, let us examine the rudiments of this type of circuit by considering the performance quantities at low frequencies. At this range one can neglect the capacitors, and the equivalent circuit appears as in Figure 16-5.

Note that the forward transfer function is given by g_m (the mutual

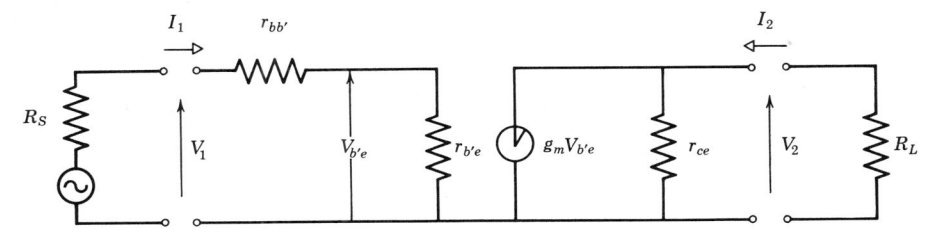

Fig. 16-5. Low-frequency hybrid-π circuit.

transconductance). The g_m is related to the real part of the y_f parameter, and its unit is *mhos*. The g_m function here should be compared to the h_f function in the h parameter treatment. The g_m representation is useful in high-frequency circuits (where the y parameters are convenient) and in high input impedance devices. It may be remembered that g_m is the crucial parameter in vacuum tubes. In the next chapter we will see it is also used in field effect transistors.

In order to find the basic performance quantities for the low frequency model of Figure 16-5 we will use two nodal equations. These appear as

$$\left(\frac{1}{r_{b'e}}\right) V_{b'e} + 0\, V_2 = I_1$$
$$g_m V_{b'e} + \left(\frac{1}{r_{ce}} + \frac{1}{R_L}\right) V_2 = 0 \tag{15}$$

It can immediately be seen that the R_{in} and the R_o are given by

$$R_{\text{in}} = R_s + r_{bb'} + r_{b'e}$$
$$R_{\text{out}} = r_{ce} \tag{16}$$

For the voltage gain, we will assume that $r_{ce} \gg R_L$, and neglect r_{ce}. The voltage gain is

$$A_v = \frac{V_2}{V_1} = -g_m R_L \frac{r_{b'e}}{r_{bb'} + r_{b'e}} \tag{17}$$

The current gain can be found by using $V_1 = I_1(r_{bb'} + r_{b'e})$ and $V_2 = I_2 R_L$. The current gain is found to be

$$A_i = g_m r_{b'e} \times \frac{r_{ce}}{R_L + r_{ce}} \tag{18}$$

If $R_L \ll r_{ce}$, then the A_i becomes effectively the short-circuit gain h_{fe}.

Thus it is seen that the relation between the h parameter forward current gain and the current gain of this (low-frequency) hybrid-π model is given by

$$h_{fe} = g_m r_{b'e} = \beta \tag{19}$$

Also note that the A_v is approximately given by

$$A_v \approx -g_m R_L \tag{20}$$

This is the basic gain relation for vacuum tubes.

High-frequency description of transistors

We now consider the hybrid-π model in the high-frequency region. Referring to Figure 16-4, we can write the two following node equations:

$$\left(\frac{1}{r_{b'e}} + jwC_{b'e} + jwC_{b'c}\right) V_{b'e} - jwC_{b'c}V_2 = I_1$$
$$(g_m - jwC_{b'c})V_{b'e} + \left(\frac{1}{r_{ce}} + \frac{1}{R_L} + jwC_{b'c}\right) V_2 = 0 \quad (21)$$

To verify Equation (21) the reader should refer to Chapter 6 for a review of treating capacitive reactances.

Before proceeding we will note the role of $C_{b'c}$ in the second equation. The $C_{b'c}$ term multiplying $V_{b'e}$ is the signal "feed-forward" term due to the capacitor, and is negligible compared to the g_m. The $C_{b'c}$ term multiplying V_2 in the second equation represents the capacitive loading on the output. This too is negligible for the usual range of R_L. The important role of $C_{b'c}$ is in the "feedback" term multiplying V_2 in the first equation.

Neglecting the $C_{b'c}$ terms in the second equation, then, the current gain (using $V_2 = -I_2R_L$) is found to be:

$$A_i = \frac{I_2}{I_1} = \frac{g_m r_{b'e}}{1 + jw[C_{b'e} + C_{b'c}(1 + g_mR_L)]}$$
$$= \frac{h_{fe}}{1 + jw[C_{b'e} + C_{b'c}(1 + g_mR_L)]} \quad (22)$$

One interpretation of Equation (22) is that we have derived the current gain as a function of frequency. Thus, in terms of the hybrid-π parameters (related to the physical structure), this expression is a derivation for the h_{fe} expression of Equation (8). Note that if R_L is very low, the effective capacitance is simply $C_{b'e} + C_{b'c}$.

If R_L approaches zero, the f_{hfe} is given by

$$f_{hfe} \approx \frac{1}{2\pi r_{b'e}(C_{b'e} + C_{b'c})} \approx \frac{1}{2\pi r_{b'e}C_{b'e}} \quad (23)$$

If the g_mR_L term cannot be ignored, the f_{hfe} is given by

$$f_{hfe} = \frac{1}{2\pi r_{b'e}[C_{b'e} + C_{b'c}(1 + g_mR_L)]} \quad (24)$$

Finally, the f_t of Equation (9) can be shown to be

$$f_t = \frac{g_m}{2\pi(C_{b'e} + C_{b'c})} = \frac{h_{feo}}{2\pi r_{b'e}(C_{b'e} + C_{b'c})} \qquad (25)$$

In effect, then, the current gain (h_{fe}) drop-off with frequency is represented by capacitances in this equivalent circuit. We can now reexamine the high-frequency calculation of Chapter 10. The treatment there consisted of separately analyzing the effects of $C_{b'e}$ and of $C_{b'c}$. It is seen that the effective output capacitance (C_{oe}) of the common-emitter stage is given by $g_m r_{b'e} C_{b'c}$, which equals $h_{fe} C_{b'c}$. This multiplication of a basic capacitance is related to the Miller effect. If the load is resistive the two $C_{b'c}$ terms can be neglected in the input impedance calculation (as they were above). Then the input impedance has the same form as the A_i. Solving Equation (21) for $V_{b'e}$ and using $V_{b'e}/I_1$ (and neglecting $r_{bb'}$) the Z_in is

$$Z_\text{in} = \frac{r_{b'e}}{1 + jwr_{b'e}[C_{b'e} + C_{b'c}(1 + g_m R_L)]} \qquad (26)$$

The fact that the capacitance seen by the input is increased by the term $(1 + g_m R_L)$ is called the *Miller effect*.

Using Equation (26) one can work with a simplified circuit wherein the effective capacitance is lumped in the input circuit. The resulting circuit is shown in Figure 16-6. Note that one can use

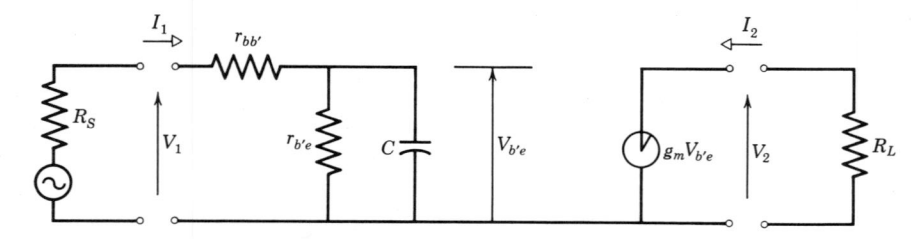

Fig. 16-6. Simplified circuit lumping the capacitance.

the circuit of Figure 16-6, as a more tractable equivalent circuit, for general gain calculations with the hybrid-π circuit. Its great advantage is that there is now no coupling between input and output.

The basic methods in this section can be used to find the frequency response of any given circuit. In particular, one can write complete equations to find the influence of the coupling capacitors, the bypass capacitors, and any other reactive elements. Here we have simply looked at the high-frequency description of the transistor. We found how to derive the f_{hfe} and f_t points in terms of physical parameters of the transistor.

In comparing the methods here to those of the previous matrix methods, we note that the equations here quickly become complex. However, their use is necessary in any derivation. An essential difference is that each matrix parameter represents a combination of physical elements, while the physical equivalent circuit has one quantity per physical element.

17

Circuit aspects of field effect transistors

The field effect transistor, as was noted in Chapter 5, is an old device which has found renewed application because of new manufacturing techniques. It was noted that the field effect transistor differs drastically from the (bipolar) junction type transistor studied previously in this book. There are also sufficient differences in design aspects and terminology to warrant a separate chapter devoted to the circuit aspects of field effect transistors.

Ever since the introduction of transistors, those applications that required a high input impedance have been difficult to solve with the low input impedance bipolar transistors. The field effect transistor (FET) is a natural solution for these applications. The modern FET's offer high input impedances with very low noise levels. Therefore, one can expect to see many applications where the first stage is a high input impedance FET followed by a cascade of bipolar junction transistors. In addition, one can expect to see the field effect transistor exploited in the thin film implementation of integrated circuits.

The reader is referred to Chapter 5 for the basic theory and operation of the FET. Here we will simply summarize the major

Circuit aspects of field effect transistors

points. The field effect transistor basically operates by varying the conductivity in a main channel semiconductor. This conductivity is controlled by the effects of the "gate" on the carrier action. One end of the main channel semiconductor is called a *source*; the other end is called the *drain*. The element which controls the conductivity in the channel is called the *gate*. In comparison to a vacuum tube, the source is comparable to the cathode, the drain is comparable to the collector, and the gate is comparable to the grid.

There are two types of FET's. The newest and most promising is the metal-oxide semiconductor (MOS) version of the FET. This is also called the *insulated-gate* FET. The other FET is the *junction-type*, in which the conductivity is controlled by reverse-biased P-N junctions.

There are also two types of insulated-gate FET's: the depletion type, which has a positive and negative swing in its characteristics, and the induced channel type (also called the enhancement type), which has a positive or a negative swing, depending upon the channel semiconductor type.

Although there are obviously a variety of FET's, they are sufficiently similar in a circuit sense to permit treating the crucial circuit

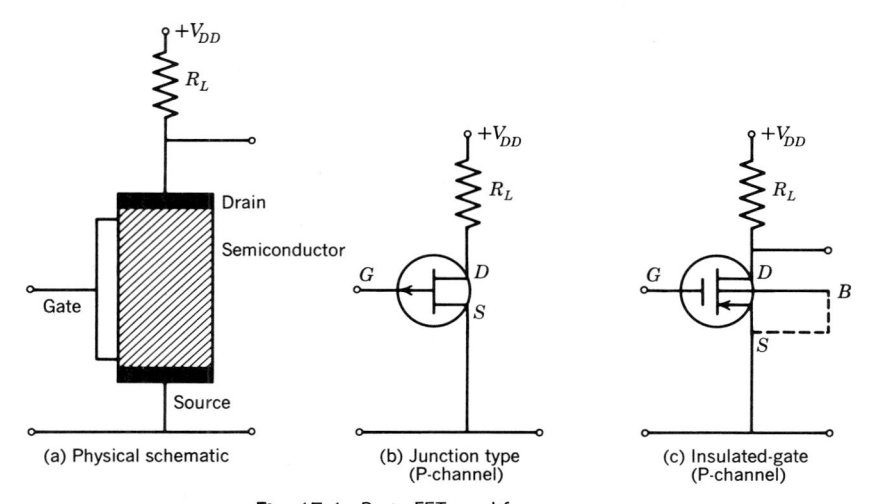

Fig. 17-1. Basic FET amplifier circuit.

aspects as a common entity. Figure 17-1 shows a basic FET amplifier (without bias circuitry). Part (a) depicts a simple physical representation; (b) shows the circuit symbol for a P-channel junction

FET; and (c) shows the circuit symbol for a P-channel insulated-gate FET. The fourth terminal on the insulated-gate type (marked B) refers to a connection made to the substrate. This is often connected to the source and can be ignored at low frequencies.

Figure 17-2 shows some typical FET characteristics. The char-

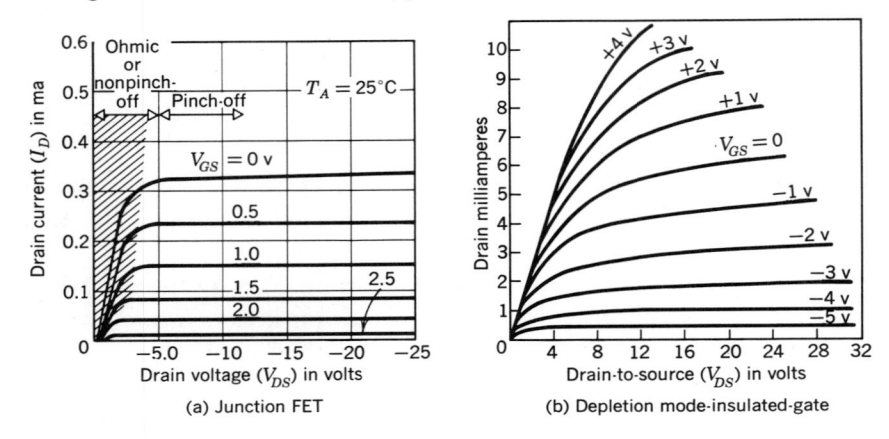

Fig. 17-2. Static characteristics of FET's.

acteristics of part (a) are for a junction FET, while part (b) shows those of a depletion-mode insulated-gate FET. Referring to these characteristics, there are a few static parameters which play a role in all FET applications. They are:

I_{DSS} (in junction-type) = drain-to-source current at zero gate voltage. In the junction-type I_{DSS} occurs when the drain current becomes nearly saturated. This current is a measure of the total dynamic range possible with the given junction FET.

I_{DSB} (in insulated-gate type) = drain-to-source current at zero gate voltage. In the enhancement mode variety it is related to the gate-voltage dynamic range. In this case the FET is "off," and the drain current is very small.

V_p (pinch-off voltage) = gate voltage for which the channel is completely depleted and the source-to-drain current goes to zero. This specifies the "off" end of the dynamic range. V_p is used both for junction and insulated-gate types.

V_t (threshold voltage) = similar to V_p above, but is used in insulated-gate types.

Circuit aspects of field effect transistors

Other static characteristics are also given by the manufacturer but the above are the most important for our purposes.

The load line analysis used previously in this book may of course be used on the FET characteristics. Such tools apply regardless of the device. Having considered the basic static characteristics, we will now study the a-c incremental behavior of the FET's.

SMALL SIGNAL PERFORMANCE QUANTITIES. The objective here will be to consider the performance quantities of the basic FET connections. First we will need to consider the equivalent circuit of the FET. Figure 17-3 shows a relatively complete equivalent circuit for

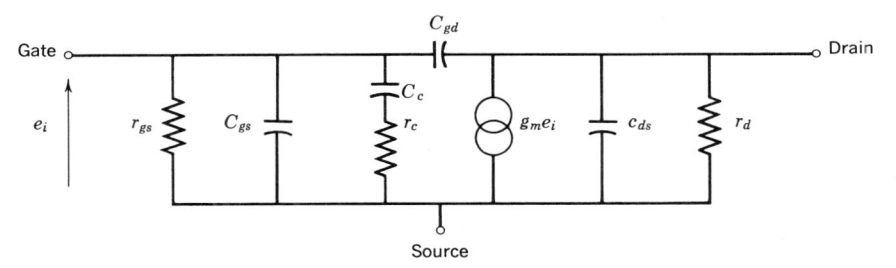

Fig. 17-3. A-c equivalent circuit of insulated-gate FET.

the insulated-gate field effect transistor (without substrate connections). The subscripts of the elements identify the terminals to which the element is attached. This circuit contains more elements than are necessary for most design calculations.

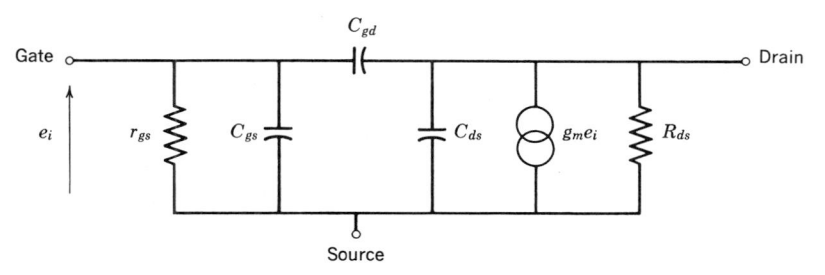

Fig. 17-4. Equivalent circuit for junction FET.

Figure 17-4 shows the equivalent circuit suitable for the junction type FET. As seen, this is the same as the circuit of Figure 17-3 except that the branch containing C_c and r_c is deleted. We will consider the circuit of Figure 17-4 to be an approximate equivalent circuit for the insulated-gate FET. Hence we will refer to this circuit for both FET types.

It is seen that the equivalent circuit of Figure 17-4 is a hybrid-π equivalent circuit similar to the high-frequency version that we treated in the previous chapter.

Thus all of the considerations derived there will apply here to the FET. For example, we note that the forward transfer function is given by g_m, an admittance function. This is certainly sensible for any high input impedance device. It would not make sense to specify a current gain h_{fe}, since the input current is extremely small. These same factors hold for the vacuum tube, and g_m is the basic parameter for it.

In general, manufacturers of FET's will usually specify the hybrid-π parameters of Figure 17-4. In some cases the set of y parameters are given.

Because of the very high input impedance, the important performance quantities are the voltage gain and the input capacitance. These factors, too, are similar to the vacuum tube.

For any detailed analysis regarding the circuit of Figure 17-4, one can use the equations developed for the hybrid-π circuit in the previous chapter. Here we will resort to a simplification, which is justified, and is commonly used in vacuum tube analysis.

In any high impedance circuit the frequency response is limited by the input capacitance. Therefore, in Figure 17-4, the capacitor C_{dg} affects the frequency response through the Z_{in} long before it affects the voltage gain. Therefore we can convert the "coupled" circuit of Figure 17-4 to the "no-feedback" circuit of Figure 17-5.

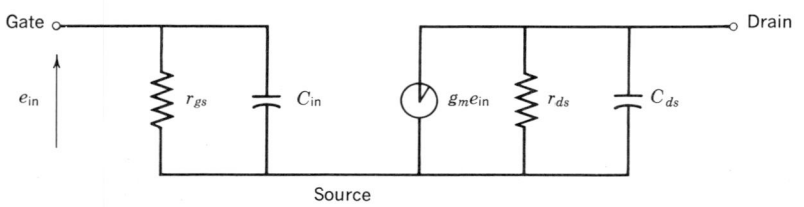

Fig. 17-5. Simplified circuit for FET analysis.

We note, though, that the C_{in} must account for the entire capacitance seen by the input (including C_{dg}). Use of this simplification is a standard procedure in vacuum tube design, and was discussed in the

Circuit aspects of field effect transistors

previous chapter (Miller effect). The alternative is to deal with quite complex equations. We will now note the performance quantities for two basic FET connections.

COMMON SOURCE CONNECTION. The common source arrangement is depicted in Figure 17-1. Using the equivalent circuit of Figure 17-5, the low-frequency voltage gain is found to be

$$A_v = \frac{g_m R_L r_{ds}}{r_{ds} + R_L} \tag{1}$$

If r_{ds} is much greater than R_L, as is usually the case, then the A_v is given approximately as

$$A_v \approx g_m R_L \tag{2}$$

The relation of Equation (2) is familiar in the vacuum tube area.
The input capacitance can be found to be

$$C_{\text{in}} = C_{gs} + (1 - A_v)C_{dg} \tag{3}$$

It is seen that the feedback capacity is increased by approximately the voltage gain of the stage. This was called the Miller effect in vacuum tube design.

An important consideration in any actual amplifier is bias stability. Bias stability is more important for the junction-type FET than for the insulated-gate type. In any case one will need a gate resistor (R_G) similar to the grid resistor used with the vacuum tube. In addition, a resistor in series with the source (R_S) will contribute to bias stability in the same way as an emitter resistance does for the bipolar junction transistor. Although any such series source resistance may be bypassed, it may be desirable to retain an un-bypassed R_S for a-c feedback. Given the circuit of Figure 17-6, the new voltage gain A_v' will be

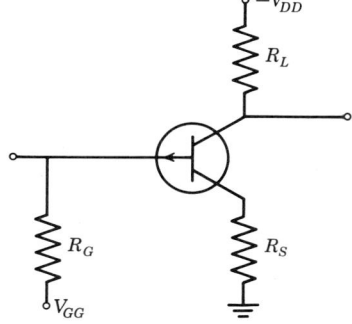

Fig. 17-6. Bias stabilized circuit.

$$A'_v = \frac{A_v}{1 + A_v \dfrac{R_S}{R_L}} = \frac{g_m R_L}{1 + g_m R_S} \tag{4}$$

If one had $g_m R_S \gg 1$ the feedback voltage gain would appear as

$$A'_v = \frac{R_L}{R_S} \tag{5}$$

This is the typical way in which the gain is made independent of the device parameters by feedback.

COMMON DRAIN CONDITION. Another useful circuit is the FET in the common drain (or source follower) connection. (This is equivalent to the cathode follower in vacuum tubes or the emitter follower with bipolar transistors.) In this case the following performance equations can be established:

$$A_v = \frac{g_m r_{dg} R_L}{r_{dg} + (1 + g_m r_{dg}) R_L} \tag{6}$$

$$C_{\text{in}} = C_{dg} + (1 - A) C_{gs}$$

The FET can also be used in the common gate connection. The above are the most basic circuit aspects of the field effect transistor. Although the FET was fairly slow in developing, it now appears certain that it will be an important semiconductor device. One can expect the FET's to appear in conjunction with bipolar transistors.

In this chapter we have seen that the hybrid-π equivalent circuit and the y parameter circuit are appropriate for field effect transistors. It appears that the h parameter circuit will continue to be used at low frequencies, and for design bandwidth calculations. Any serious analysis at high frequencies will involve the hybrid-π or the y parameter method.

REFERENCES

1. Griswold, David M., "Understanding and Using the MOS FET," *Electronics*, December 14, 1964, Vol. **37**, No. 31, p. 66.

2. Wallmark, J. T., "The Field Effect Transistor—An Old Device With New Promise," *IEEE Spectrum*, March 1964, p. 182.

APPENDIX I

Determinants

Much of the electric circuit analysis consists of solving simultaneous equations. Such equations result when either the mesh or the nodal analysis is used. Hence, in electronic circuits, simultaneous equations appear whenever the equivalent circuit concept is used. Chapter 8 was concerned with simultaneous equations.

There are two general ways to solve such simultaneous equations: (1) the method of elimination, and (2) the method of determinants. The two methods are related, but differ in procedure. Essentially, "determinants" represents an organized, consistent procedure, whereas "elimination" is less organized and more flexible.

In this text the method of determinants was used throughout. The reason for this is because it allowed a consistent portrayal for each case. We will present the method of elimination first, however, since it is probably more intuitive. Since we usually encountered two simultaneous equations, the methods will be illustrated by the use of two equations. It should be remembered that in simultaneous equations there are as many equations required as there are unknowns.

Two general simultaneous equations can be written

$$a_1 x + b_1 y = c_1, \qquad a_2 x + b_2 y = c_2 \qquad (1)$$

By convention, the first letters of the alphabet (a, b, c, etc.) represent the constants of the system, and such letters as x, y, etc., represent the unknowns. The parameters of the system being considered determine the constants, whereas the unknowns are those variables which are sought. For example, in transistors the constants will be given by the h parameters, and the unknowns will be the currents or the voltages. Note that if currents are the unknowns, the known voltages will be the c's of Equation (1), and vice versa.

The method of elimination consists generally of combining the two equations in such a manner as to eliminate one variable. The value of this variable is then found; following this, the known variable is substituted back into either of the original equations and the remaining unknown is evaluated.

To illustrate this procedure, we eliminate the y variable from Equations (1). To accomplish this, we multiply the first equation by b_2 and the second equation by b_1. The result is

$$a_1 b_2 x + b_1 b_2 y = c_1 b_2, \qquad a_2 b_1 x + b_1 b_2 y = c_2 b_1 \qquad (2)$$

If we now subtract one equation from the other, it is seen that the y variable is eliminated since its coefficient is zero. Hence we have an equation for x:

$$(a_1 b_2 - a_2 b_1) x = c_1 b_2 - c_2 b_1, \qquad x = \frac{c_1 b_2 - c_2 b_1}{a_1 b_2 - a_2 b_1} \qquad (3)$$

If we now substitute this value of x into *either* equation of (1) we obtain

$$y = \frac{a_1 c_2 - a_2 c_1}{a_1 b_2 - a_2 b_1} \qquad (4)$$

Note that this process could have been reversed; the x variable could have been eliminated first and the y found by substitution. To do this, the first equation is multiplied by a_2 and the second equation by a_1. In this case, the unknown y is found first. The result, of course, would be identical to that above.

As illustrated above, then, the method of elimination consists of removing one variable by combining the equations. The remaining variable is then found by substituting the evaluated variable back into an original equation.

This method, illustrated for two equations here, can be extended to any number of simultaneous equations. The procedure is to take two equations at a time, and eliminate one variable between them. Pairs of equations must be thus treated, and the resulting equations

Determinants

combined until one variable remains. Then one begins working in reverse to evaluate the other variables. The elimination method quickly becomes very tedious when more than three equations are involved.

As mentioned, the determinants method essentially consists of *organizing* the above procedure into a compact form. Also, it is possible to generalize the determinants method for large numbers of equations with relative simplicity.

The essential idea in the determinants method is to arrange the *constants* of the simultaneous equations in arrays (called a determinant), and then to evaluate these arrays. The variable, it can be shown, is equal to the ratio of two such determinants.

If we have two simultaneous equations, they can be written as before:

$$a_1 x + b_1 y = c_1$$
$$a_2 x + b_2 y = c_2 \quad (5)$$

Then it can be shown that the unknowns x and y can be written as the ratio of two determinants:

$$x = \frac{\begin{vmatrix} c_1 & b_1 \\ c_2 & b_2 \end{vmatrix}}{\begin{vmatrix} a_1 & b_1 \\ a_2 & b_2 \end{vmatrix}}, \quad y = \frac{\begin{vmatrix} a_1 & c_1 \\ a_2 & c_2 \end{vmatrix}}{\begin{vmatrix} a_1 & b_1 \\ a_2 & b_2 \end{vmatrix}} \quad (6)$$

This is, of course, only a symbolic representation of the solution. We have now to see how the arrays that form the determinants are achieved, and how to evaluate the determinants.

First, we note that the denominator determinant is the same for both variables. This denominator is formed by arranging the *coefficients of the unknowns* in the same positions as they occur in the equation. This assumes, of course, that the original equations are arranged as in (5) above, with the unknowns appearing in a vertical line. For the numerator determinant in the x solution, we first *replace the x coefficients by the constants of the right side (c's)*. Then the resulting coefficients are formed into an array. Likewise for the y numerator; the coefficients of y are replaced by the c's. The resulting array of constants forms the numerator of y.

To evaluate a determinant, one multiplies the elements along a diagonal, including both downward and upward diagonals. The downward diagonals are positive, and the upward diagonals are preceded by a negative sign. The value of the determinant is consequently formed by subtracting the upward diagonal value (product of the elements in the diagonal) from the downward diagonal value. This procedure can be illustrated by a representation:

$$\begin{vmatrix} d & u \\ & \end{vmatrix} = \text{value of } d - \text{value of } u \tag{7}$$

If this is applied to both numerator and denominator determinants of Equation (6), we find

$$x = \frac{\begin{vmatrix} c_1 & b_1 \\ c_2 & b_2 \end{vmatrix}}{\begin{vmatrix} a_1 & b_1 \\ a_2 & b_2 \end{vmatrix}} = \frac{c_1 b_2 - c_2 b_1}{a_1 b_2 - a_2 b_1}$$

and (8)

$$y = \frac{\begin{vmatrix} a_1 & c_1 \\ a_2 & c_2 \end{vmatrix}}{\begin{vmatrix} a_1 & b_1 \\ a_2 & b_2 \end{vmatrix}} = \frac{a_1 c_2 - a_2 c_1}{a_1 b_2 - a_2 b_1}$$

As seen, these results are identical to those of Equations (3) and (4), where the method of elimination was used.

We can now summarize the steps:

1. Arrange the equations so that like unknown variables appear in a vertical line.

2. Form the denominator determinant (for either unknown) by putting the coefficients of the variables in an array.

3. Form the numerator determinant by substituting the right-side constants for the coefficients of the sought unknown, using the same relative positions and again forming the array.

4. Evaluate the determinants by taking products along the diagonal; subtract the upward diagonal product from the downward diagonal product.

Thus the use of determinants results in an orderly, consistent procedure for solving simultaneous equations.

The above procedure can be generalized, with some caution, to the cases of more than two equations. For any number of simultaneous equations, the unknown can be written as a ratio of two determinants:

Determinants

$$x_1 = \frac{N_1}{D}, \quad x_2 = \frac{N_2}{D}, \quad x_3 = \frac{N_3}{D}, \quad \ldots \tag{9}$$

where x_1, x_2, etc. are the unknown variables.

The determinants in these ratios are formed exactly as illustrated for the two-equation case. There is a difference in evaluating the determinants, however. *Only two- and three-equation sets can be evaluated by the "diagonal" method.* If the determinant is greater than a three-by-three, a procedure involving co-factors must be used. The reader is referred to any standard mathematics textbook for this latter procedure.

The diagonal method of evaluation for the case of three equations is similar to that of the two-equation case and is depicted below. The main difference is that now all possible diagonals are used; this is most easily accomplished by repeating the first two columns as shown.

$$\begin{vmatrix} a_1 & b_1 & c_1 \\ a_2 & b_2 & c_2 \\ a_3 & b_3 & c_3 \end{vmatrix} = \begin{vmatrix} a_1 & b_1 & c_1 & a_1 & b_1 \\ a_2 & b_2 & c_2 & a_2 & b_2 \\ a_3 & b_3 & c_3 & a_3 & b_3 \end{vmatrix}$$

$$= a_1 b_2 c_3 + b_1 c_2 a_3 + c_1 a_2 b_3 - a_3 b_2 c_1 - b_3 c_2 a_1 - c_3 a_2 b_1$$

To reemphasize, if a determinant is larger than three-by-three, the diagonal method can no longer be used for evaluating the determinant.

APPENDIX II

Parameter conversions

For a two-terminal pair device, such as the transistor, there are a number of forms in which the parameters can be specified. Based on the black-box concept (see Chapter 6), different sets of parameters may be specified depending on which currents and voltages are assumed known and which ones are unknown. Also, parameters may be specified according to a given equivalent circuit. If the parameters are based on the black-box concept, they are often called *matrix* parameters, since they lend themselves to matrix manipulations. Parameters based on an equivalent circuit may or may not be of the matrix type, depending on the equivalent circuit.

When transistors first appeared, it was the practice to specify the *T-equivalent circuit* parameters (see Chapter 7). The parameters specified for this circuit are r_e, r_b, r_c, and α or r_m, which consist of three resistance values and a current gain or resistance, respectively. Because of the particular impedance values in a transistor, the parameters are most easily *measured* in terms of the h matrix parameters. For this reason most manufacturers in the past years have been specifying the transistor h parameters. These are the parameters used primarily in this text.

Nevertheless, many times, parameters other than the h parameters

Parameter conversions

are given. It is the purpose here to show the relationship between the parameters.

Consider the transistor in terms of a black box (see Fig. A-1), i.e.,

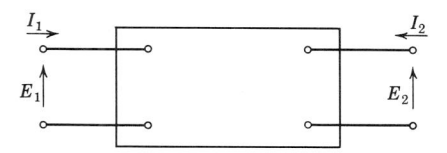

Fig. A-1. The transistor as a black box.

in terms of input and output voltages and currents. If we regard the input current and the output voltage as the unknowns, the equations for the transistor appear as

$$E_1 = h_{11}I_1 + h_{12}E_2$$
$$I_2 = h_{21}I_1 + h_{22}E_2$$
h parameters (1)

This is the basic set of equations used in this book. Other possible forms are the following:

$$E_1 = z_{11}I_1 + z_{12}I_2$$
$$E_2 = z_{21}I_1 + z_{22}I_2$$
z parameters

where I_1 and I_2 are the unknowns.

$$I_1 = y_{11}E_1 + y_{12}E_2$$
$$I_2 = y_{21}E_1 + y_{22}E_2$$
y parameters (2)

where E_1 and E_2 are the unknowns.

$$I_1 = g_{11}E_1 + g_{12}I_2$$
$$E_2 = g_{21}E_1 + g_{22}I_2$$
g parameters

where E_1 and I_2 are the unknowns.

It should be stressed that, for a single circuit, each of the above representations is equally valid. If circuits are to be combined, however, one form is preferred over the others, based on the manner in which the circuits are connected. As stated previously, the h parameters are usually given for the transistor. Each of the parameter types listed above is of the matrix type.

Parameter conversions

Given any one set of parameters, we can find any of the other sets. Table 1 shows the relationship between each of the various

Table 1

Given → To find:	→ h		→ z		→ y		→ g	
→ h	h_{11}	h_{12}	$\dfrac{\Delta^z}{z_{22}}$	$\dfrac{z_{12}}{z_{22}}$	$\dfrac{1}{y_{11}}$	$\dfrac{-y_{12}}{y_{11}}$	$\dfrac{g_{22}}{\Delta^g}$	$\dfrac{-g_{12}}{\Delta^g}$
	h_{21}	h_{22}	$\dfrac{-z_{21}}{z_{22}}$	$\dfrac{1}{z_{22}}$	$\dfrac{y_{21}}{y_{11}}$	$\dfrac{\Delta^y}{y_{11}}$	$\dfrac{-g_{21}}{\Delta^g}$	$\dfrac{g_{11}}{\Delta^g}$
→ z	$\dfrac{\Delta^h}{h_{22}}$	$\dfrac{h_{12}}{h_{22}}$	z_{11}	z_{12}	$\dfrac{y_{22}}{\Delta^y}$	$\dfrac{-y_{12}}{\Delta^y}$	$\dfrac{1}{g_{11}}$	$\dfrac{-g_{12}}{g_{11}}$
	$\dfrac{-h_{21}}{h_{22}}$	$\dfrac{1}{h_{22}}$	z_{21}	z_{22}	$\dfrac{-y_{21}}{\Delta^y}$	$\dfrac{y_{11}}{\Delta^y}$	$\dfrac{g_{21}}{g_{11}}$	$\dfrac{\Delta^g}{g_{11}}$
→ y	$\dfrac{1}{h_{11}}$	$\dfrac{-h_{12}}{h_{11}}$	$\dfrac{z_{22}}{\Delta^z}$	$\dfrac{-z_{12}}{\Delta^z}$	y_{11}	y_{12}	$\dfrac{\Delta^g}{g_{22}}$	$\dfrac{g_{12}}{g_{22}}$
	$\dfrac{h_{21}}{h_{11}}$	$\dfrac{\Delta^h}{h_{11}}$	$\dfrac{-z_{21}}{\Delta^z}$	$\dfrac{z_{11}}{\Delta^z}$	y_{21}	y_{22}	$\dfrac{-g_{21}}{g_{22}}$	$\dfrac{1}{g_{22}}$
→ g	$\dfrac{h_{22}}{\Delta^h}$	$\dfrac{-h_{12}}{\Delta^h}$	$\dfrac{1}{z_{11}}$	$\dfrac{-z_{12}}{z_{11}}$	$\dfrac{\Delta^y}{y_{22}}$	$\dfrac{y_{12}}{y_{22}}$	g_{11}	g_{12}
	$\dfrac{-h_{21}}{\Delta^h}$	$\dfrac{h_{11}}{\Delta^h}$	$\dfrac{z_{21}}{z_{11}}$	$\dfrac{\Delta^z}{z_{11}}$	$\dfrac{-y_{21}}{y_{22}}$	$\dfrac{1}{y_{22}}$	g_{21}	g_{22}

matrix parameters. This table is to be read in the horizontal direction. Although we are interested mainly in the first row, showing how to obtain the h parameters from the other matrix quantities, the other relations are included for completeness. Row 2 shows how to obtain the z parameters, etc. The quantity Δ in this table means, in each case, the determinant value of the parameters. The table is used by simply equating the desired parameter to the quantity in the corresponding position of the other parameters. For example,

$$h_{11} = \frac{\Delta z}{z_{22}}; \quad h_{22} = \frac{1}{z_{22}}; \quad z_{12} = \frac{-y_{12}}{\Delta y}; \quad \text{etc.} \qquad (3)$$

Although this table relates the general matrix-type parameters, it is of interest to relate the parameters of the T equivalent circuit to the h matrix parameters used in this book.

Parameter conversions

The T equivalent circuit is repeated (from Figure 7-9) in Figure A-2. First of all (as stated in Chapter 7) we note the relation between

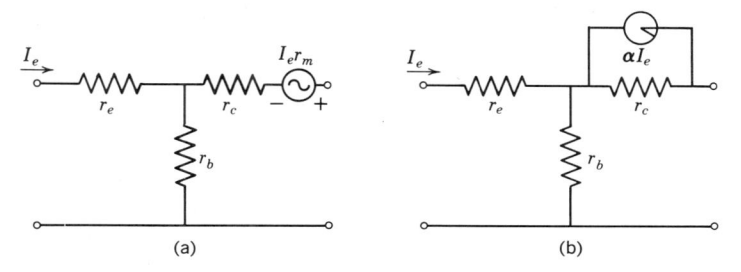

Fig. A-2. T-equivalent circuits for transistors: (a) T-equivalent circuit with voltage generator; (b) T-circuit with current generator.

this simplified T equivalent circuit and the basic one which preceded it (given in Figure 7-8). These relations are

$$r_b = g_{ec}r_{cc}r_e + r_{b'}$$
$$r_c = r_{cc}(1 - g_{ec}r_e)$$
$$r_e = r_e[1 - g_{ec}r_{cc}(1 - \alpha - g_{ec}r_e)] \quad (4)$$
$$\alpha = \alpha$$

Now, dealing with the T parameters of Figure A-2, we first note that these parameters are closely related to the (common-base) z parameters:

$$z_{11} = r_e + r_b, \quad z_{21} = r_b + r_m$$
$$z_{12} = r_b, \quad z_{22} = r_b + r_c \quad (5)$$
$$\alpha = \frac{r_b + r_m}{r_b + r_c} \approx \frac{r_m}{r_c}$$

To find the h^b parameters from the T parameters we have the relation

$$h_{ib} = r_e + r_b\left(1 - \frac{r_b + r_m}{r_b + r_c}\right) = r_e + r_b(1 - \alpha)$$

$$h_{rb} = \frac{r_b}{r_b + r_c}$$

$$h_{fb} = -\left(\frac{r_b + r_m}{r_b + r_c}\right) = -\alpha \approx -\frac{r_m}{r_c} \quad (6)$$

$$h_{ob} = \frac{1}{r_b + r_c} \approx \frac{1}{r_c}$$

Since we have used the h^e parameters throughout this book, it is helpful to be able to find the h^e parameters in terms of both the T equivalent parameters and the h^b parameters:

$$h_{ie} = \frac{h_{ib}}{(1+h_{fb})(1-h_{rb})+h_{ob}h_{ib}} \simeq \frac{h_{ib}}{1+h_{fb}}; \quad h_{ie} \simeq r_b + \frac{r_e}{1-\alpha}$$

$$h_{re} = \frac{h_{ib}h_{ob} - h_{rb}(1+h_{fb})}{(1+h_{fb})(1-h_{rb})+h_{ob}h_{ib}} \simeq \frac{h_{ib}h_{ob}}{1+h_{fb}} - h_{rb}; \quad h_{re} \simeq \frac{r_e}{(1-\alpha)r_c} \qquad (7)$$

$$h_{fe} = \frac{-h_{fb}(1-h_{rb}) - h_{ob}h_{ib}}{(1+h_{fb})(1-h_{rb})+h_{ob}h_{ib}} \simeq \frac{-h_{fb}}{1+h_{fb}}; \quad h_{fe} \simeq \frac{\alpha}{1-\alpha}$$

$$h_{oe} = \frac{h_{ob}}{(1+h_{fb})(1-h_{rb})+h_{ob}h_{ib}} \simeq \frac{h_{ob}}{1+h_{fb}}; \quad h_{oe} \simeq \frac{1}{(1-\alpha)r_c}$$

Also, it is of interest to know the relation between the h^c and the h^b parameters:

$$h_{ic} = \frac{h_{ib}}{(1+h_{fb})(1-h_{rb})+h_{ob}h_{ib}} \simeq \frac{h_{ib}}{1+h_{fb}}$$

$$h_{rc} = \frac{1+h_{fb}}{(1+h_{fb})(1-h_{rb})+h_{ob}h_{ib}} \simeq 1$$

$$h_{fc} = \frac{h_{rb}-1}{(1+h_{fb})(1-h_{rb})+h_{ob}h_{ib}} \simeq -\frac{1}{1+h_{fb}} \qquad (8)$$

$$h_{oc} = \frac{h_{ob}}{(1+h_{fb})(1-h_{rb})+h_{ob}h_{ib}} \simeq \frac{h_{ob}}{1+h_{fb}}$$

Finally, it is of interest to know the T equivalent parameters in terms of the h^b and h^e parameters:

$$r_e = h_{ib} - (1+h_{fb})\frac{h_{rb}}{h_{ob}} = \frac{h_{re}}{h_{oe}}$$

$$r_b = \frac{h_{rb}}{h_{ob}} = h_{ie} - \frac{h_{re}(1+h_{fe})}{h_{oe}}$$

$$r_c = \frac{1-h_{rb}}{h_{ob}} = \frac{h_{fe}+1}{h_{oe}} \qquad (9)$$

$$\alpha = -h_{fb} \simeq \frac{h_{fe}}{1+h_{fe}}$$

Table 1 and the above relations allow the conversion of any set of parameters to the h type, so that the results found within the text can be applied consistently, no matter what parameters are specified.

APPENDIX III

Transistor parameters

The following is a selected sample of transistor characteristics. These characteristics are included for two reasons; to give an indication of the parameters of available transistors and to serve as a source for parameters of commercial transistors for use in solving the problems included in this text.

RCA 2N270 GERMANIUM P-N-P ALLOY TYPE JUNCTION TRANSISTOR
for large-signal audio-frequency applications

GENERAL DATA

Electrical:

Maximum DC Collector Current for dc collector-to-base voltage of -25 volts with emitter open, and at ambient temperature of 25° C.	-16	μa
Maximum DC Emitter Current for dc emitter-to-base voltage of -12 volts with collector open, and at ambient temperature of 25° C.	-12	μa
Maximum Junction-Temperature Rise (With transistor in free air)	0.24	°C/mw

Mechanical:

Operating Position	Any	
Maximum Length (Excluding flexible leads)	0.375"	
Maximum Diameter	0.360"	
Case	Metal	
Envelope Seals	Hermetic	
Leads, Flexible	3	
Minimum length	1.5"	
Orientation and diameter	See Dimensional Outline	

Lead 1 — Emitter
Lead 2 — Base
Lead 4 — Collector

AUDIO-FREQUENCY AMPLIFIER — Class A

Maximum Ratings, *Absolute-Maximum Values*:

PEAK COLLECTOR-TO-BASE VOLTAGE	-25 max.	volts
DC COLLECTOR-TO-BASE VOLTAGE	-25 max.	volts
PEAK EMITTER-TO-BASE VOLTAGE	-12 max.	volts
DC EMITTER-TO-BASE VOLTAGE	-12 max.	volts
PEAK COLLECTOR CURRENT	-150 max.	ma
DC COLLECTOR CURRENT	-75 max.	ma
PEAK EMITTER CURRENT	150 max.	ma
DC EMITTER CURRENT	75 max.	ma
TRANSISTOR DISSIPATION:		
At an ambient temperature of 25° C.	250 max.	mw
At an ambient temperature of 55° C.	150 max.	mw
At an ambient temperature of 71° C.	60 max.	mw
AMBIENT TEMPERATURE (During operation)	71 max.	°C
STORAGE-TEMPERATURE RANGE	-65 to +85	°C

↑ Indicates a change.

Characteristics, *At Ambient Temperature of 25° C*:

Common-Emitter Circuit, Base Input

DC Collector-to-Emitter Voltage	-1	volt
DC Collector Current	-150	ma
Large-Signal DC Current Gain	70	

Typical Operation, *At Ambient Temperature of 25° C*:

Common-Emitter Circuit, Base Input

DC Supply Voltage	-9	volts
DC Collector-to-Emitter Voltage	-6.7	volts
Emitter Resistor	100	ohms
Emitter-Bypass Capacitor	50	μf
DC Collector Current	-19	ma
DC Base-to-Emitter Voltage	-0.19	volt
Input Resistance	400	ohms
Load Impedance	400	ohms
Signal Frequency	1	kc
Power Gain◆	35	db
Total Harmonic Distortion	10▲ max.	%
Max.-Signal Power Output◆	60	mw
Transistor Dissipation	128	mw

AUDIO-FREQUENCY AMPLIFIER — Class B

Maximum Ratings, *Absolute-Maximum Values*:

PEAK COLLECTOR-TO-BASE VOLTAGE	-25 max.	volts
DC COLLECTOR-TO-BASE VOLTAGE	-25 max.	volts
PEAK EMITTER-TO-BASE VOLTAGE	-12 max.	volts
DC EMITTER-TO-BASE VOLTAGE	-12 max.	volts
PEAK COLLECTOR CURRENT	-150 max.	ma
DC COLLECTOR CURRENT	-75 max.	ma
PEAK EMITTER CURRENT	150 max.	ma
DC EMITTER CURRENT	75 max.	ma
TRANSISTOR DISSIPATION:		
At an ambient temperature of 25° C.	250 max.	mw
At an ambient temperature of 55° C.	150 max.	mw
At an ambient temperature of 71° C.	60 max.	mw
AMBIENT TEMPERATURE (During operation)	71 max.	°C
STORAGE-TEMPERATURE RANGE	-65 to +85	°C

Characteristics, *At Ambient Temperature of 25° C*:

Common-Emitter Circuit, Base Input

DC Collector-to-Emitter Voltage	-1	volt
DC Collector Current	-150	ma
Large-Signal DC Current Gain	70	

◆, ▲: See next page.   ↑ Indicates a change.

Transistor parameters

Typical Push-Pull Operation, At Ambient Temperature of 25° C:
Common-Emitter Circuit, Base Input

Unless otherwise specified, values are for 2 transistors

DC Supply Voltage	-12	volts
Emitter Resistor	5	ohms
DC Base-to-Emitter Voltage (Zero-signal)	-0.11	volt
Peak Collector Current (Per transistor)	-110	ma
Zero-Signal DC Collector Current (Per transistor)	-2	ma
Max.-Signal DC Collector Current (Per transistor)	-35	ma
Signal-Source Impedance (Base to base)	4000	ohms
Load Impedance (Collector to collector)	600	ohms
Signal Frequency	1	kc
Circuit Efficiency	75	%
Power Gain ◆	32	db
Total Harmonic Distortion	10 ■ max.	%
Max.-Signal Power Output ◆	500	mw

● Measured at the primary of the output transformer.
▲ This value is 4 per cent maximum at max.-signal power output of 10 milliwatts.
■ This value is 5 per cent maximum at max.-signal power output of 10 milliwatts.

OPERATING CONSIDERATIONS

The 2N270 should not be connected into or disconnected from circuits with the power on because high transient currents may cause permanent damage to the transistor.

The *flexible leads* of the 2N270 are usually soldered to the circuit elements. Soldering of the leads may be made close to the glass stem provided care is taken to conduct excessive heat away from the lead seal. Otherwise, the heat of the soldering operation will crack the seals of the leads and damage the transistor.

When dip soldering is employed in the assembly of printed circuitry using the 2N270, the temperature of the solder should not exceed 230° C for a maximum immersion period of 10 seconds.

In class B service, when the 2N270 is operated at ambient temperatures other than 25° C, the base-to-emitter voltage should be reduced or increased by approximately 0.002 volt for each degree the ambient temperature is above or below 25° C, respectively. When this transistor is operated under varying ambient temperatures, some form of temperature compensation may be used in the base-to-emitter circuit to hold the operating point constant.

500 Transistor parameters

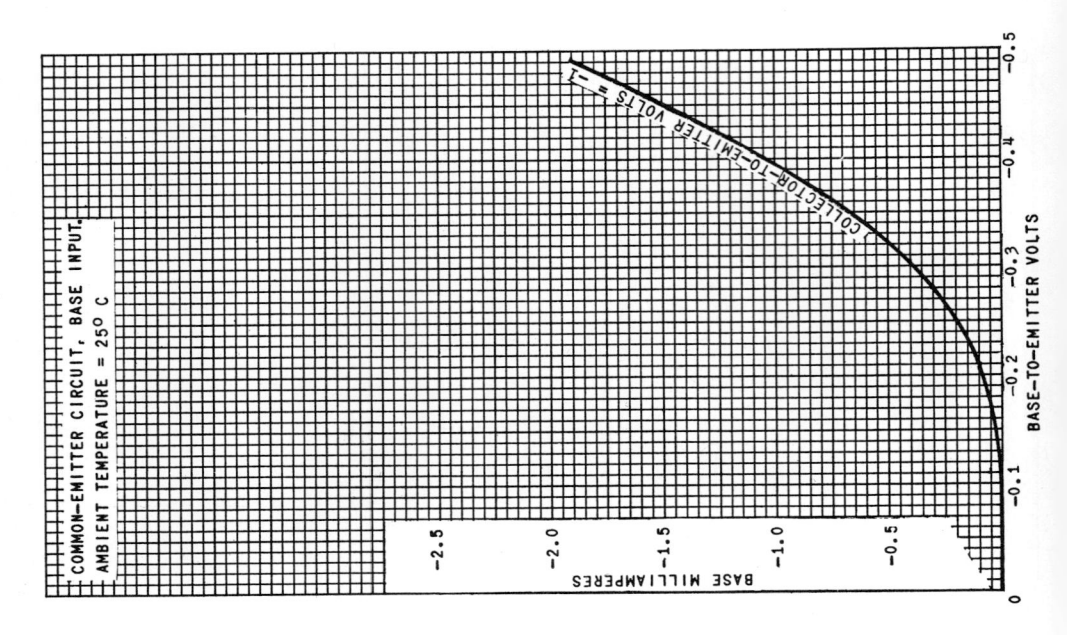

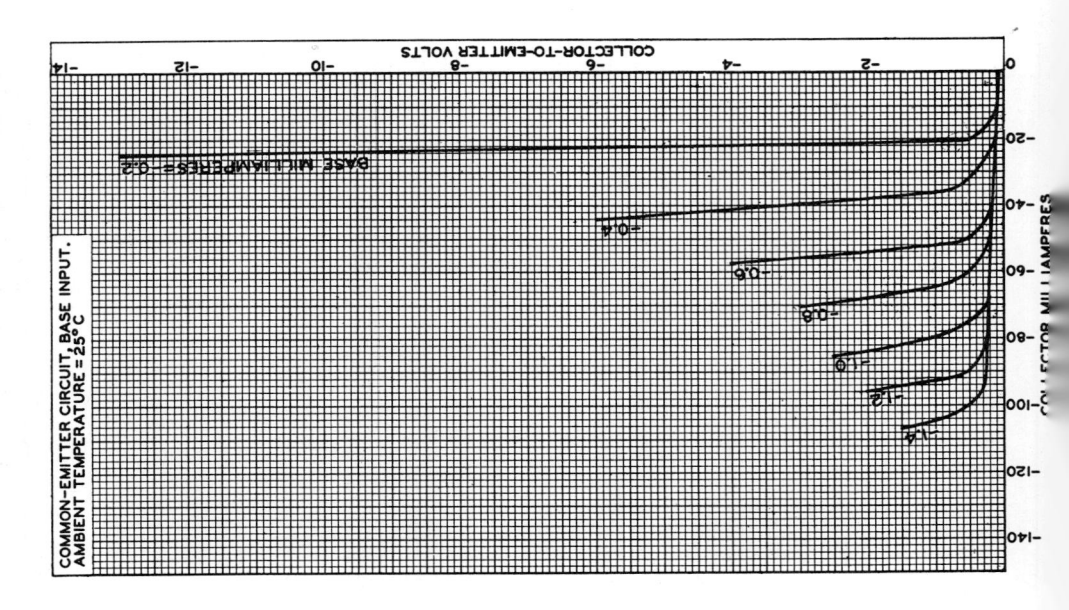

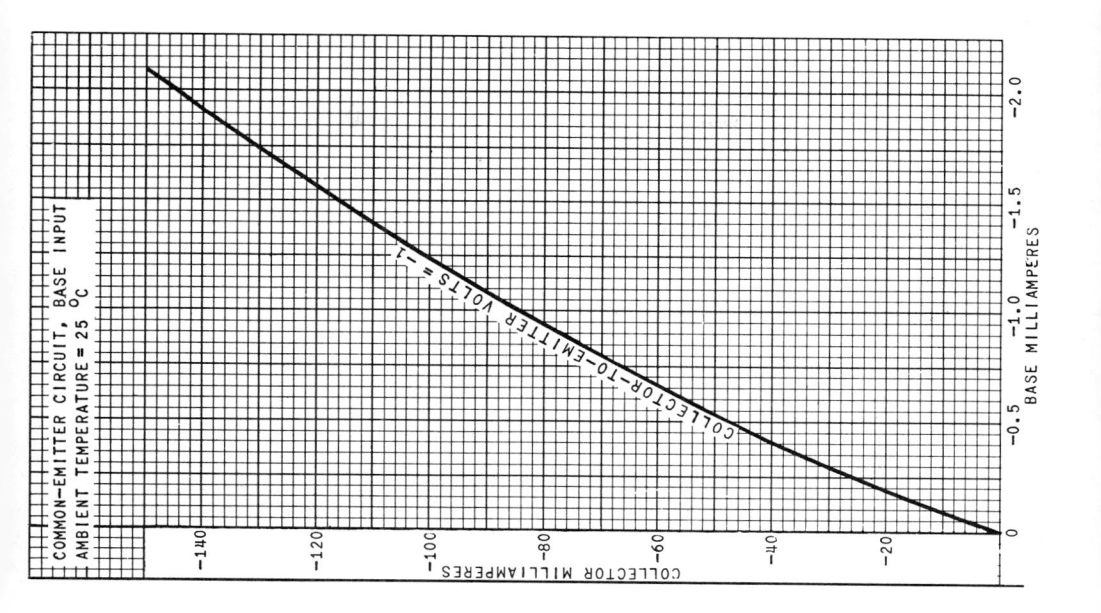

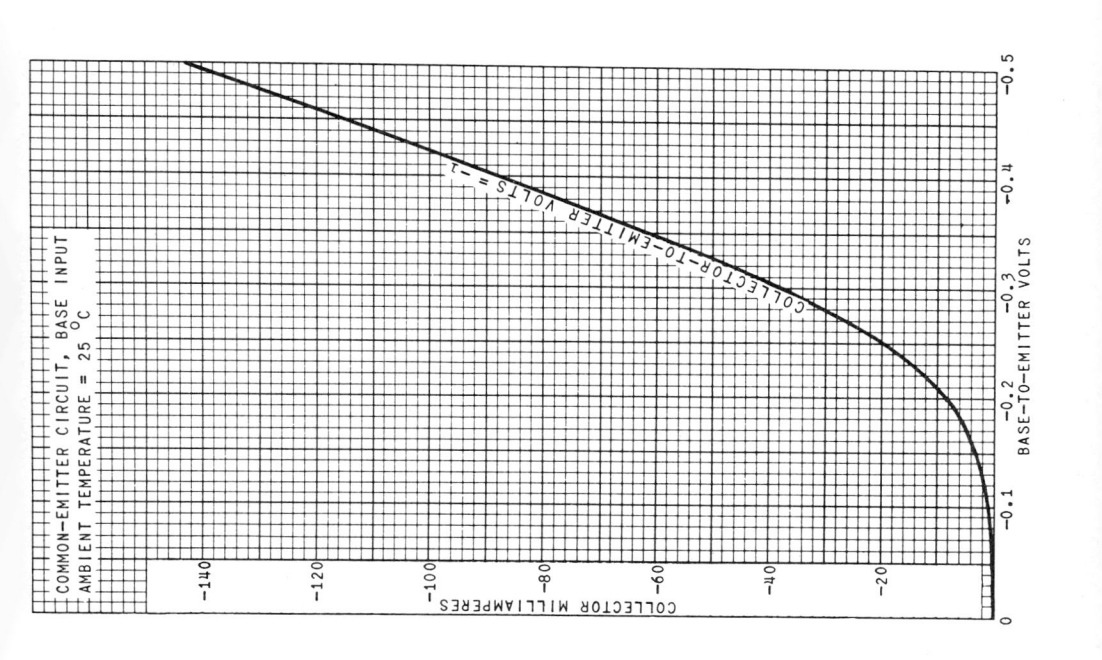

Transistor parameters

GENERAL ELECTRIC 2N322, 2N323, 2N324, 2N1097, 2N1098 P-N-P JUNCTION TRANSISTORS

The General Electric Types 2N322, 2N323, 2N324, 2N1097 and 2N1098 are PNP alloy junction transistors designed for audio driver and power output applications. These units are similar to the higher voltage 2N1414 series. Higher gain is available with the 2N508.

Processing includes storage for a minimum of 100 hours at 100°C and a hermetic seal test on each unit. To control thermal runaway, the transistor base is internally connected to the case. This assures a conservative junction temperature at maximum power ratings.

absolute maximum ratings (25°C)

Voltage
Collector to Base	V_{CBO}	−18	volts
Collector to Emitter ($R_{BE} \leq 5$ kohms)	V_{CER}	−18	volts
Emitter to Base	V_{EBO}	−5	volts

Current
Collector	I_C	−200	ma

Dissipation
Total Transistor*	P_T	200	mw
Total Transistor at 55°C**	P_T	140	mw

Temperature
Storage	T_{STG}	−65 to +100	°C
Operating Junction	T_J	−65 to +85	°C
Lead Temperature, 1/16″ ±1/32″ from case for 10 seconds maximum	T_L	260	°C

* (Derate 2.0 mw/°C increase in ambient from 25°C to 55°C)
** (Derate 4.7 mw/°C increase in ambient from 55°C to 85°C)

DIMENSIONS WITHIN JEDEC OUTLINE TO-5

NOTE 1: This zone is controlled for automatic handling. The variation in actual diameter within this zone shall not exceed .010.

NOTE 2: Measured from max. diameter of the actual device.

NOTE 3: The specified lead diameter applies in the zone between .050 and .250 from the base seat. Between .250 and .5 of these zones the lead diameter is held. Outside maximum of .021 diameter is held. Outside controlled. Leads may be inserted, without damage, in .031 holes while transistor enters .371 hole concentric with lead hole circle.

APPROX WEIGHT .05 OZ
ALL DIMENSIONS IN INCHES

502

electrical characteristics: (25°C)

DC CHARACTERISTICS

		2N322			2N323			2N324		
		Min.	Typ.	Max.	Min.	Typ.	Max.	Min.	Typ.	Max.
Forward Current Transfer Ratio ($V_{CE}=-1v, I_C=-20$ ma)	h_{FE}	34	50	65	53	80	121	72	100	198
Base to Emitter Voltage ($V_{CB}=-1v, I_C=-20$ ma)	V_{BE}	−0.18		−0.32	−0.18		−0.32	−0.18		−0.32	volts
Collector Cutoff Current ($V_{CB}=-16v$)	I_{CBO}		−6	−16		−6	−16		−6	−16	μa
Emitter Cutoff Current ($V_{EB}=-3v$)	I_{EBO}		−3	−16		−3	−16		−3	−16	μa
Collector to Emitter Voltage ($R_{BE}=5$ kohms, $I_C=-600$ μa)	V_{CER}	−18			−18			−18			volts

SMALL SIGNAL CHARACTERISTICS
($V_{CE}=-5v, I_E=1$ ma, $f=1$ kc except as noted.)

Forward Current Transfer Ratio	h_{fe}		44			70			88		
Input Impedance	h_{ie}		1400			1700			2600		ohms
Output Admittance	h_{oe}		30			35			40		μmhos
Reverse Voltage Transfer Ratio	h_{re}		4.5			6.5			7.0		$\times 10^{-4}$
Cutoff Frequency ($V_{CB}=-5v, I_E=1$ ma)	f_{hrb}	1.0	3.0		1.5	3.5		2.0	4.0		mc
Output Capacity ($V_{CB}=-5v, I_E=1$ ma, $f=1$ mc)	C_{ob}		18	35		18	35		18	35	pf

DC CHARACTERISTICS

		2N1097			2N1098		
		Min.	Typ.	Max.	Min.	Typ.	Max.
Forward Current Transfer Ratio ($V_{CE}=-1v, I_C=-20$ ma)	h_{FE}	34	55	90	25	50	90
Base to Emitter Voltage ($V_{CB}=-1v, I_C=-20$ ma)	V_{BE}	−0.18		−0.32	−0.18		−0.32	volts
Collector Cutoff Current ($V_{CB}=-16v$)	I_{CBO}		−6	−16		−6	−16	μa
Emitter Cutoff Current ($V_{EB}=-3v$)	I_{EBO}		−3	−16		−3	−16	μa
Collector to Emitter Voltage ($R_{BE}=5$ kohms, $I_C=-600$ μa)	V_{CER}	−18			−18			volts

SMALL SIGNAL CHARACTERISTICS
($V_{CE}=-5v, I_E=1$ ma, $f=1$ kc except as noted.)

Forward Current Transfer Ratio	h_{fe}		48			44		
Input Impedance	h_{ie}		1500			1400		ohms
Output Admittance	h_{oe}		32			30		μmhos
Reverse Voltage Transfer Ratio	h_{re}		5.0			4.5		$\times 10^{-4}$
Cutoff Frequency ($V_{CB}=-5v, I_E=1$ ma)	f_{hrb}	1.0	3.0		1.0	3.0		mc
Output Capacity ($V_{CB}=-5v, I_E=1$ ma, $f=1$ mc)	C_{ob}		18	35		18	35	pf

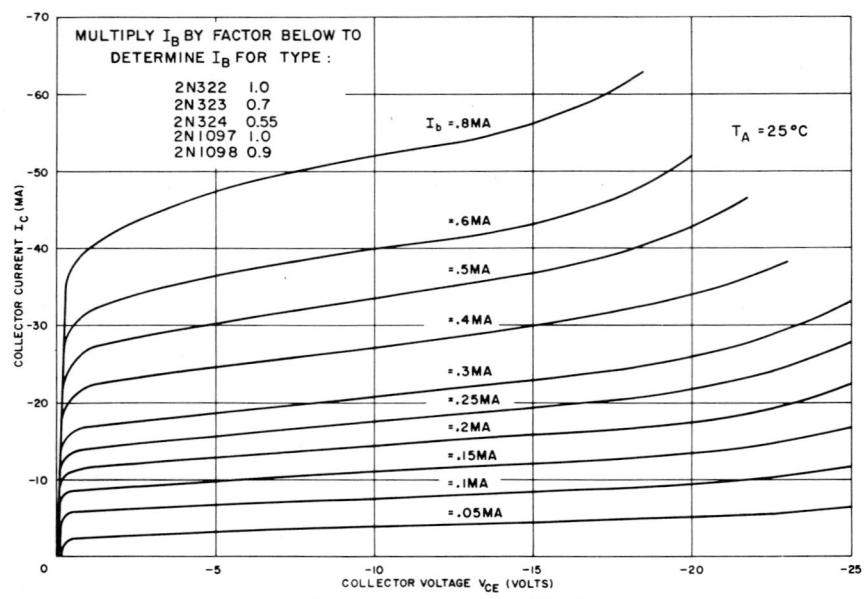

COMMON EMITTER COLLECTOR CHARACTERISTICS

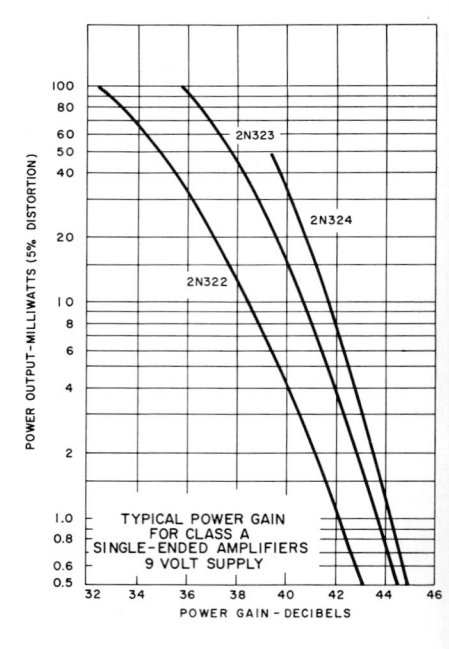

MULTIPLY I_B BY FACTOR BELOW TO DETERMINE I_B FOR TYPE:

Type	Factor
2N322	1.0
2N323	0.7
2N324	0.55
2N1097	1.0
2N1098	0.9

$T_A = 25°C$

COLLECTOR CUTOFF CURRENT VS TEMPERATURE
$V_{CB} = -10$ VOLTS

TYPICAL POWER GAIN FOR CLASS A SINGLE-ENDED AMPLIFIERS 9 VOLT SUPPLY

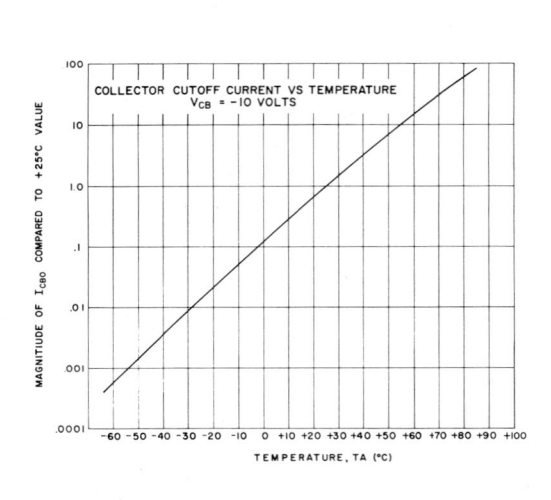

504

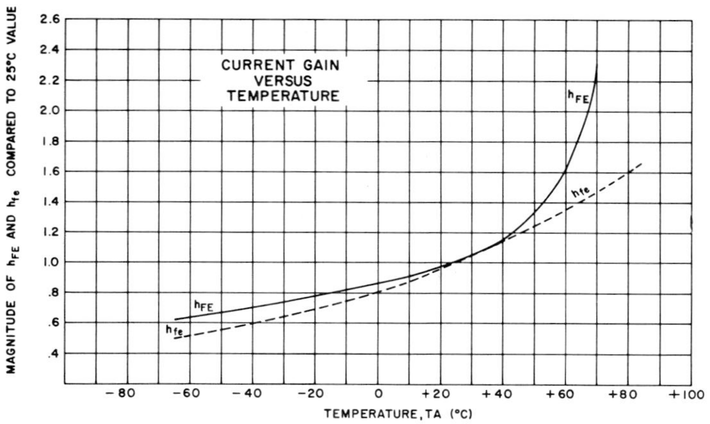
CURRENT GAIN
VERSUS
TEMPERATURE
MAGNITUDE OF hFE AND hfe COMPARED TO 25°C VALUE
hFE
hfe
2.6
2.4
2.2
2.0
1.8
1.6
1.4
1.2
1.0
.8
.6
.4
-80
-60
-40
-20
0
+20
+40
+60
+80
+100
TEMPERATURE, TA (°C)

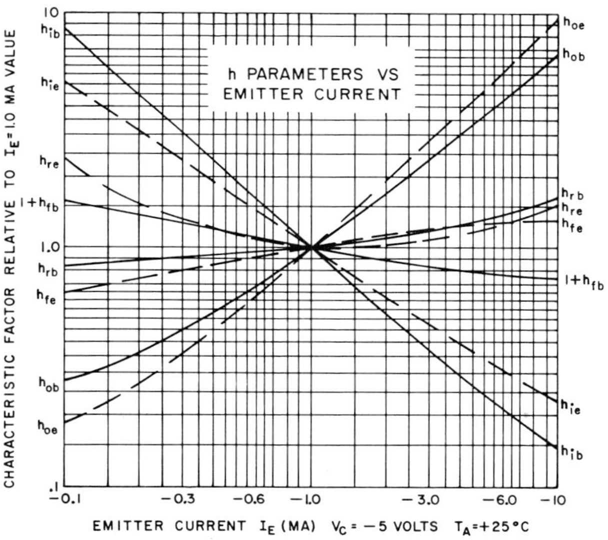
h PARAMETERS VS
EMITTER CURRENT
CHARACTERISTIC FACTOR RELATIVE TO IE=1.0 MA VALUE
hib
hie
hre
1+hfb
hrb
hfe
hob
hoe
10
1.0
.1
-0.1
-0.3
-0.6
-1.0
-3.0
-6.0
-10
EMITTER CURRENT IE (MA) VC = -5 VOLTS TA=+25°C

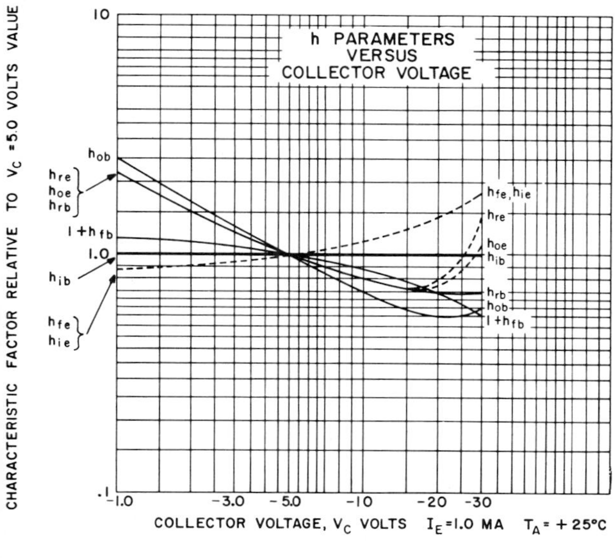
h PARAMETERS
VERSUS
COLLECTOR VOLTAGE
CHARACTERISTIC FACTOR RELATIVE TO VC =5.0 VOLTS VALUE
hob
hre
hoe
hrb
1+hfb
hib
hfe
hie
hfe, hie
hre
hoe
hib
hrb
hob
1+hfb
10
1.0
.1
-1.0
-3.0
-5.0
-10
-20
-30
COLLECTOR VOLTAGE, VC VOLTS IE=1.0 MA TA= +25°C

GENERAL ELECTRIC 2N3392, 2N3393, 2N3394 N-P-N SILICON TYPE TRANSISTORS

The General Electric 2N3392, 2N3393 and 2N3394 are NPN silicon planar passivated transistors designed as small signal consumer and industrial amplifiers. These devices feature tight beta control at an extremely low price.

NOTE 1. The specified lead diameter applies to the zone between .050 and .250 from the base of the seat. Between .250 and end of lead a maximum of .021 diameter is held. Outside of these zones the lead diameter is not controlled.

ALL DIMEN. IN INCHES

3 LEADS .017 +.002 −.001 (NOTE 1)

absolute maximum ratings (25°C) unless otherwise specified

Voltages
Collector to Emitter	V_{CEO}	25	V
Emitter to Base	V_{EBO}	5	V
Collector to Base	V_{CBO}	25	V

Current
Collector (Steady State)[1]	I_C	100	ma

Dissipation
Total Power (free air at 25°C)[2]	P_T	200	mw
Total Power (free air at 55°C)[2]	P_T	120	mw

Temperature
Storage	T_{stg}	−30 to +125	°C
Operating	T_J	+100	°C
Lead Temperature, 1/16″ ± 1/32″ from case for 10 seconds max.	T_L	+260	°C

[1] Determined from power limitations due to saturation voltage at this current.
[2] Derate 2.67 mw/°C increase in ambient temperature above 25°C.

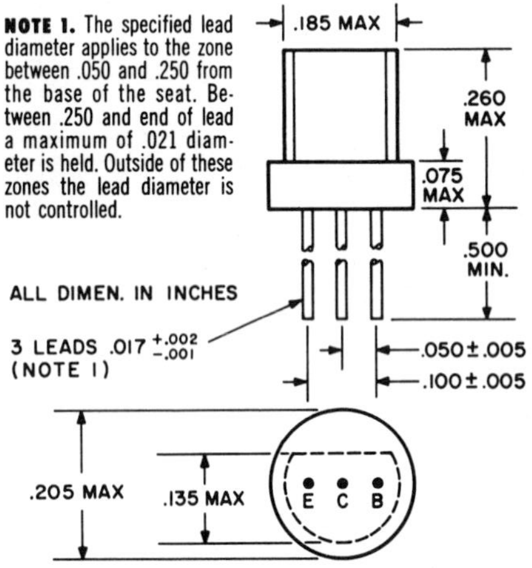

electrical characteristics (25°C) unless otherwise specified

DC CHARACTERISTICS

			Min.	Typ.	Max.	
Collector Cutoff Current		I_{CBO}			0.1	μa
($V_{CB} = 25V$, $I_E = 0$)		I_{CBO}			10	μa
($V_{CB} = 25V$, $T_A = 100°C$)						
Emitter Cutoff Current		I_{EBO}			0.1	μa
($V_{EB} = 5V$, $I_C = 0$)						
Collector to Emitter Voltage		V_{CEO}	25			volts
($I_C = 1$ ma)						
Forward Current Transfer Ratio	2N3392	h_{FE}	150		300	
($V_{CE} = 4.5V$, $I_C = 2$ ma)	2N3393	h_{FE}	90		180	
	2N3394	h_{FE}	55		110	

SMALL SIGNAL CHARACTERISTICS

		Min.	Typ.	Max.	
Output Capacitance	C_{ob}	4.5	7	12	pf
($V_{CB} = 10V$, $I_E = 0$, $f = 1$ mc)					
Input Impedance	h_{ib}		15		ohms
($V_{CE} = 10V$; $I_C = 2$ ma; $f = 1$ kc)					
Gain Bandwidth Product	f_t		140		mc
($I_C = 4$ ma; $V_{CB} = 5V$)					
Forward Current Transfer Ratio	h_{fe}		15		mc
($I_C = 20$ ma; $V_{CB} = 5V$, $f = 20$ mc)					

		2N3392	2N3393	2N3394	
Forward Current Transfer Ratio	h_{fe}	208	150	100	
Input Impedance	h_{ie}	6000	3400	2750	ohms
Output Admittance	h_{oe}	14.0	10.0	7.7	μmhos
Voltage Feedback Ratio	h_{re}	.33	.225	.175	x10^{-3}

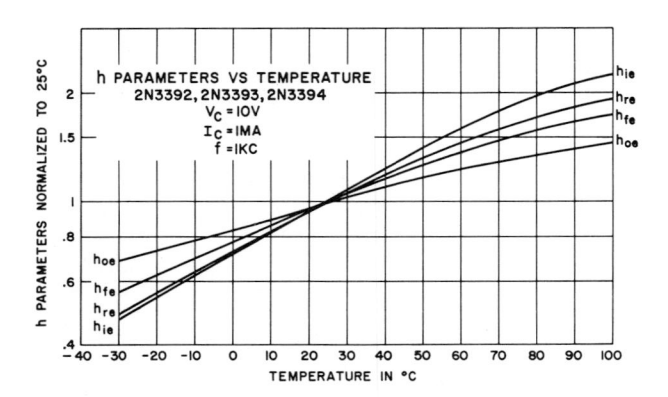

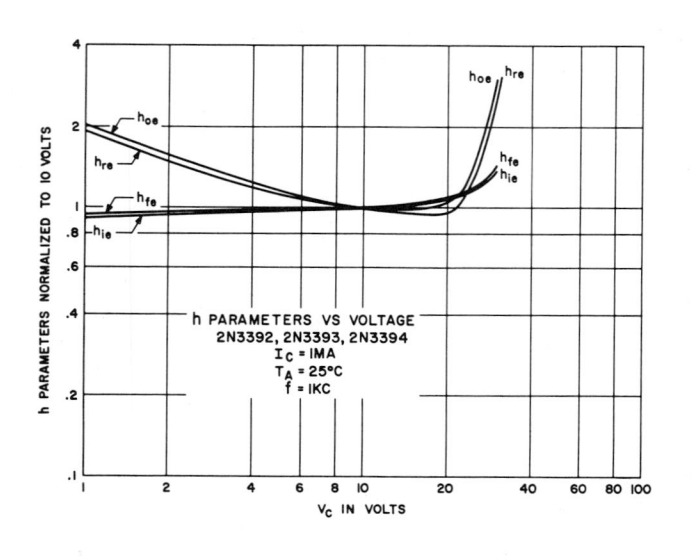

h PARAMETERS VS TEMPERATURE
2N3392, 2N3393, 2N3394
V_C = 10V
I_C = 1MA
f = 1KC

h PARAMETERS VS VOLTAGE
2N3392, 2N3393, 2N3394
I_C = 1MA
T_A = 25°C
f = 1KC

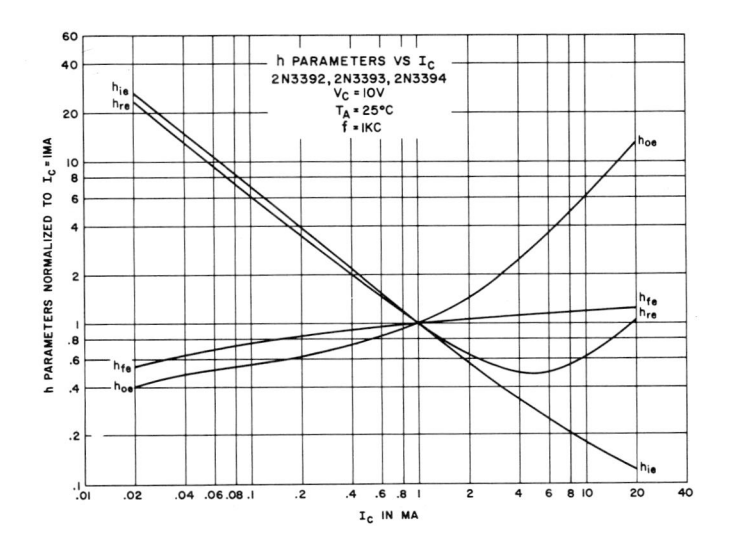

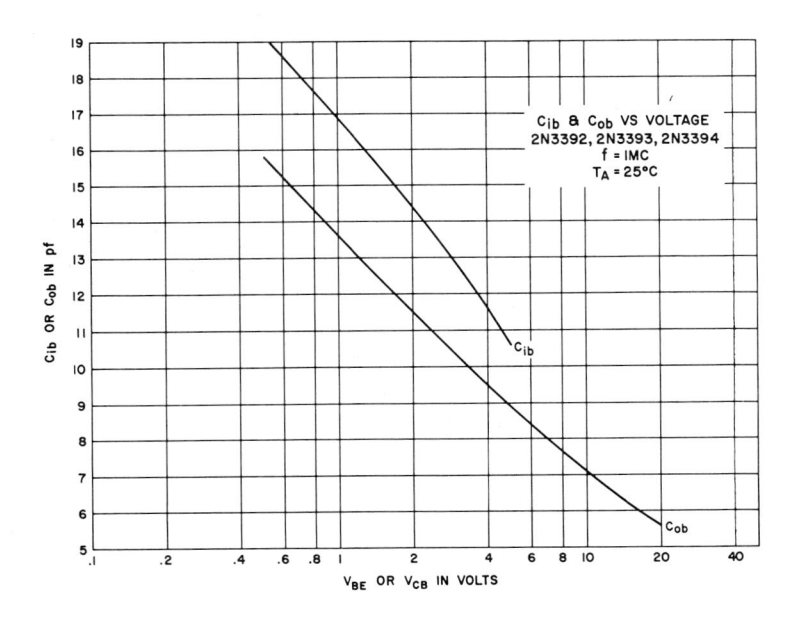

Transistor parameters

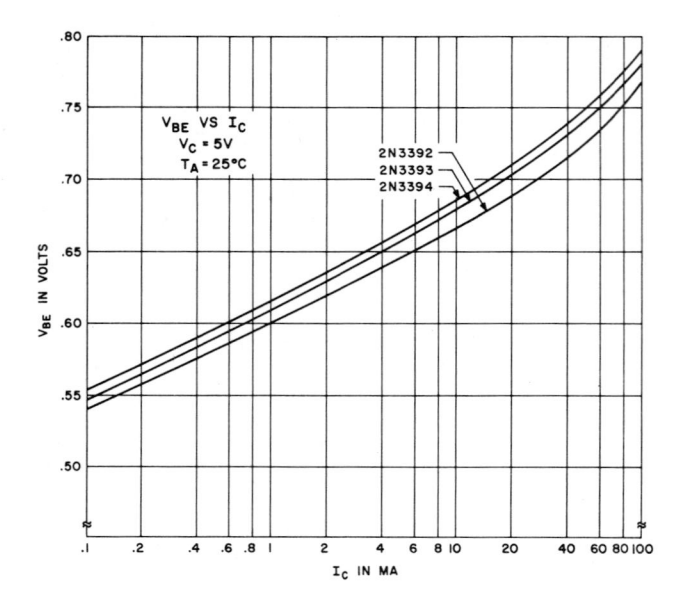

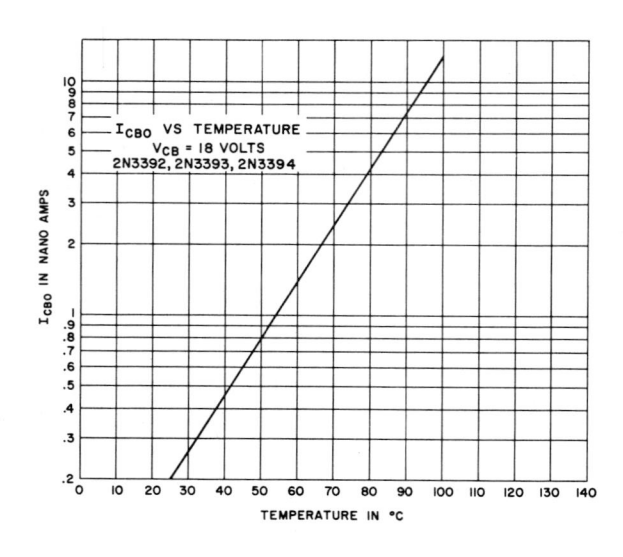

Transistor parameters

V_{BE} VS I_C for 2N3392, 2N3393, 2N3394 at $V_C = 5V$, $T_A = 25°C$

I_{CBO} VS TEMPERATURE at $V_{CB} = 18$ VOLTS for 2N3392, 2N3393, 2N3394

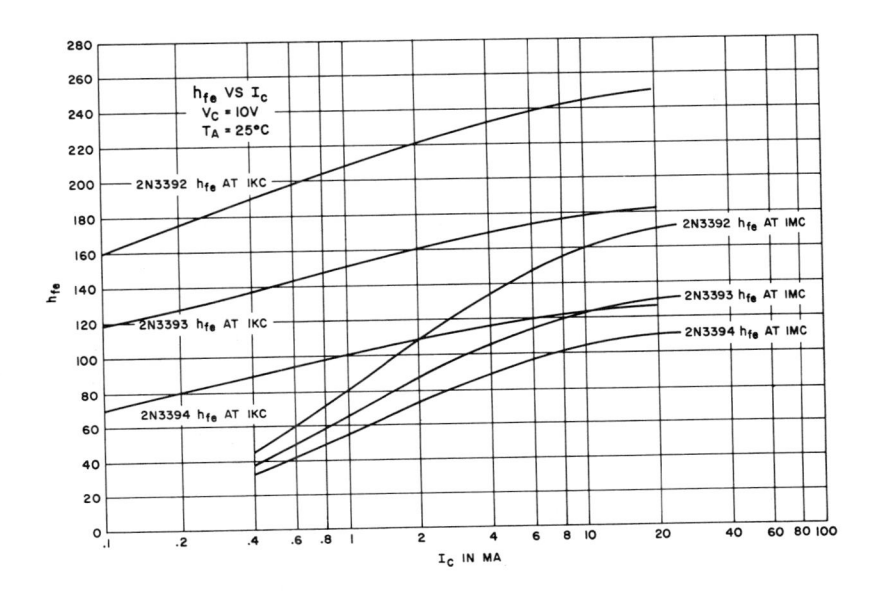

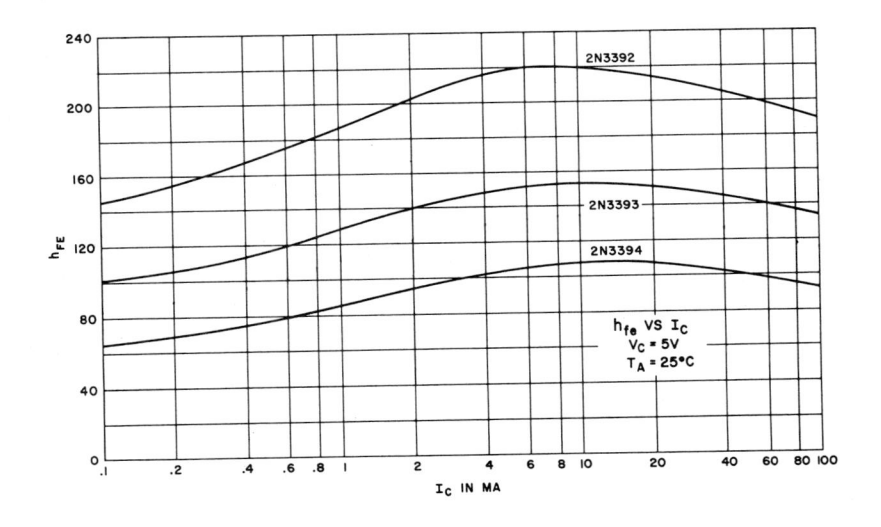

Transistor parameters

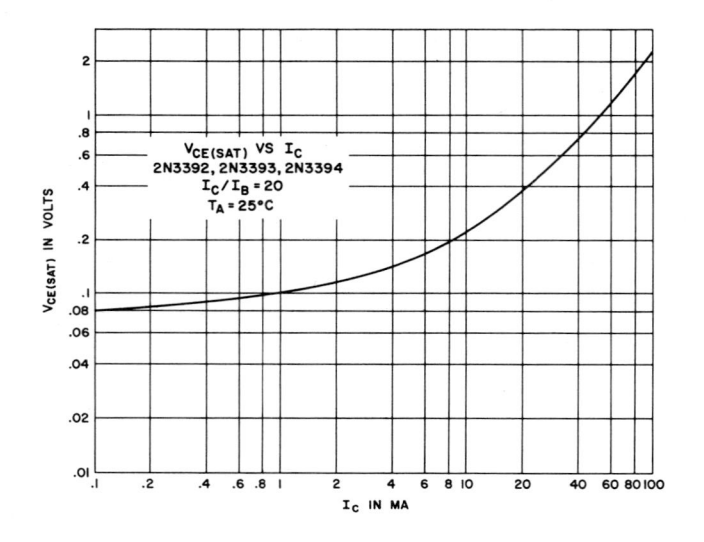

Transistor parameters

$V_{CE(SAT)}$ vs I_C
2N3392, 2N3393, 2N3394
$I_C/I_B = 20$
$T_A = 25°C$

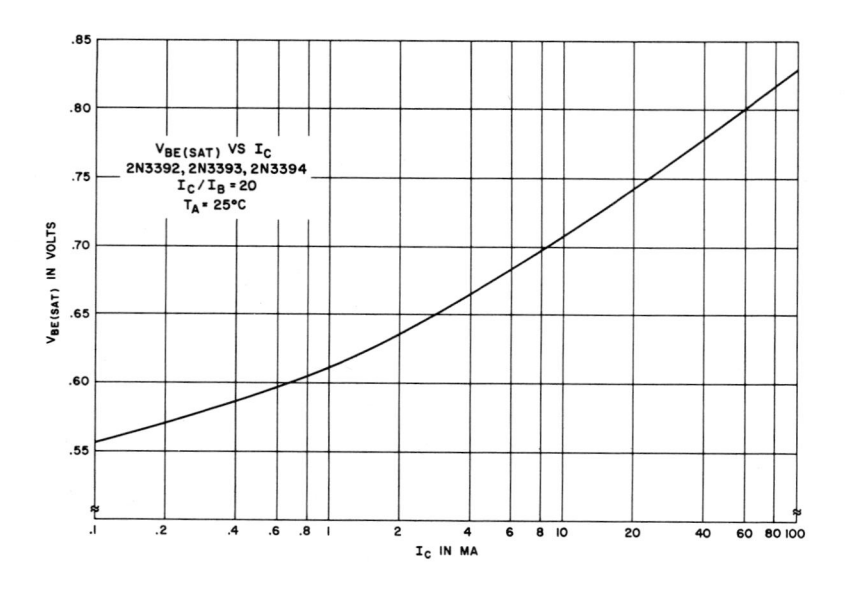

$V_{BE(SAT)}$ vs I_C
2N3392, 2N3393, 2N3394
$I_C/I_B = 20$
$T_A = 25°C$

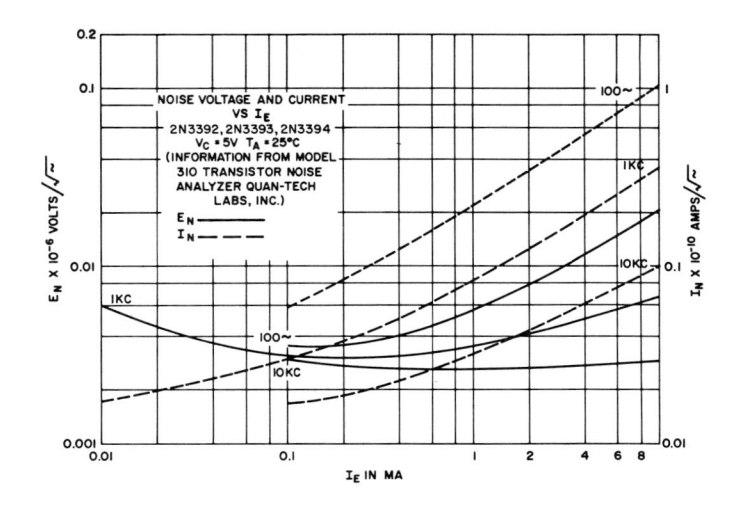

Transistor parameters

NOISE VOLTAGE AND CURRENT VS I_E
2N3392, 2N3393, 2N3394
V_C = 5V T_A = 25°C
(INFORMATION FROM MODEL 310 TRANSISTOR NOISE ANALYZER QUAN-TECH LABS, INC.)

E_N ———
I_N — — —

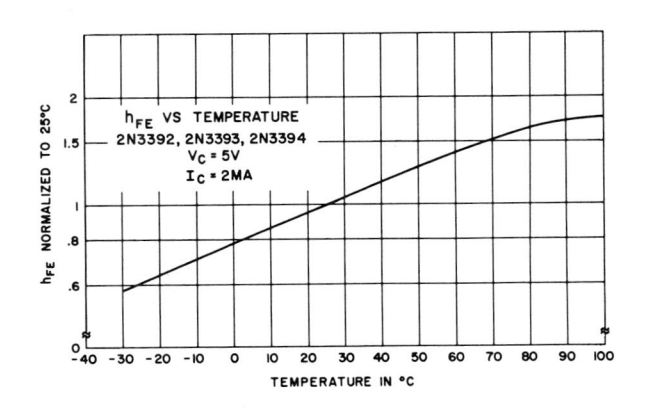

h_{FE} VS TEMPERATURE
2N3392, 2N3393, 2N3394
V_C = 5V
I_C = 2MA

FAIRCHILD 2N3638 P-N-P HIGH CURRENT SWITCH—DIFFUSED SILICON PLANAR EPITAXIAL TRANSISTOR

The 2N3638 is a PNP silicon PLANAR epitaxial transistor designed for digital applications at current levels to 500 milliamperes. The high gain-bandwidth product, f_T, at high currents, makes it an excellent unit for line driving and memory applications.

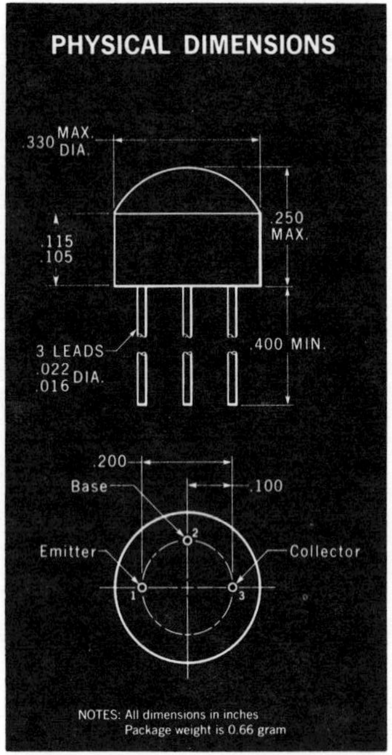

ABSOLUTE MAXIMUM RATINGS [Note 1]

Maximum Temperatures

Storage Temperature	-55°C to +125°C
Operating Junction Temperature	+125°C Maximum
Lead Temperature (Soldering, 10 sec time limit)	+260°C Maximum

Maximum Power Dissipation

Total Dissipation at 25°C Case Temperature (Notes 2 and 3)	0.7 Watt
at 25°C Free Air Temperature (Notes 2 and 3)	0.3 Watt

Maximum Voltages and Current

V_{CBO}	Collector to Base Voltage	-25 Volts
V_{CES}	Collector to Emitter Voltage	-25 Volts
V_{CEO}	Collector to Emitter Voltage (Note 4)	-25 Volts
V_{EBO}	Emitter to Base Voltage	-4.0 Volts
I_C	Collector Current (Note 2)	500 mA

ELECTRICAL CHARACTERISTICS (25°C Free Air Temperature unless otherwise noted)

Symbol	Characteristic	Min.	Typ.	Max.	Units	Test Conditions
V_{CE}(sat)	Collector-Emitter Saturation Voltage (pulsed, Note 5)		-0.38	-1.0	Volts	I_C = 300 mA, I_B = 30 mA
V_{CE}(sat)	Collector-Emitter Saturation Voltage (pulsed, Note 5)		-0.08	-0.25	Volts	I_C = 50 mA, I_B = 2.5 mA
h_{fe}	High Frequency Current Gain (f = 100 Mc)	1.0	1.5			I_C = 50 mA, V_{CE} = -3.0 V
C_{obo}	Common-Base, Open-Circuit Output Capacitance		12	20	pf	I_E = 0, V_{CB} = -10 V
V_{CEO}(sust)	Collector to Emitter Sustaining Voltage (Notes 4 and 5)	-25			Volts	I_C = 10 mA, I_B = 0 (pulsed)

Additional Electrical Characteristics on page 2

Copyright 1964 by Fairchild Semiconductor, a division of Fairchild Camera and Instrument Corporation

NOTES:

(1) These ratings are limiting values above which the serviceability of any individual semiconductor device may be impaired.
(2) These are steady state limits. The factory should be consulted on applications involving pulsed or low duty cycle operations.
(3) These ratings give a maximum junction temperature of 125°C and junction-to-case thermal resistance of 143°C/Watt (derating factor of 7.0 mW/°C); junction-to-ambient thermal resistance of 333°C/Watt (derating factor of 3.0 mW/°C).
(4) Rating refers to a high-current point where collector-to-emitter voltage is lowest. For more information send for Fairchild Publication APP-4.
(5) Pulse Conditions: length = 300 μsec; duty cycle = 1%.
(6) See switching circuit for exact values of I_C, I_{B1}, and I_{B2}.

515

ELECTRICAL CHARACTERISTICS (25°C Free Air Temperature unless otherwise noted)

Symbol	Characteristic	Min.	Typ.	Max.	Units	Test Conditions
BV_{CBO}	Collector to Base Breakdown Voltage	-25			Volts	$I_C = 100\ \mu A$, $I_E = 0$
BV_{CES}	Collector to Emitter Breakdown Voltage	-25			Volts	$I_C = 100\ \mu A$, $V_{EB} = 0$
h_{FE}	DC Pulse Current Gain (Note 5)	30	67			$I_C = 50\ mA$, $V_{CE} = -1.0\ V$
h_{FE}	DC Pulse Current Gain (Note 5)	20	40			$I_C = 300\ mA$, $V_{CE} = -2.0\ V$
h_{FE}	DC Pulse Current Gain (Note 5)	20				$I_C = 10\ mA$, $V_{CE} = -10\ V$
t_{on}	Turn On Time (Note 6)		28	75	nsec	$I_C \approx 300\ mA$, $I_{B1} \approx 30\ mA$
t_{off}	Turn Off Time (Note 6)		110	170	nsec	$I_C \approx 300\ mA$, $I_{B1} \approx 30\ mA$, $I_{B2} \approx -30\ mA$
$V_{BE}(sat)$	Base-Emitter Saturation Voltage (pulsed, Note 5)	-0.9		-1.1	Volts	$I_C = 50\ mA$, $I_B = 2.5\ mA$
$V_{BE}(sat)$	Base-Emitter Saturation Voltage (pulsed, Note 5)	-0.8	-1.25	-2.0	Volts	$I_C = 300\ mA$, $I_B = 30\ mA$
BV_{EBO}	Emitter to Base Breakdown Voltage	-4.0			Volts	$I_E = 100\ \mu A$, $I_C = 0$
I_{CES}	Collector Reverse Current		0.1	35	nA	$V_{CE} = -15\ V$, $V_{EB} = 0$
$I_{CES}(65°C)$	Collector Reverse Current		0.002	2.0	μA	$V_{CE} = -15\ V$, $V_{EB} = 0$
C_{ibo}	Common Base, Open Circuit Input Capacitance		65		pf	$I_C = 0$, $V_{EB} = -0.5\ V$

TYPICAL ELECTRICAL CHARACTERISTICS

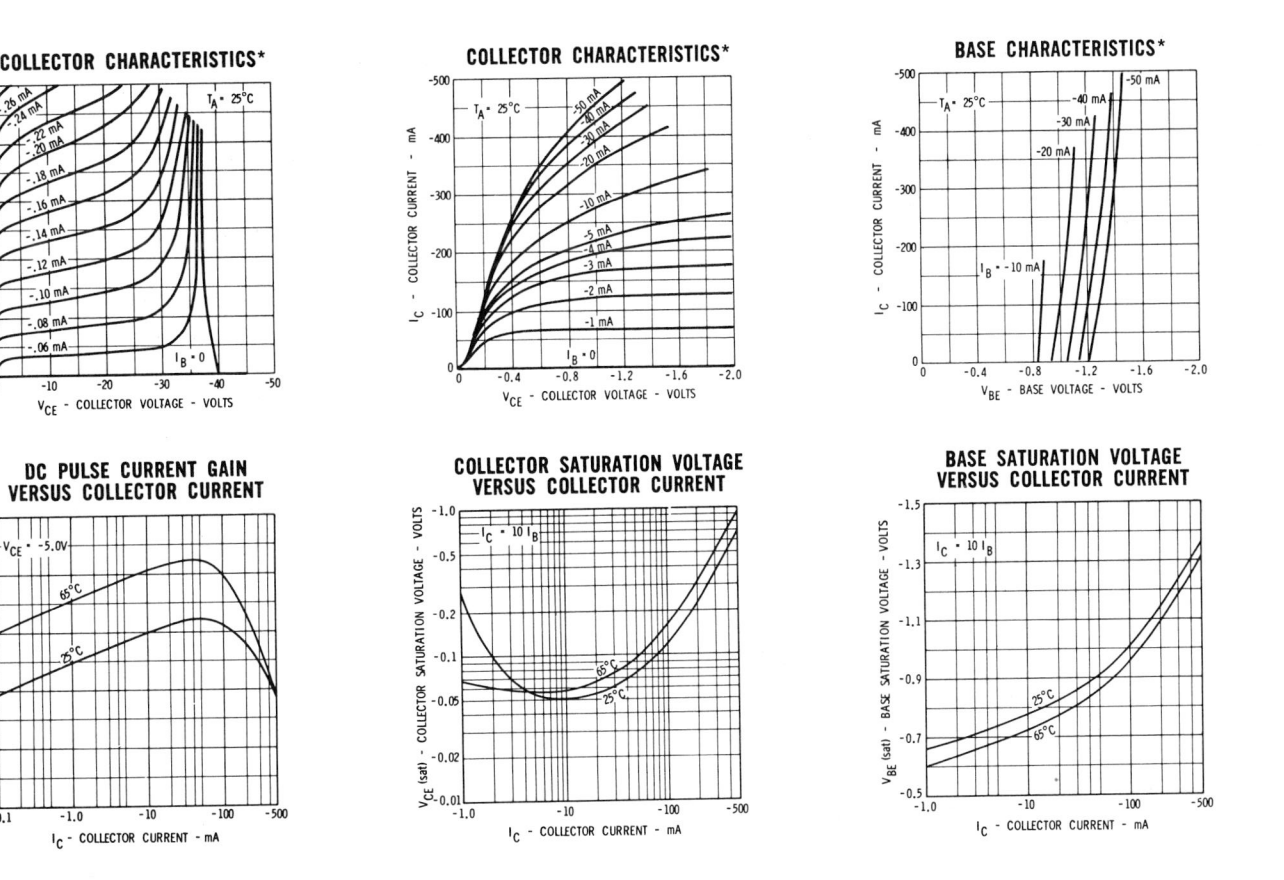

*Single family characteristics on Transistor Curve Tracer.

COLLECTOR-BASE REVERSE CURRENT VERSUS REVERSE BIAS VOLTAGE

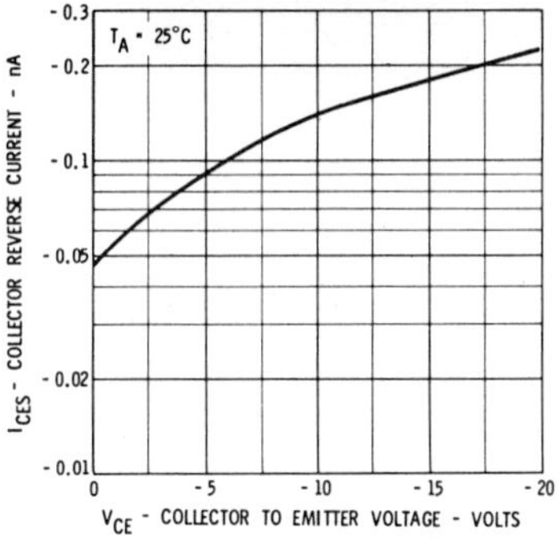

COLLECTOR-BASE DIODE REVERSE CURRENT VERSUS TEMPERATURE

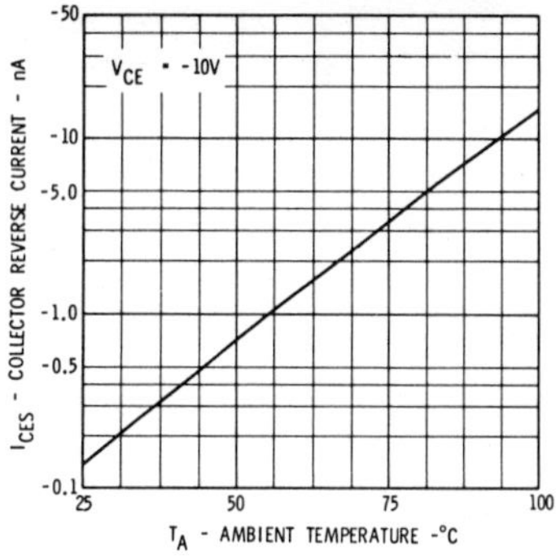

INPUT AND OUTPUT CAPACITANCE VERSUS REVERSE BIAS VOLTAGE

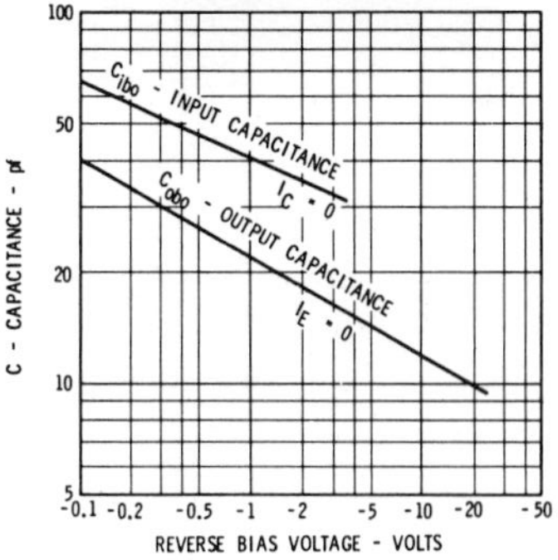

CONTOURS OF CONSTANT GAIN BANDWIDTH PRODUCT (f_T)

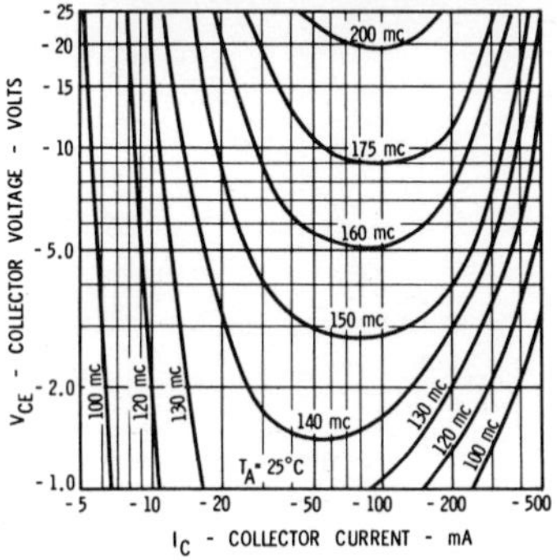

SWITCHING TIMES VERSUS COLLECTOR CURRENT

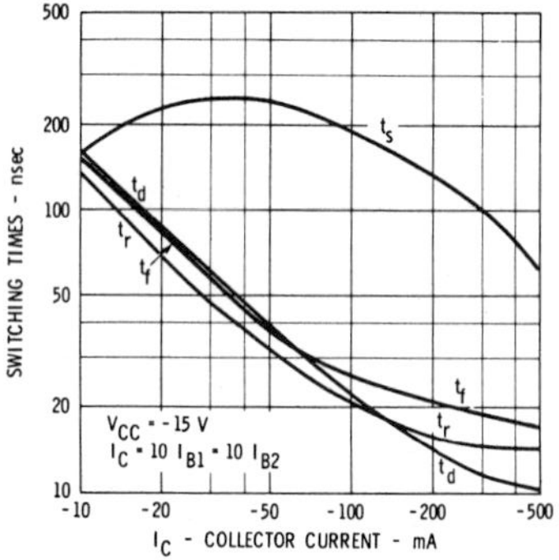

SWITCHING TIMES VERSUS TEMPERATURE

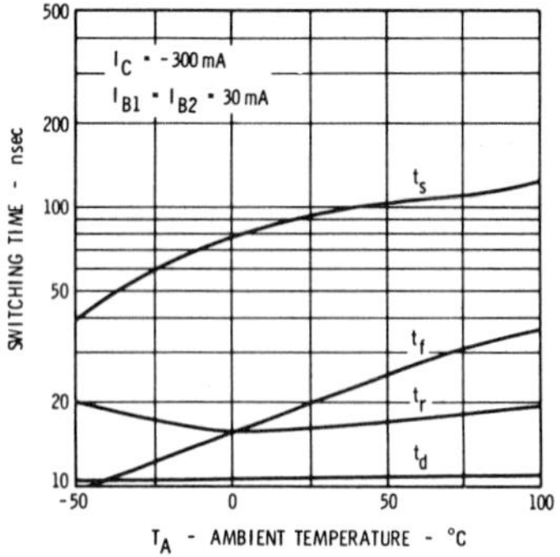

DELAY TIME VERSUS TURN ON BASE CURRENT AND REVERSE BASE EMITTER VOLTAGE

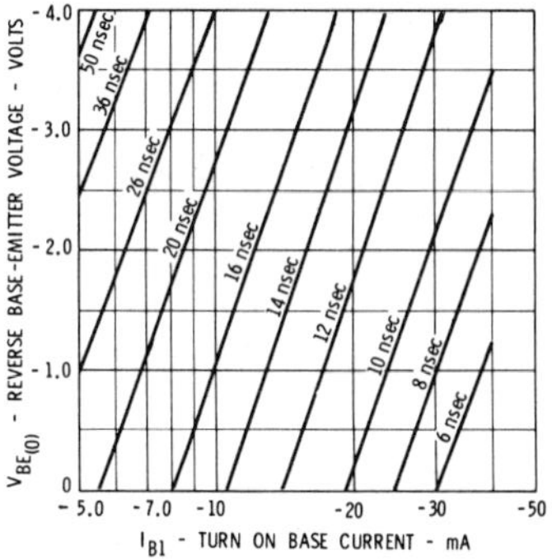

RISE TIME VERSUS TURN ON BASE CURRENT AND COLLECTOR CURRENT

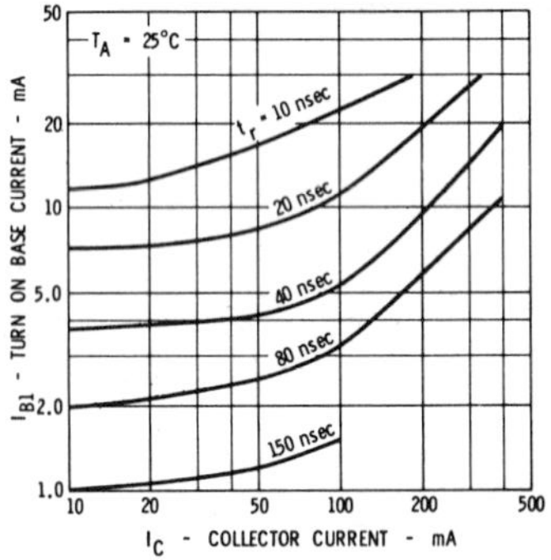

519

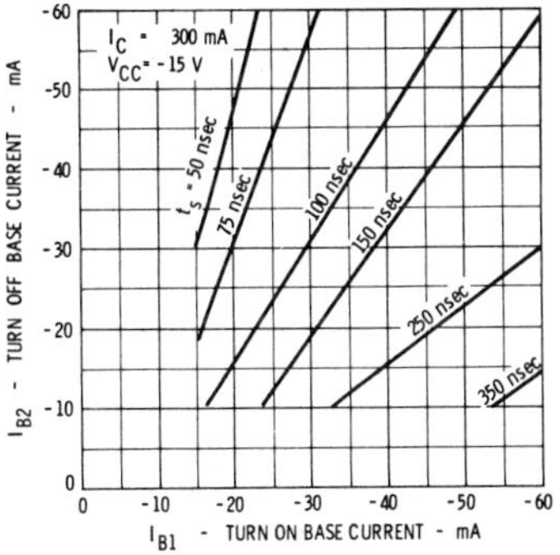

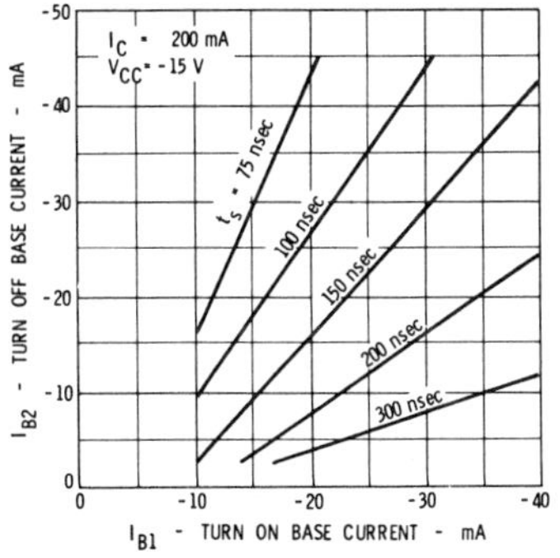

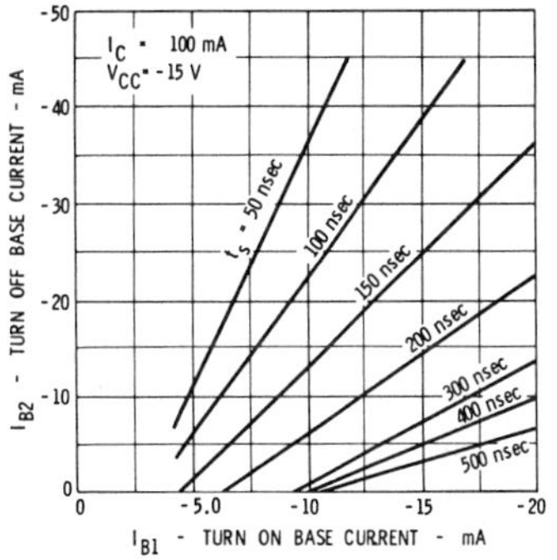

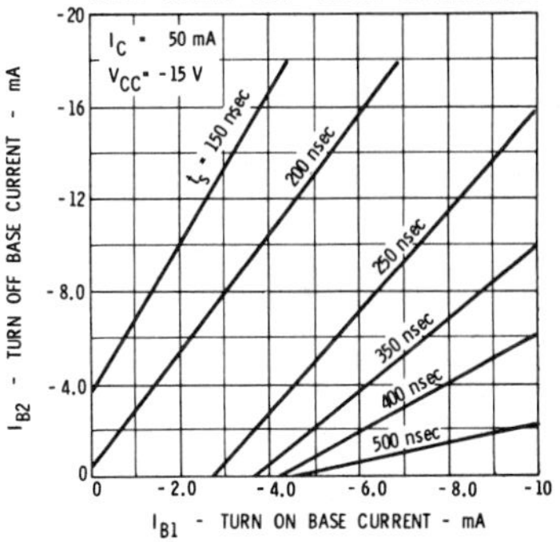

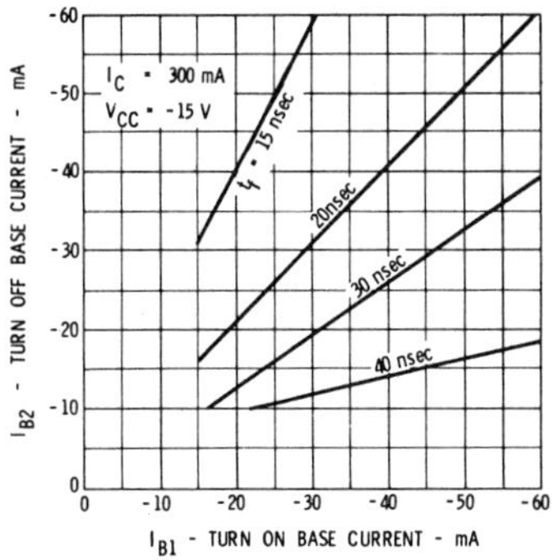

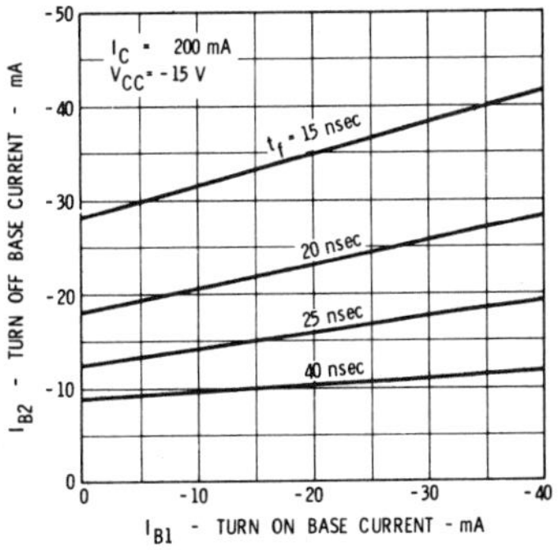

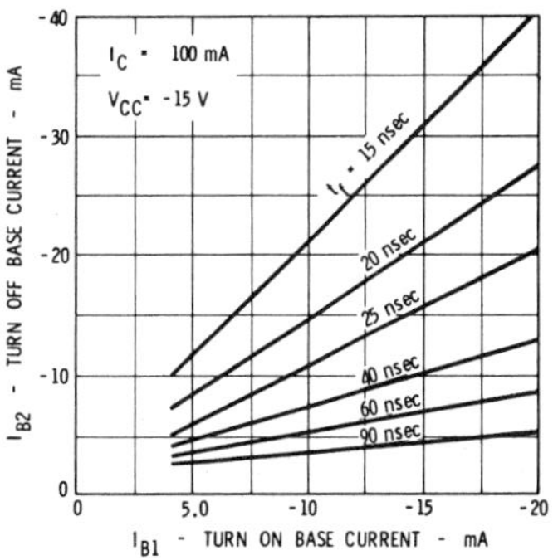

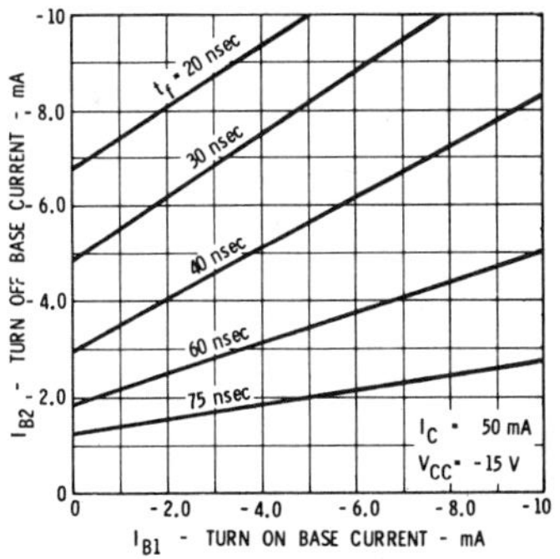

SMALL SIGNAL CHARACTERISTICS

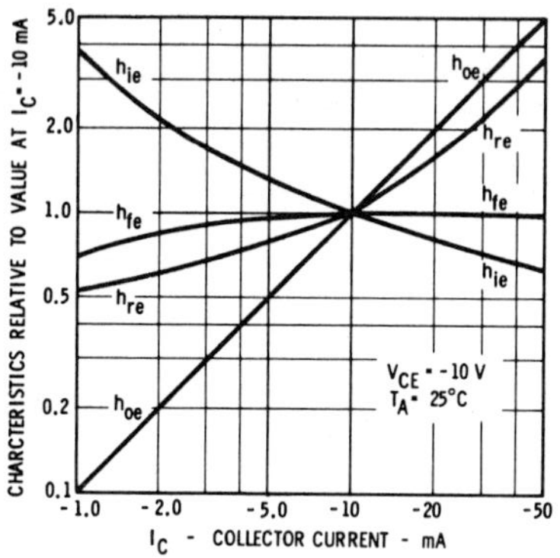

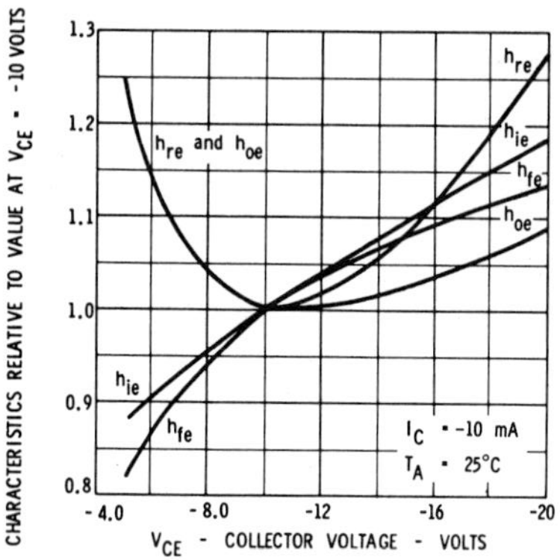

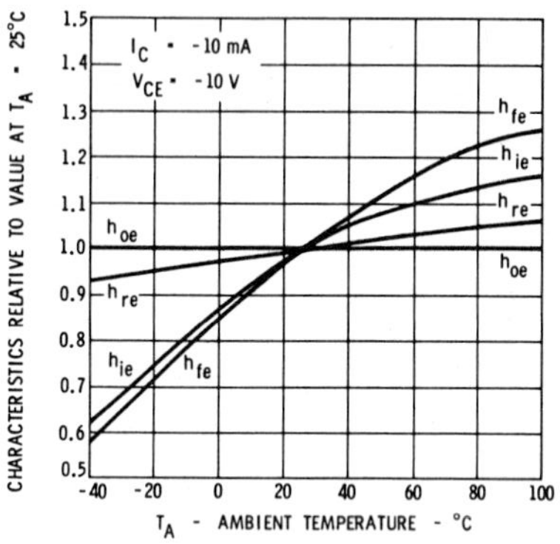

h PARAMETERS (f = 1 kc)

SYMBOL	CHARACTERISTICS	MIN.	TYP.	MAX.	UNITS	TEST CONDITIONS
h_{ie}	Input Resistance		480	2000	ohms	$I_C = 10$ mA $V_{CE} = -10$ V
h_{oe}	Output Conductance		80	1200	µmhos	$I_C = 10$ mA $V_{CE} = -10$ V
h_{re}	Voltage Feedback Ratio		162	2600	x10⁻⁶	$I_C = 10$ mA $V_{CE} = -10$ V
h_{fe}	Small Signal Current Gain	25	74			$I_C = 10$ mA $V_{CE} = -10$ V

T_ON and T_OFF TEST CIRCUIT

$V_{BB} = +3.1$V $\quad V_{CC} = -10$V

TO SAMPLING SCOPE
$t_r < 1.0$ nsec
$Z_{IN} \geq 100$K

$V_{IN} = -9.0$V
$t_r, t_f < 6.0$ nsec
PULSE WIDTH = 0.5 µsec
$Z_{IN} = 50\Omega$

TEXAS INSTRUMENTS 2N1302, 2N1304, 2N1306, 2N1308 N-P-N AND
2N1303, 2N1305, 2N1307, 2N1309 P-N-P COMPLEMENTARY
ALLOY JUNCTION GERMANIUM TRANSISTORS

High-Frequency Transistors for Computer and Switching Applications

- **Complementary Families**
- **Proven Reliability and Stability**

environmental tests

To ensure maximum integrity, stability, and long life, finished devices are subjected to the following tests and conditions prior to thorough testing for rigid adherence to specified characteristics.

- All devices receive a 100°C stabilization bake for 100 hours.
- The hermetic seal for all devices is verified by helium leak testing.
- Production samples are life tested at regularly scheduled periods to ensure maximum reliability under extreme operating conditions.
- Continuous Quality Control checks on in-process assembly are maintained.

***mechanical data**

The transistors are in a JEDEC TO-5 hermetically sealed welded package with glass to metal seal between case and leads. Approximate weight is one gram.

THE BASE IS IN ELECTRICAL CONTACT WITH CASE

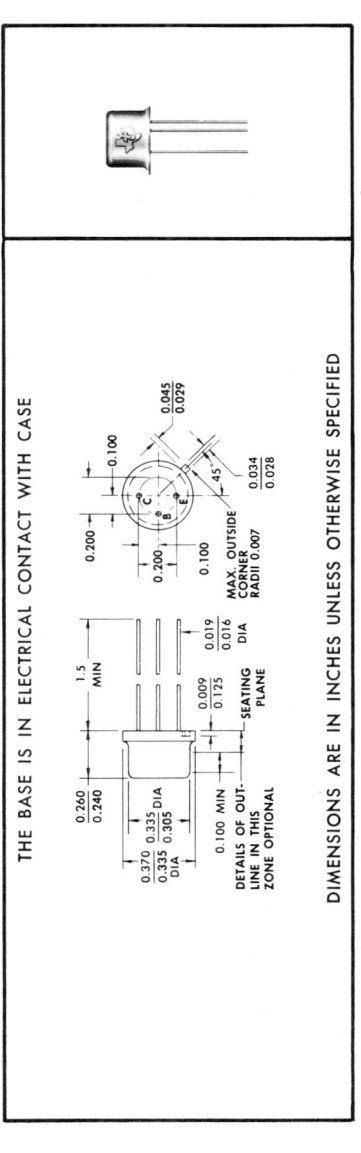

DIMENSIONS ARE IN INCHES UNLESS OTHERWISE SPECIFIED

***absolute maximum ratings at 25°C free-air temperature (unless otherwise noted)**

	2N1302, 2N1304, 2N1305, 2N1306, 2N1308	2N1303, 2N1307, 2N1309
Collector-Base Voltage	25 v	30 v
Emitter-Base Voltage	25 v	
Collector Current	300 ma	
Total Device Dissipation at (or below) 25°C Free-Air Temperature (See Note 1)	150 mw	
Operating Collector Junction Temperature	85°C	
Storage Temperature Range	−65°C to 100°C	

NOTE: 1. Derate linearly to 85°C free-air temperature at the rate of 2.5 mw/C°.
*Indicates JEDEC registered data.

electrical characteristics at 25°C free-air temperature

N-P-N types 2N1302, 2N1304, 2N1306, and 2N1308

PARAMETER		TEST CONDITIONS		2N1302 MIN	2N1302 TYP	2N1302 MAX	2N1304 MIN	2N1304 TYP	2N1304 MAX	2N1306 MIN	2N1306 TYP	2N1306 MAX	2N1308 MIN	2N1308 TYP	2N1308 MAX	UNIT
BV_{CBO}	Collector-Base Breakdown Voltage	$I_E = 100\ \mu a$,	$I_E = 0$	25	—	—	25	—	—	25	—	—	25	—	—	v
BV_{EBO}	Emitter-Base Breakdown Voltage	$I_E = 100\ \mu a$,	$I_C = 0$	25	—	—	25	—	—	25	—	—	25	—	—	v
*V_{PT}	Punch Through Voltage†	$V_{EBfl} = 1\ v$		25	—	—	20	—	—	15	—	—	15	—	—	v
*I_{CBO}	Collector Cutoff Current	$V_{CB} = 25\ v$,	$I_E = 0$	—	3	6	—	3	6	—	3	6	—	3	6	μa
*I_{EBO}	Emitter Cutoff Current	$V_{EB} = 25\ v$,	$I_C = 0$	—	2	6	—	2	6	—	2	6	—	2	6	μa
*h_{FE}	Static Forward Current Transfer Ratio	$V_{CE} = 1\ v$,	$I_C = 10\ ma$	20	100	—	40	115	200	60	130	300	80	160	—	—
		$V_{CE} = 0.35\ v$,	$I_C = 200\ ma$	10	100	—	15	110	—	20	125	—	20	140	—	—
*V_{BE}	Base-Emitter Voltage	$I_B = 0.5\ ma$,	$I_C = 10\ ma$	0.15	0.22	0.40	0.15	0.22	0.35	0.15	0.22	0.35	0.15	0.22	0.35	v
*$V_{CE(sat)}$	Collector-Emitter Saturation Voltage	$I_B = 0.5\ ma$,	$I_C = 10\ ma$	—	0.07	0.20	—	0.07	0.20	—	—	0.20	—	—	0.20	v
		$I_B = 0.25\ ma$,	$I_C = 10\ ma$	—	—	—	—	—	—	—	—	—	—	—	—	v
		$I_B = 0.17\ ma$,	$I_C = 10\ ma$	—	—	—	—	—	—	—	0.07	0.20	—	0.07	—	v
		$I_B = 0.13\ ma$,	$I_C = 10\ ma$	—	—	—	—	—	—	—	—	—	—	—	—	v
h_{ib}	Small-Signal Common-Base Input Impedance	$V_{CB} = 5\ v$,	$I_E = -1\ ma$	—	28	—	—	28	—	—	28	—	—	28	—	ohm
		$f = 1\ kc$														
h_{rb}	Small-Signal Common-Base Reverse Voltage Transfer Ratio	$V_{CB} = 5\ v$,	$I_E = -1\ ma$	—	5×10^{-4}	—	—	5×10^{-4}	—	—	5×10^{-4}	—	—	5×10^{-4}	—	—
		$f = 1\ kc$														
h_{ob}	Small-Signal Common-Base Output Admittance	$V_{CB} = 5\ v$,	$I_E = -1\ ma$	—	0.34	—	—	0.34	—	—	0.34	—	—	0.34	—	μmho
		$f = 1\ kc$														

PARAMETER		TEST CONDITIONS									UNIT
h_{fe}	Small-Signal Common-Emitter Forward Current Transfer Ratio	$V_{CE} = 5$ v, $I_C = 1$ ma $f = 1$ kc		—	105	—	—	120	—	—	135	—	—	170	—	—
*f_{hfb}	Common-Base Alpha-Cutoff Frequency	$V_{CB} = 5$ v, $I_E = -1$ ma		3	12	—	5	14	—	10	16	—	15	20	—	mc
*C_{ob}	Common-Base Open Circuit Output Capacitance	$V_{CB} = 5$ v, $I_E = 0$ $f = 1$ mc		—	14	20	—	14	20	—	14	20	—	14	20	pf
C_{ib}	Common-Base Open-Circuit Input Capacitance	$V_{EB} = 5$ v, $I_C = 0$ $f = 1$ mc		—	13	—	—	13	—	—	13	—	—	13	—	pf

†V_{PT} is determined by measuring the emitter-base floating potential V_{EBfl}. The collector-base voltage, $V_{CB'}$ is increased until $V_{EBfl} = 1$ volt; this value of $V_{CB} = (V_{PT} + 1\text{ v})$.

switching characteristics at 25°C free-air temperature

PARAMETER		TEST CONDITIONS††	2N1302			2N1304			2N1306			2N1308			UNIT
			MIN	TYP	MAX	MIN	TYP	MAX	MIN	TYP	MAX	MIN	TYP	MAX	
t_d	Delay Time	$I_C = 10$ ma, $I_{B(1)} = 1.3$ ma	—	0.07	—	—	0.07	—	—	0.06	—	—	0.06	—	µsec
t_r	Rise Time	$I_{B(2)} = -0.7$ ma, $V_{BE(off)} = -0.8$ v	—	0.20	—	—	0.20	—	—	0.18	—	—	0.15	—	µsec
t_s	Storage Time	$R_L = 1$ kΩ (See Fig. 1)	—	0.70	—	—	0.70	—	—	0.64	—	—	0.64	—	µsec
t_f	Fall Time		—	0.40	—	—	0.40	—	—	0.36	—	—	0.34	—	µsec
Q_{sb}	Stored Base Charge	$I_{B(1)} = 1$ ma, $I_C = 10$ ma (See Fig. 2)	—	800	—	—	760	—	—	720	—	—	680	—	pcb

††Voltage and current values shown are nominal; exact values vary slightly with device parameters.

operating characteristics at 25°C free-air temperature

PARAMETER		TEST CONDITIONS	2N1302			2N1304			2N1306			2N1308			UNIT
			MIN	TYP	MAX	MIN	TYP	MAX	MIN	TYP	MAX	MIN	TYP	MAX	
NF	Spot Noise Figure	$V_{CB} = 5$ v, $I_E = -1$ ma $f = 1$ kc, $R_G = 1$ kΩ	—	4	—	—	4	—	—	3	—	—	3	—	db

*Indicates JEDEC registered data (typical values excluded).

COMMON-EMITTER COLLECTOR CHARACTERISTICS

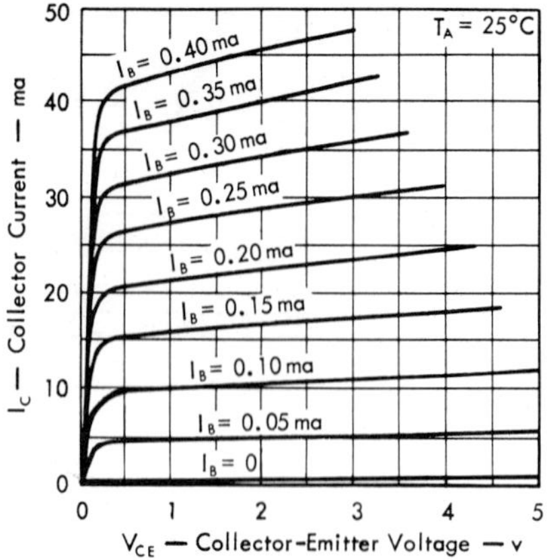

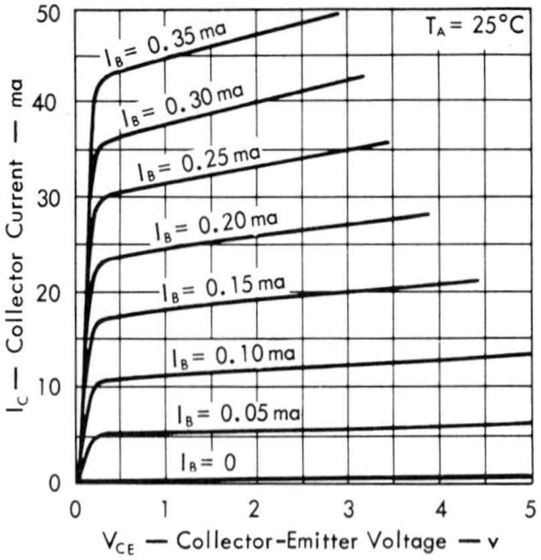

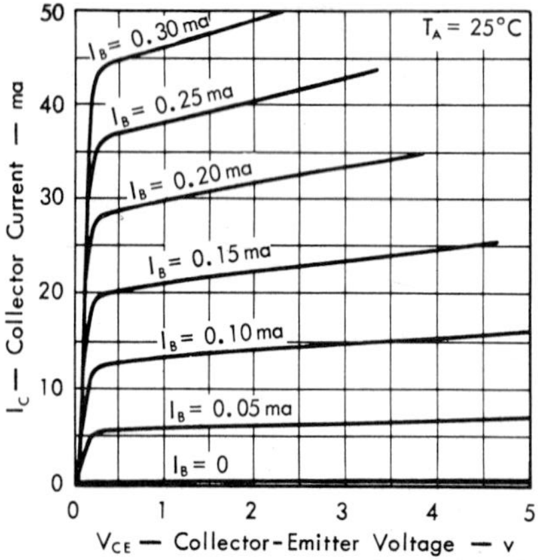

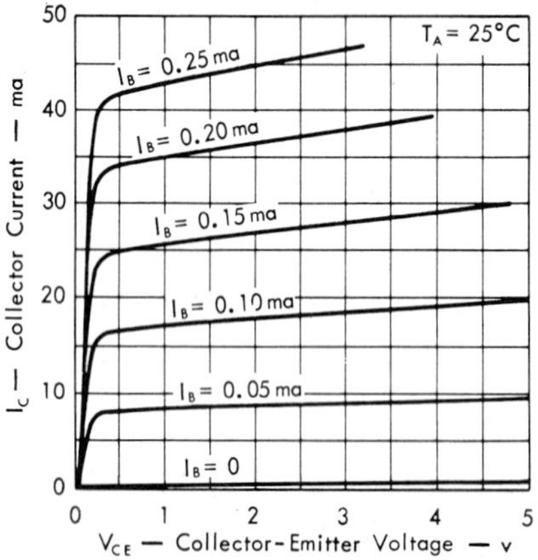

PARAMETER MEASUREMENT INFORMATION

FIGURE 1 SWITCHING TIMES
(POLARITIES SHOWN APPLY TO N-P-N)

TEST CIRCUIT

VOLTAGE WAVEFORMS

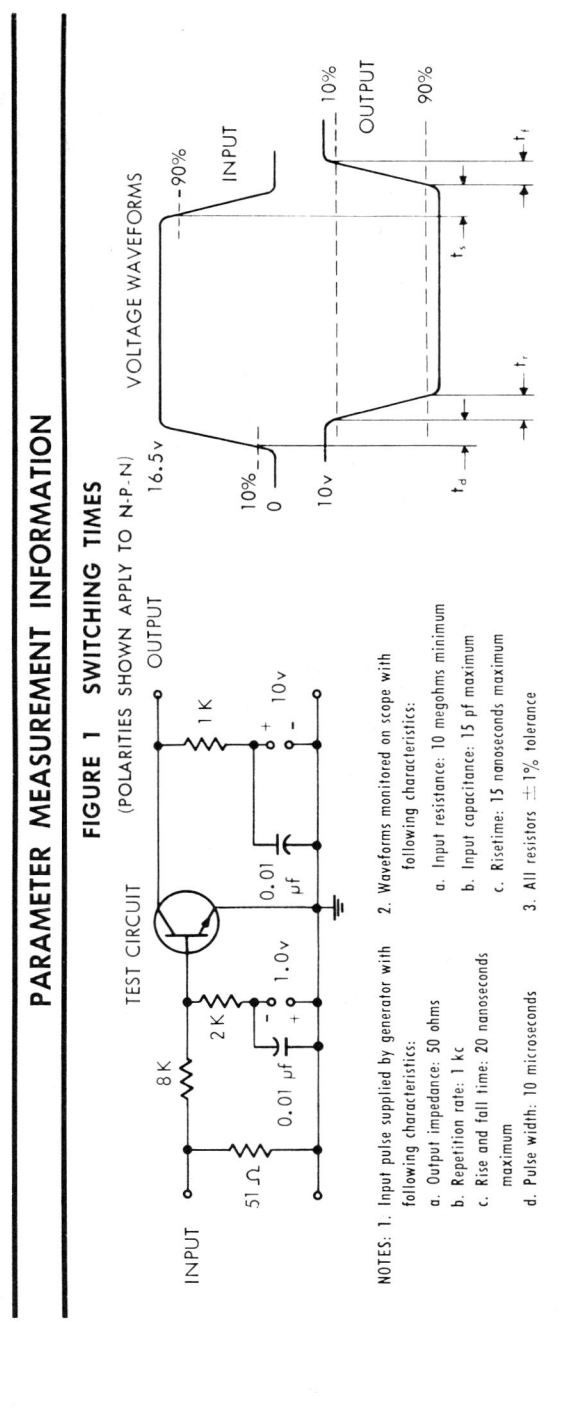

NOTES:
1. Input pulse supplied by generator with following characteristics:
   a. Output impedance: 50 ohms
   b. Repetition rate: 1 kc
   c. Rise and fall time: 20 nanoseconds maximum
   d. Pulse width: 10 microseconds

2. Waveforms monitored on scope with following characteristics:
   a. Input resistance: 10 megohms minimum
   b. Input capacitance: 15 pf maximum
   c. Risetime: 15 nanoseconds maximum

3. All resistors ±1% tolerance

P-N-P types 2N1303, 2N1305, 2N1307, and 2N1309

electrical characteristics at 25°C free-air temperature

PARAMETER		TEST CONDITIONS	2N1303 MIN	2N1303 TYP	2N1303 MAX	2N1305 MIN	2N1305 TYP	2N1305 MAX	2N1307 MIN	2N1307 TYP	2N1307 MAX	2N1309 MIN	2N1309 TYP	2N1309 MAX	UNIT
BV_{CBO}	Collector-Base Breakdown Voltage	$I_E = -100\ \mu a,\ I_E = 0$	−30	—	—	−30	—	—	−30	—	—	−30	—	—	v
BV_{EBO}	Emitter-Base Breakdown Voltage	$I_E = -100\ \mu a,\ I_C = 0$	−25	—	—	−25	—	—	−25	—	—	−25	—	—	v
*V_{pt}	Punch Through Voltage†	$V_{EBf} = -1\ v$	−25	—	—	−20	—	—	−15	—	—	−15	—	—	v
*I_{CBO}	Collector Cutoff Current	$V_{CB} = -25\ v,\ I_E = 0$	—	−2	−6	—	−2	−6	—	−2	−6	—	−2	−6	μa
*I_{EBO}	Emitter Cutoff Current	$V_{EB} = -25\ v,\ I_C = 0$	—	−1.5	−6	—	−1.5	−6	—	−1.5	−6	—	−1.5	−6	μa
*h_{FE}	Static Forward Current Transfer Ratio	$V_{CE} = -1\ v,\ I_C = -10\ ma$	20	100	—	40	115	200	60	130	300	80	160	—	—
		$V_{CE} = -0.35\ v,\ I_C = -200\ ma$	10	45	—	15	55	—	20	65	—	20	75	—	—
*V_{BE}	Base-Emitter Voltage	$I_B = -0.5\ ma,\ I_C = -10\ ma$	−0.15	−0.25	−0.40	−0.15	−0.25	−0.35	−0.15	−0.25	−0.35	−0.15	−0.25	−0.35	v
		$I_B = -0.5\ ma,\ I_C = -10\ ma$	—	−0.08	−0.20	—	—	—	—	—	—	—	—	—	v
*$V_{CE(sat)}$	Collector-Emitter Saturation Voltage	$I_B = -0.25\ ma,\ I_C = -10\ ma$	—	—	—	—	−0.08	−0.20	—	—	—	—	—	—	v
		$I_B = -0.17\ ma,\ I_C = -10\ ma$	—	—	—	—	—	—	—	−0.08	−0.20	—	—	—	v
		$I_B = -0.13\ ma,\ I_C = -10\ ma$	—	—	—	—	—	—	—	—	—	—	−0.08	−0.20	v
h_{ib}	Small-Signal Common-Base Input Impedance	$V_{CB} = -5\ v,\ I_E = 1\ ma$ $f = 1\ kc$	—	29	—	—	29	—	—	29	—	—	29	—	ohm
h_{rb}	Small-Signal Common-Base Reverse Voltage Transfer Ratio	$V_{CB} = -5\ v,\ I_E = 1\ ma$ $f = 1\ kc$	—	7×10^{-4}	—	—	7×10^{-4}	—	—	7×10^{-4}	—	—	7×10^{-4}	—	—
h_{ob}	Small-Signal Common-Base Output Admittance	$V_{CB} = -5\ v,\ I_E = 1\ ma$ $f = 1\ kc$	—	0.40	—	—	0.40	—	—	0.40	—	—	0.40	—	μmho

		TEST CONDITIONS					
h_{fe}	Small-Signal Common-Emitter Forward Current Transfer Ratio	$V_{CE} = -5$ v, $I_C = -1$ ma $f = 1$ kc	—	115	—	130	—
*f_{hfb}	Common-Base Alpha-Cutoff Frequency	$V_{CB} = -5$ v, $I_E = 1$ ma	3	12	—	5	14
*C_{ob}	Common-Base Open-Circuit Output Capacitance	$V_{CB} = -5$ v, $I_E = 0$ $f = 1$ mc	—	10	20	—	10
C_{ib}	Common-Base Open-Circuit Input Capacitance	$V_{EB} = -5$ v, $I_C = 0$ $f = 1$ mc	—	9	—	—	9

(continued)

						UNIT
	—	150	—	—	190	—
	—	16	—	15	20	mc
	20	—	10	—	10	pf
	—	—	—	—	9	pf

†V_{PT} is determined by measuring the emitter-base floating potential V_{EBf1}. The collector-base voltage, V_{CB}, is increased until $V_{EBf1} = -1$ volt; this value of $V_{CB} = (V_{PT} - 1$ v$)$.

switching characteristics at 25°C free-air temperature

PARAMETER		TEST CONDITIONS††	2N1303			2N1305			2N1307			2N1309			UNIT
			MIN	TYP	MAX	MIN	TYP	MAX	MIN	TYP	MAX	MIN	TYP	MAX	
t_d	Delay Time	$I_C = -10$ ma, $I_{B(1)} = -1.3$ ma	—	0.06	—	—	0.06	—	—	0.06	—	—	0.05	—	μsec
t_r	Rise Time	$I_{B(2)} = 0.7$ ma, $V_{BE(off)} = 0.8$ v	—	0.18	—	—	0.18	—	—	0.14	—	—	0.14	—	μsec
t_s	Storage Time	$R_L = 1$ kΩ (See Fig. 1)	—	0.80	—	—	0.80	—	—	0.78	—	—	0.76	—	μsec
t_f	Fall Time		—	0.38	—	—	0.38	—	—	0.36	—	—	0.30	—	μsec
Q_{sb}	Stored Base Charge	$I_{B(1)} = -1$ ma, $I_C = -10$ ma (See Fig. 2)	—	960	—	—	920	—	—	880	—	—	800	—	pcb

††Voltage and current values shown are nominal, exact values vary slightly with device parameters.

operating characteristics at 25°C free-air temperature

PARAMETER		TEST CONDITIONS	2N1303			2N1305			2N1307			2N1309			UNIT
			MIN	TYP	MAX	MIN	TYP	MAX	MIN	TYP	MAX	MIN	TYP	MAX	
NF	Spot Noise Figure	$V_{CB} = -5$ v $I_E = 1$ ma $f = 1$ kc, $R_G = 1$ kΩ	—	4	—	—	4	—	—	3	—	—	3	—	db

*Indicates JEDEC registered data (typical values excluded).

COMMON-EMITTER COLLECTOR CHARACTERISTICS

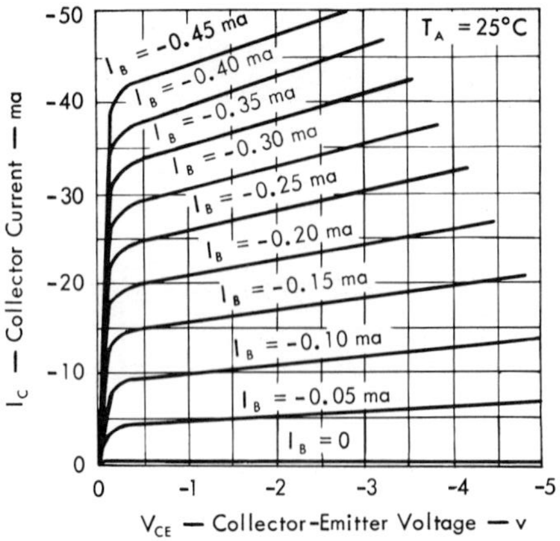

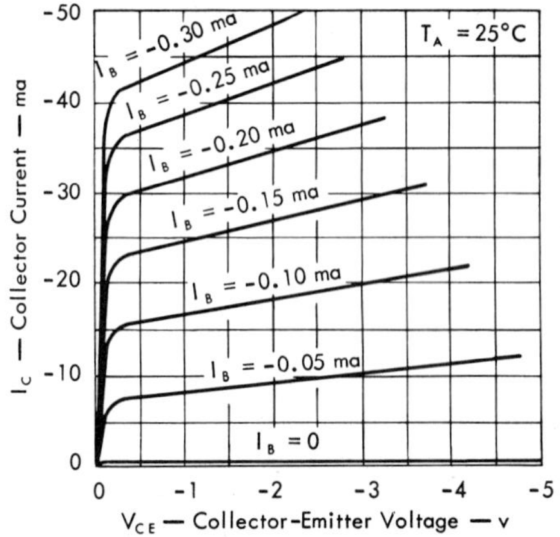

NOTE: These Characteristics are measured by the sweep method using a 575 Tektronix Curve Tracer (or equivalent).

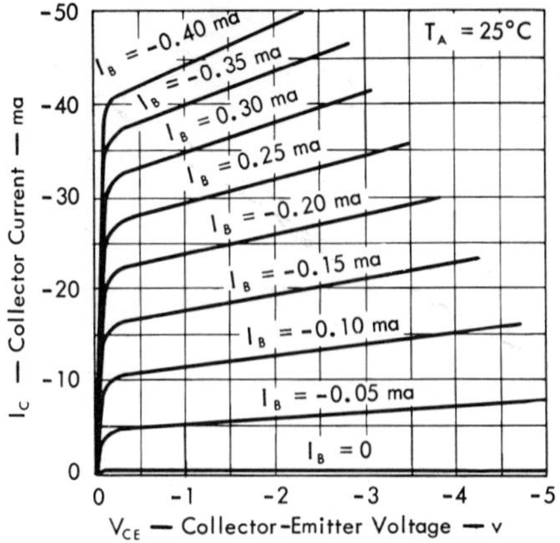

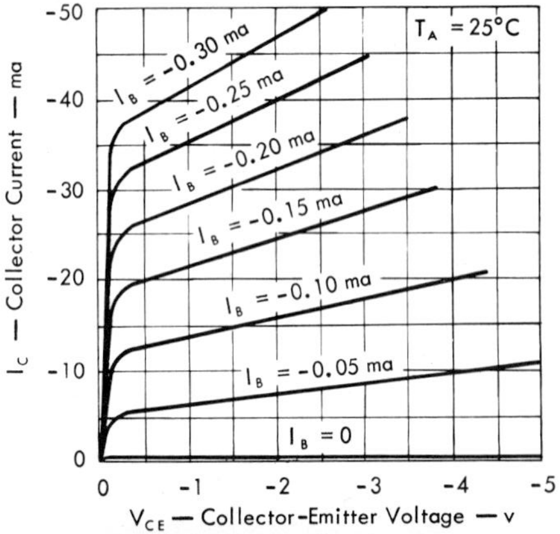

PARAMETER MEASUREMENT INFORMATION

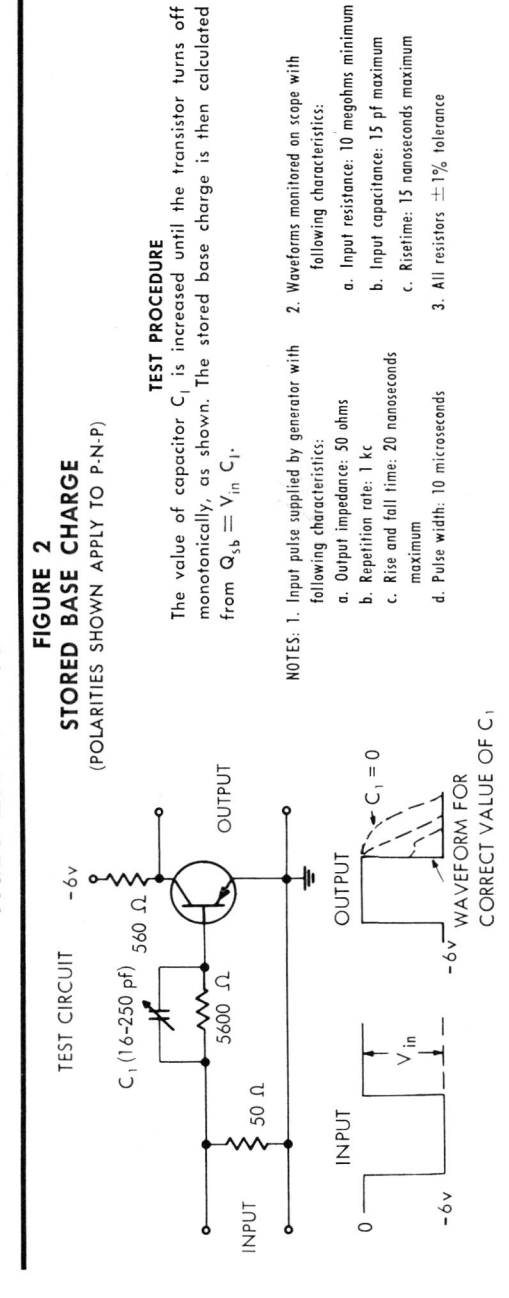

FIGURE 2
STORED BASE CHARGE
(POLARITIES SHOWN APPLY TO P-N-P)

TEST CIRCUIT

C₁ (16–250 pf), 560 Ω, 5600 Ω, 50 Ω, −6v

TEST PROCEDURE

The value of capacitor C_1 is increased monotonically, as shown. The stored base charge is then calculated from $Q_{sb} = V_{in} C_1$.

NOTES:
1. Input pulse supplied by generator with following characteristics:
   a. Output impedance: 50 ohms
   b. Repetition rate: 1 kc
   c. Rise and fall time: 20 nanoseconds maximum
   d. Pulse width: 10 microseconds

2. Waveforms monitored on scope with following characteristics:
   a. Input resistance: 10 megohms minimum
   b. Input capacitance: 15 pf maximum
   c. Risetime: 15 nanoseconds maximum

3. All resistors ±1% tolerance

N-P-N types 2N1302, 2N1304, 2N1306, and 2N1308; P-N-P types 2N1303, 2N1305, 2N1307, and 2N1309

NORMALIZED STATIC FORWARD
CURRENT TRANSFER RATIO
vs
FREE-AIR TEMPERATURE

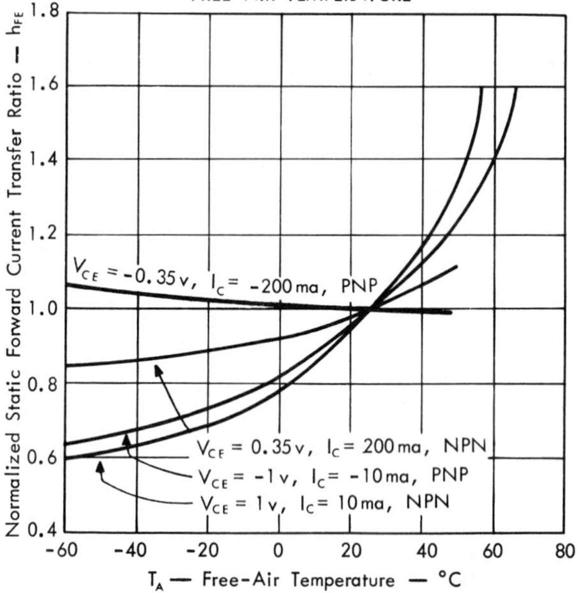

NORMALIZED STATIC FORWARD
CURRENT TRANSFER RATIO
vs
COLLECTOR CURRENT

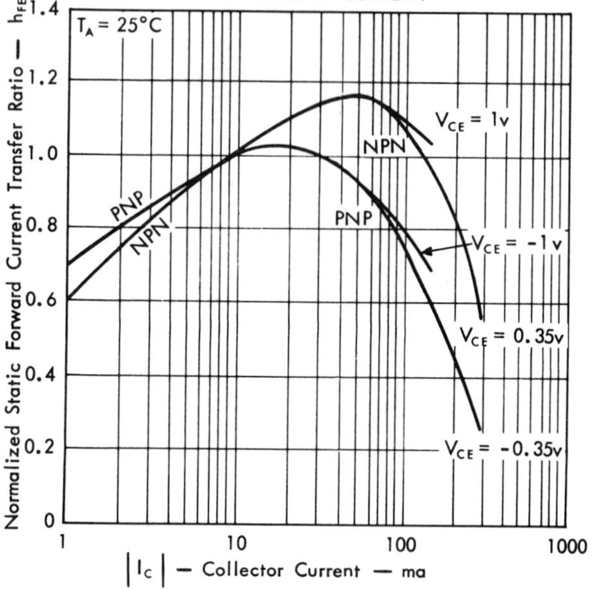

532

BASE-EMITTER VOLTAGE
vs
COLLECTOR CURRENT

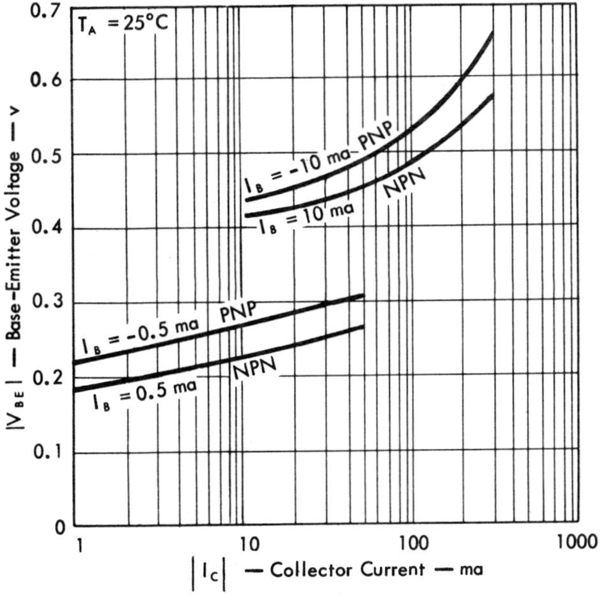

BASE-EMITTER VOLTAGE
vs
FREE-AIR TEMPERATURE

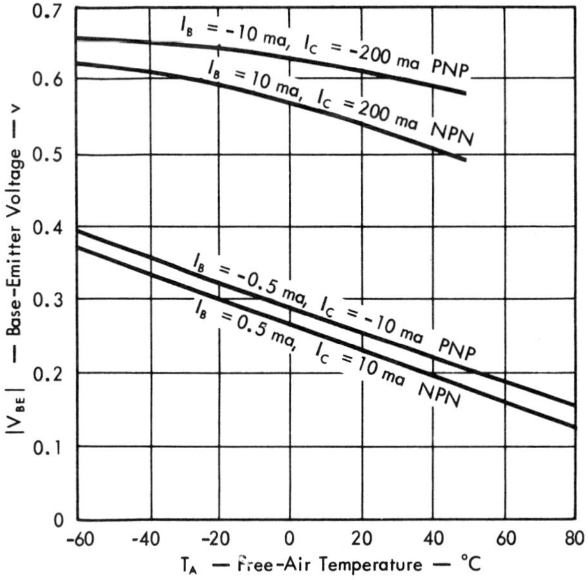

534

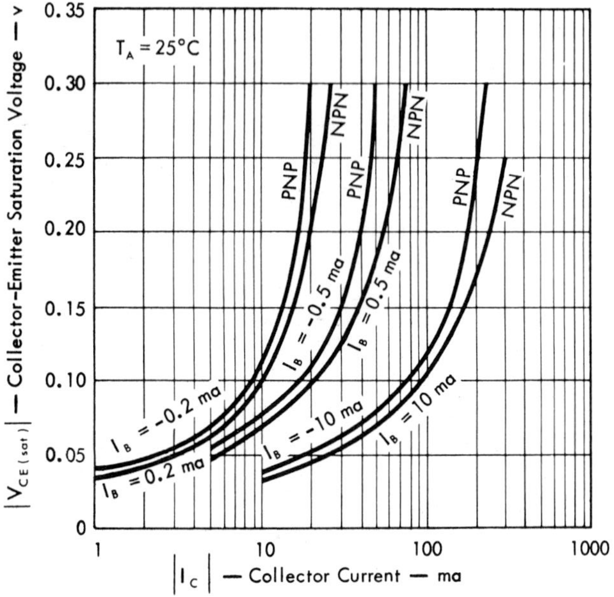

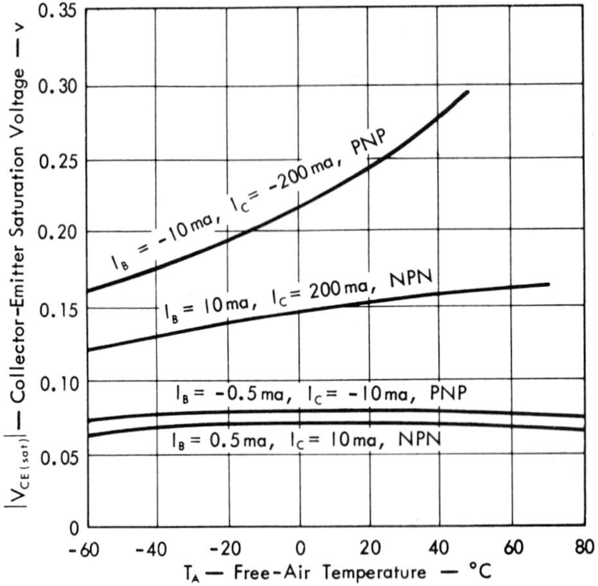

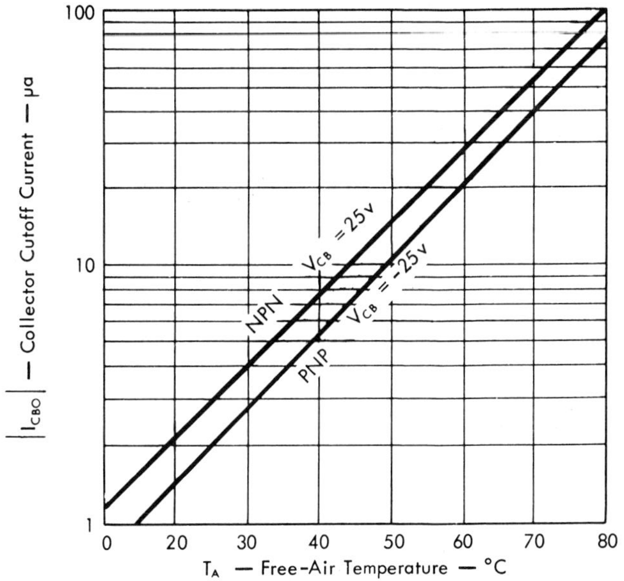

COMMON-BASE OPEN-CIRCUIT OUTPUT CAPACITANCE
vs
COLLECTOR-BASE VOLTAGE

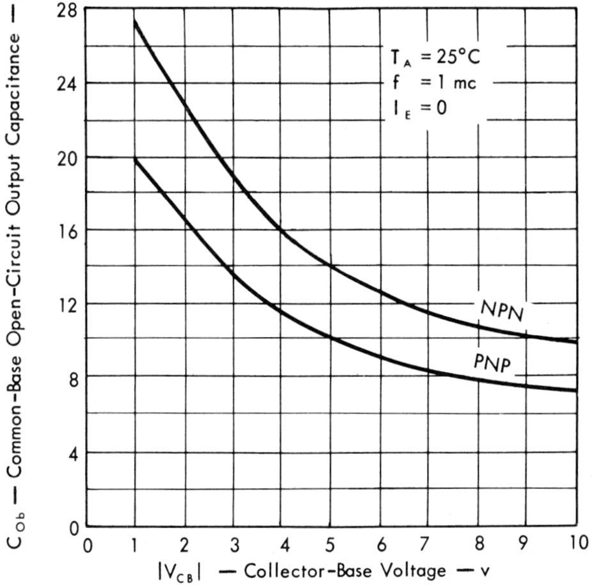

$T_A = 25°C$
$f = 1\ mc$
$I_E = 0$

COLLECTOR CUTOFF CURRENT
vs
FREE-AIR TEMPERATURE

536

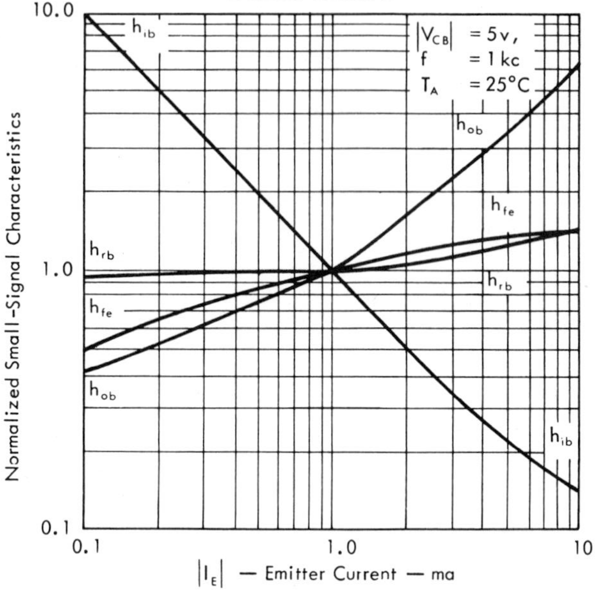

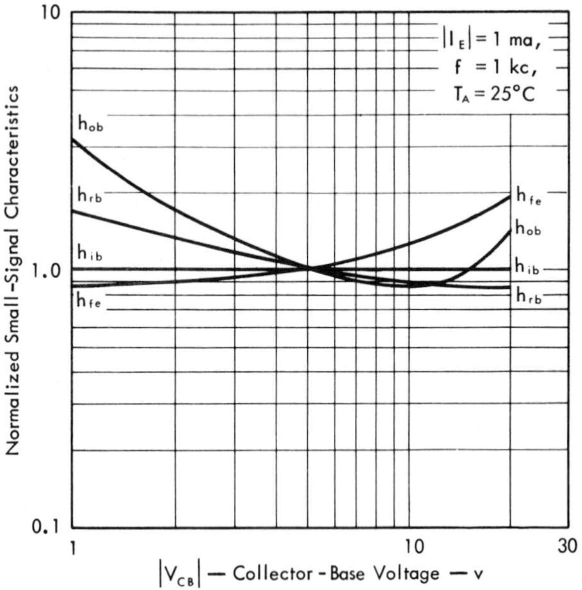

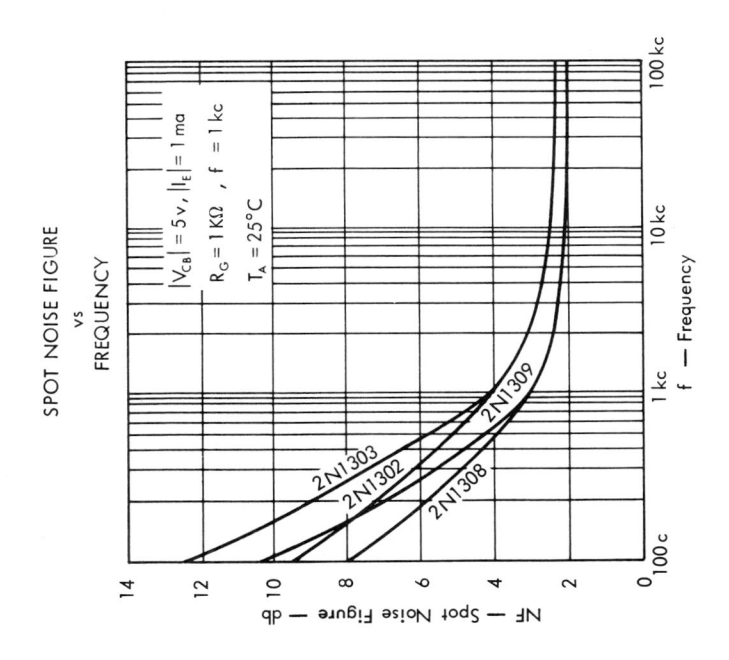

SPOT NOISE FIGURE
vs
FREQUENCY

Index

Acceleration, 12, 13, 17
Acceptor, 48
A-c feedback, Chap. 12 (see Feedback amplifiers)
Action and reaction, 13, 14, 17
Active networks, 143
   defined, 113
Active region, 142, 430, 461
Admittance, 104
Alloy junction transistor, 73, 75–77
Alpha (α), 66, 69, 145, 160
   junction transistor, 145
Alpha cutoff frequency, 278, 291, 294–297
Alternating current
   defined, 94
   feedback, Chap. 12
Aluminum, 49
Amplifier
   cascade, Chap. 10
   d-c, 349–355
   graphical analysis of, 149–154
   physical operation of, 64–69
   power, Chap. 9
   small-signal, Chaps. 8, 17
      common base, 184–190
      common collector, 191–194
      common drain (FET), 486
      common emitter, 179–183
      common source (FET), 485, 486
      comparison of configurations, 194–199
Amplifier design, examples of, 235–239, 249–253, 298–317

Analysis of circuits, 113–127
   equivalent circuit, 155–164
   examples, 203–209
   frequency, 128–133, 276–297, Chap. 16
   graphical, 143–154
Analytical expression for transistor, 460–463
AND circuits, 455, 458, 459
Astable multivibrator, 444–449
Atoms, 10, 16
   binding forces of, 28, 29
   in association to form crystals, 28–31
   isolated atom (the), 20–27
Available gain, defined, 201
Available noise power, defined, 384

Back current (see Cutoff current)
Bandwidth
   defined, 109, 132
   noise, 384, 385
Bardeen, J., 5
Barrier of P-N junction, 58
Base, 61–68
   defined, 61
Base resistance, 156–158, 495, 496
Beta (β), 146, 147
   cutoff frequency, 291–296, 471, 472, 477, 478
   defined, 69, 146
Bias (device), 61–65, 143
   field effect transistor, 83–85
   junction transistor, 60–62, 267, 430

539

Index

Bias (device) (cont.)
  P-N junction, 59
Biasing circuits, 267–275, 335–349
Bias stability, Chap. 11
  defined, 333
  stabilized circuits, 345–349
Binding forces
  between atoms, 28, 29
  in atoms, 21–28
Bipolar, 81, 480
Bistable circuit, 438–444
  defined, 428
Black box concept, 120–124
Brattain, W. H., 5

Capacitance, 97–99
  coupling, 153, 266, 267, 277, 284–290
  diffusion, 467
  input, 478, 484
  transition, 432, 467
Carbon, 27
Carriers (see Charge carriers)
Cascade amplifiers, Chap. 10
  biasing circuits, 267–275
  design example, 298–317
  frequency response, 276–297
Channel (in FET), 82, 85
Characteristics, App. III
  common base, 144
  common emitter, 146
  defined, 144
  dynamic, 406
  Ebers-Moll's description of, 460–463
  field effect transistor, 482
  negative impedance input, 412–419
  temperature variation, 325–330
Charge, electronic, 21
Charge carriers in a semiconductor, 41, 42
  N-type, 46
  P-type, 48
Chemical bonding, 76
Circuit analysis
  comparison of methods, 164, 165
  equivalent, 155–164
  examples of, 203–209
  frequency calculations, 128–133
  graphical, 143–155
  linear of oscillators, 407–411, 419–421
  mesh, 113, 114
  methods of, 113–117
  nodal, 115–117

Circuit theorems, 117–120
Circuits, Chap. 6
  basic connections, 100–111
  biasing, 267–276
  bias stabilized, 335–349
  d-c amplifier, 349–355
  digital switching, Chap. 15
  equivalent of noise source, 386–387
  field effect transistor, Chap. 17
  power and large signal, Chap. 9
Clamping diodes, 443
Class A power amplifier, 222–238, 254–255
  design examples, 235–238
  distortion, 231–234
  operating point, 226
  performance equations, 227–231
Class B power amplifier, 239–253
  complementary symmetry, 255–258
  design examples, 249–253
  distortion, 247–248
  operating point, 239
  performance equations, 242–247
  single-ended circuits, 258–261
Clipping, 233
Collector, 61–69
  defined, 61
  efficiency, 221
Collector capacitance, 291, 292, 467
  common base, 292, 296
  common emitter, 292, 296, 467
  high frequency effect, 290–296
  hybrid-π circuit, 467, 468, 477–479
Collector characteristic curves, App. III
  common base, 144
  common emitter, 146
  defined, 144
  power transistor, 220
  temperature variation, 325–330
Collector current, 66, 144
  limitation, 216
Collector dissipation (see Power dissipation)
Collector junction, 61–63
Colpitts oscillator, 405, 410–411
Common base
  alpha cutoff, 295
  characteristics, 144
  collector capacitance, 292
  equivalent circuit, 156, 158, 174, 184
  h parameters, 187–189, 194
  performance quantities, 190, 195–197
Common base amplifier, 64–67, 184–191

Index

Common base amplifier (*cont.*)
  a-c feedback, 373
  bias circuit, 268, 274
  current gain, 177, 190, 195, 196
  equivalent circuit, 174, 185
  input resistance, 190, 195, 197
  output resistance, 190, 195, 198
  physical operation of, 63–68
  power gain, 190, 195, 196
  voltage gain, 190, 195
Common base power amplifier, 248
Common collector
  equivalent circuit, 191–192
  h parameters, 191–193, 194–199
Common collector amplifier, 191–194
  a-c feedback, 372
  bias circuit, 268
  current gain, 194, 195, 196
  equivalent circuit, 174, 191, 192
  h parameters, 193–195
  input resistance, 193, 195, 197
  output resistance, 194, 195, 198
  power gain, 194, 195, 196
  voltage gain, 194, 195
Common collector hybrid parameters (see h parameters)
Common drain (FET), 486
Common emitter
  characteristics, 146, 148, 153, 154
  collector capacitance, 291, 292, 467, 475–477
  equivalent circuits, 159, 162, 174, 180, 182, 468, 470, 473, 475
  h_{fe} cutoff, 291, 295, 296, 471, 472, 477
  h parameters, 161, 162, 173, 194, 470–472
  hybrid-π parameters, 475, 476
  input characteristics, 413
  y parameters, 473, 474
Common emitter amplifier
  a-c feedback, 367, 368, 370
  bias circuits, 267–276
  current gain, 180, 181, 195, 196
  equivalent circuits, 159, 162, 174–184, 468, 470, 473, 475, 478
  input resistance, 180, 182, 195, 197, 368, 371, 476
  output resistance, 180, 182, 195, 198, 369, 372, 476
  physical operation of, 68
  power gain, 181, 195, 196, 471, 474
  voltage gain, 181, 195, 471, 474, 476

Common-emitter hybrid parameters (see h parameters)
Common-emitter power amplifier
  Class A, 223–224, 228, 254
  Class B, 239, 249, 258, 259
  design examples, 235–238, 249–253
Common source (FET), 485, 486
Comparison of vacuum tube and transistor, 4, 63, 69, 171, 176, 208
Complementary symmetry, 255–258
Compounds, 23
Conductance, defined, 105
Conduction band
  defined, 31
  in germanium, silicon, 35–38
  in P-N junctions, 57–59
Conduction electrons, 38, 41
Conductivity, 40
Convention, current, 144, 270, 431
Copper oxide, 35
Coulomb's law, 21
Covalent binding forces, 28, 29
Covalent bonds
  defined, 36
  in N-type crystal, 44, 46
  in P-type crystal, 46–48
  in semiconductors, 36, 41–43, 49–52
Criterion
  for power amplifiers, 214–222
  for power transistors, 216–218
  for small-signal amplifiers, 169–172
Crossover distortion, 247, 248
Crystal detector, 86
Crystals
  formed by atoms, 28–32
  manufacture, 75, 76, 79
  N-type, 44–46
  P-type, 46–49
  structure, properties of, 35–43
  with impurities, 43–49
Current
  conduction in semiconductors, 40–43
  defined, 93
  in N-type material, 46
  in P-type material, 48
  in solid materials, 40
  limitation of transistors, 216
  noise, 382
Current, alternating (see Alternating current)
Current convention, 144, 270, 431
Current, direct (see Direct current)

Current feedback
  a-c, 366–370
  d-c, 335–341
Current gain (A_i), 171, 176-179
  cascade amplifier, 279, 280
  common base, 190, 194–196
  common collector, 194–196
  common emitter, 180, 194–196
  defined, 171
  of transistor, 66, 69, 145–147, 177, 187, 192
  versus frequency, 295, 296, 471, 474, 477
  with feedback, 360–363, 371, 374
Current mode, 437, 438–439
Current source
  defined, 112
  for transistor drive, 152, 232–233
Cutoff current, 63, 219, 243
  defined, 60
  in digital switching circuits, 431, 432, 439
  in stability factor, 333, 334
  temperature effect on, 325–330
Cutoff region, transistor characteristics, 219, 220, 231–233, 430–433, 460–463
  defined, 220, 430

DCTL, 457–460
Delay time, 433
Depletion field effect transistor, 84, 481
Depletion mode, 84
Depletion region, defined, 60
  in FET, 83
Design considerations, 297, 298, 334
  astable multivibrator, 449
  flip-flops, 442
  power amplifier, 235–238, 249–253
  small-signal amplifier, 299–317
Design curves
  high frequency, 294
  low frequency, 289
Design examples
  cascade amplifier, 298–317
  Class A power amplifier, 235–239
  Class B power amplifier, 249–253
Determinants, 114–117, 163, 164, App. I
  oscillator criterion, 407
Diamond, 27
Dielectric effect in impurity crystals, 44–45
Differential d-c amplifier, 353–376
Diffusion, 43, 62–63
  in manufacture, 78

Diffusion capacitance, 467
Diffusion recombination noise, 387
Digital
  circuits, Chap. 15
  defined, 428
Digital switching circuits, Chap. 15
Diode, 60, 86
  clamping, 443
  photodiode, 87, 88
  temperature sensitive, 347
  tunnel, 88, 89, 422–423
  Zener, 87
Direct-coupled transistor logic, 457–460
Direct current, 94
Direct-current amplifiers, 349–355
Direct-current equivalent circuit, 330–332, 337, 342, 343
Direct-current feedback, 335–341
Direct-current load lines (see Load lines)
Dissipation, collector (see Power dissipation)
Distortion, 221
  Class A, 231–234
  Class B, 247–248
  with feedback, 365
Donor, defined, 44
Drain, 81, 82, 481
Drift transistor, 78
Driver stage, 215

Ebers-Moll equations, 443, 461–463
Effective value of sine wave, 94–95
Efficiency
  collector, 221, 229, 242–244
  of sources, 200
Electric field
  in conducting materials, 41
  in P-N junctions, 58
Electrochemical etched and plated transistors, 77, 78
Electromagnetic energy, absorbed by an atom, 26
Electrons
  diffusing, 62
  in isolated atom, 20–27
  in junction transistor, 65
  in N-type crystal, 44–46
  in P-type crystal, 46–49
  in semiconductor current, 39
  orbits, 20–27
Electron energy
  in isolated atom, 24–27

Index

Electron energy (*cont.*)
  in N-type crystal, 44–46
  in P-type crystal, 46–49
  in semiconductors, 37–39, 41–43, 49
Electron-hole pairs
  defined, 42
  effected by temperature, 50
Electron-pair bonds, defined, 36 (see Covalent bonds)
Electron shells, 22–23, 29
Electrostatic forces, 21
  between atoms, 29
Emitter, 61–69
  defined, 61
Emitter junction, 61
Emitter resistance, 156–158, 495, 496
Energy, 17–20
  levels in crystals, 28–31
  levels in germanium, silicon, 38
  light, 52
  of electrons in an atom, 24–27
Energy bands, 28–31
  conduction, 31
  germanium, silicon, 37
  junction transistor, 61
  tunnel diode, 89
  valence, 31, 59
Energy diagram
  for an N-P-N transistor, 61
  for a P-N junction, 57, 59, 61
  for a P-N-P transistor, 70
  of germanium, silicon, 38
Enhancement mode, 84
Epitaxial transistor, 78
Equivalent circuit
  common base, 158, 174, 185
  common collector, 174, 192
  common emitter, 159, 174, 180, 182, 468, 473, 475, 478
  d-c, 330–332, 337, 342, 343
  general h parameter, 123–124, 160
  hybrid-π, 468, 475, 478, 483
  method of, 120–124, 155–165
  mid-frequency, 278–281
  of FET, 483, 484
  of junction field effect transistor, 483, 484
  of noise source, 386–387
  of oscillator, 403, 405, 407, 412, 420
  of physical device, 121
  T-equivalent circuit, 156, 158, 159, 495
  y parameter, 473

Equivalent circuit method of analysis, 155–164
Etching, 76
Examples
  of cascade amplifiers, 298–317
  of circuit analysis, 203–209
  of Class A design, 235–239
  of Class B design, 249–253
  of stability factor, 334
External noise, 381

Face-centered cubic lattice, 36, 37
Fall time, 436
Feedback
  a-c amplifiers, Chap. 12
  d-c current, 335–341
  d-c voltage, 341–346
  external, 335–346, Chap. 12
  internal, 160
Feedback amplifiers, Chap. 12
  general effects of using, 360–365
  methods of treating, 365–366
  multistage feedback, 373–376
  series feedback, 366–370
  shunt feedback, 370–372
Feedback oscillators, 402, 404
  conditions for oscillation, 404
  description, 404
  mathematical analysis, 406–411
Fermi-level, 39, 43
  defined, 39
  in N-type crystal, 45
  in P-type crystal, 49
  in P-N junctions, 56
  relation to temperature, 51–52
FET (see Field effect transistor)
Field effect transistor, 80–86, Chap. 17
  circuit aspects of, Chap. 17
  insulated gate, 83–86, 481
  junction type, 81–83, 481
  physical construction, 85–86
  small-signal equations, 484–486
Flip-flop, 438–444
Forbidden energy band
  defined, 31
  germanium, silicon, 37, 38
  N-type crystal, 45
  P-type crystal, 48, 49
Forward bias, 59
  of emitter junction, 61, 64
  of P-N junction, 57–59
Forward current, 57–59

Four-terminal networks
  black box concept, 120–125
  defined, 121
Frequency response
  amplifier, high-frequency, 290–297
  amplifier, low-frequency, 284–290
  current gain, 295, 476
  general, 128–134
  of transistors, 290–297, Chap. 16
  with feedback, 364

Gain (see Current; Power; Voltage)
  available, 201–202
  maximum available, 202–203
  transducer, 200–201
Gain stability with feedback, 363
Gallium, 49
Gate, 81, 82, 481
Germanium, 27, 36
  crystal structure, 30, 36–38
  energy bands, 30, 38
g parameters, App. II
Grain boundary, 28, 36
Graphical analysis
  Class A push-pull, 254–255
  method of, 143–155
  power amplifiers, 222–253
Gravitation, 11–15, 19
  comparison to electrostatic forces, 21
Grown junction transistor, 73–75

h_{fb} (see Alpha), 124, 160–161, 177, 187, 194–195
  defined, 123, 124, 185
  high-frequency cutoff, 295
  variation with operating point, 183
h_{fe} (see Beta), 124, 160–161, 177, 194–195
  defined, 123, 124, 476
  high-frequency cutoff, 295, 471, 477
  temperature variation, 327, 328
  variation with operating point, 183
Half-power points, 288, 294, 471, 477
  defined, 131–132
Hartley oscillator, 405–410
Heat energy, 18–19
  applied to isolated atom, 25
  applied to semiconductors, 49–52
High frequency
  general calculations, 130–131
  transistor response, 266, 277, 290–297, 471, 477

High-frequency description of transistors, 291–296, Chap. 16
High temperature
  effect on characteristics, 325–330
  effect on h parameters, 325–330
History of transistor, 5–7
Hole
  conduction by, 42–49
  energies in P-type materials, 48
  in junction transistor, 69–70
  mass of, 42
Hole-electron pairs (see Electron-hole pairs)
h parameters, 122–124, 159–164, 173–178
  common base, 184–191
  common collector, 191–194
  common emitter, 179–184
  conversions, App. II
  defined, 124, 160, 161, 185
  feedback, 369, 372
  temperature variation, 327–330
  variation with operating points, 183
Hybrid-π parameters, 468, 475–477, 483, 484

I_{CBO}, (I_{CO}), 60, 234, 243, 431
  defined, 60, 234
  stability factor, 333–334
  temperature variation, 326–330
I_{CEO}, 243, 327–328
  defined, 219, 243
I_{CES}, 432
I_{DSB}, 482
I_{DSS}, 482
Impedance
  defined, 100
  matching, 127
Impurities in crystals, 43–49
  acceptor, 48
  donor, 44
Impurity atoms
  aluminum, 49
  antimony, 46
  arsenic, 46
  gallium, 49
  indium, 49
  in N-type crystals, 44–46
  in P-type crystals, 46–49
Indium, 49, 75, 76
Induced channel field effect transistor, 85
Inductance, 99–100

Index

Inductive reactance, 99–100
Inertia, 12
Input resistance
  cutoff region, 413
  defined, 172
  nonlinearity of, 232
  saturation region, 414
Input resistance of amplifiers
  common base, 190, 195, 197
  common collector, 193, 195, 197
  common emitter, 179, 180, 195, 197
  FET amplifier, 484
Input resistance with feedback, 368, 371
Insulated gate field effect transistors, 83–85
  characteristics, 482
  depletion type, 84, 481
  equivalent circuit, 483
  induced channel-type, 85, 481
Insulators, defined, 31
Internal noise, 381–389
  defined, 381
Interstage, 128, 266, 281–283
  loss in, 281–290, 293–297
Interstage gain, 281–297
Intrinsic semiconductor
  defined, 43
  relation to temperature, 43
Inverter, 437
Ionic binding forces, 28–29
Ionized atom, 23
  in P-type crystal, 48–49

Junction (see P-N junctions)
  collector, 61–64
  emitter, 61–64
Junction capacitance, 291, 432, 435
Junction diode, 60, 86–89
  temperature sensitive, 346–347
Junction field effect transistor, 81–83, 481
  characteristics, 482
  equivalent circuit, 483
Junction type transistor, 73
  alloy junction, 73, 75–77
  diffusion, 73, 78
  electrochemical etching and plating, 73, 77–78
  epitaxial, 73, 78, 79
  grown junction, 73–75

Kinetic energy, 18
Kirchhoff's laws, 113

Large-signal analysis, 143, 146, Chap. 9
  Class A amplifiers, 222–239
  Class B amplifiers, 239–253
Lattice, of crystal, 36
Life of transistors, 8
Light, 52–53
Linear, 118, 121, 144
  amplifier analysis, Chaps. 8, 10
  equivalent circuit (see Equivalent circuit)
  oscillator analysis, 406–413, 420–421
Linear network analysis, 113–127, 155–164, Chaps. 8, 10, 11, 12, 13, 14, 15, 16, 17
Load line, 149–153, 219–220, 222–225, 228, 237, 241, 247
  a-c, 153, 222–225
  construction of, 149, 154
  input characteristic, 414
Logical gating circuits, 454–460
Logic circuits, 454–460
  diode, 458
  direct-coupled transistor, 457–460
  resistor transistor, 455–457
Low frequency
  calculations, 129
  response, 266, 276–278, 284–290

Majority carrier
  in FET, 81, 82
  in N-type material, 46
  in P-type material, 48
  of biased P-N junctions, 60
Manufacture of transistors, Chap. 5
  field effect transistors, 80–86
  junction transistors, 73–80
Mass, 12–15
Matrix parameters, 468–469
Maximum available gain, 202–203, 297
Maximum power transfer, 125–127, 171, 219
Mesa transistor, 79
Mesh equations, 113–115
Metallic binding forces, 28, 29–30
Metal oxide semiconductor, 481
Metals, 29
Micro-alloy transistor, 78
Mid-frequency, 130–132, 278–284
Minimum detectable signal, 399
Minority carrier
  in base region, 62, 81

Minority carrier (*cont.*)
  in N-type material, 46
  in P-type material, 48
  of biased P-N junctions, 60
Molecule, 28
Monostable circuit, 449-452
  defined, 428
MOS, 481
Multistage feedback, 373-376
Multivibrators, Chap. 15
  astable, 444-448
  bistable (flip-flop), 438-444
  monostable, 449-452
Mutual resistance, 158, App. II

NAND circuits, 455, 458, 459
Negative feedback
  a-c amplifier, Chap. 12
  d-c (in amplifier), 335-346
Negative resistance, 412-422
  multivibrator, 416
  oscillator, 402, 403, 412, 416-422
Negative resistance characteristics, 413-419
Network representation of transistors, 120-125, 156, 160, 161, Chaps. 8, 16
Neutrons, 21-22
Newtonian physics, 11-17
Newton's laws of physics, 14-17
  applied to solar system, 14-17
Nodal equations, 115-117
Noise
  equivalent circuit of, 386
  general considerations of, 381-387
  noise figure, 389-392
  1/f, 383, 387
  thermal, 382-386
  transistor sources, 387
  white, 383, 387
Noise figure, 389-392, 398
  dependance on R_g, 397
  direct measurement, 394
  integrated, 391-392
  methods of measuring, 392-395
  spot, 391-392
  two-generator measurement, 392
  use of, 395-398
Noise power, 390
  defined, 384
Noise sources, transistor, 387-389
Nonlinearity, 145, 157, 221
  of input resistance, 232
  oscillator analysis, 406

NOR circuits, 455, 458, 459
Normal region (see Active region)
Norton's theorem, 117-120
  applied to transistor, 118-120
  related to mesh, nodal, 117-120
N-P-N junction transistor, 60-69, 73-76
N-type crystal, defined, 44-46
N-type semiconductor, 44-46
Nucleus, 21
Nyquist, H., 384

OFF condition, 431-432, 439
  defined, 429
Ohm's law, 40, 97, 104
ON condition, 432-433, 439
  defined, 429
One-shot circuit, 449-452
Open-circuit stable, defined, 417
Operating characteristics (see Characteristics)
Operating point, d-c, 157, 219, 222, 226, 298
  common emitter amplifier, 154
  complete bias equations, 337-345
  input equations for, 270-276
  limitation, 220, 226
  of Class A, 226
  of Class B, 239, 240
  on input characteristic, 416, 417
  oscillators, 418, 419
  variation with temperature, 325-330
OR circuits, 455, 458, 459
Oscillator, Colpitts, 411
Oscillator, Hartley, 405-410
Oscillator, negative-resistance, 402, 403, 412, 416-422
Oscillators, Chap. 14
  feedback, 402-411
  general considerations, 402
  general description, 401-404
Oscillators, feedback (see Feedback oscillators)
Output characteristics (see Characteristics)
Output power (see Power output)
Output resistance, defined, 172
Output resistance of amplifiers
  common base, 190, 195, 198
  common collector, 194, 195, 198
  common emitter, 180, 195, 198
Output resistance with feedback, 365, 369, 372

Index

Parallel circuit, 104–108
   Q of, 109–111
   resonance, 108–111
Parameters
   conversion, App. II
   d-c, 326, 327, 331, 332
   feedback, 369, 372
   h, 123, 124, 159–164, 173, 470–472, Chap. 8
   hybrid-π, 468, 475–477, 483, 484
   matrix, 468–469
   variation with operating point, 183
   variation with temperature, 325–330
   Y, 159, 472–474
   Z, 159
Parameters, transistor (see h parameters; Hybrid-π parameters)
Passive circuit elements, 97–100
Performance equations
   Class A power amplifiers, 227–231
   Class B power amplifiers, 242–246
   FET amplifiers, 483–485
   small-signal amplifiers, 179, 195
Phase inverter
   for single-ended circuit, 259, 260
   transformer as, 240
Phasor diagram, 102–107
Photodiodes, 87
Physical construction of transistors, 79, 80
   alloy, 77
   mesa, 79
   planar, 80
Physics
   review of, Chap. 2
   summary, 32
Planar transistor, 80
P-N junctions, 55–60
   effect of bias on, 59–60
P-N-P junction transistor, 69–70
Point contact transistor, 5, 403
Polycrystalline material, 36
Positive feedback, 362
   in oscillator, 402–406
   in switching circuits, 440
Potential barrier, defined, 58
Potential energy, 18–19
Power, 96–97
Power amplifier, Chap. 9
   Class A, 222–239
   Class A push-pull, 254–255
   Class B, 239–253
   complementary symmetry, 253, 255–258

Power amplifier (*cont.*)
   design example, 235–239, 249–253
   distortion, 221, 231–234, 247–248
   efficiency, 221, 227, 243
   performance quantities, 215–222
   single-ended Class B circuits, 258–261
Power dissipation, 216
   allowable in Class A, 226–231
   allowable in Class B, 242–247
   versus temperature, 217, 218
Power efficiency (see Efficiency, collector)
Power gain
   available, 201–202
   cascade amplifier, 276–297
   common base, 190, 195, 196
   common collector, 194, 195, 196
   common emitter, 181, 195, 196, 470, 474
   defined, 170
   in decibel, 278, 281–289, 294–297
   transducer, 199–201
Power output, 219–221
   Class A, 226–231
   Class B, 242–247
Power spectrum, noise, defined, 383
Power transistor, requirements of, 215
Protons, 21
P-type crystal, defined, 46–49
P-type semiconductor, 46–49
Push-pull
   Class A amplifiers, 254–255
   Class B amplifiers, 240–253

Q of circuit
   defined, 109
   parallel, 111
   series, 110
Q point (see Operating point, d-c)
Quantum mechanics, 32
Quantum of energy, 26, 32

Rate grown junction transistor, 74, 75
Reactance
   capacitive, 99
   inductive, 99
Regions, transistor
   active (normal), 142, 430, 461
   cutoff, 219, 220, 430
   saturation, 219, 220, 430
Resistance, 97
   equivalent of noise, 389
   feedback, 371
   in transistor equivalent circuit, 157

Resistance (*cont.*)
  negative, 415–418
  saturation, 433
Resistor-transistor logic, 455–457
Resonance, 108–111
  parallel, 110
  series, 108
Reverse bias, 65, 83, 87
  of P-N junction, 59–60
Reverse current, 59–60 (see Cutoff current)
Rise time, 433–434
rms (root mean square) value of sine wave, 95
RTL, 455–457

Saturated flip-flop, 438–439
Saturation mode, 437, 439
Saturation region transistor characteristics, 142, 430
  defined, 219–220
Saturation resistance, 433
Schmitt trigger, 452–454
Selenium, 35
Self-bias circuit, 274
Semiconductor, Chap. 3
  charge carriers of, 42
  defined, 31
  devices, 86–89
  effect of heat, light on, 49–53
  intrinsic, 43
  noise, 387
  N-type, 44–46
  P-type, 46–49
Series circuit, 100–104
  Q of, 109
  resonance in, 108–111
Series feedback, 366–370
Shockley, W., 5
Short-circuit current gain (see Alpha; h_{fb}, h_{fe})
Short circuit stable, 417
Shot noise, 391
Shunt-fed circuit, 223–225
Shunt feedback, 370–373
Signal-to-noise ratio, 398, 399
Silicon, 27
  crystal structure, 36
Single-battery common emitter bias, 271–272
Single crystal (see Crystals)
Single-ended Class B circuit, 258–261

Single-stage amplifiers
  feedback amplifiers, Chap. 12
  field effect transistor, Chap. 17
  high frequency, Chap. 16
  power amplifiers, Chap. 9
  small-signal, Chaps. 8, 12
Solar system
  analogy to the atom, 20–21
  application of Newton's laws to, 16–17
Source, 81, 82, 481
Stability, bias (see Bias stability)
Stability factor
  common emitter circuits, 335–341
  d-c amplifiers, 350–352
  defined, 333
  unstabilized circuit, 333
Stabilized circuits, 335–346
Static collector characteristics (see Collector characteristics)
Steering network, 439
Storage time, 435–436
Substrate, 84, 85, 482
Surface-barrier transistor, 77
Susceptance, defined, 110
Switch, transistor, 429–437
Switching circuits, Chap. 15
Switching time, 433–437
  delay time, 433
  full time, 436
  rise time, 433–434
  storage time, 435–436

Table of
  h parameters, 173, 194
  parameter conversions, App. II
  performance values, 179, 195
  typical parameter values, 195
Temperature
  effect on characteristics, 324–330
  effect on dissipation, 217–218, 226
  effect on parameters, 325–327, 363
  effect on semiconductors, current, 43
  relation to electron energies, 50–51
Temperature compensation, 346–347 (see Bias stability)
Temperature-sensitive devices, 346–347
TFT, 85
Thermal noise, 383–386
Thermistors, 87
Thevenin's theorem, 117
  applied to transistor, 117–120
  relation to mesh, nodal, 119–120

Index

Thin film transistor (TFT), 85
Transducer gain, defined, 200
Transformers, 136–137, 222–225, 240–242, 255–261
  coupling, 267, 268, 275, 299–305
Transients
  general, 134–136
  transistor, 433–437
Transistor
  analytical expressions for, 460–462
  bias for, 61, 62, 268, 430
  characteristics, 144–149, 220, 326, 482
  FET, 80–86
  junction, 73–80
  manufacture, 73–86
  negative resistance characteristic, 415–416
  noise sources, 387–389
  N-P-N, 60–69
  physical action in, 61–69
  physical limitations, 216–218
  P-N-P, 69–70
  power dissipation, 226
  switch, 429–437
Transistor applications, 7
Transistor, basic concepts of, 63–69
Transistor characteristics, App. III (see Characteristics)
Transistor, history of, 5–7
Transistor, junction-type, 73
  alloy junction, 73, 75–77
  diffusion, 73, 78
  epitaxial, 73, 78, 79
  electrochemical etching and plating, 73, 77–78
  grown junction, 73–75
Transistor, neutron bombardment of, 7
Transistor noise sources, 387–389
Transistor, power, 214–219
Transition capacitance, 467
Triggered digital circuits, 438–454
Two-battery bias supply
  common-base amplifier, 268
  common-collector amplifier, 268
  common-emitter amplifier, 268
Two-terminal networks, Norton's and Thevenin's theorem, 119–120

Two-terminal oscillators, 413–422
  mathematical analysis, 406
Two-terminal pair networks
  black box concept, 120–125
  defined, 120
Tunnel diode, 88, 89, 422–423

Unipolar transistors, 81

Vacuum tube, comparison to, 4, 63, 64, 67, 170, 484
Valence bond band
  defined, 31
  in germaniums, silicons, 37–38
  in P-N junctions, 57
  in semiconductor current, 41
Valence electrons, 23
  in compounds, 23
  of germaniums, silicons, 38
Variation of operating characteristics with temperature, 324–330
Varistors, 86
Voltage, 95–97
  limitation of transistors, 216–219
  noise, 382
Voltage feedback
  a-c, 370
  d-c, 341–345
Voltage gain (A_v), 172, 179
  common base, 190–195
  common collector, 194, 195
  common drain (FET), 485, 486
  common emitter, 181, 195
  common source (FET), 485, 486
  defined, 172
Voltage source, defined, 111–113

Weight, 11–16
White noise, 383–386
  defined, 383

Y parameters, 159, 472–474

Zener
  diodes, 86–87
  effect, 87
Z parameters, 159, App. II